Fuad A. Abdullah
University of Nebraska at Omaha

Financial Management for the Multinational Firm

Prentice-Hall, Inc., Englewood Cliffs, New Jersey 07632

Library of Congress Cataloging-in-Publication Data

Abdullah, Fuad A. (Fuad Abdul-Kader) (date)
Financial management for the multinational firm.

Includes bibliographies and index.
1. International business enterprises—Finance.
2. International business enterprises—Finance—Case studies. I. Title.
HG4027.5.A23 1987 658.1'599 86-25226
ISBN 0-13-316340-7

Editorial/production supervision
and interior design: **Cheryl Lynn Smith**
Cover design: **George Cornell**
Manufacturing buyer: **Ed O'Dougherty**

Printed in the United States of America

10 9 8 7 6 5 4 3

ISBN 0-13-316340-7 01

Prentice-Hall International (UK) Limited, *London*
Prentice-Hall of Australia Pty. Limited, *Sydney*
Prentice-Hall Canada Inc., *Toronto*
Prentice-Hall Hispanoamericana, S.A., *Mexico*
Prentice-Hall of India Private Limited, *New Delhi*
Prentice-Hall of Japan, Inc., *Tokyo*
Prentice-Hall of Southeast Asia Pte. Ltd., *Singapore*
Editora Prentice-Hall do Brasil, Ltda., *Rio de Janeiro*

To Marithe

Contents

PART II THE FOREIGN EXCHANGE MARKET AND FOREIGN EXCHANGE EXPOSURE MANAGEMENT

PART III MULTINATIONAL WORKING CAPITAL MANAGEMENT

Preface

The last two decades witnessed a growing interest, both on the operational and academic levels, in the workings of international finance, and in particular the financial activities of the multinational firm. This growing interest has reflected the spread of multinational business activity and also an accelerated movement toward integrated international financial markets.

These developments are significantly impacting the fortunes of an increasing number of large and medium-sized businesses in almost every country and also millions of investors throughout the world. Firms which until recently had little or no international exposure are realizing that their operations are influenced by this multinational phenomenon, even if their base of operation remains primarily domestic.

In recognition of this trend, firms with multinational activities have been strengthening their organizational ability to manage their resources in the changing environment. Increasing emphasis and greater human resources are being directed to such areas as international cash management, foreign exchange exposure management, and multinational capital budgeting. Business school programs throughout the world have also recognized this trend. International business finance is now regarded as an essential part in the training of business students by an increasing number of schools and colleges in the United States and abroad. Familiarity with international financial management has become indispensable for all students pursuing a degree and a career in business.

International finance textbooks have frequently devoted extensive coverage to many areas that fall within the scope of international economics. A number of them dwelled on international finance theory or had a significant macroeconomic orientation, neglecting the operational aspects of the interface between the multinational firm and international financial markets.

The focus of this book is on multinational financial management as viewed and practiced by the multinational firm. Familiarity with certain areas of the firm's environment, such as the international monetary system and determination of exchange rates under alternative regimes, is essential to the international financial manager. These areas are developed only to the extent necessary to achieve their understanding by the manager. Material that overlaps with international economics is kept to a minimum, but key economic concepts that impact the financial process are not overlooked.

The topical sequence of this book parallels closely the one generally followed in business finance texts. In essence, the financial decision-making process is extended to an international setting. After examining the environment of the multinational firm, exchange markets, and the international monetary order, the book addresses working capital management and the management of fixed investments in that order. Factors bearing on the international investment or financing decision, such as the political risk and international taxation issues, are given adequate coverage as they impact this decision to a significant degree.

International financial theory is explained in an understandable format without encumbering the presentation by an overdose of quantitative and highly abstract formulations. Major topical areas such as foreign exchange risk management, the borrowing, investment and capital budgeting decisions, and positioning of funds and cash management, are written with a substantial emphasis on practices and conventions of the marketplace. Basic theory in an understandable format supplemented by ample illustrations are the strongest aspect of this work.

Another strong quality in this work is the case studies, which are intended to highlight the decision-making process in each major topical area. Although all these case studies are hypothetical, they were designed to simulate, as closely as possible, true marketplace situations and the real-life options available to the financial manager. Each case study is closely linked to the material in the chapter or chapters to which it relates, and is carefully interwoven with the major issues raised in the text material. In a few cases, the text material itself is built around a case study.

Students generally find this approach of integrating the case studies with the text material more effective as a learning device than the alternative of supplementing the textbook with cases chosen from other sources.

This book is primarily intended for use in undergraduate courses in international business finance offered by business school programs. Students who have completed basic courses in financial management, economics, and accounting principles should be able to comprehend the material without difficulty. Exposure to a course on financial institutions should further enhance the understanding of the covered material. It is also suitable, when supplemented by a selection of appropriate readings, for MBA students. Students pursuing an MBA degree, irrespective of their previous exposure to international finance, will find the material in this book as opening a window to the world of multinational financial management. The practical and illustrative approach adopted throughout the book and the focus on the firm itself should appeal to students contemplating careers in firms that engage in any form of multinational business activity.

The author would like to acknowledge the contribution of the Research Support Center of the College of Business Administration of the University of Nebraska at Omaha, particularly that of Jackie Lynch, who word processed several drafts of the manuscript. The book benefited from the valuable comments made by the reviewers (Professor Susan E. Moeller of Northeastern University, Professor Jacobus T. Severiens of Kent State University, and Professor Jim Hugon of Portland State University). The author is also grateful for the help and support received throughout the project preparation from Linda Frascino and Cheryl Smith of Prentice-Hall. Credit also is due to my students for their endurance and for their helpful comments on some of the problems and cases used in this book.

While acknowledging the contribution of these and others who in some way or another helped in shaping the final product, the author assumes responsibility for any errors or weaknesses that remain in it.

F. A. A.

1

The Multinational Company and Its Environment

INTRODUCTION—A HISTORICAL PERSPECTIVE

The focus of this book is on the functions of the financial manager of a multinational company (MNC). Alternatively stated, the primary emphasis will be on the various financial management functions viewed from the standpoint of the MNC.

The MNC is not a recent creature. Major companies of colonial powers extended their operations in the occupied countries and territories, and developed a substantial base of political and economic power in these areas. One of the earliest was the East India Company, which was established in 1600, and was given the monopoly of trade with the East Indies. The early history of MNCs took primarily the form of alliance with the parent country's military or political power in extending their activities to foreign areas. From the rubber plantations in Malaya to banana farms in Latin America, these firms established a strong foothold, enjoying the protection of their home countries and developing, in some instances, into major political powers themselves.

A group of international oil and mining companies obtained lucrative concessions to prospect for oil and minerals, particularly in the Middle East and Latin America, during the second half of the nineteenth century and the early part of the twentieth century. This was, perhaps, the most significant development in the annals of the MNC, for it produced the seeds of significant political and economic developments that took place later in this century.

Multinational companies still suffer from the negative image produced by their former association with colonial powers, or strong political presence of their home governments in the foreign territories. The peoples in those areas, rightly or wrongly, viewed this association as the primary source of their economic and social problems. Those feelings were heightened by the rise of nationalism, which culminated in political independence for most occupied countries in Asia and the Middle East during the inter-war period, and Africa following the end of World War II. This development also set the stage for the nationalization of foreign interests, particularly in the oil and other extractive industries, which peaked in the 1950s and 1960s.

Although MNCs existed probably as far back as the early civilizations, a new breed of dynamic and aggressive MNCs emerged over the last three decades and dotted the map of the world. The bulk of multinational activity today takes place in industrial countries where the absence of restrictions and the development of technology and communication have made this activity both feasible and profitable. In the Third World, these MNCs are no longer associated with colonialism or need the protection of their governments. They have cast off the stigma which long characterized their predecessors, and have thrived on being able to achieve profitability, and at the same time to contribute to the economic development of their host countries.

Financial institutions, particularly large banks, insurance companies, and accounting firms, have traditionally followed their clients wherever their services were needed. Today a relatively small number of international banks, sometimes referred to as multinational banks, dominate the financial markets in every corner of the world. From the Caribbean to Hong Kong, and from the sleepy villages of North Yemen to the financial money centers of Switzerland, the presence of these banks is an unmistakable sign of the growth and coming into maturity of the MNC.

WHAT IS AN MNC?

The question that has always puzzled writers in the field of multinational financial management is simply, what is an MNC? In a sense, there is hardly a business venture or an undertaking which is completely immune to international commodity prices or to economic and political developments elsewhere in the world. The farmer in Iowa has to worry about world corn and soybean prices; a baker in Kuwait has to keep an eye on imported wheat or flour prices, and even a shoe shine boy in Singapore is impacted by changes in the price of boot shine.

Academicians and the international business and financial community have long sought a definition for an MNC that uses an objective and measurable yardstick. The one most commonly used is the proportion of overall revenue generated from foreign operations. But then the question arises, what proportion of foreign-generated revenue to overall income makes a firm multinational? Does it have to be 50 percent? Indeed not. Most large U.S. firms generally recognized as leading MNCs do not even approach that proportion. What about five or ten percent? These proportions are generally considered too low to characterize the firm as an MNC. There seems to be some kind of a consensus that the proportion of foreign-based income has to be at least 25 to 30 percent of total income for the firm to qualify as an MNC.

The search for that proportion of foreign-based revenue which separates an MNC from a domestic firm seems futile. Perhaps the key to resolving this issue is to ask the opposite question: What is not an MNC? A good intuitive answer is a firm whose degree of involvement in foreign operation does not figure in the managerial decision-making process. Alternatively stated, a firm is not multinational if its management does not consider it as such. The paramount consideration seems to be whether or not the degree of the firm's involvement in external activities (manufacturing, export, distribution, financing, and the like) warrants management's attention. If the management considers such activities as crucial to its successful operation, and if these activities impact the decision-making process, then the firm must be considered as an MNC, irrespective of what proportion of total revenue is generated from foreign operations. Foreign-based manufacturing or distribution operations, the hallmark of most well-known MNCs, is not a necessary condition for a firm to be characterized as an MNC.

According to this operational definition, a firm which exports ten percent of its output may be considered an MNC if such exports are crucial to its survival—and if the management has to weigh political, exchange, and other risks involved in such operations. On the other hand, another firm which exports a larger proportion of its output may not be so considered, if such exports represent few large transactions annually which are denominated in the firm's own currency. The key factor here is that the second firm does not find itself preoccupied with or concerned about exposure to exchange rate and political risks. These considerations, therefore, do not continuously figure in the management's decision-making process.

A firm may become an MNC by virtue of its substantial involvement in international financial markets, on the borrowing and/or investing sides, despite its limited foreign manufacturing or distribution activities. A domestic company, on the other hand, does not qualify as multinational just because it occasionally obtains loans from foreign countries or from the Eurocurrency markets.

These examples illustrate the difficulty of arriving at a definition of an MNC based on objective and measurable criteria. Even if such criteria can be developed, there will still be disagreement as to what really constitutes an MNC. Further insight into the distinguishing features of MNCs will be developed in Chapter 12, which examines some common characteristics of these firms which impel them to undertake direct foreign investment outside their home countries.

THE ENVIRONMENT OF THE MNC

MNCs' managers have to understand the environment in which they function if they are to achieve their objective in maximizing the value of their firms, or the rate of return from foreign operations. The environment consists of:

1. The international financial system, which consists of two segments: the official part represented by the accepted code of behavior by governments comprising the international monetary system, and the private part, which consists of international banks and other multinational financial institutions that participate in the international money and capital markets.
2. The foreign exchange market, which consists of multinational banks, foreign exchange dealers, and organized exchanges where currency futures are regularly traded.
3. The host country's environment, consisting of such aspects as the political and socioeconomic systems, and people's cultural values and aspirations. Understanding of the host country's environment is crucial for successful operation and essential for the assessment of the political risk.

The multinational financial manager has to realize that the presence of his firm in a number of countries and the diversity of its operations present challenges as well as opportunities. The challenges are the unique risks and variables the manager has to contend with which his or her domestic counterpart does not have to worry about. One of these challenges, for example, is the multiplicity and complexity of the taxation systems which impact the MNC's operations and profitability. But this same challenge presents the manager with opportunities to reduce the firm's overall tax burden, through transfer of funds from high- to low-tax affiliates and by using tax havens.

The financing function is another such challenge, due to the multiplicity of sources of funds or avenues of investment available to the financial manager. The manager has to worry about the foreign exchange and political risks in positioning funds and in mobilizing cash resources. This diversity of financial sources enables the MNC at the same time to reduce its cost of capital and maximize the return on its excess cash resources, compared to firms that raise and invest funds in one capital market.

In a real sense MNCs are particularly situated to make the geographic, currency, and institutional diversity work for them. This diversity, if properly managed, helps to reduce fluctuations in their earnings and cash flows, which would translate into higher stock market values for their shares. This observation is especially valid for the well-diversified MNCs.

This is not to suggest that the job of the manager of an MNC is easier, or less demanding, than if he or she were to operate within the confines of one country. The challenges and the risks are greater, but so are the rewards accruing to intelligent, flexible, and forward-looking management. The key to such a management is to make the diversity and complexity of the environment work for the benefit of the firm and to lessen the adverse impact of conflicts on its progress.

Conflict with the Environment

The conflict between the MNC and its environment is real and frequently very intense. This conflict takes many forms. The most important, and perhaps the most crucial, is the conflict between its goals and policies and those of the host country. Frequent conflicts arise within the MNC itself, which are often manifested in differing policies and strategies adopted by the head office management as opposed to the local management of the affiliate. Fierce competition occurs among rival MNCs trying to establish footholds in the same markets. Occasionally the goals of MNCs also clash with the policies of their home governments.

The conflict with the goals and policies of the host government has been the most celebrated, and parenthetically, the most documented. The annals of multinational financial management are replete with accounts of such diametrically opposite goals, as dramatized by the highly publicized confiscation and nationalization of foreign enterprises by a number of host governments. It is not difficult to see how the profit- or share-price-maximizing policy of the MNC runs counter at times to the economic and financial policies of the host country. The financial objectives of the MNC are circumscribed by such constraints relating to the host country as:

1. Economic development policies and objectives.
2. Monetary policies and credit restraints.
3. Fiscal and taxation policies.
4. Balance of payments policies and exchange controls.
5. Others, such as employment and labor policies.

Most host countries, particularly among the developing countries (LDCs), have ongoing economic development programs which specify, *inter alia,* priorities in the use of economic resources. Although some of these programs may be ill conceived, they embody the official policies adopted by the governments of these countries. Conflict will be minimized if the MNC's affiliate fits in the general framework of the host's developmental policies, and if the former avoids actions that would disrupt or impede the country's development objectives. National planning priorities are conditions that the MNC has to learn to live with, even if it happens to disagree with them.

The conflict between the MNC's financial objectives and national economic priorities of the host country is not an inescapable situation. The affiliate may be engaged in activities that make a real contribution to the country's development, such as firms engaged in manufacturing agricultural implements and other capital goods, or firms in the communication and data processing industries. The most common area of disagreement is the proportion of profits remitted as dividends, or in other forms, to the parent company, which would determine how much resources are left for reinvestment locally. Capital formation is the *sine qua non* of economic growth, and the host government expects foreign firms to contribute their share to this process.

Most developing countries attempt to influence availability and cost of credit to various sectors of the economy, although they lack a well-developed institutional framework that makes for effective monetary policy. Authorities expect local affiliates of MNCs to conform to the same credit and other restraints that apply to local national firms. In practice, foreign affiliates are often able to circumvent credit controls by their access to external resources available from the parent company, sister affiliates, or the Eurocurrency markets. In certain situations, conversion of a large amount of foreign currency into local currency by a foreign affiliate could cause a substantial increase in the money supply, thus frustrating national monetary policy. The host country's central bank, however, has the option of neutralizing the influx of foreign exchange, thus avoiding the ensuing inflationary impact.

The most visible aspect of fiscal policy that impacts local affiliates of MNCs is the host country's taxation system. Taxation is an area which presents the MNC with the challenge of working with two or more taxing jurisdictions, as well as the opportunity to use its flexibility and wide geographical presence to reduce its overall tax burden. A number of foreign firms enjoy substantial tax concessions granted by host countries to attract foreign investment. The most objectionable aspect of tax behavior on the part of MNCs is the use of transfer pricing and other mechanisms to evade or avoid the payment of taxes due to the host country.

Another aspect of fiscal policy objectives of the host country that may conceivably clash with MNCs' profit-maximization behavior is their contribution to social overhead capital. The presence of relatively large foreign firms on their soil with substantial manpower requirements often necessitates vast investments in public utility, transportation, educational, and health facilities. While host governments regard such investments as part of their development programs, they often require foreign affiliates to contribute to their financing.

The most vexing and troubling aspect of host governments' policies to MNCs are exchange controls and import restrictions, particularly those imposed subsequent to the commencement of operation of the foreign firm. Host governments often justify these measures as necessary to correct balance of payments disequilibria and to conserve their scarce foreign exchange resources. MNCs contend that such restrictive measures impede their operations and contravene their rights, as spelled out under the concession agreements, to make just transfers to the parent companies. Sharp conflicts often arise as MNCs attempt to circumvent these restrictions through transfer pricing and working capital management techniques. These practices in turn invite the animosity of domestic enterprises that have to live with restrictive measures, as they do not possess the tools and resources to get around them. This scenario sometimes leads to temporary or permanent blockage of transfers, and may eventually culminate in the expropriation of foreign firms.

Host countries have also been traditionally critical of foreign affiliates' local employment policies. Their complaints generally center on the affiliates' heavy reliance on foreign personnel for technical and managerial positions, and the nonexistence, or the inadequacy, of training programs for the local work force. Once again, we witness a clash of interests: MNCs' desire to hire the best personnel to further their financial objectives, and the country's aspirations to train their people with the requisite technical and managerial skills essential for the process of economic development.

The preceding analysis should not suggest that conflicts between MNCs and their host countries are confined to operations in LDCs. Although conflicts with the host environment in developed industrial countries are relatively infrequent and less intense, they are, nevertheless, real. Operations of Japanese automobile manufacturing facilities in the United States, for example, draw sharp objections from domestic manufacturers, as well as from the states and communities where domestic facilities are concentrated, and even from organized labor. The Swiss monetary authorities, to cite another example, impose regulations on MNCs' borrowing in the Swiss money and capital markets. These regulations, such as the queue technique (which forces foreign borrowers to wait for their turn to tap the funds markets) are justified by the need to have orderly markets and to prevent adverse impact on domestic monetary and credit policies.

Understanding the Cultural and Religious Values of the Host Country

Equally important as the desirability of adapting to the host government's economic and development policies, is the ability of the MNC to understand and respect the cultural and religious heritage of the host country. The ability to blend with the host environment is not an easy matter, particularly in countries where cultural values and codes of behavior differ sharply from those prevailing in its home country. This is not merely good public relations, but is often essential to the smooth and successful operation of foreign firms. MNCs which flagrantly violate the established code of ethics or behavior in the host country, or offend the people's religious or traditional values, will have to face an increasingly hostile environment. It is not uncommon for such firms to face consumers' boycott of their product, or public opinion's clamor for government intervention to correct their practices.

United States firms which have had long experience in operating in Saudi Arabia (such as Aramco, Northrup Corporation, Raytheon Corporation, and the Whittaker Corporation) have learned to understand the deeply religious and conservative values of the country. Personnel of these and other firms operating in that country are adequately briefed about these values before assuming their posts. Violation of the personal code of conduct, or behavior which offends the cultural and religious traditions of the country, is often sufficient grounds for terminating the employment of persons involved.

Conflict within the MNC

Conflict sometimes arises between the management of the affiliate company and that of the parent company. This is particularly the case if the decision-making process is largely centralized at the head office level. Local managers feel that they are left out of major decisions, and that policies and strategies are mapped out by executives who are not in touch with the realities of the local environment. If decision making is highly decentralized, head office managers may disagree with the actions taken by local management. In either case, animosities and tensions would develop within the enterprise to the detriment of smooth and efficient operation.

The parent company and local affiliate may develop different approaches over a wide number of management areas, but there are certain highly sensitive areas where differences are likely to be sharp and, at times, disruptive to overall operations. These include financing requirements (transfers to parents as against retention of earnings for expansion and growth), foreign exchange exposure management, personnel policies, and conduct of relations with host country authorities.

MNCs differ widely in the degree to which the decision-making process is centralized and the flexibility to deal with emerging situations in the field. Certain areas, such as cash management and cash positioning strategies, exchange risk exposure management, changes in the original concession agreement, and top personnel appointments are typically highly centralized. However, within the framework of overall strategies determined by the head office, managers of affiliates are sometimes given substantial flexibility in day-to-day operations. For example, the local manager may be given the power to decide whether or not to hedge foreign exchange positions of less than the equivalent $50,000, while the decision to hedge positions involving larger amounts remains vested with the financial manager at the head office.

Conflict with the Home Country

MNCs may sometimes find themselves at odds with the policies of their own home country toward the host countries where they operate. United States firms operating in Arab countries, for instance, have been asked to observe the rules of boycott of Israel imposed by their hosts, while the U.S. government itself has never recognized the validity or legality of this boycott. Some of these firms faced the difficult choice of losing their established markets in Arab countries, or observing the boycott rules and, thus, acting in a manner contrary to the policies of their own country in the Middle East.

Another example is the position of the U.S. government on the Siberian Gas Pipeline Project, which will enable Western European markets to use gas produced in Soviet fields. While many large firms from the European Economic Community are participating in several construction phases of this project, U.S. firms have been denied such participation by their own government.

MNCs generally respect and attempt to abide by the policies of their country, even when their managements disagree with the reasons or the motivation behind these policies. Some question the loyalty and patriotism of the MNCs on the grounds that they are, by definition, multinational, and owe no particular loyalty to any flag. Moreover, the profit-maximization motive is often strong enough to supersede any sense of loyalty to the flag country. Most, if not all, of MNCs' managers disagree with what they consider as their perennial critics and detractors. Nevertheless, MNCs have found ways to get around the restrictive policies of their own governments, as they have always found ways to circumvent restrictions imposed by host governments. There does not seem to be a limit to their ingenuity, their versatility, and their adaptive power to new situations and challenges.

ORGANIZATION OF THE TEXT

The text is divided into six parts reflecting in logical sequence the financial management functions facing the MNC. Part I introduces the MNC and explains its interaction and conflicts with its environment. It also includes a review of the evolution of the international monetary system within which the MNC functions. Part II explains the organization and functioning of foreign exchange markets, and measurement and management of foreign exchange exposure. Part III deals with multinational working capital management, which includes receivables and inventory management, foreign trade financing, fund positioning, and international cash management.

Part IV examines the MNC's financing decision, international banking, and the growth and functioning of the Eurocurrency and Eurobond markets. Part V deals with strategies motivating direct foreign investment, and explores the principles governing the evaluation of foreign projects and multinational national capital budgeting procedures. It also includes cost of capital theory as it applies to the multinational firm, as well as the assessment and management of the political risk. Part VI is devoted to a number of other issues impacting multinational financial management, including the taxation of the MNC, and the principles of international accounting and the control of foreign operations. That part concludes with an examination of the global debt issue and its implications to the international financial system.

The text also contains a number of case studies highlighting the financial decision-making process in simulated but realistic situations. One case study is devoted to each of the following areas of multinational financial management: measurement of the foreign exchange risk, management of foreign exchange exposure, multinational working capital management, international cash management, the external financing decision, cost of capital theory, and management of the political risk. Two case studies are devoted to each of the following topics: the application of the capital budgeting techniques to the evaluation of foreign projects, multinational banking and the borrowing-investment decision, and international accounting and control of foreign operations.

REVIEW QUESTIONS

1. Why is there so much disagreement over an operational definition of the multinational firm? Is such a definition really necessary?
2. There is so much emphasis in the literature on MNCs' operations in developing countries and the conflict with their host environment. How do you reconcile this emphasis with the fact that the bulk of multinational business is conducted in industrial countries?
3. Union Pacific, a major railroad company based in Omaha, Nebraska, has raised funds from international capital markets, including a loan from Kuwait. Does that make Union Pacific a multinational firm?
4. A number of state governments (in the United States) restrict the purchase of real estate or businesses by foreign investors within their states. How do you justify these restrictions? Could these activities, if unregulated, prove harmful or injurious to the economic and social interests of the affected communities?

5. If you were a manager of an affiliate of a U.S. firm in a foreign country which just adopted an economic development program setting priorities and goals with which you happen to disagree, what strategy would you formulate to function under these conditions? Would you consider resigning your position?
6. Is decentralization of the decision-making process an effective means of reducing the affiliate's conflict with its local environment? If you were just appointed as a manager of your firm's affiliate in a certain country, would you consider yourself better equipped to deal with conflict situations than the management at home which has had longer experience of operating in that particular country?
7. Are the objectives and interests of MNCs and their host countries necessarily irreconcilable? As a local manager, what flexibility do you have to reconcile these objectives? Would you be tempted to think that conceding to restrictions imposed by the host government might be beneficial to your firm in the long run?
8. Could conflict arise between the parent company's goal to maximize the welfare of the company's stockholders and the goal to maximize the rate of return on its investment in a foreign affiliate? If you were in charge of the affiliate's operations, would you object to measures that hurt your own profitability, but help to benefit the firm as a whole?
9. Can there be any justification for MNCs' managers to circumvent restrictions on their operations abroad imposed by their home governments? Do you agree with the contention that multinational managers have little loyalty to any government, even their own?

BIBLIOGRAPHY

AHARONI, YAIR, "On the Definition of a Multinational Corporation," *Quarterly Review of Economics and Business Studies* (Spring-Summer 1980), pp. 98–104.

AJAMI, R. A., "Multinational Firms and Host Arab Society: Areas of Conflict and Convergence," *Management International Review,* No. 1 (1980), pp. 16–27.

ARBOSE, J., "The Men Behind the Multinationals," *International Management* (November 1983), pp. 20–21.

BALIGA, B. R., "World-views and Multinational Corporations' Investments in the Less Developed Countries," *The Columbia Journal of World Business* (Summer 1984), pp. 80–84.

BARDSLEY, R. G.,"How a Multinational Ought to Invest its Surplus Cash," *Euromoney* (March 1980), p. 104.

BARTLETT, C. A., "How Multinational Organizations Evolve," *Journal of Business Strategy* (Summer 1982), pp. 20–32.

BRANDT, W. K., "Pitfalls in Planning for Multinational Operations," *Long Range Planning* (December 1980), pp. 23–31.

Business Week, "How the Multinationals Help Rather Than Hurt," June 30, 1980, p. 112.

Business Week, "Drastic New Strategies to Keep U.S. Multinationals Competitive," October 8, 1984, p. 168.

CRAY, D., "Control and Coordination in Multinational Corporations," *Journal of International Business Studies* (Fall 1984), pp. 85–98.

DANIELS, J. D., "Strategy and Structure of U.S. Multinationals: An Exploratory Study," *Academy of Management Journal* (June 1984), pp. 292–307.

DANIELS, J. and S. PATIL, "U.S. Foreign Acquisitions: An Endangered Species?" *Management International Review,* Vol. 2 (1980), pp. 25–34.

DOZ, Y. L., "Strategic Management in Multinational Companies," *Sloan Management Review* (Winter 1980), pp. 27–46.

______, "Multinational Strategy and Structure in Government Controlled Businesses," *The Columbia Journal of World Business* (Fall 1980), pp. 14–25.

DRAKE, R. L., and L. M. CAUDILL, "Management of the Large Multinational: Trends and Future Challenges," *Business Horizons* (May/June 1981), pp. 83–91.

DYMSZA, W. A., "Trends in Multinational Business and Global Environments: A Perspective," *Journal of International Business Studies* (Winter 1984), pp. 25–46.

GENDRON, M., "Simple Approach to International Business [Financial Management of Foreign Operations]," *Managerial Planning* (May/June 1985), pp. 56–60.

HAHLO, H. R., J. G. SMITH, and R. W. WRIGHT, EDS., *Nationalism and the Multinational Enterprise.* Leiden: A. W. Sithoff, 1973, and Dobbs Ferry, N.Y.: Oceana, 1973.

HILL, J. S. and R. R. STILL, "Cultural Effects of Technology Transfer by Multinational Corporations in Lesser Developed Countries," *The Columbia Journal of World Business* (Summer 1980), pp. 40–51.

______, "Effects of Urbanization on Multinational Product Planning: Markets in Lesser-developed Countries," *The Columbia Journal of World Business* (Summer 1984), pp. 62–67.

HILL, R., "Are Multinationals Aliens in the Third World?" *International Management* (January 1981), pp. 12–16.

JAIN, H. C., "Disinvestment and the Multinational Employer—A Case History from Belgium," *Personnel Journal* (March 1980), pp. 201–205.

JAIN, H. C., and Y. PURI, "Role of Multinational Corporations in Developing Countries: Policy Makers Views," *Management International Review,* No. 2 (1981), pp. 57–66.

KATZ, A., "Lively Decade for Multinationals," *Business America* (October 1980), pp. 18–20.

LITVAK, I. and C. MAULE, EDS., *Foreign Investment: The Experience of Host Countries.* New York: Praeger, 1970.

MASON, R. H., "Conflicts Between Host Countries and the Multinational Enterprise," *California Management Review* (Fall 1974), pp. 5–14.

PEARSON, J. and L. HELM, "For Multinationals, It Will Never Be the Same: Companies Are Rethinking the Costs and Risks of Worldwide Business," *Business Week* (December 1984), p. 57.

PRAHALAD, C. K., "Patterns of Strategic Control Within Multinational Corporations," *Journal of International Business Studies* (Fall 1984), pp. 55–72.

RAIZADA, V. K. V., "Multi-ethnic Corporations and Inter-ethnic Conflict," *Human Resource Management* (Fall 1981), pp. 24–27.

ROBINSON, J., "Future for Multinations in Europe," *Management Review* (February 1980), pp. 39–40.

SETHI, N. K., "Strategic Planning System for Multinational Companies," *Long Range Planning* (June 1982), pp. 80–89.

SPEAR, A. S., "Role of the Multinational Corporation in World Trade," *American Import/Export Bulletin* (August 1980), p. 10.

STULL, J. B., "Communication in Multinational Companies," *Supervisory Management* (August 1983), pp. 2–9.

TEECE, D. J., "Multinational Enterprise, Internal Governance, and Industrial Organization," *American Economic Review* (May 1985), pp. 233–238.

ULMER, M. J., "Multinational Corporations and Third World Capitalism," *Journal of Economic Issues* (June 1980), pp. 453–471.

VERNON, R., *Sovereignty at Bay: The Multinational Spread of U.S. Enterprises.* New York: Basic Books, 1971.

______, *Storm Over the Multinationals.* Cambridge, Mass.: Harvard University Press, 1977.

WATANABE, S., "Multinational Enterprises, Employment and Technology Adaptations," *International Labour Review* (November/December 1981), pp. 693–710.

WELGE, M. K., "Comparison of Managerial Structures in German Subsidiaries in France, India, and the United States," *Management International Review,* No. 21 (1981), pp. 5–21.

WILKINS, M., *The Maturing of Multinational Enterprise.* Cambridge, Mass.: Harvard University Press, 1974.

WRIGHT, P., "The Developing World to 1990: Trends and Implications for Multinational Business," *Long Range Planning* (August 1982), pp. 116–25.

2

Evolution of the International Monetary and Financial Systems

INTRODUCTION

The international monetary and financial environment in which MNCs operate today is the outcome of a long period of evolution dating back, perhaps, to the early days of the Industrial Revolution. Four phases may be distinguished in the evolutionary process:

1. The International Gold Standard: 1880–1914 and 1919–1933 (for the United States)
2. The Interwar Period: 1918–1939
3. The Bretton Woods System: 1944–1971
4. The Floating Exchange Rates Regime: 1973–Present

This chapter will discuss briefly the first three phases before examining in some depth the current international monetary system, which has had a profound impact on all facets of operation of the multinational firm. Essential to the understanding of any international monetary system is the nature and mechanism of the adjustment process to international disequilibria which is inherent in that system. Although a detailed account of this process belongs more appropriately to textbooks in international economics, financial managers of MNCs must be able to comprehend the relationship between disequilibria in the balance of payments and movements in exchange rates under alternative systems.

This chapter will conclude with a review of the stresses and problems which confront the present system and proposals to improve its functioning or, alternatively, to return to some form of a managed or a fixed exchange rate regime.

THE INTERNATIONAL GOLD STANDARD

The gold standard had its origin in England in the seventeenth century, when the value of one pound sterling was defined in terms of gold, and a gold coin with a value of one pound was struck. England, however, did not officially adopt the gold standard until 1816, when gold became legal tender for payment of public and private debt. The United States, France, and a number of European countries were either on a silver or a bimetallic standard (the currency unit was defined both in terms of gold and in terms of silver) until the latter part of the nineteenth century. Following William McKinley's victory over William Jennings Bryan, a silver advocate, in the 1896 presidential elections, the U.S. adopted the gold standard officially in 1900.

Automatic Adjustment Mechanism

An international gold standard is said to exist when two or more countries (a) define their currency unit in terms of a stated weight of gold, (b) guarantee full convertibility of all forms of money into gold, (c) allow unrestricted circulation, export, and import of gold, and (d) allow unrestricted melting and minting of gold and gold coins at the option of the holder. An essential feature of the gold standard is that countries adhere to *the rules of the game,* so that its built-in adjustment mechanism would insure (1) domestic price stability and (2) fixed exchange rates between the currencies of countries observing the rules of the gold standard.

The domestic price adjustment mechanism is based on the direct relationship between the quantity of gold and the quantity of money on the one hand, and the direct relationship between the quantity of money and the price level, as explained by the quantity theory of money, on the other hand.[1] If an increase in the quantity of money causes the price level to rise, the price of gold as a commodity will exceed its monetary value. Some gold will be withdrawn from circulation and put into other uses, since it fetches a higher value in those nonmonetary applications. As a consequence of this

[1]There are several versions of the quantity theory of money. In its classical—the so-called crude—form it postulates a proportionality between the change in the money stock and the general price level. Expressed in the format of the equation of exchange $MV = PT$, an increase in the money supply M will result in a proportionate rise in prices P, if it is assumed that both V (velocity of circulation of money) and T (goods and services exchanged for money) remain constant, at least in the short run.

withdrawal, the quantity of money will decline and, subsequently, so does the general price level. A deflationary process caused by a decline in the quantity of money will be also corrected via the flow of gold from other uses into the monetary use. As the price of gold as a commodity falls in tandem with other prices, its monetary value will begin to exceed its commodity value, causing the owners of gold to bring it to the mint.

The international automatic adjustment process of the gold standard, which links exchange rates among currencies in a fixed relationship, is accomplished by the price-specie flow mechanism. To understand the working of this mechanism, let us assume that the gold parities of the U.S. dollar and the pound sterling were established as follows:

$1.00 = 23.22 grains of gold (one troy ounce of gold is valued at $20.67)

£1.00 = 116.10 grains of gold (one troy ounce of gold is valued at £4.1675)

These parities established an exchange rate between the dollar and the pound sterling of £1.00 = $5.00. This fixed rate between the two currencies could only fluctuate within a very narrow band determined by the cost of shipping (and insuring) gold between the United States and Britain. For example, if it costs $0.10 to ship and insure 116.1 grains of gold from the United States to Britain, the maximum range of fluctuation in the exchange rate between the two currencies would be established as follows:

£1.00 = $5.10 (U.S. gold export point)

£1.00 = $4.90 (U.S. gold import point)

American merchants and tourists, under the assumptions outlined above, would not pay more than $5.10 to acquire one pound sterling, for if the pound increased above this level, it would pay them to buy 116.1 grams of gold for $5.00 in the United States, ship to Britain at a cost of $0.10, and then exchange it there for one pound sterling. This established the *gold export point* for the United States. Similarly, British merchants and tourists would not accept less than $4.90 in exchange for one pound sterling. When the exchange rate for the pound dropped below that level, they were better off buying 116.1 grams of gold in Britain, shipping it to the United States at a cost of $0.10, and exchanging it there for $5.00. This established the *gold import point* for the United States.

The price-specie flow mechanism insured that any disequilibrium in trade, and subsequent payments imbalances between the United States and Britain were corrected by the flow of gold to the surplus country. In Phase I (Exhibit 2-1), Britain sold more goods and services to the United States than it imported, which was paid for by a net flow of gold to Britain (the surplus country). The gold inflow inflated the money supply in Britain and caused a rise in the price level, while the outflow of gold from the United States

Exhibit 2-1. The Price-Specie Flow Mechanism

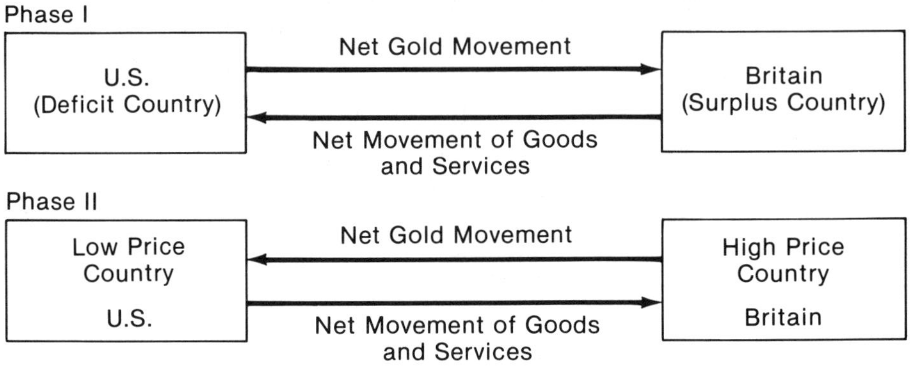

reduced the money supply there and caused a deflationary movement in prices. The disequilibrium was corrected in Phase II, which reversed the movements pattern in Phase I. Since the inflation in Britain caused its goods and services to become more expensive, and therefore less competitive than American goods and services, the United States became a net exporter of goods and services and a net importer of gold.

Decline of the Gold Standard

The automatic adjustment mechanism of the gold standard, which tended to insure at one and the same time domestic price stability and international equilibrium with fixed exchange rates, won for it many admirers among economists, statesmen, and businesses engaged in international trade. However, it should be pointed out that for the gold standard to produce such an outcome, monetary authorities must observe the rules of the game and refrain from intervention that impedes working of the adjustment mechanism. Moreover, since adjustments required time, a prolonged period of inflation in surplus countries (subject to gold inflow) and deflation in deficit countries (subject to gold outflow) must be tolerated.

While the gold standard was credited for a sustained expansion of world trade, many countries, particularly those whose economies were subjected to unemployment and other consequences of the deflationary process, became more and more disenchanted with the regime. There were other drawbacks in the gold standard which became visible in time. The gold standard did not stabilize all prices; it stabilized only the price of gold. Thus it was possible for a country to undergo rapid inflation even while the gold standard was in effect. A discovery of rich gold deposits in one country provided the basis not only of producing inflation in that country, but also of that country's exporting inflation, via the price-specie-flow mechanism, to other countries. Moreover, while world trade benefited from the regime of stable exchange rates, its growth was subject to the increase in gold production devoted to monetary uses, since gold provided the only means of international settlement.

As world statesmen grew more and more impatient of subjecting their economies to the vagaries of gold production and the price-specie flow mode of reestablishing equilibrium, World War I dealt a devastating blow to the gold standard. The war considerably strained international relations and led many countries to impose restrictions on gold exports. Adversaries inflated their economies to finance the cost of the war, which tested and strained existing currency parities. Country after country imposed restrictions on imports and capital movements, while hostilities at sea severely disrupted international trade. By the time the war ended, the gold standard was virtually dead.

THE INTERWAR PERIOD 1918–1939

During World War I, most countries had inflated their economies to pay for the war effort, which made it difficult, if not impossible, for most of them to return to the gold standard on the basis of the original parities. The United States reinstated the gold standard, on the basis of the original parity, in 1919. Britain also reinstated the gold standard with the original gold parity in 1925, an act which was widely criticized by many economists, including John Maynard Keynes, since the country underwent substantial inflation during the war. Such an action severely hampered British export performance in the postwar period, and contributed to the fading out of the pound sterling as the eminent currency of world trade and payments. By 1931 the strains on the pound proved irreversible, which resulted in its being declared inconvertible into gold. This development shifted the pressure from the pound to the U.S. dollar, the only remaining currency convertible into gold, and which eventually culminated in the suspension of dollar convertibility into gold in 1933.

The interwar period was generally characterized by the rising tide of nationalism and protectionism, as well as by widespread chaos in international monetary relations. Countries engaged in competitive devaluation of their currencies in an attempt to promote their exports, and imposed tariffs and other restrictions on imports. The prevailing exchange rate regime was a mixture of widely fluctuating rates and rates maintained by elaborate exchange control devices. The era was also characterized by runaway inflations in some countries, particularly in Germany, an event which contributed to the rise of the National Socialists to political leadership in that country.

World War II inflicted a heavy toll on the economies of the warring nations and substantially disrupted international trade and monetary relationships. Anticipating the end of hostilities, monetary and economic policy leaders of the victorious powers began to reshape the international monetary order. There was a need for a system which would contribute to the reconstruction of the devastated economies and reestablish the necessary environment for the growth in international trade and investments. Restoration of the gold standard in its original form was not only unthinkable, but was thought to be undesirable as well. Yet there was a yearning among these leaders and a number of eminent economists for the orderly regime of stable exchange rate environment that contributed significantly to the prosperity of the world.

THE BRETTON WOODS INTERNATIONAL MONETARY SYSTEM (1944–1971)

The 1944 meeting of world powers and their monetary experts in Bretton Woods, New Hampshire produced a workable formula which paved the way for the resumption of growth in world trade and the reconstruction of economies badly ravaged by the war. The agreement, initialed by the conferees on behalf of their nations,[2] produced a blueprint of what came to be known as the Bretton Woods System.

The Parity System

The international monetary order which emerged from the Bretton Woods agreements placed the U.S. dollar, the world's leading currency of world trade and payments, as the linchpin of the system, and expressed currencies of all other participant nations at a fixed parity with the dollar. The parity of the U.S. dollar, the only currency to be fully convertible into gold, was established at $35 per troy ounce. This was backed by the undertaking of the United States government to guarantee unconditionally the international convertibility of its currency.

The exchange rates of all signatory countries were pegged to the U.S. dollar at parities which reflected, at that time, appropriate conversion rates against the U.S. dollar, given weight to changed economic and financial conditions in each country since the suspension of the gold standard. Under the agreements, the monetary authorities of signatory nations undertook to maintain the parities of their currencies vis-a-vis the dollar, and limit deviations of exchange rates from respective parities within a narrow band of

[2]Although the U.S.S.R. and some of its East European allies took part in the proceedings, they did not initial the Bretton Woods agreement, nor did they join the International Monetary Fund. However, subsequently, Yugoslavia, Romania, and Hungary joined. Switzerland, because of its professed neutrality, which precludes joining international bodies such as the United Nations, is not an IMF member. Peoples' Republic of China replaced China (Taiwan) in 1981.

one percent above and below established parities. Such undertaking envisaged that countries must pursue appropriate economic and financial policies to maintain the established parities, and must intervene in exchange markets, if necessary, to insure that actual exchange rate would be maintained within the defined band.

The working of the Bretton Woods parity system described above is illustrated in Exhibit 2-2.

Suppose that the market demand for French francs, whose parity with the dollar was established at FF 1.00 = \$0.25, is represented by *DD*. The demand for French francs originates primarily from importers of French goods who wish to pay for these imports. This demand intersects the market supply schedule of French francs *SS* at parity (French francs are supplied to the market primarily by French importers who wish to buy other currencies to pay for imports of goods and services from the rest of the world). The demand and supply schedules of currencies as shown in Exhibit 2-2 conform to the normal shape of such schedules for commodities. As the exchange rate of the French franc, the price of the franc in terms of the dollar, decreases, more francs will be demanded to pay for goods and services imported from France, thus the downward slope of the demand curve. The supply curve slopes upward, because as the exchange rate for the franc appreciates, French importers will supply more francs in

Exhibit 2-2. Working of the Bretton Woods Parity System

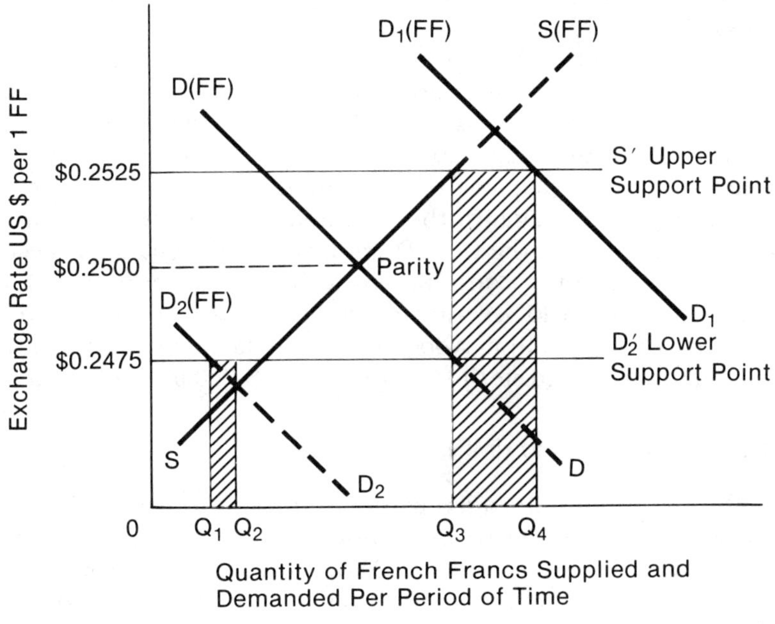

order to buy larger quantities of other currencies to pay for increased imports of goods and services from the rest of the world.

Let us assume that for some reason, the demand for French goods, such as wines and perfumes, increases sharply. To pay for sharply higher imports from France, importers in other countries will have to buy (demand) more French francs. The demand curve for francs shifts to the right and is depicted in the chart as D_1D_1. If market demand depicted by D_1D_1 is allowed to intersect market supply SS without intervention on the part of French monetary authorities, the exchange rate will go above the upper limit of \$0.25 plus one percent or \$0.2525 per franc. However, that situation should not be allowed to take place under the Bretton Woods system. In order to prevent this, Bank de France, France's central bank, must intervene at the upper support point by supplying whatever quantity of francs is necessary to prevent the exchange rate from going over the upper support point. The supply curve of French francs thus becomes perfectly elastic at the exchange rate of \$0.2525 per French franc. The quantity of francs supplied by the central bank is shown by the shaded area above Q_3Q_4.

A sharp decrease in the demand for French goods will shift the demand curve for French francs to D_2D_2. Such a shift, if allowed to manifest itself in the marketplace, will produce an equilibrium exchange rate below the lower support point. This outcome is avoided by the obligation of Bank de France to intervene in the exchange markets to buy whatever quantities of francs that are needed to prevent the exchange rate from falling below support point (shown by the shaded area above Q_1Q_2). The demand for French francs thus becomes perfectly elastic at the lower support point, as shown by D_2D_2'.

The Bretton Woods system provided for adjustment of the original parities if the economic and financial circumstances of a member country warranted such an adjustment. This feature, which earned the system the nickname of the "adjustable peg," allowed a member to devalue (lower its currency's parity against the U.S. dollar) or revalue its currency (raise its currency's parity against the U.S. dollar) up to five percent without prior consultations with the IMF. Devaluation or revaluation exceeding five percent required prior consultations with, and tacit approval of, the executive board of the IMF. Several such adjustments were made over the 30-year history of the Bretton Woods system, notable among which is the devaluation of the pound sterling in 1967 from \$2.80 to \$2.40, or by 14.3 percent.

The International Monetary Fund (IMF)

The Bretton Woods agreements gave birth to two international financial institutions: the International Monetary Fund (IMF) and the International Bank for Reconstruction and Development (IBRD), commonly referred to as the World Bank. The IMF was entrusted with the broad function of overseeing the new international monetary order, while the World Bank was to play a major role initially in the postwar reconstruction effort and, subsequently, in furthering the development and economic growth of the less-developed countries, now commonly referred to as developing countries or LDCs.

The IMF, whose original membership included signatories of the Bretton Woods agreements,[3] was envisioned as a pool of currencies contributed by members which are available to members encountering balance of payments difficulties[4] in the form of temporary short-term assistance. The pool was formed by having each country contribute 25 percent of its quota in gold and 75 percent in its own currency in the form of noninterest-bearing notes. The original quota for each country was established by a formula which took into account several variables such as GNP, global trade, population, and other macroeconomic and financial criteria. The quotas were revised upward several times, the latest round of which was approved in March 1983 and raised the global quotas to over SDR90 billion.[5] A country's quota as a ratio of the global quota determines its voting power.

The voting power of some countries, particularly the large ones, had to be reshuffled several times and were reduced to make room for new members, and to reflect the ascending economic and financial power of OPEC countries. As of April 30, 1984, the United States' share of total quotas was 19.32 percent, followed by the United Kingdom (6.70 percent), the Federal Republic of Germany (5.84 percent), France (4.85 percent), Japan (4.57 percent) and Saudi Arabia (3.47 percent).[6] United States voting power, though it declined over the years, still gives it a veto power, since amendments to the articles of agreement and other major decisions require total votes representing 85 percent of the total quotas. The IMF is managed by a 22-member executive board, six of whom are appointed by governments of the countries listed above holding the largest quotas. The remaining executive directors are elected annually by the rest of member countries combining quotas of individual countries to form, for the most part, regional groupings of members. The managing director is appointed by the executive board for a five-year term. The managing director, by tradition a western European banker or a statesman, is the chairman of the executive board. The supreme governing body of the IMF is the board of governors, on which all member countries are represented normally by either the minister of finance (Secretary of Treasury for the United States)

[3]Membership increased from the original 45 members to 149 members as of December 31, 1985.

[4]The balance of payments of a country lists payments for and receipts from all foreign transactions, giving rise to supply for or demand of its currency during a period of time, normally a year. See Appendix B to this chapter.

[5]International Monetary Fund, *Annual Report* (1984), p. 74. The Special Drawing Right (SDR) is defined in a later section in this chapter.

[6]*Ibid.*, p. 154.

or governor of the central bank. The board of governors convenes once a year to deliberate and resolve major policy issues.

Providing short-term balance-of-payments support for member countries, to enable them to maintain their currencies' parities, takes the form of drawings in tranches (each tranche is equal to 25 percent of a country's quota) from the available pool of currencies. The drawing, technically termed a "purchase" of foreign currencies, is paid for by that country's own currency in the form of noninterest-bearing notes. Thus, each successive drawing of a tranche will increase the amount of the member's currency held by the IMF by 25 percent of the quota. The "purchase" is reversed in three to five years, unless rescheduled, by having the borrowing country "repurchase" its currency with foreign exchange. Drawing successive credit tranches is subject to increasing degree of conditionality. Conditionality means that successive drawings of tranches will be subject to increasing restrictions and conditions imposed by the IMF to ensure that the borrowing country is taking corrective policy measures.

Access to IMF resources has been expanded over the years from the original short-term advances under regular tranche policies by the creation of several specialized facilities. These facilities include:

1. *Compensatory Financing Facility.* Established in 1963 to provide financial assistance to members experiencing temporary export shortfalls. This facility was later extended to countries experiencing temporary sharp increases in the cost of their imports.
2. *Buffer Stock Financing Facility.* Established in 1969 to assist members in balance of payments need for financing their contributions to approved international buffer stocks of primary products.
3. *Extended Facility.* Established in 1974 to provide medium-term assistance to members to overcome serious structural, as contrasted with temporary, balance of payments disequilibria. This three-year stabilization program contrasts with IMF's earlier practice of supporting member countries' short-term financial programs, usually carried out over a one-year period.
4. *Oil Facility.* Established in 1974 to assist members most seriously affected by oil price increases instituted by OPEC countries. This facility was terminated.
5. *Trust Fund.* Established in 1976 to provide balance-of-payments assistance on concessional terms to the 25 members with the lowest per capita income. Resources for this fund were derived from part of the profits realized from the sale of gold held by the IMF for member countries, following the demonitization of gold in 1976. This facility was terminated in 1981.
6. *Supplementary Financial Facility.* Established in 1977 to provide additional financing to members suffering serious balance of payments difficulties, particularly those with substantial foreign debt. This facility was made necessary by the policy of enlarging access of members to the resources of the institution.

Total access of members to IMF resources under tranche drawings and the facilities described earlier has been considerably enlarged over the years. Access by members during 1984 was subject to an annual limit of 125 percent of quota, three-year limit of 375 percent of quota, and a cumulative limit of 500 percent of quota.[7]

Special Drawing Rights (SDRs)

There was some concern in the late 1960s that international reserves, consisting at that time of gold, IMF gold tranche positions, and convertible currencies, were not growing at a pace consistent with the expansion of international trade and consequent greater need for liquidity. To supplement these reserves, the IMF decided in 1967 to create a new international asset (SDRs) and allocate them to member countries in proportion to their quotas. SDRs are used only by official agencies of member government for international settlements. Total SDRs in existence on April 30, 1985 amounted to SDR 21.4 billion (about 6 percent of global reserves) allocated in several issues which took place between 1971 and 1981. Proposals to allocate further SDR issues have not been favored by a sufficient majority of the total voting power (85 percent).

When the SDR was first issued in 1971, it was defined as having the same gold parity as the U.S. dollar, that is, 0.888571 gram or 1/35 ounce. However, with the subsequent devaluations of the dollar, and the flotation of major currencies, the SDR was redefined as an average value of a basket of 16 major currencies weighted according to their importance in world trade. The basket was simplified on January 1, 1981 to five major currencies (the U.S. dollar, the Deutsch mark, the French franc, the Japanese yen, and the pound sterling) comprising a trade weighted index. The basket and the weights are to be revised every five years. The value of the SDR is computed daily by the IMF in terms of the U.S. dollar and all major currencies.[8]

The value of the SDR appreciated against the U.S. dollar in the late 1970s and the early 1980s due to the appreciation of the other components

[7]International Monetary Fund, *Annual Report 1984*, p. 78.

[8]The SDR value is computed by summing up the values in U.S. dollars, based on market exchange rates, of a basket of five currencies, using the weights established in the last revision effective January 1, 1986. Below is the calculation of the SDR value on February 10, 1986.

CURRENCIES	AMOUNT	EXCHANGE RATE IN FOREIGN CURRENCY PER U.S. $ ON FEBRUARY 10, 1986	U.S. DOLLAR EQUIVALENT
U.S. dollar	0.4520	1.0000	0.4520
Deusche mark	0.5270	2.3820	0.2212
French franc	1.0200	7.2990	0.1397
Japanese yen	33.4000	187.6000	0.1780
Pound sterling	0.08930	1.4120	0.1261
			1.1170

Thus the SDR unit was worth $1.1170 on February 10, 1986, or U.S. $1.00 = SDR 0.8953.

of the basket against the U.S. dollar. However, with the sharp rise in the value of the dollar against the other four currencies in the basket in 1984 and early 1985, the value of the SDR dropped below parity with the U.S. dollar.

As the SDR is a composite of currencies that are not likely to move in the same direction or in the same degree, its value is likely to be more stable than any of the components. This relative stability of the SDR, as a unit of account, has had wide appeal in international financial markets. There have been issues of SDR-denominated Eurobonds as well as SDR-denominated syndicated loans and SDR-denominated deposits (see Chapter 9). OPEC countries seriously considered switching from the dollar to the SDR as the pricing unit for their marker crude oil in late 1970s, but eventually discarded the idea. In addition to being the unit of account for IMF operations and transactions, a large number of international and regional organizations also use the SDR as a unit of account, or as the basis for a unit of account.[9]

Strains on the Bretton Woods System

The gold-exchange dollar standard created by the Bretton Woods agreements had been deservedly credited with providing a stable foreign exchange and payments environment which served the world needs very well during the three decades that it lasted. World trade and international investment flourished under this regime, and the economies of a large number of newly independent nations were helped by the facilities and assistance made available to them by the IMF.

There were, however, a number of inherent drawbacks in the system which manifested themselves over the years, as well as events that jolted the international monetary and financial system, particularly in its later years. In the first place, the "adjustable peg" provided a safety valve for changing currency parities whenever underlying economic and financial circumstances of the country in question warranted it. This type of situation, described as a fundamental disequilibrium in the balance of payments of a certain country, provided speculators with a one-way option, which contributed to a further exacerbating of the imbalance in its international payments. Speculators in foreign exchange markets take positions on the future course of a currency, hoping to realize profits if future exchange rate

[9]The international and regional organizations using the SDR as a unit of account, or as the basis for a unit of account, as of April 30, 1985 were the African Development Bank, African Development Fund, Arab Monetary Fund, Asian Clearing Union, Asian Development Bank, Great Lakes States Development Bank, East African Development Bank, Economic Community of West African States, European Conference of Postal and Telecommunications Administrations, International Centre for Settlement of Investment Disputes, International Development Association, International Fund for Agricultural Development, International Telecommunication Union, Islamic Development Bank, Nordic Investment Bank, and the Universal Postal Union. See the International Monetary Fund, *Annual Report 1984,* p. 88.

movements coincide with their expectations. Selling short a currency under pressure did not involve much of a risk to speculators, since it was unthinkable that countries in this position would revalue their currencies in the face of substantial losses of reserves. Such speculation on a massive scale could force the hand of governments and in some instances, as in the 1967 devaluation of the pound sterling, hastened such an outcome. This kind of speculation, generally described by economists as destabilizing, turned against the U.S. dollar in the late 1960s and early 1970s when it became increasingly evident that the linchpin currency of the system itself was vulnerable.

The system also suffered from some internal structural problems; the most widely recognized was the imbalance or the assymetry of the roles and the responsibilities of the surplus and the deficit nations. Countries experiencing persistent deficits in their balance of payments had no real option but to undergo belt tightening and painful economic policy measures, if they wanted to stop the drain on their reserves. Moreover, these countries had to accept the policy prescriptions of the IMF if they were to use the institution's resources. On the other hand, surplus countries felt no such immediate compulsion to take corrective action. Although sustained increases in their international reserves meant that they might have to put up with some inflationary consequences, their options were much more comfortable than those of the deficit nations. Moreover, there were mechanisms whereby an increase in reserves could be neutralized and prevented from resulting in undue expansion in the domestic money supply. The IMF had little or no clout with these countries, since they were net lenders to the institution rather than net borrowers.

The IMF has also been widely faulted for its rigid approach to payments disequilibria experienced by member countries, particularly among the LDCs. The heart of the controversy revolves around the conditionality issue,[10] which refers to the set of policies that a member country is required to pursue as a condition to the use of IMF's resources. These policies are mainly designed to ensure that the use of resources by needing members is appropriate and temporary. The IMF distinguishes between two levels of conditionality. Low conditionality requires only that a member, desirous of making a drawing, represents that it has a balance of payments need and is taking appropriate measures to resolve its deficit. High conditionality, which is involved in drawings at high credit tranches and/or gaining enlarged access to the Fund's resources, involves the formulation of a formal financial program containing specific measures designed to eliminate the country's payments disequilibrium. Use of IMF's resources under these circumstances requires IMF concurrence that the stabilization program is

[10]See Institute for International Economics, *IMF Conditionality* (1983). The volume contains 21 papers presented on the subject at a conference held by the Institute of International Economics in March 1982 in Virginia.

adequate for the achievement of its objectives, and a commitment by the member to implement it.

The controversy over IMF conditionality centers on the disagreement over the source of payments disequilibria and, therefore, appropriate remedies to deal with them. The IMF has traditionally maintained that balance of payments difficulties are frequently associated with the prevalence of excess demand pressures. Inflationary pressures are induced mainly by expansionary financial policies, and demand management, in the form of deflationary policies and other austerity measures, has been the centerpiece of IMF policies.[11] While it is true that excessive demand, arising mainly from public sector deficit financing, has been the major cause of payments imbalances among most countries, cost-push induced inflation should not be neglected.[12] Some IMF critics concede that its diagnosis of the root of payments imbalances has been generally correct, but charge that the IMF has shown disdain for gradualism in the application of the medicine, and a decided preference for shock treatment.[13] This approach, it is contended, has often caused recessionary trends, unemployment, underutilization of the industrial sector, and political disorders.

THE CRISIS OF 1971–73; ATTEMPTS TO SAVE THE FIXED EXCHANGE RATES SYSTEM

The seeds of destruction of the Bretton Woods system were sown in the immediate post-World War II era, when the United States undertook substantial commitments under the Marshall Plan and other schemes to reconstruct and revitalize the economies of its allies and other countries ravaged by the war. Partly due to the pressures of these commitments, its balance of payments swung into deficit in the late 1950s.

The continuing deficits in the U.S. balance of payments in the early 1960s were a welcome development, since these deficits provided the means of increasing international reserves. With a sustained rapid increase in world trade and investments, and virtually all newly mined gold going into hoards and industrial uses, deficits incurred by the major reserve-currency country (the U.S.) provided needed liquidity for international payments. However, as these deficits grew, and problems affecting other reserve-currency countries such as the United Kingdom and France developed, confidence in the system began to weaken. Successive crises which led to the devaluation of the pound sterling (1967) and the French franc (1969), as well as wide fluctuations in the price of gold in the London market, aggravated the situation.

[11]William B. Dale, "Financing Adjustments of Payments Imbalances," *IMF Conditionality, op. cit.,* p. 4.

[12]Dragaslav Avramovic, "The Role of the International Monetary Fund: The Disputes, Qualifications, and Future," *IMF Conditionality, op. cit.,* p. 593.

[13]Sidney Dell, "Stabilization: The Political Economy of Overkill," *IMF Conditionality, op. cit.,* p. 21.

The United States adopted a series of measures during the 1960s to stem the rising deficits in its balance of payments. These measures included the Interest Equalization Tax of 1963, voluntary controls on new capital outflow in 1965, and mandatory controls imposed in 1968 which limited new dollar outflows to a given percentage of a base year figure. The worsening in the U.S. external payments situation despite these measures threw into doubt its ability to honor the gold conversion commitment, the centerpiece of the Bretton Woods system. This doubt was heightened by the growing realization that gold held at that time by the United States could meet only a small fraction of dollar claims held by foreign official monetary institutions, if holders of such claims insisted on conversion.

Expectation of a record deficit in 1971 led to massive selling of the U.S. dollar in world financial markets, and a rise in the free market price of gold. Responding to the inevitable, on August 15, 1971, President Nixon suspended official purchases and sales of gold by the U.S. Treasury, thus terminating *de facto* the Bretton Woods fixed-exchange rate system. Currencies of most of the leading trading countries were allowed to float in relation to the dollar. Exchange rates, adjusting to market forces and speculative "hot money" movements, resulted in a *de facto* depreciation of the dollar vis-a-vis currencies of most of its trading partners.

An international monetary conference was held in Washington D.C. in December 1971 to salvage the fixed-exchange rate system. The outcome of this conference was the Smithsonian Agreement, which provided for:

1. A change in the gold parity of the U.S. dollar from $35 to $38.02 per troy ounce, or a devaluation of about 8.57 percent. Currencies of surplus countries were revalued upwards by percentages ranging from 7.4 percent for the Canadian dollar to 16.9 percent for the Japanese yen. The purpose of these exchange rate adjustments was to produce a realignment of currencies which reflected better the realistic values of these currencies.
2. The band of fluctuations from par values was widened from Bretton Woods' one percent to 2 ¼ percent above and below parity. Widening of the band of fluctuations was intended to give countries more flexibility in managing their exchange rates and their financial policies.

The objective of the Smithsonian Agreement was not to save the Bretton Woods system, since convertibility of the U.S. dollar into gold was no longer an undertaking of the U.S. government. It was rather an attempt to arrive at a compromise which would give the world a somewhat more flexible fixed exchange rate system. However, these adjustments, significant as they were, failed to stem the tide of speculation against the weak currencies (the U.S. dollar and the pound sterling) and the massive capital inflow to the strong currencies (particularly the deutsche mark, the Swiss franc, the Dutch guilder, and Japanese yen). Another devaluation of the U.S. dollar (by 10 percent, raising the price of gold to $42.22 per troy ounce) in February 1973 could not change the tide of currency flows in favor of the strong European currencies and the Japanese yen. Exchange markets were in turmoil and were closed during most of March 1973. When they reopened, most major currencies began to float.

In an attempt to limit exchange rate fluctuations between currencies closely linked by a common market, members of the European Economic Community (EEC) and other European countries that were likely to join the EEC entered into the European Joint Float Agreement. This arrangement, which was nicknamed "the snake," aimed at keeping values of members' currencies within a relatively narrow band of 2¼ percent with respect to each other. The band of the fluctuation of the joint float with respect to the U.S. dollar was twice as wide, or 4½ percent under the Smithsonian Agreement. The arrangement was less than a total success, although it helped stabilize exchange relationships among countries with closely allied economies. Market pressures forced both the United Kingdom and Italy to withdraw soon after the agreement was negotiated in May 1972. Monetary cooperation among EEC countries was eventually embodied in the European Monetary System, which was established in March 1978.

THE FLOATING EXCHANGE RATE REGIME, 1973—PRESENT

The turmoil in exchange markets did not cease when major currencies were allowed to float beginning March 1973. The remaining years of the decade produced events and changes that sent shock waves throughout the international monetary system and resulted in far-reaching effects on the economies of most countries. These events are explained in the following paragraphs in chronological order.

The precipitous rise in oil prices beginning in October 1973, which quadrupled within a span of a little over a year, had profound impact on the exchange market and the alignment of the world's major currencies. Ironically, though OPEC pricing policies jolted the world, it produced a temporary salutary effect on foreign exchange markets. This development strengthened the currencies of countries which were substantially self-reliant in oil and energy sources (notably the United States), and countries with recent important oil discoveries (notably the United Kingdom and Norway, which benefited from the oil and gas discoveries in the North Sea). Responding to the improvement in its balance of payments, the United States eliminated in early 1974 all remaining controls on capital outflows instituted during the 1960s.

The energy crisis adversely affected all nonoil-exporting countries, particularly LDCs, which had to divert substantial resources to finance their oil imports. The shock produced initially a worldwide recession which lasted until early 1976. When economic activity started to pick up, inflation rates in most countries rose sharply.

The oil crisis severely tested the ability of the world's financial institutions to recycle the huge balance of payments surpluses garnered by OPEC countries (the so-called petrodollars). Major multinational banks and international financial institutions must be credited with performing this essential function rather smoothly. It must be noted, however, that the massive borrowing by a large number of LDCs to pay for their oil imports was a major factor in the emergence of the global debt crisis in the early 1980s (see Chapter 20).

The volatility of exchange rates during the 1974–1977 period intensified, reflecting in part the oil price shock, differentials in inflation and interest rates, and massive speculative activity. These developments produced nonalignments in the currencies of members of the European Joint Float, "The Snake," which led to the withdrawal of France (1976), Sweden (1977), and Norway (1978).

In an attempt to bring the institutional framework of the IMF in line with the system that had actually evolved, a committee was formed in 1974 to propose needed reforms in the international monetary system.[14] These deliberations culminated in the Jamaica Agreement in 1976. The main features of the new agreement which became effective in April 1978 are (1) legalization of the *de facto* regime of floating exchange rates and affirmation of the right of each country to peg or float its currency, and (2) demonitization of gold as a reserve asset. The 25 percent of the quota of member countries which until then was payable in gold, was to be paid in the form of currencies acceptable to the IMF or SDRs. One-third of the gold held by the IMF was sold over a period of four years beginning in early 1976, and profits realized on that sale (the difference between the official and market prices) were placed in a trust fund to help the 25 members with the lowest per capita income.

The major responsiblity of the IMF under the revised system is surveillance of the exchange rate arrangements adopted by members. Surveillance is exercised in the form of annual consultations with members during which their exchange rate and financial and economic policies are reviewed.

CURRENT EXCHANGE RATE ARRANGEMENTS

The current exchange regime is generally described as a flexible or floating rate system because the exchange rates of the U.S. dollar and currencies of the major industrial countries are essentially determined by free market forces. These currencies account for the bulk of international payments. The system is sometimes referred to as a "managed float" system, since monetary authorities intervene in exchange markets on occasions to offset

[14]The Committee for the Reform of the International Monetary System and Related Issues, also known as the Committee of Twenty.

what they consider destabilizing or erratic factors, and to maintain orderly exchange markets.

The majority of countries continue to peg their currencies in one form or another. According to Exhibit 2-3, showing exchange rate arrangements as of December 31, 1985, 92 countries, out of a total IMF membership of 149, continue to peg their currencies either against a single currency or composite of currencies (33 countries peg their currencies to the U.S. dollar, 13 countries peg to the French franc, 11 peg to the SDR, 31 peg to other baskets, and four peg to other currencies). Four member countries did not report their exchange rate arrangements. The remaining countries (53) described their exchange rate arrangements as floating independently, or as adjusting according to a set of indicators (the so-called *managed float*).

The agreement which gave rise to the European Joint Float, or the "snake," was replaced by a more elaborate arrangement in 1978 when the European Monetary System (EMS) was established. Like its predecessor, the EMS, which began operating in 1979, sought to provide a measure of stability for exchange rates among its members by setting up:

1. A system of bilateral rates which permits fluctuations of up to 2¼ percent from the central rates. (The Italian lira is allowed a band of 6 percent due to its volatility.)
2. A European Currency Unit (ECU), which is a weighted cocktail of member countries' currencies, to serve as a unit of account for the system.
3. A European Monetary Cooperation Fund (FECOM), to which every member makes a contribution in domestic and international currencies based on its quota. This pool of currencies is made available to members in the form of credit facilities, in the same manner that the IMF resources are used by member countries.
4. A provision to support the economic growth of the weaker members by transfer of resources to these members.

The performance of the floating exchange rate regime since its inception in 1973 has been less satisfactory. The system has been plagued by short-term volatility, which has tended to discourage investment and trade by increasing the financial risks for participants. There is also some evidence that this volatility has hurt the export performance of LDCs and has increased the level of reserves which these countries need to cope with exchange market uncertainties. According to the report of the G-24 Working Group, the floating rate system has not been able to provide "a framework that facilitates the exchange of goods, services, and capital among countries, which sustains sound economic growth and helps develop orderly underlying conditions necessary for financial and economic stability."[15]

[15]International Monetary Fund, "Report of the Deputies of the Intergovernmental Group of 24," *IMF Survey* (September 1985), pp. 2–16. See Appendix A to this chapter for excerpts from this report.

Exhibit 2-3. Exchange Rates and Exchange Arrangements, December 31, 1985

Member (currency)	Exchange Rate Pegged to	Exchange Rate[1]	Exchange Rate Otherwise Determined[2,3]
Afghanistan (Afghani)[4]			50.60
Algeria (dinar)[4]	bskt	4.7728	
Antigua and Barbuda (EC$)[5]	$	2.70	
Argentina (austral)[4]			0.8005
Australia (dollar)			1.46864
Austria (schilling)	bskt	17.33	
Bahamas (dollar)[4]	$	1.00	
Bahrain (dinar)			0.376
Bangladesh (taka)[4]	bskt	31.00	
Barbados (dollar)	$	2.0113	
Belgium (franc)[4,6]			50.36
Belize (dollar)	$	2.00	
Benin (franc)	F	50.00	
Bhutan (ngultrum)	Re	1.00	
Bolivia (peso)[4]	$		1,692,000.00
Botswana (pula)[8]	bskt		
Brazil (cruzeiro)[4,7]			10,440.00
Burkina Faso (franc)	F	50.00	
Burma (kyat)	SDR	8.5085	7.74613
Burundi (franc)	SDR	122.7	111.706
Cameroon (franc)	F	50.00	
Canada (dollar)			1.3975
Cape Verde (escudo)	bskt	85.3971	
Central African Republic (franc)	F	50.00	
Chad (franc)	F	50.00	
Chile (peso)[4,7]			180.2
China (renminbi)[4]	bskt	3.2015	
Colombia (peso)[4,7]			172.20
Comoros (franc)	F	50.00	
Congo (franc)	F	50.00	
Costa Rica (colón)[4]			53.70
Côte d'Ivoire (franc)	F	50.00	
Cyprus (pound)[8]	bskt		
Denmark (krone)[6]			8.969
Djibouti (franc)	$	177.721	
Dominica (EC$)[5]	$	2.70	
Dominican Rep. (peso)[4]			3.00
Ecuador (sucre)[4]			95.75
Egypt (pound)[4]	$	0.70	
El Salvador (colón)[4]	$	2.50	
Equatorial Guinea (franc)	F	50.00	
Ethiopia (birr)	$	2.07	
Fiji (dollar)	bskt	1.120448	
Finland (markka)	bskt	5.417	
France (franc)[6]			7.561
Gabon (franc)	F	50.00	
Gambia, The (dalasi)[4]	£	5.00	
Germany, Fed. Rep. of (deutsche mark)[6]			2.4613
Ghana (cedi)	$	60.00	
Greece (drachma)			147.76
Grenada (EC$)[4,5]	$	2.70	
Guatemala (quetzal)[4]	$	1.00	
Guinea (syli)[4]	SDR	24.6853	22.4735
Guinea-Bissau (peso)[8]			
Guyana (dollar)	bskt	4.15	
Haiti (gourde)	$	5.00	
Honduras (lempira)[4]	$	2.00	
Hungary (forint)[4]	bskt	47.347	
Iceland (króna)			42.06
India (rupee)			12.316545
Indonesia (rupiah)			1125.00
Iran, Islamic Rep. of (rial)[4]	SDR	92.30	84.0298
Iraq (dinar)	$	0.310857	
Ireland (pound)[6]			0.804182
Israel (shekel)[4]			1499.5
Italy (lira)[6]			1678.5
Jamaica (dollar)[4]			5.48
Japan (yen)			200.5
Jordan (dinar)	SDR	0.387747	0.353004
Kampuchea, Democratic (riel)[8,9]			
Kenya (shilling)	SDR	17.887	16.2843
Korea (won)			890.20
Kuwait (dinar)	bskt	0.28901	
Lao People's Dem. Rep. (kip)[4]	$	10.00	
Lebanon (pound)			18.10
Lesotho (loti)	R	1.00	
Liberia (dollar)	$	1.00	
Libya (dinar)	$	0.296053	
Luxembourg (franc)[4,6]			50.36
Madagascar (franc)	bskt	635.79	
Malawi (kwacha)	bskt	1.6792	
Malaysia (ringgit)	bskt	2.4135	
Maldives (rufiyaa)		7.1286	
Mali (franc)	F	50.00	
Malta (lira)	bskt	0.386757	
Mauritania (ouguiya)[4,8]	bskt	77.07	
Mauritius (rupee)	bskt	14.31	
Mexico (peso)[4]			371.70
Morocco (dirham)			9.62125
Mozambique (metical)	bskt	41.587	
Nepal (rupee)[4]	bskt	20.70	
Netherlands (guilder)[6]			2.772
New Zealand (dollar)			2.002002
Nicaragua (córdoba)[4]	$	10.00	
Niger (franc)	F	50.00	
Nigeria (naira)[4,8]			
Norway (krone)	bskt	7.5825	
Oman (rial Omani)	$	0.345395	
Pakistan (rupee)			15.9878
Panama (balboa)	$	1.00	
Papua New Guinea (kina)[8]	bskt		
Paraguay (guaraní)[4]	$	240.00	
Peru (sol)[4,7]		13,942.77	
Philippines (peso)			19.0015
Portugal (escudo)[7]			157.487
Qatar (riyal)			3.64
Romania (leu)[4]	bskt	11.23	
Rwanda (franc)	SDR	102.71	93.5070
St. Christopher and Nevis (EC$)[5]	$	2.70	
St. Lucia (EC$)[5]	$	2.70	
St. Vincent (EC$)[5]	$	2.70	
São Tomé and Principe (dobra)	SDR	45.25	41.1955
Saudi Arabia (riyal)			3.645
Senegal (franc)	F	50.00	
Seychelles (rupee)	SDR	7.2345	6.58628
Sierra Leone (leone)[4]	SDR	5.74119	5.22677
Singapore (dollar)	bskt	2.105	
Solomon Islands (dollar)	bskt	1.61264	
Somalia (shilling)[4,8]			
South Africa (rand)			2.55754
Spain (peseta)			154.15
Sri Lanka (rupee)			27.4075
Sudan (pound)[4]	$	2.50	
Suriname (guilder)	$	1.785	
Swaziland (lilangeni)	R	1.00	
Sweden (krona)	bskt	7.6155	
Syrian Arab Rep. (pound)[4]	$	3.925	
Tanzania (shilling)	bskt	16.41475	
Thailand (baht)	bskt	26.65	
Togo (franc)	F	50.00	
Tonga (pa'anga)	A$	1.00	
Trinidad and Tobago (dollar)	$	3.609	
Tunisia (dinar)	bskt	0.758217	
Turkey (lira)[4]			576.855
Uganda (shilling)[4]			1400.00
United Arab Emirates (dirham)			3.671
United Kingdom (pound)			0.692281
United States (dollar)			1.00
Uruguay (new peso)			124.875
Vanuatu (vatu)[8]	SDR	110.14	100.271
Venezuela (bolívar)[4]	$	7.50	
Viet Nam (dong)[4]	SDR	10.37883	9.44887
Western Samoa (tala)			2.30627
Yemen Arab Rep. (rial)	$	6.485	
Yemen, People's Dem. Rep. (dinar)	$	0.345399	
Yugoslavia (dinar)[4]			312.805
Zaïre (zaïre)			55.7925
Zambia (kwacha)[4,8]	bskt		
Zimbabwe (dollar)	bskt		1.64123

$ U.S. dollar; £ pound sterling; F French franc; P Spanish peseta; R South African rand; bskt currency basket other than SDR; Re Indian rupee; A$ Australian dollar

1 Rates as reported to the Fund and in terms of currency units per unit listed; rates determined by baskets of currencies are in currency units per U.S. dollar.

2 Market rates in currency units per U.S. dollar.

3 Under this heading are listed those members that describe their exchange rate arrangements as floating independently or as adjusting according to a set of indicators (see footnote 7) and certain other members whose exchange arrangements are not otherwise described in this table. In addition, U.S. dollar quotations are given for the currencies that are pegged to the SDR and for those that participate in the European Monetary System (see footnote 6).

4 Member maintains multiple currency practices and/or dual exchange market. A description of the member's exchange system as of December 31, 1984 is given in the *Annual Report on Exchange Arrangements and Exchange Restrictions, 1985.*

5 East Caribbean dollar.

6 Belgium, Denmark, France, the Federal Republic of Germany, Ireland, Italy, Luxembourg, and the Netherlands are participating in the exchange rate and intervention mechanism of the European Monetary System and maintain maximum margins of 2.25 percent (in the case of the Italian lira, 6 percent) for exchange rates in transactions in the official markets between their currencies and those of the other countries in this group. No announced margins are observed for other currencies.

7 Exchange rates adjusted according to a set of indicators.

8 Exchange rate data not available.

9 Information on exchange arrangements not available.

Source: International Monetary Fund, Washington, D.C., *IMF Survey,* (February 3, 1986), p. 42.

REVIEW QUESTIONS

1. How does the gold standard interfere with a domestic economic objective, such as the maintenace of full employment? Does the burden of adjustment fall equally on deficit and surplus nations?
2. Explain how a large discovery of gold in the United States affects its economy and those of its trading partners, under the gold standard. If the United States takes steps to offset the monetary impact of the newly discovered gold, would it be observing the "rules of the game?"
3. Where did the Bretton Woods System borrow the idea of defining the band of fluctuations from the established parities for any two currencies within two percent? Did this narrow band prove to be a problem later when substantial changes in economic and financial conditions in major industrial countries caused the parities to become unworkable?
4. What is meant by an adjustable peg? Did the Bretton Woods System contain an effective and readily usable mechanism for adjusting parities?
5. Compare the adjustment process (to balance of payments disequilibria) under the gold standard and under the fixed-exchange regime introduced by Bretton Woods. Does the latter also lack the symmetry in requiring both deficit and surplus nations to share the burden of adjustment equally?
6. Why was the availability of sufficient international liquidity a major concern in the late 1960s? What was the solution that was adopted by the IMF membership to alleviate this concern?
7. Students of international monetary relations and international monetary authorities distinguish between "stabilizing" and "destabilizing" speculation in currency markets. What is meant by this distinction? Why was the Bretton Woods System more susceptible to destabilizing speculation than the current flexible rates regime?
8. Define the principle of "conditionality" as applied by the IMF. Is the IMF still applying this principle under the current international monetary system? Why do a large number of countries find it difficult to accept the IMF prescription as a cure for their ailments?
9. Does a flexible exchange rate regime allow domestic policy objectives to be pursued, irrespective of developments in the international sector? If that is the case, why do statesmen argue during international conferences about appropriate domestic policies that would insure orderly exchange markets? (For example, why did the United States urge its trading partners in the mid-1980s to pursue domestic economic policies (including higher interest rates) designed to weaken the U.S. dollar vis-a-vis their currencies)?

10. Which of the following groups favors a flexible rate system, as against a fixed-rate regime? Indicate in each case the main arguments of each group for or against the two systems.
    a. Professional economists and university economic professors.
    b. Exporters of corn and soybeans in Iowa and Nebraska.
    c. Multinational financial managers.
    d. Chief executive officers of large multinational banks.
    e. Statesmen and central bankers.
    f. Consumer advocates.
11. If the onus of adjustment in the current international floating system falls on exchange rates themselves, why have central bankers frequently intervened in foreign exchange markets? In view of these interventions (sometimes of massive scale) can we say that exchange rates under this system are truly market determined?
12. What are some of the major weaknesses of the floating rates regime that lead some to propose changing to a new international monetary order? What are the alternatives that have been proposed?
13. Why is the current international monetary system referred to as a floating or a flexible rates system, despite the fact that the majority of countries have been pegging their currencies either to other currencies (such as the U.S. dollar or French franc) or to a basket of currencies (such as the SDR)? Why would a country like the Ivory Coast in West Africa find it in its best interests to continue pegging its currency to the French franc?
14. Indicate where (in which section of the U.S. Balance of Payments) each of these transactions will appear, and whether they are debit (−) or credit (+) entries. (Disregard counterpart of each transaction.)
    a. An American tourist buys gifts in Neverneverland.
    b. IBM opens an office in Neverneverland financed by funds from the home office.
    c. A Neverneverlander purchases U.S. Treasury bill.
    d. An American firm receives dividends from its subsidiary in Neverneverland.
    e. U.S. Treasury transfers SDRs to the Bank of England.
    f. U.S. investors buy Eurobonds denominated in deutsche marks.

BIBLIOGRAPHY

Banker, "Bretton Woods Orphans" (September 1981), p. 7.

BLADEN, A., "Developing International Financial Crisis," *Forbes* (October 27, 1980), p. 210.

BOARMAN, P. N., and D. G. TUERCK, eds., *World Monetary Disorder: National Policies vs. International Imperatives.* New York: Praeger, 1976.

BRENNER, M. J., *The Politics of International Monetary Reform.* Cambridge, Mass.: Ballinger, 1976.

CROCKETT, A. D., and M. GOLDSTEIN, "Inflation Under Fixed and Flexible Exchange Rates," *IMF Staff Papers* (November 1976), pp. 509–544.

DINI, L., "Where the International Financial System Needs Strengthening," *Banker* (September 1983), pp. 29–30.

Economist, "Floating Currencies and Choppy Trade" (March 24, 1984), p. 67.

FLEMING, J. M., "Floating Exchange Rates, Asymmetrical Interventions, and the Management of International Liquidity," *IMF Staff Papers* (July 1975), pp. 263–283.

GERSTEIN, A. S., "Reflections on the International Monetary System," *Finance and Development* (September 1980), pp. 40–41.

GOLSTEIN, M., "Whither the Exchange Rate System?," *Financial Executive,* June 1984, pp. 2–6.

GUDAC, T., "Pricing and Exchange Rates in Planned Economies," *Finance and Development* (September 1984), pp. 40–43.

Institute for International Economics, *IMF Conditionality,* a compendium of 21 papers presented on the subject at a conference held by the Institute in Virginia in 1982 (Washington, D.C.), 1983.

International Monetary Fund, *Annual Report 1984* (Washington, D.C.), 1984.

JOHNSON, R. S., C. W. HULTMAN, and R. A. ZUBER, "Currency Cocktails and Exchange Rate Stability," *Columbia Journal of World Business* (Winter 1979), pp. 117–126.

KERN, D., "Not a Prophecy, But a Guide to Action," *Euromoney* (July 1980), pp. 137–138.

KORTEWEG, PIETER, "Exchange-Rate Policy, Monetary Policy, and Real Exchange-Rate Variability," *Essays in International Finance,* No. 140. Princeton, N.J.: International Finance Section, Department of Economics, Princeton University, December 1980.

KROLL, S., "Comparing Currencies," *Financial World* (February 5, 1985), pp. 66–67.

MAKIN, J. H., "Fixed Versus Floating: A Red Herring," *Columbia Journal of World Business* (Winter 1980), pp. 7–14.

MCCALLUM, J. S., "International Financial System: In Crisis," *Business Quarterly* (Spring 1980), pp. 64–67.

McKINNON, R. I., *Money in International Exchanges (The Convertible Currency System)*. New York and Oxford: Oxford University Press, 1979.

PINSKY, N. J., and J. G. KVASNICKA, "The European Monetary System," *Economic Perspectives*. Chicago: Federal Reserve Bank, November-December 1979, pp. 3–10.

PRINGLE, R., "Shape of Currency Crisis in the 1980's," *Banker* (February 1981), pp. 29–33.

PRUNTEL, J. R., "Can We Make Floating Exchange Rates Easier to Live With?" *Banker* (January 1985), pp. 15–18.

RHOMBERG, R. R., "Indices of Effective Exchange Rates," *IMF Staff Papers* (March 1976), pp. 88–112.

RODRIGUEZ, C. A., "Managed Float: An Evaluation of Alternative Rules in the Presence of Speculative Capital Flows," *American Economic Review* (March 1981), pp. 256–260.

SALOP, J., "Divergence Indicator: A Technical Note," *IMF Staff Papers* (December 1981), pp. 682–97.

SCAMMEL, W. M., *International Monetary Policy: Bretton Woods and After.* New York: Wiley, 1975.

SOLOMON, A. M., "Toward a More Resilient International Financial System," Federal Reserve Bank of New York, *Quarterly Review* (Autumn 1983), pp. 1–5.

TEETERS, N., "The Role of Banks in the International Financial System," *Journal of Banking and Finance* (December 1983), pp. 453–466.

TINBERGEN, J., coordinator, *Reshaping the International Order: A Report to the Club of Rome.* New York: Dutton, 1976.

WESTERFIELD, J. M., "Empirical Properties of Foreign Exchange Rates Under Fixed and Floating Rate Regimes," *Journal of International Economics* (June 1977), pp. 181–200.

WHITMAN, M., "The Payments Adjustment Process and the Exchange Rate Regime: What Have We Learned?" *American Economic Review* (May 1975), pp. 133–146.

WILLIAMSON, J., "On the System in Bretton Woods," *American Economic Review* (May 1985), pp. 74–79.

WITTEVEEN, H. J., "The Emerging International Monetary System," *Finance and Development* (September 1976), pp. 7ff.

WOOD, G. E., "Do We Need World Monetary Reform?", *Banker* (July 1980), p. 29.

APPENDIX A

The Functioning of the Present Exchange Rate Systems

Excerpts from the Report of the Deputies of the Intergovernmental Group of 24 on the International Monetary System released in August, 1985, for consideration by the Board of Governors of the IMF in the annual meetings held in Seoul, Korea (October 8–11, 1985). International Monetary Fund, *IMF Survey,* Washington, D.C., September 1985, pp. 7–10.

Floating exchange rates were adopted by major industrial countries in the early Seventies, as the par value system established by Bretton Woods could not cope with the stresses generated by divergent national macroeconomic policies in an environment of increasing capital mobility. It had been anticipated at that time that market forces, aided by stabilizing capital flows, would keep exchange rates close to the levels required to achieve current account equilibrium and free other macroeconomic instruments to deal with domestic economic priorities. It was also hoped that floating exchange rates would assist the adjustment process and growth of world trade and output.

THE EXPERIENCE WITH FLOATING RATES

The experience with floating exchanges rates has not been up to the original expectations. Both in terms of short-term volatility and long-term misalignment, exchange rate variability has increased since the abandonment of the Bretton Woods system. The increase in volatility, referring to short-term fluctuations, since the adoption of floating rates is well documented. Exchange rate volatility has not declined as markets became used to dealing with the flexible exchange rate system, as was anticipated when floating was first adopted.

Wide fluctuations in exchange rates have tended to bring about greater uncertainty about future exchange rates. Evidence from forward markets indicates that most exchange rate fluctuations are unanticipated. Volatility has contributed to expansion of financial transactions and greater capital movements not directly related to trade flows. It has discouraged investment and trade by adding to financial risks for investors and traders.

Misalignment, referring to a persistent deviation of the exchange rate from the equilibrium level, has been severe and, according to some studies, it has also become larger in the recent period than under the Bretton Woods system. Much of the medium-term movement in real exchange rates in recent years reflects not the changing pattern of competitiveness but rather the result of differences in fiscal and monetary policies, in which industrial countries have chosen macroeconomic policies independently, without serious consideration of their impact on the world economy. Misalignment inevitably produces either idle resources or wasteful shifts of resources back and forth between tradables and nontradables. It becomes a potent source of pressures for protectionism.

Exchange rate variability has, as the 1984 G-24 Revised Program had put it, "especially hurt the developing countries." Exporters and importers in these countries are exposed to high exchange risks in the absence of well-developed financial markets, especially forward cover arrangements. The destabilizing uncertainties of floating rates have increased the reserve and capital needs of developing countries from the levels which would otherwise exist.

The functioning of the present floating-rate system has thus not been able to provide, as Article IV, Section 1 of the Articles of Agreement of the IMF puts it, "a framework that facilitates the exchange of goods, services, and capital among countries," which sustains sound economic growth and helps develop orderly underlying conditions necessary for financial and economic stability.

PROPOSALS FOR IMPROVING EXCHANGE RATE STABILITY

The 1984 G-24 Revised Program stated that an exchange rate system should be devised to overcome the recognized rigidities of a par value system and the destabilizing uncertainties of floating rates. Besides, the improved functioning of the exchange rate system requires the recognition of major countries that both the floating-rate and the fixed-rate systems need rules of the game relating to domestic macroeconomic policies. The Revised Program categorically stated that "this implies greater effort on the part of the developed countries to achieve a substantial degree of discipline and coordination in the conduct of their national policies." Exchange rate stability should be an important objective of policy instead of being a residual of other policy actions of individual countries, as is the case at present.

The principle behind the concept of "target zones" for exchange rates of major countries, commitment to which would promote greater international policy consistency, is in line with the approach of the 1984 G-24 Revised Program. Adoption of target zones for the exchange rates of major currencies could help achieve the objective of exchange rate stability and a sustainable pattern of payments balances. The proposal needs to be further studied and pursued to gain general acceptance. In the meantime, a mechanism has to be devised to enforce policy coordination among the developed, especially the key currency, countries. Although the role of the developing countries in influencing such an exchange rate system is necessarily limited—and therefore the related mechanism of coordination and surveillance will be essentially concerned with the developed countries—it is important, as the 1984 G-24 Revised Program states, "that this coordination should take account of the needs of developing countries."

Policy coordination in this context implies that monetary policy for exchange rate stability should complement the use of fiscal policy to counter inflationary and deflationary pressures as well as the use of other policy instruments. Intervention, for instance, could be used on a meaningful scale, without confining it to "leaning against the wind," towards the end of exchange rate stability, as a complementary measure to other policies, and sometimes in coordination with other countries.

A framework for such a policy coordination already exists under Article IV of the IMF, according to which "each member undertakes to collaborate with the Fund and other members to assure orderly exchange arrangements and to promote a stable system of exchange rates" (Section 1) and "the Fund shall exercise firm surveillance over the exchange rate policies of members, and shall adopt specific principles for the guidance of all members with respect to those policies" [Section 3(b)]. Over and above the regular multilateral consultations, a mechanism or procedure that would trigger consultations among the concerned countries and between them and the Fund is necessary whenever the indicators available suggest that excessive short-term movements of one of more major currencies are taking place, or that any major currency is already, or is in the process of becoming, seriously misaligned.

Since the concept of misalignment is central in this process of surveillance, it should be clearly spelled out in operational terms. Although the term misalignment was not used in 1970, the IMF's report on the "Role of Exchange Rates in the Adjustment of International Payments" of that year provided an authoritative definition of the concept of fundamental disequilibrium, which was the Bretton Woods term for the same thing.

> "A basic feature of the concept of fundamental disequilibrium is that although its ultimate focus is on the balance of payments it is related to a general condition of the member's economy and does not require that an imbalance must have developed in the balance of payments. This, in turn, reflects the underlying philosophy of the Bretton Woods system that while attainment of balance in international payments must be a focal point of concern for the international financial community, it is not to be regarded as an objective in isolation from other objectives of the international monetary system. These objectives include the expansion and balanced growth of international trade on the basis of a liberal and nondiscriminatory regime of trade and payments, to contribute to the promotion of high levels of employment and real income and to the development of the productive resources of all the Fund's members as primary objectives of economic policy. In this conception, attainment of payments balance through the use of measures destructive of national or international prosperity would clearly not comprise a durable payments equilibrium."

The alignment or misalignment of an exchange rate thus has to be judged in the light of a country's overall economic performance and its impact on the international economy and not merely its balance of payments performance. For example, in many developing countries with relatively undiversified economies, protection of infant industries, judiciously applied, may be an indispensable element in the process of diversification and development, as recognized by GATT. On the other hand, for countries with diversified economies and relatively high mobility of factors of product, substantial or increasing restrictions on trade could well be a major symptom of exchange rate misalignment.

Exchange rates of developing countries are not of any great significance in relation to the international alignments of exchange rates, and assessment of the appropriateness of a developing country's exchange rate does not generally involve systematic considerations comparable to those applicable to the exchange rate of a major industrial country.

APPENDIX B

A Primer in Balance of Payments Analysis

The balance of international payments, which embodies a record of all transactions between a country and the rest of the world, represents an important part of the environment in which MNCs operate. Understanding balance of payments accounting is crucial to the multinational financial manager in several areas of decision making.

Borrowing and investment decisions, as well as hedging operations, are especially impacted by balance of payments developments and prospects in the countries whose currencies are involved in these decisions. Although the balance of payments is a historical record of past transactions, a proper analysis of these data can reveal trends in the factors that underlie the value of a currency in international markets. Financial managers of MNCs strive to discern these trends in order to use them to the advantage of their firms. These techniques are developed in later chapters as part of an overall multinational financial strategy which aims at achieving the goals of the particular firm.

Although the direct foreign investment decision is influenced mainly by longer-term factors, such as the expected rate of return and the political risk, it is also impacted by balance of payments prospects of the host countries. These prospects help determine the course of exchange rate changes over the horizon of the projects' life cycle. Balance of payments developments also determine, to some extent, a nation's ability to marshal resources for the achievement of peoples' needs and aspirations, and are therefore a factor in shaping that nation's economic and political stability.

WHAT IS A BALANCE OF PAYMENT?

The balance of payments is simply a record of *all* transactions that take place between a certain country and the rest of the world during a period of time. The time-frame is usually a year, but most countries compile and publish balance of payments data quarterly. While all *recorded* transactions appear in the balance of payments, some transactions, particularly illegal ones, escape recording and, consequently, do not appear in the officially compiled data. These transactions are exemplified by smuggling of goods to escape tariffs or trade restrictions, and by capital flight, where funds flow out of countries that impose restrictions on capital movements and transfers, seeking safety and/or more favorable returns in other countries.

The balance of payments is compiled by using the double-entry accounting principle in recording international transactions. Each transaction gives rise to an equivalent debit and credit entries in the balance of payments of the two countries involved in the transaction.

To illustrate this principle, suppose that a U.S. firm exports goods worth $1000 to a French firm against a draft payable in 90 days. If we assume an exchange rate of $1.00 = FF 8.00, this transaction will appear in the U.S. and French balance of payments as shown in Table 2-1.

Suppose that the French firm paid for the transaction by a check drawn on its account in a U.S. bank prior to the preparation of the balance of payments accounts; then we have the recording in Table 2-2.

In either illustration, exports represented a credit entry in the U.S. balance of payments, while the counterpart debit was in the form of an increase in claims on France, or a decrease of French claims against the U.S. The transaction is just the opposite viewed from the standpoint of France.

Table 2-1.

U.S. BALANCE OF PAYMENTS			BALANCE OF PAYMENTS OF FRANCE		
	Credit (+)	Debit (−)		Credit (+)	Debit (−)
Exports	$1000		Imports		FF 8000
Claims on foreigners (short-term investment in France)		$1000	Claims by foreigners (short-term borrowing from the U.S.)	FF 8000	

Table 2-2.

U.S. BALANCE OF PAYMENTS			BALANCE OF PAYMENTS OF FRANCE		
	Credit (+)	Debit (−)		Credit (+)	Debit (−)
Exports	$1000		Imports		FF 8000
Foreign assets in the U.S.		$1000	French assets in foreign countries	FF 8000	

Export of securities gives rise to the same type of entries in the balance of payments as the export of goods and services. Suppose that a U.S. investor buys $500 worth of bonds issued by a French firm and pays for them by drawing a check on his or her U.S. bank account in favor of the seller, who deposits the check to his or her account in a U.S. bank; then we have the entries in Table 2-3.

Note that the purchase of French bonds by a U.S. investor is a debit entry for the U.S. (an import of securities) which is financed by an increase in foreign assets in the U.S. (the amount of $500 in U.S. banks transferred from the investor's account to the account of the French firm that sold the bonds). For France, the sale of bonds is a credit entry (export of securities), the counterpart of which is an increase in French assets abroad (balances held in U.S. banks).

As a rule of thumb, a transaction which results in an *increase in the demand* for the U.S. dollar (such as exports of goods and services, and securities) are credit entries in the U.S. balance of payments. Conversely, transactions which increase the supply of U.S. dollars (such as import of goods, services, and securities) are debit entries in the U.S. balance of payments. If all international transactions involving the United States are accounted for, the amounts of U.S. dollars supplied and demanded in currency markets during a certain period of time are thus determined.

Table 2-3.

U.S. BALANCE OF PAYMENTS			BALANCE OF PAYMENTS OF FRANCE		
	Credit (+)	Debit (−)		Credit (+)	Debit (−)
Investments abroad		$500	Foreign investments in France	FF 4000	
Foreign assets in the U.S.	$500		French assets in foreign countries		FF 4000

Supply and demand forces arising from international transactions are the major determinants of currency values in a flexible exchange rate system.

STRUCTURE AND INTERPRETATION OF THE BALANCE OF PAYMENTS

If each international transaction results in equal debit and credit entries, then the balance of payments, which is merely a record of all such transactions, must also balance. Although this is a truism, it nevertheless embodies a basic concept of finance. Nations, just like individuals, can spend more than current income only by drawing down their previously accumulated savings, or by borrowing from other entities. When they eventually deplete their savings and run out of further borrowing opportunities, they will have to retrench.

Another important concept in balance of payments analysis is that, while total debits equal total credits by necessity, it matters how an excess of debits in one section is financed by an excess of credits in other sections of the account. This distinction gives meaning to such terms as a "deficit" or a "surplus," "strengthening" or "weakening" in the balance of payments, despite the inevitable equality of the overall balance.

The balance of payments is traditionally divided into three sections or accounts: (1) the current account, (2) the capital account, and (3) the reserves account, sometimes also called "monetary movements." Transactions taking place in the third section are said to be settling transactions, that is, outflows or inflows of reserves in settlement of transactions *above the line* in the current and capital accounts. Although there are no conceptual problems as to what constitutes current account transactions, there is some disagreement as to whether certain short-term capital movements should be above or below the line. Consequently, there are questions as to what is the appropriate measure of the overall balance of payments outcome, depending on which transactions are deemed to be settling transactions, rather than bona fide capital movements above the line.

Table 2-4 is a balance of payments for a mythical country measured in millions of units of the currency of the country. The structure of the balance of payments, as well as the interpretations of the various balances, are given below:

1. *Current Account.* The country experienced a deficit in the balance of trade of 55 million currency units representing excess of merchandise imports over exports. This was partly offset by a net credit of 11 million currency units in services (representing earnings from such services as shipping, insurance, tourism, and other services rendered to residents of other countries in excess of use of such services rendered by other countries to its own residents), as well as by a credit of 20 million currency units derived from

Table 2-4. Name of Country, Balance of Payments—1985 (in millions of currency units)

	Credit (+)	Debit (−)	Balance
I. *Current Account*			
Merchandise exports	65		
Merchandise imports		120	
Balance of trade			−55
Services (net)	11		
Unilateral transfers (net)	20		
Balance on current account			−24
II. *Capital Account*			
Long-term			
Direct investment abroad		2	
Direct foreign investment in the country	12		
Securities (net) [portfolio investment]		5	
Loans (official and private net of repayments)	7		
Balance on long-term capital transactions			+12
Basic balance (balance on current a/c + balance on long-term capital movements)			−12
Short-term (private)			
Residents' holdings of short-term funds abroad	2		
Other short-term transactions		1	
Overall balance (basic balance + short-term private capital movements)			−11
Errors and omissions (statistical discrepancy)			− 3
III. *Official Reserves*			
SDR allocations			
IMF position	5		
Net official monetary reserves (− increase)	9		

Summary

Balance on current a/c	−24	
Basic balance	−12	
Overall balance	−11	
Statistical discrepancy	− 3	−14
Official reserve movements		+14

unilateral transfers. The latter includes grants and aid received from other countries and transfers made by the country's citizens who are working abroad. As a result, the deficit on current account was 24 million currency units.

2. *Capital Account.* Long-term capital movements consist of direct investment, portfolio investment, and long-term loan transactions.[1] The country achieved a credit balance of 12 million currency units overall in long-term capital transactions during 1985. Foreign investors committed 12 million currency units in direct equity investment in that country. In addition, the country borrowed 7 million currency units from the rest of the world net of repayments on previous loans. This inflow of capital was partly offset by direct investment made by the country's residents abroad, and by a net purchase of foreign securities in the amounts of 2 and 5 million currency units, respectively.

   The net long-term capital inflow narrowed the gap in current transactions to a deficit 12 million currency units. This is referred to as the *basic balance,* representing the outcome of transactions motivated primarily by economic and commercial considerations. These are sometimes referred to as autonomous transactions to differentiate them from *accommodating* transactions, which take place in the form of short-term capital and official reserve movements. The difficulty with the concept of the basic balance is that some short-term capital inflows and outflows are also motivated by economic factors, such as when funds move across boundaries to seek higher rates of return. A considerable proportion of such movements, however, is carried out to settle transactions that have taken place in the current and long-term capital accounts, or for speculative purposes.

   Short-term capital movements take primarily the form of changes in bank balances held abroad and in ownership of foreign short-term money market instruments. For this particular country, residents' holdings of short-term funds abroad decreased by 1 million currency units (a decrease is a financing or a credit item), thus resulting in an overall balance of payment deficit of 11 million currency units.

3. *Official Reserve Movements.* Transactions below the line in Table 2-4 (the item "errors and omissions" will be explained below) represent purely settling or accommodating flows. They consist of changes in the country's chest of foreign convertible currencies, net drawings (or repayments) on the IMF, and allocations of Special Drawing Rights (SDRs). SDRs are international

[1]Direct foreign investment represents acquisition of real assets abroad and/or financial assets for the purpose of controlling foreign enterprises (see Chapter 12). Portfolio investment, on the other hand, refers to acquisition of securities of foreign governments or firms for purely investment purposes, primarily income. The distinction between acquisition of foreign securities for income purposes and acquisition with control intentions, is often arbitrary.

reserves created periodically by the IMF (see Chapter 2) and allocated to member countries in proportion to their respective quotas in the organization (none was allocated in 1985).

This particular country had a net drawing of the equivalent of five million currency units from the IMF, and its reserves of foreign currencies declined by the equivalent of nine million currency units (both representing sources of funds or credit transactions). Total financing items or monetary movements thus amounted to 14 million currency units, whereas the gap or the overall deficit in the balance of payments was only 11 million currency units. The difference of three million units in net debits is a statistical discrepancy, as the balance of payments as a whole must balance. This discrepancy, which is often referred to as "errors and omissions," is explained by unrecorded and "illegal" transactions both on the debit and credit sides. Often, particularly for countries with unstable political systems and excessive exchange and trade controls, the debit discrepancy is primarily accounted for by illegal capital outflow or capital flight.

ADJUSTMENTS TO DISEQUILIBRIA IN THE BALANCE OF PAYMENTS

The country whose balance of payments is depicted in Table 2-4 is obviously experiencing a disequilibrium in the balance of payments. Transactions in the current and capital accounts produced a fairly sizable gap which required financing in the form of a *decrease* in the country's foreign reserves, and an *increase* in its drawings on IMF resources. A country, like individuals and households, cannot indefinitely live beyond its means before its financing capacity in the form of past accumulated savings and borrowings is exhausted. Sooner or later some adjustment in the form of corrective action or retrenchment will have to take place.

The mechanisms of the adjustment process explained in Chapter 2 vary according to the exchange rate regime in effect. Under the gold standard, the price-specie flow mechanism insured restoration of external equilibrium through inflating the economies of surplus countries while deflating those of deficit countries.

The onus of adjustment under the Bretton Woods fixed-parities system fell primarily on deficit countries, which experienced a drain on their reserves unless effective corrective policies (mainly demand management and contractionary monetary policies) were vigorously pursued by such countries. Surplus countries, which experienced swelling in their international reserves, were less impelled to pursue corrective policies, particularly when restoring equilibrium implied inflating their economies. The adjustment process under this regime focused on domestic economic and financial policies. Countries that failed to take appropriate measures, or where such measures did not produce adequate results, had their parities adjusted through devaluation or revaluation.

Under the prevailing floating exchange rates regime, the burden of adjustment falls primarily on the exchange rates themselves, while countries are able to pursue domestic economic goals more freely. Even countries which continue to peg their currencies to the U.S. dollar (or to other currencies or a basket of currencies) adjust their exchange rates frequently to insure proper currency alignment with their major trading partners. The system, however, cannot be described as working smoothly relying only on market forces to reverse balance of payments disequilibria. The United States and major industrial countries have often intervened in exchange markets, while the IMF has continued to exercise close surveillance of exchange rate policies of member countries. The purpose of this surveillance is to insure that countries pursue economic and financial policies which are conducive to an orderly international monetary system. The major objective of interventions in the exchange markets has been to moderate the excessive volatility that has characterized these markets.

An example of intervention in exchange markets to correct a balance of payments disequilibrium is the accord reached in October 1985 among the United States and four of its major trading partners (Japan, Germany, the United Kingdom, and Canada) to exert a downward pressure on the U.S. dollar. Massive intervention by the central banks of the five countries followed, which resulted in a steep decline in the U.S. dollar rate against major currencies. The accord sought to reverse a substantial and sharply deteriorating U.S. trade deficit, which reached $148 billion in 1985.

3

Exchange Rates and Exchange Markets

An exchange rate is a price of a currency expressed in terms of units of another currency. As any price, it is determined by market forces, as well as by other factors and influences which interfere with or circumvent the working of market forces. This chapter does not address itself to the determination of exchange rates under alternative international monetary regimes. Rather, it deals with the mechanics of exchange rate quotations and describes the functioning of exchange markets and the role of participants in these markets.

EXCHANGE RATE QUOTATIONS

The exchange rate for any particular currency may be quoted in terms of *all other* currencies. Alternatively, the exchange rate of all other currencies may be quoted in terms of that *particular* currency. Thus for n currencies, the number of possible exchange rates equals $n(n - 1)$. Note that the first set of quotations is the reciprocal of the second set. For example, SF/$ (the U.S. dollar expressed in units of Swiss francs) is the reciprocal of $/SF (the Swiss franc expressed in units of U.S. dollars). Note also that only $n - 1$ exchange rates need to be known to derive the entire set of rates. The rest of the rates, which are derivable from the original known set, are said to be *redundant* since they are either *reciprocals* or *cross rates* of the original known rates. To illustrate, assume a mythical world with only five currencies: the

U.S. dollar, the pound sterling, the deutsche mark, the Swiss franc, and the Japanese yen. All possible exchange rates between any pair of these currencies are presented in the matrix in Exhibit 3-1.

Of the 20 possible exchange rates [(5(5 − 1)], only four rates (encircled) are needed to derive the entire set. The remaining 16 are redundant, since four (underlined) are merely the reciprocal of the original four, and 12 are cross rates which can be derived from the original four. The deutsche mark in terms of the pound sterling (DM/£), for example, is a cross rate derived by multiplying $/£ × DM/$.

Due to the dominance of the U.S. dollar in international trade and investments, it is conventional to quote exchange rates as U.S. dollars per one unit of foreign currency (usually called U.S. $ equivalent or the direct method), or alternatively, foreign currency units per one U.S. dollar (usually called the indirect or European system of quotation). Exhibit 3-2, reproduced from *The Wall Street Journal,* presents the dollar quotations (for December 6, 1984) against major foreign currencies. Note that these quotations are the selling rates (*ask price*) charged by the seller (Banker's Trust Company of New York) for wholesale transactions involving amounts of $1 million or more. Rates for smaller transactions, which usually interest the tourist or small traders and investors, are not given, but they are less favorable; that is, they provide fewer units of foreign currency per dollar sold, or alternatively, require more U.S. currency per unit of foreign currency purchased.

As indicated in Exhibit 3-2, the quoted rates are prices *asked* by the dealer (Banker's Trust Company) for clients who want to purchase foreign currencies against dollars. Not shown in the exhibit are rates at which the same dealer is willing to buy foreign currencies from its customers for U.S. dollars (the bid price). Bid quotations would have shown more foreign currency units per U.S. dollar than ask prices, since the dealer's margin represents the *spread* between bid and ask quotes. Usually, an exchange rate is quoted both ways with the bid quotation preceding the ask or offer quotation.

Exhibit 3-1.

	$	£	DM	SF	Y
$	1.00	$/£	$/DM	$/SF	$/Y
£	£/$	1.00	£/DM	£/SF	£/Y
DM	DM/$	DM/£	1.00	DM/SF	DM/Y
SF	SF/$	SF/£	SF/DM	1.00	SF/Y
Y	Y/$	Y/£	Y/DM	Y/SF	1.00

Exhibit 3-2. Foreign Exchange Quotations

Foreign Exchange

Thursday, December 6, 1984

The New York foreign exchange selling rates below apply to trading among banks in amounts of $1 million and more, as quoted at 3 p.m. Eastern time by Bankers Trust Co. Retail transactions provide fewer units of foreign currency per dollar.

Country	U.S. $ equiv. Thurs	U.S. $ equiv. Wed	Currency per U.S. $ Thurs	Currency per U.S. $ Wed
Argentina (Peso)	.007084	.007084	141.17	141.17
Australia (Dollar)	.8425	.8550	1.1869	1.1696
Austria (Schilling)	.04660	.04632	21.46	21.59
Belgium (Franc)				
Commercial rate	.01621	.01618	61.70	.61.82
Financial rate	.01606	.01609	62.25	62.15
Brazil (Cruzeiro)	.0003488	.0003488	2867.00	2867.00
Britain (Pound)	1.2090	1.2025	.8271	.8316
30-Day Forward	1.2086	1.2020	.8274	.8319
90-Day Forward	1.2084	1.2018	.8275	.8321
180-Day Forward	1.2097	1.2026	.8267	.8315
Canada (Dollar)	.7565	.7568	1.3219	1.3213
30-Day Forward	.7554	.7558	1.3238	1.3231
90-Day Forward	.7539	.7543	1.3264	1.3258
180-Day Forward	.7528	.7531	1.3283	1.3278
Chile (Official rate)	.008293	.008293	120.59	120.59
China (Yuan)	.3611	.3611	2.7693	2.7693
Colombia (Peso)	.009007	.009007	111.03	111.03
Denmark (Krone)	.09091	.09050	11.0000	11.0500
Ecuador (Sucre)				
Official rate	.01489	.01489	67.18	67.18
Floating rate	.008295	.008295	120.55	120.55
Finland (Markka)	.1563	.1565	6.4000	6.3900
France (Franc)	.1068	.1062	9.3650	9.4200
30-Day Forward	.1066	.1060	9.3790	9.4345
90-Day Forward	.1063	.1057	9.4030	9.4580
180-Day Forward	.1059	.1054	9.4425	9.4920
Greece (Drachma)	.007905	.007937	126.50	126.00
Hong Kong (Dollar)	.1278	.1278	7.8250	7.8295
India (Rupee)	.08183	.08210	12.22	12.18
Indonesia (Rupiah)	.0009372	.0009372	1067.00	1067.00
Ireland (Punt)	1.0190	1.0140	.9814	.9862
Israel (Shekel)	.001694	.001694	590.45	590.45
Italy (Lira)	.0005288	.0005277	1891.00	1895.00
Japan (Yen)	.004062	.004056	246.20	246.55
30-Day Forward	.004071	.004065	245.66	246.02
90-Day Forward	.004092	.004085	244.35	244.78
180-Day Forward	.004129	.004121	242.20	242.65
Lebanon (Pound)	.1285	.1285	7.785	7.785
Malaysia (Ringgit)	.4149	.4149	2.4105	2.4100
Mexico (Peso)				
Floating rate	.004630	.004739	216.00	211.00
Netherlands (Guilder)	.2895	.2878	3.4540	3.4750
New Zealand (Dollar)	.4870	.4885	2.0534	2.0471
Norway (Krone)	.1126	.1124	8.8800	8.9000
Pakistan (Rupee)	.06689	.06689	14.95	14.95
Peru (Sol)	.0002108	.0002108	4743.60	4743.60
Philippines (Peso)	.05021	.05021	19.917	19.917
Portugal (Escudo)	.006135	.006098	163.00	164.00
Saudi Arabia (Riyal)	.2809	.2808	3.5600	3.5610
Singapore (Dollar)	.4618	.4620	2.1655	2.1645
South Africa (Rand)	.5455	.5435	1.8332	1.8399
South Korea (Won)	.001220	.001220	820.00	820.00
Spain (Peseta)	.005882	.005879	170.00	170.10
Sweden (Krona)	.1144	.1139	8.7400	8.7800
Switzerland (Franc)	.3968	.3918	2.5200	2.5525
30-Day Forward	.3983	.3932	2.5108	2.5435
90-Day Forward	.4011	.3959	2.4930	2.5258
180-Day Forward	.4061	.4006	2.4625	2.4960
Taiwan (Dollar)	.02535	.02535	39.45	39.45
Thailand (Baht)	.03708	.03708	26.97	26.97
Uruguay (New Peso)				
Financial	.01474	.01474	67.86	67.86
Venezuela (Bolivar)				
Official rate	.1333	.1333	7.50	7.50
Floating rate	.07918	.07918	12.63	12.63
W. Germany (Mark)	.3273	.3238	3.0550	3.0885
30-Day Forward	.3283	.3247	3.0464	3.0802
90-Day Forward	.3303	.3266	3.0273	3.0620
180-Day Forward	.3338	.3300	2.9955	3.0305
SDR	0.991257	0.993025	1.00882	1.00702
ECU	0.726697	0.729208	....	....

Special Drawing Rights are based on exchange rates for the U.S., West German, British, French and Japanese currencies. Source: International Monetary Fund.

ECU is based on a basket of community currencies. Source: European Community Commission.

Source: Reprinted by permission of *The Wall Street Journal*, ©Dow Jones & Company, Inc. (1984). All Rights Reserved.

Forward vs. Spot Quotations

A *spot* exchange rate for a certain currency quotes the price of immediate delivery (usually within two business days) of that currency, effected through cable, wire, or electronic transfer. The *forward* rate is a price quotation for delivering that currency sometime in the future. Forward rates are quoted by foreign exchange dealers and banks for any future delivery which suits their clients up to two years.[1] However, as shown in Exhibit 3-2, they are usually quoted for delivery in 30 days, 90 days, and 180 days. Published quotations are usually given for major currencies; however, dealers and banks provide forward quotations for other currencies requested by their clients. Forward rates for currencies of most LDCs are not available, as no forward market exists for these currencies.

[1]Forward contracts with maturities exceeding two years are arranged, though infrequently, by banks to meet the requirements of their clients.

A forward rate for a certain currency may be higher or lower than the spot rate. In the first case, market participants expect the currency to appreciate vis-a-vis the U.S. dollar, and the currency is said to be trading at a *forward premium.* In the second case, participants expect the currency to depreciate vis-a-vis the U.S. dollar and it is said to be trading at a *forward discount.* In Exhibit 3-2 the Canadian dollar was quoted at a forward discount, while the Swiss franc was quoted at a forward premium. Forward premiums (or discounts) are usually calculated in percentage per annum to enable comparison with the *interest rate differential* between the two countries whose currencies are quoted. The forward premium (or discount) may be calculated by the following formula:

$$\text{Forward premium (or discount) in percent per annum}$$
$$= \frac{\text{forward rate} - \text{spot rate}}{\text{spot rate}} \times \frac{12}{n} \times 100$$

where n stands for the number of months till maturity of the forward contract. The forward discount on the Canadian dollar and the forward premium on the Swiss franc for the quotations provided in Exhibit 3-2 are

$$\text{Canadian dollar (30 days)}$$
$$= \frac{.7554 - .7565}{.7565} \times \frac{12}{1} \times 100 = -1.74\% \text{ (discount)}$$

$$\text{Swiss franc (180 days)}$$
$$= \frac{.4061 - .3968}{.3968} \times \frac{12}{6} \times 100 = +1.86\% \text{ (premium)}$$

A forward quote by an exchange dealer for the Swiss franc may be given as follows:

.3968/78 15/17 33/38 93/103

The customer will recognize that the dealer is quoting one Swiss franc as equivalent to \$.3968 bid and \$.3978 asked, his spot buying and selling price for the Swiss franc, respectively. The numbers to the right are called the *swap points* for forward quotations of 30 days, 90 days, and 180 days, respectively. He or she will further recognize that the Swiss franc is being quoted at a premium (the customer should know that by familiarity with the current quotes in currency markets) because the swap points are in ascending order; that is, the numbers after the obliques are progressively higher than the numbers before the obliques. The swap points in this case should be added to the spot bid/ask quotations to arrive at the following quotations:

spot bid/spot ask	30 days bid/ask	90 days bid/ask	180 days bid/ask
\$.3968 – \$.3978	.3983/.3995	.4001/.4016	.4061/.4081

Had the swap points been quoted in a descending order (the number after the oblique is smaller than the number before the oblique), the customer should conclude that the currency was being quoted at a forward discount, and that swap points should be subtracted. Adding the swap points in this case could result in higher bid than ask quotations, which is, of course, out of the question.

The reader should have realized that the procedure outlined above applies to exchange rates quoted in U.S. dollar equivalent terms. When rates are quoted in European terms (units of foreign currency per U.S. dollar), exactly the reverse procedure applies.

PARTICIPANTS IN EXCHANGE MARKETS

The foreign exchange market has no centralized meeting place where transactions are conducted. The market consists of trading desks at major commercial banks, as well as a small number of foreign exchange brokers in the United States and abroad connected by wire or electronic communication devices to enable swift conclusion of exchange transactions. In this respect it is similar to the over-the-counter market for trading securities. Transactions are normally concluded by wire or by electronic communication systems and are subsequently confirmed in writing.

Participants in the foreign exchange market consist of large commercial banks in the United States and abroad, a handful of exchange brokers, U.S. and foreign multinational companies, central banks, and individuals and small businesses who enter the exchange market either as investors or speculators, or otherwise for the purpose of meeting personal or business requirements for foreign currencies.

Large commercial banks in financial centers in the United States and abroad maintain foreign exchange trading desks, primarily to meet the requirements of their clients, who are mainly multinational companies, exporters, and importers. They also conduct foreign exchange business at the retail level for tourists and others. These banks, sometimes referred to as multinational banks, maintain an active interbank market in foreign exchange either directly or through specialized foreign exchange brokers. The latter, about half a dozen of them in the United States, operate discreetly at the wholesale level to protect the anonymity of their client banks until the deal is concluded in return for a commission. A broker, when contacted by a client bank to purchase 10 million pounds sterling, will approach other banks and brokers to shop for the best possible rate for his client without tipping his hand, that is, without revealing whether the client is interested in buying or selling.

As indicated above, banks operate in the foreign exchange market as intermediaries to sell or buy foreign exchange for their clients and, normally, avoid taking positions in the market. A bank that has committed itself to buy a certain currency in amounts exceeding its commitments to sell that particular currency is said to have a *long position* in that currency. A *short position* arises when the bank is committed to selling amounts of that currency exceeding its commitments to purchase it. Unless banks desire to speculate on foreign currencies, they strive to *square* their positions, that is, to bring their commitments to buy and to sell each foreign currency into approximate equality, chiefly through the interbank market.

Central banks of all countries maintain a balance of foreign currencies as the major constituents of their international reserves, particularly since gold was demonetized in 1976. Central banks, like the Federal Reserve System, enter the foreign exchange market to buy or sell their currencies in exchange for other currencies to maintain certain desired levels of exchange rates for their currency, or to smooth out unwanted fluctuations in these rates.

The role of speculators in the foreign exchange market is vital, yet often misunderstood. A speculator can be a financial institution, or a nonfinancial business, or an individual, though most often the last. What they have in common is their willingness to deliberately assume short or long positions in either the spot or forward exchange market in order to realize a profit, since they have no known or anticipated receipt or payment in foreign currencies to hedge or offset. Because of their special role in the market, their activities are discussed in a later section in this chapter.

RELATION OF SPOT RATE TO FORWARD RATES

The fact that a certain currency is trading at a forward premium (or discount) vis-a-vis another currency conveys the collective judgment of participants in the exchange market to the effect that the future spot rate of that currency is expected to appreciate (or depreciate) against the other currency. This may or may not materialize depending on a host of factors which include, *inter alia,* the interest rate differential between the two countries, the inflation rate differential between the two countries, and the degree to which inflation rate differential is translated into interest rate differential in the expected time horizon. Other factors which could influence the outcome include the efficiency of the financial and exchange markets in the two countries, and absence of controls, restrictions, or other forms of intervention which can impede the adjustment of the exchange rate, during that time horizon, to interest rate and inflation differentials.

The crucial question that both theoreticians and operators in the foreign exchange market have been trying to answer is *whether* and to *what extent* the forward rate is an *accurate predictor* of the expected future spot rate. Theoreticians maintain that if markets are efficient, in the absence of intervention or controls in the exchange or financial markets, the forward rate is an accurate predictor of the future spot rate. What they mean is that the forward rate of currency A in terms of currency B is an accurate predictor of the future spot rate if three conditions are met:

1. *Interest rate parity* will hold; that is, the forward premium (or discount) on currency A vis-a-vis currency B will be exactly offset by the interest rate differential between countries A and B, with the currency of the country where the interest rate is lower being quoted at a forward premium and vice versa.
2. *Purchasing power parity principle* will hold; that is, the differential in the rate of inflation between countries A and B will translate itself into currency A's depreciating vis-a-vis currency B, during the expected time horizon, by a percentage roughly equal to the excess of the inflation rate in country A over country B.
3. *The International Fisher effect* will hold; that is, interest rate differentials between countries A and B will reflect the inflation rate differential between the two countries, with the high-interest country experiencing the higher inflation rate.

If these three relationships hold, and they usually do not, unless financial and exchange markets are efficient and unencumbered by controls and regulations, it can be proven that the forward rate is an accurate predictor of the future spot rate. This does not mean, however, that the future spot rate will be identical with the forward rate. It just means that the former will be as likely above as below the latter and that the deviations between the two are random.

We now proceed to discuss and illustrate these relationships in numerical or graphic terms.

Interest Parity and Covered Interest Arbitrage

Assume the following terms:

R US	Interest rate per annum in the United States (say 12 percent)
R Lit	Interest rate per annum in Italy (say 18 percent)
S($/Lit)	Spot exchange rate of Italian lira in terms of U.S. $ (0.0005288)
$F_{1/2}$($/Lit)	180 days forward rate of Italian lira (.00005182)

Using the formula for calculating the forward premium (or discount) on the Italian lira against the U.S. dollar expressed in percent per annum, we find that the lira is selling at a forward discount of 4 percent calculated as follows:

Forward premium (or discount −)

$$= \frac{F_{1/2}(\$/\text{Lit}) - S(\$/\text{Lit})}{\text{S}(\$/\text{Lit})} \times \frac{12}{n} \times 100$$

$$= \frac{0.0005182 - 0.0005288}{0.0005288} \times \frac{12}{6} \times 100$$

$$= -4 \text{ percent}$$

The situation depicted by this illustration presents an opportunity to realize an assured profit by:

1. Borrowing U.S. dollars in the U.S. at 12 percent.
2. Converting the dollars into liras at the spot rate.
3. Investing the liras for 180 days in short-term money market instruments in Italy.
4. Selling the liras forward against the U.S. dollar at the quoted forward rate for 180 days.
5. Receiving U.S. dollars 180 days from now by delivering Italian liras realized from liquidating the money market investment in Italy.
6. Paying back U.S. dollar loan.

Since the interest rate differential is six percent in favor of the Italian money market, while the annualized forward discount on the lira is four percent, the transactions outlined above should net two percent of the amount borrowed in the United States, disregarding transaction costs. Moreover, there is no exchange risk involved, since the trader starts with borrowed U.S. dollars today and ends with dollars to pay the loan 180 days later. These transactions are referred to as *covered interest arbitrage* as the trader or arbitrager took advantage of the differential in interest rates between the United States and Italy, while covering the exhange risk in the forward market.

The arbitrage process described above will continue as long as it remains profitable, that is, as long as there is a positive interest rate differential in favor of Italy which more than offsets the annualized forward discount on the Italian lira. Arbitrage, however, tends to narrow this advantage, causing a movement towards interest parity, the point at which no further arbitrage is profitable. The reason for this movement may be explained in terms of the behavior of the four variables listed at the beginning of this section which will cause the *interest rate differential* to *narrow* and the *forward discount* on the Italian currency to *widen* as explained below:

Factors causing interest rate differential to narrow:

- Borrowing in United States will increase U.S. interest rates.
- Investing in Italy will lower interest rate by increasing the supply of investible funds.

Factors causing forward discount on Italian lira to widen:

- Buying liras in the spot market will increase the spot rate $S(\$/\text{Lit})$.
- Selling the lira forward will depress the forward rate $F_{1/2}(\$/\text{Lit})$.

The interest parity relationship is depicted in the diagram in Exhibit 3-3. The parity is represented by a band, rather than a line, to allow

Exhibit 3-3. Interest Rate Parity Diagram

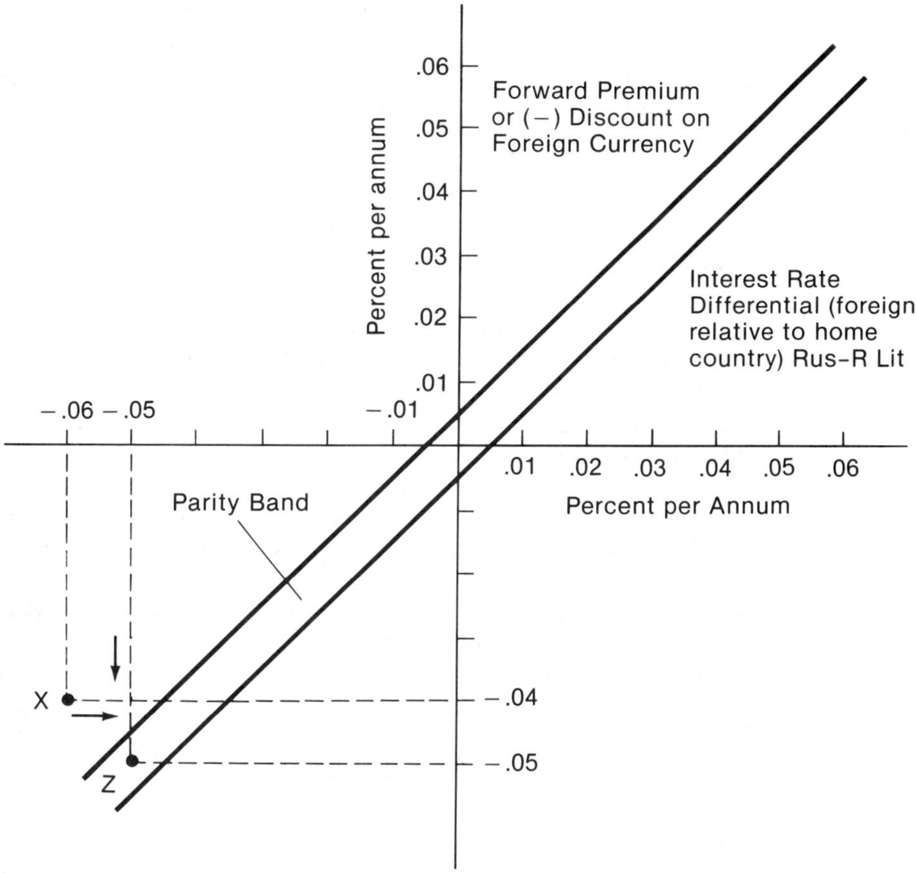

for transaction cost involved in arbitrage operations. Points located inside the band, such as point *Z*, present no opportunity for successful arbitrage since the interest rate differential in favor of Italy is exactly offset by the forward discount on the lira, taking into account transaction costs. Point *X*, which illustrates the situation given earlier in this section, lies outside the parity band and presents an opportunity for profitable arbitrage. When arbitrage is undertaken, it will trigger changes in the variables involved, as explained earlier, which will move point *X* toward point *Z*.

Purchasing Power Parity

Purchasing power parity simply states that exchange rates among currencies adjust to the rate of inflation experienced by the respective countries. Countries with high inflation rates are likely to experience depreciation in their currency values relative to countries with lower inflation rates. Goods and services produced by the former become more expensive in world markets, leading to trade deficits (caused by lower exports and increased imports). These deficits, unless corrected or offset in the capital account, will result in balance of payment difficulties and, consequently, downward pressure on exchange rates.

The above version of purchasing power parity is often referred to as the *relative* version to differentiate it from the *absolute* version which states that the exchange rate between currency A and currency B will be determined so that commodity prices will be equal in both markets. If the exchange rate settles at $1B = 2.5A$, then one unit of currency B will buy in country B the same basket of goods and services which can be bought in country A by 2.5 units of currency A. The basis of this theory is that if the price of a particular commodity is not equal everywhere, arbitrage in goods, that is, buying goods in one market and selling them in other markets to achieve profit, will insure eventual equality. The absolute or static form of purchasing power parity theory has limited usefulness and has been difficult to verify empirically due to the existence of factors inhibiting commodity arbitrage, such as shipping costs, differential tariffs, quotas, and other quantitative restrictions on trade.

The relative version of purchasing power parity has been tested empirically by several studies.[2] The major problems involved in testing the validity of the relationships are the choice of appropriate measures for the general price level or inflation rates in the countries being studied, as well as the time period used. The choice of the time period is critical, not only because the length of such a period has a profound impact on the outcome, but also because of the different exchange regimes (flexible or fixed) prevailing during a chosen time period. Overall, the relationship has been found to hold over the long run, but sharp departures could occur for shorter time periods. Moreover, evidence seems to point out that parity holds more closely when the price indices used measure price movements of tradable goods, as against overall price indices or indices covering non-tradable goods.[3] However, a study by Hans Genberg, which used the period 1967–1976, in which exchange rates became more volatile, concluded that there were greater variations from the parity relationships under these conditions than during periods of fixed exchange rates.[4] He also discovered

[2]See Lawrence H. Officer, "The Purchasing-Power-Parity Theory of Exchange Rates: A Review Article," *IMF Staff Papers* (March 1976), pp. 1–60. See also "Purchasing Power Parity: A Symposium," *Journal of International Economics,* Vol. 8, no. 2 (May 1978), and J. David Richardson, "Some Empirical Evidence on Commodity Arbitrage and the Law of One Price," *ibid.,* pp. 341–351.

[3]Irving B. Kravis and Richard E. Lipsey, "Price Behavior in the Light of Balance of Payments Theories," *Journal of International Economics,* Vol. 8, no. 2 (May 1978), pp. 193–246.

[4]Hans Genberg, "Purchasing Power Parity Under Fixed and Flexible Exchange Rates," *Journal of International Economics,* Vol. 8, no. 2 (May 1978), pp. 247–267.

that most of the departures from purchasing power parity resulted from movements in exchange rates rather than from changes in price levels.

Empirical evidence aside, it can be shown that under efficient and flexible exchange markets, with no quantitative or other restrictions on trade, and in the absence of any form of price control, the movement in the exchange rate between any two countries' currencies tends to equal the difference between the inflation rate in the two countries. For example, if Italy experiences an inflation rate of 10 percent compared to five percent in the United States over a certain period of time, then the exchange rate for the lira in terms of the U.S. dollar should be expected to decline by about five percent over the same time period.[5] This purchasing power parity relationship may be illustrated in a diagram similar to the one shown for interest parity, with the difference in inflation rate (Italy relative to United States) plotted on the horizontal axis and the expected or forecast change in the rate of exchange of Italian lira in terms of the U.S. dollar (\$/Lit) plotted on the vertical axis.

The International Fisher Effect

Irving Fisher, an illustrious American economist known for his contribution to interest rate and price theories, demonstrated that the nominal interest rate R is equal to the real interest rate r plus the expected inflation rate $\dot{P}$ plus the product of the last two variables, or

$$R = r + \dot{P} + r\dot{P}$$

This relationship, which, as Fisher stated, holds for any one country, could be generalized to apply on an international basis. He postulated that the differential in nominal interest rates between any two countries should reflect the difference in the rate of inflation between the two countries, since real interest rates are equal in the absence of restrictions. The Fisher Effect has been found to hold particularly well for short-maturity government securities issued by different countries. When comparisons are made with respect to longer-term government and private securities, the outcome has been found to be distorted by price fluctuations of government bonds prior to maturity and by the default risk of private issues of securities.

[5]More precisely, if $\overset{*}{P}$ Lit is the expected rate of inflation in Italy and $\overset{*}{P}$ US is the expected rate of inflation in the United States, then the exchange rate of the lira against the U.S. dollar is expected to depreciate by 4.5 percent, as shown below:

$$\overset{*}{S}(\$/\text{Lit}) = \frac{\overset{*}{P}\text{ US} - \overset{*}{P}\text{ Italy}}{(1 + \overset{*}{P}\text{ Italy})}$$

or

$$= \frac{0.05 - 0.10}{1.10} = \frac{-0.05}{1.10} = -0.045 \quad \text{or} \quad -4.5\%$$

This relationship, sometimes referred to as the *Fisher-Open Condition,* can be derived from interest rate and purchasing power parities when these two relationships are expressed in an *expectant* form, that is, *ex ante* as contrasted with *ex post* or realized form.

Interest parity may be rewritten as follows:

$$R\ \text{US} = R\ \text{Lit} + \mathring{e}(\$/\text{Lit})$$

Where R US and R Lit stands for borrowing cost in the United States and Italy, respectively, and $\mathring{e}$ ($/Lit) is the *expected* annual rate of change in the exchange rate. At equilibrium, or parity, the *expected* yield or borrowing cost at home (United States) is equal to the yield or interest rate abroad (Italy), plus the annual rate of appreciation (or minus the annual depreciation rate) of the foreign currency (Italian lira).

Purchasing power parity may be rewritten as follows:

$$\dot{P}\ \text{US} - \dot{P}\ \text{Lit} = \mathring{e}(\$/\text{Lit})$$

Where $\dot{P}$ US and $\dot{P}$ Italy are the annual inflation rates which are expected to occur in the United States and Italy, respectively. The formula states that the *expected* change in the lira/dollar exchange rate is equal to the difference in the rate of inflation that is *expected* to occur.

We thus obtain:

$$R\ \text{US} - R\ \text{Lit} = \dot{P}\ \text{US} - \dot{P}\ \text{Lit}$$

Therefore, *ex ante* the difference in interest rates between the United States and Italy is equal to the difference in the expected inflation rates, which is the *Fisher-Open Effect.* By rearranging we get:

$$R\ \text{US} - \dot{P}\ \text{US} = R\ \text{Lit} - \dot{P}\ \text{Lit} \quad \text{or} \quad r\ \text{US} = r\ \text{Lit}$$

The last formulation demonstrates Fisher's condition of the equality of real *interest rates* in different countries. Recasting the relationships in this form shows that not only are interest rate parity, purchasing power parity, and the Fisher Effect interrelated, but also each parity is derivable from the other two parities.

EXCHANGE RATE FUTURES AND OPTIONS

In addition to the forward market, where foreign exchange contracts can be transacted by multinational corporations or individuals with banks and brokers, future exchange contracts may be bought or sold for hedging or speculative purposes at the International Monetary Mart (IMM), which is part of the Chicago Mercantile Exchange. The IMM was organized in 1972 to facilitate future trading in foreign currencies which represent the major currencies of international trade and investment.

Eight currency futures (pound sterling, Canadian dollar, Dutch guilder, German mark, Japanese yen, Mexican peso, Swiss franc, and French franc) are traded in units of specified contracts patterned after the commodity future contracts at the Chicago Board of Trade. The contract specifications are shown in Exhibit 3-4 as compiled by the International Monetary Market.

As is the case in the commodity future market, both hedgers and speculators participate in the currency futures market, impelled by different motivations. The hedger is covering an existing or a prospective payable or receivable in a certain currency to cover his or her exposure, while the speculator is creating a position to realize a profit. A speculator buys a futures contract with the intention of selling it at a higher price, or conversely, sells a futures contract with the intention of buying it back at a lower price. Both types of participants are essential for efficient functioning of the futures market.

Options on currency futures are traded at the Chicago Merchantile Exchange for three currencies: the deutsche mark, British pound, and Swiss franc (see Exhibit 3-5). These instruments track changes in the prices of the underlying futures, thus facilitating spreading and arbitrage between the options and the futures. As in stock options, buying a call DM option, for example, is buying the right to acquire one DM future contract (covering DM125,000) at a certain striking price any time prior to a specified expiration date. A put DM option, conversely, is the right to sell one underlying DM futures contract.

Options on six currencies (British pound, Canadian dollar, deutsche mark, French franc, Japanese yen, and Swiss franc) are also traded on the Philadelphia Exchange. The Philadelphia options (Exhibit 3-6) are for spot currencies, rather than futures in bundles half the size of the IMM futures contracts shown in Exhibit 3-4. The use of currency options by multinational financial managers is illustrated in a later section of this chapter.

Although the forward exchange market and the futures exchange contracts made available by the IMM serve essentially the same purposes, there are a number of important differences between the two markets. These differences are summarized below:[6]

1. The forward market is a worldwide market where transactions are conducted by banks and exchange dealers connected by wire and electronic communication devices, mainly to accommodate the needs of their clients, the multinational corporations. The futures market provides a specific arena or location where contracts in specific currencies may be traded. The clientele are typically individual speculators, relatively small importers and exporters, and small businesses exposed to the foreign exchange risk.

[6]See also Exhibit 3-7 for comparison between the two markets.

Exhibit 3-4. International Monetary Market Contract Specifications

(1) Contract	(2) Size	(3) Hours[a]	(4) Months	(5) Minimum Fluctuation in Price	(6) Equals Contract
Pound sterling	25,000	7:30[d] 1:24 (9:20)	Jan., Mar., Apr., Jun., Jul., Sep., Oct., Dec., spot mo.	0.0005 (5 pt.) ($2.50/pt.)	$12.50
Canadian dollar	100,000	7:30[d] 1:22 (9:19)	Jan., Mar., Apr., Jun., Jul., Sep., Oct., Dec., spot mo.	0.0001 (1 pt.) ($10/pt.)	$10.00
Dutch guilder	125,000	7:30[d] 1:30 (9:23)	Jan., Mar., Apr., Jun., Jul., Sep., Oct., Dec., spot mo.	0.0001 (1 pt.) ($12.50/pt.)	$12.50
German mark	125,000	7:30[d] 1:20 (9:18)	Jan., Mar., Apr., Jun., Jul., Sep., Oct., Dec., spot mo.	0.0001 (1 pt.) ($12.50/pt.)	$12.50
Japanese yen	12,500,000	7:30[d] 1:26 (9:21)	Jan., Mar., Apr., Jun., Jul., Sep., Oct., Dec., spot mo.	0.000001 (1 pt.) ($12.50/pt.)	$12.50
Mexican peso	1,000,000	7:30[d] 1:18 (9:17)	Jan., Mar., Apr., Jun., Jul., Sep., Oct., Dec., spot mo.	0.00001 (1 pt.) ($10/pt.)	$10.00
Swiss franc	125,000	7:30[d] 1:16 (9:16)	Jan., Mar., Apr., Jun., Jul., Sep., Oct., Dec., spot mo.	0.0001 (1 pt.) ($12.50/pt.)	$12.50
French franc	250,000	7:30[d] 1:28 (9:22)	Jan., Mar., Apr., Jun., Jul., Sep., Oct., Dec., spot mo.	0.00005 (5 pt.) (2.50/pt.)	$12.50

[a]Times in parentheses indicate close on last day of trading.

[b]I refers to initial margins; M refers to maintenance margins.

[c]Margin on intercommodity spreads: The margin on all intercommodity spreads is the higher nonspread margin of the two commodities. Allowable IMM intercommodity spreads are gold vs. Swiss franc, domestic CDs vs. 90-day T bill, Eurodollar time deposit vs. domestic CDs, Eurodollar time deposit vs. 90-day T bill, and spreads between British pound, Dutch guilder, German mark, Swiss franc, and French franc. Exception: domestic CDs vs. 90-day T bill is $500 (I), $400 (M). Eurodollar time deposit vs. domestic CDs is $500 (I), $400 (M), and Eurodollar time deposit vs. 90-day T bill is $700 (I), $600 (M). Dutch guilder vs. German mark nondelivery month spread is $500, Swiss franc vs. German mark spread rate is $1,000 (I), $700 (M). Delivery month spread margins apply to spreads involving the lead month.

Exhibit 3-4. *(continued)*

(7) Limit	(8) Last Day Trading	(9) Delivery Date	(10) Minimum Margin[b]	(11) Spread Margin[c]	(12) Delivery Month Margin	(13) Delivery Month Spread Margin
0.05[e] (500 pt.) ($1,250)	2 bus. days bef. 3rd Wed.	3rd Wed.	I $1,500 M $1,000	Market	I $2,200[f] M $1,500	I $1,000[f] M $ 700
0.0075[e] (75 pt.) ($750)	2 bus. days bef. 3rd Wed.	3rd Wed.	I $ 900 M $ 700	Market	I $1,200[f] M $ 900	I $1,000[f] M $ 700
0.0100[e] (100 pt.) ($1,250)	2 bus. days bef. 3rd Wed.	3rd Wed.	I $1,200 M $ 900	Market	I $2,200[f] M $1,500	I $1,000[f] M $ 700
0.0100[e] (100 pt.) ($1,250)	2 bus. days bef. 3rd Wed.	3rd Wed.	I $1,500 M $1,000	Market	I $2,200[f] M $1,500	I $1,000[f] M $ 700
0.000100[e] (100 pt.) ($1,250)	2 bus. days bef. 3rd Wed.	3rd Wed.	I $1,500 M $1,000	Market	I $2,200[f] M $1,500	I $1,000[f] M $ 700
0.00150[e] (150 pt.) ($1,500)	2 bus. days bef. 3rd Wed.	3rd Wed.	I $5,000 M $4,000	I $5,000 M $4,000	I $5,000[f] M $4,000	I $5,000[f] M $4,000
0.0150[e] (150 pt.) ($1,875)	2 bus. days bef. 3rd Wed.	3rd Wed.	I $2,000 M $1,500	Market	I $3,000[f] M $2,000	I $1,500[f] M $1,000
0.00500[e] (500 pt.) ($1,250)	2 bus. days bef. 3rd Wed.	3rd Wed.	I $1,200 M $ 900	Market	I $2,200[f] M $1,500	I $1,000[f] M $ 700

[d]Central Time. On the last day of trading, currency contracts close in rotation starting at 9:16 A.M. Currency contracts open on call with Swiss franc opening at 7:30 A.M.

[e]Spot month to start trading without limits on the last trading day of the previous month; for example, February '81 would start trading without limits on the last trading day of the January '81 contract.

[f]Spot month margins start on the last trading day of the prior contract month.

Source: Chicago Merchantile Exchange, *Trading and Hedging with Currency Futures and Options,* (January 1982).

Exhibit 3-5. Contract Specifications*

	TRADING UNIT	STRIKE PRICE	PREMIUM QUOTATIONS	TICKER SYMBOLS	MINIMUM PRICE FLUCTUATION (TICK SIZE)	TRADING HOURS
Options on DM Futures	One Deutsche mark futures contract (covering DM125,000) of the specified contract month	Numbers in whole cent intervals	Quotations are cents per Deutsche mark. A quote of .50¢ represents an option price of $625. ($.0050 × DM125,000)	Calls: CM Puts: PM	.01 ($.0001), equal to $12.50 (same as DM futures)	7:30 a.m. to 1:20 p.m. Central time (same as DM futures)
Options on BP Futures	One British pound futures contract (covering BP25,000) of the specified contract month	Intervals of 2.5¢ (e.g., $1.200, $1.225, $1.250)	Quotations are cents per British pound. A quote of 1.25¢ represents an option price of $312.50. ($.0125 × BP25,000)	Calls: CP Puts: PP	.05¢ ($.0005), equal to $12.50 (same as BP futures)	7:30 a.m. to 1:24 p.m. Central time (same as BP futures)
Options on SF Futures	One Swiss franc futures contract (covering SF125,000) of the specified contract month	Numbers in whole cent intervals	Quotations are cents per Swiss franc. A quote of .50¢ represents an option price of $625. ($.0050 × SF125,000)	Calls: CF Puts: PF	.01¢ ($.0001), equal to $12.50 (same as SF futures)	7:30 a.m. to 1:16 p.m. Central time (same as SF futures)

*Contract specifications are subject to change. Check with your broker to confirm this information.

Exhibit 3-5. *(continued)*

Specifications Common to All CME Options on Currency Futures

Months Traded March, June, September, December

Daily Price Limit None

Strike Prices When a new contract month is listed for trading, there will be five put and call strike prices: the nearest strike to the underlying futures price, the next two higher and the next two lower. For example, if the March DM price closes at $.3651 on the previous day, the strikes listed for March puts and calls will be: 35¢, 36¢, 37¢, 38¢, 39¢.

A new strike price will be for both puts and calls when the underlying futures price touches within half a strike price interval of either the second highest or second lowest strike prices. As an example, if the March DM futures price touches .3751 after the options are listed as in the above example, then a new strike price at 40¢ will be listed for puts and calls the next day. (No new options will be listed, however, with less than 20 calendar days until expiration.)

Last Day of Trading Two Fridays before the third Wednesday of the contract month. If that Friday is an Exchange holiday, the last trading day will be the next business day.

Minimum Margin No margin required for put or call option buyers, but the full premium must be paid in cash. Check with your broker for margin on short option positions and combination option, futures positions.

Exercise Procedure Option buyers may exercise on any trading day. Check with your brokerage firm for its exercise procedure.

Exercise results in a long futures position for a call buyer or a put seller, and a short futures position for a put buyer or a call seller. The futures position is effective on the trading day immediately following exercise, and is marked-to-market to the settlement that day. If the futures position is not offset prior to the expiration of trading in the futures contract, delivery of physical currency will result or be required.

Expiration Options expire at 5:00 p.m. on the last trading day. However, your broker may set a considerably earlier cut-off time for exercising expiring options. Always check with your broker for exercise deadlines.

There is *no* automatic exercise of the expiring in-the-money currency options by the CME clearing house.

Source: Chicago Mercantile Exchange, *Options on Currency Futures: An Introduction* (Chicago, 1984), pp. 8–9.

Exhibit 3-6.

FOREIGN CURRENCY OPTIONS

Friday, Feb. 21

Option & Underlying	Strike Price	Calls–Last			Puts–Last		
		Feb	Mar	Jun	Feb	Mar	Jun
12,500 British Pounds-cents per unit.							
BPound	120	s	r	r	s	r	0.10
145.32	.130	r	r	r	r	r	0.60
145.32	.135	r	9.80	r	r	0.10	1.50
145.32	.140	r	5.10	5.80	r	0.40	2.75
145.32	.145	r	1.80	3.60	r	2.20	5.70
145.32	.150	r	0.30	1.75	r	5.90	r
145.32	.155	r	0.05	r	r	r	r
50,000 Canadian Dollars-cents per unit.							
CDollr	...71	r	r	r	r	0.15	1.00
72.00	...72	r	0.41	0.80	r	0.69	1.55
62,500 West German Marks-cents per unit.							
DMark	..35	s	8.29	r	s	r	r
43.47	...37	r	r	6.75	r	r	r
43.47	...38	r	r	r	r	r	0.06
43.47	...39	r	4.30	4.68	r	r	r
43.47	...40	r	3.40	r	r	r	r
43.47	...41	r	2.31	2.93	r	r	0.33
43.47	...42	r	1.60	2.30	r	0.11	0.50
43.47	...43	r	0.81	1.65	r	0.32	0.87
43.47	...44	r	0.37	1.13	r	0.82	1.44
43.47	...45	s	0.10	0.73	s	r	r
43.47	...46	s	r	0.46	s	r	r
125,000 French Francs-10ths of a cent per unit.							
FFranc	.110	s	30.50	r	s	r	r
6,250,000 Japanese Yen-100ths of a cent per unit.							
JYen	... 48	r	r	6.96	r	r	r
54.69	...50	r	4.75	4.98	r	r	0.18
54.69	...52	r	2.60	r	r	0.10	0.40
54.69	...53	r	1.91	r	r	0.19	0.67
54.69	...54	s	1.01	2.00	s	0.41	1.04
54.69	...55	s	0.54	1.43	s	0.80	1.50
54.69	...56	s	0.23	1.08	s	1.58	r
54.69	...57	s	0.12	0.73	s	r	r
54.69	...58	s	0.08	r	s	r	r
62,500 Swiss Francs-cents per unit.							
SFranc	..47	r	4.71	r	r	r	r
51.99	...48	r	3.74	r	r	r	0.21
51.99	...49	r	r	3.49	r	r	r
51.99	...50	r	1.95	3.03	r	0.16	0.57
51.99	...51	r	1.34	r	r	0.33	0.89
51.99	...52	s	0.58	1.64	s	0.78	1.43
51.99	...53	s	0.28	r	s	r	r
51.99	...54	s	0.14	0.87	s	r	r

Total call vol. 12,377 Call open int. 251,232
Total put vol. 7,358 Put open int. 239,378

Chicago Board Options Exchange

Friday, Feb. 21

Option & Underlying	Strike Price	Calls–Last			Puts–Last		
		Feb	Mar	Jun	Feb	Mar	Jun
25,000 British Pounds-cents per unit.							
BPound	140	r	r	r	r	1.08	r
100,000 Canadian Dollars-cents per unit.							
CDollar	..68	s	r	r	s	r	0.18
72.00	...69	s	r	r	s	r	1.02
125,000 West German Marks-cents per unit.							
DMark	..40	r	r	r	r	r	0.15
43.47	...41	r	r	r	r	r	0.26
43.47	...42	r	r	r	r	r	1.16
43.47	...44	s	1.01	r	s	r	r
43.47	...45	s	0.11	2.08	s	r	r
12,500,000 Japanese Yen-100ths of a cent per unit.							
JYen	... 52	r	r	10.22	r	0.10	r
54.66	...53	r	r	r	r	0.19	r
54.66	...54	s	3.04	r	s	1.06	3.04
54.66	...55	s	1.26	r	s	2.17	4.30
125,000 Swiss Francs-cents per unit.							
SFranc	..50	r	r	r	r	0.15	r
51.98	...51	r	r	r	r	r	3.00
51.98	...52	s	2.00	r	s	2.03	r
51.98	...54	s	0.12	r	s	r	r

Total call volume 286. Total call open int. 19,741.
Total put volume 1,161. Total put open int. 15,313.
r–Not traded. s–No option offered.
Last is premium (purchase price).

2. The forward market theoretically enables the participants to buy and sell any foreign currency in any amount and for any desired maturity. In practice, however, trading is confined to about 20 major currencies for maturities usually not exceeding two years. The IMM offers futures contracts only in eight major currencies for specified maturities or delivery dates. (Delivery date is the third Wednesday of January, March, April, June, July, September, October, and December.) Moreover, the size of each contract is specified in whole units of each of the currencies being traded.

Exhibit 3-7. Comparison of the Forward and Futures Markets

	FORWARD	FUTURES
Size of Contract	Tailored to individual needs.	Standardized.
Delivery Date	Tailored to individual needs.	Standardized.
Participants	Banks, brokers, and multinational companies. Public speculation not encouraged.	Banks, brokers and multinational companies. Qualified public speculation encouraged.
Security Deposit	None as such, but compensating bank balances or lines of credit required.	Small security deposit required.
Clearing Operation	Handling contingent on individual banks and brokers. No separate clearinghouse function.	Handled by exchange clearinghouse. Daily settlements to the market price.
Marketplace	Over the telephone worldwide.	Central exchange floor with worldwide communications.
Regulation	Self-regulating.	Commodity Futures Trading Commission; National Futures Association
Liquidation	Most settled by actual delivery. Some by offset, at a cost.	Most by offset: very few by delivery.
Transaction Costs	Set by "spread" between bank's buy and sell price.	Negotiated brokerage fees, quoted for entry and exit.

Source: Chicago Mercantile Exchange, *Understanding Futures in Foreign Exchange* (Chicago, 1984), p. 8.

3. While participants in the forward market deal with each other, traders in currency futures make contracts with the exchange itself. Future exchange contracts are commodity futures and, thus, are subject to certain specified margin and maintenance requirements, as well as specified daily price fluctuation limits. The forward market contracts are not subject to these requirements or limits. Banks normally require no deposit from their larger clients, although generally they reduce the client's line of credit by the value of the contract, or require a deposit equivalent to a certain percentage (5–10 percent) of the value of the contract.
4. Like commodity futures, a currency future contract is almost never exercised, but is rather closed by reversing the contract prior to the delivery (maturity) date. Forward contracts are normally exercised by the buyer or the seller at the maturity date, although a forward contract can be offset by entering a reverse agreement with the bank or the dealer.

Although the futures and forward markets are separate markets subject to different rules and requirements, arbitrage operations insure that price quotations remain roughly in line. If, for example, the 6-month forward buying price of Swiss francs is \$0.3654 while the selling rate on the same date on the Chicago IMM is \$0.3660, an arbitrager would buy forward from a bank and sell Swiss francs futures on the same date. The arbitrager could make a profit of \$0.0006/SF or \$75 for each contract of SF125,000. He must, however, pay out of that a commission for selling francs on the IMM. Moreover, positions in the futures market require a margin as well as maintenance funds as daily contract prices vary. These factors permit differentials to persist between forward and futures market rates. However, arbitrage will ensure that the ask price of forward currency does not significantly exceed the bid price of the same currency in the futures market.

HEDGING AND SPECULATION IN THE FOREIGN EXCHANGE MARKET

Both the forward and futures markets afford participants in these markets the opportunity to engage in hedging or speculative transactions. Hedging consists of covering a present or an anticipated position in a foreign currency, thus substituting a presently known cost for an open-ended outcome of the uncovered position. Speculation, on the other hand, entails creating a position in a foreign currency for the purpose of realizing profit.

Hedging by Importers and Exporters

Any foreign trade transaction involves an exchange risk either to the exporter or the importer, depending on the currency of denomination of the transaction. The time lag between the date of placing the order and the date of settlement may be as long as one year or even longer, due in part to the prevalence of three to six months' trade credit in such transactions. The party which is exposed to the exchange risk, the importer if the transaction is denominated in the exporter's currency, faces the choice of remaining uncovered or buying the exporter's currency forward with a delivery date coinciding with the date of settlement. If the importer chooses not to hedge because of inertia, or because he or she expects the exchange rate to remain virtually unchanged or move in his or her favor in the duration, a *speculative* position is created. In this case, the importer is betting that his or her expectation of the movement of exchange rates is superior to that of the exchange market as reflected by the spread between the spot and forward rates. In other words, the importer is taking the position that the forward rate quoted presently is not an accurate predictor of the future spot rate.

If the importing firm can source its requirements from suppliers in a number of countries, its decision to import from one supplier or another should be governed not by unit cost based on today's spot rate, but rather by the unit cost based on covering the foreign currency payable in the forward market. Even if it decides against hedging, its choice of supplier should be governed by the spot rates for the respective currencies that it expects to prevail on the date of settlement.

To illustrate the nature of this decision, let us assume that a U.S. firm about to issue an order to import 1000 units of a certain commodity receives the quotations in Table 3-1. For the sake of simplifying comparison, let us also assume that the prices quoted are delivered prices and that delivery from all suppliers would take three months (terms: sight draft upon delivery).

The relevant cost and exchange rate data are shown in Table 3-1.

To ascertain the lowest cost supplier in each case, one must express all costs in U.S. dollars. This is shown in Table 3-2.

If the decision is to be based on the spot rate prevailing at the time the order is placed, the Swiss supplier offers the lowest cost. On the other hand, if the U.S. firm were to choose the supplier on the basis of exchange rates that it expects to prevail three months later, its choice will be the Italian supplier. The Italian supplier is also the lowest if the U.S. firm decides to hedge the transaction by buying the supplier's currency forward. As it turned out, Italy provided the lowest cost based on the exchange rates that

Table 3-1.

	ITALY	SWITZERLAND	FRANCE
Delivered cost of 1000 units	LIT 8,000,000	SF 10,500	FF 40,000
$S(\$/j)$ Spot exchange rate	\$0.000627	\$0.4712	\$0.1256
$\overset{*}{S}_{1/4}(\$/j)$ Spot exchange rate expected to prevail in 3 months	\$0.000600	\$0.4800	\$0.1240
$F_{1/4}(\$/j)$ Three months forward rate quoted today	\$0.000590	\$0.4850	\$0.1200
$S_{1/4}(\$/j)$ Spot rate that actually prevailed 3 months hence	\$0.000575	\$0.4650	\$0.1250

Table 3-2.

	ITALY	SWITZERLAND	FRANCE
$S(\$/j)$	\$5016	\$4947	\$5024
$\overset{*}{S}_{1/4}(\$/j)$	\$4800	\$5040	\$4960
$F_{1/4}(\$/j)$	\$4720	\$5092	\$4800
$S_{1/4}(\$/j)$	\$4600	\$4882	\$5000

actually prevailed three months later on the date of settlement. You would normally expect the choice based on the forward cover to be the same as the one based on actual future rates, since the forward rate is said to be an accurate predictor of the future spot rate. Note, however, that this is not the case with the Swiss franc, which actually depreciated contrary to market expectations. Note also that the U.S. supplier would have fared best if it had decided to wait to buy the foreign currency (Italian liras) at the date of settlement rather than covering in the forward market. If it had elected to do so, it would have taken the risk that exchange rates might have moved against it; that is, the dollar might have depreciated vis-a-vis the three foreign currencies.

Parties to an international trade transaction have options other than denominating the transaction in either the currency of the importer or the exporter. The price per unit, for example, may be set in a mixture of the two currencies, or in a third currency, or in units of Special Drawing Rights (SDRs), or in any generally accepted composite units based on "baskets" or "cocktails" combining a number of currencies.[7] These arrangements are sometimes resorted to in order to reduce and/or split the currency risk between the parties to the transaction. In the case of SDRs and currency cocktails, the primary purpose is to limit this risk, since the movements of currencies in the composite unit are expected to partially offset each other. In practice the bulk of world trade, because of convention and convenience, is conducted in U.S. dollars. This in effect relieves U.S. traders from shouldering the exchange risk and relegates it to the other party to the transaction. American exporters, however, must weigh the decision to set prices in U.S. dollars against the risk of losing business to other competitors who may be willing to invoice in the importers' currencies.

Hedging by Borrowers and Investors

Earlier in this chapter, it was explained that borrowers in foreign money markets, attracted perhaps by lower interest rates prevailing there, have the option to hedge in the forward market to generate the foreign currency with which to repay their obligations abroad. It was also pointed out that such borrowing ceases to be profitable at the point of interest rate parity, that is, when the forward premium on the foreign currency equals the differential in the cost of borrowing. Likewise, investors attracted by the higher return on money market investments abroad can hedge by selling foreign currency forward. At parity, these operations cease to generate a higher rate of return than domestic investments.

Hedging by MNCs on their borrowing and investing operations outside their home country is usually conducted in the context of their overall policies governing exchange risk exposure management, as discussed in

[7]SDRs and other composite units are discussed in Chapters 2 and 9.

Chapter 5. It should be pointed out here that hedging foreign currency receivables and payables can be conducted with a variety of techniques in addition to the forward and futures exchange markets. These techniques are discussed in Chapter 5.

Use of the forward and futures markets for hedging long-term loans and investments is somewhat limited. Although forward currency contracts can be negotiated for periods exceeding two or three years, such operations are rather uncommon due to the reluctance of banks to undertake such commitments, particularly in an environment of volatile exchange rates.

Speculation in Foreign Exchange Markets

By definition a speculator does not have an existing or anticipated foreign currency receivable or payable. Speculators' stock in trade is their presumed ability to outsmart other participants in the foreign exchange market. When exchange markets are efficient, that is, when relevant information is equally available to all participants in the market, in the absence of restrictions or controls, the forward rate will tend to be an accurate predictor of the future spot rate. Under these circumstances, the role of the speculator is rather circumscribed. If parities do not prevail, allowing a profit to be frequently made from interest arbitrage, the foreign exchange market is inefficient. Tests conducted to determine whether it is efficient, that is, whether the forward rate is an accurate predictor of the future spot rate, concluded that it is an "unbiased" but poor predictor of the eventual spot rate. By "unbiased" it is meant that it is as likely to be above as below the future spot rate.[8]

Speculation may be conducted in either the spot or the forward market, although in terms of volume most speculation takes place in the forward market. Speculators will take a long position, that is, buy the foreign currency if they expect that currency will gain in value. Conversely, a short position is assumed by selling the currency if the expectation is that it will depreciate against a speculator's own currency or other currencies.

If the speculator expects the Italian lira to appreciate against the U.S. dollar within a certain time horizon, say six months, he or she will buy the lira in the spot market today, using borrowed dollars, and will invest the proceeds in Italy. Thus, every Italian lira the speculator wants to have six months later will cost now:

$$\frac{S(\$/\text{Lit})}{(1 + R\ \text{Lit})^{1/2}}$$

[8]Maurice Levi, *International Finance, Financial Management and the International Economy* (New York: McGraw Hill, 1983), pp. 293–295. See also Richard M. Levich, "The Efficiency of Markets for Foreign Exchange. A Review and Extension," reprinted in *International Finance, Concepts and Issues,* edited by Gerald D. Gay and Robert W. Kolbe, Robert F. Dame, Inc. (Richmond, VA 1983), pp. 397–428.

The amount to be paid in dollars six months from now equals:

$$S(\$/\text{Lit}) \cdot \frac{(1 + R\ \text{US})^{1/2}}{(1 + R\ \text{Lit})^{1/2}}$$

The speculator will realize a profit if:

$$\overset{*}{S}_{1/2}(\$/\text{Lit}) > S(\$/\text{Lit}) \cdot \frac{(1 + R\ \text{US})^{1/2}}{(1 + R\ \text{Lit})^{1/2}}$$

that is, if the dollars realized six months from now from changing liras into dollars, at the spot rate prevailing then, exceed the number of dollars borrowed now to buy liras in the spot market.

Forward speculation enables speculators to act on the basis of the spread between the quoted forward exchange rates and their own prediction of the future spot rates. Speculators will go long on the Italian lira if they expect the future spot rate to be above the forward rate, that is, $\overset{*}{S}(\$/\text{Lit}) > F(\$/\text{Lit})$. They will buy the currency at the forward rate quoted today, take delivery of the liras at the maturity of the contract, and sell them at the higher spot rate prevailing then, pocketing the difference. Conversely, if the future spot rate is expected to be lower than the forward rate, that is, $\overset{*}{S}(\$/\text{Lit}) < F(\$/\text{Lit})$, liras sold today in the forward market will be bought back at the cheaper rate prevailing at the maturity of the contract.

To illustrate speculation in the forward market, using the data given earlier for importing from alternative sources, we hypothesize that a speculator wants to go *long* on the Italian lira and the French franc and *short* on the Swiss franc. The outcome of this speculation after three months using the spot rates that actually prevailed then is tabulated in Table 3-3.

The speculator lost money on the lira contract because it depreciated, whereas the expectation was for it to appreciate, since $\overset{*}{S}_{1/4}(\$/\text{Lit}) > F_{1/4}(\$/\text{Lit})$ or \$0.000600 > \$0.000590. The actual rate three months later turned out to be \$0.000575. The speculator realized profit on the other two contracts, because the eventual spot rates corresponded with his or her expectations.

Table 3-3.

Currency	Bought/Sold Forward	1 million units at $F_{1/4}$ (\$/j)	Sold/Bought Spot at $S_{1/4}$ (\$/j)	Profit (loss)
Italian lira	Bought	\$ 5,900	\$ 5,750	\$ (150)
Swiss franc	Sold	\$485,000	\$465,000	\$20,000
French franc	Bought	\$120,000	\$125,000	5,000
			Overall	\$24,850

USE OF CURRENCY OPTIONS BY MULTINATIONAL FINANCIAL MANAGERS

Multinational corporate treasurers have been recently attracted by the versatility of the currency option instrument both as a complement to the forward and futures market and as an effective hedging device for managing risks in itself. The use of the device is still limited, partly because of managements' resistance to the use of this instrument due to preconceived notions as to its speculative nature. Nevertheless, its emerging popularity with corporate treasurers and financial managers warrants attention. This section illustrates the benefits and limitations of the currency option as a hedging technique in a highly volatile currency environment.[9]

A currency option is a contract specifying the right to buy (call) or sell (put) foreign exchange (Philadelphia options) or foreign exchange futures (Chicago options) within a specified period. There are four ways to trade an option: buy a call, sell (write) a call, buy a put, sell (write) a put. The buyer has the opportunity to take advantage of buying or selling foreign currency at a prearranged price if the market provides it. If the market does not provide the opportunity, the buyer will just let the option expire. For this privilege the buyer must pay the seller some premium. This premium is the maximum amount the buyer can lose upon the expiration of the option.

To illustrate the use of currency options as a hedging alternative to the forward market, let us assume that a U.S. importing firm has to make a payment of FF10 million in six months. The treasurer of the firm desires to fix the cost of imports in dollars today. One way to accomplish this objective is to buy FF10 million in the forward market for delivery in six months. This commits the firm to sell a known number of dollars to a bank at a rate that is in effect at the time of the hedge.

By buying sufficient French franc call options with the desired maturity, the importing firm makes no such commitment. If the franc rises above the strike price specified in the option contract, the importer will find it advantageous to exercise the option, using the proceeds to make the payment to the French exporter. If the franc fails to reach the preset strike price, the firm can let the option lapse, losing only the premium money paid for the option. To make settlement in francs, the treasurer will take advantage of the lower prices in the spot market. The currency option thus allows the importer, in return for a known maximum cost (the premium), to protect the firm against a rising franc, while allowing it to cash in on a falling currency.

[9]The author wishes to acknowledge the contribution of Maureen Svagera of the Commercial Federal Savings and Loan Association of Nebraska in developing some of the illustrations in this section.

In addition to managing risks, some sophisticated and aggressive corporate treasurers are finding ways to generate additional income with currency options. For example, a U.S. corporation that has a constant inflow of Swiss francs can earn premiums from writing options against its franc inventory. If the currency erodes in value, the option will never be exercised and the premium will be pure profit.

On the other hand, if the franc rises and the option is exercised, the corporation already owns the currency it is giving up. The chance for additional profit if the franc moved even higher is all that is sacrificed by this transaction.

Another transaction that is a spin-off from the traditional hedging techniques is one where a company that needs to pay for British imports in three months will buy British pounds on the interbank forward market. If the pound rallies, the importer can lock in that profit by purchasing options to sell the currency at the improved exchange rate. If the pound moves lower by the time the payment comes due, the company exercises its option and receives the higher price. Then to pay for the imports, the company buys pounds in the spot market at the depressed rate.

The preceding illustrations present the use of options as a complement to the forward market. But in some cases the foreign exchange risk of a multinational company can be hedged only through the use of options. This is the case when a corporation bids on a foreign contract or an acquisition in a foreign currency. While unsure of successfully winning the contract, the bidding firm would want to guarantee that the exchange rate does not move against it, should they win the contract. If the company hedges in the forward market and loses the bid, it would still have to take possession of the currency, which it would have to sell on the spot market, possibly at a big loss. By using options, the maximum risk is known at the outset and limited to the premium paid on buying the call options.

Despite the flexibility of the currency option as an instrument of risk management, a large number of MNCs' treasurers are still skeptical. Some agree that the premium for options to protect bids can be costly if they fail to receive many bids. Some traditional managers continue to look upon this instrument as too speculative for their style of management. A foreign currency trader at a major investment banking house assessed the hedging potential of currency options by stating, "... in a highly volatile currency environment, the options hedge will always underperform what turns out to be the best alternative, but only by a small margin. On the other hand, the options position will substantially outperform the worst alternative."[10]

Buyers and writers of foreign currency options are subject to special risks in addition to the recognized risks associated with options positions.

[10]Michael Sesit, "Foreign Currency Options Grow Popular But Pose Risks for Banks," *The Wall Street Journal,* April 29, 1984, p. 17.

These special risks include:

1. Foreign currency transactions in the forward market involve dollar amounts that are likely to be substantially larger than amounts involved in the exercise of options. Consequently, investors who buy or write the options may have to deal in the odd lot market for the underlying currency at prices that are less favorable.
2. There is no systematic reporting of last sale information for foreign currencies. While the bid and offer information is available on the exchange floor and in the bankers' and brokers' offices, there is no regulatory requirement stating that rates be quoted on a current basis. This may prohibit investors from receiving timely and accurate data. In addition, the data that is available is quoted for large transactions which may not be representative of the prices for foreign currency options.
3. The hours of trading in foreign currency options do not conform to the round-the-clock trading of the underlying currencies in the interbank market. This means that significant price and rate movements can take place that will not be reflected in the options market until the following day. This may deprive traders in currency options of the chance to make quick and timely decisions to liquidate their positions.

Trading in options is expanding at a rapid pace. The typical option is for the equivalent of \$5–10 million for a maturity of three to six months. The premium for such a contract normally costs 1.5 to 1.75 percent of the option value. Large MNCs such as Texaco, Inc., IBM, Intel Corporation, Hercules, Inc., Ford Motor Co., and Nestle S.A. are active participants in this market.[11]

While the Philadelphia Exchange provides the arena for trading options on foreign currencies, large financial firms such as Citibank, Chemical Bank, Merrill Lynch, and Goldman Sacks & Co. are in the business of writing over-the-counter options for their clients. Over-the-counter options are custom tailored in maturity and size to fit the requirements of the customer, unlike Exchange options, which are standardized. As more and more institutions begin to write options, premiums have tended to decrease, thus attracting more corporate treasurers to the options market.

REVIEW QUESTIONS

1. Compare and contrast the international money markets and foreign exchange markets as to centers or localities of operation, methods or channels of communicating prices and quotations, participants, and overall size.

[11]Michael Sesit, "Foreign Currency Options Grow Popular," p. 17.

2. How many exchange rates exist in a fictitious world where there are only seven currencies? How many exchange rates are needed to derive the whole set of exchange rates? Explain how the other "redundant" rates are derivable from the original set.
3. If currency X is quoted at a forward discount against currency Y, what can be said about currency Y in terms of X? What behavior in the future spot rate X/Y is being anticipated by participants in the exchange market? What factors underlie or justify such expectations? Can the participants prove wrong?
4. What are swap points in exchange rate quotations? Explain when swap points must be added to the respective bid/ask spot prices to arrive at forward bid/ask quotations, if exchange rates are quoted in U.S. dollar equivalent terms (U.S. dollar per unit of foreign currency)? How do the calculation of the forward premium (discount) and the treatment of the swap points differ when exchange rates are expressed in European terms (foreign currency units per 1.00 U.S. dollar)?
5. What is meant by the forward rate being an "accurate" predictor of the future spot rate? Is that different from being an "unbiased" predictor? What conditions should be satisfied for the first relationship to be valid?
6. Why is interest parity more realistically represented by a band rather than a line? List at least three reasons that could explain persistent differentials in money market interest rates among countries on a covered basis (that is, when the exchange risk is covered in the forward market).
7. What are broken exchange rates? Would this situation persist in efficient exchange markets? Explain how three-cornered or "triangular" arbitrage eliminates broken rates.
8. Distinguish between the "absolute" and the "relative" versions of purchasing power parity (PPP) theorem. Does available empirical evidence lend support to either version? What is the most important contribution of PPP to international finance, and under what circumstances is it expected to hold?
9. What is the basis of the Fisherian (after Irving Fisher) postulate that "real" interest rates tend to be equal in different countries? How does Fisher Open Condition explain the differentials in nominal interest rates among countries?
10. a. List the major requirements or conditions for efficient money and foreign exchange markets.

    b. If these markets were truly efficient, summarize the relationships that would exist between or among:

(1) Forward and future exchange rates.
(2) Forward premiums (discounts) and interest rate differentials.
(3) Inflation rate differentials between any two countries and the expected future exchange rate between their currencies.
(4) Inflation and nominal interest rate differentials between any two countries.

11. How does speculation in the forward exchange market differ from speculation in the spot market? What is meant by going "long" or "short" in the currency market? Under what conditions would you sell a certain currency forward?

REVIEW PROBLEMS

1. A foreign exchange dealer quoted the following rates for the pound sterling on Friday, November 30, 1985.

Spot	\$1.4710/\$1.4810
30-day forward	65/44
90-day forward	145/123
180-day forward	290/222

   a. Determine the outright quotations for the pound sterling.
   b. Was the pound sterling selling at a forward premium or a forward discount on that date? Calculate the forward premium (or discount) on the 90-day forward contract. Use ask (offer) rate to answer this question.
   c. How many U.S. dollars would it cost you to buy £1,000,000 on November 30, 1985?
   d. If you expect to receive £1,000,000 in 180 days from the quotation date, how many U.S. dollars would you expect to realize by selling them forward?

2. Using data in Problem 1, and assuming that the yield on a six-month CD of major banks in the United States is 9 percent, what should be the yield on a comparable CD in the United Kingdom to insure interest parity between the two countries? Are covered yield differentials likely to persist under efficient money and exchange markets?

3. A U.S. distributor purchases goods from France in the amount of French francs (FF) 50 million. Payment in French francs is due in three months. Market data is as follows:

Exchange rates (\$/FF)	**French francs**
Spot	\$0.118850
3-month forward	\$0.118140

Interest rates (percent per annum)	
United States	9.00%
France	10.25%

a. What is the premium or discount on the forward franc? Is there an incentive for interest arbitrage? Explain how arbitrage operations will eventually eliminate profit opportunities.
b. Assume that the interest rate in France is 11.4 percent instead of 10.25 percent, that is, a condition of virtual interest parity. Show how the U.S. firm can hedge this transaction in (1) the money market, (2) the forward market. (Show all calculations, ignoring transaction cost.)
c. If the actual spot rate in 90 days turned out to be $0.160735, how did the U.S. firm fare under the options listed in section (b) compared to an unhedged position? (Show all calculations, ignoring transaction cost.)
d. Which hedging technique in section (b) would you prefer to execute if you take into account transaction cost? What transaction costs are involved in either technique? Are transaction costs likely to be higher in one technique than the other?

4. Suppose that the interest rate in Sandland is 24 percent per annum, whereas it is only 8 percent per annum in the United States. You are considering investing $10,000 for 180 days in Sandland securities but are concerned about the exchange risk. Sandland's currency is *camel.* You find the following quotations in the newspaper in U.S. dollar terms:

Sandland (camel)	$0.1000
30-day forward	0.0980
90-day forward	0.0970
180-day forward	0.0950

a. Calculate the forward premium (discount) of the camel against the U.S. dollar (based on the 180-day quotation).
b. What is the net gain in U.S. dollars from investing in Sandland securities relative to U.S. securities if it is assumed that the exchange rate in 180 days equals today's spot rate?
c. Suppose the camel depreciates by 10 percent relative to the dollar in the next 180 days; what is your net gain (or loss) from an uncovered position relative to investment in the United States?
d. What is your net gain (or loss) from a covered position? (Ignore transaction cost.)

5. A U.S. firm about to issue an order to import 1000 widgets received the following C.I.F. quotations in local currency. Delivery from all suppliers would take three months (terms of payment: sight draft upon delivery).

	ITALY	SWITZERLAND	FRANCE
Local cost	Lit8,000,000	SF10,500	FF40,000
So ($/j)	0.000627	0.4712	0.1256
$\overset{*}{S}_{1/4}$ ($/j)	0.000600	0.4800	0.1240
$F_{1/4}$ ($/j)	0.000590	0.4850	0.1200
$S_{1/4}$ ($/j)	0.000575	0.4650	0.1250

a. Which country would you import from if you based your decision on today's rates?
b. Which country would you import from if you decided on forward hedging?
c. Which country actually provided the best price at the time of delivery?
d. If you were a speculator, in which currency or currencies would you go long? In which currency or currencies would you go short? What is the overall profit/loss from your positions per *one million units* of foreign currencies? (Ignore transaction cost.)

6. Given the following data about countries A and B, and given that interest rate parity, purchasing power parity, and the international Fisher Effect hold for both countries,

	COUNTRY A	COUNTRY B
Spot exchange rate	1A = 5B	1B = .20A
Yield on 12-month Treasury bills	7.5%	
Expected inflation rate during the next 12 months	4%	6%

a. Calculate the yield on 12-month Treasury bill in country B.
b. Calculate the 12-month forward exchange quote for currencies of both countries.
c. How is the differential in the rate of inflation related to the forward premium (discount) expressed in percentage per annum?
d. If the yield on 12-month Treasury bills in country B were given as 10 percent, which of the parity equilibria given above would be violated? Under what circumstances would you expect such a situation to prevail?

BIBLIOGRAPHY

ADLER, M. "Forget Hedging Costs," *Euromoney* (September 1983), pp. 137–138.

ADLER, M. and B. DUMAS, "Portfolio, Choice and the Demand for Forward Exchange," *American Economic Review* (May 1976), pp. 332–339.

Banker, "Foreign Exchange Markets: Is There a Case for Intervention?" (May 1983), pp. 25–27.

BARON, D. P., "Flexible Exchange Rates, Forward Markets, and the Level of Trade," *The American Economic Review* (June 1976), pp. 253–266.

Business Week, "Getting Into the Foreign Exchange Game" (May 25, 1981), pp. 182–183.

CALLIER, PHILIPPE, "Speculation and the Forward Foreign Exchange Rate: A Note," *Journal of Finance* (March 1980), pp. 173–176.

CHRYSTAL, K. A., "A Guide to Foreign Exchange Markets," *Federal Reserve Bank of St. Louis Review* (March 1984), pp. 5–18.

CORNELL, B., "Spot Rates, Forward Rates, and Exchange Market Efficiency," *Journal of Financial Economics* (August 1977), pp. 55–65.

———, "Determinants of the Bid-Ask Spread on Forward Exchange Contracts Under Floating Exchange Rates," *Journal of International Business Studies* (Fall 1978), pp. 33–41.

———, "Relative Price Changes and Deviations from Purchasing Power Parity," *Journal of Banking and Finance,* no. 3 (1979), pp. 263–279.

CORNELL, B. and J. K. DIETRICH, "The Efficiency of the Foreign Exchange Market Under Floating Exchange Rates," *Review of Economics and Statistics* (February 1978), pp. 111–120.

CROCKETT, A., "Determinants of Exchange Rate Movements: A Review," *Finance and Development* (March 1981), pp. 33–37.

DEARDORFF, A., "One-Way Arbitrage and Its Implications for Foreign Exchange Markets," *Journal of Political Economy* (April 1979), pp. 351–364.

DENIS, J., JR., "How Well Does the International Money Market Track the Interbank Forward Market?" *Financial Analysts Journal* (January-February 1976), pp. 50–54.

DUFEY, G. and I. GIDDY, "Forecasting Exchange Rates in a Floating World," *Euromoney* (November 1975), pp. 28–35.

DUFEY, G. and R. MIRUS, "Forecasting Foreign Exchange Rates: A Pedagogical Note," *Columbia Journal of World Business* (Summer 1981), pp. 53–61.

EATON, J. and S. J. TURNOVSKY, "The Forward Exchange Market, Speculation, and Exchange Market Intervention," *Quarterly Journal of Economics* (February 1984), pp. 45–69.

Economist, "Why Exchange Rates Change," November 24, 1984, pp. 66–67.

ENSOR, R., "The World's Best Foreign Exchange Dealer," *Euromoney* (September 1980), pp. 92–99.

Federal Reserve Bank of New York Quarterly Review, "The Changing Role of the Foreign Currency Futures Market" (Summer 1984), p. 43.

FEIGER, G., and B. JACQUILLAT, "Currency Option Bonds, Puts and Calls on Spot Exchange and the Hedging of Contingent Foreign Earnings," *Journal of Finance* (December 1979), pp. 1129–1139.

FRENKEL, J. A., "The Forward Exchange Rate, Expectations and the Demand for Money: The German Hyperinflation," *American Economic Review* (September 1977), pp. 653–670.

———, "The Purchasing Power Parity: Doctrinal Perspective and Evidence from the 1920's," *Journal of International Economics* (May 1978), pp. 169–192.

———, "Efficiency and Volatility of Exchange Rates and Prices in the 1970's," *Columbia Journal of World Business* (Winter 1979), pp. 15–27.

GENBERG, H., "Effects of Central Bank Intervention in the Foreign Exchange Market," *IMF Staff Papers* (September 1981), pp. 451–476.

GHANEM, A. M. S., "Purchasing Power Parity: A Test of Validity in Today's Markets," *Management International Review,* no. 4 (1982), pp. 19–33.

GIDDY, I. H., "Measuring the World Foreign Exchange Market," *Columbia Journal of World Business* (Winter 1979), pp. 36–48.

———, "Research on the Foreign Exchange Markets," *Columbia Journal of World Business* (Winter 1980), pp. 4–6.

GIDDY, I. H. and G. DUFEY, "The Random Behavior of Flexible Exchange Rates: Implications for Forecasting," *Journal of International Business Studies* (Spring 1975), pp. 1–32.

GUDAC, T., "Pricing and Exchange Rates in Planned Economies," *Finance and Development* (September 1984), pp. 40–43.

GUPTA, S., "A Note on the Efficiency of Black Markets in Foreign Currencies," *Journal of Finance* (June 1981), pp. 705–710.

HEKMAN, C. R., "Measuring Foreign Exchange Exposure: A Practical Theory and Its Application," *Financial Analysts Journal* (September/October 1983), pp. 59–63.

HILL, J. and T. SCHNEEWEIS, "Forecasting Effectiveness of Foreign Currency Futures," *Business Economics* (May 1981), pp. 42–46.

HILLEY, J. L., "Why There Is No Long Forward Market in Foreign Exchange," *Euromoney* (January 1981), pp. 94–103.

JACQUE, L. L., "Why Hedgers Are Not Speculators," *Columbia Journal of World Business* (Winter 1979), pp. 108–116.

KERN, D., "Currency Forecasting: Not a Prophecy, But a Guide to Action," *Euromoney* (July 1980), pp. 137–147.

KING, D., "Exchange Market Efficiency and the Risk-Taker of Last Resort," *Columbia Journal of World Business* (Winter 1979), pp. 28–35.

KOHLHAGEN, S. W., "The Performance of the Foreign Exchange Markets: 1971–1974," *Journal of International Business Studies* (Fall 1975), pp. 33–39.

———, *The Behavior of Foreign Exchange Markets—A Critical Survey of the Empirical Literature.* New York: New York University Monograph Series in Finance and Economics, no. 3, 1978.

———, "The Forward Rate as an Unbiased Predicator of the Future Spot Rate," *Columbia Journal of World Business* (Winter 1979), pp. 77–85.

KORTEWEG, P., "Exchange-Rate Policy, Monetary Policy, and Real Exchange-Rate Variability," *Essays in International Finance,* no. 140. Princeton, N.J.: International Finance Section, Department of Economics, Princeton University, December 1980.

KRUGMAN, P., "Vehicle Currencies and the Structure of International Exchange," *Journal of Money, Credit and Banking* (August 1980), pp. 513–526.

LEVICH, R. M., "Are Forward Exchange Rates Unbiased Predicators of Future Spot Rates?" *Columbia Journal of World Business* (Winter 1979), pp. 49–61.

———, "Analyzing the Accuracy of Foreign Exchange Forecasting Services: Theory and Evidence," in *Exchange Risk and Exposure: Current Developments in International Finance,* edited by Clas Wihlborg and Richard Levich. Lexington, Mass.: Heath, 1980.

LOGUE, D. E., R. SWEENEY, and T. WILLETT, "The Speculative Behavior of Exchange Rates During the Current Float," *Journal of Business Research,* Vol. 6, no. 2 (1978), pp. 147–158.

MCKINNON, R. I., *Money in International Exchanges: The Convertible Currency System.* New York and Oxford: Oxford University Press, 1979.

NORRIS, J. F., and M. K. EVANS, "Beating the Futures Market in Foreign Exchange Rates," *Euromoney* (February 1976), pp. 62–71.

PANTON, D. B., and O. M. JOY, "Empirical Evidence on International Monetary Market Currency Futures," *Journal of International Business Studies* (Fall 1978), pp. 59–68.

PAPADIA, F., "Forward Exchange Rates as Predictors of Future Spot Rates and the Efficiency of the Foreign Exchange Market," *Journal of Banking and Finance* (June 1981), pp. 219–240.

PRYCE, V., "Foreign Exchange Market: One Step Forward," *Banker* (January 1981), p. 95.

SOENEN, L. A., and E. G. F. VAN WINKEL, "Real Cost of Hedging in the Forward Exchange Market," *Management International Review,* no. 1 (1982), pp. 53–59.

SOLNIK, B., "International Parity Conditions and Exchange Risk," *Journal of Banking and Finance* (August 1981), pp. 281–293.

STOKES, H. H. and H. NEUBURGER, "Interest Arbitrage, Forward Speculation, and the Determination of the Forward Exchange Rate," *Columbia Journal of World Business* (Winter 1979), pp. 86–98.

WILLETT, T. D., "It's Too Easy to Blame the Speculators," *Euromoney* (May 1979), pp. 111–120.

APPENDIX C

An Anecdote: The Foreign Exchange Speculation Game

Somewhere in the back alleys of steaming Singapore in a modest one-room apartment lived Tsu Ping Huang. For a man in his late fifties, Mr. Huang looked youthful with sure footing, boyish face, and an indelible smile. Little was known about him except that he was kind and considerate to the neighbors, particularly children, who eagerly waited for the candy he would bring to them every Saturday morning.

Mr. Huang's seemingly docile personality and uneventful life hid a tumultuous preoccupation in the roller coaster game of foreign exchange speculation. During the ten years since he started betting his money on currency fluctuations just before Christmas 1974, he had managed to parlay a modest life savings of $10,000 into several million dollars.

Coming from a poor Chinese family, he had very little formal education and spent most of his youthful years as kitchen help in restaurants where his father worked as a cook. He was, however, an avid reader, and even in his late teens he developed a strong fascination for the workings of the financial markets in Singapore. He was determined to become one day involved in some capacity in the fascinating world of finance side by side with the other players who occupied the tall buildings in downtown Singapore.

The opportunity finally presented itself in 1960, when he was offered a job as a messenger in one of Singapore's largest banks. He spent almost ten years in this job, which brought him close to the people he had always admired. During these years he tried to understand banking and the money game, not only by keenly observing his surroundings, but also by reading the financial press almost religiously. It was during his last year with the bank that he developed a keen interest in the foreign exchange department of the bank, where foreign currencies are bought and sold in the spot and forward markets.

Huang's second break came in early 1971, when he got a job with a large stock and commodities brokerage house as a filing clerk. By that time his knowledge about banking and financial markets was so vast that brokers were often impressed and puzzled over his observations on the condition of the market and the accuracy of his forecasts. Cautiously but determinedly he started to play the stocks and commodities, using an account which he discreetly opened with a rival brokerage house. He committed his entire savings, about $10,000, to this account, trading mostly stock options and his favorite commodity, pork bellies.

Although his fascination with foreign currencies continued to increase, the limited band of fluctuations (two percent centered at the parity established by the Bretton Woods system) failed to ignite sufficient speculative fervor. He was dreaming of a world in which currency rates can move up and down freely. As the cracks in that system became more and more obvious in the late 1960s, Mr. Huang knew that the floating currency rates era was not far away. His wishes came true on August 15, 1971, when the announcement by President Nixon to terminate the dollar convertibility into gold dealt a death blow to the fixed-exchange-rate system. By 1973 most of the world's major currencies were floating.

Mr. Huang's delight with the onset of the floating currencies era turned into a disappointment when he realized that he lacked the mechanism or the forum to participate in the game. The only arena for the currency game at that time was the interbank market and foreign exchange dealers, commonly known as the forward market. Forward purchase or sale of foreign currencies in this market involved transactions of at least $10 million. Petty currency speculators like him had no outlet. Well, these speculators did not have to wait very long. On May 16, 1972, the Chicago Mercantile Exchange commenced trading in currency futures at the IMM, using standardized contracts fashioned after the commodities contracts traded at Chicago's Board of Trade.

However, for over a year following currency future trading in Chicago, Mr. Huang could not find a brokerage house in Singapore to allow him to trade on these futures. In the meantime, he was avidly following daily contract price movements and open interest statistics. When he finally was in a position to trade in currency futures, the OPEC exploded the oil price bomb. Its impact on the world's economy and its inflationary implications were touching everybody's life in every corner of the world.

While Huang continued to be bearish on the U.S. dollar and the pound sterling and bullish on the yen and the mark, his cultivated analytical sense led him to conclude that the sharp rise in oil prices engineered by OPEC would work, at least for some time, in favor of the dollar and the pound, and against the yen and the mark. The United States was much less dependent on imported oil than Japan and Germany, while the United Kingdom's balance of payments should improve dramatically with oil exports from North Sea wells.

1974 was a banner year for Huang. At the Christmas party for the staff of the brokerage house where he worked, very few people knew that the modest man wearing a rumpled grey suit and a cheap blue tie was already a millionaire. Hardly anything else changed for him. He kept his job as a clerk and his old one-room apartment in a low-rent district. He had only one close friend and confidant, Tom Ty, an account executive with the brokerage house who handled his accounts.

The next three years were a mixed bag for Huang. While his fortune and the scale of his operations continued to grow, there were some serious setbacks which he blamed mostly on bad luck and bad judgment. His personal resources were still not sufficient to switch his speculation venue from the circumscribed currency futures market to the flexible and made-to-order transactions in the interbank market. As he was eager to make this transformation and move up to the world of high finance, his friend Mr. Ty introduced him to Ali Rajab, a businessman from the United Arab Emirates who owned a controlling interest in Gulf Trading and Investment Company. As it happened, Mr. Rajab himself was deeply involved in currency speculation.

Mr. Huang was persuaded by Mr. Rajab to buy a minority interest in his company with the understanding that the two would pool their resources to speculate on currency movements in the forward market. Their first plunge was in June 1976, when they sold yen on a 15-day forward contract amounting to the equivalent of $20 million. The bank required a safety deposit of $2 million, since neither had had previous dealings with that particular bank. Mr. Huang was persuaded against his better judgment by Mr. Rajab's insistence that he had reliable information that the U.S. monetary authorities were about to take strong measures to shore up the troubled dollar. The measures never came about, and the dollar continued to slide. The loss on buying back the yen to close the forward contract wiped out a substantial part of the security deposit.

Dismayed by his first plunge into the big league, Mr. Huang informed his partner that in the future he had to call the shots, or he would no longer join him in his speculative ventures. Mr. Rajab reluctantly agreed. Despite persistent rumors in the financial community that the dollar was overdue for a strong rebound, Mr. Huang's gut feeling was that the dollar slide was far from over. He prevailed on his partner to repeat their transaction on the same scale, now buying Swiss francs forward against the dollar. The dollar fell sharply during the duration of the contract and the partners emerged with a handsome profit, which more than offset their loss in the previous transaction.

While Huang moved his major operations to the interbank market, he kept playing the Chicago currency futures with remarkable success. His scale of involvement in currency speculation finally proved too burdensome and time-consuming for him to continue his duties with the brokerage house. At the insistence of Mr. Rajab, he accepted a position as an assistant general manager with Gulf Trading and Investment Company. The position was mostly ceremonial with few substantive functions. In the course of the farewell party given to him by his colleagues, the general manager offered him a position as an account executive specializing in commodity and currency brokerage. He politely declined.

In the fall of 1978 Huang fulfilled his most cherished lifetime dream. He visited the trading pits of the IMM and the Chicago Board of Trade, which for twenty years had been the object of his adoration and fascination. Watching the frenzy of trading, the shouting and the howling, and the intriguing hand signals, he felt as if his heart were leaping out of his chest. He felt like a kid visiting Disneyland for the first time.

Fate had it that Mr. Huang was in the United States at a time of momentous decision on the value of the dollar. By early fall 1978, the dollar exchange rate hit record lows against most major currencies, particularly against the German mark, the Swiss franc, and the yen. Even before he embarked on his trip to the United States, he had had a strong feeling that the time was ripe for a sharp recovery of the dollar. While in New York in mid-October, there were some faint signs that the U.S. monetary authorities were about to make a major effort to support the dollar. These signs were largely dismissed by the international financial community, mostly because such signals in the past had proved to be a false alarm. Mr. Huang's keen sense of perception told him that something serious and momentous was about to happen. He took considerable dollar positions both on the interbank and futures market, using the bulk of his financial resources.

On November 1, 1978 the United States announced massive measures to defend the dollar. The package included increased swap lines with central banks of major trading partners, drawings from the IMF, sales of

SDRs and gold, and bond issues in the Euro-markets. Following the announcements, the dollar recovered sharply. When the dust settled, Mr. Huang realized that he had a big one—a masterpiece, a profit of $10 million in a few weeks.

Mr. Huang's currency speculation batting average during 1980 to 1983 was considerably less impressive than his achievements in the earlier years. Like many other speculators (individual and institutional) who flourished in the era of the dollar's decline, he misjudged the duration and the magnitude of the dollar's appreciation. The dollar started a spectacular climb in 1981 which continued, with minor corrections, to mid-1985. The dollar's appreciation during this period was sharpest during 1984 and early 1985, and was most pronounced against the European currencies. The deutsche mark, for example, declined by 13 percent against the U.S. dollar, from a rate of DM2.75 per dollar in December 1983 to DM3.17 in January 1985; the pound sterling depreciated by over 20 percent to $1.11 during the same period.

The amplitude of day-to-day fluctuations in exchange rates was considerable during this period, particularly in September 1984, and again in March 1985. Mr. Huang was caught by a merciless widely gyrating market, with seemingly no end in sight to the underlying strength of the dollar. His basic problem was probably his total immersion in the game, which robbed him of that fine perceptive and intuitive judgment which had worked for him so well for so many years. Perhaps part of the problem was that he uncharacteristically started to listen to the technical analysts whose charts could not explain why the dollar was gaining when it should have been declining.

1985 was a very bad year for Huang. Early in January the Gulf Trading and Investment Company went bankrupt, and his friend Rajab was in court answering accusations of hiding the company's assets from the creditors. Two fairly large forward transactions negotiated by Huang in January, in which he bought pounds sterling and deutsche marks against dollars, resulted in heavy losses. Like a general whose soldiers were in disarray, he decided to mobilize all his remaining resources and make one last stand. On a nice day early in April he decided to go all out for the dollar, selling pounds sterling and marks 60-days forward. It just happened that this particular timing coincided with a nose dive of the dollar.

On a Saturday morning in June 1985 the neighborhood kids were anxiously awaiting the candy that Mr. Huang brought them every week. He did not show up that Saturday or any Saturday thereafter. On the night before, he ended all speculation. He took his own life.

4

Measurement of Foreign Exchange Exposure

In a Quandary

Mr. A.W. Baker, Vice President in charge of Foreign Operations of Instruments International (A U.S. MNC) has just received word from the manager of the foreign exchange desk of one of the company's banks that the rupee was depreciating rapidly. Country A, where Instruments International recently established an affiliate to manufacture household appliances, has been experiencing political turmoil in recent months. Mr. Baker was worried about the company's foreign exchange exposure both in Country A and in Country B, where a subsidiary was also recently set up to assemble widgets for household and industrial uses.

As Instruments International has not had a long experience in managing the foreign exchange risk, Mr. Baker asked his senior staff, which included a foreign exchange operations manager, to meet with him the following day in order (1) to assess the exposure and (2) to map out a strategy for minimizing the impact of foreign exchange fluctuations on the company's overall operation and profitability. He asked Mr. Newman, manager of foreign exchange operations, to prepare a memorandum sketching out the different types of exposure the company was subject to, as well as statements showing the amount of exposure for each affiliate and each currency.

In his memorandum, Mr. Newman stated that there were three types of foreign exchange exposure encountered by any MNC, namely, (1) *trans-*

lation (accounting) exposure, (2) *transaction* exposure, and (3) *economic* (cash flow) exposure.

TRANSLATION EXPOSURE

Translation or accounting exposure is encountered when financial statements of subsidiaries or affiliates are combined with the parent's data to form consolidated financial statements at the end of each accounting period. The process of consolidation would require translating the accounts of each affiliate into the parent company's currency (the U.S. dollar in the case of Instruments International). Due to changes in the dollar exchange rates of the rupee (Rp) and the peso (Ps), the currency units of country A and country B, respectively, consolidation would result in bookkeeping gains (or losses). While these gains (or losses) are not actual or realized gains (or losses), established uniform accounting standards require that they must be measured and reported in accordance with FASB (Financial Accounting Standard Board) Rule #52.

What Is FASB Rule #52?

Rule #52, which became effective for fiscal years beginning on or after December 15, 1982, requires that any U.S. firm with foreign operations should provide information disclosing effects of foreign exchange rate changes on the enterprise consolidated financial statements and equity. The translation of each affiliate's financial statements measured in foreign currency[1] into the reporting currency (the currency in which the combined statements are reported—the U.S. dollar in the case of U.S. MNCs) should follow the following procedure:

1. Assets and liabilities are to be translated at the *current exchange rate*, that is, the rate prevailing at the date of the consolidated statements.
2. All revenues and expenses are to be translated at the *actual exchange rates* prevailing on the date of the transactions. However, for items occurring numerous times during the accounting period, *weighted averages* for exchange rates may be used.
3. Translation adjustments (gains or losses) are not to be charged to the net income of the reporting company. Instead, these adjust-

[1]The foreign currency in which the accounts of the affiliate are expressed is called the "functional" currency, defined as the currency of the primary economic environment in which a foreign entity operates (that is, the environment in which the entity generates and spends cash). This is usually the currency of the foreign domicile of the entity. The U.S. dollar could be considered the functional currency for a foreign-based affiliate of a U.S. firm if the foreign entity's operations are closely integrated with those of the parent so that buying and selling activities are primarily in the parent's country and/or the parent's currency.

ments are accumulated and reported in a separate account shown in the shareholders' equity section of the balance sheet, where they remain until the foreign entity is disposed of.

Mr. Newman explained that FASB #52 superseded FASB #8, which had been in effect since 1976, as well as a number of other rules and interpretations. Rule #8 provided for translating monetary assets and liabilities at the current rate, and nonmonetary assets (such as inventory and fixed assets), as well as capital stock, at the historical rate. He also indicated that FASB #52 contained other provisions which dealt with the handling of transaction exposure, including forward exchange contracts.

Instruments International Translation Exposure

The balance sheet for affiliate A in Exhibit 4-1 was prepared and translated into U.S. dollars first at the rate of Rp1.00 = US $.35, and subsequently at the depreciated rate of $.25 both at the current (FASB Rule #52) and temporal (FASB Rule #8) methods.

Translation exposure may be measured by (Exposed assets − exposed liabilities) (the change in the exchange rate), thus for the current method it was equal to (Rp20,860 − Rp10,200) (−$.10) = −$1066. For the temporal method, it was equal to (Rp7100 − 10,200) (−$.10) = +$310. It was also noted that, unlike the temporal method, where the translation loss was charged to current income and shown as a deduction from retained earnings, the loss under the current method was shown in a special account designated as "adjustment to owners' equity," leaving retained earnings unchanged.

TRANSACTION EXPOSURE

Transaction exposure reflects the impact of settling *outstanding* obligations entered into before a change in the exchange rate, but settled after the change. Exposure would include all unsettled *payables* and *receivables* which appear on the balance sheet, as well as off-balance sheet items which represent *commitments* already entered into, and which will create future receivables and payables. These include contracts to buy or sell foreign exchange forward, unfilled customers' orders, purchase commitments from suppliers, obligations under a leasing arrangement when not reflected in the balance sheet.

According to FASB Rule #52 all transaction gains (losses) should be accounted for and included in the entity's net income in the reporting period to which they pertain. Unlike translation gains (losses), which require only a bookkeeping adjustment, transaction gains (losses) are realized as soon as the exchange rate changes.

Exhibit 4-1. Balance Sheet of Affiliate A

		U.S. $(000 OMITTED)		
			Rp1.00 = $0.25	
Assets	*Rp (000)*	*Rp1.00 = $0.35*	*Current*	*Temporal*
Cash	2,500	875	625	625
Accounts receivable	4,600	1,610	1,150	1,150
Inventory	8,200	2,870	2,050	2,870
Prepaid expenses	700	245	175	245
Fixed assets net of depreciation	4,860	1,701	1,215	1,701
Total assets	20,860	7,301	5,215	6,591

LIABILITIES AND NET WORTH

		U.S. $(000 OMITTED)		
			Rp1.00 = $0.25	
	Rp (000)	*Rp1.00 = $0.35*	*Current*	*Temporal*
Accounts payable	3,200	1,120	800	800
Accrued taxes	500	175	125	125
Bank loan (short-term)	2,000	700	500	500
Long-term debt	4,500	1,575	1,125	1,125
Capital stock	5,000	1,750	1,750	1,750
Retained earnings	5,660	1,981	1,981	2,291
Adjustment to owners' equity			(1,066)	
Total liabilities and net worth	20,860	7,301	5,215	6,591
Translation gain (loss)			(1,066)	310

ANALYSIS OF TRANSLATION EXPOSURE

Balance Sheet Item	Current (Rule #52)	Temporal (Rule #8)
Assets	All exposed	All exposed except fixed assets, inventory, and prepaid expenses
Liabilities	All exposed	All exposed
Capital stock	Not exposed	Not exposed
Retained earnings	Not exposed	Exposed

Transaction Exposure of Instruments International Affiliates

Mr. Newman prepared a statement of transaction exposure for each of the two affiliates of Instruments International: affiliate A and affiliate B. (See Exhibits 4-2 and 4-3). The statements reflected the transaction exposure arising from the depreciation of the rupee from $0.35 to $0.25, and the appreciation of the peso, the currency of unit of country B, from $0.10 to $0.12.

To construct a transaction exposure report for affiliate A, Mr. Newman needed a breakdown of the affiliate's exposed assets and liabilities by currency. He also needed information on the off-balance sheet items. This report is presented in Exhibit 4-2.

The exposure report could be interpreted either from the standpoint of the affiliate or that of the parent company. An entity cannot have an exposure in the currency in which its transactions are measured. Thus, affiliate A does not have an exposure in rupees. However, it has a net exposure of ($75,000) in pounds sterling and a net exposure of ($1,000,000) in U.S. dollars; that is, it has a short position on both the U.S. dollar and the pound sterling. From the viewpoint of the parent company,

Exhibit 4-2. Transaction Exposure Report for Affiliate A (thousands of U.S. dollars)

ASSETS AND LIABILITIES	RUPEES	POUNDS STERLING	U.S. DOLLARS
Cash			
Accounts receivable	800	200	150
Other exposed assets	175		
Forward currency purchase contract		500	
Unfilled customers orders	325	225	
Exposed assets	1300	925	150
Accounts payable and taxes	750		175
Bank loan (short-term)	500		
Long-term debt	125	500	500
Forward currency sale contract		200	
Future purchase commitments and leases		300	700
Exposed liabilities	1375	1000	1375
Net Position	(75)	(75)	(1225)

Exhibit 4-3. Transaction Exposure Report of Affiliate B (thousands of U.S. dollars)

ASSETS AND LIABILITIES	PESOS	POUNDS STERLING	DEUTSCHE MARKS	RUPEES	U.S. DOLLARS
Cash					
Accounts receivable	400	200			750
Other exposed assets					
Forward currency purchase contract			500		
Unfilled customers orders	600	400			200
Exposed Assets	1000	600	500		950
Accounts payable and taxes	350			200	700
Bank Loan (short-term)			1000		
Long-term debt	1500				500
Forward currency sale contract					
Future purchase commitments and leases	300	500			350
Exposed Liabilities	2150	500	1000		1550
Net Position	(1150)	100	(500)	(200)	(600)

the affiliate has a net exposure of $325,000 in rupees and net exposure of ($75,000) in pounds sterling.

Exhibit 4-3 shows the transaction exposure for affiliate B prepared along the same lines as Exhibit 4-2. According to this report, affiliate B has a long position of $100,000 in pounds sterling, a long position in deutsche marks of $75,000, and a short position of $260,000 in U.S. dollars. The exposure report for both affiliates includes intracompany transactions. Affiliate A owes the parent company $150,000 for components delivered and also has a $500,000 in lease rental commitments. Both of these commitments wee denominated in U.S. dollars. In addition, it carries as accounts receivable $200,000 from affiliate B, denominated in rupees. The latter, in addition to the obligation just indicated, carries an unfilled order of $200,000 placed by the parent company and also owes the parent $250,000 in long-term debt.

Preparation of a Transaction Report for Instruments International and Affiliates

A transaction report for Instruments International and affiliates is shown in Exhibit 4-4. Unlike translation exposure, which is properly measured

Exhibit 4-4. Transactions Exposure Report for Instruments International and Affiliates (thousands of U.S. dollars)

ENTITY	CURRENCY			
Instruments International (U.S. Parent)	**Rp**	**Ps**	**£**	**DM**
Accounts receivable			+835	+1035
Current liabilities			−935	− 875
Bank loan (short-term)		−1000		
Long-term debt				
Forward exchange contracts		+ 750		
Unfilled customers' orders net of future purchase commitments				
Future lease rentals net of lease commitments				
Net Exposure		− 250	−100	+ 165
Affiliate A	**U.S.$**	**Ps**	**£**	**DM**
Accounts receivable	+ 150		+200	
Current liabilities	− 175			
Bank loan (short-term)				
Long-term debt	− 500		−500	
Forward exchange contracts			+300	
Unfilled customers' orders net of future purchase commitments			− 75	
Future lease rentals net of lease commitments	− 700			
Net Exposure	−1225		− 75	
Affiliate B	**U.S.$**	**Rp**	**£**	**DM**
Accounts receivable	+ 750		+200	
Current liabilities	− 700	− 200		
Bank loan (short-term)				−1000
Long-term debt	− 500			
Forward exchange contracts				+ 500
Unfilled customers' orders net of future purchase commitments	− 150		−100	
Future lease rentals net of lease commitments				
Net Exposure	− 600	− 200	+100	− 500

only by currency and only from the perspective of the parent, transaction exposure is measured by entity as well as by currency. A few observations regarding Exhibit 4-4 are in order:

1. An entity cannot have a transaction exposure measured in its own currency. By definition, transaction exposure can only be in terms of other currencies.
2. Cash balances do not contribute to transaction exposure. These balances do not represent future receivables or payables in foreign currency.
3. Unlike translation exposure, intracompany transactions do not cancel out. Affiliate B payable to affiliate A of $200,000 denominated in rupees represents an exposure to the former but not the latter. Also, liabilities and commitments of the two affiliates to the parent company denominated in U.S. dollars are shown in their dollar exposure column. However, they do not appear as exposure items for the parent, since it cannot have exposure in U.S. dollars.
4. For each entity, forward exchange purchase contracts are netted against forward exchange sales contracts, while unfilled customers' orders are netted against future purchase commitments in each currency. Similarly, future lease rental receipts are netted against lease payments commitments for each currency.
5. Forward exchange contracts for each entity are intended in part to offset potential receipts or payments in each currency. However, while hedging appears to be the primary purpose of these transactions, maturities and amounts may not exactly match.

Exhibit 4-5 shows the overall transaction exposure position of Instruments International and affiliates by currency with the exception of the U.S. dollar, the parent company's reporting currency. Note that the rupee and peso positions represent a transaction risk to the company as a whole, although they do not entail such a risk for the respective affiliates.

Exhibit 4-5. Instruments International and Affiliates Overall Transaction Exposure (thousands of U.S. dollars)

CURRENCY	NET LONG POSITION	NET SHORT POSITION
Rupees		75
Pesos		1150
Pounds sterling		75
Deutsche mark		335

Note: The overall position for transaction exposure in rupees is obtained by subtracting the exposed payables of affiliate A from the exposed receivables (disregarding cash) or 1300 − 1375 = −75. Transaction exposure in pesos is computed in the same manner: 1000 − 2150 = −1150. Net exposure of the three entities are summed up to obtain overall exposure in pounds sterling and deutsche marks.

Cash Flow Exposure Statement

Although Exhibit 4-5 represents a meaningful summary of Instruments International's overall transaction exposure, it does not take into consideration the continuous nature of the company's operation in the various markets. To overcome the static nature of the exposure report, a quarterly (or monthly) near-term cash flow schedule by currency would be more useful for purposes of exposure management policies. Exhibit 4-6 shows budgeted receipts from existing accounts receivable and anticipated credit sales, as well as other anticipated receipts such as lease rentals, disposal of assets, security sales, and insurance proceeds. Budgeted disbursements, likewise, reflect not only payments of existing accounts payables, but also anticipated payments on future purchases on credit, amortization of debt, purchase of supplies and equipment, and so forth. Obviously, the periodic

Exhibit 4-6. Cash Flow Report—Instruments International and Affiliates (equivalent thousands of U.S. dollars)

CURRENCY	1st QTR	2nd QTR	3rd QTR	4th QTR	Year Total
U.S. Dollars ($)					
Budgeted receipts	2,500	3,000	3,800	2,700	12,000
Budgeted disbursements	4,600	1,700	2,500	1,800	10,600
Net position	(2,100)	1,300	1,300	900	1,400
Affiliate A (Rp)					
Budgeted receipts	480	570	550	450	2,050
Budgeted disbursements	450	500	650	500	2,100
Net position	30	70	(100)	(50)	(50)
Affiliate B (Ps)					
Budgeted receipts	620	650	800	520	2,590
Budgeted disbursements	605	750	1,800	560	3,715
Net position	15	(100)	(1,000)	(40)	(1,125)
Pounds Sterling (£)					
Budgeted receipts	300	250	250	750	1,550
Budgeted disbursements	100	150	100	250	600
Net position	200	100	150	500	950
Deutsche marks (DM)					
Budgeted receipts	—	150	—	150	300
Budgeted disbursements	200	400	150	350	1,100
	(200)	(250)	(150)	(200)	(800)
Net receipts (payments) all currencies	(2,055)	1,120	200	1,110	375

cash flow report by currency is superior to the combined exposure report for purpose of exposure management action for two reasons:

1. In addition to *existing commitments,* the report includes *anticipated* cash flows.
2. Its periodicity permits better timing of exposure management strategies.

The cash flow report shows that conclusions based on Exhibit 4-5 as to which currencies were in short or long positions would have led to erroneous exposure management posture. According to Exhibit 4-5, Instruments International had a relatively small negative exposure in pounds sterling. However, if all anticipated receipts and disbursements are accounted for, as they are in Exhibit 4-6, the company actually had a sizable long position in that currency.

ECONOMIC EXPOSURE

Economic exposure of Instruments International to changes in exchange rates goes beyond the impact of these changes on balance sheet items in the accounting period in which they occur (translation exposure), or the gains or losses arising from the impact of these changes on existing or anticipated payables and receivables in foreign currencies (transaction exposure). Economic exposure encompasses the immediate and potential impact of unexpected exchange rate changes on the cash flow generated by affiliates, and consequently on the earning power of the company as a whole beyond the accounting period when these changes occurred.

In theory, economic exposure can arise only from unexpected changes in exchange rates. Expected changes would be factored in by the financial markets, and would be reflected in inflation and interest rate differentials between the country of the parent company (the United States) and the country of the affiliates in accordance with the purchasing power parity theory and the International Fisher Effect. If financial markets are not efficient to permit these adjustments to be made, the impact of expected exchange rate changes would have been already reflected in the expected cash flows generated by the affiliates and on the market value of the parent company.

Measuring economic exposure arising, for instance, from an unexpected depreciation of affiliate A's currency against the parent company's currency is an exercise of tracing the impact of this depreciation on its sales both in the local and export markets, as well as on its cost structure. This impact is discussed under the following subheadings.

Revenue from Sales and Pricing Strategies

Local market (Country A). Revenue from sales in the affiliate's local market depends on the change in the volume of sales and its pricing strategy following the depreciation of the rupee. It also depends on the degree of competition the affiliate had been facing prior to the depreciation. Appliances produced by the affiliate have a competitive advantage over imports, which would cost more in terms of rupees. The percentage increase in sales volume, however, hinges on the company's pricing strategy and the elasticity of demand for the products in country A. If the affiliate faces relatively elastic demand, the best policy would be to maintain the existing price schedule. If, on the other hand, it faces relatively inelastic demand, it may choose to raise its prices up to the full percentage of the depreciation. The student will recognize that to lower the unit price (in case of elastic demand) or raise it by more than the percentage of the depreciation of the rupee would suggest that the affiliate was not following profit-maximizing behavior prior to the depreciation.

In the absence of import competition, the affiliate has no latitude in its pricing strategy in its local market. Depreciation of the local currency would offer no basis for changing its price schedule. As a result, its sales revenue will remain constant in local currency, but will decrease by the full percentage of the depreciation in terms of U.S. dollars.

Export markets. Affiliate A has more latitude in the export markets now that the rupee has depreciated in terms of the U.S. dollar and other currencies. Export prices could be raised by up to the percentage of depreciation, or by about 29 percent,[2] without suffering a competitive disadvantage in relation to foreign products. The optimal strategy, if the affiliate was maximizing profits (or minimizing losses) prior to the change, is to raise its export prices sufficiently to produce the maximum possible gain in revenue. Reaction of competitors will have to be taken into account, as they may choose to lower their prices to prevent affiliate A from claiming a larger share of their markets.

These various strategies may be illustrated by the behavior of affiliates of Japanese and German automobile manufacturers in the United States during 1982 and 1983, when the dollar appreciated sharply vis-a-vis the Japanese yen and the deutsche mark. This development accorded the affiliates substantial latitude in their strategy to gain a larger share of the U.S. car market. Realizing that they were in a highly differentiated product market with intense promotional competition (conditions of relatively inelastic demand), they elected not to lower prices. Instead, they generally matched the moderate price increases instituted by domestic manufacturers. In early 1978, when both the yen and the mark were appreciating sharply vis-a-vis the U.S. dollars, GM and Ford took advantage of price increases on competitive foreign cars to raise prices on their Chevette and Pinto models.

[2]A depreciation of the rupee from U.S. \$0.35 to U.S. \$0.25 represents a decline of (\$0.35 − \$0.25)/(\$0.35) × 100, or 28.6 percent.

Cost Structure

Domestic inputs are not likely to be impacted significantly in the initial phase by the decline in the value of the rupee. However, a country whose currency is losing value is likely to have an inflation problem, which can be aggravated by the depreciation of the currency. The rise in the cost of imports, particularly foodstuffs and commodities that are widely used by the public, will exert an upward pressure on the cost of living, which in turn translates into increases in wages and prices of other domestic inputs.

Imported inputs are likely to rise by a significantly higher rate than local inputs, perhaps by as much as the rate of depreciation of the local currency, if it is assumed that the dollar price of imported inputs stays the same. This is particularly true if country A represents a small market, since foreign producers will not be incurring a high risk by raising the local price of their raw materials or components by the full amount of depreciation of the local currency.

Overall, it is reasonable to conclude that the cost structure of the affiliate will rise, but by less than the depreciation of the local currency. The increase in the costs of production depends on the distribution of the total cost per unit between the domestic and import components, and the ability of the affiliate to adjust its mix of inputs as relative costs change. Reflecting the rise in the sales volume and production costs, overhead expenses and working capital requirements will also increase. The probable impact of a decline in the value of the affiliate's currency on the parent company's company cash flow pattern is schematically presented in Exhibit 4-7.

Measuring Economic Exposure

To trace the process of measuring economic exposure, a hypothetical illustration based on the operations of affiliate A before and after the depreciation of the rupee will be presented in this section. The purpose of the exercise is to determine the quantitative impact of depreciation of the affiliate's currency on the parent's dollar cash flow under different scenarios of price, volume, and cost changes over a three-year period. Exhibit 4-8 shows cash flow generated by affiliate A before the depreciation of the rupee.

Analysis of Instruments International economic exposure will be worked out in terms of the following scenarios:

1. The least likely scenario: All variables remain unchanged.
2. A highly favorable scenario: Sales increase significantly in both home and export markets, while costs increase only moderately.
3. A highly unfavorable scenario: Sales increase moderately in export markets and remain unchanged in the home markets, but costs rise sharply.

Exhibit 4-7. Schematic Presentation of Probable Impact of Depreciation of Affiliate's Currency (Rupee) on Parent Company's Cash Flow in U.S. Dollars

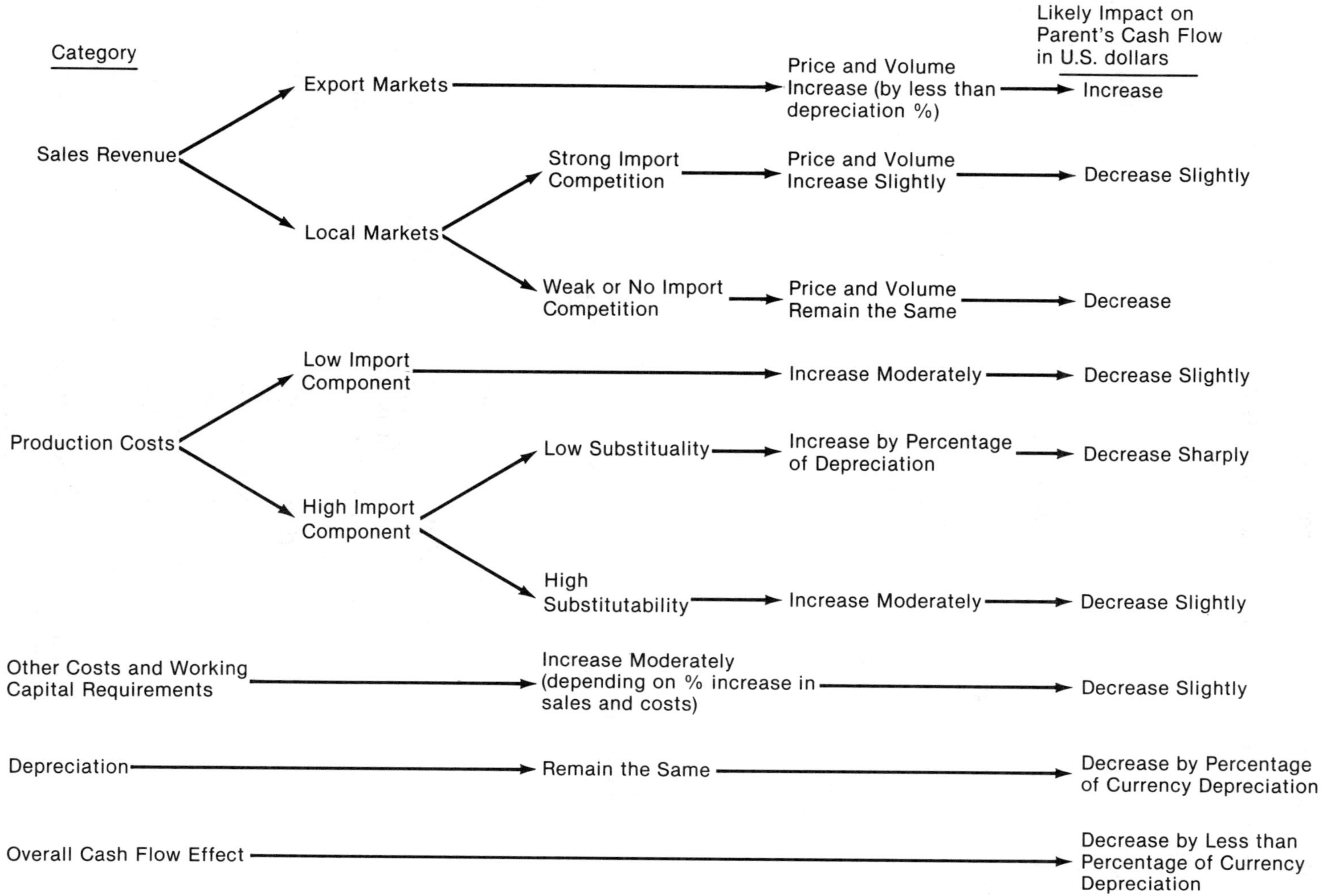

Exhibit 4-8. Cash Flow Generated by Affiliate A Prior to Depreciation of the Rupee

SCENARIO 1:

The Base Case	Units	Unit price (Rp)	Total (Rp million)	
Export sales	350,000	4.00	1.40	
Domestic Sales	450,000	5.00	2.25	
Total sales revenue			3.65	
PRODUCTION COSTS				
Local labor	200,000 man-hours	6.00	1.20	
Local inputs	700,000 units	0.50	0.35	
Imported inputs	900,000 units	1.00	0.90	
Total production costs				2.45
Net operating income				1.20
Overhead costs			0.25	
Depreciation			0.35	
Total other expenses				0.60
Net profit before tax				0.60
Income tax at 25%				0.15
Profit after tax				0.45
Add back depreciation				0.35
Cash flow in rupees				0.80
Cash flow in U.S. dollars (rupee 1 = U.S. $0.35) = $280,000				

4. The most likely scenario: Sales increase somewhat in the home market and by a higher ratio in the export markets (prices may rise, or remain the same, depending on the elasticity of demand). Cost of domestic inputs will rise moderately, while cost of imported inputs will be unchanged in dollar terms, that is, rise in terms of local currency by the same percentage of currency depreciation.

Calculation of *cash flow impact* for each scenario will now be worked out.

Scenario 1. Cash flow will remain at Rp800,000, equivalent to $200,000, resulting in a net decline of $80,000 in parent's company cash flow in each of the three years.

Scenario 2. The following changes are assumed to occur:

Export sales: 20 percent increase in volume, 20 percent increase in price

Domestic sales: 15 percent increase in volume, 10 percent increase in price

Local costs: No change in unit price

Imported component: 10 percent increase in unit price

Overhead expenses: 5 percent increase

Working capital requirement: Rise by 50 percent of the increase in sales in year 1 only

Calculation of the net cash flow in U.S. dollars for scenario 2 is shown in Exhibit 4-9.

Cash flow in year one will be reduced by $152,500, the amount of the increase in working capital requirements (50 percent of the increase in sales). Cash flow in each of year 2 and year 3 would amount to $327,500, representing a sizable increase from the cash flow level generated in the base case.

Scenario 3. The following changes are assumed to take place:

Export sales: 15 percent increase in volume, no increase in price

Domestic sales: No increase in volume, no change in price

Local costs: Increase by 5 percent in unit price due to inflationary pressures

Imported components: Increase by 28.6 percent in unit price, or by the full percentage of depreciation of the rupee, with no flexibility in substituting local inputs for imported components

Exhibit 4-9. Cash Flow Generated by Affiliate A following Depreciation of the Rupee

SCENARIO 2:

	Units	Unit price Rp	Total (Rp million)	
Export sales	420,000	4.80	2.02	
Domestic sales	517,500	5.50	2.85	
Total sales revenue				4.87
PRODUCTION COSTS				
Local labor	234,380 man-hours	6.00	1.41	
Local inputs	820,330 units	0.50	.41	
Imported inputs	1,054,710 units	1.10	1.16	
Total production costs				2.98
Net operating income				1.89
Overhead costs			.26	
Depreciation			.35	
Total other expenses				.61
Net profit before tax				1.28
Income tax at 25%				.33
Profit after tax				.96
Add back depreciation				.35
Cash flow in rupees				1.31
Cash flow in U.S. dollars (rupee 1 = U.S. $0.25) $327,500				

Overhead expense: Increase by 10 percent

Working capital requirement: Increase by the same amount as the increase in sales in year 1 only

Calculation of the net cash flow in U.S. dollars for scenario 3 is shown in Exhibit 4-10.

Cash flow in year 1 will be reduced by $52,500, the amount of increase in working capital requirements (same as the increase in sales). Cash flow in each of year 2 and year 3 would amount to $137,500, representing a substantial decline from the cash flow generated in the base case.

Scenario 4. The following changes are assumed to take place:

Export sales: 15 percent increase in volume, 10 percent increase in price

Domestic sales: 10 percent increase in volume, 5 percent increase in price first year, 10 percent second year, and 12.5 percent third year

Local costs: No change first year, 5 percent second year, 10 percent third year (reflecting increasing inflationary pressure)

Imported components: Increase by same rate as depreciation of rupee vis-a-vis U.S. dollar (same as scenario 3)

Exhibit 4-10. Cash Flow Generated by Affiliate A following Depreciation of Rupee

SCENARIO 3:

	Units	Unit Price Rp	Total (Rp million)	
Export sales	402,500	4.00	1.61	
Domestic sales	450,000	5.00	2.25	
Total sales revenue				3.86
PRODUCTION COSTS				
Local labor	213,120 man-hours	6.30	1.34	
Local inputs	745,920 units	0.525	0.39	
Imported inputs	959,040 units	1.286	1.23	
Total production costs				2.96
Net operating income				0.90
Overhead costs			0.28	
Depreciation			0.35	
Total other expenses				0.63
Net profit before tax				0.27
Income tax at 25%				0.07
Profit after tax				0.20
Add back depreciation				0.35
Cash flow in rupees				0.55
Cash flow in U.S. dollars (rupee 1 = U.S. $.025) $137,500				

Overhead expenses: No increase in first year, increase by 5 percent in second year, and 10 percent in third year

Working capital requirements: Increase by 75 percent of the increase in sales in year 1 only

Calculation of the net cash flow in U.S. dollars for scenario 4 is shown in Exhibits 4-11 and 4-12. Cash flow in year 1 is to be reduced by $135,000, the amount of increase in working capital requirements representing 75 percent of the increase in sales. It should be noted that in scenario 4, the underlying assumption is that country A will experience an acceleration in the inflation rate following depreciation of its currency. Consequently, unit price of domestic sales and local costs are shown to rise gradually from year 1 to year 3. This is a realistic consequence of currency depreciation, particularly if imported goods constitute a significant proportion of the basic components of the cost of living. Rising prices of imported goods will translate to cost-of-living increases, which in turn will lead to higher wages and costs of production.

The impact of the four scenarios on Instruments International's market value, which sums up the overall economic exposure, may be shown by

Exhibit 4-11. Cash Flow Generated by Affiliate A following Depreciation of the Rupee in Year 1

SCENARIO 4:

	Unit	Unit price (Rp)	Total (Rp million)	
Export sales	402,500	4.40	1.77	
Domestic sales	495,000	5.25	2.60	
Total sales revenue				4.37
PRODUCTION COSTS				
Local labor	224,380 man-hours	6.00	1.35	
Local inputs	785,330 units	0.50	0.39	
Imported inputs	1,009,710 units	1.286	1.30	
Total production costs				3.04
Net operating income				1.33
Overhead costs			0.25	
Depreciation			0.35	
Total other expenses				0.60
Net profit before tax				0.73
Income tax at 25%				0.18
Profit after tax				0.55
Add hock depreciation				0.35
Cash flow in rupees, year 1				0.90
Cash flow in U.S. dollars, year 1 (rupee 1.00 = U.S. $0.25) = $225,000				

Exhibit 4-12. Calculation of Cash Flow in Years 2 and 3

SCENARIO 4:	(Rp MILLION)			
	Year 2		Year 3	
Export sales	1.77		1.77	
Domestic sales	2.72		2.78	
Total sales revenue		4.49		4.55
PRODUCTION COSTS				
Local labor	1.41		1.48	
Local inputs	0.41		0.43	
Imported inputs	1.30		1.30	
Total production cost		3.12		3.21
Net operating income		1.37		1.34
Overhead costs	0.26		0.28	
Depreciation	0.35		0.35	
Total other expense		0.61		0.63
Net profit before tax		0.76		0.71
Income tax at 25%		0.19		0.18
Profit after tax		0.57		0.53
Add back depreciation		0.35		0.35
Cash flow (Rp million)		0.92		0.88
Cash flow in U.S. dollars (rupee 1.00 = U.S. $0.25)		$230,000		$220,000

finding the present value of changes in cash flow over the three-year period. The present value of these changes discounted at the company's cost of capital (18 percent) is shown in Exhibit 4-13. It is assumed that the incremental working capital required to support the increase in sales in year 1 will be recovered at the end of year 3.

Exhibit 4-13 shows that, depending on what assumptions are postulated with respect to sales volume and prices in the domestic and export markets as well as cost structure, a sharp depreciation of the currency of the affiliate against the parent's currency (in this case 28.6 percent) could affect the value of the company as a whole by an amount ranging from a decline of about $322,000 to an increase of about $67,000. It is to be noted that the results are tilted toward the negative side, as the most favorable scenario generates only a modest increase in value, while the highly unfavorable scenario generates a substantial decline in value. The most likely scenario (scenario 4) results in a sizable decline in value. However, the decline is considerably smaller than scenario 1, which assures that all variables remain unchanged, a very unlikely situation. The conclusion to be drawn from this exercise is that a sharp decline in the affiliate's currency is likely to result in

Exhibit 4-13. Changes in Cash Flow by Year from Base Case (U.S. dollars)

	(PV) Factor at 18%	Scenario 1	Scenario 2	Scenario 3	Scenario 4
Year 1	.8475	−80,000	−105,000	−195,000	−190,000
	PV	−67,800	−88,988	−165,263	−161,025
Year 2	.7182	−80,000	+47,500	−142,500	−50,000
	PV	−57,456	+34,115	−102,344	−35,910
Year 3	.6086	−80,000	+47,500	−142,500	−60,000
	PV	−48,688	+28,909	−86,726	−36,516
Add recovery of working capital Year 3	.6086	—	+152,500	+ 52,500	+135,000
	PV	—	+ 92,812	+ 31,952	+ 82,161
Aggregate PV at 18% (overall change in the value of the firm)		−$173,944	+$ 66,848	−$322,381	−$151,290

a negative overall economic exposure to the parent company. This can be explained by the failure of increased cash flow in dollar terms generated mainly by the export markets to offset the decline in cash flow from the domestic market. However, an offshore affiliate producing entirely or mainly for the export markets may experience positive cash flow effect under these circumstances in the absence of retaliatory price cutting by the competitors.

Summary

Accounting (translation) exposure reflects the changes in the dollar value of balance sheet items resulting from fluctuations in the exchange rates of currencies in terms of which the accounts of the affiliates are measured. The amount of the exposure depends on which assets or liabilities are considered exposed by the method or standard of exposure measurement being used. The method or standard also determines the impact of the measured exposure on the quarterly (or yearly) income statement. According to the current method (FASB #52), which became applicable to U.S. MNCs at the end of 1982, all assets and liabilities are exposed and are translated at the current rate. Translation adjustments (gains or losses) are accumulated and reported in a separate account shown in the shareholders' equity section of the balance sheet.

Transaction exposure reflects the impact of settling all outstanding obligations (including off balance-sheet receivables and payables) at a different exchange rate from the rate prevailing when these obligations were made. According to FASB #52, all transaction gains (losses) should be accounted for and included in the entity's net income in the reporting period to which they pertain.

Economic exposure measures the immediate and potential impact of unexpected exchange rate changes on the cash flow generated by an MNC's affiliates, and on the earning power of the company as a whole, beyond the accounting period when the changes occur. The overall impact on the value of the company as a whole depends on a host of factors relating to the distribution of sales between the domestic and export markets, elasticity of demand for the product in each market, the cost structure of the affiliate, particularly the proportion of the imported component and the degree of substitutability between domestic and imported inputs. Another factor is the extent to which the situation deviates from the purchasing power parity principle, that is, to what extent inflationary pressures in the country of the depreciating currency will offset the sales and cost benefits arising from currency depreciation. A typical scenario for a U.S. MNC would have the overall cash flow decline in the intermediate term, following a sharp depreciation in the currency of the company's affiliate or affiliates.

STUDY PROJECT

The following article appeared in *The Wall Street Journal* on February 23, 1984.

Dollar's Continuing Slide in Currency Markets Could Give a Boost to Multinational's Stocks by Gary Butka*

The dollar continued its month-long slide against major foreign currencies yesterday—and that could be good news for the stocks of many U.S. multinational corporations.

The weakening dollar has figured strongly in arguments that the stock market will go lower, as analysts reason that foreign investors will be averse to possible currency losses and stay away from U.S. shares.

The bullish side of the dollar's weakness is the substantial earnings gains that multinationals would realize when their foreign profits are translated into dollars. The dollar will have to drop further before quarterly profits abroad start to look better than a year ago. But the multinationals also could get another boost if analysts' earnings estimates—based on a flat, or even stronger, U.S. currency—come up short.

Beneficiaries of a weaker dollar could include major pharmaceutical, drug and cosmetic concerns—such as Schering Plough, SmithKline, Gillette and International Flavors and Fragrances. Other companies recently mentioned on Wall Street in this vein are Polaroid, Dow Chemical, Pan Am, Coca Cola, Ogilvy & Mather and Philbro-Salomon.

Before rushing off to buy these stocks, investors should be aware that foreign-earnings swings based on currency translations tend to be less pronounced than they were a couple of years ago. That's because new accounting standards eliminate the profit impact of changes in foreign-asset values. Also, reports of the dollar's imminent demise (including one in this column) have been greatly exaggerated in the past.

That said, it's been hard for stock market pundits to ignore the foreign-exchange developments of the past six weeks. Since Jan. 9, when the dollar hit records against many currencies, it has fallen 6.4% against the West German mark, 5.2% against the French franc, 4.3% against the British pound and 3% against the Swiss franc. It has remained on par since then with the Japanese yen.

"I think the dollar's weakness will be a major factor in the way market leadership develops in the next two years." said Francis Kelly, director of research at Oppenheimer & Co.

Doing well, he feels, won't only be sectors with big foreign profiles such as drugs, major technology concerns, auto makers and construction-machine makers. A waning dollar also should push up U.S. inflation, Mr. Kelly says, meaning investors could start pining again for the precious metal and real-estate plays of yesteryear. Gold stocks have been soaring lately.

Until recently, Mr. Kelly worked at Dean Witter Reynolds, where he compiled a list of companies that would realize the biggest earnings gains if the dollar were to stage a 10% retreat. He was a little early then, because the dollar gained smartly immediately after his report. Its recent losses, however, have just about made up for those gains, and Dean Witter will stand behind the list, according to its research boss, Lee Idleman.

At the top of the list is Polaroid, with a projected 30% earnings rise from what it otherwise would make in the next 12 months, followed by Dow Chemical, with a 20% boost, and Philbro-Salomon, which Dean Witter believes would gain by 10% to 15%. Other names high on the list are Burroughs, Kodak and Gillette.

A team at Salomon Brothers also has sized up which companies might be affected most by foreign-currency swings. Rather than make any predictions that might come out wrong, however, Salomon ranked the companies based on which had the highest percentage of currency-transaction changes relative to sales in 1982, the last year of complete results.

Leading its list of 140 companies were Asarco, ASA Ltd., Mesa Petroleum and Ranger Oil, all commodity extractors. They were followed by Crown, Cork and Seal, Scott Paper and Timken. The Solomon tally included only companies with more than $300 million in stock-market value.

Some analysts urge caution on those expecting to make a buck out of any company with foreign exposure. Deepak Raj, who follows cosmetics concerns for Merrill Lynch, recently identified Gillette, International Flavors and Richardson-Vicks as potential beneficiaries of the dollar's fall. He ignored other companies with bigger foreign exposure in Latin America, where the dollar has stayed stronger than it has against European currencies. He also said speculators on the dollar's fall would do well to focus on companies where unit sales also should increase abroad.

1. Explain why a decline in the value of the dollar vis-a-vis the deutsche mark, French franc, Swiss franc, and the pound sterling would improve the earnings and stock prices of a number of U.S. MNCs listed in the article.
2. Why were "foreign earnings swings based on currency transactions" expected to be less pronounced than they were two years earlier? Why does FASB Rule #8 result in wider swings in reported earnings than FASB Rule #52 for the same fluctuations in exchange rates?
3. Why are MNCs dealing with natural resources or commodity base (for instance, Asarco, ASA Ltd., Mesa Petroleum, and Ranger Oil) likely to have a higher degree of exposure than other MNCs listed in the article?
4. The U.S. dollar declined sharply against major currencies during 1985. Investigate the impact of this decline on any three U.S. multinational firms mentioned in this article.

REVIEW QUESTIONS

1. Why did financial managers of MNCs object to the use of FASB #8 for consolidating the accounts of their subsidiaries or affiliates, particularly during the 1979–1982 period?
2. Which of the following transactions of affiliate A of a U.S. parent company results in transaction exposure to the parent company? Explain in each case the reasoning behind your answer.
   a. Affiliate A enters into a long-term lease agreement denominated in country A's currency.
   b. Affiliate A acquires new equipment payable in cash in country A's currency.
   c. Affiliate A sells goods on credit terms to residents of country A.
   d. Affiliate A buys equipment from the parent company denominated in U.S. dollars.
   e. Affiliate A enters a contract to provide raw materials to affiliate B over a period of time (transaction denominated in currency A).
   f. Affiliate A enters a contract to provide components to affiliate B over a period of time (transaction denominated in currency B).
   g. Affiliate A expedites collection of its local accounts receivables.
   h. Affiliate A executes a forward contract to sell currency A forward against U.S. dollars.
   i. Affiliate A executes a forward contract to sell currency A forward against Japanese yens.

j. Affiliate A leases equipment to another company operating in country A specifying that lease rates are payable in U.S. dollars.
k. Affiliate A declares a dividend to the parent company payable immediately.
l. Affiliate A declares a dividend to the parent company payable in three months.

3. Explain why economic exposure cannot arise from expected changes in the exchange rates. Does this hold true even if exchange markets are not efficient?
4. Show how each of the following factors may impact the economic exposure of a U.S. parent company resulting from the operations of its affiliate in country A, whose currency has depreciated against the U.S. dollar.
   a. The cost structure of affiliate A.
   b. The elasticity of demand for A's products in country A.
   c. Competition to affiliate A's products in third-country markets.
   d. Ability of affiliate A to substitute local inputs for components sourced from the parent company.
   e. The time value of money.
5. Why is economic exposure difficult to measure? Suggest a scenario where an expected decline in the present value of a firm (due to negative economic exposure) may actually turn out to be beneficial to the firm.

REVIEW PROBLEMS

1. Translate the following balance sheets of the two subsidiaries of ABC, Inc. (a U.S. MNC) into U.S. dollars, using: (a) monetary-nonmonetary method, and (b) the current method of translation.

	U.K. SUBSIDIARY (MILLIONS OF POUNDS STERLING)		FRENCH SUBSIDIARY (MILLIONS OF FRENCH FRANCS)	
	12/31/84	12/31/85	12/31/84	12/31/85
Cash & marketable securities	120	143	2,143	1,915
Accounts receivable	315	407	4,020	3,775
Inventories	612	750	3,950	3,850
Fixed assets (net)	1,350	1,300	7,010	6,850
Total assets	2,397	2,600	17,123	16,390

Bank loans	500	450	3,000	2,800
Accounts payable	490	553	4,873	4,658
Long-term debt	650	700	4,250	4,000
Net worth	757	897	5,000	4,932
Total liabilities & net worth	2,397	2,600	17,123	16,390

Assume the following exchange rates

12/31/85 £1.00 = U.S. $1.40 U.S. $1.00 = FF7.25

12/31/84 £1.00 = U.S. $1.05 U.S. $1.00 = FF9.00

Show also how the parent company will reflect the exchange gains (losses) in its consolidated statements, using the monetary-nonmonetary method (FASB Rule #8) as against the current method (FASB Rule #52).

2. Show the impact on the cash flow of ABC, Inc., a U.S. MNC in years 1–3, arising from the appreciation of the French franc from U.S. 1.00 = FF9.00 to U.S. 1.00 = FF7.25, given the following data:

BASE CASE SCENARIO

Sales	Units	Unit Price (FF)	Total (FF million)
Domestic	5,000,000	3.50	
Export	1,500,000	4.50	
Total sales revenue			
PRODUCTION COSTS			
Local labor	500,000 man-hours	12.00	
Local inputs	6,500,000 units	0.75	
Imported inputs (from parent co.)	4,500,000 units	1.25	
Total production costs			
Net operating income			
Overhead costs			1.25
Depreciation			1.00
Net profit before tax			
Income tax at 40%			
Profit after tax			
Add back depreciation			
Cash flow in French francs			
Cash flow in U.S. dollars			

OTHER ASSUMPTIONS

Scenario 1	Scenario 2	Scenario 3
All variables remain unchanged. Sale price in export markets remain fixed in foreign currencies, which depreciated vis-a-vis the French franc by an average of 10 percent.	Unit price for domestic sales decreases by 5 percent in year 1 and by another 5 percent in year 3. • Foreign sales decline by 10 percent and unit price (in French franc equivalent) decreases by 5 percent to offset in part the appreciation of the franc against currencies of export markets. • Labor cost increases by 5 percent annually. Unit price of imported inputs reflects the full impact of the depreciation of the U.S. dollar vis-a-vis the French franc.	No change in domestic sales and unit price. • Foreign sales remain unchanged both in volume and unit price (the consumers in those markets absorb the full price increase in terms of their local currencies). • Due to lower cost of inputs imported from the parent company, 1,000,000 units of imported inputs are substituted in each of year 2 and 3 for 1,500,000 units of local inputs. • ABC, Inc., uses a cost of capital of 15 percent to evaluate capital investments abroad. • No changes in working capital requirements are assumed in this problem.

BIBLIOGRAPHY

ADLER, M., and B. DUMAS, "Should Exposure Management Depend on Translation Accounting Methods?" *Euromoney* (June 1981), pp. 132–138.

AGGARWAL, R., "FASB No. 8 and Reported Results of Multinational Operations: Hazard for Managers and Investors," *Journal of Accounting, Auditing and Finance* (Spring 1978), pp. 197–216

______, *Financial Policies for the Multinational Company: The Management of Foreign Exchange.* New York: Praeger, 1976.

ALIBER, R. Z. and C. P. STICKNEY, "Accounting Measures of Foreign Exchange Exposure: The Long and Short of It," *Accounting Review* (January 1975), pp. 44–57.

BARNETT, J. S., "Corporate Foreign Exposure Strategy Formulation," *Columbia Journal of World Business* (Winter 1976), pp. 87–97.

BEAVER, W., and M. WOLFSON, "Foreign Currency Translation Gains and Losses: What Effect Do They Have and What Do They Mean?" *Financial Analysts Journal* (March-April 1984), pp. 282–289.

BURNS, J. M., *Accounting Standards and International Finance.* Washington, D.C.: American Enterprise Institute for Public Policy Research, 1976.

CHOI, F. D. S. and A. SONDHI, "Accounting for Floating Currencies: An International Perspective," *Journal of Accounting, Auditing and Finance* (Summer 1985), pp. 335–340.

CHOI, F. D. S., H. D. LOWE, and R. G. WORTHLEY, "Accountors, Accountants, and Standard No. 8," *Journal of International Business Studies* (Fall 1978), pp. 81–87.

COLLINS, S., "They're Burying Statement No. 8, Long Live Statement No. 52," *Euromoney* (January 1982), p. 122.

COOPER, K., D. FRASER, and R. M. RICHARDS, "The Impact of SFAS #8 on Financial Management Practices," *Financial Executive* (June 1978), pp. 26–31.

DEUPREE, M. M., "Is FASB #8 the Best Approach?" *Financial Executive* (January 1978), pp. 24–29.

DIETEMANN, G. J., "Evaluation of Multinational Performance Under FASB No. 8," *Management Accounting* (May 1980), pp. 89–93.

DONALDSON, H. and A. REINSTEIN, "Implementing FASB No. 52: The Critical Issues," *Financial Executive* (June 1983), pp. 40–42.

EAKER, M. R., "The Numeraire Problem and Foreign Exchange Risk," *Journal of Finance* (May 1981), pp. 419–426.

EUN, C. S., "Global Purchasing Power View of Exchange Risk," *Journal of Financial and Quantitative Analysis* (December 1981), pp. 639–650.

FANTL, I. L., "Problems with Currency Translation—A Report of FASB No. 8," *Financial Executive* (December 1979), pp. 33–36.

FINANCIAL ACCOUNTING STANDARDS BOARD, *Foreign Currency Translation,* Statement of Financial Accounting Standards No. 52 (December 1981). Stamford, Conn.: Financial Accounting Standards Board, 1981.

GEORGE, A. M., "Cash Flow Versus Accounting Exposures to Currency Risk," *California Management Review* (Summer 1978), pp. 50–55.

GERNON, H., "The Effect of Translation on Multinational Corporations Internal Performance Evaluation," *Journal of International Business Studies* (Spring-Summer 1983), pp. 103–112.

GIANNOTTI, J. B., "FASB 52 Gives Treasurers the Scope FASB 8 Denied Them," *Euromoney* (April 1982), pp. 141–142.

GIDDY, I. H., "Measuring the World Foreign Exchange Market," *The Columbia Journal of World Business* (Winter 1980), pp. 36–48.

GRAY, D., "Corporate Preferences for Foreign Currency Accounting Standards," *Journal of Accounting Research* (Autumn 1984), pp. 760–764.

LEVI, M. D., "Underutilization of Forward Markets or Rational Behavior," *Journal of Finance* (September 1979), pp. 1013–1017.

MAKIN, J. H., "Flexible Exchange Rates, Multinational Corporations and Accounting Standards," *Federal Reserve Bank of San Francisco Economic Review* (Fall 1977), pp. 44–45.

RAYBURN, F. R. and G. M. CROOCH, "Currency Translation and the Funds Statement: A New Approach," *Journal of Accountancy* (October 1983), pp. 51–52.

RODRIGUEZ, R. M., "FASB No. 8: What Has It Done For Us?" *Financial Analysts Journal* (March-April 1977), pp. 40–47.

SHANK, J. K., J. F. DILLARD, and R. J. MURDOCK, *Assessing the Economic Impact of FASB No. 8.* New York: Financial Executives Research Foundation, 1979.

______, "FASB No. 8 and the Decision-Makers," *Financial Executive* (February 1980), pp. 18–23.

SHERWIN, J. T., "Foreign Exchange Exposure Management," *Financial Executive* (May 1979), pp. 18–23.

TAUSSIG, R. A., "Impact of SFAS No. 52 on the Translation of Foreign Financial Statements of Companies in Highly Inflationary Economies," *Journal of Accounting, Auditing and Finance* (Winter 1983), pp. 142–156.

WENTZ, R., "Towards a General Foreign Exchange Risk Consciousness," *Columbia Journal of World Business* (Winter 1979), pp. 127–135.

WYMAN, H. E., "Analysis of Gains and Losses from Foreign Monetary Items: An Application of Purchasing Power Parity Concepts," *Accounting Review* (July 1976), pp. 545–558.

5

Management of Foreign Exchange Exposure

INTRODUCTION

The advent of the floating exchange rate regime since the early 1970s has heightened the interest of multinational firms in developing techniques and strategies for foreign exchange exposure management. Although multinationals obviously differ in their exposure management motivation and objectives, the primary goal is to protect corporate profits from the negative impact of exchange rate fluctuations. However, the goals as well as strategies or techniques of management depend on whether the focus is on accounting exposure or economic exposure.

Preoccupation with the impact of currency fluctuations on balance sheet and income statements brought about by FASB #8 created a disproportionately strong involvement in hedging the translation exposure risk. After January 1, 1976, when the provisions of this rule became effective, exchange gains and losses, though unrealized, were required to be passed through the quarterly income statement, thus influencing quarterly as well as annual income and earnings per share.

Financial managers of multinationals, fearful of reporting substantial exchange losses and adverse impact on market share prices, focused on risk management policies with a view to insulating reported earnings from exchange rate gyrations. This emphasis on short-run operating results led to excessive exchange risk aversion behavior among the MNCs, which engaged in hedging and risk offsetting techniques, irrespective of the cost, and regardless of the impact of this behavior on their long-term performance.

FASB #52, which adopted current rate translation for all fiscal years beginning on or after December 15, 1982, relieved the financial managers of MNCs from their preoccupation with cosmetic accounting to improve the quarterly operating results. This rule relegates exchange gains or losses to an equity adjustment account which does not impact reported income until such gains or losses are actually realized. Consequently, an increasing emphasis has been placed since then on management of long-term economic exposure.

Organizational Policies for Managing Exposure

An important aspect of management of foreign exchange risk is the degree of centralization of foreign exchange transactions and responsibility for developing and implementing hedging strategies. Three levels or degrees of centralization may be distinguished. At the first level, policy making is maintained at the headquarters level, and the responsibility for developing and implementing strategies is delegated to the operating level. This arrangement has the advantage of lower administrative cost, but is likely to result in an uncoordinated exposure strategy, since interdivisional netting cannot take place.

A second level of centralization is to maintain both policy and formulation of strategy at the headquarters level and leave implementation to the operating units. This will result in a more effective and better coordinated strategy, but is likely to involve higher administrative costs. Maximum centralization may be achieved when all three functions are performed by the head office, thus permitting the MNC to utilize all available exposure management techniques. This level of centralization, however, involves relatively high administrative costs and requires frequent reporting by the operating units.

Aside from the organizational aspect, an exposure management strategy must delineate the types of exposure to be monitored and formulate corporate objectives and a follow-up system for evaluating exchange risk management activities.

Statement of Objectives

The overriding objective of foreign exchange risk management is commonly expressed as eliminating or reducing the variability of the consolidated earnings of an MNC which is attributable to unexpected currency fluctuations. While this is an expression of the overall objective, MNCs usually formulate more specific objectives related to the type of exposure being managed. The objective of translation exposure management, for instance, may be stated as *minimizing* quarter-to-quarter (or year-to-year) earnings fluctuations due to exchange rate changes.[1] Minimizing economic exposure, on the other hand, may require ignoring the accounting outcome of exposure and concentrating on managing cash flow fluctuations and their impact on the value of the firm. Statement of objectives will also include management's view on an acceptable cost of exposure management, including the demand which such management may have on the MNC's senior staff. Transamerica defines its exposure management objective as protecting "future stream of income without, however, engaging in excessive speculation, incurring undue costs or preempting an inordinate amount of management time."[2]

MANAGING TRANSACTION AND TRANSLATION EXPOSURE

Hedging in its various forms provides the centerpiece in MNC's management of transaction and translation foreign exchange exposure. Hedging refers to a wide variety of transactions or activities which offset or counterbalance, in whole or in part, the risk of loss from a change in foreign exchange rates. The hedger in essence substitutes a presently known cost of a hedging operation for an open or indeterminate future exchange risk.

MNCs practice, in varying degrees, the following types of hedging operations which are listed by the frequency of their overall use.[3]

1. Forward market hedge
2. Financial market hedge (borrowing/lending)
3. Leading and lagging and working capital adjustments
4. Currency selection and exposure netting
5. Currency and credit swaps
6. Transfer price adjustments

Another way of classifying hedging operations is based on the nature of the strategy adopted to produce the counterbalancing operations. Under this basis of classification, one may list the following hedging postures:

1. Active strategy, which includes primarily the forward market hedge and the money market hedge.

[1]See David B. Zenoff, "Applying Management Principles to Foreign Exchange exposure." *Euromoney* (September 1978), pp. 123–130.

[2]As stated in "Firm's Exposure Management Mixes Strong HQ Control with Decentralization," *Business International Money Report* (December 1977), pp. 401–402.

[3]A study conducted in 1976 by the Wharton School, the University of Pennsylvania, lists forward contracts as the most widely used hedging techniques resorted to in varying degrees of frequency by over 90 percent of the MNCs polled. It was followed closely by leading and lagging receivables and payables, and the financial or money market hedge. See Wolfram Nolte, *Empirical Study of Corporate Foreign Exchange Risk Management Practices.* Wharton School, University of Pennsylvania, December 1976.

2. Defensive measures, which consist mainly of working capital adjustments. This includes measures to influence the level of the affiliate's net working capital by leading and lagging amounts receivable from or payable to (a) other entities outside the MNC and (b) the parent company and other affiliates (intracompany transactions).

   Under (a), the following practices may be listed, assuming an expected depreciation of the affiliate's currency.

   Reduce level of local currency cash and marketable securities.

   Tighten credit and speed up collection to reduce local currency receivables.

   Delay payments of local accounts payable.

   Delay collection of hard-currency receivables.

   Speed up payments of hard-currency payables.

   Under (b), the following practices may be listed:

   Speed up dividend and fee remittances to parent.

   Speed up payment of intersubsidiary accounts payable.

   Delay collection of intersubsidiary accounts receivable.

3. Export-import strategy which consists, *inter alia,* of invoicing exports in foreign currency and imports in local currency (wherever possible), as well as stepping up imports of hard-currency goods and components.

Forward Market Hedge

The forward market hedge consists of offsetting an anticipated receivable/payable dominated in foreign currency by concluding at the outset a forward contract to sell/buy that currency with delivery set at a determinate future date so as to coincide with the date of anticipated receipt/payment of foreign currency (see example on page 122). The forward hedge in effect substitutes a presently known quantum representing the cost of the hedge for an open-ended future outcome in the absence of the hedge. When the forward contract reverses existing or contemplated receivables/payables in foreign currency, it affords the MNC a complete or "covered" hedge against the foreign exchange risk; that is, the forward contract perfectly matches the future funds to be received or paid in foreign currency. The forward market hedge provides a perfect cover for transaction exposure.

Offsetting translation exposure by the forward hedge still leaves a residual risk, because funds to fulfill the forward contract have to be purchased in the future in the spot market. This is called an "open" or "uncovered" hedge, because the hedger is taking the risk of reversing the future contract in the spot market at a rate which may differ (and usually does) from the forward rate. Only when the future spot rate (at the time of the maturity of the contract) equals the forward rate does hedging against a translation exposure afford a complete or a perfect hedge (see example on page 122).

Evaluation of the Forward Hedge

A financial manager can use the forward market either to avoid (minimize) the foreign exchange risk or to take a position in the foreign exchange market, that is, speculate. In the latter case, the management acts on the belief that it can outguess the market on the direction of exchange rate changes.

Undertaking hedging operations in the forward market presumes that the management believes that the exchange markets are efficient, that is, that the forward rate is an accurate predictor of the future spot rate (see Chapter 4). It is, of course, conceivable that the management may perceive the markets as efficient and may still elect not to buy the forward market "cover." Being an accurate predictor of the future spot rate does not mean that the future spot rate will be identical with the forward rate. It means only that the former will be as likely above as below the latter.

Forward hedging operations must also be balanced against the cost of these operations. These consist of transaction costs (the spread between the bid and the ask quotations). In the case of using the forward market for counterbalancing translation exposure, the cost is measured by the difference between forward and future spot rates. For an MNC that has frequent exposure in many currencies, hedging every transaction is counterproductive, since the likely outcome of the gains and losses under an unhedged position will approach zero, particularly under a floating rate regime. Unless the exchange market is perceived to be grossly distorted, due to political risk or otherwise, a policy to hedge all exposure is likely to be as costly as the expected exchange rate changes. If hedging a large number of transactions will produce the same outcome as the unhedged position, then the overall gain from hedging operations is slightly negative because of the cost of arranging the protection.

It must also be pointed out that the forward hedge is available only for few major currencies and only for certain maturities. The bulk of international transactions, however, is denominated in these currencies, and most maturity needs for the MNCs are covered by available contracts in the forward market. This aspect of the foreign exchange markets renders exposure management more difficult for MNCs with substantial exposure in developing countries.

Money Market Hedge

The money market hedge consists of reversing the foreign currency receivables/payables by creating matching payables/receivables in the respective foreign currency through borrowing in the money markets. If a

U.S. firm is committed to pay FF1,000,000 in three months, it could hedge the exchange risk by borrowing U.S. dollars now, converting the dollars into French francs at the spot rate, and investing the proceeds in French money market instruments. The proceeds of these instruments upon maturity in three months will be used to meet the FF1,000,000 commitment. The amount of the U.S. dollar loan depends on: (1) spot exchange rate between dollars and French francs (S_0(\$/FF), and (2) the yield (or interest rate) on the investment in French money market instruments (see example below). In this manner, the U.S. firm has substituted a fixed amount of obligation denominated in U.S. dollars for a commitment denominated in French francs which will translate into an unknown amount of dollars.

The reader will recognize that if forward cover is available and interest rate parity holds, the interest rate differential between the two countries (the Unites States and France in this case) will be exactly offset by the forward premium/discount of the French franc against the U.S. dollar. In situations where this parity does not hold and interest rate differentials exceeding transaction costs exist, arbitrage operations are profitable. Whenever such opportunities exist, they should be taken by the MNC irrespective of its exchange exposure position or exposure management policies.

A variation of the money market hedge is the so-called *balance sheet hedge* or balancing exposed assets and liabilities, a position of zero net exposure. If the MNC translates according to the "temporal" method (the method which underlay FASB #8), such a hedge would entail bringing monetary debt up to the level of monetary assets. Under the "current" method of translation which is presently in effect (as embodied by FASB #52), a complete balance sheet hedge is impracticable. Such a hedge would imply eliminating net worth, since all assets and liabilities are exposed.

Example Illustrating Alternative Use of the Forward Market Hedge and the Money Market Hedge vs. the Unhedged Position

Instruments International, Inc. has just imported a shipment of chemicals from a German firm valued at DM5,000,000 payable in 180 days. The company has three options as to the uncovered position it now has in deutsche marks:

1. Do nothing, that is, remain unhedged, particularly if the management is of the opinion that the spot rate in 180 days will be substantially unchanged from today's spot rate, or that the spot rate in 180 days will be about equal to today's 180-day forward rate, or, better still, if it believes that the deutsche mark will depreciate vis-a-vis the U.S. dollar. Irrespective of its belief, it will be taking a *speculative* position.
2. Hedge in the forward market

3. Hedge in the money market

In order to undertake the forward or the financial hedge, the management needs the following data:

Spot exchange rate: S_0(DM/\$) = 2.6600
180-day forward rate: F(DM/\$) = 2.5802
(a 6 percent premium)
U.S. interest rate: 13 percent per annum
German interest rate: 8 percent per annum

Option 1. Unhedged Position

Instruments International will wait for 180 days and exchange an unknown amount of U.S. dollars, depending on the spot rate in 180 days, for DM5 million to pay for the shipment.

Option 2. The Forward Hedge

Instruments International will enter a 180-day forward contract to buy DM5,000,000 for dollars today. In 180 days it will exchange \$1,937,834 (5,000,000/2.5802) for DM5,000,000 to pay for the shipment. In this manner it fixed today the amount of dollars it needs to pay for the shipment.

Option 3. The Financial Hedge

Instruments International has to borrow today sufficient dollars, which when exchanged today for deutsche marks and invested for 180 days in Germany, will generate exactly DM5,000,000.

$$\frac{\text{DM}5{,}000{,}000}{1.04} = \text{DM}4{,}807{,}692$$ needs to be invested today in Germany

$$\frac{\text{DM}4{,}807{,}692}{S_0(\text{DM}/\$)} = \frac{4{,}807{,}692}{2.6600} = \$1{,}807{,}403$$ amount of dollars which needs to be borrowed today in U.S.

$$\$1{,}807{,}403 \times (1.065) = \$1{,}924{,}884$$ amount of dollars which the company has to pay its bankers in the U.S. 180 days from now

The financial hedge fixes today the cost of the shipment in U.S. dollars (\$1,924,884) and provides, through the liquidation of the investment in Germany in 180 days, exactly DM5,000,000 to pay for the shipment.

To complete this illustration let us see how Instruments International would have fared under each of the alternative options, assuming that each of the following spot rates prevailed in 180 days:

$\overset{*}{S}_0(DM/\$) = 2.5802$ (exactly equal to the 180 forward rate at the date of the transaction)

$\overset{*}{S}_0(DM/\$) = 2.5550$ (the deutsche mark premium against the U.S. dollar turned out to be more than expected)

$\overset{*}{S}_0(DM/\$) = 2.7200$ (the deutsche mark depreciated against the U.S. dollar contrary to market expectations)

Exhibit 5-1 dramatizes the fact that while each of the hedged positions fixed today in terms of U.S. dollars the cost of imports, the cost of the shipment under the unhedged position was really open-ended, and ranged from \$1,838,235 to \$1,956,947 under the alternative spot rates which were assumed to prevail in 180 days. Under the hedged options, the firm will be completely insulated from future exchange rate fluctuations. However, the firm fared better under the financial hedge than under the forward hedge, because exchange and interest rate data given above created a situation of profitable covered arbitrage in favor of borrowing in the U.S. and investing in Germany.

$$R_{us} - R_{Germany} < \frac{S_0(DM/\$) - F_{1/2}(DM/\$)}{S_0(DM/\$)}$$

or in other words, the interest rate differential is 5 percent per annum, or 2.5 percent for 180 days, while the forward premium on the deutsche mark is 6 percent per annum, or 3 percent for 180 days. As stated earlier, if such an opportunity exists, management should avail itself of profitable covered arbitrage irrespective of its exposure position or its exposure management policies.

The forward market does not provide a "covered" hedge against the translation risk, because the hedger will still be exposed to the future rate in the spot market. Currency bought/sold forward has to be sold/bought in the spot market at maturity to fulfill the contract. The final outcome of the hedge depends on the spot rate at the maturity of the forward contract.

Exhibit 5-1. Cost of Goods Imported by Instruments International, Inc. from Germany Under Different Hedging Positions and Different Assumed Future Spot Rates (U.S. dollars)

FUTURE SPOT RATE	UNHEDGED POSITION	FORWARD HEDGE	FINANCIAL HEDGE
$\overset{*}{S}_0(DM/\$)$ 2.5802	1,937,834	1,937,834	1,924,884
2.5550	1,956,947	1,937,834	1,924,884
2.7200	1,838,235	1,937,834	1,924,884

To illustrate this principle, let us assume that Instruments International has a German affiliate with net exposed assets of DM5,000,000 under the current rate exposure method. Exhibit 5-2 shows the net gain (loss) from hedging this translation risk, by entering a 180-day forward contract to sell this amount of deutsche marks, under several assumed future spot rates.

Exhibit 5-2 reveals that hedging the translation risk by a forward contract, that is, by selling DM5,000,000 forward against the dollar, entails taking a speculative position. The net gain (loss) on the forward transaction can be determined only after entering the spot market 180 days later to fulfill the forward commitment. Should the spot rate 180 days later turn out to be equal to today's 180-day forward rate, the profit (loss) on the forward transaction will be zero, and the company will still have a translation exposure gain (loss) equal to the same gain (loss) had the company not entered into the forward contract. The effect of the hedge is to lock in the forward premium quoted for the mark.

Thus it would seem that the translation risk is not amenable to be hedged by the forward market, and that other hedging techniques may be more appropriate. Leading and lagging, working capital adjustments, and currency swaps provide a far superior hedge for the translation risk than the forward market. The following section addresses other hedging techniques:

Other Hedging Techniques Against the Transaction and Translation Risks

Leading and lagging and working capital adjustments

To the extent possible, and subject to the limitations imposed by various host countries,[4] the MNC has some latitude to reduce its overall exposure

Exhibit 5-2. Hedging Translation Risk in the Forward Market Overall Outcome Under Alternative Future Spot Rates (U.S. dollars)

Assumed Future Spot Rate $\dot{S}_0$(DM/$)	Profit (Loss) on Forward Transaction (actual)	Translation Gain (Loss) (bookkeeping)	Net Gain (Loss)
2.5550	(18,637)	76,772	58,135
2.5802	0	58,135	58,135
2.6600	58,135	0	58,135
2.7200	99,599	(41,464)	58,135

[4]See Appendix D for list of country limitations on leading and lagging.

to transaction and translation risks by taking steps to reduce its net exposure in soft currencies (currencies that are expected to depreciate against the parent's reporting currency) and, if it so wishes, to increase its net exposure in hard currencies (currencies that are expected to appreciate against the parent's reporting currency).

In general, the affiliate with the "soft" currency must reduce its net working capital in local currency by reducing cash and marketable securities to a feasible minimum, tighten its credit policies, accelerate the collection of receivables, reduce the level of inventories, and speed up transfers to other affiliates and to the parent company. It must also lead, to the extent possible, payments of accounts payable to suppliers in other countries and delay the collection of receivables from customers outside its domicile. The affiliate with the "hard" currency must strive to do the opposite. It must be pointed out, however, that these measures are to be taken with a view to lessening the degree of exposure rather than taking speculative positions with a view to achieving foreign exchange profit. Moreover, the actions must be coordinated on a company-wide basis, with other hedging operations that the MNC has instituted being taken into account. Use of "transfer pricing," the pricing of goods, services, and technology exchanged among the affiliates and the parent company to alter the working capital position of the operating units, will be discussed in Chapter 6 dealing with current asset management.

Currency Selection and Exposure Netting

Hedging against exposure to currency fluctuations can be reduced by judicious selection of currencies so as to minimize net exposure. A long position in currencies A and B, for example, would tend to reduce overall net exposure if the two currencies are negatively correlated, that is, if one is likely to appreciate vis-a-vis the U.S. dollar, while the other one is likely to depreciate. If, on the other hand, currencies A or B are positively correlated, that is, they move fairly in unison vis-a-vis the U.S. dollar, then a long position in A must be counterbalanced by a short position in B, or vice versa. Another strategy involving currency selection for MNCs engaged in foreign trade is to denominate exports insofar as possible in a strong currency and denominate imports in a weak currency. This, of course, involves shifting the exchange risk to the other side of the international trade transaction, and its success depends on the relative bargaining positions of the two sides. A firm instituting such a policy may lose export sales to competitors who are willing to continue to bill exports in local (importer's) currency.

The last ten years provided many examples of currency switching brought about by substantial shifts in currency values with the advent of the floating rate regime in the early nineteen-seventies. Several European and

Japanese exporters, which used to bill their customers in U.S. dollars, demanded payment in their own currencies with the sharp decline in the value of the dollar. OPEC members considered seriously dropping the U.S. dollar as a basis for pricing crude oil in favor of a more stable monetary unit such as the SDR.

Use of currency selection and switching by the MNC as a hedging device is inextricably related to the overall policy of working capital management and funds positioning, which are discussed in Chapters 6 and 8.

Parallel Loans and Currency Swaps

Another method of reducing foreign exchange exposure practiced with some frequency by MNCs is to circumvent the exchange market altogether through the use of parallel loans and currency swaps.

A parallel loan is an arrangement whereby two MNCs agree to finance each other's affiliate by extending a loan in local currencies. These loans are then reversed, also in local currencies, at the agreed maturity date. Although the spot rate is used as a reference value to determine the corresponding values of the loan, no currencies are converted in the exchange markets, See Exhibit 5-3.

It should be noted that parallel loans bear interest at rates which are negotiated by the two parties. The two rates used are usually different and reflect the cost of money in each country.

A currency swap is an exchange of an equivalent amount of two different currencies by two firms in two separate countries which is reversed at an agreed date in the future. It differs from a parallel loan

Exhibit 5-3. Illustration of Parallel Loan (Assuming a Spot Reference Rate of £1.00 = $1.50)

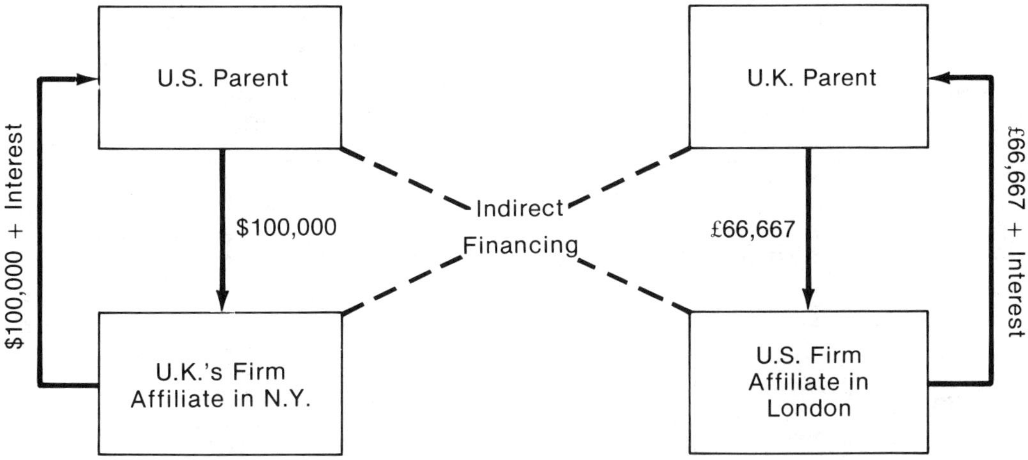

arrangement in that no interest is involved, and no record of the transactions appears on the balance sheet of the contracting firms. Since the transaction does not create receivables or payables in foreign currencies, translation and transaction risks are avoided. A variation of this arrangement, where one party to the transactions is a bank (often a central bank), is called a *credit swap.* An example of a credit swap is shown in Exhibit 5-4.

As in parallel loans, the exchange market is completely circumvented both at the inception and at the reversal of the transaction. Only the spot exchange rate is used as a reference to determine amounts to be exchanged.

MANAGING ECONOMIC EXPOSURE

The primary goal of economic exposure risk management is to protect corporate profits from the negative impact of exchange rate fluctuations. The diversified MNC stands in this respect in a much better position than the relatively undiversified firm. Diversification reduces the variability of the overall cash flow. When changes in foreign exchange rates negatively impact one portion of a firm's market, the same change can result in a positive impact to operations in a different market segment of the firm, thereby offsetting the loss. Moreover, a broadly diversified firm can recognize changes in exchange rates and react to them more decisively than the undiversified firm.

The impact of foreign exchange fluctuations on the cash flow of the company as a whole has been found to be a function of a number of variables, such as price sensitivity of demand in the various markets served by the operating units, pricing flexibility in these markets, ability of the

Exhibit 5.4. Illustration of a Credit Swap Arrangement (Assuming a Spot Exchange Rate of LE1.00 = $1.40)

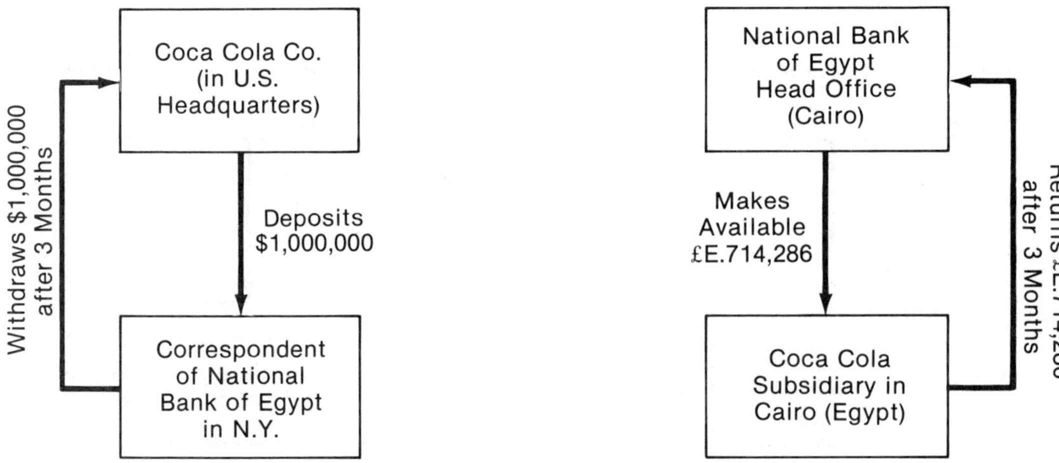

operating units to adjust their mix of inputs as relative costs change, and subsequent inflation in the countries which devalued their currencies. There is also lack of any necessary relationship between accounting-derived measures of exposure and the true impact of currency changes on the firm's economic value. It has also been shown that the change in an affiliate's cash flow arising from currency depreciation or appreciation will not necessarily match in direction nor in magnitude the net impact on the cash flow of the MNC as a whole.[5]

Several studies on economic exposure distinguished between impact of exchange rate fluctuations on nominal and real cash flows. Where exchange rates adjust to changes in relative prices (purchasing power parity holds), there is, in real terms, no exchange risk. Real exposure occurs when relative prices of firm's inputs and outputs change as a result of exchange rate movements, causing a shift in the firm's competitive position and in noncontractual cash flows.[6] The problem is that purchasing power parity does not hold for a number of reasons, or does not hold within the time frame which is operationally meaningful for exposure management purposes.

Managing economic exposure has led multinationals to reassess their reporting and internal control systems to cope with unpredictable markets and floating exchange rates. A strategy of reacting to exchange rate fluctuations is not adequate. Multinational firms need an anticipatory strategy[7] which requires projections of future cash flows under alternative exchange rate scenarios. Effects of exchange rate exposure on all the company's operations and entities needs to be ascertained, not just the consolidation effect.

Laurent L. Jacque suggested an optimal solution to economic exposure management by adjusting the sales-inputs currency mix so that changes in future sales revenue will be neutralized by changes in the cost of inputs. However, he thought that a neutral economic exposure can seldom be brought about by this process of adjustment alone. The MNC will probably need to supplement changes in the real sector by manipulating the currency mix of short-term and long-term financing.[8]

[5]Gunter Dufey, "Corporate Finance and Exchange Rates Variations," *Financial Management* (Summer 1972), pp. 51–57.

[6]See, for example, Alan C. Shapiro, "Exchange Rate Changes, Inflation, and the Value of the Multinational Corporations," *The Journal of Finance* (May 1975), pp. 485–502.; Bradford Cornell, "Inflation, Relative Price Changes, and Exchange Risk," *Financial Management* (Autumn 1980), pp. 30–35; and Clas Wihlborg, "Currency Exposure: Taxonomy and Theory," in *Exchange Risk and Exposure: Current Development in International Financial Development,* co-edited with Richard M. Levich (Lexington, Mass.: 1980) D. C. Heath.

[7]See Andrew R. Prindle, "International Money Management: Systems and Techniques," *Euromoney* (October 1971).

[8]Laurent L. Jacque, "Management of Foreign Exchange Risk: A Review Article," in *International Finance: Concepts and Issues,* edited by Gerald D. Gay and Robert W. Kolbe (Richmond, Va.: Robert F. Dame, Inc., 1983), pp. 477–478.

An economic exposure management strategy obviously depends on the nature of the firm and the frequency of its exposure to exchange rate risk. A strategy which suits the requirements of an occasional exporter will not be adequate to the habitual exporter or an MNC with extensive foreign operations. Moreover, a well-diversified MNC must weigh the cost of exposure management against the benefit, in the form of an increment to the value of the firm, which can accrue from such management. It can follow a passive approach to exposure management hoping or anticipating that different segments of the firm react differently to exchange rate fluctuations, resulting in little departure from the desired cash flow pattern. Alternatively, it can engage in an aggressive exposure management strategy that seeks to neutralize the impact of unexpected exchange rate changes on net cash flows.

In an effort to neutralize or lessen economic exposure, the well-diversified MNC may attempt to effect adjustments in: (1) marketing management and (2) production management.

Marketing Management

Whether reacting to or anticipating foreign exchange rate changes, the MNC and its affiliates can offset the impact of relative price changes by effecting changes in its pricing strategies in various markets and in market selection.

Revising marketing strategy can be feasible only in situations where deviations from purchasing power parity persist. In these situations, the affiliate whose local currency was devalued ought to consider penetrating new markets where it has become more competitive. Needless to say, revision of marketing strategy must be closely coordinated with the pricing strategy. An affiliate facing a depreciating local currency gains a considerable pricing latitude in export markets. If demand for the product is inelastic, such as the case in highly differentiated products, the affiliate will be able to raise prices in local currency by up to the full percentage of depreciation of the local currency to maximize revenues from these markets. At the other extreme, if these markets are extremely competitive and demand is price sensitive, the affiliate will lower export prices in terms of foreign currencies, thus realizing an increase in home currency revenues somewhat less than the percentage of depreciation of the exchange rate. There is much less pricing latitude in the local market, particularly if no strong foreign competition existed prior to the decline in the value of the local currency. If it is assumed that the affiliate was following profit maximization behavior prior to the decline, its best strategy is to maintain domestic prices unchanged. If strong prior competition existed from foreign imports, the affiliate gains a competitive advantage over them. Domestic prices may be raised or maintained, depending on such factors as price sensitivity of demand and economies of scale in production.

The experience of most U.S. MNCs in the early 1970s following the devaluation of the dollar illustrates some aspects of these strategies. The devaluation of the dollar gave them a substantial latitude in pricing their exports in foreign markets. Realizing that they were dealing in most cases with highly differentiated product, they elected for the most part to maintain their prices in foreign currency terms and even raised them in certain instances. In the domestic market, where they faced competition, such as in the automobile industry, they reacted to the increase in the prices of West German and Japanese imports by raising prices on models competitive with these imports, such as the Chevette and the Pinto. This strategy on the part of U.S. manufacturers paid off, because they improved their profit margins while keeping U.S. cars competitive with their foreign rivals.

Production Management

The MNC and its affiliates can offset the adverse impact of currency fluctuations on cash flows by adapting their production strategies to the new situation. Increasing the degree of differentiation of the product, or expanding their product line to include higher-quality items, for example, are appropriate strategies to offset the impact of local currency appreciation on revenues from foreign markets. Shapiro suggested that Volkswagen, faced with a sharply appreciating mark against the dollar, was forced to abandon its policy of depending on the price appeal of the "bug" in U.S. markets, and introduced higher-priced models to appeal to middle-income buyers on the basis of prestige and styling.[9]

Adjustment can also be effected in the cost structure. An affiliate with a depreciating currency and with a high import content may face a sharp increase in its cost structure. The degree to which it can substitute less expensive local inputs for the now higher-priced foreign inputs could enable it to sustain its cash flow. This is illustrated by the experience of some U.S. manufacturing companies in the early 1970s. Faced with successive devaluations of the U.S. dollar, they reversed their policy of sourcing parts and components abroad in favor of buying these products in the U.S. Ford, for example, which used to import engines for the Pinto model from the U.K. and Germany, built domestic facilities to produce these engines.[10]

MNCs, faced with a substantially different currency alignment situation, may decide to locate new plants or subsidiaries in countries with appreciably lower production costs. Several German firms found it feasible to establish production and assembly facilities in the U.S., as a sharply appreciating mark during the 1970s threatened their ability to compete effectively in the United States. The same circumstances induced Mercedes Benz in 1973 to switch the sourcing of its diesel trucks destined for the U.S.

[9]Alan C. Shapiro, *Multinational Financial Management* (Boston, Mass.: Allyn & Bacon, 1981), pp. 200–201.

[10]*Ibid.* p. 202.

market from West Germany to Brazil. Brazil at that time provided a relatively lower-cost location, particularly for labor intensive production in view of the prospect of further monetary alignments. However, these cost advantages were later eroded by a sharply accelerating inflation rate.

Summary

Management exposure strategies have gained a prominent place in MNCs' financial planning since the advent of the floating exchange rate system in the early 1970s. MNCs have reacted by strengthening and centralizing their exposure management organization, and have attempted new techniques to minimize net exposure.

Hedging includes a variety of techniques designed to substitute a known present cost for an open-ended future risk. Hedging through the forward and money markets are the most widely used approaches to neutralize or minimize transaction and translation exposure. Other techniques such as leading and lagging, adjustment of working capital, swaps, and transfer pricing are also frequently used by MNCs. An optimal hedging strategy depends on the extent and frequency of the firm's foreign exchange exposure. For firms that have continuing receipts or outflows in a number of foreign currencies, repeated forward hedging is of dubious value. Such firms would do just as well in the long run by exchanging foreign currencies in the spot market as they would by entering into forward contracts. Unless the firm's risk aversion is such that it must cover all positions, and since the forward rate appears to be on average an unbiased predictor of the future spot rate, there is no long-run net gain from using the forward market. As a matter of fact, hedging by the forward "cover" may involve higher transaction costs, since the bid-ask spreads are usually larger in forward markets than in spot markets. However, there is no strong disincentive to use the forward market, since transaction costs represent a very small percentage of the size of currency transactions. The same conclusions apply to the money market hedge if interest parity prevails, that is, when interest rate differentials are equated to the forward premium or discount through arbitrage operations.

Managing economic exposure poses a more serious challenge for the MNC, particularly as the impact of exchange rate fluctuations on net cash flows extends well beyond the accounting period in which these fluctuations occur. Moreover, under a regime of freely fluctuating rates, such management is rendered extremely difficult from the operational point of view as rates become more volatile. A well-diversified MNC with respect to currencies, products, and sources of inputs can afford to take a passive attitude toward risk management. The diversity of its cash flows from independent origins can be relied upon in the long run to dampen the volatility of the overall net cash flow. On the other hand, an MNC relying heavily on a limited number of cash flow sources from two or three affiliates must develop a dynamic exposure management strategy to protect its profitability. Such a strategy usually involves adjustments in production and marketing policies to offset the adverse impact of currency fluctuations on cash flows.

REVIEW QUESTIONS

1. Select one U.S. MNC that has a highly centralized exchange exposure management strategy and another which has a highly decentralized approach. Contrast the two approaches and indicate why multinational financial managers may pursue one or the other.
2. Among the three types of exposure: translation, transaction, and economic, which is the easiest to manage? Which is the most difficult? Explain your reasoning.
3. Inasmuch as consolidation of subsidiary accounts with those of the parent is now governed by FASB Rule #52, should MNCs' managers be preoccupied with managing translation exposure? Explain why such exposure is not amenable to being completely eliminated.
4. Contrast an aggressive vs. a defensive strategy in hedging transaction exposure. Can the latter strategy achieve a perfect hedge?
5. Explain how a flexible policy of leading and lagging accounts receivable from or payable to other entities might work to reduce the transaction exposure of an affiliate. Why do some countries, particularly LDCs, impose limits on leading and lagging for import payments, for export receipts, and other types of transfers?
6. Contrast the forward market hedge and the money market hedge as to (a) cost, (b) convenience, and (c) effectiveness. Under what conditions would the second hedge become the only viable option?
7. Your affiliate is located in a developing country that has a soft currency with no forward exchange market, and where there is no organized money market. Assume additionally that parallel loans and credit swap opportunities are not available. Suggest an optimum strategy to minimize transaction exposure.
8. Draw up a strategy for a Japanese MNC manufacturing and distributing cars from locations in the United States to manage economic exposure arising from a sharp decline in the value of the Japanese yen against the U.S. dollar.
9. How would your answer to Question 8 differ if the Japanese firm conducts operations involving the manufacture and distribution of a number of items (such as motorcycles, snowmobiles, and the like) in addition to cars, in a number of countries in addition to the U.S. market?

10. A South Korean firm is exporting subcompacts to the U.S. market, relying on low production cost in South Korea to penetrate the U.S. market primarily on the basis of price appeal. Faced with a combination of stiffening competition from Japanese cars in the same category and a sharp depreciation of the U.S. dollar against its own currency, what production and marketing adjustments are advisable to protect its market in the United States?

REVIEW PROBLEMS

1. Prepare an exposure management strategy for Instruments International and affiliates based on data given in Chapter 4. In particular, be prepared to discuss the following aspects of the recommended strategy during the meeting called by Mr. Baker.
   a. What would be an optimal hedging strategy against the translation and transaction risks in each of the currencies where there is an exposed position?
   b. Is the company diversified enough to rely on offsetting cash flow movements to reduce its net economic exposure? If not, what are the basic elements of an economic exposure management policy which would suit the requirements of the company?
2. A French firm has contracted to buy parts from Japan worth ¥15 billion payable in three months. The firm has receivables for goods sold to a Japanese firm valued at ¥5 billion, also due in three months. It is the policy of the firm to hedge all residual currency positions. Given the following exchange and interest rates data:

Exchange rates: Spot	**3-month forward rate**
¥/FF FF1.00 = ¥27.00	¥/FF FF1.00 = 26.65

Interest rates (% per annum)

France	13.2%
Japan	8.0%

   a. Show how the firm can execute the desired hedge in the forward market.
   b. If, instead, the hedge is executed in the money market, what steps need to be taken? (*Hint:* The amount borrowed in French francs should be such that when it is invested in Japan for three months, it will result in sufficient proceeds to pay off the obligation in Japanese yens.)
   c. Calculate the foreign exchange gains (losses) of an unhedged position (compared to a hedged position) if the spot rate in three months is FF1.00 = ¥26.50.

Show all calculations in a, b, and c, disregarding all transaction costs.

3. Your affiliate in the Philippines declared a dividend of 50,000,000 pesos which is transferable in six months to the parent company in the United States. You are worried about adverse economic and political developments in the Philippines that could trigger a sharp depreciation of the peso during the next six months. Your attempts to hedge in the forward market were unsuccessful, as your bankers were not able to quote you a forward rate for the peso. You are looking at two options:
   a. Invest the peso funds in Philippine government securities yielding 10 percent per annum, and take the risk of the exchange rate that will prevail six months from now.
   b. You were approached by a U.S. firm operating in the Philippines which needed local funds. They expressed their willingness to borrow ₱50,000,000 from your affiliate against a payment in U.S. dollars of $2,250,000 to your bank in the United States in six months.

   You asked your staff to research the prospects of the peso/dollar exchange rate in the next six months. They compiled the following data:

EXCHANGE RATE—PESOS PER U.S. DOLLAR

	Spot Rate in Six Months		
Current Spot Rate	*No Change*	*Best case scenario*	*Worst case scenario*
18.5	18.5	20.0	24.0

   The no-change case assumes that the Central Bank of the Philippines will support the rate at the current level during the next six months.
   a. Which course of action will you take in each of the three scenarios? (Show all calculations.)
   b. Which course of action will you take, assuming that you assign the following probabilities to the future spot rate scenarios?

No Change	10%
₱/$20.0	25%
₱/$24.0	65%

4. If you were the financial manager of a multinational corporation in charge of foreign exchange operations, explain how you would minimize the risk to your firm in each of the following situations.
   a. Your firm has modest amounts of receivables and payments in currencies A, B, C, D, E, F, and G not coincident in timing.
   b. Your firm has a fairly large 3-month receivables in currency A, but it also has a subsidiary in country A to which you intend

to make a transfer in four months equivalent to one-half of your receivables.

c. Your firm has a receivable in currency Y maturing in six months and an equivalent payable in currency X for payment about the same time. Currencies Y and X are positively correlated against the dollar.

d. Answer c if currencies X and Y are negatively correlated against each other.

e. Your firm has to meet a tax payment in country Z three months from now.

BIBLIOGRAPHY

ADLER, M. and B. DUMAS, "International Portfolio Choice and Corporation Finance: A Synthesis," *Journal of Finance* (June 1983), pp. 925–984.

ANTL, B. and A. G. HENRY, "The Case for a Coordinated Hedge," *Euromoney* (May 1980), pp. 109–119.

ANTL, B. and R. ENSOR, eds., *Management of Foreign Exchange Risk,* 2nd ed. London: Euromoney Publications, 1982.

AUBEY, R. T. and R. H. CRAMER, "Use of International Currency Cocktails in the Reduction of Exchange Rate Risk," *Journal of Economics and Business* (Winter 1977), pp. 128–134.

BABBELL, D. F., "Determining the Optimum Strategy for Hedging Currency Exposure," *Journal of International Business Studies* (Spring-Summer 1983), pp. 133–139.

BIGER, N., "Exchange Risk Implications of International Portfolio Diversification," *Journal of International Business Studies* (Fall 1979), pp. 64–74.

BOOTH, L. D., "Hedging and Foreign Exchange Exposure," *Management International Review,* no. 1 (1982), pp. 26–42.

BOOTHE, R. and J. MADURA, "Reducing Exposure to Exchange Rate Risk: A Case Study," *Long Range Planning* (June 1985), pp. 98–101.

CALDERON-ROSSEL, J. R., "Covering Foreign Exchange Risks of Single Transactions: A Framework for Analysis," *Financial Management* (Autumn 1979), pp. 78–85.

DONALDSON, J. A., *Corporate Currency Risk.* London: Financial Times Business Information, Ltd., 1980.

______, "Managing Currency Exposures After the End," *Banker* (August 1980), pp. 77–78.

EAKER, M. R., "Denomination Decision for Multinational Transactions," *Financial Management* (Autumn 1980), pp. 23–29.

EAKER, M.R. and D. GRANT, "Optimal Hedging of Uncertain and Long Term Foreign Exchange Exposure," *Journal of Banking and Finance* (June 1985), pp. 221–231.

EATON, J. and S.J. TURNOVSKY, "The Forward Exchange Market, Speculation, and Exchange Market Intervention," *Quarterly Journal of Economics* (Fall 1984), pp. 45–69.

EVERETT, R.M., A.M. GEORGE, and A. BLUMBERG, "Appraising Currency Strengths and Weaknesses: An Operational Model for Calculating Parity Exchange Rates," *Journal of International Business Studies* (Fall 1980), pp. 80–91.

FERCHAT, R., "Managing Foreign Exchange Risks," *CA Magazine* (January 1981), pp. 26–29.

FITZSIMONS, R.B., "Exposure Management Is Too Important to be Left to the Treasurer," *Euromoney* (March 1979), pp. 103–112.

FOLKS, W.R., JR., "Optimal Foreign Borrowing Strategies with Operations in the Forward Exchange Markets," *Journal of Financial and Quantitative Analysis* (June 1978), pp. 245–254.

GEORGE, A., "Cash Flow versus Accounting Exposures to Currency Risk," *California Management Review* (Summer 1978), pp. 50–54.

GIDDY, I.H., "Why It Doesn't Pay to Make a Habit of Forward Hedging," *Euromoney* (December 1976), pp. 96–100.

GILLETT, P., "Managing Foreign Exchange Exposure," *Accountancy* (May 1985), p. 67.

GRAY, S.J., "The Impact of International Accounting Differences from a Security-Analysis Perspective: Some European Evidence," *Journal of Accounting Research* (Spring 1980), pp. 64–76.

HAGEMANN, HELMUT, "Anticipate Your Long-Term Foreign Exchange Risks," *Harvard Business Review* (March/April 1977), pp. 81–88.

HAYES, P., "Exposure Management: A Look at How Foreign Exchange Transactions Affect Earnings for the Overseas Trader," *American Import/Export Management* (May 1982), p. 26.

HEYWOOD, J., *Foreign Exchange and the Corporate Treasurer.* London: A. & C. Black, Ltd., 1979.

HOLLIS, M., "A Decentralized Foreign Exchange Risk Model," *Management International Review,* Vol. 3 (1980), pp. 53–60.

HUME, J.G., "Remaining Calm in Troubled Markets: The Growth of Risk Hedging Vehicles," *Journal of Commercial Bank Lending* (December 1984), pp. 36–44.

JACQUE, L.L., "Management of Foreign Exchange Risk," *Journal of International Business Studies* (Spring/Summer 1981), pp. 81–101.

JILLING, M., *Foreign Exchange Management in U.S. Multinational Corporations.* Ann Arbor, Mich.: UMI Press, 1980.

JOHNSON, L. J. and C. H. WALTHER, "New Evidence of the Effectiveness of Portfolio Hedges in Currency Forward Markets," *Management International Review,* no. 2 (1984), pp. 15–23.

KOENIG, P., "Using a Captive to Cope with Currency Exposure," *Institutional Investor* (November 1981), pp. 191–194.

KOHLHAGEN, S. W., "A Model of Optimal Foreign Exchange Hedging Without Exchange Rate Projections," *Journal of International Business Studies* (Fall 1978), pp. 9–19.

LEVICH, R. M. and C. G. WIHLBORG, eds., *Exchange Risk and Exposure.* Lexington, Mass.: Lexington Books, 1980.

LOGUE, D. E. and G. S. OLDFIELD, "Managing Foreign Assets When Foreign Exchange Markets Are Efficient," *Financial Management* (Summer 1977), pp. 16–22.

MCRAE, T. W. and D. P. WALKER, *Foreign Exchange Management.* Englewood Cliffs, N.J.: Prentice-Hall, Inc., 1980.

MATHUR, I., "Managing Foreign Exchange Risk Profitability," *The Columbia Journal of World Business* (Winter 1982), pp. 23–30.

MATTLIN, EVERETT, "Playing the Currency Game," *Institutional Investor* (May 1976), pp. 83–96, 124.

MEIRJOHANN, F. W., "Multinational's Currency Management Philosophy," *Euromoney* (September 1981), pp. 29–30.

NAIDU, G. N. and T. S. SHIN, "Effectiveness of Currency Futures Market in Hedging Foreign Exchange Risk," *Management International Review,* no. 4 (1981), pp. 5–16.

PRINDLE, A. R., "Guidelines for MNC Money Managers," *Harvard Business Review* (January 1976), pp. 73–80.

PRUNTEL, J. R., "Can We Make Floating Exchange Rates Easier to Live With?" *Banker* (January 1985), pp. 15–18.

RODRIGUEZ, R. M., *Foreign Exchange Management in U.S. Multinationals.* Lexington, Mass.: Lexington Books, 1980.

______, "Corporate Exchange Risk Management: Theme and Aberrations," *Journal of Finance* (May 1981), pp. 427–439.

______, "The Increasing Attraction of the SDR to Business Corporations," *Euromoney* (December 1981), pp. 168–179.

SERFASS, W. D. JR., "You Can't Outguess the Foreign Exchange Market," *Harvard Business Review* (March/April 1976), pp. 134–137.

SOENEN, L. A., "The Optimal Currency Cocktail: A Tool for Strategic Foreign Exchange Management," *Management International Review,* no. 2 (1985), pp. 12–22.

———, and E. G. F. VAN WINKEL, "Real Cost of Hedging in the Forward Exchange Market," *Management International Review,* no. 1 (1982), pp. 53–59.

SRINIVASULU, S. L., "Strategic Response to Foreign Exchange Risks," *Columbia Journal of World Business* (Spring 1981), pp. 13–23.

———, "Classifying Foreign Exchange Exposure," *Financial Executive* (February 1983), pp. 36–44.

———, "Strategic Response to Foreign Exchange Rates," *The Columbia Journal of World Business* (Spring 1983), pp. 42–47.

STANLEY, M. T., "Portfolio Diversification of Foreign Exchange Risk: An Empirical Study," *Management International Review,* Vol. 1 (1980), pp. 83–92.

SUHAR, V. V., "The Export Hedger Needs to be Where the Central Management Is," *Euromoney* (June 1980), pp. 111–123.

TRAN, V. Q., *Foreign Exchange Management in Multinational Firms.* Ann Arbor, Mich.: UMI Press, 1980.

WALDNER, S. C., "How to Borrow in a Foreign Currency," *Euromoney* (June 1980), pp. 96–103.

WATERS, S. R., "Exposure Management Is a Job for All Departments," *Euromoney* (December 1979), pp. 79–82.

WIHLBORG, C., "Economics of Exposure Management of Foreign Subsidiaries of Multinational Corporations," *Journal of International Business Studies* (Winter 1980), pp. 9–18.

APPENDIX D

Limits on Leads, Lags and Netting in Selected Countries

COUNTRY	EXPORT LAG	EXPORT LEAD	IMPORT LAG	IMPORT LEAD	NETTING
Argentina	180 days	180 days/360 days	120 days	Permission required	Permission required
Australia	Allowed–no limit	Allowed–no limit	Allowed–no limit	Allowed–no limit	Allowed
Belgium	180 days	90 days	180 days	30 days	Depends on transaction
Brazil	Permission required	Allowed–no limit	180 days to 8 years	Not allowed	Not allowed
Canada	Allowed–no limit	Allowed–no limit	Allowed–no limit	Allowed–no limit	Allowed
Chile	90 days	90 days	120 days	Not allowed	Not allowed
Denmark	30 days	Allowed–no limit	Allowed–no limit	30 days	Allowed
France	180 days	Allowed–no limit	Allowed–no limit	Permission required	Allowed
Germany	Allowed–no limit	Allowed–no limit	Allowed–no limit	Allowed–no limit	Allowed
Greece	90 days	Allowed–no limit	Allowed–no limit	Permission required	Allowed
Hong Kong	Allowed–no limit	Allowed–no limit	Allowed–no limit	Allowed–no limit	Allowed
India	180 days	Allowed–no limit	180 days	Permission required	Permission required
Ireland	180 days	Allowed–no limit	Allowed–no limit	Not allowed	Permission required
Italy	360 days	5 years	5 years	120 days	Allowed
Japan	360 days	360 days	360 days	360 days	Depends on transaction
Korea	180 days	180 days	90 days	Not allowed	Allowed only in exceptional cases
Malaysia	180 days	Allowed–no limit	Allowed–no limit	Allowed–no limit	Allowed
Mexico	30 days	Allowed–no limit	Allowed–no limit	Allowed–no limit	Permission required
Netherlands	Allowed–no limit	Allowed–no limit	Allowed–no limit	Allowed–no limit	Allowed
Nigeria	90 days	Allowed–no limit	270 days	Permission required	Not allowed
Norway	Allowed–no limit	Allowed–no limit	Allowed–no limit	Allowed–no limit	Permission required
Philippines	60 days	Allowed–no limit	Variable	Permission required	Permission required

Source: Business International Corporation, *Business International Money Report,* November 9, 1984, pp. 358–359. Reprinted with permission from the Business International Corporation (New York). Data in the table is compiled by an annual survey conducted by Business International Corporation. Footnotes have been omitted.

APPENDIX D ***(continued)***

COUNTRY	EXPORT LAG	EXPORT LEAD	IMPORT LAG	IMPORT LEAD	NETTING
Singapore	Allowed–no limit	Allowed–no limit	Allowed–no limit	Allowed–no limit	Allowed
South Africa	180 days	Allowed–no limit	Allowed–no limit	Permission required	Permission required
Spain	180 days	Allowed–no limit	90 days	90 days	Permission required
Sweden	Allowed	Allowed	Allowed	Permission required	Permission required
Switzerland	Allowed–no limit	Allowed–no limit	Allowed–no limit	Allowed–no limit	Allowed
Taiwan	180 days	180 days	180 days	Not allowed	Permission required
Thailand	180 days	180 days	270 days	Permission required	Permission required
UK	Allowed–no limit	Allowed–no limit	Allowed–no limit	Allowed–no limit	Allowed
US	Allowed–no limit	Allowed–no limit	Allowed–no limit	Allowed–no limit	Allowed
Venezuela	Allowed–no limit	Allowed–no limit	Allowed–no limit	Allowed–no limit	Allowed

CASE STUDY

Foreign Exchange Risk Management Strategies Multinational Equipment and Accessories, Inc.

Thomas McGuigan, C.E.O. of Multinational Equipment and Accessories (ME&A) Inc., has been telling his senior staff for some time that the time has come for ME&A to formulate and centralize foreign exchange risk management strategies, in view of recent setbacks in subsidiary operations, and the increasing volatility and complexity of foreign exchange markets in recent years. He and Frank Boulard, Vice President of Financial Operations, have become increasingly apprehensive of the diverse and uncoordinated policies being followed at the local level. There has been inadequate reporting by the operating units and lack of centralized review of hedging strategies that are needed to minimize ME&A's exposure to currency fluctuations.

Background

ME&A was incorporated in 1957 in Omaha, Nebraska as Midwestern Equipment and Accessories Co. to manufacture farm equipment and implements primarily for the Midwestern markets. During the first ten years, the company had an erratic record of growth and profitability competing with giant farm implement firms, such as International Harvester, Massey Ferguson, and Deere & Co., which dominated the Midwestern, Southern, and Southwestern agricultural belt. In 1969, fueled by a major financing package of about $125 million in equity and convertible debenture issue underwritten by the First Chicago Corporation, a major investment banking firm in the Midwest, ME&A embarked on a major expansion and streamlining of its operations in both the Omaha and Phoenix, Arizona plants. The expansion and modernization program was designed to make the company more competitive in the farm machinery and implements market by streamlining its assembly lines and increasing the overall efficiency of operations. Farm equipment produced by the company included tractors, combines, and agricultural implements such as tillage tools, seeding machinery, harvesting machinery, and crop-handling equipment. Lawn and garden equipment as well as snowmobiles were also manufactured.

During the early 1970s ME&A had a sustained growth in its established regional market, and managed to negotiate several sizable export contracts, mainly to Brazil, Argentina, and Turkey. The export business was sparked by the intense competition in the home market, increased production capacity, and the appointment of Mr. Pablo Gonzales as Vice President of Marketing. Mr. Gonzales had a long experience with International Harvester (IH) in exports to Latin American markets and for a number of years managed IH's subsidiary in São Paulo, Brazil.

In early 1978, at the urging of Mr. Gonzales, ME&A acquired a plant in Manitoba, Canada from Massey Ferguson for $40 million in cash and notes. The acquisition was deemed to be extremely valuable for increasing the export capacity of the company, and was effected at highly favorable terms, as Massey Ferguson was undergoing a financial crisis at the time of the acquisition. Shortly thereafter, the company, availing itself of attractive tax and other concessions from the government of Brazil, decided to set up an assembly plant in Brazil, mainly to serve the Brazilian and neighboring markets. In June 1980, the company floated $50 million in subordinated debentures to finance the Brazilian project, and was then renamed Multinational Equipment and Accessories. The Brazilian subsidiary, Brazil Equipment and Accessories, started production in mid-1981.

Recent Sales and Operational Performance (1977–1982)

During the period 1978–1982, ME&A had a healthy though erratic growth rate in sales, particularly in export markets. Although the overall record could not be described as impressive, it was nevertheless encouraging. The period was characterized by several unfavorable international and domestic developments which adversely affected the performace of major farm implement firms, and drove at least one major producer to the verge of bankruptcy. These developments may be summarized as follows:

1. A recession in the United States and major industrial countries, which depressed the agricultural sector and adversely affected the demand for agricultural machinery.
2. Demand for capital goods, including agricultural implements, by third-world countries, particularly the Latin American and Middle Eastern markets, decreased sharply owing to new rounds of sharp increases in oil prices, increasing burden of third-world debt to major international banks, and the decline in LDCs' exports to the industrial countries.
3. Increasing volatility in the foreign exchange markets due to the rise in oil prices, the high inflation rate experienced by most industrial and developing countries, and increasing pressure on heavily indebted countries like Brazil, Argentina, Chile, Turkey, among others, to devalue their currencies.

Financial conditions and operating results for the period 1977–1982 are summarized in Exhibits 1 and 2. Sales in 1982 by country and by affiliate are shown in Exhibit 3.

The near-term prospects for sales appear to be moderately favorable due in part to the economic recovery which has been taking hold since

Exhibit 1. Multinational Equipment and Accessories, Inc. (Consolidated Balance Sheet 1977–1982) (millions of U.S. dollars)

ASSETS	1977	1978	1979	1980	1981	1982
Cash and bank deposits	23.5	17.8	42.4	58.9	43.4	34.5
Marketable securities	15.0	8.2	13.7	25.9	14.3	19.5
Accounts receivable	28.4	24.4	19.4	35.0	42.3	36.1
Prepaid items	5.2	14.9	7.3	8.2	17.9	17.8
Inventories (work in process and finished products)	80.0	82.9	65.8	85.4	89.2	95.0
Property, plant, and equipment (net of depreciation)	16.4	45.4	46.7	49.6	69.5	77.4
Total Assets	168.5	193.6	195.3	263.0	276.6	280.3
LIABILITIES AND NET WORTH						
Bank loans (Short-term)	15.0	15.0	16.5	15.0	20.0	25.0
Accounts payable	11.9	12.9	17.8	22.0	18.5	20.5
Notes payable	–	15.0	15.0	15.0	12.0	12.0
Accrued taxes	3.2	2.8	2.8	5.2	2.8	7.5
Other accrued items	10.5	11.5	9.8	12.3	14.6	12.9
Subordinated debentures	–	–	–	50.0	50.0	50.0
First mortgage bonds	20.0	18.0	16.0	14.0	12.0	10.0
Stockholders' equity	107.9	118.4	117.4	134.5	146.7	142.4
Total Liabilities and Net Worth	168.5	193.6	195.3	263.0	276.6	280.3

Exhibit 2. Multinational Equipment and Accessories Operating Highlights, Year ending December 31, 1977–1982 (millions of U.S. dollars)

OPERATING RESULTS	1977	1978	1979	1980	1981	1982	1983 (Projected)
Net sales	157.8	148.0	160.2	190.9	185.3	225.0	300.00
Profit before tax	9.3	15.5	(7.8)	23.3	17.0	(9.0)	25.0
Taxes	3.5	5.0	(6.8)	6.2	4.8	(4.7)	9.0
Profit after tax	5.8	10.5	(1.0)	17.1	12.2	(4.3)	16.0
SHAREHOLDER INFORMATION (IN DOLLARS)							
Earnings per share	$1.16	$2.10	$(0.20)	$3.42	$2.44	$(0.86)	$3.20
Dividends per share	0.40	0.50	0.50	0.50	0.50	0.50	0.60
Stock price range (L–H)	14–32	20–39	11–25	16–40	17–28	12–19	
Price earning ratio (L–H)	12–28	10–19	–	5–12	7–11	–	
SELECTED RATIOS							
Current ratio	3.7	2.6	2.4	3.1	3.1	3.6	
Long-term debt as percentage of total assets	.12	.09	.08	.24	.22	.21	
Sales/total assets (asset turnover)	.94	.76	.82	.73	.70	.80	
Net profit/stockholders' equity	.0534	.089	(.009)	.127	.083	(.030)	

Exhibit 3. Multinational Equipment and Accessories Summary of Sales in 1982 (millions of U.S. dollars)

	U.S. PARENT	CANADIAN SUBSIDIARY	BRAZILIAN SUBSIDIARY	TOTAL
Sales in home market	80.7	30.8	20.0	131.5
Exports to Latin American markets	11.5		21.0	32.5
Exports to Turkey and Middle Eastern markets	22.1			22.1
Exports to Australia and Far Eastern markets		18.5		18.5
Other exports	8.7	11.7		20.4
Total	123.0	61.0	41.0	$225.00
1983 Projection	150.0	80.0	70.0	300.00

mid-1983 in the United States and major industrial countries. Demand for farm products and income received by farmers have tended to rise recently. Moreover, LDCs' demand for farm machinery is projected to rise as their exports to industrial countries recover from recession levels. Projections for 1984 show that farm equipment sales are expected to improve significantly from the depressed level in recent years, reflecting increased farm income, greater planting activity, and the need for farmers to improve efficiency by upgrading machinery. Higher crop prices, the result of the Payment-in-Kind program and 1983's drought, are bolstering farmers' income and optimism. Profit margins on equipment sales should also improve, as price discounting to reduce high levels of inventories becomes less necessary under better market conditions.

While the domestic and international sales outlook appears to be relatively bright, there are still big question marks. The farm machinery industry is plagued by a substantial excess capacity, increasing the intensity of competitive behavior among major producers. This led over the past two years to frequent discount and price cutting practices. Moreover, earnings of farm equipment companies continue to be adversely affected by high interest rates, as well as by a strong dollar, which has hurt sales abroad.

The farm implement machinery market is dominated by few large firms: Deere and Co., the largest domestic manufacturer of farm equipment, International Harvester (a leading manufacturer of medium and heavy trucks, with such trucks accounting for about one-half of total sales, the other half accounted for by agricultural equipment), Massey Ferguson (based in Canada), and Caterpillar Tractor. Exhibit 4 contains comparable data on farm equipment companies, including Multinational Equipment and Accessories, for 1982.

Exhibit 4. The Farm Implements Industry Selected Comparative Data—1982

	DEERE & CO.	1 H[1]	MASSEY FERGUSON[2]	CATERPILLAR TRACTOR	ME&A
Sales ($ million)	3968	3601	2058	6469	225
Net income ($ million)	53	(1266)	(205)	(180)	(4.3)
Earning per share ($)	0.78	(20.44)	(8.95)	(2.04)	(0.86)
Dividend per share ($1)	2.00	0.30	–	2.40	0.50
Return on equity	2.2%	NM[3]	−86.6%	−4.9%	−3%
Long-term debt/total assets	.15	.54	.60	.32	.21
Share Price ($) High	37	26	$2\frac{3}{4}$	$55\frac{1}{4}$	19
Low	22	6	$1\frac{5}{8}$	$33\frac{1}{8}$	12
P/E Ratio High	47	NM	NM	NM	NM
Low	28	NM	NM	NM	NM
Percentage of total sales accounted for by foreign sales (outside U.S. & Canada)	23	29	75	57	50

[1]International Harvester has been operating under financial duress since 1980. Operations in 1982 were cut back to about one-half of the 1980 level. Lenders have recently approved to refinance $3.5 billion of the company's debt.

[2]Year ended October 31.

[3]Note meaningful.

Export Terms and Currency Exposure

Exports from the U.S. plants (with the exception of exports to Turkey) are against irrevocable letters of credit payable in U.S. dollars against a draft 90 days from acceptance of draft by importer's bank. Exports to Turkey (which account for about 50 percent of total exports to Middle Eastern countries) are invoiced in Turkish liras and are insured by the Foreign Credit Insurance Corporation.

Exports from the Canadian subsidiary are invoiced in Canadian dollars and are payable by a 90-day draft issued against an irrevocable letter of credit. Exports from the Brazilian subsidiary to the Latin American market are invoiced in U.S. dollars, with the exception of exports to Argentina (about the equivalent of $10 million in 1982), which are invoiced in Argentinian australs. All exports from the Brazilian subsidiary are against 180-day notes guaranteed by a bank in the country of the importer.

Sales of the Canadian and Brazilian subsidiaries in their respective home markets, as shown in Exhibit 3, represent an additional currency exposure for the company as a whole, since these sales are effected in domestic currencies.

Recent Exchange Markets' Behavior

Mr. McGuigan has been deeply concerned about the volatility of exchange rate movements in the recent past, and by the strong resurgence in the value of the U.S. dollar, particularly in late 1982 and early 1983. The strengthening of the U.S. dollar, he figured, would adversely affect the foreign operations of ME&A by: (1) making exports denominated in U.S. dollars more expensive in foreign markets and, therefore, less competitive, and (2) causing substantial translation and transaction losses in subsidiary operations, thus reducing net cash flows from these operations in terms of U.S. dollars.

The greatest concern of the management, particularly Mr. Gonzales, the Marketing Vice President, is the deteriorating economic and political situation in Brazil. Brazil's huge external debt ($86 billion at the end of 1982) and accelerating inflation rate led to a sharp depreciation in the exchange rate of the cruzado. Brazil interrupted scheduled payments on its external debt in the last quarter of 1982, and renegotiated, in early 1983, its external debt with a consortium of international banks. While it was hoped that the rescheduling agreement and the financial program recently negotiated with the International Monetary Fund would lead to some economic and financial stability, further turbulence in the exchange markets seems likely (Exhibit 5).

Brazilian inflation and balance of payments problems are also shared by Argentina, which also has a huge external debt ($39 billion at the end of 1982). Argentina's inflation rate in 1982 was over 150 percent, compared with about 100 percent for Brazil. Consequently, the austral depreciated even more sharply against the U.S. dollar than the Brazilian cruzado. The political and economic outlook for these two countries in the next two to three years points to continued instability, astronomical rates of inflation, and fast decline in currency values. Servicing of the massive external debt owed by these two countries will continue to pose a serious threat to their economic and financial stability.

Although the situation in Turkey is not alarming, its economy and finances also suffered a serious deterioration in recent years. Large budget deficits and fast rates of monetary expansion have resulted in high and rising inflation rates. These, together with external debt servicing difficulties, have led to a sharp depreciation of the Turkish lira. There is hope, however, that the measure of political stability which Turkey has achieved recently, together with the successful renegotiation of Turkey's external debt just recently completed, will result in some improvement in the economic and financial situation.

While Mr. McGuigan is not worried about ME&A operations in Canada, the continuing weakness of the Canadian dollar against the U.S. dollar has hurt the company's consolidated financial picture due to trans-

Exhibit 5. Exchange Rates of Argentinian Austral, Brazilian Cruzado, and Turkish Lira against U.S. Dollar (period averages)

Period	Argentinian australs per U.S. dollar	Canadian dollars per U.S. dollar	Brazilian cruzados per U.S. dollar	Turkish liras per U.S. dollar
1980				
1st Q	.168	1.1643	45.01	61.59
2nd Q	.180	1.1703	49.83	75.53
3rd Q	.190	1.1586	54.70	80.09
4th Q	.196	1.1893	61.33	86.93
1981				
1st Q	.220	1.1936	70.83	94.59
2nd Q	.376	1.1986	83.89	102.84
3rd Q	.513	1.2117	99.72	118.89
4th Q	.652	1.1918	118.08	128.56
1982				
1st Q	1.026	1.2089	137.87	142.25
2nd Q	1.367	1.2447	160.18	153.27
3rd Q	3.773	1.2499	189.65	171.86
4th Q	4.203	1.2314	230.36	182.84
1983				
Jan.	5.141	1.2284	263.20	188.89
Feb.	5.718	1.2273	315.54	194.78
March	6.399	1.2262	400.56	198.79
April	7.166	1.2322	435.26	207.13
May	7.772	1.2287	474.63	198.64
June	8.521	1.2322	517.78	221.55

International Monetary Fund, *International Financial Statistics* (several issues).
Figures taken from several issues of *International Financial Statistics,* International Monetary Fund.

lation and transaction losses encountered in converting Canadian to U.S. dollars. These exchange losses have been a major depressing factor to the company's share prices in the market.

Mr. McGuigan asked Mr. Gonzales and Mr. David Whitley, a foreign exchange specialist in the Financial Division, to prepare a report outlining the strategies which are appropriate for ME&A to manage its foreign exchange exposure. He planned to submit major policy recommendations in this area to the board of directors after consultations with the company's bankers, particularly the manager of Foreign Exchange Operations.

6

Multinational Working Capital Management

In this section the principles and policies relating to working capital management for the multinational firm will be examined. This chapter is devoted to the strategic differences between domestic and multinational working capital management, with special emphasis on intersubsidiary transfer of funds, as well as transfers from the affiliates to the parent company. This would entail a review of the obstacles—legal, administrative and others—which hinder the transfer process, and mechanisms available to the MNC to overcome or alleviate these obstacles. Chapter 7 covers receivables and inventory management, as well as export-import financing. Chapter 8 will examine positioning of funds and cash management strategies. International financial markets and international banking are discussed in Chapters 9, 10, and 11.

DOMESTIC VS. MULTINATIONAL WORKING CAPITAL MANAGEMENT

The fundamental decisions facing financial managers in a domestic or a multinational context are essentially the same. Stated briefly, they should maintain adequate working capital to insure smooth and trouble-free functioning of the firm, while avoiding unnecessary funds tied in cash balances, receivables, inventories, and marketable securities. Funds tied up in current assets are costly because of the foregone income that could have been earned if these funds were invested. Income-earning current assets, such as marketable securities, yield a rate of return substantially below the firm's cost of capital. The objective of the financial manager is, therefore, to *optimize,* rather than *minimize,* investment in each of the four categories of current assets: cash, marketable securities, receivables, and inventories. A corollary function is to minimize the cost of borrowed funds, and to maximize the rate of return on excess funds invested in the money market.

Multinational management of working capital, however, differs in five key respects from domestic management.

1. International financial managers have a wider choice of options available for meeting the MNC's or its affiliates' requirements for funds. For instance, an affiliate may be self-financing, or it may seek financing from the parent. Alternatively, it may obtain funds from local banks or other local sources. Eurocurrency markets provide another source of meeting the financial needs of the affiliates or the parent company. It should be noted, however, the Eurocurrency loans (or Eurocurrency deposits for investment) may be availed by domestic firms which are attracted to these markets by lower rates on loans and higher yield on invested funds than are available from the domestic markets.[1]
2. The financial manager of an MNC, while having wider options for formulating working capital policies, faces risks which are peculiar to multinational sourcing and investing of funds, namely the exchange rate risk and the political risk.
3. Financial managers of MNCs have more latitude than their counterpart in domestic firms in their ability to move funds about the different parts of the system so as to attain optimal utilization of the resources at their disposal. Cash mobilization, discussed in Chapter 8, has its limitations and costs, but it provides more flexibility in meeting the requirements of the deficit units from the excess resources of the surplus units, thus reducing the overall resort to external financing.
4. International financial managers have to make tougher decisions and face more obstacles than their counterparts in purely domestic firms. The units comprising an MNC are widely separated geographically, and the circumstances of the affiliates and the local financial markets are not readily familiar to them. Although developments in international communication facilities and electronic funds transfers, as well as the services of multinational banks, make their job easier, the decision-making process remains a complex one, and they have to contend with weighing the impact of a host of variables, tangible and intangible.
5. Insofar as their financing decisions involve tax considerations, international financial managers face not only different taxation systems, but differential tax rates. Some aspects of the impact of taxes on the financing decision will be examined later in this chapter. A complete review of the taxation-related strategies of

[1]Union Pacific Railroad, which is not classified as an MNC, raised a syndicated Eurodollar loan from a Kuwaiti financial institution in 1982.

MNCs, incorporating the latest changes in the IRS and major countries taxation codes for the multinational firms, are presented in Chapter 18.

Criteria for choosing among financing sources involve, as in domestic working capital management, essentially a trade-off among cost, risk, and return. The only difference is that for the international financing decision the risk factor is accentuated by the currency exposure and political risks. Tax considerations, as stated earlier, are further complicated by differential tax codes and taxation rates. For the MNC, therefore, working capital policy must take into account the following:

1. Cost in the form of interest rates prevailing in different markets, compensating requirements, and other hidden charges levied by financial institutions.
2. Currency exposure risk and the need to dovetail each financing decision with the company's overall exposure management policy.
3. Differential tax considerations, with a view to minimizing the overall tax burden of the company.
4. Need to maintain maximum flexibility to meet the future requirements of the parent company and its affiliates, subject to cost and risk constraints.
5. Firm's degree of aversion to political risk, and its overall political risk management policies.

INTRACORPORATE TRANSFER OF FUNDS

Intracorporate transfer of funds, particularly transfers from the affiliates to the parent and interaffiliate transfers, are subject to a number of constraints. The most important is the political constraint ranging from limitations on certain types of transfers, such as dividends, to outright blockage of funds and currency inconvertibility. These transfers are also constrained by differential tax rates on affiliate and parent company profits, as well as by taxation (or tax withholding policies) of transferred dividends. The third constraint on mobility of funds among the units of the MNC is in the form of transaction costs involved in fund transfers and in converting funds from one currency to another.

Transfer of funds from affiliates to parent companies and from one affiliate to another takes many forms. These comprise royalties, fees, payment for inputs and components, interest on loans, repayment of principal of loans, dividends, and repatriation of the original or subsequent investments. A number of these transfers require some elaboration.

A *royalty* is a payment in return for the use of patents, technology, or a trade name. Royalties thus represent a payment, usually by an affiliate to the parent, for the right to use the company's name or special processes, usually under a licensing arrangement. Licensing arrangements ought to state clearly and specifically the rights of the licensee to manufacture and sell the product or service, the markets where these may be sold, and the obligations of the licensee (the affiliate in this case) to reimburse the parent company. Royalties are in most instances stated as a specified *amount* per unit sold, or as a specified *percentage* of the sale price. This will not only establish clearly the rights and obligations of the parties and prevent incursion on markets not covered by the agreement, but also facilitate the eventual transfer of funds. Host countries are less likely to impede or restrict funds transferred in payment for royalties under a clear and articulated licensing agreement than under an ambiguous one.

Fees are compensation for professional services and expertise, usually rendered by the parent to the affiliates. While the amounts of such payments are less specific and are open to more dispute (between an affiliate and the government of the host country) than royalties, the scale of these fees and the obligations of the affiliate to compensate the parent need to be spelled out in a specific agreement at the outset. Host countries have habitually objected to what they consider inflated renumeration for the services of visiting executives or maintenance personnel from the parent company. This problem has always been exacerbated by the significantly higher scale of compensation used by U.S. MNCs compared to other countries. However, the host country is less likely to object to transfers requested by the affiliate if the scale of fees has been established in a written agreement between the parent and the affiliate at the outset.

Servicing loans advanced by the parent does not normally present serious transfer problems to the affiliate, unless the host country happens to be experiencing foreign exchange difficulties. In countries where strict foreign exchange controls are in place or likely to be imposed, "fronting"[2] loans through an international banking institution would result in smoother debt servicing by affiliates, since the host country is less likely to take action that would damage its international credit standing.

Remittance of dividends to the parent company is subject to restrictions and limitations in most LDCs. Most host countries require a minimum retention of profits generated by foreign enterprises with a view to furthering the process of economic development. Transfer of all or most of locally generated earnings is viewed by host governments as a policy which is inimical to the goal of economic development. In general, dividend transfer policies established at the outset and consistently followed are likely to encounter less difficulties than variable payout ratios, that is, ratios of "gross dividends" to "earnings."

[2]"Fronted" loans are loans made to the affiliate by a banking institution (usually a well-known multinational bank) backed by a deposit of an equivalent amount made by the parent with the same bank. See Exhibit 3.

"Unbundling" of Transfers

"Unbundling"[3] is the policy followed by most MNCs of breaking up total intracorporate transfer of funds into separate flows, corresponding to the nature of payment. Viewed from the standpoint of transfers from an affiliate to the parent, *royalties* represent payment for technological know-how and patents, *fees*[4] are compensation for professional services, *prices* represent reimbursement for inputs and components shipped to the affiliate, *interest* and *repayment* of *principal* represent debt servicing obligations, and *dividends* designate the part of earnings that the parent receives from the affiliate.

Unbundling provides the MNC with a fair and flexible mechanism to recover funds from its affiliates without incurring the risk of host country limitations on dividend remittances. In addition, unbundling reduces the overall tax liability, since certain transfers such as royalties, fees, and interest are tax deductible in the host country. This is particularly true if affiliates' earnings are subject to different tax rates, in that it permits the matching of forms of transfers with the tax position of each affiliate. A related advantage of unbundling is that it permits the effective use of the "transfer pricing" mechanism explained in the next section.

TRANSFER PRICING

Pricing of intracorporate exchange of goods and services provides the MNC with an effective tool of achieving its overall corporate objectives of maximization of profits and/or the value of the company as a whole. Yet it is the most sensitive and probably the most misunderstood area in multinational financial management. Transfer pricing enables the MNC to influence the amounts and direction of intracorporate transfers to achieve a number of important yet conflicting corporate objectives. While it represents a potent weapon in the hands of the management of the parent company, the effective utilization of this tool in furthering its objectives has been increasingly circumscribed by legal and administrative constraints both in the parent and host countries.

Transfer pricing is used by MNCs to accomplish one or more of the following objectives:

1. Minimizing the total tax paid by the company as a whole.
2. Positioning of funds in locations that will suit the management's working capital policies.

[3]The term is also used when MNCs sell technology under licensing arrangements or management service under management contracts, as contrasted with the outright establishment of an operating affiliate or a subsidiary.

[4]*Licensing fees* and *royalties* are sometimes used interchangeably to denote payment for technology, patents, or trade names.

3. Reducing exchange risk exposure and circumventing exchange controls.
4. Reducing tariffs and overcoming quantitative and administrative restrictions on imports.
5. Maximizing the transfers from affiliates to the parent.
6. "Window dressing" operations designed to improve an affiliate credit status with a view to influencing financial institutions and suppliers.

Large MNCs have often used reinvoicing centers located at tax havens to coordinate transfer pricing policy. These centers take title to goods and services sold by the parent to its affiliates, or by one affiliate to other affiliates, and invoice receiving affiliates at prices set administratively to accomplish one or more of the corporate objectives listed above. Setting up an invoicing center in no way changes the physical flow of goods and services from the producing units to the receiving units, and invoices issued by the center often do not reflect the true cost of production of the items exchanged. The basic purpose of this arrangement is obviously to funnel the profits arising from these transactions to lower tax affiliates, and away from the higher-taxed parent or affiliate. Another related purpose is to position funds in countries which have strong or stable currencies and/or no exchange controls, and away from countries which have soft currencies and/or foreign exchange restrictions.

Reinvoicing centers, which were popular with U.S. MNCs prior to 1962, were discouraged by the passage of U.S. Revenue Act of 1962, which declared profits realized by these centers as part of the total taxable income of the U.S.-based MNC. A 1977 ruling by the IRS, however, revived the use of such centers by allowing allocation to a firm's foreign affiliates parent expenses that previously could be written off only in the United States. Thus, the ruling allowed the generation of additional foreign tax credits that can only be utilized against U.S. taxes owed on foreign source income, thus enhancing the value of tax havens and reinvoicing centers.

CASE STUDY

Transfer Pricing of Westmore Electric, Inc.

The use of transfer pricing in conjunction with an invoicing center is illustrated in Exhibit 6-1. Westmore Electric, Inc., a U.S.-based manufacturer of household appliances, operates from plants located in the U.S. and in countries A, B, and C, and uses a reinvoicing center located in an

Exhibit 6-1. Westmore Electric, Inc. Direction of Financial and Real Flows Illustrating a Transfer Pricing System with a Reinvoicing Center

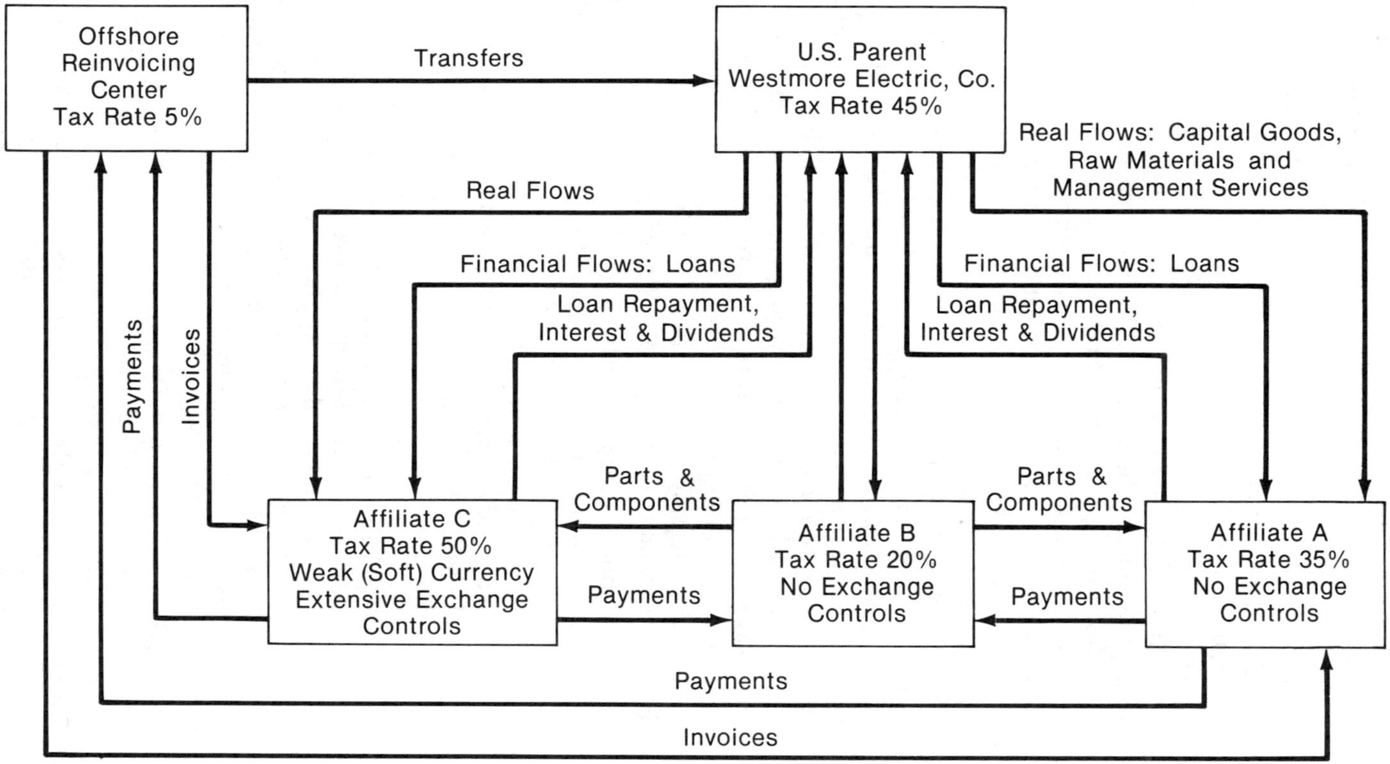

offshore tax haven. This illustration is designed to dramatize the impact of substantial differences in tax rates (45 percent at home, 5 percent in the offshore invoicing center, 35 percent in country A, 20 percent in country B, and 50 percent in country C), as well as currency exposure risk (mainly in country C, whose currency is expected to depreciate and where elaborate exchange controls are in effect) on the pricing of goods and services exchanged among the units of Westmore Electric, Inc.

Exhibit 6-1 shows the full range of goods and services exchanged among the units of the company. The parent company provides real flows in the form of capital goods, raw materials, technology, and management services to affiliates A and C, as well as financial flows (loans) to affiliates A, B, and C. Affiliate B sells inputs and components to affiliates A and C. While real flows move directly from the parent to affiliates A and C, the receiving units are billed by the reinvoicing center in accordance with the pricing strategy determined by the parent. Settlement of invoices is effected by payments to the invoicing center, which are then transferred to the parent as requested. Since no real transfers are made to affiliate B, no invoices are forwarded to it from the center. Inputs and components shipped from B to the other two affiliates are billed directly to them by B rather than through the reinvoicing center. All three affiliates make financial transfers periodically to the parent in the form of loan repayment, interest, and dividends.

The arrangements shown in Exhibit 6-1 allow Westmore Electric considerable flexibility in using transfer pricing to:

1. Siphon off profits away from affiliates A and C, which have high corporate income tax rate, to affiliate B and the reinvoicing center, which have low tax rates.
2. Minimize the amount of funds held by affiliate C as that country maintains extensive exchange controls and may conceivably block future transfers. Moreover, the currency risk is relatively high, since currency C is expected to depreciate. If the exchange risk is deemed unacceptably high, the reinvoicing center may invoice affiliate C in other than its local currency.
3. Affiliate B, which manufactures parts for electric appliances for local assembly, also supplies the other two affiliates with these parts, thus providing additional flexibility to insure smooth operations. Due to its low tax rate (20 percent) and the absence of exchange controls, its transactions are not handled by the reinvoicing center.

Exhibit 6-2 illustrates the principles of transfer pricing and its impact on total taxes paid and net profits realized by Westmore Electric, Inc. The illustration assumes that all invoicing and transfers are made in U.S. dollars; thus it abstracts from the exchange exposure risk to concentrate on transfer pricing. It also assumes that all net profits realized by the operating affiliates and the reinvoicing center are transferred to the parent company in the

Exhibit 6-2. Westmore Electric, Inc. Impact on Taxes and Profits of Transfer Pricing (U.S. dollars)

ALTERNATIVE 1—NO REINVOICING CENTER

Uniform 30% Markup	Cost of Inputs	Assembly and Other Expenses	Sale Proceeds	Taxable Income	Taxes	Amount Transferred to Parent
300 units shipped to A at $130	39,000	6,000	60,000	15,000	5,250	48,750
300 units shipped to C at $130	39,000	8,000	75,000	28,000	14,000	47,400
				Total transferred to parent		$96,150

ALTERNATIVE 2—NO REINVOICING CENTER

Different Markups	Cost of Inputs	Assembly and Other Expenses	Sale Proceeds	Taxable Income	Taxes	Amount Transferred to Parent
300 units shipped to A at $120 (low markup)	36,000	6,000	60,000	18,000	6,300	47,700
300 units shipped to C at $140 (high markup)	42,000	8,000	75,000	25,000	12,500	49,500
				Total transferred to parent		$97,200

ALTERNATIVE 3—A & C BILLED BY

Reinvoicing Center	Cost of Inputs	Assembly and Other Expenses	Sale Proceeds	Taxable Income	Taxes	Amount Transferred to Parent
300 units shipped to A invoiced at $150	45,000	6,000	60,000	9,000	3,150	50,850
300 units shipped to C invoiced at $180	54,000	8,000	75,000	13,000	6,500	57,900
			Total transferred to reinvoicing center			$108,750
			Less operating and overhead costs of center			5,000
				Taxable income		$103,750
				Taxes at 5%		5,188
				Amount transferred to parent		$ 98,562

Exhibit 6-2. *(continued)*

SUMMARY OF NET PROFIT REALIZED BY WESTMORE ELECTRIC, INC. (U.S. dollars)

	Proceeds of Shipment of parts	Cost of Shipment	Overhead Expenses	Profit Before Tax	Dividends Received	Taxable Income	Taxes Due
Alternative 1	78,000	60,000	10,000	8,000	18,150	26,150	11,768
Alternative 2	78,000	60,000	10,000	8,000	19,200	27,250	12,263
Alternative 3	98,562	60,000	10,000	28,562		28,562	12,853

The following summary demonstrates the impact of transfer pricing on funds received by Westmore Electric, Inc. under the three alternatives, as well as overall taxes paid by the company and its affiliates.

(U.S. dollars)

	Total Funds Transferred to Parent	Taxes Paid by Parent*	Funds Received by Parent net of taxes	Total Taxes Paid by Co. as a Whole	Funds Retained by Affiliate C
Alternative 1	96,150	(—)	96,150	19,250	5,600
Alternative 2	97,200	(—)	97,200	18,800	5,000
Alternative 3	98,562	(—)	98,562	18,041	2,600

*Taxes due, less credit for taxes paid by affiliates. Taxes paid by affiliates are creditable up to the amount of the U.S. tax liability on foreign source income (no refunds).

form of dividends, except that country C restricts dividend transfers to 60 percent of net profit. Operating affiliates, in addition, transfer the invoiced value of the parts received to the parent (in alternatives 1 and 2), or to the reinvoicing center (alternative 3). To simplify the illustration, it is further assumed that no taxes are withheld by countries A and C and the offshore locality on profits transferred to the parent company.

Other assumptions in Exhibit 6-2

- Parent ships 300 units monthly to each of affiliate A and C.
- Parent's cost is $100 per unit delivered to affiliates.
- Affiliates pay no tariff on imported parts.
- Affiliate A sells the finished product at $200 per unit.
- Affiliate C sells the finished product at $250 per unit.

Applicable tax rates

- Affiliate A, 35 percent
- Affiliate C, 50 percent
- Offshore reinvoicing center, 5 percent
- Parent, 45 percent

Exchange controls and restrictions on transfers

- Country A None
- Country B None
- Country C Extensive exchange control system. Only 60 percent of profit may be remitted to parent company.
- Offshore (location of reinvoicing center) None

Westmore Electric achieved the best outcome in alternative 3, which resulted in maximum funds received from affiliates net of taxes paid by the parent, minimum taxes paid by the company as a whole, and minimum amount retained by affiliate C, which is subject to high currency risk exposure and likelihood of future blocking of transfer. Two observations should, however, be made:

1. Alternative 2 enabled Westmore Electric, Inc. to achieve a better outcome, without employing a reinvoicing center, by adopting a low markup for the affiliate with the lower tax rate (A) and a high markup for the affiliate with the higher tax rate (C).
2. Westmore Electric could have achieved even better results by using directly the differential markup used by the reinvoicing center. It would have saved the operating expenses, as well as the modest tax paid by the offshore center. However, it would have been difficult to justify the markup policies under the criteria usually established by the tax authorities. Reinvoicing centers are

valuable to MNCs' transfer pricing strategies, primarily because they seem to disguise profitability and to avoid the scrutiny of governments.

The conflicting nature of objectives sought by transfer pricing strategies may also be illustrated by the Westmore Electric case. It is likely that country C, which apparently suffers from scarcity of foreign exchange resources, maintains both a high tariff and an import quota system, or other quantitative restriction on imports. If it is the parent company's objective to reduce the amount of custom duties paid by affiliate C (assuming ad valorem rather than specific duties), a low markup policy, producing lower invoiced prices, would have been appropriate. Similarly, to get around import quotas established in value terms, and to insure that the affiliate's operations will not be jeopardized by lack of component parts, lower invoice prices would have been the answer. This transfer pricing strategy, however, would have clashed with the objective of siphoning off funds from affiliate C, which has both a high tax rate and a high currency exposure risk.

Another corporate objective which can be influenced by the transfer pricing mechanism is the desire of some MNCs to improve the credit standing of an affiliate to impress lenders and/or suppliers. If this were the goal of Westmore Electric with respect to affiliate A, for instance, transfer pricing should have been used to strengthen the financial position and to enhance, genuinely or by mere window dressing transactions, the profitability of the affiliate. Again, this goal would have been in conflict with the overall objective pursued by the company of diverting profits from the operating affiliates to the offshore reinvoicing center located in a tax haven.

CONSTRAINTS ON TRANSFER PRICING

In practice, the latitude of MNCs in achieving corporate objectives through the transfer pricing mechanism is constrained by: (1) tax regulations in the parent and host countries, (2) the desire of MNCs to maintain smooth working relationships with the authorities in the host countries, and (3) the need to consider the interests and goals of local joint venture partners.

MNCs' use of transfer pricing to reduce overall corporate income tax is constrained by tax provisions in the United States and in most industrial countries. Typical of these provisions is section 482 of the U.S. Internal Revenue Code, which gives the I.R.S. the right to reallocate gross income, deductions, credit, or allowances among the parent company and its affiliates so as to prevent tax evasion. Guidelines issued under these provisions attempt to establish an objective basis for ascertaining a "correct price" for intracompany transactions. This price is based on the price used in the sale of the same goods to outside customers in an "arm's length" transaction.

United States tax authorities have established three methods for determining arm's length prices for intracompany transactions: comparable uncontrolled price, resale price, and cost-plus. The first, the most straightforward and most objective, is the price used in a similar transaction between two unrelated firms. If this price cannot be identified, or is rejected as inapplicable, the sale price charged by the distribution affiliate less an appropriate profit margin is deemed as the arm's length price. The cost-plus price, to be used when the first two methods are rejected, is based on the cost incurred by the manufacturing affiliate plus an appropriate markup based generally on the industry's average margin.

The arm's length test often encounters problems in precisely identifying comparable uncontrolled prices (or resale and cost-plus prices), particularly for specific transfers of technology or administrative services for which there are no market counterparts. Furthermore, what happens to be acceptable to one country's tax authorities may not be acceptable to the tax officials of the other country in which the transaction originated. Many countries consider the scale of fees charged for engineering or managerial services charged by U.S. MNCs to their affiliates to be exorbitant. These problems have brought out the need to establish international standards that go beyond the ambiguous arm's length concept. Tax treaties between major industrial nations (see Chapter 18) attempt, among other objectives, to provide objective remedies to the problems raised by transfer pricing and resolution of conflicts that may arise among tax authorities of different nations in monitoring MNCs practices.

Other Constraints

Apart from tax authorities in host countries, transfer pricing practices by MNCs are carefully monitored by exchange control departments, which approve transfers in most developing countries. As foreign exchange resources are scarce in many LDCs, transfers by MNCs are subject to scrutiny so as to thwart attempts by the latter to circumvent restrictions on capital outflows.

Another important limitation on the use of transfer pricing is the presence of joint-venture partners in the host country. Joint-venture arrangements are mandatory in a number of developing countries, where a 50 percent limitation is imposed on foreign ownership. Where such arrangements exist, economic and development policies are oriented toward controlling abuse of transfer pricing practices. MNCs' affiliates in these countries are usually subject to close scrutiny to insure the interests of local partners, as well as to promote national economic interest. In this environment transfer pricing practices are severely constrained, although developing countries have generally been flexible with respect to the transfer of funds in the form of royalties and fees for managerial and technical skills.

Transfer Pricing in Practice

Empirical data on use of the transfer pricing mechanism by MNCs are relatively scarce. This scarcity is understandable, as MNCs generally refrain from publicizing their intracorporate pricing strategies to avoid the scrutiny of tax authorities and to maintain smooth working relationships with governments in host countries. In view of the sensitive nature of the transfer pricing decision, it is very difficult to attach much credence to surveys conducted to ascertain the relative importance of the several variables influencing the decision.

A number of surveys conducted in the early nineteen seventies attempted to probe the major factors affecting international transfer pricing decisions by U.S. multinational firms operating mostly in advanced industrial countries. These surveys singled out the income tax liability as the major factor behind international transfer pricing decisions.[5]

A more recent survey was conducted by Kim and Miller among U.S. firms having at least one subsidiary in two of eight specified developing countries: Korea, Malaysia, Philippines, Taiwan, Brazil, Colombia, Mexico, and Peru.[6] The overall response rate to the questionnaire (15 percent) indicates that the majority of firms declined to reveal what they considered sensitive or confidential information. The major findings of this survey are[7]

1. The three most important factors influencing the transfer pricing decision are profit repatriation restrictions within the host country, exchange controls within the host country, and joint-venture constraints within the host country. Income tax liability within the host and parent countries, which was the dominating factor in earlier surveys, were ranked fifth and sixth (among nine factors), respectively.
2. International transfer pricing policies are shaped by long-term considerations relating to the firm's profitability objectives, rather than short-term factors, such as taxes and tariffs.

MANAGING BLOCKED FUNDS

Blockage of funds by actions of host country authorities is a common phenomenon in many LDCs which normally face chronic or temporary external payments disequilibria. Blockage ranges from restrictions on some types of transfers, typically depreciation allowances and dividends, to the

[5]See Richard D. Robinson, *International Business Management: A Guide to Decision Making*, 2nd ed. (New York: Holt, Rinehart and Winston, 1978), p. 498; and *Setting Intercorporate Pricing Policies* (New York: Business International Corporations, 1973), pp. 5–9.

[6]Seung H. Kim and Stephen W. Miller, "Constituents of the International Transfer Pricing Decision," in *International Finance: Concepts and Issues*, edited by Gerald D. Gay and Robert W. Kolbe (R. F. Dame, Inc. Finance Series, Richmond, VA, 1983), pp. 620–631.

[7]See also the author's findings in a survey of MNCs' cash and exchange exposure management policies in Appendix E, Chapter 8.

extreme case of outright prohibition of all transfers to the parent. While the underlying motivation behind most restrictions is the shortage of foreign exchange, many LDCs justify them on grounds of furthering the goal of economic development in requiring that a minimum proportion of generated funds be reinvested locally. Expropriation or nationalization have often been justified on the grounds of national sovereignty and the necessity for a country to control areas of critical or strategic economic activity.

MNCs strategies to deal with transfer blockage may be discussed under three headings: (1) defensive strategy against blockage or restrictions anticipated at the outset (before undertaking the foreign project), (2) measures to deal with recurrent partial blockage of funds, and (3) strategies to handle total and prolonged blockage of funds.

Defensive Strategy for Anticipated Blockage

Problems with respect to future transfer of funds from a foreign affiliate yet to be established may be anticipated in the light of economic and political climate in the host country. In these cases, the parent firm should pursue a defensive strategy to minimize the impact of future blockages by building a number of safeguards into the proposed foreign investment. These safeguards consist of such features as relying heavily on local financing for the foreign project (both for part of the initial fixed investment and for financing working capital requirements), taking in local partners from the private sector, or organizing the project as a joint venture with an organization representing the host government. Other measures discussed earlier consist of unbundling services at the outset to insure that particular transfers (such as royalties or fees) are not lumped together with other transfers which are most likely to be restricted.

While the measures suggested above do not afford complete protection against blockage of funds, they tend to lessen its financial impact on the parent firm. Certain aspects, such as the joint-venture arrangement as well as heavy indebtedness to local financial institutions, would act as a deterrent to possible drastic measures by the local authorities. These authorities are less likely to take measures that will inflict harm on local investors or threaten the integrity of local financial institutions. Unbundling spelled out in a specific and clear licensing agreement for the affiliate, which includes the rate of compensation for technical and managerial services provided by the head office, will avoid possible disagreements on the nature of transfers in the long run, and thus minimize the impact of restrictive policies.

Measures to Cope with Partial and Temporary Blockage of Funds

When an MNC faces a situation of recurrent but temporary restrictions on transfers (which were totally or largely unanticipated at the time of the foreign investment decision), it has access to several devices or mechanisms to deal with this situation. The most obvious, and perhaps the most controversial, is to use transfer pricing mechanism to siphon off funds from that affiliate. Potent as this mechanism is, it has its limitations, which were discussed earlier in this chapter. Of particular importance are government interface problems and the risk of worsening what may be already a strained relationship with the host country.

Another possible remedy for this situation is the use of interaffiliate leading and lagging to accelerate transfers out of the problem affiliate, and to delay the payments due that affiliate from other units. This mechanism, however, is a one-shot affair and may run into the host country's limitations on such practices. Indeed, in a country with extensive foreign exchange controls, leading and lagging are either totally prohibited or severely constrained.[8] A related strategy is to effect working capital adjustments for the affiliate in question, while avoiding further infusion of funds from the parent. If it proves impossible to obtain local financing of working capital needs, the parent should "front" its loans to the subsidiary, that is, channel the loan through an international financial institution, which acts as an intermediary, as shown in Exhibit 6-3.

"Fronting" loans in the manner described has a number of advantages over direct loans to the affiliate. The host country's authorities are less likely to permit default of an obligation to an international bank, thus damaging its credit standing in the world financial markets, than to allow a situation of default to parent's loans. Moreover, the cost of granting a loan channeled through an international bank may be lower than the cost of a direct loan, due to the interest earned on the time deposit placed with the bank. Better still, if the deposit in the intermediary bank has been placed by a finance affiliate of the parent located in a tax haven country, the arrangement would generate tax savings for the parent. This is because interest payments on the loan by the affiliate are tax deductible, while interest receipts on

Exhibit 6-3. "Fronting" a Loan to an Affiliate through an International Financial Institution

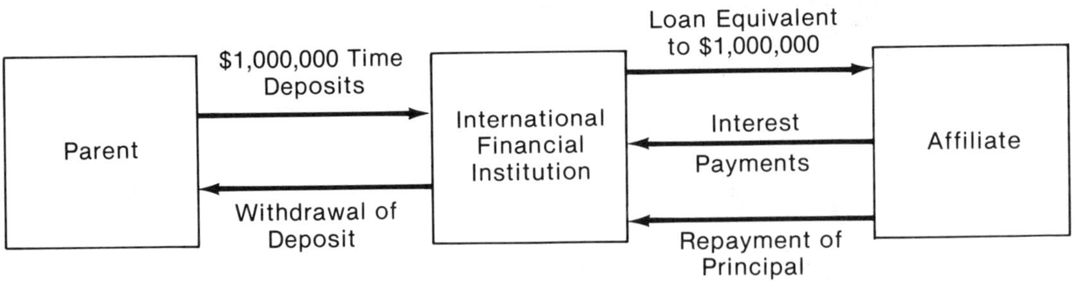

[8]For a list of the current limitations on payments leading and lagging in a number of countries, see pages 140–141.

the deposit placed by the finance affiliate with the intermediary bank are tax free.

Use may also be made of parallel loans to a local affiliate of another firm, if such one can be located, with the interest payable in foreign currency. Such an opportunity, however, is unlikely, since the same circumstances confront all MNCs operating in the problem country.

For the duration of the restriction on transfers, excess funds, if any, at the disposal of the affiliate should be placed in local short-term investments. If such investments are unavailable to utlilize excess cash until the restrictions are eased, use may be made of some of the devices described in the following section.

Strategy to Deal with Permanent or Prolonged Blockage

Situations in which an MNC finds itself confronting a permanent or prolonged blockage of funds calls for long-term, and perhaps more imaginative, strategies. MNCs with long experience in operating in problem countries have developed over the years a number of measures designed to overcome host countries' prohibition of transfers and to reduce the opportunity cost of blocked funds. These measures have in common the setting up of long-term arrangements often requiring fixed investment and/or reordering of the parent's firm policies and strategies. Some of the most widely used practices are

1. Using the production facilities of the affiliate, or altering such facilities with additional investment from the blocked funds, to generate exports which are often not directly related to the original activities of the affiliate. These exports benefit the host country (let us say India) by generating scarce foreign exchange which is not otherwise forthcoming. Consequently, a deal may be struck with the authorities to transfer profits realized on these operations. These exports may be invoiced in Indian rupees and sold to other affiliates of the MNC. These other affiliates can pay for them by buying rupees (often at a substantial discount from the official rate) from unofficial markets, thereby realizing handsome profits of reexporting goods imported from India. The host country is not likely to object to these practices, because buying rupees in the unofficial market will narrow the spread between the rate in such markets and the official exchange rate for the rupee.
2. Alternatively, export items created by the subsidiary may be bartered for goods which the host country needs, so it is, therefore, willing to part with foreign exchange to obtain them. Barter arrangements, as difficult as they are to negotiate and conclude, have reemerged in the early 1980s after declining in importance in the previous two decades. In 1983, for instance, Japanese firms involved in the construction of industrial projects in Iraq accepted

Iraqi products, primarily oil, in lieu of the transfers which had been delayed on account of foreign exchange problems Iraq was experiencing.

3. The MNC can use all or part of the blocked funds locally by switching part of its worldwide supporting functions to the country with blocked funds, or by using the services of that country. The MNC in this example may locate certain corporate functions, such as research and development, in India. It may also hold its conferences in New Delhi instead of other cities and may use India's national airline for the travel of its staff wherever possible.
4. If the previous measures are impracticable, or insufficient to utilize all blocked funds, the MNC's last resort is to undertake fixed investments in the host country which are essentially unrelated to its main activities.This course of action is especially advisable if viable local money market and other securities are unavailable or are highly risky. A company assembling cars and other vehicles in India may purchase local businesses selling at depressed prices, or a hotel accommodating the tourist business, or even real estate if such an investment looks attractive in local terms. While these investments do not alleviate the blockage problem, they reduce the potential opportunity cost of such blockage, pending negotiations with the host government, or eventual relaxation of exchange controls.

REVIEW QUESTIONS

1. Some managers believe that multinational working capital management is just an extension of domestic management policies. Do you agree? Should an MNC develop a set of working capital policies for its international operations that is different from its guidelines for domestic operations?
2. If multinational working capital management calls for new policy guidelines, which variables or factors should the manager consider in formulating these guidelines?
3. Why are multinational financial managers keen on *unbundling* payments made by affiliates to the parent company? Is unbundling a panacea for all transfer restrictions and blockage problems?
4. If you are negotiating an agreement with the government of a developing country regulating the operations of the affiliate that you are about to set up in that country, what particular provisions would you like to include in that agreement? Would you insist that the same type of agreement should apply to your affiliates in other countries?
5. Why is the transfer of dividends from affiliates to parent companies the most restricted type of transfers by host governments? Should a

financial manager of an MNC endeavor to conceal such transfers by negotiating artificially inflated royalty or service payments?

6. "Transfer pricing is a potent and flexible tool which managements of MNCs can use freely to circumvent transfer restrictions imposed by host governments." Comment on this statement, highlighting particularly the mechanisms used by such governments (as well as the parent country's government) to blunt the effectiveness of this tool.
7. Transfer pricing, in the opinion of some managers, is not as effective a tool as it may seem in managing intracorporate transfers. What are the reasons behind this position? How do you reconcile it with the reluctance of most MNCs to reveal the full extent of transfer pricing operations?
8. How effective is the "arm's length" test adopted by U.S. tax authorities (Section 482 of the U.S. Internal Revenue Code) in controlling illegal practices by U.S. MNCs? Are these guidelines adequate to control tax avoidance or evasion practices by large MNCs with worldwide operations? Should the same guidelines be extended to cover domestic intersubsidiary transactions of large corporations?
9. Outline a strategy to deal with the problem of an imminent blockage of transfers by the host government in a country where your affiliate is operating. Would your strategy be different if the expected blockage is deemed to be of a temporary nature? Explain.
10. Is the technique of "fronting loans" effective in discouraging governments of developing countries from blocking loan service payments by affiliates located within their boundaries? (Consider in your answer high-debt LDCs experiencing problems in servicing their obligations to international banks.)

BIBLIOGRAPHY

ARPAN, J. S., *International Intracorporate Pricing.* New York: Praeger, 1972.

______, "International Intracorporate Pricing: Non-American Systems and Views," *Journal of International Business Studies* (Spring 1972), pp. 1–8.

BARRETT, M. E., "Case of the Tangled Transfer Price," *Harvard Business Review* (May-June 1977), pp. 20–36, 176–178.

BENKE, R. L., "Applying an Opportunity Cost General Rule for Transfer Pricing," *Management Accounting* (June 1982), pp. 43–51.

BENKE, R. L. and J. D. EDWARDS, "Transfer Pricing: Techniques and Uses," *Management Accounting* (June 1980), pp. 44–46.

BURNS, J. O., "How IRS Applies the Intercompany Pricing Rules of Section 482: A Corporate Survey," *Journal of Taxation* (May 1980), pp. 308–314.

———, "Transfer Pricing Decisions in U.S. Multinational Corporations," *Journal of International Business Studies* (Fall 1980), pp. 23–29.

BURNS, J. O., and R. S. ROSS, "Establishing International Transfer Pricing Standards for Tax Audits of Multinational Enterprises," *The International Journal of Accounting* (Fall 1981), pp. 161–179.

COBURN, D. L., "Dilemmas in MNC Transfer Pricing," *Management Accounting* (November 1981), pp. 53–58.

CONTRACTOR, F. J., "The 'Profitability' of Technology Licensing by U.S. Multinationals—A Framework for Analysis and an Empirical Study," *Journal of International Business Studies* (Fall 1980), pp. 40–63.

DRUMM, H. J., "Transfer Pricing in the International Firm," *Management International Review,* no. 4 (1983), pp. 32–43.

EDMUNDS, J. C., "Working Capital Management in Multinational Companies: An Integrated Approach," *Management International Review,* no. 3 (1983), pp. 73–80.

FOWLER, D. J., "Transfer Prices and Profit Maximization in Multinational Enterprise Operations," *Journal of International Business Studies* (Winter 1978), pp. 9–26.

GRANICK, D., "National Differences in the Use of Internal Transfer Prices," *California Management Review* (Summer 1975), pp. 28–40.

GREENE, J. and M. G. DUERR, *Intercompany Transactions in the Multinational Firm.* New York: The Conference Board, 1970.

KEEGAN, W. J., "Multinational Pricing: How Far is Arm's Length?" *Columbia Journal of World Business* (May-June 1969), pp. 57–66.

KIM, S. H. and S. W. MILLER, "Constituents of the International Transfer Pricing Decision," *Columbia Journal of World Business* (Spring 1979), pp. 69–77.

KOPITS, G. F., "Intra-Firm Royalties Crossing Frontiers and Transfer-Pricing Behavior," *Economic Journal* (December 1976), pp. 791–805.

LALL, S., "Transfer Pricing by Multinational Manufacturing Firms," *Oxford Bulletin of Economics and Statistics* (August 1973), pp. 173–195.

LEFF, N. H., "Multinational Corporate Pricing Strategy in the Developing Countries," *Journal of International Business Studies* (Fall 1975), pp. 55–64.

LESSARD, D. R., "Transfer Prices, Taxes, and Financial Markets: Implications of International Financial Transfers within the Multinational Firm" in Robert G. Hawkins, ed., *The Economic Effects of Multinational Corporations.* Greenwich, Conn.: JAI Press, 1979.

NESS, W. L., JR., "U.S. Corporate Income Taxation and the Dividend Remittance Policy of Multinational Corporations," *Journal of International Business Studies* (Spring 1975), pp. 67–77.

OBERSTEINER, E., "Should the Foreign Affiliate Remit Dividends or Reinvest?" *Financial Management* (Spring 1973), pp. 88–93.

PETTY, J. W., II, and E. W. WALKER, "Optimal Transfer Pricing for the Multinational Firm," *Financial Management* (Winter 1972), pp. 74–87.

PLASSCHAERT, S. R. F., "Multiple Motivation for Transfer Pricing Modulations in Multinational Enterprises and Governmental Counter-Measures: An Attempt at Clarification," *Management International Review,* no. 1 (1981), pp. 49–63.

RUTENBERG, D. P., "Maneuvering Liquid Assets in a Multinational Company," *Management Science* (June 1970), pp. B-671–684.

SANGSTER, B., "International Funds Management," *Financial Executive* (December 1977), pp. 46–52.

SUMMA, D., "Remittances by U.S. Owned Foreign Corporations: Tax Considerations," *Columbia Journal of World Business* (Summer 1975), pp. 40–45.

WEIGEL, D., "Restrictions on Dividend Repatriations and the Flow of Direct Investment to Brazil," *Journal of International Business Studies* (Fall 1970), pp. 35–50.

YUNKER, P. J., "A Survey Study of Subsidiary Autonomy, Performance Evaluation, and Transfer Pricing in Multinational Corporations," *Columbia Journal of World Business* (Fall 1983), pp. 51–64.

7

Export-Import Financing and Receivables and Inventory Management

The multinational firm, like the domestic firm, has to establish and reassess policies and strategies relating to receivables and inventory management. While the nature of these decisions is essentially similar to those facing the domestic firm, it is complicated by the geographic distance and multiplicity of political jurisdictions characterizing the operations of the multinational firm. Moreover, in addition to currency exposure implications of such decisions, the MNC's receivables management is complicated by the distinction between receivables from outsiders and intracorporate receivables, while inventory management is more difficult due to international sourcing of raw materials and components. On the other hand, management's decisions in these areas benefit from the advantage of the natural hedge afforded by the diversity of its operations, which permits judgmental errors to cancel out to some degree.

Export-import transactions are closely tied to receivables and inventory management. In the first place, credit policy, a major variable determining the size, turnover, and quality of receivables, is at the same time the most important factor in the export decision and subsequently in the documentations that are generated by that decision. Second, the size and location of inventories of raw materials, semi-finished goods, and finished goods are closely linked with the export (and import) activities of the parent company and its affiliates.

The first part of this chapter is devoted to an examination of export and import financing, the documents that are currently used to facilitate foreign trade and to accommodate the financing process, and available credit insurance schemes designed to reduce certain risks facing the participants in these transactions. The second part examines receivables and inventory management decisions in a multinational context.

EXPORT-IMPORT FINANCING

Invoicing and Credit Decisions

An exporting firm has to reach a decision on two points before proceeding with the transaction: the *currency* of invoicing, and whether or not to extend *credit* to the importer. Related to the second point is the duration of credit and the form which the credit extended would take.

By deciding on the currency in which the export transaction is invoiced, the exporter is able to determine which party will bear the exchange rate risk. Invoicing in the exporter's currency will shift the risk to the importer, whereas invoicing in the importer's currency leaves the exporter exposed to this risk. Alternatively, choosing a third country's currency is likely to saddle the importer with the greater part of the risk, as the exporter is likely to select a "hard" country, that is, one that is expected to appreciate vis-a-vis the importer's currency during the duration of credit. Choosing the currency of invoicing, however, has to be viewed as one aspect of the overall terms of the transaction, and should reflect the relative competitive positions of the parties involved in the transactions, as well as prevailing world market conditions for the commodity being traded. Japanese firms, for example, have been known to consent to invoicing in weaker LDCs' currencies rather than the Japanese yen, to gain access to third-world markets at the expense of their competitors from other industrial countries.

The credit decision is more difficult and more complex than in domestic trade, because the exporter is not always in a position to assess the creditworthiness of the importer and is often unfamiliar with credit and business practices in foreign countries. Although the services of credit-reporting agencies are available, financial and other relevant data are not as accurate or as timely as similar data relating to firms in the same country. Credit extension is not a necessary condition for the conclusion and consummation of an export transaction. If competitive conditions in the industry permit, an exporter might insist on cash terms, such as cash against documents, or payment of a sight draft against documents.[1] Competitive conditions in the world markets for most traded commodities, however, have been such that short-term credit (typically 3-6 months) is an important

[1]These and other terms are explained later in this chapter.

feature of the bulk of international trade transactions. In most cases, credit terms conform to the established norms for the industry or the type of merchandise being traded.

DOCUMENTATION OF FOREIGN TRADE TRANSACTIONS

A foreign trade transaction, as the one illustrated in Exhibit 7-1, typically involves two distinct considerations: financing the transaction, and facilitating the completion of the transaction to the satisfaction of both parties—the exporter and the importer—in accordance with the terms agreed upon. To achieve these objectives, a number of documents are drawn and exchanged by the parties shown in Exhibit 7-1. These are the

Exhibit 7-1. The foreign trade financing cycle

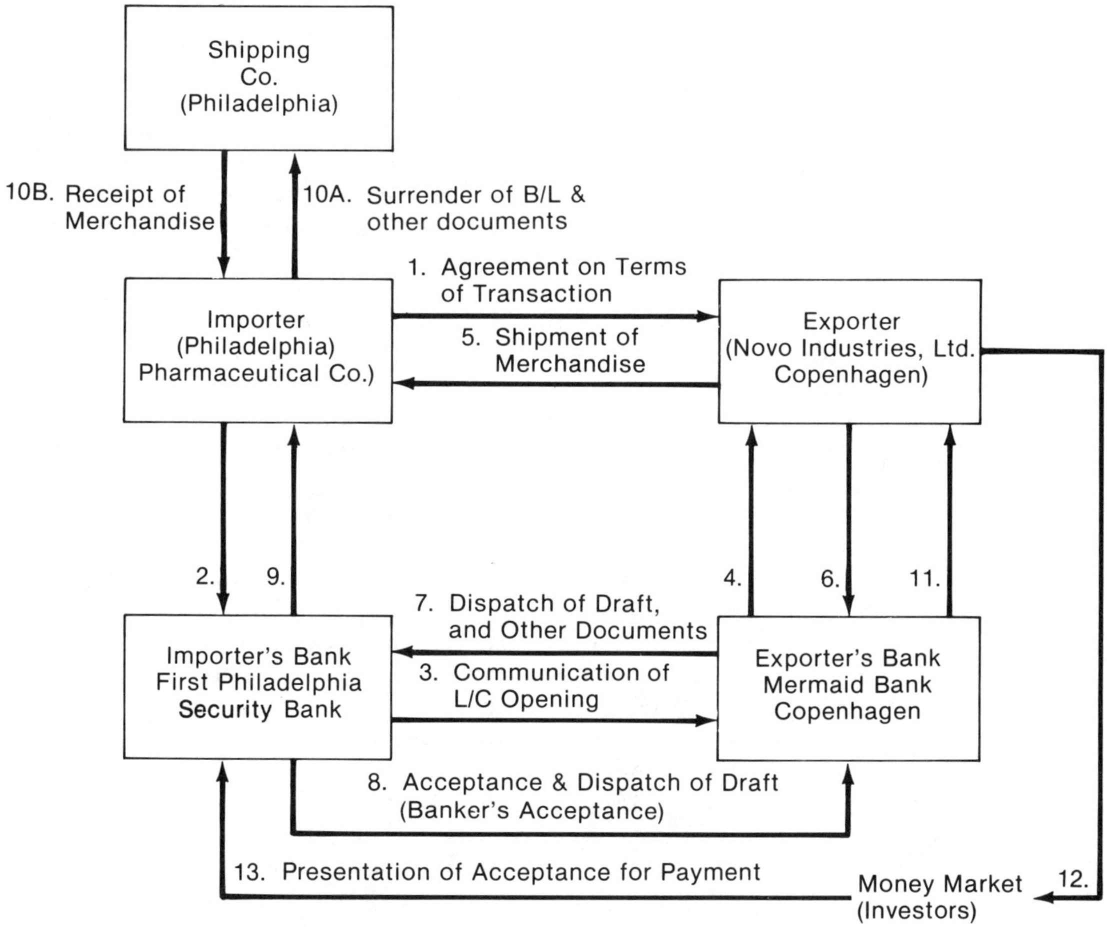

letter of credit (*L/C*), the bill of exchange (*draft*), the bill of lading (*B/L*), and the insurance policy and other documents requested by the importer. These documents are briefly explained in the following section.

A *letter of credit (L/C)* is an instrument negotiated by the importer with his bank (step 2) which embodies the terms agreed upon with the exporter (step 1), and assures the latter that payment for the shipped merchandise will be forthcoming. It is essentially a promise by the importer's bank to pay a definite sum to a designated beneficiary (usually the exporter) upon the fulfillment of the terms of the transactions as specified in the L/C. The basic function of this document is to substitute the credit of the importer's bank for that of the importer.

Letters of credit may be drawn in any one of several forms, depending primarily on the terms of the transaction and the nature of the relationship between the importer and the exporter. The L/C in Exhibit 7-1 is *irrevocable;* that is, it cannot be cancelled or altered by the issuing bank for any reason other than a breach by the exporter of the agreed terms of the transaction. An L/C, if so required or arranged by the exporter may be *confirmed* by his or her own bank, in which case the latter adds its promise to pay to that of the importer's bank. This arrangement would further assure the exporter of payment for the goods that are about to be shipped. Confirmation of the L/C by the exporter's bank signifies the bank's readiness to honor a draft issued on the L/C, when the draft is accompanied by the required documents. Letters of credit are normally issued for one specific transaction, but in some instances *revolving L/Cs* are issued, covering several transactions between the parties over a period of time. Revolving L/Cs are typically of the revocable type because of the additional risks arising from the open-ended nature of the issuing bank's undertaking.

When advice of the opening of the letter of credit is communicated to the exporter by the bank (steps 3 and 4), the exporter proceeds with the shipment of the merchandise (step 5), draws a draft (a bill of exchange), and forwards this document together with the bill of lading, a properly executed insurance policy, and other required documents to his or her bank (step 6).

A *draft* or a *bill of exchange* is typically an order issued by the exporter (drawer) addressed to the importer (drawee) instructing the latter to pay a specific stated sum (value of transaction) on a specified date to either the drawer or a designated third party (the exporter's bank). The date of payment could be upon presentation to the importer (in which case it is called a *sight draft*), or after the lapse of a specified time from the date of presentation and acceptance, or alternatively from the date of shipment of goods (*time draft*). A properly drawn draft would entitle its holder, who received it in *due course,* to receive payment irrespective of disagreements among the maker and the earlier holders, or any challenges to the underlying commercial transaction.

The draft illustrated in Exhibit 7-2 was forwarded by the exporter's bank to the importer's bank (step 7), and was accepted by the latter (step 8) in accordance with the terms of the transaction. The draft thus became a *bank draft,* in contrast with its being accepted by the importer himself, in which case it would become a *trade draft.* A bank draft, or a *banker's acceptance,* a versatile and highly negotiable money market instrument, has thus been created. Being an unconditional promise by a banking institution to make the payment on the draft at maturity, should the importer fail to honor the commitment to pay, a banker's acceptance is a marketable instrument which can be discounted. Discounting is selling the draft to a financial institution or an investor prior to maturity at a price determined by subtracting the amount of discount (discount rate per annum charged by the financial institution times the number of days to maturity/365 days) from the face value. In the illustration shown in Exhibit 7-1, the banker's acceptance created in the transaction was discounted by the exporter (Novo Industries, Ltd.) with investors in the money market (step 12). These investors in turn presented it on the date of maturity (120 days following acceptance on May 12, 1984—Exhibit 7-2) to Philadelphia Security Bank for payment (step 13). On that date, or on a prior date if so arranged, Philadelphia Security Bank charged the account of Philadelphia Pharmaceutical Co. with the face value of the draft plus bank charges.

The importer, Philadelphia Pharmaceutical Co., was able to obtain physical possession of the goods before the settlement described in the previous paragraph took place. To do so, the importer must have been in possession of the shipping documents specified in the L/C. In Exhibit 7-1, the bill of lading (B/L) and other required documents were forwarded to the importer by Philadelphia Security Bank on the day of the acceptance of the draft by the bank or shortly thereafter (step 9). With these documents in hand, the importing company or its agents were able to obtain possession of the merchandise from the agents of the shipping company in the Port of Philadelphia and clear them through customs authorities (steps 10A and 10B).

The importer could not have obtained physical possession of the goods without surrendering the original B/L and other required documents to the shipping company. The B/L is a document issued by the carrier transporting the merchandise attesting to the fact that the goods described on the face of the document have been placed with them by the exporter. The B/L serves not only as a receipt for merchandise entrusted with the carrier, but also as a contract between the exporter and the carrier, binding the latter to provide transportation and other services in return for payment of freight and other charges by the former. The paramount obligation of the carrier is to see to it that the merchandise is not released to the consignee (the importer or his or her agents) prior to unconditional surrender of the original B/L and other required documents as specified in the

Exhibit 7-2. The draft and its acceptance by a bank

No X13897 Copenhagen, Denmark May 5, 1984

120 days after sight of this bill

First Bill of Exchange
(duplicates unpaid)

Pay to the

Order of Mermaid Bank, Copenhagen U.S. $500,000

The Sum of Five Hundred Thousand U.S. Dollars only.

Value received and charge to a/c of

Philadelphia Pharmaceutical Co. Philadelphia, PA, (U.S.A.)
Drawn under Philadelphia Security Bank L/C #05970 issued April 3, 1984

To:

Philadelphia Security Bank
Broad & Chestnut Streets
Philadelphia, Pennsylvania

Signed for Johannes Jergens
Managing Director
Novo Industries, Inc.

Inscription on Face of Draft Signifying Acceptance

For value received by Philadelphia Pharmaceutical Co. covering imports of drugs and pharmaceutical products from Copenhagen, Denmark.

Value: $500,000
Accepted
May 12, 1984

Payable at

Philadelphia Security Bank
Broad & Chestnut Streets
Philadelphia, Pennsylvania

By____________________
Authorized Signature

L/C. Therefore, it serves an important function of being a document which vests title of the goods with the exporter during shipment and until they are released to the importer. The document can thus serve as a collateral against which funds may be advanced to the exporter by his or her bankers while the goods are in transit.

Bills of lading may be issued in many forms. A typical B/L customarily used in international trade is a *clean* B/L made to the *order* of the exporter. This would indicate that goods were placed with the carrier in apparently good condition,[2] and that the carrier is instructed to deliver the goods to the order of a certain designated party (usually the importer or an agent). Unlike a B/L made to order, a *straight* B/L does not constitute a legal title to the goods and is, therefore, not needed by the consignee to obtain possession of them.

In addition to the B/L, other documents are drawn in the process of shipping and delivering merchandise across national boundaries. The importer must also be in possession of an *insurance policy* issued by an insurance company or by an underwriter covering the risks specified in the L/C. This is usually issued in the name of the exporter and is subsequently endorsed by him or her to the consignee. To be valid, the policy must be issued in the same currency as the L/C and must not be dated later than the date of the matching shipping documents. A *commercial invoice* issued by the exporter containing description of merchandise, unit prices, and terms of sale, is also required. Other optional documents, which are usually specified in the L/C, include a *certificate of origin,* attesting that the goods originated or were manufactured in the country of export, a *consular invoice* issued by the consulate of the importing country to help prevent false declarations of value, and a *packing list* issued by the exporter or by an independent packing company to enable customs authorities to identify the shipped merchandise.

OTHER SOURCES OF FOREIGN TRADE FINANCING

The typical foreign trade transaction described in the earlier sections is financed by the importer's bank and financial institutions and investors operating in the money market. Most countries provide other means of financing foreign trade transactions through a variety of private and public institutions and financial arrangements. These sources are discussed briefly in this section.

[2]The carrier is not obligated to ascertain the contents of the shipped merchandise beyond visual inspection of the pieces shipped. In general, the transaction described in this chapter is an illustration of a typical foreign trade transaction, thus sidetracking the intricate legal rights and obligations of the parties, particularly when the nature of the documents used departs from the ones described here.

Government Export Promotion and Financing Programs

The United States, as well as most industrial countries and a number of developing countries, offer a variety of government export promotion and financing programs. Export financing is normally offered at subsidized terms, thus entailing an element of cost to the taxpayer. Most of these programs also involve export credit guarantees and insurance. Typical of these programs are the facilities offered by Export-Import Bank of the United States (The EX-IM Bank), and the Exports Credit Guarantee Department (E.C.G.D.) of the United Kingdom.

The EX-IM Bank, established in 1934 and rechartered in 1945, is entrusted with the function of facilitating foreign trade transactions between the United States and foreign countries. It is an autonomous agency of the U.S. government with its five full-time directors appointed by the President with the advice and consent of the Senate. Its resources consist of $1 billion of nonvoting stock fully paid in by the U.S. Treasury, and an option to borrow from the Treasury in amounts up to the authorized limits when needed to carry out its functions.

The major function of the EX-IM Bank is to provide a supplementary source for financing exports as a backup to funds advanced by commercial banks, thereby enhancing the liquidity of these banks, particularly in the area of medium-term financing (181 days to five years). Export credit obligations of such maturities acquired by U.S. commercial banks are guaranteed by EX-IM Bank if they meet the criteria established by it. Approval is granted upon verification of applications made by banks on behalf of their exporter clients to ascertain that such exports meet the criteria of maintaining employment and output levels in the United States, and are necessary to overcome competition from exporters in other countries.

EX-IM Bank also provides long-term (5–12 years) direct lending to borrowers outside the United States for the purpose of purchasing U.S. goods. The Bank requires private participation in these direct loans, primarily because of its role as a supplementary source of export financing rather than competitive with private sources. The Bank also extends loans on a partly subsidized basis to foreign financial institutions, which in turn make credit available to medium-sized and small business firms in their countries to purchase U.S. equipment. Other activities of the Bank include guaranteeing lease transactions, financing in part preinvestment outlays by U.S. firms abroad, and providing political risk coverage on U.S. equipment used outside the United States.

The British E.C.G.D. dates back to 1919 and offers essentially medium- and long-term financing in support of British exports. Financing takes the form of participation with private lending institutions, as well as direct loans to foreign institutions and guarantees of foreign trade obligations acquired by British banks. Most of the U.S. major trading partners have comparable export financing and foreign credit insurance programs.[3] The role of these government programs has been increasing in recent years, reflecting the need to supplement medium-term suppliers' credit provided primarily by private financial institutions. These facilities are particularly crucial for capital goods of high unit value (the so-called large ticket items) which have been increasingly supplied on a long-term basis. The growth of these programs also reflects the intensification of competition among industrial countries for Third World markets.

Industry-Banking Financing Schemes

An example in the area of collaboration between exporters and banks in providing export credit with government support is the Private Export Funding Corporation (PEFCO). PEFCO is a private corporation whose stockholders consist of 54 commercial banks, one investment banking firm, and seven manufacturing companies with a major concentration in aircrafts and aircraft equipment. All PEFCO foreign obligations, consisting of medium- to long-term obligations of foreign importers, are unconditionally guaranteed by EX-IM Bank. Consequently, PEFCO does not evaluate credit risks or appraise country risk, as these functions are performed by EX-IM Bank. It obtains the bulk of its resources from sale of secured notes and long-term securities in the capital market.

Factoring and Forfaiting

Factoring, or selling accounts receivables on a nonrecourse basis, is discussed in more detail in the section relating to accounts receivable management. Factoring is especially important for foreign sales on an open account basis which represent a relatively small proportion of global foreign trade transactions.

Forfaiting[4] is a variation of factoring designed to attract investors' funds for medium-term export financing, particularly for technology and capital goods destined to East European countries and LDCs. The process consists of the forfaiter's (usually a subsidiary of a European bank) buying, or discounting on a nonrecourse basis, promissory notes issued for the exporter by the importer (usually a government or a government firm in the importing country). The exporting firm under this arrangement is relieved of the political and commercial risks inherent in the transactions, as these risks are assumed by a specialist (the forfaiter). However, it remains responsible for other trade-related risks, such as the quality of goods.

[3]United Kingdom, Belgium, Norway, Denmark, Netherlands, Italy, France, Spain, Japan, Sweden, Germany, Canada, and Switzerland.

[4]From the French *a forfait,* meaning to "forfeit or surrender a right."

Promissory notes issued by the importing firm are guaranteed by a bank in the importing country, which becomes the primary obligor in the eyes of all subsequent holders of the notes. When these notes are received by the exporter, they are endorsed "without recourse" and are discounted with the forfaiter in accordance with terms previously arranged. The proceeds of discounting the notes consist of their face value minus discount charges (discount rate per annum already agreed upon × number of days until maturity/365) and an additional fee of about 0.1 percent per month of the unused part of the original commitment. The forfaiter usually turns around and sells the notes, which at that point carry two names (importer's bank and forfaiting firm), to investors in the European money market to free the funds for another round of forfaiting. The buyers of these notes rely primarily on the endorsement of the forfaiting firm, which is presumed to have assessed carefully commercial as well as country risk. The firm thus bears the risk that the notes will eventually be honored by the importing firm or its bank.

Export Credit Insurance

Export credit insurance is to be distinguished from insuring shipments across national boundaries while in transit, mainly against sea perils, commonly referred to as *marine* or *maritime insurance.* Export credit insurance protects the exporter, or the financial institution which bought or discounted foreign trade obligations, against commercial and political risks. The existence of this coverage induces banks to provide nonrecourse financing of capital goods items normally sold with medium to long maturities extending up to 12 years.

Foreign Credit Insurance Association (FCIA), an association of some fifty private insurance companies and EX-IM Bank, offers a variety of export credit insurance schemes. Coverage is offered for short-term contracts (up to 180 days from date of shipment) and medium-term contracts (181 days to five years). Comprehensive policies cover both commercial risk (up to 90 percent of the value of the transaction) and political risk (up to 95 percent of the value of the transaction), or insurance against political risk only may be purchased (90 percent coverage). Insurance rates are primarily based on the terms of the export transaction and the country of destination. To qualify for FCIA coverage, exporters must have legal residence in, and ship from, the United States or its territories, and at least 50 percent of the value of shipment must have originated in the U.S.[5]

MULTINATIONAL RECEIVABLES MANAGEMENT

Managerial decisions dealing with appropriate levels of receivables and inventory for the multinational firm are parallel to those faced by the

[5]See Appendix G, Chapter 17.

domestic firm. Multinational receivables and inventory management is, however, rendered more complex by currency fluctuations, exchange restrictions, differential inflation rates among countries, longer delivery and lead times, and greater risk of disruption of supplies. This section examines briefly these decisions stressing the factors or aspects that are peculiar to the multinational firm as contrasted with its domestic counterpart.

Receivables Management

It was pointed out earlier in this chapter that creation of receivables is inextricably related to the credit decision process. Shipment on a cash basis (such as cash against documents or sight draft) entails receivables creation for a short duration, that is, while goods are in transit, or the time which lapses between the drawing of the draft and its payment by the importing firm or its banker. Goods shipped against L/Cs on which time drafts are drawn and accepted by the issuing bank shift the credit function from the exporter to financial institutions and the money market.

Receivables arise mainly from shipments on open account, consignment shipments, and shipments of goods and services between parent and affiliates, as well as among the latter. In addition to export sales on credit, local sales on credit by affiliates and subsidiary units create receivables for the selling units, as well as for the MNC as a whole.

The criterion for the credit decision which gives rise to accounts receivable is identical to that faced by the domestic firm, that is, comparing incremental profits with incremental costs, so as to arrive at the credit policy or credit terms which would maximize the firm's profit. A complicating factor for the MNC is the possible foreign exchange loss on sales on credit made by one of its subsidiaries.

To illustrate the process of optimizing the level of accounts receivable, let us assume that a subsidiary of a U.S. MNC in Egypt is considering a relaxation of its credit policy so as to allow sale on credit to a lower credit class group. Existing sales amount to £E (Egyptian pounds) 5,000,000 on the basis of selling on credit to groups A, B, and C. Extending credit to group D will increase sales to £E5,500,000. Additional sales have the same contribution to profit as existing sales (say 10 percent); group D customers are estimated to have an incremental bad debt experience of 4 percent, and the cost of financing or carrying incremental accounts receivables is 12 percent per annum. All sales on credit are made on a 90-day basis with no cash discount allowed. The relaxation of the present credit policy should be instituted, provided that:

$$\text{Incremental profits} > \text{incremental costs}$$

or

$$\text{£E}500{,}000(.10) > \text{£E}(500{,}000)(.04) + (500{,}000)(.03) + (500{,}000)(0.96)(d)$$

where (d) stands for the expected rate of depreciation of the foreign currency against the home currency.

$$£E50{,}000 \geqq £E20{,}000 + 15{,}000 + 480{,}000d$$
$$d = 3.1\%$$

It would thus prove profitable for the Egyptian subsidiary to extend credit to group D customers provided that the expected devaluation of the Egyptian pound against the U.S. dollar in 90 days is less than 3.1 percent. Barring an unforeseen sharp deterioration in Egypt's international payments situation or the country's political risk, a depreciation of this magnitude in three months is unlikely. Consequently, the current credit policy should be eased.

Factoring

Receivables arising from export credit sales or credit sales by affiliates and subsidiaries may be factored on a *nonrecourse* basis; that is, the factor assumes all credit and political risks except for disputes between the original contracting parties with respect to defects in the merchandise or service exchanged, or noncompletion of the transaction as contracted.

Factoring export receivables is in many respects similar to the forfaiting facility that was discussed earlier in this chapter, except that the latter usually involves a government agency on the importing side, with a government bank or a financial institution in the importing country guaranteeing the notes issued by the importing agency to the forfaiter.

Factoring can offer several advantages to the exporter or the MNC. It permits the exporter to quote more competitive terms, or to ship goods on open account rather than insisting on cash terms or shipment against a letter of credit. It relieves the exporting firm from the costs of credit investigation and collection, as well as from the cost of assessing the political risk. The factoring firm is better placed to assess these risks and, by virtue of its diversified credit portfolio in many countries, its loss experience is likely to be lower than that of the exporting firm. As a result, the factor may pass on part of these cost savings to its clients.

International factoring, however, is still an expensive proposition. Export factoring fees differ depending on the size, quality, and the annual turnover of the underlying receivables. A typical fee would consist of about 2 percent of credit sales plus a discount rate of 1 to 2 percent above the benchmark lending rates of commercial banks (the Eurodollar rate or the London Interbank Offering Rate, "LIBOR").

Most of the international factoring of accounts receivables is effected by the International Factoring Group, which has an extensive network of agencies in most industrial countries. The absence of agencies of this group in most LDCs limits the usefulness of this service to firms dealing with these countries. Even for firms exporting or conducting business in industrial countries where factoring services are available, factoring is not necessarily advisable for each and every exporting firm. It is especially adaptable to small firms that cannot afford the cost of credit-checking and risk evaluation process, and firms which have only occasional exports to few geographically dispersed countries. Firms which are habitual and substantial exporters to a large number of countries can rely on their diversified portfolio of accounts receivable to produce the same cost savings and limited loss experience which the international factor is able to realize. Management of intracompany receivables is subject to a different set of criteria related mostly to exposure management, which was covered in Chapter 5.

MULTINATIONAL INVENTORY MANAGEMENT

The inventory management decision, that is, the determination of the optimal level of stocks of finished goods, work in process, raw materials, parts, and components to be kept on hand, is generally identical for the domestic and the multinational firm. The same techniques also apply to the determination of the level of required safety stocks.[6] However, the MNC faces greater problems in controlling the underlying variables. Complicating factors include the diverse inventories maintained in several widely separated locations, longer and more variable transit time, lengthy custom proceedings, frequently changing import controls and tariffs, and supply disruptions due to dock strikes and political strife. Superimposed on these frequently changing variables is the currency fluctuation risk.

To illustrate the impact of these complicating variables on the basic inventory solution, assume that a purely domestic firm is faced with the following data:

$$\text{Economic order quantity (EOQ)}^7 = 1200 \text{ units} = \text{monthly sales}$$
$$\text{Safety stock}^7 = 100 \text{ units}$$
$$\text{Lead time} = 10 \text{ days}$$

On the basis of these data, the *reordering point* is determinable and equal to:

$$\text{Reorder point} = \text{safety stock} + (\text{daily sales} \times \text{lead time})$$
$$= 100 + (40 \times 10) = 500 \text{ units}$$

Exhibit 7-3 portrays the basic inventory solution for this firm. A new order of 1200 units is triggered as soon as the level of inventory reaches 500 units. The safety stock and allowance for lead time (the estimated time

[6]For a detailed discussion of inventory management models, consult standard financial management or industrial management textbooks.

[7]The EOQ as well as the optimum level of safety stock are determined by the models referred to in footnote 6.

Exhibit 7-3. Basic inventory management solution (the domestic firm)

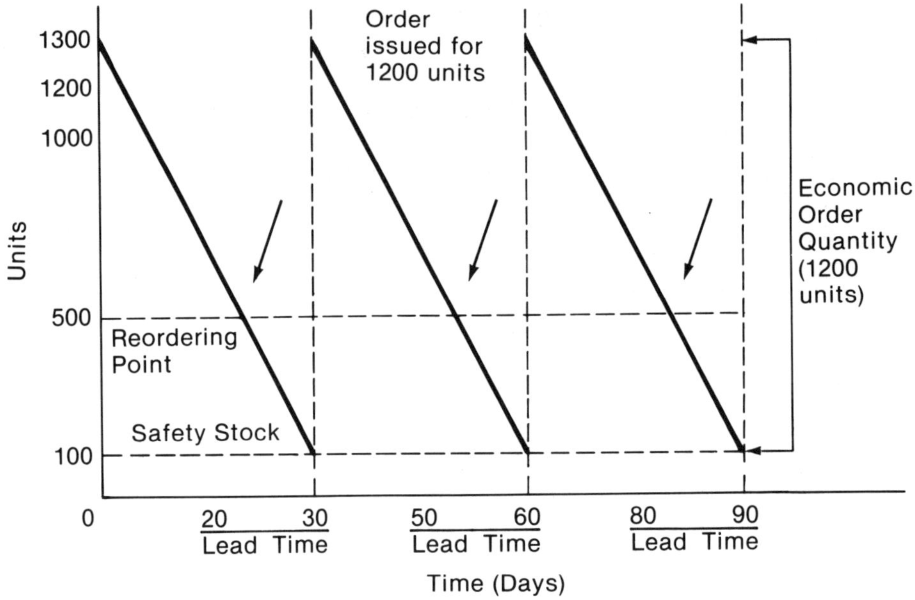

which elapses between placing the order and receiving it) provide a built-in cushion to accommodate possible variability in the rate of sales per day and the time necessary to issue new orders and having them filled. In this simplified model, the first order is issued for 1300 units to cover the monthly requirement and the establishment of the safety stock, with all subsequent orders issued for 1200 units.

Let us now assume that the firm facing the data used in the illustration is a subsidiary of an MNC which sources its finished products or components from the parent company or from another affiliate. The impact of the geographic distance between the supplying unit and the point of sale, and possible delays in transit time and customs proceedings will require a revision of both the level of safety stock and in lead time. The level of safety stock, which is determined by an optimum solution equalizing stockout costs and the cost of carrying the safety stock, would probably have to be revised upward, due to the higher frequency of estimated stockouts. Similarly, lead time would also have to be lengthened to offset a higher probability of unexpected delays in transit or in clearance from customs. With a recalculated safety stock level of 150 units and a revised lead time of 15 days, the new reordering point will be 750 units [150 + (40 × 15)]. These changes will produce the effects shown in Exhibit 7-4.

It should be pointed out that the changed assumptions underlying Exhibit 7-4 do not affect the original EOQ determination. The inputs which

Exhibit 7-4. Basic inventory management solution (a subsidiary of an MNC)

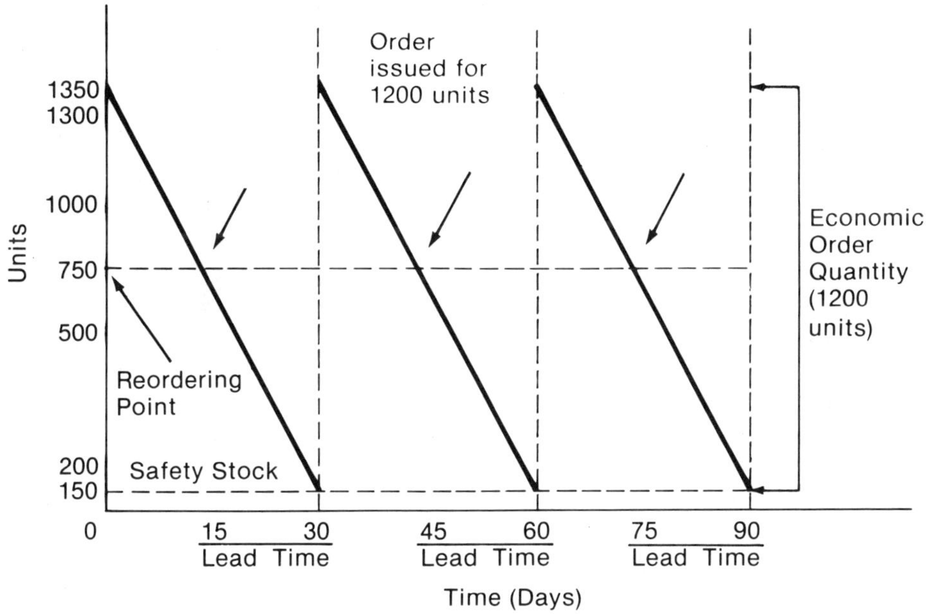

go into that solution, namely, total sales per year, ordering costs, carrying costs, and unit price have been assumed to remain unchanged. If any of these variables were to be influenced by factors affecting the inventory solution for the multinational firm, then the original EOQ determination will have to be reworked to reflect new values for the inputs.

Stockpiling

MNCs not only sell their products and services in many countries, but often source their raw materials and components on a worldwide basis. Stockpiling is resorted to when the supply of raw materials or components is likely to be disrupted due to anticipated strikes, political turmoil, or other destabilizing factors. Similarly, an affiliate operating in a country where restrictions on transfers are expected to be imposed, or whose currency is expected to depreciate, would need to engage in anticipatory purchases of imported parts and components.

An inventory policy of hedging against anticipated transfer restrictions and/or currency depreciation by stockpiling needed raw materials and components must balance a number of conflicting variables. Most important among these are

1. Anticipated (or projected) rate of depreciation of the local currency against the home (parent company) currency.

2. Anticipated increase in the price of imported parts and components in terms of the supplier's currency.
3. Holding costs of inventories which includes capital (investment) costs, insurance, warehousing, and spoilage.
4. Opportunity cost of local funds, i.e., rate earned on short-term investments of liquid funds if not used in financing stockpiles of imported parts and components.

To illustrate the stockpiling solution, suppose that Ford Motor Company is attempting to establish for its affiliate in Argentina an inventory management system for components sourced in the United States. Such a solution must take into account the estimated increase in the price of the components, the projected depreciation of the Argentinian peso vs. the United States dollar, and the holding costs of inventories. In addition, the opportunity cost of peso balances held in Argentina, as measured by the rate of return on liquid investments in that country, must be factored in. Given the following data:

- Price (of components) = $25.00 per unit rising at 1% monthly
- Holding costs (in U.S. $) = 2% per month
- Excess peso balances held in Argentina earn 3% monthly in marketable securities
- The peso is projected to depreciate against the United States dollar by 5% in each of the next two months, 3% in the third month and 2% in each of the following three months

The optimum stockpiling solution may be determined from the following tabulation by equating the estimated increase in the unit price of the component with the cumulative carrying cost:

Table 7-1.

Month	Opportunity Cost of Local Funds (%) (Rate of Return − Dep. of the Peso)	Holding Costs (%)	Total Monthly Carrying Cost (%)	Cumulative Carrying Cost (%)	Cumulative Price Increase (%)
1	−2	2	0	0	0.0
2	−2	2	0	0	1.0
3	0	2	2	2	2.0
4	1	2	3	5	3.0
5	1	2	3	8	4.0
6	1	2	3	11	5.0

Components should be stockpiled, therefore, to cover the affiliate's requirements for three months. Stockpiling in excess of three months' requirements will be counterproductive as, beginning with the fourth month, cumulative carrying costs exceed the expected increase in the price of the component. It is evident that a higher expected rate of increase in the component price or a faster rate of depreciation in the peso exchange rate (other variables remaining unchanged) will cause the stockpile to rise in terms of coverage of future months. On the other hand, the higher the rate that can be earned in local short-term investment of the peso (again, other variables remaining the same), the smaller will be the stockpile.

Should the stockpiling have been warranted by possible disruption in the supply of components or by imminent import or foreign exchange controls to be imposed by the host country (Argentina), then the parent company may decide to stockpile in excess of the optimum solution worked out in the illustration. Although that decision would be judgmental in nature, the probability of the occurrence of total interruption of supplies should be considered.[8] As the probability of disruptions increases (other variables remaining unchanged), more inventory should be stockpiled. If the disruption is expected to last for a considerable period of time, or is deemed to be permanent, alternative sources of supply should be cultivated. As a matter of hedging against such eventualities, multinational firms usually develop more than one source of supply to meet the needs of their affiliates, particularly if the main supply source is subject to frequent interruptions.

REVIEW QUESTIONS

1. Show how export-import transactions are closely related to receivables and inventory management for the multinational firm. In particular, explain the link between the choice of an invoicing currency and the credit decision.
2. Are the L/C and banker's acceptance instruments that are exclusively used in financing foreign trade? Why are these two instruments especially adapted to foreign trade? State the advantages that each instrument provides for the exporter and importer in a typical foreign trade transaction (such as the one illustrated in Exhibit 7-1).
3. Why have major capital goods exporting countries found it necessary to establish government export financing programs, instead of relying on banking and other private financing facilities? Does EX-IM Bank subsidize U.S. exports?
4. Distinguish between factoring and forfaiting as techniques for managing receivables arising from exports. Which particular situations lend themselves best to forfaiting?

[8]A formalized mathematical solution could be worked out for this situation taking into account, in addition to the variables indicated above, the probability of the occurrence of stockouts and the cost of such stockouts. This solution is beyond the scope of this book.

5. Distinguish between marine and export credit insurance. Which particular risk or risks are covered under each type?
6. How does the management of receivables generated by affiliate sales differ from the management of intracompany receivables? For example, what measures are appropriate if the currency of the affiliate is expected to depreciate?
7. Why is international factoring of accounts receivable relatively more costly than factoring domestic receivables? Would you advise a highly diversified MNC which regularly generates substantial receivables in a large number of countries to resort to factoring?
8. What is stockpiling? Under what circumstances is stockpiling strategy recommended for affiliates' operations?
9. The inventory management solution for the MNC does not differ from that of a typical domestic firm and can be determined by the same techniques. Comment on the statement, pointing out differences, if any, between the two situations.

REVIEW PROBLEMS

1. A subsidiary of a U.S. MNC in Egypt is considering relaxation of its credit policy in an attempt to increase sales and to use unutilized capacity. The new policy calls for extending credit to lower credit class groups, and extending the credit period from 90 days to 120 days to all accounts with no cash discount allowed.

CURRENT SITUATION		NEW POLICY
Sales (Egyptian pounds)	£E1,000,000	£E2,000,000
Contribution margin to profits	10%	15% (all sales)
Bad debt experience	4%	5% (on all accounts)
Cost of financing receivables	12% per annum	12% per annum
Credit period	90 days	120 days

a. Should the new credit policy be instituted if it is assumed that the Egyptian pound is not expected to depreciate against the U.S. dollar in the next four months?

b. Should the new credit policy be instituted if the Egyptian pound is expected to depreciate by one percent per month against the U.S. dollar?

c. Calculate the monthly rate of depreciation of the Egyptian pound against the U.S. dollar that would leave the management of the U.S. firm indifferent as to whether or not to adopt the new credit policy.

2. Would the subsidiary in Problem 1 be better off by expanding sales up to £E1,500,000, given the following changes?

Contribution margin	15% (on additional sales only)
Bad debt experience	5% (on additional sales only)
Financing cost	6% per annum (on additional sales only through subsidized local financing)
Depreciation of the Egyptian pound	1% per month
Credit period	90 days (unchanged)

3. A U.S. firm is attempting to determine the optimal amount of stockpiling of components which are shipped from the parent company (in terms of months' requirements) for its affiliate in the Philippines. The relevant data are given below:

    - Price of components is $15.00 per unit, rising at 1.5 percent per month.
    - Holding costs are two percent per month.
    - Excess peso balances held in the Philippines and invested in marketable securities earn 24 percent per annum.
    - The peso/U.S. dollar exchange rate is expected to remain unchanged in the first two months, and to depreciate thereafter by three percent per month.

    a. Calculate the optimal stockpiling requirement for the Philippine affiliate.

    b. Rework the optimal solution if the peso is projected to depreciate against the U.S. dollar by three percent in each of the next two months, two percent in the third month, and one percent in each of the subsequent months.

    c. Would you answer to (a) or (b) be different if the parent company expects imminent controls imposed by the Philippine government on imports of raw materials and components?

4. XYZ Trading Co. of the United Kingdom receives $1,000,000 in payment for exports to ABC Electronics of Philadelphia, Pa. (XYZ Co. banks with Barclays-London, and ABC banks with Philadelphia Security Bank. S_0 \$/£ = 1.25.)

    a. XYZ Trading Co. keeps amount in deposit in Philadelphia Security Bank.

    b. XYZ Trading Co. asks its bank to transfer export proceeds to its account in pounds sterling.

    c. Instead of (b), XYZ Trading Co. transfers dollar proceeds from Philadelphia Security Bank, and places it with its own bank as a time deposit denominated in dollars.

    Show the above transactions in T accounts of Barclays and Philadelphia Security Bank.

BIBLIOGRAPHY

ALEXANDER, E. D., "One Other Way to Get Paid for Your Exports [Factoring]," *American Import/Export Bulletin* (February 1981), p. 40.

BAKER, J. C., and R. J. WAYMAN, "Forfaiting: A Little-Known Method of International Trade Financing," *Journal of Commercial Bank Lending* (December 1983), pp. 41–51.

BAROVICK, R. L., "Export Credit Insurance: An Important Marketing Tool," *Business America* (August 23, 1982), pp. 6–7.

BAYALIS, A. E., "The Documentation Dilemma in International Trade," *Columbia Journal of World Business* (Spring 1976), pp. 15–22.

BLEIBERG, R. M., "Thunder on the Right: The Export-Import Bank Does More Harm Than Good," *Barrons* (July 12, 1982), p. 11.

BLOCK, H. S., "Export Financing Emerging as a Major Policy Problem," *Columbia Journal of World Business* (Fall 1976), pp. 85–95.

BOWEN, D., "Getting Paid Used to Be So Simple," *Euromoney* (January 1984), pp. 118–119.

BRADY, D. L., and W. O. BEARDEN, "The Effect of Managerial Attitudes on Alternative Export Methods," *Journal of International Business Studies* (Winter 1979), pp. 79–84.

CHASE MANHATTAN, *Methods of Export Financing,* 2d ed. New York: Chase World Information Corporation, 1976.

CURTIN, D., "The Uncharted $4 Billion World of Forfaiting," *Fortune* (August 1980), pp. 62–70.

Export-Import Bank: Financing for American Exports—Support for American Jobs. Washington, D.C.: Export-Import Bank of the United States, 1980.

FEINBERG, R. E., *Subsidizing Success: The Export-Import Bank in the U.S. Economy.* Cambridge: Cambridge University Press, United Kingdom, 1982.

Forfaiting. Zurich, Switzerland: Credit Suisse, 1980.

GAETA, J. J., "How to Choose the Right Bank for Export Finance," *American Import/Export Management* (February 1985), p. 30.

GMUR, C. J., ed., *Trade Financing.* London: Euromoney Publications, 1981.

GUILD, I., "Forfaiting as a Tool for International Bankers," *Banker* (May 1982), p. 131.

______, "Forfaiting Widens Its Appeal," *Banker* (April 1984), pp. 45–46.

HARRINGTON, J. A., *Specifics on Commercial Letters of Credit and Bankers Acceptances.* Jersey City, N.J.: Scott Printing Corporation, 1974.

HELFRICH, R. T., "Trading in Bankers' Acceptances: A View from the Acceptance Desk of the Federal Reserve Bank of New York," *Monthly Review, Federal Reserve Bank of New York* (February 1976), pp. 51–57.

HOLLIS, S. E., *Guide to Export Credit Insurance.* New York: Foreign Credit Insurance Association, 1971.

HUSZAGH, S. M., and M. R. GREENE, "How Exporters View Credit Risk and FCIA Insurance—The Georgia Experience," *Journal of Risk Insurance* (March 1985), pp. 117–132.

LYONS, M. S., "EXIM Bank: Where U.S. Exports Get a Big Boost," *Duns Review* (July 1981), p. 23.

MCNAMEE, J. W., "Export Payment Letters—They're to Your Credit," *American Import/Export Management* (November 1981), p. 36.

MELTON, W. C., and J. M. MAHR, "Bankers Acceptances," *Federal Reserve Bank of New York, Quarterly Review* (Summer 1981), pp. 39–52.

PLAUT, S. E., "Export-Import Follies," *Fortune* (August 25, 1980), pp. 74–77.

POSNER, A. R., "The States and Overseas Export Promotion," *MSU Business Topics* (Summer 1980), pp. 43–49.

RABINO, S., "An Additional Evaluation of an Export Incentive Program: The Cost of DISC," *Columbia Journal of World Business* (Spring 1980), pp. 61–65.

ROBERTS, R. W., "Let's Hear It For the Export-Import Bank," *Fortune* (November 3, 1980), pp. 123–124.

SCHUSTER, F., "Barter Arrangements with Money: The Modern Form of Compensation Trading," *Columbia Journal of World Business* (Fall 1980), pp. 61–66.

SHAPIRO, A. C., "Optimal Inventory and Credit-Granting Strategies Under Inflation and Devaluation," *Journal of Financial and Quantitative Analysis* (January 1973), pp. 37–46.

SHAPIRO, A. C., H. KUNREUTHER, and P. LANG, "Planning Horizons for Inventory Stockpiling," working paper, University of Pennsylvania, 1976.

SHARP, H. L., "Controlling Risk in Global Trade," *Financial Executive* (April 1980), pp. 14–17.

STOLZ, R., "Eximbank: What It Does for American World Traders," *Cashflow* (November-December 1980), pp. 34–39.

Uniform Customs and Practices for Documentary Credits. New York: United States Council of the International Chamber of Commerce, 1974.

WALVOORD, R. W., "Alternative Ways of Getting Paid for Your Exports," *American Import/Export Bulletin* (October 1980), pp. 48–50.

WEIGAND, R. E., "International Trade Without Money," *Harvard Business Review* (November-December 1977), pp. 28–30, 34, 38, 42, 166.

WHITING, D. P., *Finance of Foreign Trade,* 3rd ed. London: MacDonald and Evans, 1973.

8

Cash Positioning and International Cash Management Strategies

INTRODUCTION

International Data Processing Technology, Inc. (IDPT) is a diversified computer and minicomputer U.S. multinational corporation with worldwide sales offices and manufacturing and assembly affiliates in a number of countries. Although its total sales in 1982 (about $150 million) puts it in the category of small to medium-sized firms in its industry, IDPT has attracted a considerable interest among investors and investment analysts due to the recent high growth rate in its operations and the dynamic quality of the management.

Mr. John W. Reardon, C.E.O. of the company, has been reviewing in the past few months IDPT's cash management policies on a worldwide basis, particularly in view of the company's relatively strong dependence on foreign sales, which in 1982 accounted for over 40 percent of total sales. Mr. Reardon has recently been leaning toward evolving a more comprehensive cash positioning and management strategy for IDPT which has the following major objectives:

1. Minimizing cash and liquid asset balances held by affiliates and sales offices abroad.
2. Minimizing currency exposure and transaction costs of currency conversion operations by a well-designed multilateral netting system.

3. Speeding up collection of checks and drafts to permit a more effective cash mobilization to the point where it is needed without undue delays.
4. Centralizing of investment of excess cash balances so as to generate the best available return.

IDPT has been relying heavily since 1979 on the services of Global Hanover and Trust Co., a leading New York multinational bank, which maintains branches or affiliates in most countries where IDPT does business. Services provided by the bank include overdraft facilities to IDPT's affiliates and sales offices, electronic transfer of funds, and, in some locations, lockbox arrangements to speed up the collection of customers' checks. Although these arrangements have been adequate for IDPT requirements in the early years of its growth, Mr. Reardon is of the opinion that a more formalized and perhaps a more sophisticated system of global cash management is now in order.

In a meeting with Mr. Alan S. Ray, a senior vice president of Global Hanover in charge of MNCs' operations, Mr. Reardon outlined the objectives of the desired program and solicited Mr. Ray's recommendations. The latter indicated that his bank had on many occasions designed cash positioning and management systems for large and medium-sized MNCs in cooperation with design and consulting firms that specialize in these services. He recommended to Mr. Reardon that IDPT retain Automatic Data Network, Inc. to study IDPT's requirements and design an appropriate cash management system for the company.

Following an extensive review of IDPT's operations during 1979–1982 and several interviews with Mr. Reardon and his senior staff (including a number of key affiliate managers), Automatic Data Network submitted the following preliminary report. The consulting firm asked Mr. Reardon and Mr. Ray to review the report with a view to pinpointing the key areas of cash savings and other economies in cash management. This review was deemed essential to the final formulation of a program that suits the requirements of IDPT, taking into account the projected growth in the company's operations during 1984–1988.

Automatic Data Network's report consisted of four parts. The first part dealt with principles and guidelines governing the development of cash management systems for MNCs, as well as the mechanisms and services available to these companies to put these systems into effect. The second part covered the techniques of expediting the collection process. The third part dealt with design of cash management systems in general. The fourth part dealt with a preliminary design of a system that suited the present needs and future requirements of IDPT.

THE REPORT

Part One—Principles and Guidelines

THE CASH POSITIONING DECISION

The cash positioning decision of an MNC, as contrasted with a purely domestic corporation, is three-dimensional because it involves a choice of (a) currency of location, (b) the type of liquid assets held, that is, currency and coins, demand and time deposits, and marketable securities, and (c) maturities, yields, and liquidity characteristics. Handling of worldwide cash balances of the MNC differs from the domestic firm not only because of the currency choice, but also because of the greater array of possible choices or forms of liquid assets and maturities afforded by international financial markets.

The primary objectives of any effective cash management system involving worldwide operations are

1. Minimizing the overall cash requirements of the company as a whole without impinging on the smooth operation of the company and each affiliate or subsidiary.
2. Minimizing the currency exposure risk.
3. Minimizing the political risk.
4. Minimizing the transaction costs, that is, the cost of currency conversions, borrowing and investments transactions, and forward exchange transactions.
5. Taking full advantage of the economies of scale, as well as the benefit of superior knowledge of market conditions, both in borrowing and investment operations.

The complexity of the cash positioning decision arises from the conflicting nature of these objectives. For example, eliminating (or minimizing) the political risk dictates that all receipts in foreign currencies be converted to the home currency (the currency of the parent). This might, and in many cases does, interfere with the requirements of the affiliates, which need a minimum working capital to ensure efficient operations. Moreover, such operations require that cash or liquid assets should be maintained in the currency in which payments are to be effected, rather than the home currency. On the other hand, minimizing transaction costs of currency conversions would require that cash balances be kept in the currency in which they are received, which conflicts with both the currency and political exposure criteria. As another illustration of the conflicting nature of the primary objectives, consider the need to maintain cash balances in a developing country in anticipation of future payments due to the time required to transfer funds to such a country. Obviously, maintenance of such balances in excess of immediate requirements may impinge on the goal to benefit from economies of scale in earning the highest possible rate of return from investing these funds.

CENTRALIZATION

Despite the conflicting nature of the objectives of a cash management system, the key to developing an optimum system is centralization of cash management. Centralization in this context does not necessarily entail the pooling of overall liquid resources, although some degree of pooling would take place, but rather the centralization of reports, information and, most importantly, the decision-making process as to cash mobilization, movement, and investment outlets.

A carefully centralized system can afford the MNC the following advantages:

1. Holding cash balances maintained throughout the system to a minimum.
2. Enabling the center, to which all cash positions are periodically reported by affiliates, to invest all excess cash resources to obtain the maximum possible return.
3. Enabling the center, to which all information of future needs is relayed by affiliates, to respond expeditiously to liquidity requirements throughout the system.
4. Permitting the center to make full utilization of a multilateral netting system, both interaffiliate and between the MNC and other corporations, so as to minimize transaction costs and currency exposure.
5. Enabling the center to use in an optimum fashion the various hedging strategies available to the firm so as to ensure enforcement of the MNC's foreign exchange exposure policies.
6. Enabling the MNC to achieve maximum utilization, within legal and administrative constraints, of the transfer pricing mechanism to enhance the profitability and the growth of the firm.

Some of the advantages cited above for a centralized cash management system need some elaboration. The next section of the report addresses itself to these points.

HOW DOES A CENTRALIZED SYSTEM HOLD OVERALL CASH BALANCES TO A MINIMUM?

Cash balances held by the parent and each of the affiliates are required to meet expected and anticipated cash disbursements. This *transaction* demand for cash balances, as it is called by economists, needs to be supplemented by a liquidity cushion to meet unexpected outlays, the *precautionary* demand for funds, as it is often called. In a decentralized system, each entity would reach its own decision as to the appropriate level of cash balances to meet the transaction and precautionary demands for funds. The affiliates are in most cases better equipped to make a decision as to what constitutes adequate balances in view of their intimate knowledge of their circumstances. This, however, does not mean that the cash positioning decision ought to be made in the field. Affiliates can obviously convey their estimates to the center, so that the final decision made then would take into account local requirements and circumstances.

The basic factor in reducing overall cash balances in a centralized system is a statistical principle which states that the variance of the whole is smaller than the sum of the variances of the parts. To illustrate, let us assume than an MNC has two affiliates, A and B, with the mean cash requirements and dispersions around the mean shown in Table 8-1, as measured by the standard deviation.

If it is assumed that the cash requirements in each location are normally and independently distributed, and that, as a policy, the MNC in question maintains in each location an additional precautionary balance equal to three standard divisions above the expected requirements, then the company as a whole must maintain total balances equivalent to $3,000,000. Maintaining three standard deviations above the mean virtually insures that all cash needs can be met.[1]

The same level of confidence (99.87 percent) can be achieved if all cash balances are maintained in a centralized depository, say the parent's, with a joint balance of $2,617,191. This sum represents the total expected cash needs of the three entities plus three standard deviations of the joint distribution. The variance of the aggregate probability distribution is the

Table 8-1.

LOCATION	EXPECTED CASH NEEDS	STANDARD DEVIATION	EXPECTED CASH NEEDS + 3 STANDARD DEVIATIONS
Parent	$1,000,000	$250,000	$1,750,000
Affiliate A	500,000	90,000	770,000
Affiliate B	300,000	60,000	480,000
Total	$1,800,000		$3,000,000

[1]Three standard deviations above and below the mean cover 99.87 percent of the area under a normal probability distribution. Thus, the chance of not being able to meet cash needs is only .13 percent.

sum of the individual variances, since the probability distributions are independent, as shown below:

$$\sqrt{(250{,}000)^2 + (90{,}000)^2 + (60{,}000)^2} = \$272{,}397$$

Thus centralizing cash balances in one depository will generate a total cash savings of $382,809, representing the difference between $3,000,000 and $1,800,000 + (3)($272,397). This is illustrated in Exhibit 8-1.

Most cash management systems have one or two central depositories or currency clearing centers located in prominent financial centers with well-developed financial markets and international banking facilities. Large U.S. multinational companies with two-center systems usually have one located in New York and the other in a European city such as Geneva or London. A one-center cash management system realizes more fully the benefits of centralization than a two-center system. However, the latter has the advantage of flexibility in responding more readily to the unexpected requirements of affiliates operating in the same general region.

It should be noted that MNCs sometimes maintain cash balances in locations where they have no affiliates or sales operations, if these locations are better situated to serve affiliates located in developing countries. Such is the case if these countries lack well-developed financial markets, or if they involve unacceptable exchange or political risks. In these situations, balances are usually kept in a financial center in the region and transferred in time to meet maturing obligations.

MULTILATERAL NETTING

Centralization of cash balances in a center to which all positions are reported periodically by affiliates permits the MNC to make full use of mul-

Exhibit 8-1. Total Cash Requirements—Centralized Depository (Parent)

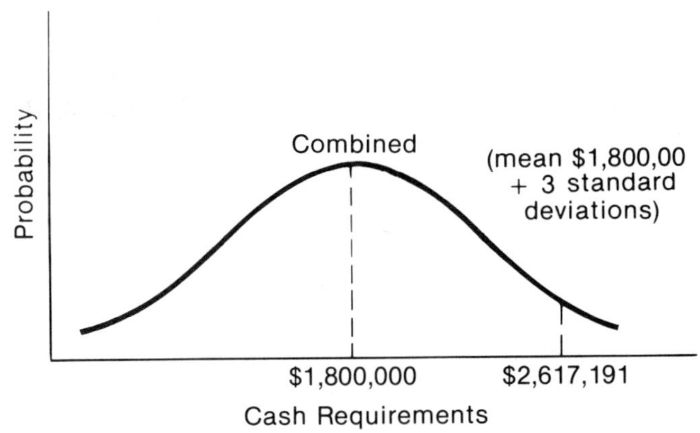

tilateral netting. Netting involves offsetting receivables against payables of the various entities, so that only the net amounts are eventually transferred among affiliates. An MNC can also utilize multilateral netting with outside firms and agencies.

Multilateral netting reduces overall transaction costs by eliminating a number of unnecessary conversion and transfer of currencies. Netting, therefore, entails a saving in both exchange conversion costs and transfer costs. It also entails a reduction of the unnecessary float, funds that are in the process of being transferred among affiliates instead of being invested by the center. It has also been argued that multilateral netting can help avoid the possibility of *mislocated funds,* that is, funds placed in the wrong currency, by enabling the center to monitor current and short-term anticipated cash needs, and to devise an effective cash mobilization system. The essence of an effective cash mobilization system is the use of information available to the center in the form of near-term cash budgets to cover deficits throughout the system, and to reach appropriate borrowing/investing decisions in light of expectations about future cash needs, interest rates, and possible currency fluctuations. Computerized techniques have been developed to provide MNCs with optimal solutions for cash management problems under varying circumstances.[2]

To illustrate multilateral payments netting system, let us assume that IDPT has at a certain point of time the payments shown in the matrix in Exhibit 8-2.

Exhibit 8-2. IDPT Illustrative International Payments Matrix (thousands of dollars)

RECEIVING AFFILIATES	PAYING AFFILIATES				TOTAL RECEIPTS
	U.S.	Mexico	Taiwan	South Korea	
United States	–	700	250	500	1450
Mexico	700	–	300	250	1250
Taiwan	100	300	–	700	1100
South Korea	300	250	400	–	950
Total Payments	1100	1250	950	1450	4750

	Payment	Receipt	Net Payment	Net Receipt
United States	1100	1450	–	350
Mexico	1250	1250	–	–
Taiwan	950	1100	–	150
South Korea	1450	950	500	–
Total	4750	4750	500	500

[2]See: Business International Corporation, *Computerized Corporate Statistical Tables, New Techniques in International Exposure and Cash Management,* Vol. 5 (New York, 1976).

If all positions are communicated to the central depository (assumed to be the parent in this illustration), settlement will be effected by having the center (in the U.S.) instructing the affiliate in South Korea to pay the equivalent of $350,000 to the parent and $150,000 to the affiliate in Taiwan. Netting in this theoretical illustration has the following advantages:

1. Transaction costs involved in 12 conversions of currencies in the spot market were reduced to two transactions.
2. Transfer costs on the equivalent of $4,750,000 of funds were reduced to the cost of transferring only the equivalent of $500,000.
3. IDPT reduced considerably the float in the form of needless transfers and, thus, could generate some return on these funds in the form of interest earned or avoided.

CASH MOBILIZATION

As a by-product of centralization, the center will be in possession of valuable information relating to the cash position of each affiliate, as well as each affiliate's need for liquid resources in the near term, say during the next week or fortnight. This information provides the basis for a short-term periodical cash budget, or cash forecast, which will enable the manager of the central pool to reach decisions relating to:

1. Breaking down the aggregate inflows and outflows of each affiliate by currency. This will facilitate netting operations.
2. Determining the timing and amount of funds required by the deficit units. This will make possible an efficient mobilization of cash.
3. Determining the need for borrowing and required maturities.
4. Determining the amount and duration of balances available for investment.

To illustrate a periodic cash forecast for IDPT's three affiliates shown in Exhibit 8-2 earlier, let us assume that the manager of the currency clearing center in New York requested and received the weekly cash reports from each affiliate as shown in Exhibit 8-3.

All balances in the cash forecasts shown in Exhibit 8-3 are reported in U.S. dollars, with local currencies translated at exchange rates designated by the central depository. The managers of the central depository are now in position to assemble the individual reports into a composite report for the system as a whole in order to ascertain the amount and direction of cash mobilization. This is shown in Exhibit 8-4.

Deficit units may be asked to cover their positions by drawing on their local banking overdraft facilities, while surplus units may be asked to transfer the excess cash to the center for investment. Alternatively, depending on the ground rules under which the managers of the central depository

Exhibit 8-3. Weekly Cash Reports Submitted by Affiliates of IDPT (thousands of U.S. dollars)

AFFILIATE: MEXICO

Cash Position on May 1, 1985, −300 Forecast Activity during May	Deposit	Disburse	Net
Week 1	175	50	125
Week 2	150	200	− 50
Week 3	300	120	180
Week 4	50	175	−125
Net for Period			+130

AFFILIATE: TAIWAN

Cash Position on May 1, 1985, +225 Forecast Activity during May	Deposit	Disburse	Net
Week 1	200	300	−100
Week 2	180	280	−100
Week 3	375	205	+170
Week 4	80	120	− 40
Net for Period			− 70

AFFILIATE: SOUTH KOREA

Cash Position on May 1, 1985, +50 Forecast Activity during May	Deposit	Disburse	Net
Week 1	200	20	180
Week 2	325	175	150
Week 3	80	100	− 20
Week 4	175	150	+ 25
Net for Period			+335

Exhibit 8-4. IDPT's Central Depository (U.S.) Reported Weekly Cash Position of Affiliates (thousands of U.S. dollars)

	CASH POSITIONS MAY 1, 1985			CASH FORECASTS (MAY)				
Affiliate	Available	Required	Diff	1st wk	2nd wk	3rd wk	4th wk	4 wk total
Mexico	−300	100	−400	125	− 50	180	−125	+130
Taiwan	+225	100	+125	−100	−100	+170	− 40	− 70
South Korea	+ 50	100	− 50	180	150	− 20	+ 25	+335
All reporting affiliates	− 25	+300	−325	+205	0	+330	−140	+395

operate, cash may be mobilized directly from a surplus to a deficit unit. For instance, at the beginning of the period, the Mexican and South Korean affiliates will cover their positions by local overdrafts, while the affiliate in Taiwan may be asked to keep its cash, since it is anticipating a deficit during the first week of May. The South Korean affiliate will probably be asked to transfer its surplus cash during the first and second weeks in May. The position of the Taiwan affiliate will swing nearly into balance after the first week in May, while the Mexican affiliate will be able to pay back the equivalent of $125 million in bank overdrafts.

The system as a whole is forecast to generate a cash surplus of $395 million, part of which will be used to correct the overall deficit position recorded on May 1, while the balance will be received throughout the month of May by the center for investment. If the system as a whole had been forecast to sustain a sizable deficit during the month of May, then some borrowing by the center would have been necessitated. In that eventuality cash would have been mobilized from the center to the affiliates to redress their deficit positions.

The system described in this illustration was somewhat simplified in order to highlight the working of the cash mobilization system. In particular, forecasts would have included breakdown by currency (for hedging purposes) and interaffiliate transactions (for netting purposes).

HEDGING STRATEGY

Centralized cash management permits optimal utilization of the hedging techniques described in Chapter 5 in line with overall hedging strategy which the MNC has adopted. This should not imply, however, that all hedging operations are or should be undertaken by the manager of the centralized depository. The center needs accurate and complete information to formulate an overall strategy. Implementation of the strategy, or parts of it, is often delegated to the operating units.

Data such as presented in Exhibits 8-3 and 8-4 should be in detailed form, including currency breakdown to help determine to what extent forward market hedging is desirable or feasible, whether exposure can be reduced by leading and lagging transfers, and to what extent borrowing in certain markets can contribute to lessening currency exposure.

TRANSFER PRICING

A centralized cash management system, with the vast amount of reports and information available to the managers of the central depository, also permits the full utilization of the transfer pricing mechanism to further the objectives of the MNC.[3] Transfer pricing, the establishment of prices for the

[3]Transfer pricing was covered in detail in Chapter 6.

intracorporate exchange of inputs, services, and technology, provides an effective tool for positioning of funds. A parent company wishing to remove funds from a particular affiliate can follow a high-markup policy for inputs and components supplied to that affiliate. Transfer pricing also provides alternative means of transferring funds from affiliates located in countries with restrictive foreign exchange control systems.

Part Two — Expediting the Collection Process

PROBLEMS OF INTERNATIONAL CASH MANAGEMENT

International cash management for the MNC is complicated by the absence, in most locations, of effective tools to expedite transfers and by the great variations in the practices of financial institutions. Many of the services and systems that are used by domestic cash managers in the U.S. are not available abroad. Balance reporting systems are generally primitive and lockbox collection services are not available in most countries. Moreover, many international banks view float as part of their compensation structure, forcing the cash managers to endure exceptionally long delays in collecting and moving funds. There are certain areas, however, of cash management abroad which are more advanced than U.S. cash management. A large proportion of corporate-to-corporate payments in Europe, the Middle East, and Asia are electronic, in contrast to the paper-based payment system, which is still predominant in the United States.[4]

Cash collection and fund transfers between the company's foreign subsidiaries are expedited by a number of services and systems. Wherever available, the cash manager should seriously weigh the benefits which his firm can derive from using them against their cost. These systems and services are explained briefly below:

Electronic funds transfer systems. Most banks abroad offer their clients electronic funds transfer facilities and transfers by telex. Since the geographic spread of customers is rather diverse, mail times for receiving check payments can be very long. Exhibit 8-5, which is based on a recent independent study, indicates mail times between New York and major financial centers abroad, as well as between these centers. Because of the relatively long time involved, payments of large amounts by check are discouraged by most MNCs.

Electronic funds transfer systems have their pitfalls. There are diverse interrelationships among domestic and foreign banks, and, in most instances, the actual transfer route is unknown to the corporate cash man-

[4]See Steven F. Maier, "International Cash Management Problems: An Overview," *Journal of Cash Management,* Vol. 3, no. 1 (February-March 1983), pp. 14–15.

Exhibit 8-5. Some Examples of International Mail Times (in days)

MAILING POINTS	RECEIVING POINTS						
	New York	London	Brussels	Frankfurt	Hong Kong	Tokyo	Panama
London	7.0		4.5	6			
Paris	6.0	3.5	4.0	4			
Brussels	5.0	4.5	2.5	3			
Rome	10.0	9.0	10.0	11.5			
Geneva	5.0	4.0	3.0	3.0			
Amsterdam	7.0	4.0	3.0	3.0			
Madrid	6.5	3.5	4.0	5.5			
Milan	8.0	4.5	3.5	4.0			
Athens	10.0	9.0	5.5	7.5			
Taipei	11.0				6.0	5.0	
Hong Kong	6.5				2.5	5.0	
Tokyo	7.5				5.0	2.5	
Seoul	9.5				8.0	4.0	
Singapore	11.5				9.0	4.5	
Sydney	8.0				8.0	6.5	
San Pavlo	7.0						7.5
Rio de Janerio	6.5						7.0
Buenos Aires	12.5						5.5
Lima	9.5						6.5
Mexico City	8.0						6.0

Source: Kenneth L. Parkinson, "Dealing With the Problems of International Cash Management," *Journal of Cash Management,* Vol. 3, No. 1 (Feb/Mar 1983), p. 18.

ager. This circuitous transfer path, often involving several banks in different locations, increases the possibility of a processing error, resulting in misrouted transfers. Incoming receipts (transfers to the U.S. in dollars) are less likely to be misrouted than outgoing transfers, since the final step of the incoming transfer is made through the Clearing House Interbank Payment System (CHIPS). CHIPS is owned and operated by the New York Clearing House Association, comprised of twelve New York banks.

Lockbox systems. A lockbox system is a device used widely in the U.S. to expedite the check clearing process by having customers forward their checks to a designated postal box in the company's name. Mail received in these boxes is collected one or more times daily by a local bank or a branch of a multinational bank. Checks are processed expeditiously so that the MNC is given credit for the funds at the currency mobilization center usually in one or two days, thus reducing the check clearing process by as much as three to four days. Lockbox arrangements are not as widely used abroad, due in part to the use of noncheck means of payment, such as notes or drafts in many overseas locations. As a result, banks overseas have not yet attained the degree of sophistication attained by their U.S. counterparts in developing effective cash management services for MNCs.

Value dating. Value dating is a negotiated banking service whereby the bank credits the account of the MNC with the value of deposited checks after the lapse of a specified number of days (depending on the location on which the checks are drawn), irrespective of how long it would take to clear them. On the disbursement side, European banks establish a back value date for all items disbursed in international transactions, that is, banks debit a company's account usually two days before foreign funds are made available.

Value dating of checks and drafts deposited for collection is illustrated in Exhibit 8-6 for a sample of countries. The striking feature of the arrangements shown in this exhibit is the wide range of services offered even within the same city. This, however, is not surprising given the nature of value dating as a negotiated arrangement.

Unlike U.S. banks, most European banks charge a company's account immediately for local disbursements, and back-date one to two days for foreign disbursements. This practice gives the bank, instead of the company, the advantage of the float. In addition, most banks charge their customers for transfer services based on a percentage of the amount being transferred. These charges are also negotiable, and may be waived for large clients. Both U.S.- and European-based MNCs surveyed by Business International Corporations cited value-dating practices as their main complaint about international banking services.[5]

Exhibit 8-6. Examples of Typical Value-dating Arrangements for Receipts in Days

	CHECKS		NOTES/DRAFTS	
Country	Local	Outside	Local	Outside
Italy (Rome)	1	2–3	7–13	10–14
United Kingdom	1–3	1–3	N/A[1]	N/A[1]
France	1–2	3–5	2–4	4–5
Brazil	0–1	0–1	7	N/A[1]
Malaysia	1	2	N/A[1]	N/A[1]

[1]N/A — Not available.

Source: Kenneth L. Parkinson, "Dealing with the Problems of International Cash Management," *Journal of Cash Management,* Vol. 3, No. 1 (February/March 1983), p. 20.

[5]Business International Corporation, *Computerized Corporate Statistical Tables,* Table 5.

Other procedures for expediting the collection process. By prior arrangement, some MNCs debit their customers' accounts held with their banks (the MNC's bank) directly. This is done usually in the form of preauthorized periodic payments up to a maximum amount. This arrangement does not only eliminate mail delay, but also saves clearing time by initiating the debiting to the customer's account a stated number of days before the due date. It is usually resorted to when there are only a limited number of large accounts, particularly in locations where the check-clearing process is quite lengthy.

Part Three—Design of Cash Management Systems

Cash management systems, spurred by the high interest rate environment of the late 1970s and the early 1980s, have become the vogue among medium and large corporations, both domestic and multinational. Large multinational banks as well as specialized firms are now providing corporations with customized cash management systems designed to suit their needs and requirements.

A typical cash management system combines elements of the services offered by banks, such as those discussed in the previous section, with an international communication network, based on the latest state of the arts developments in funds transfer and balance reporting. An essential part of this system is international balance and transaction detail reporting available through many multinational U.S. banks, as well as a number of large banks abroad. Balance transaction reporting is yet to catch on among overseas banks, partly because the most popular international communication networks were not designed to include this service.

A customized cash management system for reporting and monitoring overseas cash management activities is shown in Exhibit 8-7. This system combines balance reporting capabilities with the documentation reporting process. This combination enables central cash managers, who will be the recipient of these pieces of information, to devote the bulk of their efforts to analytical activities, such as comparison of bank costs in the same country, or comparison of bank costs among countries. Review should also be made of the adequacy of reports from the field, so that missing information may be included in future reports.

Part Four—Designing a Cash Management System for IDPT

Data Network, Inc. is of the opinion that neither current need of IDPT nor potential requirements within the next four or five years justify an elaborate and highly sophisticated cash management system. An adequate system can be best built around the services now provided to IDPT by Global Hanover and Trust Co. and its branches and correspondents abroad where IDPT has

Exhibit 8-7. Macrologic of System for Reporting and Monitoring Overseas Cash Management Activities

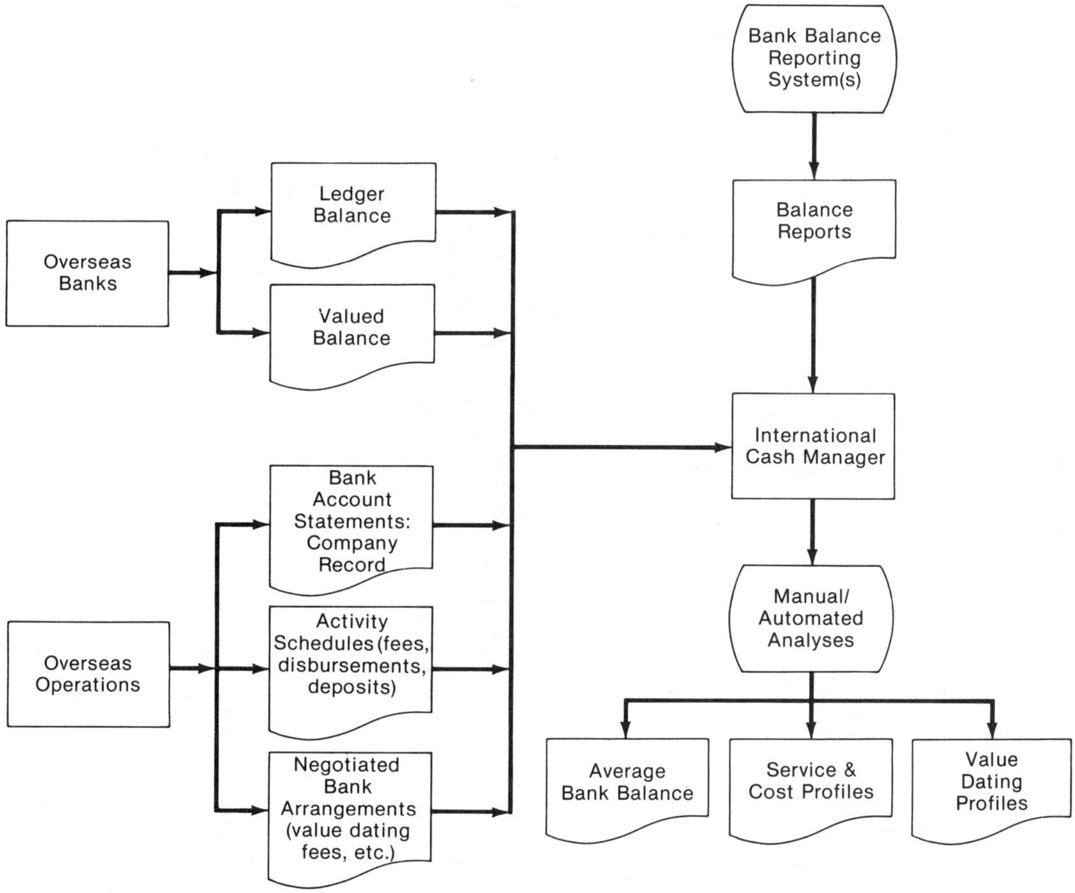

Source: Kenneth L. Parkinson, "Dealing with the Problems of International Cash Management," *Journal of Cash Management,* Vol. 3, No. 1 (February/March 1983), p. 24.

operations. The proposed system shown in Exhibit 8-8 has the following features which quote excerpts from Data Networks, Inc.'s report to IDPT.

1. An international cash management center located in New York, where IDPT is based. The international cash manager is to coordinate closely with the domestic cash manager. Lack of such coordination is one of the drawbacks of the current arrangement.

   We have not proposed an overseas cash or currency clearing center, which many MNCs maintain, due to the fact that IDPT's major overseas operations, located in Mexico, South Korea, and Taiwan, are so geographically scattered that they are best served

Exhibit 8-8. IDPT Proposed International Cash Management System

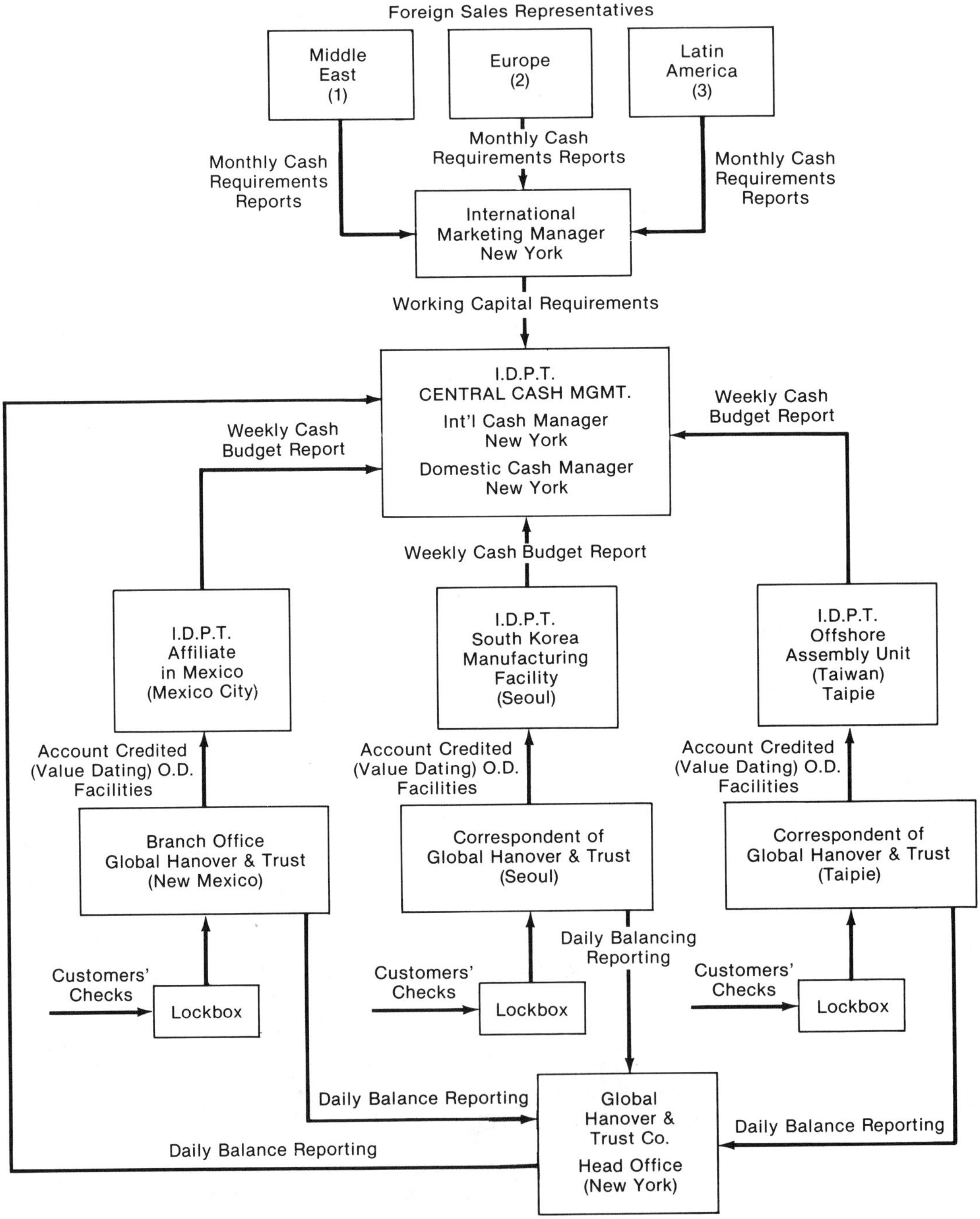

by a center located in New York. Moreover, we do not recommend at this stage linking IDPT's sales representations in Europe, the Middle East, and South America into the cash management system. The existing arrangements, whereby these representations are supervised by the marketing division, and your policy of invoicing exports in U.S. dollars payable against an irrevocable letter of credit seem to be functioning satisfactorily. The International Marketing Manager, however, should screen and communicate the modest working capital requirements of these offices to the International Cash Manager.

2. Each of the three affiliates requires that all customers in the country or the region in which it operates make payment by check to a designated lockbox in the city where the affiliate is located. These lockboxes are to be opened daily by the representative of IDPT's bankers in each city (Global Hanover branch office in Mexico City and Global Hanover's correspondents in Seoul and Taipei). The checks are to be processed and the account of the respective affiliate is to be credited with the proceeds in accordance with the value dating system agreed upon by IDPT and Global Hanover and Trust Co. Such a system is now operational for the Mexican affiliate, and a similar arrangement needs to be worked out for the other two affiliates.

   All temporary cash requirements of the affiliates are to be met by drawing on an overdraft facility arranged with their respective local bank. Each affiliate must file a weekly report (by cable or telex) with the international cash manager covering the following points:

   a. Cash position on the date of the report, including bank balances.
   b. Cash budget for the week ahead, including anticipated use of overdraft facilities.
   c. Any intracompany or interaffiliate receivables or payables, and any currency exposure (other than the local currency) on the date of the report.

3. Global Hanover head office in New York receives daily balance and transaction reports from their branch in Mexico City and correspondents in Seoul and Taipei. These reports are to be communicated immediately to the International Cash Manager. All balances deemed in excess of anticipated near-term requirements of the affiliates are to be electronically transferred to IDPT's account with the head office at the request of the International Cash Manager.

4. The International Cash Manager, being the repository of daily balance and transaction reports from the bank, weekly cash budget reports from affiliates, and monthly cash requirement reports of the sales representative offices, are always in a position to mobilize cash effectively throughout the system. This manager's

close coordination with the Domestic Cash Manager will help optimize the management of liquid funds for the entire company. Moreover, the weekly cash budgets of affiliates will make possible netting of intracompany and interaffiliate claims with a view to minimizing currency exposure and transaction costs. An illustration of multilateral netting system, patterned with some modifications after the system used by International Harvester, is presented in Exhibit 8-9.

Exhibit 8-9. Suggested Fortnightly Multilateral Netting System for IDPT

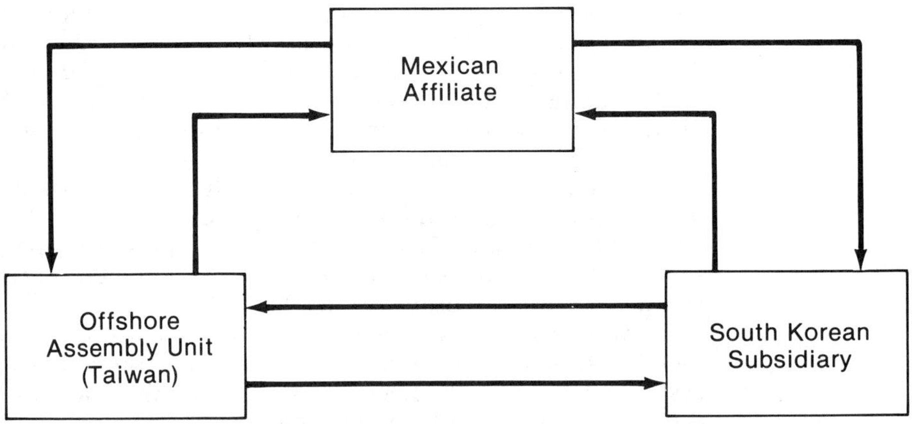

(a) Receivables and payables reported to currency center in New York on the 5th and 25th of each month.

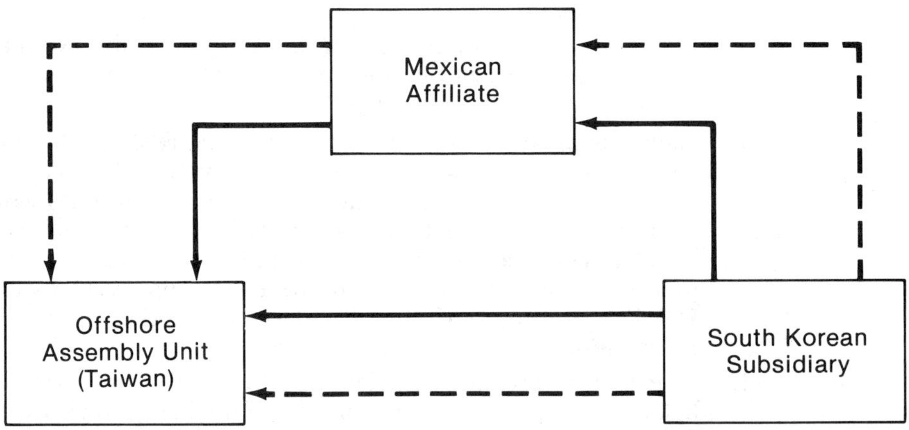

(b) Net payables/receivables (broken lines) and actual cash flows (solid lines) made on the 10th and 30th of each month.

The proposed multilateral netting system works as follows:

a. Twice each month (on the fifth and twenty-fifth of each month), affiliates report their receivables from and payables to each other to the International Cash Manager in New York.
b. The International Cash Manager converts all receivables and payables into U.S. dollars at the exchange rates prevailing on the fifth and twenty-fifth of each month.
c. After netting receivables against payables, the International Cash Manager instructs the affiliates with net payables as to how much they owe and to whom. The paying affiliates then make settlement on the tenth and thirtieth of each month. Net receiving affiliates need not take any action.
d. This fortnightly netting and settlement arrangement may be used with some flexibility, depending on the judgment of the International Cash Manager. For example, leading and lagging may be permitted up to one week.
e. Parent-affiliate receivables and payables are not handled through this netting arrangement. As indicated earlier, all sales proceeds and overdraft requirements of affiliates are handled through the local banks. Excess balances are transferred electronically, at the request of the International Cash Manager, to IDPT's account with the head office of Global Hanover and Trust Co. Other affiliate transfers for royalties, fees, interest, and dividends are also handled through the banking arrangements.

REVIEW QUESTIONS

1. What are the major prerequisites of an effective cash management system? Could such a system be developed without incorporating the firm's exchange exposure and financing policies?
2. What strategy should the international financial manager follow with respect to positioning of funds if his objectives were
   a. to minimize transaction costs?
   b. to minimize foreign exchange risk?
   c. to minimize the political risk?
   d. to insure that payments due from affiliates are effected on time?
   e. to maximize the rate of return on investment of liquid assets?
3. What is meant by "cash mobilization"? Why is centralization of cash management a necessary prerequisite to effective cash mobilization?
4. Given the following data about the cash requirements of an MNC and its affiliates:

LOCATION	MEAN EXPECTED CASH NEEDS ($ MILLIONS)	STANDARD DEVIATION ($ MILLIONS)
Parent	350	50
Affiliate X	75	15
Affiliate Y	120	34
Affiliate Z	95	25

Assuming that the MNC wishes to insure that all cash needs of the parent and affiliates can be met on time;

a. How much cash would be needed by each entity under a decentralized cash management system?

b. How much savings would accrue from a centralized system? Show how these savings are possible.

5. Show how an intracorporate multilateral netting is a necessary component of an effective cash mobilization system. Identify the savings that would accrue from multilateral netting conducted by a central depository.

6. How does value dating fit in an MNC's cash management system? What measures can be taken by the firm to overcome the limitations imposed by the practices of the banking community in the countries where it operates?

7. How would you adapt the system proposed for IDPT (see Exhibit 8-8) to suit the requirements of a U.S. MNC which has three affiliates all located in Western Europe? Sales are confined to the countries where the affiliates are located and are denominated in the currency of the affiliate. (*Hint.* Consider setting up a currency center in Europe, London for example.) Would the role of the firm's bank differ in this case from IDPT's bank?

REVIEW PROBLEMS

A U.S. multinational firm maintains a multilateral interaffiliate netting system, with netting operations conducted by a currency center, which is also in charge of investing the excess cash resources of all affiliates. The affiliates report their payables to other affiliates on the fifteenth of each month. The currency center issues instructions to net paying affiliates on the twentieth of each month, using market exchange rates on that date. Given the data in Table 8-2,

Table 8-2.

AFFILIATE	AMOUNTS DUE TO OTHER AFFILIATES	FUNDS AVAILABLE	FUNDS REQUIRED FOR OPERATIONS MAY 15–31, 1985
	Position as of May 15, 1985		
Affiliate A (£)	FF2,000,000 to B DM3,500,000 to C	£10,000,000	£5,000,000
Affiliate B (FF)	£1,500,000 to A DM2,000,000 to C	FF27,000,000	FF45,000,000
Affiliate C (DM)	£3,000,000 to A FF10,000,000 to B	DM45,000,000	DM15,000,000

1. Devise a netting system for the firm showing amounts and currencies of actual transfers made on May 20, 1985.
2. The firm's cash management policy requires that all cash surplus affiliates transfer their surpluses to the center (on the fifteenth and the last day of each month). The center handles all money market investments. Deficit affiliates are asked to cover their temporary needs by drawing on their overdraft facilities with local banks. What will be the total resources (in U.S. dollars) available for investment during the second half of May? Which affiliate (or affiliates) will be using local credit lines and in what amounts?
3. Outline the advantages (and disadvantages if any) which the firm derives from the netting plan developed in Problem 1, and from the centralized investment feature covered in Problem 2. Spot exchange rates on May 20, 1985 were

£1.00 = $1.45
$1.00 = FF6.50
$1.00 = DM2.35

BIBLIOGRAPHY

BOND, G., "Is Your Company Cashing In Internationally?" *Accountancy* (September 1982), pp. 68–70.

BUSINESS INTERNATIONAL, *The State of the Art, New Techniques in International Exposure and Cash Management,* Vols. I–V. New York: Business International Corporation, 1977.

"Cash Management in Europe, Part II: What Companies are Doing," *Business Europe* (December 28, 1973), p. 416.

COHEN, F. L., "Accelerating Foreign Remittances and Collection," *Cashflow* (May 1981), pp. 36–40.

GOELTZ, R. K., "Managing Liquid Funds Internationally," *Columbia Journal of World Business* (July-August 1972), pp. 59–65.

KESSLER, J., "Cashing In on Cash Management," *Financial World* (March 15, 1982), pp. 56–59.

LEARY, N., "Minimizing Export Cash Flow Delays," *Management Accounting* (April 1984), pp. 33–35.

MATER, S. F., "International Cash Management Problems: An Overview," *Journal of Cash Management,* Vol. 3, no. 1 (February/March 1983), pp. 14–15.

MCDERMOTT, K., "International Money Management," speech to the American Management Association, February 22, 1971.

NALIN, D. F., "Cash Planning and Managing Corporate Finance," *Euromoney* (February 1976), pp. 76ff.

OBERSTEINER, E., "Should the Foreign Affiliate Remit Dividends or Reinvest?" *Financial Management* (Spring 1973), pp. 88–93.

OOSTHOEK, W. N., "International Cash Management Consulting: A Conceptual Framework for Analyzing Corporations," *Magazine of Bank Administration* (February 1985), pp. 71–75.

PAKENHAM, K. J., "New Way to Measure Money Management Performance," *Euromoney* (March 1982), p. 150.

PARKINSON, K. L., "Dealing With the Problems of International Cash Management," *Journal of Cash Management,* Vol. 3, no. 1 (February/March 1983), pp. 18–24.

PERHAM, J. C., "The Mysterious Market in Blocked Accounts," *Dun's Review* (October 1976), pp. 93ff.

PRINDL, A. R., "International Money Management II: Systems and Techniques," *Euromoney* (October 1971).

QUIJANO, C. J., and A. K. MATHRANI, "Managing Corporate Cash in Europe," *Euromoney* (October 1971).

RUTENBERG, D. P., "Maneuvering Liquid Assets in a Multinational Company: Formulation and Deterministic Solution Procedures," *Management Science* (June 1970), pp. B-671–684.

SHAPIRO, A. C., "International Cash Management: The Determination of Multicurrency Cash Balances," *Journal of Financial and Quantitative Analysis* (December 1976), pp. 893–900.

______, "Payments Netting in International Cash Management," *Journal of International Business Studies* (Fall 1978), pp. 51–58.

SILVERBERG, J. I. L., "More Effective Cash Management," *CA Magazine* (October 1982), pp. 66–68.

SIMONSON, N., "Moving Towards Cash Management in Japan," *ABA Banking Journal* (January 1981), p. 48.

WUNDERLISCH, K., "Centralized Cash Management Systems for the Multinational Enterprise," *Management International Review* (June 1973), pp. 43–57.

ZENOFF, D. B., "International Cash Management: Why It Is Important and How to Make It Work," *Worldwide Projects and Installations Planning* (July-August 1973).

APPENDIX E

Multinational Cash Management Policies A Survey*

INTRODUCTION

Financial management techniques vary among firms depending on the complexity of their multinational organizational structures. Multinational firms face volatile and highly unpredictable currency relationships which require efficient hedging strategies to counterbalance the impact of exchange rate fluctuations on their corporate cash flows and profitability. Many large multinational corporations have evolved and refined their exposure management policies and strategies over the past ten years due to the increasing volatility of the currency markets.

Financial managers have also developed highly sophisticated international cash management and fund positioning strategies. These strategies have to be carefully integrated with exchange exposure management policies to achieve corporate objectives at a minimum cost.

In a paper we presented last year at this conference, we examined the empirical results of the authors' survey of primary financial management techniques dealing with foreign exchange exposure. This paper will present the second part of the survey dealing with international cash management and fund positioning strategies of multinational companies. The paper also examines the organic and inseparable interrelation between the two sets of strategies.

*Based on a survey of 200 MNCs conducted by the authors in 1984 with the help of Professor John Wingender of Oklahoma State University. The results of the survey were presented in the 1986 meeting of the Midwest Finance Association held in Chicago (March 19–22, 1986).

AUTHORS' SURVEY

The authors sent questionnaires during April-August 1984 to 200 U.S. companies that were identified as multinational corporations according to the selection criteria. After the initial responses, a second mailing was sent to the nonrespondents. A total of 96 responses were received. Thirteen responses were discarded for a number of reasons, predominantly those corporations indicating that, as a matter of policy, they routinely refuse to answer all questionnaires except those demanded of them by law. This left 83 completed questionnaires out of 187 for an overall response ratio of 44 percent. This ratio compares favorably with MNC surveys presented in the literature. Most previous studies have had response ratios of 40 percent or less.

The second part of the questionnaire, which is the area covered in this paper, sought data relating to factors that MNCs take into account in positioning funds internationally, the degree of centralization of international cash management, techniques used in the cash management system, the extent of the use of the transfer pricing mechanism, and considerations deemed important by the MNC in making the transfer pricing decision.

Despite the heightened interest in this field, a survey of the literature indicates relative scarcity of empirical research in this area. Most of the earlier survey focused on the management of foreign exchange exposure, primarily translation and transaction exposures. These surveys, which we reviewed briefly in last year's paper, touched only peripherally corporate international cash management strategies. This is not surprising, considering that interest in such strategies and systems dates back only to the advent of floating exchange rates in 1973, coupled with the high and volatile interest rate environment of the late 1970s and early 1980s.

OBJECTIVES OF INTERNATIONAL CASH MANAGEMENT

MNCs in the survey were asked to list in the order of importance the major factors which determine positioning of funds internationally. The responses indicate that the uppermost consideration in determining fund positioning appears to be the safety of funds, reflecting mainly concern about currency exposure and political risk of the host country. This factor was ranked first or second by about 63 percent of responding MNCs, and was mentioned as an important factor by about 92 percent of total respondents. This shows that financial managers are keenly aware of the necessity of integrating cash management and exchange exposure management strategies.

Liquidity, the ability to mobilize funds to the locations where they are needed quickly at a relatively low cost, was ranked first or second by about

58 percent of respondents, and was listed as an important factor by 82 percent of the total. Liquidity, in an international cash management context, is the absence of exchange controls and restrictions on transfers, which is essentially a function of the degree of political risk and transaction costs.

The preoccupation of a number of multinational financial managers in our sample with this risk is such that, as a matter of corporate policy, foreign operating affiliates are rarely, if ever, left with excess cash positions, that is, liquid funds in excess of working capital needs. Excess funds are immediately repatriated to the parent in the United States, or transferred to a money center, or to a financial subsidiary of the MNC elsewhere. Almost one-half of responding firms indicated that they pursue such a strategy in varying degrees to minimize exchange rate as well as political exposure.

Tax considerations and yield were closely ranked as the third and fourth most important determinants of fund positioning strategies, ranked first or second by about 24 and 22 percent of respondents, respectively. Tax issues involve a number of considerations that the financial manager has to take into account. Among these are

1. The corporate income tax rate of the host country. Managers favor positioning of funds in tax havens which combine the attractiveness of low (or zero) tax rates with currency stability, and the existence of financial and communication services which would enable efficient mobilization of funds.
2. Tax withholding provisions of the host country and the existence or nonexistence of a tax treaty between the U.S. and the host country.
3. Taxability of repatriated income in the United States, and provisions with respect to tax credits for tax paid to or withheld by foreign taxing authorities.

Yield refers to comparative investment opportunities in localities where funds are positioned. Most financial managers compare yield on a fully hedged basis, that is, fully covered against the foreign exchange risk. In this sense, yield differentials reflect interest arbitrage opportunities which sometimes exist due to imperfections in exchange and money markets. Such opportunities are almost always taken advantage of by financial managers. However, since no forward market exists for most LDC currencies, no such fully hedged yield comparison is feasible in these circumstances. This also explains why this factor was ranked fourth behind safety, liquidity, and tax matters.

Ranked next are the cash needs of the U.S. parent and financial requirements of the affiliates. These two determinants are obviously closely related. Although fairly closely ranked by our respondents, financial requirements of the operating affiliates seem to outweigh the needs of the

U.S. parent companies as a determinant of cash positioning strategy. About 39 percent of respondents listed the former as an important factor, as against about 29 percent for the latter.

It must be noted that MNCs encounter conflicts not only among these factors, but also frequently within the same determinant. For example, safety and liquidity require that funds be transferred to the parent in the United States, but that may conflict with other factors such as maximizing yield, minimizing the overall tax burden, or meeting the requirements of the affiliates. Achieving liquidity may involve large transaction costs, which would decrease the sums available for fund mobilization. Minimizing transaction costs requires that funds be left in the currencies and localities where they are generated, whereas quick mobilization dictates that funds should be positioned where they will be needed.

CENTRALIZATION OF CASH MANAGEMENT POLICIES

Response to the survey section relating to the organizational structure of international cash management indicates that MNCs tend to have highly centralized cash management structures. Seventy-two percent of respondents indicated that they have such a system in place. This system is typically characterized by one or two (in some cases three or more) centralized depositories in major financial centers, serving also as currency clearing centers. Cities mentioned frequently by our respondents as such money centers are in the order of frequency: for the United States—New York, Chicago, San Francisco; for Europe—London, Frankfurt, Zurich, Amsterdam; for the Far East—Hong Kong and Singapore. Interestingly, none of the respondents listed a Latin American city as a money center, perhaps due to the high inflation rate and the external debt crisis which characterize the economies of these countries.

The increasing trend toward highly centralized depositories is in accord with financial and statistical theory, and seems to have been accelerated by the high interest rate environment of the past ten years. In addition to one or more centralized depository and currency clearing centers, such a system typically includes the following features:

1. Affiliates hold only minimum cash balances at the local level; all excess cash is remitted to the centralized depository.
2. Affiliates use local overdraft facilities to meet unexpected cash requirements.
3. Investment of all excess funds is managed by the centralized depository.
4. A cash mobilization program is in place to move funds about the organization to the locations where they are needed quickly and efficiently.

5. A multilateral netting system with all reports of positions communicated periodically to the currency clearing center is used. After netting interaffiliate claims, this center typically sends instructions to those affiliates with net paying positions to make transfers directly to net receiving affiliates. Multilateral netting reduces not only currency exposure, but also transaction costs, by cutting down both the number and amounts of transfers.

Our survey shows that about one-half of responding MNCs maintain centralized depositories which also serve as currency clearing centers. However, the frequency of respondents reporting the presence of some specialized features of a centralized system was somewhat lower. These frequencies are shown in Exhibit 1.

Exhibit 1. Respondents Reporting Certain Features of a Centralized Cash Management System

FEATURES	NO. OF RESPONDENTS	% OF TOTAL RESPONDENTS*
Respondents with centralized cash management systems	52	72.2
Respondents with centralized depositories in major financial centers	41	56.9
Respondents reporting that all investments of excess funds are effected by centralized depositories	33	45.8
Respondents having a cash mobilization system	29	40.3
Respondents reporting that all or most borrowing by affiliates is obtained through overdraft facilities from local banks	29	40.3
Respondents having a multilateral netting system	24	33.3
Respondents reporting that currency clearing centers issue instructions for making payments to net paying affiliates only	13	18.1
Respondents using interdivisional leading and lagging to facilitate the working of the "netting system"	11	15.3

*Out of 83 completed responses, only 72 completed the section dealing with centralized cash management systems.

OTHER FEATURES OF A CASH MANAGEMENT SYSTEM

An international cash management system also typically includes several other features to expedite collection of receivables and to delay, within acceptable limits, cash disbursements. These features include:

1. Electronic fund transfer systems to overcome relatively long mail time involved in international payments. A large proportion of corporate payments in Europe, the Middle East, and Asia are electronic, in contrast to the paper-based payment system which still predominates in the United States.
2. Lockbox systems which reduce the check clearing process by one to four days, depending on the location on which checks are drawn. Lockbox arrangements are not as widely used outside the United States, due in part to the use of noncheck means of payment.
3. Value dating whereby the bank credits the account of the MNC with the value of deposited checks after the lapse of a specified number of days (depending on the location on which checks are drawn), irrespective of how long it would take to clear them.
4. Preauthorized debits to customer's account held with the MNC's bank up to an agreed maximum amount.
5. Controlled disbursement to maximize the float through the use of drafts, or drawing checks on banks that are remote from the payees' location.

The 52 respondents in our survey which indicated that they had a centralized cash management system reported also the use of the facilities in Exhibit 2 to speed up the collection process.

TRANSFER PRICING

A centralized cash management system, with the vast amount of reports and information available to the managers of the central depository, also permits the full utilization of the transfer pricing mechanism to further the objectives of the multinational firm. Transfer pricing—the establishment of administratively determined prices for intracorporate exchange of inputs, services, and technology—provides an effective tool for positioning of funds. This mechanism has been used by multinational firms to achieve a number of objectives, including siphoning off funds from high-tax locations.

Most of the MNCs surveyed (about 70 percent) said either they did not use, or seldom if at all used, the transfer pricing mechanism to facilitate transfer of funds among affiliates and from affiliates to parent. Only eight percent of respondents indicated that they used it frequently. This is in line

Exhibit 2.

FEATURE	NO. OF RESPONDENTS USING THE FACILITY	% OF TOTAL RESPONDENTS*
Lockboxes	47	65.3
Electronic fund transfer systems	36	50.0
Cable remittances	35	48.6
Mobilization centers	13	18.1
Direct debiting of customers	11	15.3
Value dating	10	13.9

*Only 72 respondents answered the section dealing with centralized cash management systems.

with the findings of earlier surveys and reflects, to an unascertainable degree, the traditional reluctance of MNCs to reveal the extent or frequency of the use of transfer pricing, mainly due to implications of tax avoidance or evasion.

Exhibit 3. The "Transfer Pricing Mechanism"

FREQUENCY OF USE	NUMBER OF RESPONDENTS	MOTIVATION	NUMBER OF RESPONDENTS
Very frequently	0	Fund positioning	11
Frequently	6	Tax considerations	21
Occasionally	18	Cash flow considerations	12
Seldom if at all	17	To deal with problems relating to tariffs and quotas	3
Not used	38	Managerial incentives	1
Total	79	Bargaining power with suppliers or financial institutions	0
		Market and competitive conditions in the foreign country	6
		Other considerations	3
		Total	57*

*A number of respondents must have checked two or more motivating factors, as only 41 respondents said that they used transfer pricing with varying frequency.

Among respondents who used transfer pricing, the primary motive appears to be tax considerations, followed by cash flow and fund positioning considerations. Other motivations for the transfer pricing decision appear to be of minor importance. Responses to the questionnaire's section dealing with transfer pricing are summarized in Exhibit 3.

SUMMARY AND CONCLUSIONS

1. Multinational firms are increasingly using centralized and more sophisticated cash management systems, probably in response to the high and volatile interest environment of the late 1970s and early 1980s. Empirical evidence indicates that such systems are significantly more widely used than in the mid-1970s.
2. Positioning of funds, an integral part of any cash management system, appears to be influenced mainly by factors relating to currency exposure risk, restrictions on the worldwide mobility of funds, and tax considerations. Maximization of yield (on a fully hedged basis) does not appear to be a dominant factor, and is not feasible in many instances, due to the nonexistence of a forward exchange market in the currencies of most LDCs.
3. International cash management policies are closely coordinated to currency exposure management, primarily through the role of central depositories, which siphon off funds from high-exposure locations and reduce the overall level of exposure by the use of multilateral netting.
4. MNCs remain reluctant to reveal substantive information on the nature and motivation of the "transfer pricing decision." On the basis of the limited response to this part of the survey, the primary motivation appears to be influencing the overall tax liability of the MNC and fund positioning. This conclusion is in line with the findings reached by surveys conducted in the early and mid-1970s, but is at variance with the findings of Professors Kim and Miller, who ranked overcoming restrictions on transfers and exchange controls in the host country as the primary motivation influencing the transfer pricing decision.

9

Eurocurrency and Eurobond Markets

INTRODUCTION

Eurocurrency markets are offshore markets where financial institutions conduct transactions which are denominated in other than the currency of the country where such institutions are located. Eurodollars, by far the largest segment of this market, are dollar-denominated time deposits held by financial institutions (mainly the so-called multinational banks) located outside the continental United States, including such deposits held by branches of U.S. banks.

The origin and the growth of the Eurodollar market over the last 25 years have been greatly influenced by landmark events and developments which reshaped international financial and currency markets in the last quarter of a century. The U.S. dollar emerged as the leading reserve and international payments currency in the post-World War II era, buttressed by its role as the centerpiece of the new international monetary order negotiated in the Bretton Woods agreements in 1944.

The U.S. balance of payments, reflecting mainly the burden of postwar reconstruction commitments under the Marshall Plan, swung to substantial deficits in the early 1960s. These deficits flushed the financial markets with U.S. dollars, or dollar claims, in the hands of foreign governments, foreign central banks, and financial institutions, as well as individuals. These developments in themselves, however, were not sufficient to foster the growth of a large wholesale market where dollar deposits and dollar loans are made by financial institutions outside the United States. An incentive was needed to persuade holders of dollars and dollar claims to place their deposits in banks outside the United States, and for those wishing to borrow dollars to raise such funds from financial institutions located in Europe and elsewhere.

The incentive was provided by the restrictive and regulatory environment that prevailed in the United States during the 1960s which was aimed at controlling capital outflows. These regulations consisted of (1) the interest equalization tax imposed in 1963 to discourage foreign portfolio investments to take advantage of higher yields prevailing abroad, (2) the voluntary foreign credit restraints enforced in 1964, which sought to discourage U.S. banks and corporations from placing short-term investments abroad, and (3) mandatory guidelines imposed in 1965 by the Office of Foreign Direct Investment to discourage such investments by U.S. firms abroad.

In addition to these restrictions, the growth of the Eurodollar market was fostered by banking regulations in the United States which adversely affected the competitiveness of U.S. banks with offshore financial institutions. Regulation Q, enforced by the Federal Reserve System, placed ceilings on interest rates paid by U.S. banks on time deposits, and Regulation M required U.S. banks to keep a stipulated percentage of their deposits in nonearning assets (vault cash and deposit with Federal Reserve banks). The Eurodollar market enjoyed the advantage of offering competitive market rates to depositors subject to no ceilings, and benefited from the lower cost of funds, as it observed no mandatory reserve requirement of any sort.

The biggest boost to the market, which probably contributed more to its growth than any other single factor, was the large balance of payments surpluses realized by OPEC countries in the 1970s due to the sharp increases in oil prices in 1973–1974 and again in 1978. Although most of these dollar surpluses were retained in the United States, invested mainly in money and capital market instruments, a sizable proportion found their way to the Eurodollar market, primarily as time deposits in European banks.

The deceleration in the growth rate of the market since 1980 reflects, to some extent, a reversal of the same factors that contributed to its phenomenal growth in the 1970s. The restrictive measures on capital flows imposed in the mid-1960s were phased out by 1974 (the interest equalization tax was repealed in 1968). Regulation Q was phased out by the Depository Institution Deregulation and Monetary Control Act of 1980 and the Depository Institution Deregulation Act of 1982, over a period which ended in March 1986. The increasingly liberal environment in the financial markets in the United States, engendered for the most part by the deregulation measures, contributed to their competitiveness vis-a-vis their offshore counterparts. Another factor which contributed to the slowdown in the growth rate of the Eurodollar market has been the sharply lower payments surpluses realized by oil-exporting countries. Indeed, the balance of payments of a number of these countries, particularly the so-called "high absorbers," turned into sizable deficits in the early 1980s.

SIZE OF THE EUROCURRENCY MARKET

The size of the Eurocurrency market and its predominant component, the Eurodollar market, may be measured in a number of methods resulting in markedly different results. As Eurodollars represent liabilities of banks outside the continental United States denominated in dollars, its gross size is the sum total of these liabilities irrespective of the form they take, their maturities, or their ownership. Since a substantial part of these liabilities represent interbank deposits, netting out these deposits will reduce the size of the market substantially.

There are several sources which compile and publish statistical data relating to the overall size of the Eurocurrency market. Two sources are considered most reliable: data published by the Bank of International Settlements (BIS) in Basel, Switzerland, and those published monthly by Morgan Guaranty Trust Co., a leading multinational bank based in New York City. The latter source is more comprehensive and is generally considered a better measure of the size of the Eurocurrency market. BIS compiles and publishes data only for banks in certain countries and locations which report such data on a regular basis.[1] However, the BIS has been expanding the coverage of reporting banks in recent years, which has resulted in narrowing the gap between these two sources.

Data in Exhibit 9-1 reveal several significant characteristics relating to the size, growth, and composition of the Eurocurrency market. The gross size of the market is measured by the gross liabilities of banks to both residents and nonresidents, denominated in dollars and in other major currencies. It should be noted that these liabilities are owed by banks and financial institutions which are located outside the country or countries in whose currencies the liabilities are denominated. Defined as such, the overall size of the market at year end 1984 was $2383 billion of which $1787 billion, or 75 percent, are liabilities to other banks, indicating that the Eurocurrency market is primarily an interbank market. When all interbank deposits are netted out, the net size is reduced to $500 billion. A distinction is sometimes made between interbank deposits made by banks

[1]BIS data incorporate reports by banks in the Group of Ten countries, Luxembourg, Austria, Denmark, Finland, Ireland, Norway, Spain, Cayman Islands, Bahamas, Netherlands Antilles, Bahrain, Hong Kong, Singapore, and by branches of U.S. banks in Panama. See Bank for International Settlements, *International Banking Developments* (third quarter 1984), Basel, Switzerland (February 1985), p. 5.

Exhibit 9-1. Size of the Eurocurrency Market (in billions of U.S. dollars at end of period)

	1971	1975	1980	1981	1982	1983	1984
Gross liabilities to residents and nonresidents of which:	150	480	1554	1927	2146	2275	2383
to nonbanks	(30)	(80)	(272)	(384)	(450)	(479)	(500)
to official monetary institutions	(15)	(70)	(127)	(113)	(91)	(88)	(96)
to other banks	(105)	(330)	(1154)	(1431)	(1605)	(1708)	(1787)
In U.S. dollars	(114)	(374)	(1178)	(1520)	(1729)	(1849)	(1918)
In other currencies	(36)	(106)	(376)	(407)	(417)	(426)	(465)
Eurodollars as % of total gross Eurocurrency market	76	78	76	79	81	81	80

Source: Morgan Guaranty Trust Company of New York, *World Financial Markets* (February 1985), p. 13, and (June 1985), p. 11.

outside a particular currency area and those made by banks located in that currency area. For example, in measuring the size of the Eurodollar market, dollar deposits owned by banks located outside the Eurodollar market area, such as banks located in Singapore and Bahrain, are not netted out, because these banks are considered original suppliers of funds to the Eurodollar market just like individuals or nonbank institutions. If this distinction is made, the net size of the Eurodollar market will be considerably larger.[2]

Exhibit 9-1 also shows the continued dominance of the Eurodollar market, accounting in recent years for over 80 percent of the overall Eurocurrency market on a gross basis. This is not surprising, considering the position that the U.S. dollar continues to occupy as the major currency of international trade and payments. The nondollar portion of the market, about 20 percent, is dominated by the Euromark, Eurosterling, and Euro-Swiss franc in that order. The other components of the market are the Euro-Dutch guilder, Euro-Canadian dollar, Euro-French franc, Euro-yen and deposits denominated in the European Currency Unit.[3]

GROWTH OF THE EURODOLLAR MARKET

The origin of the Eurodollar market is rather obscure. It is generally agreed, however, that it originated in the early 1950s by the desire of the

[2]See Marvin Goodfriend, "Eurodollars," reprinted in *International Finance, Concepts and Issues,* edited by Gay and Kolb, (Richmond, VA: Robert F. Dame, Inc., 1983), pp. 54–63.

[3]The European Currency Unit is a weighted composite of the currencies of European countries which are members of the European Monetary Cooperative Fund (FECOM); see Chapter 2.

Soviet Union and Eastern European countries to place their dollar holdings in European banks to avoid the risk of such balances being blocked if deposited in U.S. banks. The creation of the market and its subsequent growth must also be attributed in part to the emergence of the U.S. dollar as the linchpin of the international monetary system in the post-World War II period, replacing the British pound as the international reserve currency and the primary instrument of exchange in world trade and payments.

The growth of the Eurodollar market was modest in its early years, as it was estimated by Morgan Guaranty at $20 billion in 1964.[4] The phenomenal growth of the market occurred during the 1965–1980 period. According to both BIS and Morgan Guaranty data, the annual growth rate during this period of dollar deposits in European banks exceeded 30 percent. The figures in Exhibit 9-1 suggest that the growth rate has declined considerably in the 1980s, which raises an interesting question as to the future prospects of this market.

Briefly, the fast growth of the Eurodollar market in the 1965–1980 period has been attributed mainly to the following four major factors:

1. Large deficits in the U.S. balance of payments, particularly during the 1960s, which resulted in the accumulation of substantial dollars held by foreign financial institutions and individuals.
2. The restrictive environment which prevailed in the United States during the 1963–1974 period to stem capital outflows. These restrictions, which took the form of both voluntary and mandatory controls, encouraged U.S. and foreign multinational companies to borrow dollars abroad.
3. The massive balance of payments surpluses realized by OPEC countries due to sharp increases in oil prices in 1973–1974 and again in 1978. A good proportion of these "petrodollars" was deposited in financial institutions outside the United States.
4. The efficiency and lower cost base of the Eurodollar market. Being a wholesale funds market, operating free of restrictions at a substantially lower cost than its counterpart in the United States, it has been able to attract dollar deposits by offering higher interest rates, as well as making dollar loans available to borrowers at lower interest rates.

While the factors listed above contributed to the growth of the market in the 1960s and the 1970s, it is generally believed that an endogenous expansion process, analogous in some respects to the domestic deposit expansion process in the banking system, must also have been at work. Sharp differences abound in the literature among academicians and inter-

[4]For an interesting and comprehensive account of the origin of the Eurodollar market and its early growth, see Gunter Dufey and Ian H. Giddy, *The International Money Market* (Englewood Cliffs, New Jersey: Prentice-Hall Inc., 1978); and Paul Einzig, *The Eurodollar System,* 5th ed. (New York: Martins Press, 1973).

national bankers, both as to whether or not a multiplier effect has been operating in Eurodollar markets and as to the value of the multiplier. The perception that a multiplier process must have been at work is based in part on the phenomenal growth of the market, which could not be explained solely in terms of initial deposits.

The Multiplier Process

There is some confusion in the literature as to the nature of the multiplier process in the Eurocurrency market, which is compounded by failing to realize that the nucleus of the expansionary process is dollar deposits in U.S. banks, whose ownership keeps changing as the deposit-lending scenario unfolds.

To illustrate the expansionary process using the traditional T accounts to show the sequence of transactions, let us assume

Step 1:

Country K, a Middle Eastern oil exporting country, earns $1 billion for crude oil shipment to Standard Oil of Indiana (S.O.I.). S.O.I. pays for the shipment by a check drawn on its account with Chase Manhattan Bank (N.Y.), and country K elects to keep the funds as a deposit in the same bank. The following T-account is a complete record of this transaction.

Chase Manhattan Bank (N.Y.)	
	($ billion)
	(1) Deposits of Country K +$1
	(1) Deposits of S.O.I. −$1

It is obvious that this transaction neither resulted in the creation of Eurodollar deposits nor affected the money supply in the United States. For Chase Manhattan Bank (N.Y.) it just is an offsetting deposit transfer between two clients of the bank.

Step 2:

Country K decided to transfer its deposit from Chase Manhattan Bank (N.Y.) and place it as a time deposit (TD) in Chase Manhattan Bank (London). The following T-accounts record this transaction.

Chase Manhattan Bank (N.Y.)
($ billion)

	(2) Deposits of Country K −$1
	(2) A/C of C.M.B. (London) +$1

Chase Manhattan Bank (London)
($ billion)

(2) A/C at C.M.B. (N.Y.) +$1	(2) TD Country K +$1

This transaction resulted in the creation of $1 billion in Eurodollars, which is represented by country K's TD in Chase Manhattan Bank (London). It also transferred the deposit in New York from country K to Chase Manhattan Bank (London). This bank now finds itself in a situation whereby it is paying interest on country K's time deposit while it maintains a noninterest-earning deposit in New York. The bank will have to search for a way to earn income on that deposit.

Step 3:

Chase Manhattan Bank (London) is not required to maintain any reserve against the deposit; however, as a matter of prudence it may decide to lend only $900 million, thus keeping $100 million in the form of cash reserves. Assume that the loan was extended to Ciba-Geigy, a Swiss firm, which places the amount received from Chase Manhattan Bank (London) with the Union Bank of Switzerland as a time deposit. The following T-accounts record this transaction:

Chase Manhattan Bank (N.Y.)
($ million)

	(3) Deposits of C.M.B. (London) −$900
	(3) Deposits of Union Bank of Switzerland +$900

Chase Manhattan Bank (London)
($ million)

(3) A/C at CMB (NY) −$900	
(3) Loan to Ciba-Geigy +$900	

Union Bank of Switzerland
($ million)

(3) A/C at C.M.B. (N.Y.) +$900	(3) TD Ciba-Geigy +$900

This transaction resulted in the creation of another $900 million in Eurodollars. Now the Union Bank of Switzerland finds itself with more lending power, which it must utilize to defray the interest costs it is paying on Ciba-Geigy's time deposit.

Step 4:

Since the Swiss banking authorities have no jurisdiction over its dollar-denominated deposits, the Union Bank of Switzerland is not obligated to maintain any set reserve against the deposit. Based on its experience with deposits of this type, it may decide to keep 15 percent in reserves and loan out the remainder. If it is assumed that a loan of $765 million was extended to Unilever Company, a Dutch firm, which placed at a time deposit with the National Bank of Netherlands, the following T-accounts record this transaction.

Chase Manhattan Bank (N.Y.)
($ million)

	(4) Deposits of U.B.S. −$765
	(4) Deposits of National Bank of Netherlands +$765

Union Bank of Switzerland
($ million)

(4) A/C at C.M.B. (N.Y.) −$765	
(4) Loan to Unliver Co. +$765	

National Bank of Netherlands
($ million)

(4) A/C at C.M.B. (N.Y.) +$765	(4) TD Unilever Co. +$765

This transaction resulted in the creation of another $765 million in Eurodollars.

Step 5:

Assume that the National Bank of Netherlands extended a loan of $700 million to Canadian Marconi, which used the proceeds of the loan to pay for imported equipment from I.B.M. Assume further that I.B.M. banks with Citibank (N.Y.). The following T-accounts record this transaction:

Chase Manhattan Bank (N.Y.)
($ million)

	(5) Deposits of National Bank of Netherlands −$700
	(5) Citibank deposits +$700

Citibank (N.Y.)
($ million)

(5) A/C with C.M.B. (N.Y.) +$700	(5) Deposits of I.B.M. +$700

National Bank of Netherlands
($ million)

(5) A/C at C.M.B. (N.Y.) −$700	
(5) Loan to Canadian Marconi +$700	

Note that this transaction did not create any Eurodollars. The process of Eurodollar creation ceased, since the loan extended to Canadian Marconi was not deposited in the Eurodollar market, but used instead to pay a U.S. exporter.

The following conclusions may be derived from this illustration:

1. Total creation of Eurodollars amounted to $2.665 billion ($1000 million + $900 million + $765 million) in three stages, yielding a multiplier of about 2.7 times the original deposit made by country K at Chase Manhattan Bank (London). Obviously, the value of the multiplier is a function of both the ratio of reserves held by depository banks against time deposits, and the number of stages or rounds of Eurodollar creation before it is terminated by the leakage of Eurodollars into the United States.
2. By tracing the process of Eurodollar creation from its inception to its termination, it is evident that the base consisted of dollar deposits in banks located in the United States [in this case Chase Manhattan Bank (N.Y.)] switching ownership at each stage of the process. The notion that Eurodollars result from funds physically transferred from the United States and deposited abroad is erroneous.
3. There was no increase in total deposits in the United States and, therefore, no change in the money supply. Most studies con-

ducted in this area demonstrated that Eurodollar transactions have no impact on the U.S. money supply. However, it has been postulated that such transactions may have an impact on the money multiplier, if such transactions involve changes in the composition of U.S. banks' liabilities, which are subject to different reserve requirements. The potential effect depends on the differential reserve requirements and on how money is measured. Balback and Resler, who constructed a Eurodollar multiplier model to examine systematically such effects over the period 1973–1979, concluded, "Eurodollar flows were shown to have only minor effects on the U.S. money stock. This evidence warrants the conclusion that the Eurodollar market does not pose a serious threat to the ability of the Federal Reserve to control the money supply."[5]

INSTRUMENTS AND RATES OF THE EUROCURRENCY MARKETS

Eurocurrency deposits are held predominantly in the form of fixed-rate time deposits with maturities ranging from overnight to several years. Most of the funds, however, are held in the one-month to six-month maturity range. As the bulk of these deposits are interbank deposits, rates paid are competitively determined at the inception, but remain fixed for the term of the deposit. The balance of these deposits is accounted for by negotiable certificates of deposit (CDs). Introduced in 1966, CDs account for a relatively small (about 15–20 percent) but growing share of Eurocurrency deposits. Eurocurrency CDs are issued in two forms: *tap* CDs and *tranche* CDs. The former are issued in relatively large denominations (commonly from \$250,000 to \$5 million) and for maturities of less than one year, whenever banks need to "tap" the market for funds. Tranche CDs are issued in large aggregate amounts (typically \$10 million to \$50 million), but are offered to investors in small certificates (typically \$10,000). All certificates which are part of one aggregate issue bear the same interest rate and have identical maturity date.[6] The volatility of interest rates since 1979 has led to the use of Eurocurrency Floating Rate CDs (FRCDs) and Eurocurrency Floating Rate Notes (FRNs). Both are negotiable bearer instruments with rates reset at every three to six months, thus protecting investors against a decline in the principal value of the paper caused by rise in interest rates.

Rates for Eurocurrency time deposits and CDs are competitively determined and are closely aligned to rates for corresponding maturities in

[5]Anatol B. Balback and David H. Resler, "Eurodollars and the U.S. Money Supply," Federal Reserve Bank of St. Louis, *Economic Review* (June/July 1980).

[6]See Marvin Goodfriend, "Instruments of the Money Market," *Federal Reserve Bank of Richmond,* 1981. For a comprehensive survey of Eurodollar instruments, also see M. S. Dobbs-Higginson, *Instrument Manual for Fixed Income Securities in the International and Major Domestic Capital Markets,* issued by Credit-Swisse-First Boston Limited, London, 1980.

the home market. Arbitrage operations insure that the rate on three-month Eurodollar CDs moves in tandem with the rate of CDs of similar maturity issued by banks located in the United States. Data in Exhibit 9-2 demonstrate the close alignment between overnight dollar rates (measured by the Federal Funds Rate) and rates on overnight Eurodollars. The latter have been slightly higher with the spread amounting to as many as 50 basis points, but typically about 25 basis points or one-fourth of one percent. Rates for three-month CDs in Germany are also closely aligned to Euromark CDs of identical maturity, with the latter being slightly lower.

The close alignment and narrow spread between Eurocurrency rates and home rates of corresponding maturity illustrate the competitive relationship between the two markets and the close substitutability between the two forms of deposit. It has been argued that the positive spread between Eurodollar deposit rates and rates of corresponding maturities quoted by banks in the United States reflects the risk differential. The risk differential is usually explained by such factors as possible interference by host countries in repatriation of Eurodollar deposits, potential of international jurisdictional disputes, and concerns about the relative soundness

Exhibit 9-2. Comparison of Eurocurrency Deposit Rates and Rates on Instruments of Corresponding Maturity in Home Money Markets (in percentage at end of period)

	OVERNIGHT U.S. DOLLARS		3-MONTH DEUTSCHE MARKS	
	Federal Funds Rate[1]	Eurodollar Rate	3-Month CDs in Germany	3-month[2] Euromark CDs
December 1975	5.20	5.13	4.20	3.81
December 1976	4.65	4.63	4.80	4.69
December 1977	6.55	7.12	3.60	2.50
December 1978	10.03	10.62	3.70	3.31
December 1979	13.78	14.00	8.70	8.56
December 1980	18.90	19.25	10.20	8.87
December 1981	12.37	12.87	10.50	10.50
December 1982	8.95	9.25	6.20	5.88
December 1983	9.47	9.50	6.30	5.88
December 1984	8.38	8.63	5.75	5.50
1985				
January	8.35	8.50	5.85	6.00
February	8.50	8.44	6.25	6.06
March	8.58	8.81	6.20	5.88
April	8.27	8.31	5.90	5.81
May	7.97	7.50	5.80	5.50

[1]Monthly averages.
[2]Bond-equivalent yields on major three-month money-market instrument.
Source: Morgan Guaranty Trust Company of New York, *World Financial Markets,* several issues.

of foreign banks compared with banks located in the United States. The consensus, however, is that the relative riskiness of Eurodollar deposits and comparable deposits in the United States is difficult to assess and depends, to some extent, on the residence of the depositor. The positive spread may also be ascribed in part to the relative efficiency and low-cost base of Eurocurrency operations—which were described earlier.

Eurocurrency Loans

The rapid growth in Eurocurrency deposits would not have been possible had the recipient banks not been able to utilize these funds at renumerative rates. A European bank receiving a Eurodollar deposit has several options in putting this deposit to use so as to generate a rate of return sufficient to cover the interest rate paid on the deposit, defray the bank's administrative cost, and produce a margin of return. The funds may be placed in the interbank market, that is, redeposited in another banking institution in Europe or elsewhere. Alternatively, it may grant short-term Eurodollar credit to an exporter or an MNC, or a longer-term credit to an LDC government which happens to be looking to raise money in the form of syndicated Eurodollar loan (see below). Eurodollars may be also swapped for local currency to enable the bank to extend domestic loans. If the recipient bank happens to be a branch of a U.S. bank abroad, Eurodollar deposits may be loaned to their U.S. home office.

Eurocurrency loans are made for maturities ranging from overnight loans to seven years and in amounts ranging from $500,000 to $500 million. Short-term Eurocurrency credits, which are extended to MNCs and firms engaged in foreign trade, are usually in the form of lines of credit. Advances under these lines of credit are normally made against notes with maturities of 90 or 180 days. Medium-term Eurocurrency loans are extended under a revolving line of credit which permits corporate clients to draw funds up to a certain specified limit for a period of three to five years. Actual advances under this arrangement are, however, made against notes with maturities of typically 180 days which also have an automatic renewal feature. Interim rates charged on such loans are adjusted every six months.

Interest rates charged on Eurodollar credits and loans are expressed as a certain spread, ranging typically from one-half of one percent to three percent, above the six-month London Interbank Offer Rate LIBOR.[7] The exact spread above LIBOR is negotiated with the lending institution and is primarily a function of the borrower's credit standing. Very infrequently Eurodollar loans may be priced as a spread above the U.S. prime rate.

For reasons indicated earlier relating to the relative efficiency and the wholesale nature of the Eurocurrency market, as well as the absence of

[7]LIBOR is the arithmetic average of the rates at which six major banks in London are willing to pay to borrow dollar funds at a certain time during the morning.

restrictions which would increase the cost of funds, Eurocurrency loans are typically priced at slightly lower rates than those charged for loans in the home market for corresponding maturities.

THE SYNDICATED EUROCURRENCY LOAN MARKET

Although short-term credit accounts for the major part of Eurocurrency lending, an important and growing part of this market is the syndicated Eurocurrency bank credits. From a modest beginning in the late 1960s, syndicated Eurocurrency bank credits reached over $133 billion in 1981, declined somewhat during the next two years, but rose again sharply during 1984 to $112 billion. The bulges in both 1981 and 1984 are attributed mainly to the sharp increase in borrowing by U.S. MNCs and financial institutions (Exhibit 9-3).

A syndicated loan is one which is arranged and extended by a group of financial institutions to a borrower on common terms. A typical syndicated loan is one in which a government of an LDC country or a public sector corporation approaches a number of banks to arrange the syndication. The so-called *lead banks* will conduct preliminary negotiations with the borrower and, if such negotiations prove promising, they will proceed to assemble a *management* group to underwrite the loan. Once the management group reaches agreement on terms with the borrower, a placement memorandum will be prepared by the lead bank to invite other banks to participate in the syndication. The placement memorandum, a document similar to the prospectus, contains detailed financial and other data pertaining to the borrower. Once the participation is closed, the loan is final-

Exhibit 9-3. Eurocurrency Bank Credits (billions of U.S. dollars)

BORROWER	1970	1975	1979	1980	1981	1982	1983	1984
Industrial countries	4.2	7.3	27.2	39.1	86.0	42.6	38.8	77.1
Developing countries	0.4	11.1	48.0	35.1	45.2	41.5	32.9	31.6
of which:[1]								
Non-OPEC LDCs	(0.3)	(8.2)	(35.4)	(24.0)	(33.4)			
OPEC countries	(0.1)	(2.9)	(12.6)	(11.1)	(11.8)			
Communist countries	–	2.5	7.3	2.8	1.8	0.7	1.2	3.4
International organizations[2]	0.1	0.1	0.3	0.4	0.3	0.2	1.3	0.3
Total	4.7	21.0	82.8	77.4	133.2	85.0	74.2	112.5

[1]Breakdowns of LDC borrowing to OPEC and non-OPEC countries are not available after 1981.
[2]Includes regional development organizations.
Source: Morgan Guaranty Trust Company of New York, *World Financial Markets,* various issues.

ized and an agent bank, usually the lead bank, is designated to finalize the agreement, compute the appropriate interest and service charges, and oversee other aspects of the administration of the loan during its life cycle. Exhibit 9-4 shows the terms of a mythical Eurocurrency syndicated loan for illustrative purposes.

Several advantages for the lending banks and the borrower account for the fast growth of the syndicated Eurocurrency loan market. For lenders the arrangement permits diversification and sharing of the unique risks involved in a market dominated by public sector borrowers. Syndication discourages default or protection afforded by sovereign immunity. As the syndicated loan is advanced by banks in several countries, failure to meet the terms of the loan could effectively preclude the borrower from entering the credit market in the future. Banks can discourage selective default by including a cross-default clause, which would have the effect of declaring all public borrowers from a certain country in default if one borrowing entity in the country fails to meet its obligations.

The syndication process also permits participation of banks of different size in the final lending, although the original underwriting may have been done by a small group of large banks. Through this wide participation process, borrowers can have access to a larger pool of funds than can be supplied by any single lender. The syndicated Eurocurrency market played a significant role in financing the requirements of nonoil LDCs. By recycling petrodollars, the market enabled these countries to finance their oil imports.

The spread over LIBOR for a Eurocurrency syndicated loan is determined by the initial negotiation between the borrower and the under-

Exhibit 9-4. Terms of a Mythical Eurocurrency Syndicated Loan

Borrower:	Public Power Corporation of Argentina
Amount:	$100 million 10-year syndicated loan to be drawn down within two years from the date of the loan (the drawdown period)
Interest rate:	¾ of one percent over LIBOR for the first five years and 1 percent over LIBOR for the next five years. LIBOR is readjusted every six months.
Commitment fee:	½ of one percent of the undrawn portion of the credit
Front-end participation fee:	¾ of one percent of the value of the loan
Repayment:	Repayments start after three years (grace period) in 14 equal half annual installments plus interest, commitment fees, and other charges as applicable.

writing group and normally remains unchanged throughout the life of the loan.[8] The spread reflects the credit standing of the borrower, and the general conditions in the Eurocurrency market and other international money and credit markets. Spreads normally widen and maturities are shortened during tight market conditions or during periods when interest rates display volatility. The spread is normally wider for low-income developing countries than borrowers from high-income LDCs, such as OPEC countries, or borrowers from industrial countries. Spreads over LIBOR, particularly for LDC borrowers widened in the early eighties to an average of 1.5 percent, reflecting the increasing debt burden of these countries and the problems experienced by a number of them in servicing their debt (Exhibit 9-5).

It should be remembered that the cost of a typical Eurocurrency syndicated loan is higher than the LIBOR rate plus the spread. The commitment fee, which is charged on the undrawn portion of the loan (typically $\frac{1}{2}$ to $\frac{3}{4}$ of one percent annually), and the one-time front-end management fee (typically $\frac{1}{2}$ of one percent to one percent of the value of the loan) raise the effective interest cost to the borrower significantly.[9]

THE INTERNATIONAL BOND MARKET

The past quarter of a century has witnessed a fast growth and important innovations taking place in international capital markets, particularly in the foreign bond and Eurobond sectors. A foreign bond is issued by foreign borrowers and is denominated in the currency of the country in which it is issued. Foreign (non-U.S.) corporate borrowers have extensively floated dollar bonds in the United States, capitalizing on the depth and versatility of the well-organized U.S. capital market. U.S. multinational companies raised substantial amounts of capital during the 1970s by issuing bonds denominated in deutsche marks in Germany and bonds denominated in Swiss francs in Switzerland, taking advantage of what they then perceived as a lower borrowing cost in these countries. A Eurobond issue is to be distinguished from a foreign bond issue in that it is denominated in a currency other than the currency of the country of the initial issue.

The Eurobond market flourished during the last two decades, benefiting from the same factors and advantages that have given impetus to the

[8]Laurie S. Goodman in his article "The Pricing of Syndicated Eurocurrency Credits," *Quarterly Review of the Federal Reserve Bank of New York* (Summer 1980) referred to the introduction of the floating spread, a recent innovation in the market. Loans so negotiated will have the original spread reviewed annually by participating banks. The new spread is determined by the weighted average of the quotes subject to a preestablished ceiling.

[9]Laurie S. Goodman, "The Pricing of Syndicated Eurocurrency Credits," estimated that a one percent front-end management fee on a loan of $100 million priced at 100 basis points over a LIBOR of 10 percent raises the effective interest rate to the borrower from 11 percent to 11.31 percent. Assuming that the banks paid 9.75 percent for their funds, this represents an increment of 25 percent in their return.

Exhibit 9-5. Terms on International Bank Lending Commitments, 1973–1983

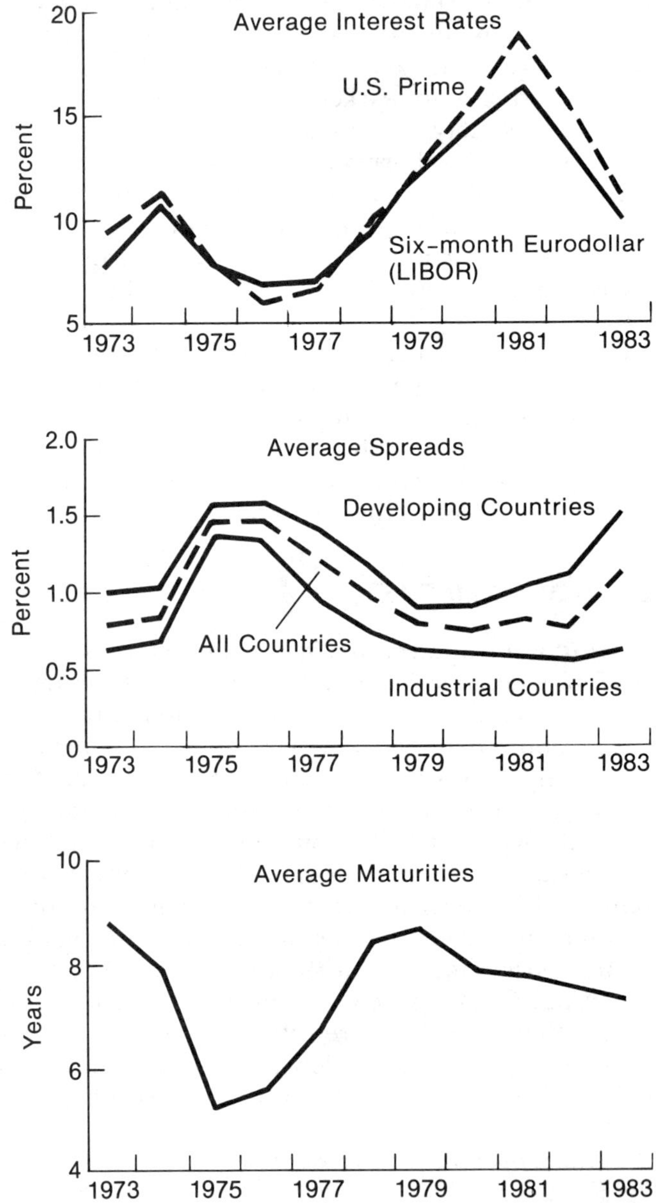

Source: International Monetary Fund, *International Capital Markets: Developments and Prospects, 1984* (Washington, D.C., 1984), p. 7.

phenomenal growth of its twin sister, the Eurocurrency market. While the size and the growth rate of this market are modest compared to the Eurocurrency market, it has established itself as a major source of long-term financing for both U.S. and non-U.S. MNCs. Since 1981, issues of international bonds have risen sharply, while the volume of international syndicated loans has declined.

The participants in the international bond market consist of leading MNCs, governments, and government enterprises on the issuing (borrowing) side, and leading multinational banks and brokerage houses on the buying (lending) side. These multinational institutions operate in a relatively control-free environment. The underwriting process is typically managed by an international syndicate representing major European banks and European and other foreign branches of U.S. banks, with participation from banks in other financial centers in Asia, the Middle East, and the Carribeans, as well as large international securities firms.

Data in Exhibit 9-6 reveal a sharp increase in issues of international bonds in the early 1980s, particularly in the Eurobond sector. The vast majority of international bonds were issued and purchased by entities in the industrial countries. The share of LDCs in this market remains fairly modest, as, apart from currency convertibility problems, borrowers in these countries generally fail to meet the minimum credit standards for successfully floating bond issues. International organizations, particularly those in the development lending field, are large borrowers, accounting in 1983 for over 17 percent of total placements.

Currency Composition and Market Share

The currency composition of international bond issues reflects, in the case of *foreign bonds,* the currency of the country of *issue,* and the currency of *denomination* in the case of Eurobonds. The major factors that influence the choice of currency for international bond issues are expectations as to movements of inflation, interest, and exchange rates, market access, and the regulatory and other features of the financial environment. In recent years these factors generally favored Switzerland as the primary country of issue for foreign bonds and the U.S. dollar as the primary currency of denomination in the Eurobond market.

The share of Switzerland in total foreign bond placement has been increasing in recent years, and accounted for almost one-half of the total market in 1983. Foreign bond issues placed in the United States, as a proportion of total foreign bond placements, have tended to decline, accounting in 1983 for only 17.5 percent of the total. Japan and Germany accounted for the bulk of the remainder, but the size of foreign bonds placed in these two countries has moved up and down erratically (Exhibit 9-7).

Exhibit 9-6. International Bond Issues and Placements[1] (millions of U.S. dollars)

	1977	1978	1979	1980	1981	1982	1983	JAN.–JUNE 1984
I. *Foreign Bonds*								
Industrial countries	10,157	10,328	13,421	11,339	14,129	16,837	18,624	11,406
Developing countries	1,609	2,583	1,431	746	1,212	726	894	775
Oil exporting	(33)	(571)	(105)	(46)	(242)	(38)	(78)	(–)
Nonoil developing	(1,576)	(2,012)	(1,326)	(700)	(970)	(688)	(816)	(775)
Centrally planned economies[2]	6		43					
International organizations	4,748	4,906	5,259	5,714	5,030	7,461	7,265	2,756
Other	90	2,896	154	125	159	191	323	125
Total foreign bonds	16,610	20,713	20,308	17,924	20,530	25,215	27,106	15,062
II. *Eurobonds*								
Industrial countries	13,167	9,774	14,212	17,206	25,210	42,816	41,013	30,255
Developing countries	2,792	3,162	1,885	1,403	3,185	3,970	2,382	1,508
Oil exporting	(453)	(1,110)	(329)	(132)	(170)	(470)	(288)	(50)
Nonoil developing	(2,339)	(2,052)	(1,556)	(1,271)	(3,015)	(3,500)	(2,094)	(1,458)
Centrally planned economies[2]	74	30		55	55		25	
International organizations	2,412	1,820	2,220	1,710	2,486	3,280	6,073	2,193
Other	1,040	175	344	75	358	263	602	557
Total Eurobonds	19,485	14,961	18,691	20,394	31,294	50,329	50,095	34,513
International Bonds (I + II)								
Industrial countries	23,324	20,102	27,633	28,545	39,339	59,653	59,637	41,661
Developing countries	4,401	5,745	3,316	2,149	4,397	4,696	3,276	2,283
Oil exporting	(786)	(1,681)	(434)	(178)	(412)	(508)	(366)	(50)
Nonoil developing	(3,615)	(4,064)	(2,882)	(1,971)	(3,985)	(4,188)	(2,910)	(2,233)
Centrally planned economies[2]	80	30	73		55		25	
International organizations	7,160	6,726	7,479	7,424	7,516	10,741	13,338	4,949
Other	1,130	3,071	498	200	517	454	925	682
Total International Bonds	36,095	35,674	38,999	38,318	51,824	75,544	77,201	49,575

[1]The country classifications are those used by the IMF.
[2]Excluding IMF member countries.
Source: International Monetary Fund, *International Capital Markets, Developments and Prospects, 1984,* Occasional Paper 31 (August 1984), p. 37.

Exhibit 9-7. Foreign Bond Issues by Country of Placement (millions of U.S. dollars, and in percent)

	1978	%	1979	%	1980	%	1981	%	1982	%	1983	%
Switzerland	7,405	35.8	9,718	47.9	7,470	41.7	8,118	39.6	11,325	44.9	13,495	49.9
United States	6,358	30.7	4,364	21.5	2,709	15.1	6,856	33.4	6,025	23.9	4,735	17.5
Japan	4,387	21.2	2,671	13.2	1,543	8.6	2,723	13.3	3,317	13.2	3,854	14.3
Germany	1,431	6.9	2,690	13.2	4,951	27.6	1,196	5.8	2,109	8.4	2,616	9.7
United Kingdom					178	1.0	911	4.4	1,129	4.5	856	3.2
Other countries	1,127	5.4	866	4.3	1,073	6.0	713	3.5	1,294	5.1	1,486	5.5
Total	20,708	100.0	20,309	100.0	17,924	100.0	20,517	100.0	25,199	100.0	27,042	100.0

Source: International Monetary Fund, *International Capital Markets, Developments and Prospects, 1984,* Occasional Paper 31 (August 1984), p. 39.

The U.S. dollar dominates the Eurobond market as the currency of denomination, accounting in recent years for over 80 percent of total issues (Exhibit 9-8). With the exception of a small decline in 1983, U.S.-dollar-denominated Eurobonds have been rising steadily both in absolute terms and as a proportion of the total market. The deutsche mark is the only other major currency of denomination, but its share of total issues, which paralleled the U.S. dollar in the mid-1970s, has declined significantly since then. There has been a noticeable increase, particularly in 1983, in Eurobond issues denominated in pounds sterling and in composite currency units. Exhibit 9-9 shows distribution of foreign bonds by country of issue, and distribution of Eurobonds by currency of issue for the period 1980–1983. It also shows breakdown by type of bond.

Special Features and Innovations in the International Bond Market

The Eurobond market has flourished due to several unique features that set it apart from the domestic bond market and the foreign bond market. These features are

1. Like the Eurocurrency market, the Eurobond market is an offshore operation not subject to national controls, which most countries have over domestic issues of securities denominated in local currency.
2. Eurobond issues are not subject to the costly and time-consuming registration procedure. Eurodollar bonds, for example, are not covered by the SEC procedures which apply to domestic and foreign bonds issued in the United States. Disclosure requirements are also less stringent than those which apply to domestic issues. This feature appeals to many MNCs, which often do not wish to disclose detailed and highly sensitive information.
3. Eurobonds are issued in bearer form, which facilitates their negotiation in the secondary market. This feature also means that the country of the ultimate owner of the bond is not a matter of public record. Although Eurodollar bonds are not available to U.S. residents when issued, investors in the U.S. could usually purchase them after a cooling-off period.
4. Eurobonds offer investors exemption from tax-withholding provisions applicable to domestic and foreign bonds. For example, holders of Eurodollar bonds are not subject to income tax withholding on the interest received (which could be as much as 30 percent) when they cash their coupons. Such withholding applies to nonresident investors in domestic and foreign bonds issued in the United States. This feature allows U.S. MNCs to reduce their borrowing cost by having their offshore financing subsidiaries issue Eurodollar bonds, with payment of interest and principal guaranteed by the parent company. Since these bonds

Exhibit 9-8. Total Eurobond Issues by Currency of Denomination (millions of U.S. dollars, and in percent)

CURRENCY	1978	%	1979	%	1980	%	1981	%	1982	%	1983	%
U.S. dollar	6,767	45.2	10,360	55.4	13,649	66.9	25,761	82.3	42,228	83.9	39,205	78.2
Deutsche mark	6,478	43.3	5,881	31.5	3,457	17.0	1,396	4.5	3,253	6.5	4,039	8.1
Composite currency units[1]	235	1.6	413	2.2	98	0.5	709	2.3	835	1.7	2,196	4.4
Pound sterling	287	1.9	291	1.6	975	4.8	535	1.7	846	1.7	2,148	4.3
Canadian dollars			481	2.6	270	1.3	688	2.2	1,200	2.4	1,066	2.1
Other currencies	1,193	8.0	1,266	6.7	1,945	9.5	2,205	7.0	1,968	3.8	1,440	3.9
Total	14,960	100.0	18,692	100.0	20,394	100.0	31,294	100.0	50,330	100.0	50,094	100.0

[1]Issues denominated in European Currency Units (ECU), European Unit of Account (EUA), and Special Drawing Rights (SDR).
Source: International Monetary Fund, *International Capital Markets, Developments and Prospects, 1984,* Occasional paper 31 (August 1984).

Exhibit 9-9. Issues and Placements by Type of Instrument. Currency of Denomination, and Country of Issue

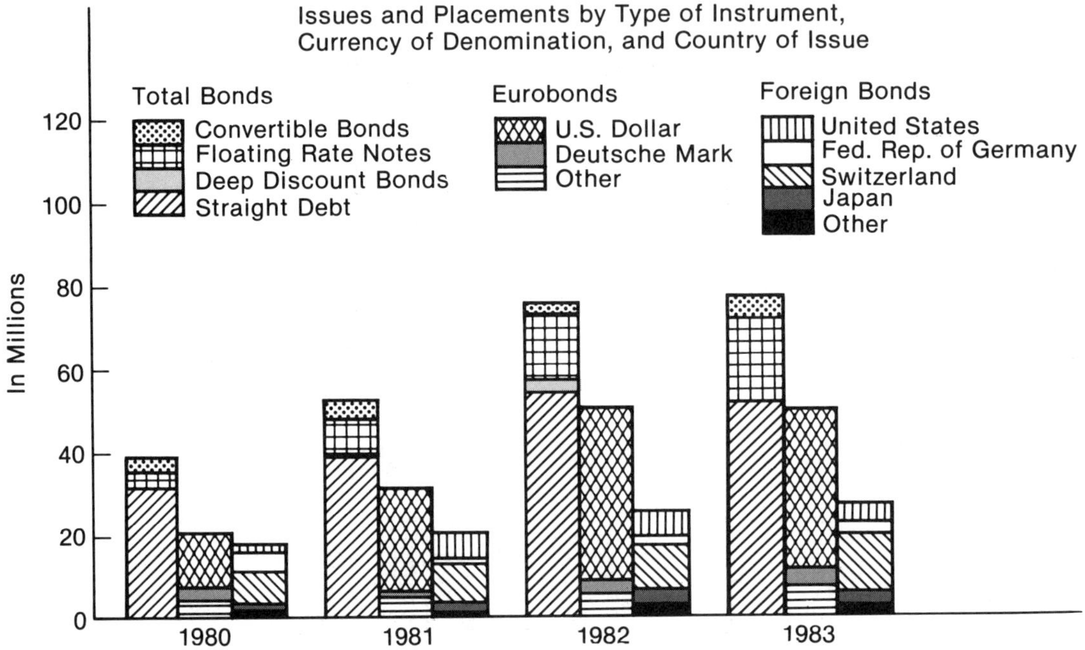

Source: International Monetary Fund, *International Capital Markets, Developments and Prospects, 1984* (Washington, D.C., 1984), p. 43.

are not subject to income tax withholding, they can be marketed at a lower yield.

The growth and popularity of both Eurobonds and foreign bonds are also attributed in part to the many innovations which have been introduced in the international bond market, particularly in the 1980s. These innovations include:

1. The issuance of convertible bonds or bonds with warrants attached. Both bonds entitle the holder to convert these bonds into common stock of the issuing corporation at a specified conversion ratio. The value of this feature in a Eurodollar bond, for example, is a function of the market price of the underlying stock and the exchange rate between the U.S. dollar and the currency of the bondholder. That this feature may prove valuable at a future point of time adds to the attractiveness and appeal of the bond.
2. Due to the volatility of interest rates in recent years, an increasing percentage of international bonds has been issued in the form of floating-rate notes. In 1983 the share of fixed-rate, straight Eurodollar bonds amounted to 55 percent of the total, while 40 per-

cent was accounted for by floating-rate notes, and 5 percent by convertibles.[10] The shift to floating-rate notes was accelerated by the spread of debt-servicing problems on international loans since mid-1982. Multinational financial institutions have tended to shun further participation in syndicated Eurocurrency loans in favor of investing in Eurodollar floating-rate notes issued by good credit risks. Floating-rate notes have been issued primarily by sovereign borrowers and multinational banks which are at both ends of the market, being both major issuers of and investors in these notes.

3. The use of multiple currency bonds and currency cocktails which are designed to attract investors interested in hedging the exchange risk. A multiple-currency bond entitles the holder to request payment of the interest and principal in any of certain specified currencies whose exchange parities are established at the outset. This arrangement thus gives the investor the option to request payment in the currency which appreciated the most or the currency that depreciated the least (if none appreciated) vis-a-vis his or her own currency. From the standpoint of the borrower, the obligation appreciates *pari passu* (at an equal rate) with the currency that appreciates the most.

International bonds denominated in a currency cocktail, such as the European Currency Unit (ECU) or Special Drawing Right (SDR), afford the investor protection against exchange rate instability, since these units are composed of a number of currencies, not all of which are likely to move in the same direction. The volatile exchange rate environment has spurred the use of currency cocktails, particularly since 1980.

Dual currency bonds, in which the principal is paid in a currency different from that of the currency of interest payment, have also been used. For example, Euro-Swiss franc bonds were issued in 1983 with interest being paid in Swiss francs and principal paid in U.S. dollars at a fixed Swiss franc/U.S. dollar exchange rate. In 1983, dual currency bond issues totaled $675 million.[11]

Another variation is combining the dual or multiple currency feature of the bond with the convertibility feature. As an example, an Italian MNC may issue a Eurodollar bond which entitles the holder to convert it, at a specified conversion ratio, into shares of the company, whose prices are expressed in Italian lira. The fortune of an investor in such a bond depends, among other things, on the movement in the U.S. dollar/Italian lira exchange rate. The value of the conversion feature increases not only with the rise in the market price of the underlying shares, but also with the appreciation of the lira against the dollar.

[10]International Monetary Fund, *International Capital Markets, op. cit.,* p. 42.
[11]International Monetary Fund, *International Capital Movements, op. cit.,* p. 45.

International Bond Yields

As in short-term Eurocurrency rates, the yield differentials among bonds denominated in different currencies reflect to a considerable degree the anticipated change in the exchange rate. However, while the process of interest arbitrage (discussed in Chapter 3) ensures that interest rate parity prevails, no such equilibrating mechanism operates in the medium and long-term capital market due to the nonexistence of forward exchange rate market for long maturities. This would suggest that yield differentials between Eurobonds denominated in different currency units could exist and persist beyond the levels that may be explainable in terms of exchange rate expectations. However, an increasing activity in swapping interest and currency in international bond markets has contributed to the ability of borrowers to arbitrage unusually large differentials in the cost of funds across countries.[12]

The data in Exhibit 9-10 show that substantial differentials exist among yields of Eurobonds denominated in different currency units, over and above what can be legitimately explained in terms of exchange rate expectations. It would be indeed very difficult to explain, for example, the wide differentials between Eurodollar bond and Swiss franc bond yields in 1983 and 1984, when the U.S. dollar was moving up strongly vis-a-vis all currencies. However, it must be remembered that at those very times, market expectation would tend to widen the forward premium in favor of the Swiss franc. Moreover, the actual yield for any particular bond holder depends on a host of variables, such as when the bond was purchased and when it was sold, the exchange rate movement in the duration between the investor's currency and the currency of denomination of the bond, and interest rate movements in the country of the currency of denomination. For example, European investors in Eurodollar bonds during 1982–1984

[12]Interest swaps are arrangements whereby two borrowers agree to swap interest payments on their respective obligations. A highly rated borrower could issue fixed-rate Eurobonds and swap interest payments with a lower-rated borrower who raised a corresponding amount of funds in the form of floating-rate notes. As an inducement for the first party to accept the swap, the second party agrees to pay a small proportion of the floating-rate interest cost. The swap arrangement thus enables the first party to lower its cost of funds, while the second party obtains essentially a fixed-rate loan at better terms than it would otherwise have to pay if it directly accessed the fixed-rate market.

Currency swaps are more complex than interest rate swaps, due to the different expectations of the parties involved in the swap as to the movement of exchange rates during the swap period. In a currency swap a highly rated borrower in the U.K. financial market, unable to access the Eurodollar bond market, could agree to swap fixed-rate, sterling obligations for fixed-rate Eurodollar obligations of the same amount. The other party to the swap arrangement would normally have the opposite credit credentials. The currency swaps thus enable both borrowers to use their good credit standing in their respective financial markets and share in the benefits therefrom.

According to IMF estimates, \$4 billion in currency swaps and \$10 billion in interest rate swaps took place in 1983. See IMF, *International Capital Movements, op. cit.,* p. 44. See also Chapter 10 for a more detailed analysis of swaps.

Exhibit 9-10. International Bond Yields[1] (percentage)

	ISSUED BY U.S. COMPANIES			ISSUED BY EUROPEAN GOVERNMENTS			
	Eurodollar	Euromark	Swiss franc	Eurodollar	Euromark	Swiss franc	ECU[2]
December 1977	7.95		5.31	8.42			
December 1978	8.55		5.70	9.12			
December 1979	10.13		6.61	10.66			
December 1980	11.76		7.27	11.83			
December 1981	12.70		7.30	13.59			
December 1982	11.16	7.24	5.70	12.53	8.10	5.40	n.a.
December 1983	11.59	7.34	5.83	12.65	8.12	5.63	11.77
December 1984	11.25	6.95	5.73	12.04	7.39	5.24	10.64
May 1985	10.58	6.90	5.69	11.20	7.37	5.20	10.10

[1]Average yield of several actively traded, high-quality issues with a maturity of 7–12 years at or near end of month.
[2]European Currency Unit.
Source: Morgan Guaranty Trust Company of New York, *World Financial Markets,* several issues.

realized high yields which reflected high nominal coupon rates, capital gains generated by declining interest rates, and the depreciation of the European currencies relative to the U.S. dollar over this period.

REVIEW QUESTIONS

1. Outline the major factors that have been responsible for the growth in the Eurocurrency markets, particularly the Eurodollar component of these markets. Which of these factors are still significant in fostering the use of these markets by investors and borrowers?
2. Under what circumstances would a financial manager of an MNC consider using Eurocurrency markets? What advantages or special features can these markets offer compared to borrowing from domestic markets? Are there drawbacks? Explain.
3. Is there a multiplier process in the placement of Eurocurrency deposits and subsequent Eurocurrency loans granted by financial institutions which receive these deposits? What are the major factors determining the size of the multiplier coefficient?
4. What forms do Eurocurrency deposits take? A financial manager is deliberating whether to place $100,000 in a domestic dollar CD or in a Eurodollar CD for three months. What issues or factors ought to be considered in making this decision? Is there a political risk involved in Eurocurrency CDs?
5. There are several methods of measuring the size of the Eurocurrency market. Comment on this statement and list the reasons for these different measurements.
6. Why are Eurocurrency deposit rates closely related to rates obtainable on instruments of corresponding maturity in home money markets? For example, why is the overnight Eurodollar rate closely aligned to the federal funds rate in the U.S. money market? Why is the former deposit rate usually (but not always) higher by some 25 to 50 basis points than the latter?
7. What is LIBOR? What determines the spread over LIBOR charged borrowers for Eurocurrency credits and loans?
8. Discuss the major advantages which the syndicated Eurocurrency loan market offers to lenders and borrowers, compared to domestic lending operations. Why is the quoted rate (spread over LIBOR) not an accurate indicator of the cost of a typical syndicated Eurocurrency loan?
9. List the major factors that are responsible for the growth of the international bond market. Indicate which of these factors (or other

considerations) explain the large number of innovations in this market.

10. Distinguish between a Eurobond and a foreign bond. List the major participants in this market. Why does the share of LDCs in this market remain fairly modest?
11. Define (a) a multiple-currency Eurobond, (b) a dual-currency convertible bond, and (c) a floating-rate Eurocurrency note. Explain in each case the distribution of risk (the exchange rate risk or the interest rate risk) between the lender (investor) and the borrower (issuer).
12. How do you explain the yield differentials among Eurobonds denominated in different currencies? Does interest parity operate in the capital market (as it does in the international money market) to eliminate these differentials on a covered basis? Do you expect an alignment between the yield on a Eurodollar bond and a dollar bond of the same risk grade and maturity?

REVIEW PROBLEM

1. a. Show the following transactions in T-accounts of the banks involved in the transactions.
   b. Indicate the total amount of Eurodollar deposits created by these transactions.
   c. What is the value of the Eurodollar deposit multiplier? Identify the factors that determine the value of the multiplier.

Transaction (1)

XYZ Co. (Netherlands) exported to ABC, Inc. (U.S.) goods valued at \$1,000,000. The importer paid by a check drawn on Citibank (N.Y.). XYZ Co. asked its bank (Algemene Bank of the Netherlands) to credit its account in Dutch guilders with the proceeds of the transaction. (The exchange rate on the value date of the transaction S_0Fl/\$ is 2.7715.)

Transaction (2)

Algemene Bank places the \$1,000,000 it has in Citibank (N.Y.) as a time deposit in Shanghai-Hong Kong Bank (Hong Kong).

Transaction (3)

Shanghai-Hong Kong Bank makes a loan of \$900,000 to Nestle Co. (Netherlands). Nestle Co. deposits the check in its account with the National

Bank of the Netherlands and asks its bank to credit its account with the equivalent in Dutch guilders. (The exchange rate on the value date of the transaction is S_0Fl/\$ = 2.7750.)

Transaction (4)

The National Bank of the Netherlands makes a loan of \$750,000 to Nova Industries (Denmark). Nova Industries uses the loan to settle an import transaction from Bristol Myers (N.Y.). Bristol Myers maintains its accounts with Chase Manhattan Bank (N.Y.).

BIBLIOGRAPHY

AHMAD, M. M., "Developing Countries and Access to Capital Markets," *Finance and Development* (December 1976), pp. 26–30.

ASHBY, D. F. V., "Will the Eurodollar Market Go Back Home?" *Banker* (February 1981), p. 93.

ASSAD, R., "How to Make the Eurobond Market More Attractive to Investors," *Euromoney* (September 1980), p. 102.

The Banker, "The Banker's Guide to World Financial Centers," May 1978, pp. 51–140.

Banker, "Eurobond Markets: Lessons for Investors," February 1981, pp. 75–77.

BHATTACHARYA, A., *The Asian Dollar Market.* New York: Praeger, 1977.

BURGESS, R., "The Competition Intensifies as the Eurobond Market Expands," *Euromoney* (February 1985), p. 117.

Business Week, "Banks Are Bailing Out as Eurobond Dealers," March 2, 1981, pp. 129–130.

Business Week, "Growing Allure of Deep-Discount Eurobonds," July 6, 1981, p. 83.

Business Week, "Safety First in the Euromarkets," August 30, 1982, p. 70.

CARROLL, J. S., "Biggest Fallacy in the Euromarkets," *Euromoney* (October 1981), p. 259.

CHOI, F. D. S., "Multinational Financing and Accounting Harmony," *Management Accounting* (March 1974), pp. 14–17.

COATS, W. L., JR., "The Weekend Eurodollar Game," *Journal of Finance* (June 1981), pp. 649–659.

CRAVEN, J. A., "Case for Change in Eurobond Issuing Techniques," *Euromoney* (November 1980), p. 94.

CROCKETT, A. D., "Eurocurrency Market: An Attempt to Clarify Some Basic Issues," *IMF Staff Papers* (July 1976), pp. 375–386.

DUFEY, G., and I. H. GIDDY, "Eurocurrency Deposit Risk," *Journal of Banking and Finance* (December 1984), pp. 567–589.

______, *The International Money Market.* Englewood Cliffs, N.J.: Prentice-Hall, Inc., 1978.

______, "Innovation in the International Financial Markets," *Journal of International Business Studies* (Fall 1981), pp. 33–51.

EADES, S., "Increasing the Options on Eurobonds," *Euromoney* (May 1985), p. 69.

ELTON, E. J., and M. J. GRUBER, eds., *International Capital Markets.* Amsterdam: North-Holland, 1976.

Euromoney, "The Bond Market's Okay If You Know the Drill" (February 1984), pp. 58–59.

Euromoney, "Should U.S. Companies Finance in the Euromarkets?" (March 1981), p. 134.

Euromoney, "Syndicated Lending—Out For the Count" (February 1983), pp. 36–38.

EVANS, R., "Can You Hedge a Eurobond?" *Euromoney* (October 1984), p. 329.

FINDLAY, M. C., III, and E. J. KLEINSCHMIDT, "Error-Learning in the Eurodollar Market," *Journal of Financial and Quantitative Analysis* (September 1975), pp. 429–443.

FINNERTY, J., "The Pluses of Zeros [Zero-Coupon Eurobonds]," *Euromoney* (May 1985), p. 67.

FINNERTY, J. E., and T. SCHNEEWEIS, "Time Series Analysis of International Dollar Denominated Interest Rates," *Journal of International Business Studies* (Spring-Summer 1979), pp. 39–52.

FINNERTY, J. E., T. SCHNEEWEIS, and S. P. HEGDE, "Interest Rates in the $Eurobond Market," *Journal of Financial and Quantitative Analysis* (September 1980), pp. 743–755.

FOLKS, W. R., and R. AVANTI, "Raising Funds with Foreign Currency," *Financial Executive* (February 1980), pp. 44–49.

FRIEDMAN, A., "International Report: The Eurobond Market Comes of Age," *U.S. Banker* (January 1984), pp. 37–38.

GILLESPIE, R. J., "Euromarket Influence on Borrowing Grows," *Pensions and Investment Age* (October 25, 1982), pp. 31–33.

GOODMAN, L. S., "Pricing of Syndicated Eurocurrency Credits," *Federal Reserve Bank of New York* (Summer 1980), pp. 39–49.

HEWSON, J. R., and E. SAKAKIBARA, *The Eurocurrency Markets and Their Implications.* Lexington, Mass.: Lexington Books, 1975.

______, "A Qualitative Analysis of Euro-Currency Controls," *Journal of Finance* (May 1975), pp. 377–400.

HODJERA, Z., "The Asian Currency Market: Singapore as a Regional Financial Center," *IMF Staff Papers* (June 1978), pp. 221–253.

HUAT, T. C., *Financial Institutions in Singapore.* Singapore: Singapore University Press Pte., 1978.

International Monetary Fund, *International Capital Markets, Recent Developments, and Short-Term Prospects,* Occasional paper No. 31, Washington, D.C., August 1984.

LEES, F. A., and M. ENG, *International Financial Markets.* New York: Praeger, 1975.

______, "Developing Country Access to the International Capital Markets," *Columbia Journal of World Business* (Fall 1979), pp. 71–84.

LEVIN, J. H., "A Financial Sector Analysis of the Eurodollar Market," *Journal of Finance* (March 1974), pp. 103–117.

LIM, Q. P., "Will the Eurodollar Bond Market Die? [Repeal of America's Withholding Taxes]," *Euromoney* (February 1985), p. 27.

LOGUE, D. E., and L. W. SENBET, "External Currency Market Equilibrium and Its Implications for Regulation of the Eurocurrency Market," *Journal of Finance* (May 1983), pp. 435–447.

LOMAX, D. F., and P. T. GUTMANN, *The Euromarkets and International Financial Policies.* New York: Halsted, 1980.

LUSZTIG, P., and B. SCHWAB, "Units of Account and the International Bond Market," *Columbia Journal of World Business* (Spring 1975), pp. 74–79.

MCKENZIE, G. W., *The Economics of the Euro-Currency System.* New York: Wiley, 1976.

MERCALDO, E. L., "Are the Euromarkets Too Competitive?" *Euromoney* (October 1981), p. 264.

MILLS, R. N., and H. S. TERRELL, "How Front-End Fees on Syndicated Euroloans are Determined," *Banker* (December 1984), pp. 27–28.

PARK, Y. S., *The Eurobond Market: Function and Structure.* New York: Praeger, 1974.

QUINN, B. S., *The New Euromarkets.* New York: Wiley, 1975.

______, "The International Bond Market for the U.S. Investor," *Columbia Journal of World Business* (Fall 1979), pp. 86–90.

REED, H. C., "The Ascent of Tokyo as an International Financial Center," *Journal of International Business Studies* (Winter 1980), pp. 19–35.

REYNOLDS, P. D., *China's International Banking and Financial System.* New York: Praeger, 1982.

RIEHL, H., and R. M. RODRIGUEZ, *Foreign Exchange and Money Markets.* New York: McGraw-Hill, 1983.

RISCHER, G., "The Role of Underwriters in the Eurocapital Market," *Euromoney* (June 1972), pp. 4–10.

STARR, D. W., "Opportunities for U.S. Corporate Borrowers in the International Bond Markets," *Financial Executive* (June 1979), pp. 50–59.

U TUN, W., and H. T. PATRICK, "Stock and Bond Issues and Capital Markets in Less Developed Countries," *IMF Staff Papers* (July 1973), pp. 253ff.

10

International Equity Markets and Recent Developments in International Capital Markets

INTRODUCTION

The first half of the present decade witnessed an increasing interest by investors in many countries in acquiring equity investments outside their countries. This tendency is particularly noticeable among U.S. institutional investors, particularly mutual funds and pension funds. The investment benefits from international portfolio diversification have been clearly demonstrated in the literature, which is summarized in Chapter 15. The increasing popularity of foreign equity investments with institutional portfolio managers suggests that there are a number of factors which have contributed to this movement beyond the diversification benefits. These benefits are derived from the low correlation between the performance of national equity markets, as deomonstrated by studies which covered periods predating the volatile exchange rate environment of the late 1970s and the early 1980s.

Due to the relative recency of this phenomenon, data on such investment activities are understandably sketchy. Nevertheless, increasing interest by investors in foreign equities portends significant implications not only for investors, but also for financial managers of multinational firms. These managers traditionally have thought of foreign financing primarily through flotations of debt securities in the form of foreign and Eurobond issues. This development, which has been described as the wave of the future, opens new vistas for these managers which have been heretofore ignored or considered as a minor aspect in the financing of their worldwide operations. This development is also of interest to the students of international finance, as it portends significant changes in the established patterns of financing foreign operations, clearly beyond the improvement in the risk/return tradeoff established in the international finance literature.

This chapter surveys the major equity markets outside the United States, their main features and characteristics, as well as their limitations. It also attempts to compare their performance over a period extending from the inception of the floating exchange regime through 1985. The increasing interest of U.S. institutional investors in these markets is highlighted, chiefly with data released by international brokerage houses. The reasons behind this trend are investigated so as to ascertain the degree of such a tendency's gaining momentum in the years ahead. The chapter concludes with the implications of this development to the multinational firm in forging a worldwide financing strategy for its operations.

FOREIGN EQUITY MARKETS

Organized stock exchanges exist in all industrial countries and in a large number of developing countries. Trading equities in well organized exchanges with relatively sufficient depth to permit participation by foreign investors may be found in Australia, Belgium, Canada, France, Germany, the Netherlands, Hong Kong, Italy, Japan, Singapore, South Africa, Sweden, Switzerland, and the United Kingdom.

Trading in stock exchanges outside of these countries poses serious problems to foreign investors. These markets are still generally primitive in nature, and lack the regulatory framework and structural safeguards that characterize equity markets in the United States and most of the industrial countries listed earlier. Trading is often shallow and price movements are, consequently, too erratic, particularly for large trades. Most of these markets are clearly inefficient, and information on the securities traded is difficult to obtain and transaction costs are relatively high.[1]

In a typical stock exchange in an LDC there are few meaningful listing requirements, only few stocks are traded, and information about the com-

[1]The author had the opportunity to observe the operations of the Bourse of Kuwait (the organized stock exchange in Kuwait) in the late 1970s. The market, a private organization, is loosely supervised by the Ministry of Trade and has a rather flexible set of informal trading rules. There are virtually no listing requirements and no machinery to insure orderly price changes (such as the specialists on the floor of the New York Stock Exchange). Share prices of a number of newly organized firms that were yet to begin operations were often driven up in a speculative frenzy. The market subsequently crashed under the impact of speculative activities in shares that often had dubious intrinsic values. The market remained closed for a considerable period of time, during which the authorities debated the financial damage sustained by a number of participants, some of whom belonged to prominent families. The government subsequently decided to bail out the Kuwaitis who sustained losses as a result of the crash. The exchange subsequently reopened after some minor changes in trading regulations were introduced.

panies whose stocks are traded is scanty. The stock exchange in Istanbul, Turkey, is perhaps typical of how stock exchanges in LDCs operate. Although it is probably overregulated by the government to prevent a repetition of the collapse of the previous exchange in 1982, potential investors lack the safeguards and information base necessary for sound investment decisions. There are 36 authorized dealers who trade the stocks of 40 listed companies which represent Turkey's largest firms. Exchange officials meet each morning to assess demand and fix prices. The price of a share is not permitted to rise or fall by more than 5 percent in any trading session. Shares in which there is buying or selling interest are displayed by exchange officials in alphabetical order using an overhead projector. Traders signify their interest (in buying or selling the displayed stock) by raising their hands and filling an order form. In a typical day only a handful of the listed stocks is traded. Bonds are traded in afternoon sessions. Foreign stocks are not traded on the Istanbul exchange, because the Turkish lira is not a convertible currency.[2]

With the exception of the United Kingdom, organized stock exchanges in the industrial countries listed earlier generally lack the depth, breadth, and resilience which characterize these markets in the United States. Trading in many exchanges is often restricted to shares of a handful of companies which dominate the market. Trading in most other listed stocks is usually thin and sporadic, thus lacking the continuous and orderly nature of price movements which are found in U.S. markets.

These limitations together with the higher perceived risk of investing in foreign stocks help explain why the internationalization of equity markets has lagged considerably behind the integration of the international money and capital markets, particularly for debt-securities and syndicated loans. It was not until 1983 that truly international equity issues were floated in three separate markets. These issues by two Canadian firms, Alcan Aluminum and Canada Enterprises, were underwritten by three separate syndications and launched simultaneously in Canada, the United States, and Europe.[3] Such issues have significant implications for financial managers of multinational firms, since they considerably widen the options available for long-term financing.

FOREIGN MULTINATIONALS' PRESENCE IN U.S. EQUITY MARKETS

Non-U.S. multinationals have long sought to avail themselves of the depth and the favorable characteristics of the U.S. equity markets to reduce their cost of capital. The major barrier has been the disclosure regulations of the

[2]Phillip Revzin, "At Stock Exchange in Istanbul, All that Is Lacking Is Stock," *Wall Street Journal,* April 4, 1986, pp. 1 and 27.

[3]*Euromoney,* "The One-World Capital Market," October 1984, p. 110.

U.S. Securities and Exchange Commission (SEC). Only a relatively small number of foreign firms have listed their securities on the organized exchanges in the United States, most of them on the New York Stock Exchange. Stiff registration requirements and extensive financial disclosure have been cited as the major impediments. Another problem is the wide difference in accounting standards and techniques in different countries. However, with the internationalization of the capital markets, greater uniformity in accounting standards and financial reporting are enabling a large number of non-U.S. multinational firms to meet the standards required by the SEC and the organized exchanges.

Most of the foreign equities are traded in the United States in the form of *American depository receipts* (ADRs). ADRs are certificates denominated in U.S. dollars issued by a U.S. bank on the basis of the foreign security which it holds in custody. The system was developed by Morgan Guaranty Trust Company of New York in 1981 to facilitate the trading of foreign securities in the United States. The ADR system allows trading foreign securities in U.S. dollars rather than the currency of the country of issue and spares the U.S. investor the cost of converting dividends received in foreign currencies to U.S. dollars. It also permits transfer of ownership of these securities in the United States without physical transfer of the underlying shares. American depository shares (ADSs) are essentially similar to ADRs in being stock ownership certificates issued in the United States by a transfer agent or a trustee acting on behalf of the foreign issuer. An ADS may be issued at a price different from that of the underlying shares to conform to norms established by the SEC and the organized exchanges.

COMPARATIVE PERFORMANCE OF EQUITY MARKETS

During the thirteen-year period since the breakdown of the Bretton Woods fixed-exchange-rate system (1971–1984), most foreign equity markets outperformed U.S. equities based on stock market indices unadjusted for changes in national currencies vis-a-vis the U.S. dollar (Exhibit 10-1). Measured by the Standard & Poors 500 index, U.S. equities outperformed only Swiss equities during this period.

When adjusted for exchange rate changes, the situation looks somewhat different. U.S. equities outperformed equity markets in Australia, Belgium, France, Italy, Switzerland, and the United Kingdom. Japanese equities have had a spectacular performance, rising about seven times faster than U.S. equities. A U.S. investor in Japanese equities during this period would have benefited not only from the sharp rise in equity prices in Japan, but also from the appreciation of the Japanese yen against the U.S. dollar. The same observation applies to the Singapore equity market and, to a lesser extent, to German equities.

Exhibit 10-1. Changes in Stock Market Indices in Fifteen Major Industrial Countries — 1971–1984

	Year End 1971 thru Year End 1984			1984		
	Stock Market Index	National Currency Parity vs. US$ % Change	Combined Change	Stock Market Index	National Currency Parity vs. US$ % Change	Combined Change
DJIA	36.10%	–	36.10%	– 3.74%	–	– 3.74%
S&P 500	63.82	–	63.82	1.40	–	1.40
Australia	113.06	−30.88	47.27	– 6.35	– 8.17	−14.00
Belgium	63.47	−29.38	15.45	16.26	−11.96	2.35
Canada	142.32	−24.10	83.93	– 5.96	– 5.75	−11.36
France	145.52	−45.89	31.78	16.40	−13.42	0.78
Germany	70.81	3.69	77.12	6.35	−13.63	– 8.14
Holland	88.69	– 8.58	72.50	17.96	−13.92	1.54
Hong Kong	251.65	−27.33	155.54	37.20	– 0.47	36.56
Italy	106.83	−69.85	– 37.65	20.28	−14.35	3.01
Japan	325.34	24.31	428.75	16.66	– 7.92	7.43
Singapore	308.98	32.26	440.92	−18.90	– 2.54	−20.97
South Africa (IND)	387.84	−61.71	86.79	– 3.25	−38.78	−40.77
Sweden	351.49	−45.87	144.38	– 6.30	−10.73	−16.35
Switzerland	0.60	50.35	51.25	0.47	−16.15	−15.76
U.K. (IND)	99.85	−54.59	– 9.24	22.77	−20.19	– 2.02
Gold						
Bullion	610.34	–	610.34	−19.19	–	−19.19
Indices						
South Africa	1154.22	−61.71	380.23	8.34	−38.78	−33.68
U.K.	879.35	−54.59	344.76	−16.81	−20.19	−33.61

Source: Drexel Burnham Lambert, Inc., *International Investment Monthly*, March 1985, p. 1. Reproduced with permission from Drexel Burnham Lambert, Inc., New York.

Equities performed poorly around the world in 1984. U.S. equities, which remained virtually unchanged during the year, fared better than most foreign equity markets on an exchange-rate adjusted basis. The sharp appreciation of the U.S. dollar against virtually all currencies more than offset the rise in foreign stock market indices during the year. Nevertheless, equity markets in Japan and Hong Kong continued to outperform U.S. equities.

Equity markets throughout the world registered sizable gains in 1985 (Exhibit 10-2). The only markets which declined on an exchange-adjusted basis were the South African and Singapore markets. The intensification of internal political strife and continued decline in the price of gold were primarily responsible for the adverse trend in South Africa. Unlike almost

Exhibit 10-2. Performance of Equity Markets—1985

		PERCENTAGE CHANGES		
	Value of Index on Dec. 31, 1985	Local Stock Market Index	National Currency Parity vs. U.S. $	Combined Change
United States				
DJIA	1546.67	27.7	–	27.7
S&P 500	211.28	26.3	–	26.3
Australia				
ASE All Ordinary	1003.70	38.2	−17.3	14.3
Belgium				
Belgian Stock Exch.	2943.48	34.6	25.9	69.4
Canada				
TSE Composite	2900.60	20.8	− 5.5	14.2
France				
CAC Generale	265.80	45.7	28.3	87.0
Germany				
FAZ Aktien	654.05	71.6	28.9	121.2
Commerzbank	1951.50	76.1	28.9	127.0
Holland				
ANP General	255.60	40.5	29.1	81.4
Hong Kong				
Hang Seng	1752.45	46.0	0.2	46.2
Italy				
Banca Commerciale	457.04	98.5	16.1	130.4
Japan				
Nikkei Dow	13113.3	13.6	25.6	42.7
Second Section	1874.16	2.8	25.6	29.2
Norway				
Oslo Stock Exchange	393.12	37.1	20.1	64.7
Singapore				
Straits Times	620.04	−23.7	3.5	− 21.1
South Africa				
ROM Industrials	1154.50	23.5	−47.9	− 35.6
Sweden				
Jacobson & P	1737.66	28.3	18.8	52.5
Switzerland				
SBC Industrials	587.90	52.5	26.4	92.7
United Kingdom				
Financial Times Ord.	1131.40	18.8	24.7	48.1
Gold				
Bullion	329.00	6.5	–	6.5
Indices				
So. Africa	1156.80	21.7	−47.9	− 36.6
U.K.	249.80	−47.8	24.7	− 35.0
Toronto	4349.09	48.9	− 5.5	40.7

Source: Drexel Burnham Lambert, Inc., *International Investment Monthly,* January 1986, p. 25. Reproduced with permission from Drexel Burnham Lambert, Inc., New York.

all currencies of industrial countries, which appreciated vis-a-vis the U.S. dollar during the year, the value of the South African rand declined against the U.S. dollar by almost 50 percent. Singapore equities lost ground on account of dislocations caused by the repercussions of the failure of a major financial institution.

With few exceptions (Australia, Canada, Singapore, and South Africa), equity markets in industrial countries considerably outperformed U.S. equities in 1985. This is particularly true of all the major trading partners of the United States, with the exception of Canada. The best performance was registered by equities in Germany, Italy, and Switzerland, while Japan and Asian markets in general had a lackluster year.

When adjusted for exchange rate changes, performance of foreign equities in 1985 was even more impressive from the standpoint of the U.S. investor. The U.S. dollar depreciated sharply against the currencies of industrial countries, ranging from 16.1 percent against the Italian lira to 28.9 percent against the deutsche mark. The only major currencies which lost ground against the U.S. dollar during the year are the Australian dollar, the Canadian dollar, and the South African rand.

A global stock index was evolved in 1986 by Euromoney and the First Boston Corporation. The index, to be known as the Euromoney/First Boston Global Stock Index, tracks the movements of 1500 equities drawn from 18 major equity markets representing the United States, Japan, the United Kingdom, Canada, Germany, France, the Netherlands, Switzerland, Australia, Sweden, Spain, Italy, Singapore, Malaysia, Hong Kong, Norway, Belgium, and Denmark. The index is calculated in two ways: The first measures overall price performance and the second measures total return. A separate index encompassing only non-U.S. stocks is also compiled. These indices appear regularly in *Euromoney.*[4]

The lesson of the comparative performance of U.S. versus foreign equity markets during this period has not been lost to U.S. investors. They have been accumulating foreign stocks in relatively large amounts over the past few years. Data in Exhibit 10-3 show that U.S. investors acquired foreign equities on a net basis in each of the years covered (1979–1984), although the amounts of net purchases have been erratic. Traditionally, net purchases of foreign securities by U.S. investors accelerate during periods characterized by a strong U.S. dollar (vis-a-vis other currencies) and dull performance by U.S. equity markets, compared to foreign markets. Conversely, new acquisition of foreign equities is discouraged by higher interest rate levels in the United States than in other major industrial countries, and by a weak dollar, which makes such acquisition more expensive.

Who is buying foreign equities? The bulk of acquisition in the period covered by Exhibit 10-3 was made by institutional investors, particularly

[4] *Euromoney,* January 1986, p. 17.

Exhibit 10-3. Net Purchases of Foreign Stocks by U.S. Investors (in millions of U.S. dollars)

	1979	1980	1981	1982	1983	1984
Europe	−137	418	816	799	2209	384
France	4	203	69	215	390	99
Netherlands	81	252	39	115	219	−113
Switzerland	− 63	25	33	75	82	56
U.K.	−171	− 45	− 38	218	1316	232
Canada	912	776	−583	− 53	333	−103
Asia	− 27	882	243	491	1247	−256
Japan	− 24	838	252	479	950	−473
Others	38	103	212	106	46	344
Total	786	2179	688	1343	3835	369

Source: Drexel Burnham Lambert, Inc., *International Investment Monthly*, March 1985, p. 3. Reproduced with permission from Drexel Burnham Lambert, Inc., New York.

Exhibit 10-4. Comparative Valuation of Equities, December 31, 1985

National Indices	Price/Earning Ratio, 1985	Price/Earning Ratio, 1986[1]	Estimated Yield	Yield of Long-Term Government Bonds
United States: S&P 500	13.3X	12.2X	3.7%	9.5%
Australia: ASE All Ordinary	11.4	10.3	4.1	15.1
Belgium: Belgian Stock Exchange	9.1	8.3	4.5	10.5
Canada: TSE Composite	13.8	12.6	3.2	10.0
France: CAC Generale	14.1	12.3	2.6	10.5
Germany: Commerzbank	13.4	12.0	1.7	6.9
Hong Kong: Hang Seng	14.1	12.9	3.5	NA[2]
Italy: Banca Commerciale	19.9	17.3	2.2	13.8
Japan: Nikkei Dow	27.5	29.3	1.0	5.8
The Netherlands: ANP-CBS General	9.6	8.6	3.8	6.9
Sweden: Jacobson & P.	NA[2]	NA[2]	NA[2]	NA[2]
Switzerland: SBC Industrials	12.4	11.2	1.9	4.5
United Kingdom: Financial Times Ordinary	11.3	10.5	4.4	10.3

[1]Estimates by Drexel Burnham Lambert, Inc.
[2]NA—Not available

Source: Drexel Burnham Lambert, Inc. *International Investment Monthly*, January 1986, p. 10. Reproduced with permission from Drexel Burnham Lambert, Inc., New York.

mutual funds and pension funds. Overseas investments of pension funds grew sharply in recent years, particularly among those which have assets exceeding $1 billion. Overseas investments of pension funds covered by ERISA (Employment Retirement Income Security Act of 1974) rose from $5.2 billion at the end of 1981, accounting for 1.3 percent of total assets, to $16.7 billion at the end of 1984, accounting for 2.4 percent of total assets. These investments were projected to rise to $40 billion at the end of 1988, accounting for 4 percent of total assets of pension funds covered by ERISA.[5] Sixty-five percent of pension funds with assets over $1 billion had assets in foreign markets in 1984 compared with 26 percent in 1979.[6]

Recent statistics on comparative market valuations by Capital International and Drexel Burnham Lambert, Inc. continue to show that U.S. equities are statistically undervalued on a comparative international basis. The gap, however, appears to have narrowed somewhat by the prolonged rise experienced by U.S. equities in 1985 and 1986. Exhibit 10-4, which is based on data compiled by Drexel Burnham Lambert, Inc., portrays comparative valuation of equities as of year end 1985. Among the countries listed, equities of six countries (Canada, France, Germany, Hong Kong, Italy, and Japan) had higher capitalization value (in terms of price/earning ratio) than the Standard & Poors 500 index.

RECENT DEVELOPMENTS AND INNOVATIONS IN INTERNATIONAL CAPITAL MARKETS[7]

International capital markets have experienced a number of significant changes and innovations during the first half of the present decade. These developments have moved these markets further toward integration and internationalization and opened new vistas of financing opportunities for MNCs. These developments are examined in this section under four headings: 1) innovations in the Eurobond markets, 2) development of the Euronote market, 3) international equities, and 4) swap transactions.

INNOVATIONS IN THE EUROBOND MARKET

Fixed rate Eurobonds (also called straights) have continued to account for over 50 percent of the total market despite the increasing popularity of the floating rate bonds. The latter accounted for about 41 percent of the market in 1985. Convertibles and bonds with warrant exchangeable into equity accounted for about 5 percent of the total market (see Exhibit 10-5).

[5] *International Investment Monthly,* March 1985, p. 4.

[6] *Ibid.,* p. 4.

[7] This section draws on material compiled and published by *Euromoney* in a special supplement to the March 1986 issue. The material and illustrations are used with special permission from *Euromoney.*

Exhibit 10.5. Eurobonds by Type of Instrument

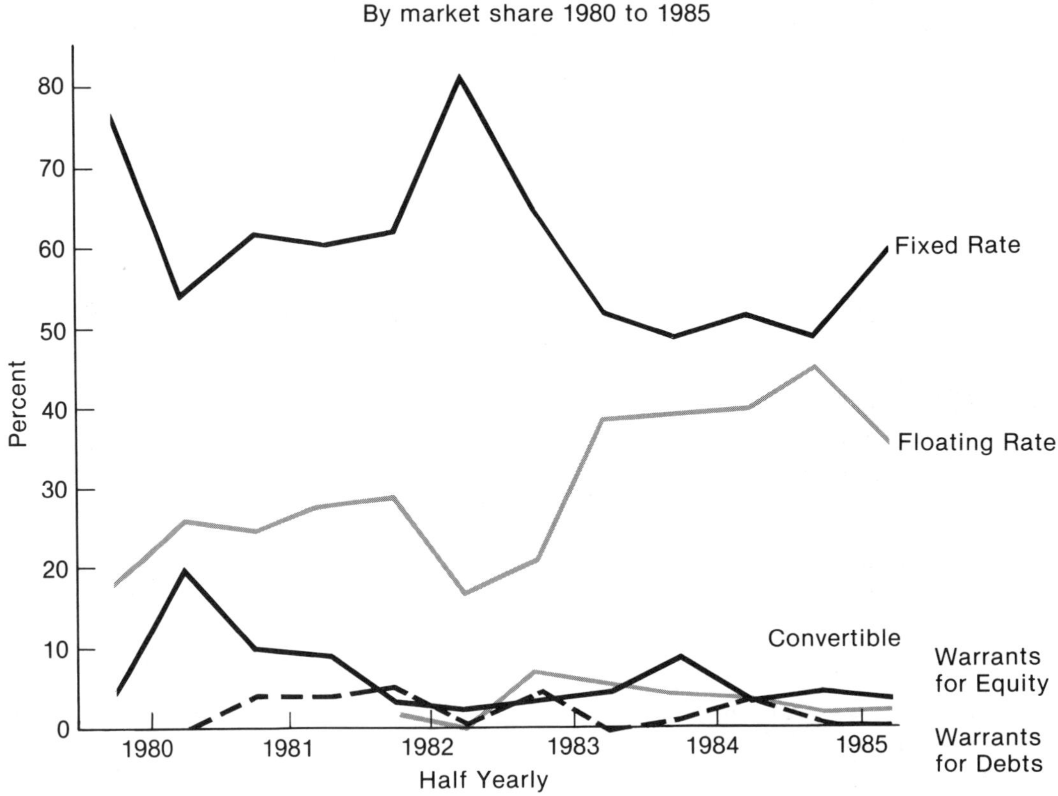

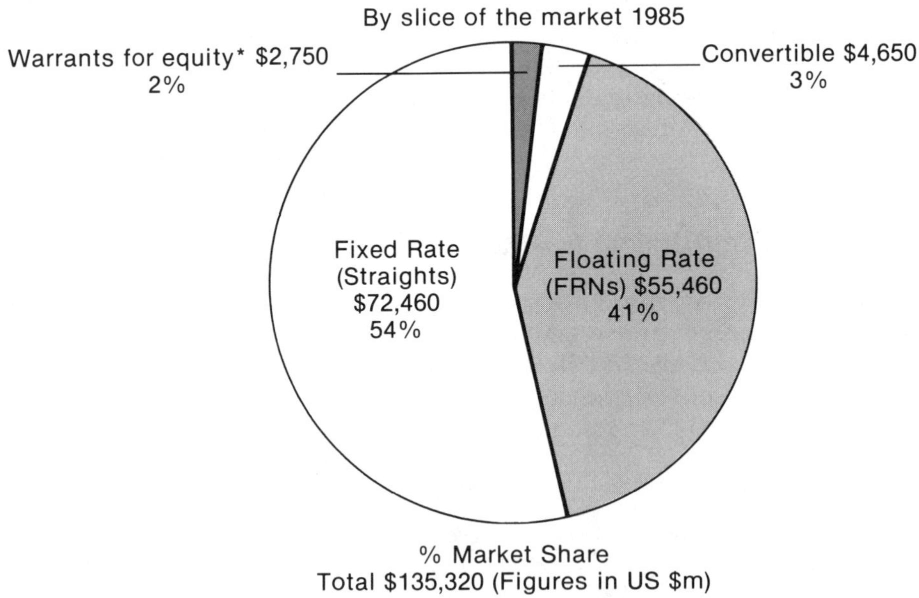

*Including both fixed rate and floating rate

Source: *Euromoney*, Annual Financing Report, March 1986. Reproduced with permission from *Euromoney*.

Convertible Eurobonds have declined somewhat in popularity following their initial success, particularly in 1980, when their share of the total market was over 20 percent. One factor behind this decline is the increasing use of international equity issued by MNCs, since convertibles are normally intended as indirect equity issues, particularly when equity markets are not favorable. Another is the introduction in the early 1980s of bond warrants. There are two types of Eurobonds issued with warrants: One type, which has long been a feature of the U.S. bond market, is exchangeable into equity of the issuing firm, and the second, which is truly innovative, is bonds with warrants that give the holder a right to exercise into the back bond (the bond issued together with, or at the same time as, the warrant). For example, the kingdom of Sweden issued in December 1980 a 13.65 percent coupon Eurobond due 1985 with warrants valid for six months, exercisable into 13.65 percent bonds due 1986.

Another innovation is the so-called *wedded warrants* illustrated by an October 1985 issue arranged for Gaz de France (the borrower) by Morgan Stanley International. The 10-year bonds are callable after five years with warrants that give the holder the option to buy identical but noncallable bonds. However, for the first five years the warrants are "wedded" to the original bonds. To exercise the warrants during this period, the holder must sell an equal amount of the original bonds back to the borrower. During the second five-year period, the bonds can be acquired for cash, since the warrants are "divorced" from the original bonds.[8]

The use of warrants has generally contributed to more market acceptability and somewhat lower coupon cost for the issuer. For the investor the wedded warrant feature means less marketability, which is compensated by higher yields and potential speculative gains.

The dual currency Eurobonds, virtually all of which are yen/dollar bonds, have been around for a few years. These are Eurobonds denominated and serviced in Japanese yen, but which are redeemable in U.S. dollars at an exchange rate fixed at the time of the issue. This feature was originally designed to attract Japanese investors with high yields (relative to domestic yen rates) in return for their taking a long-term risk (usually 10 years) on the yen-dollar exchange rate. The standard conversion rate was set in some of these issues at 208 yen per U.S. dollar. Holders of these dual currency bonds must have received a hard lesson on the dangers of speculation when the yen appreciated sharply during the first half of 1986 to about 165 yen per U.S. dollar. A number of these innovations have swap implications, which are explained later in this section.

DEVELOPMENT OF THE EURONOTE MARKET

Euronotes and their shorter-term sister Euro-commercial paper are debt instruments denominated in other than the currency of the country in

[8]*Euromoney,* special supplement, March 1986, pp. 22–23.

which they are issued and placed. From a modest beginning in 1980, the Euronote volume expanded to over $60 billion in 1985. Euronotes tap the shorter end of the Eurofunds market, being issued predominately in maturities of three or six months. As a financial instrument, it is competitive with CDs issued by financial institutions, commercial paper, and government treasury bills for the investors' funds.

The major borrowers in 1985 were U.S. and non-U.S. multinational industrial firms, accounting for well over 70 percent of total volume. Other borrowers in the order of their importance are financial institutions, governments or sovereign borrowers, and international institutions.[9] There is some evidence that the sharp rise in Euronote volume in the mid-1980s has been partly at the expense of declining Eurocredits or syndicated Eurocurrency loans. Investors have tended to shy away from the high risks associated with loans to sovereign LDCs' borrowers.

Euronotes and Euro-commercial paper are denominated almost entirely in U.S. dollars and ECUs and lack the depth of the commercial paper market in the United States. The Euro-commercial paper market is still limited to few large, well-known corporations exchanging excess liquidity among themselves, with banks acting in an intermediary role as dealers or distributors.

INTERNATIONAL EQUITIES

Few major companies today ignore equity markets outside their countries when embarking on a substantial issue of shares. Some of the large firms, particularly non-U.S. multinationals, have outstripped the resources of their domestic market and are looking for equity funds from foreign investors. Moreover, MNCs have found by experience that it is possible to raise funds at lower cost from foreign than from home equity markets. This trend has been strengthened by the increasing attention devoted by managers of institutional portfolios to foreign equities.

Among the pioneers in the Euro-equity market is Bell Canada Enterprises (a Canadian telecommunication group), which in 1975 made a simultaneous listing on six European stock exchanges: London, Zurich, Frankfurt, Paris, Brussels, and Amsterdam. Since then, the group has floated a number of Eurobond and Euro-equity issues.[10] A well-documented case is that of a Danish pharmaceutical firm, Novoindustrie A/S. In 1981 Novoindustrie successfully tapped the equity markets in London and New York. What propelled the firm to take this step was its inability to raise equity funds at home at favorable prices, and the fact that the Danish market was too small to accommodate its requirements. These conditions placed it at a competitive disadvantage vis-a-vis its rivals among U.S. and

[9]*Euromoney,* special supplement, p. 85.
[10]*Euromoney,* special supplement, p. 114.

other European multinational firms in the pharmaceutical and drugs industry. The prices that its shares were able to command in New York and London were three times what Danish investors were prepared to pay.

Another notable illustration of the internationalization of the equity base on an MNC to match its multinational operations is the experience of Phillips, a Dutch electric company. As of mid-1986, U.S. investors owned approximately one-fourth of the stock of Phillips, which does about 30 percent of its business in the United States. Phillips is accessible to U.S. investors, as it is listed both on the Over-the-Counter Market and on the New York Stock Exchange, through its U.S. subsidiary, North American Phillips Corporation.

The expansion of the Euro-equity market has been facilitated by a number of factors and innovations. These may be summarized as follows:

1. The emergence of international syndicates of banks and brokerage houses, which are capable of placing equity issues for major MNCs within time periods that are much shorter than domestic issues.
2. The relatively lower syndication and distribution fees for Euro-equities compared with domestic issues. These fees were estimated at between 2.5 and 6.5 percent of market price, compared to a discount from market prices ranging from 5 to 10 percent for domestic issues.[11]
3. The development of innovative approaches to investment in foreign equities to circumvent regulatory and physical impediments which have in the past hindered such investment.
4. The desire on the part of MNCs, particularly U.S. firms, to avoid the lengthy and costly registration requirements for home equity issues. Other firms have opted for foreign listing of their shares to escape stringent disclosure requirements, which are deemed by such firms to be harmful to their competitive position in their own industries.

Some of these points require further explanation, particularly 3 and 4. Among the innovations are the ADR and its twin sister the ADS, which represent a convenient and efficient way for U.S. investors to buy foreign equities without the actual delivery of these securities. Moreover, these investors share in dividends without incurring foreign taxes or being subject to exchange control regulations. Because the underlying stocks are not issued in the United States, the issues are not subject to the SEC registration procedure. The ADSs also make possible the sale of shares which represent a fraction of the value of the underlying foreign stocks.

Beside the ADRs, there are several forms of nonvoting stocks which allow foreign investors to receive dividends and participate in profits without enjoying the other privileges of the shareholders in the home country.

[11] *Euromoney,* special supplement, p. 121.

Convertible Eurobonds and Eurobonds with warrants exercisable into equity represent such a vehicle.

Another form of nonvoting stock is the participation certificate (PC), which has been used mainly by Swiss MNCs to attract foreign institutional investors. PCs are nonvoting certificates, issued usually in bearer form, which allow issuing companies to split their shares into more marketable portions. Nestlé, a Swiss multinational food firm, used this device in recent years to raise funds at favorable costs by having banks place the PCs directly with institutional investors, often cutting by half the time needed to obtain equity funds. The PC market is likely to become an important segment of the international equity market, as it utilizes the same cost-effective mechanisms developed by investment banks for Eurobonds.

These nonvoting quasi-equity instruments offer another attraction to investors in some countries in the form of tax advantages. As of early 1986, German companies issuing *GenuBschein,* a form of dividend-sharing security, are allowed to charge dividends paid on these shares against income. In Austria investors holding these shares are allowed to deduct 75 percent of the purchase price against taxable income.[12]

For a growing number of MNCs, seeking overseas investors has been primarily motivated by the desire to circumvent the cost and/or the disclosure rules of the stock exchanges at home. International Signals and Control Corporation (ISC), a U.S. MNC producing space and defense electronic equipment, used a specially formed holding company in the United Kingdom to raise equity funds in 1982. There were a number of factors which influenced ISC to list its stock on the London Stock Exchange rather than in New York. The cost of listing in New York is substantially higher than in London, due in part to the lengthy process of compliance with a mass of regulatory paperwork. The firm also wanted to take advantage of the higher premiums for defense stocks that British investors were willing to pay.

The primary reason, however, which prompted ISC and a large number of other U.S. multinational firms to seek listing in foreign instead of home exchanges is to avoid the full disclosure standards required by the SEC. These standards call for such details about the firm and its operations that many firms feel that disclosure would compromise their position vis-a-vis their competitors in future bidding contracts. For this reason, the SEC has been willing to relax disclosure rules for U.S. defense contractors in certain cases.

United States companies face certain limitations when seeking foreign registration and trading of their shares to avoid the SEC regulatory jurisdiction. If the number of U.S. resident shareholders exceeds a specified limit, the company has to file the same information with the SEC that it had disclosed to the regulatory authority in the foreign country. If the per-

[12]*Euromoney,* special supplement, p. 124.

centage of ownership by U.S. residents exceeds 51 percent, the company is required to apply for listing on a U.S. stock exchange.

The question of choosing an appropriate exchange for listing that would meet a firm's needs and circumstances is one that cannot be settled only by the desire to avoid compliance with costly and potentially damaging disclosure. An important consideration is to choose an exchange which gives a wider recognition for a firm's stock and expands its acceptability by investors. An interesting example is Rodime, a Scottish electronics company, which chose to list on the American Over-the-Counter Market (OTC) in the United States because it has a large number of high-tech firms seeking wider investors' recognition.[13]

Louis Vuitton, a Swiss leather goods manufacturer, issued ADRs in New York in June 1984 to boost the firm's image and sales in the United States. Four ADSs, which were sold at U.S. $15 each, make a full Vuitton share. The firm chose to list its ADRs on Over-the-Counter Market rather than on the New York Stock Exchange primarily because the cost of listing on the NYSE is approximately U.S. $30,000, compared to about five percent of this figure for listing on NASDAQ (National Association of Securities Dealers Automatic Quotation System). Furthermore, NASDAQ better suited Vuitton's needs because there are usually five or six market markers in any particular stock, compared to two on the major exchanges. Trading on NASDAQ is also possible beyond the regular hour of trading on the floors of the exchanges.[14]

SWAPS

The phenomenal growth and increased sophistication of the swap market in the mid-1980s is perhaps the most striking development in international finance in the past 25 years. From obscure and modest beginnings in the late 1970s, the total size of the market (measured by outstanding swap deals) was estimated at U.S. $200 billion at the end of 1985.

A swap is simply an exchange of assets or liabilities of an equivalent amount between two counterparties to achieve certain objectives desired by the parties. Swapping may also be thought of as a form of arbitrage whereby bankers or financial managers may take advantage of imperfections in financial markets to improve their rate of return. Even when the two parties to a swap are business corporations, banks or other financial institutions often intermediate to guarantee the fulfillment of obligations undertaken by the swap parties.

The development of financial swaps represents an imaginative response to the challenging phenomena which have characterized financial

[13] *Euromoney,* special supplement, p. 125.
[14] *Euromoney,* special supplement, p. 124.

markets in recent years. The financial environment has been tested by deregulation, increasing integration of world capital markets, and interest rate and exchange rate volatility. Swaps have themselves contributed to further integration of international money, capital, and foreign exchange markets, and have widened the options available to the participants in these markets.

Swaps meet the need of a wide range of participants, including corporate treasurers, bankers, portfolio managers, and central bankers and monetary authorities. Their needs may be a lower cost of funds, a higher rate of return, better management of interest rate exposure, or diversification of the currency risk. Irrespective of their needs and circumstances, each party to a swap operation has an objective which fits in the overall management of his or her financial resources.

The central idea behind financial swaps is that they give the parties involved access to markets at more favorable terms than are available to each acting individually. The gains achieved by having each party access the market where it has a comparative advantage are divided between the two in some fashion, depending mostly on their relative competitive position.

TYPES OF SWAPS

The types of financial swaps and their structuring are as varied as the ingenuity and creativity of the participants. There are, however, four basic swap structures which dominate the market: the interest rate swap, the fixed-rate currency swap, the currency coupon swap, and the basis rate swap. The following is a summary of these fundamental swap structures and their primary applications.

Interest Rate Swap

An interest rate swap, by far the most prevalent type, is simply an exchange between two parties of a fixed-rate interest instrument for a floating-rate interest instrument in the same currency. There is an underlying reference or "notional" principal on the basis of which interest is calculated, which normally equates to the underlying assets or liabilities being swapped. However, there is no physical exchange of the underlying assets or liabilities. Through this mechanism, an institution, let us say a savings and loan association, is able to convert an underlying asset, such as a fixed-rate mortgage, into a floating-rate asset.

This swap is primarily motivated by the arbitrage gains achieved by each counterparty's accessing the market in which it has the greatest relative cost advantage, and then entering into an interest rate swap to convert the cost of funds into the basis preferred by that party for interest rate management purposes.

This swap structure is illustrated in Exhibit 10-6. Company A has a higher credit rating than company B and can, therefore, raise funds at lower cost in both the fixed-rate and floating-rate debt markets. Company A, however, has a greater relative cost advantage over company B in the fixed-rate market than in the floating-rate market (120 basis points versus 50 basis points). It would, therefore, be mutually advantageous for company A to obtain fixed-rate funding and for company B to obtain floating-rate funding, and then to enter into a swap arrangement.

As shown in Exhibit 10-6, both companies were able to raise funds in the market which each originally desired at 35 basis points less than either could have obtained by accessing that market directly. Company A, which was in the market for floating-rate funds, was able to obtain the funds at LIBOR $-\frac{1}{10}$ of one percent instead of LIBOR $+\frac{1}{4}$ percent. Company B, which was seeking funds at a fixed rate, was able to obtain the funds at 11.65 percent instead of 12 percent.

In addition to cost advantages, interest rate swaps also provide a mechanism whereby participants may access markets which are otherwise closed to them by reason of poor credit standing, lack of name recognition by the market, or for other reasons.

The mechanism underlying the interest rate swap is versatile and can be used in a variety of interest rate exposure management situations. Let us assume that a corporate treasurer obtained fixed-rate debt, and that soon after interest rates started to decline. The treasurer can manage to reduce the firm's cost of funds by (1) swapping the fixed-rate debt to obtain LIBOR funding, (2) leaving the swap in place as interest rates decline, (3) at the end of the period of interest rate decline, entering a second swap to "lock in" the new lower fixed rate. This is illustrated in Exhibit 10-7.

Note that the underlying source of funds for company A (the fixed-rate funding at 12 percent) was left unaffected, while the treasurer took advantage of a falling interest rate market to reduce the cost funds for the firm by two percentage points.

The Fixed-Rate Currency Swap

A fixed-rate currency swap consists of exchanging a fixed-rate asset/liability denominated in one currency into a fixed-rate asset/liability denominated in another currency. There are three steps involved in a standard fixed currency swap: (1) At the outset the counterparties to the swap exchange the principal amounts at an agreed reference rate of exchange (usually the spot exchange rate). (2) During the swap period the counterparties exchange interest payments based on the outstanding principal amounts at the respective fixed interest rates agreed upon at the outset. (3) On the maturity date, the counterparties reexchange the principal amounts at the exchange rate established in step (1). The initial exchange of currencies in

Exhibit 10-6. Illustration of an Interest Rate Swap

	Company A	Company B	Comparative Advantage
Credit rating	AAA	BBB	
Cost of raising direct fixed rate funding	10.80%	12.00%	1.20%
Cost of raising direct floating rate funds	6-month LIBOR plus 1/4%	6-month LIBOR plus 3/4%	.50%
Direct funding cost			
Fixed rate funds raised directly by company A	10.80%		
Floating rate funds raised directly by company B		6-month LIBOR + ¾%	
Swap payments			
Company A pays company B floating rate interest	LIBOR	LIBOR	
Company B pays company A fixed rate interest	10.90%	10.90%	
All-in cost of funding	LIBOR − 1/10%	11.65%	
Comparable cost of equivalent direct funding	LIBOR + 1/4%	12.00%	
Savings	35 Basis points	35 Basis points	

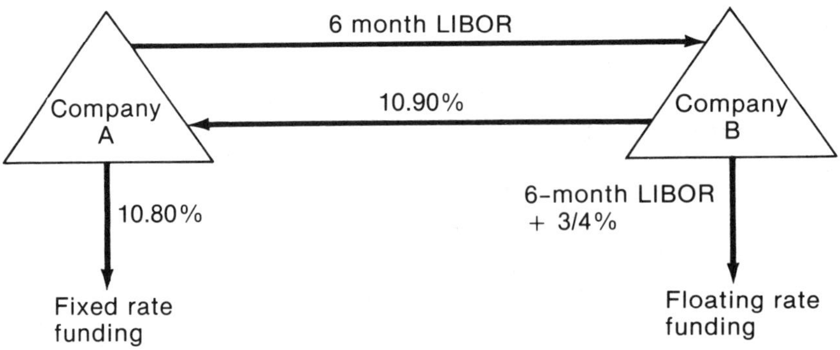

Arrows represent interest flows

Source: *Euromoney,* special supplement, March 1986, p. 95. Reproduced with permission from *Euromoney.*

Exhibit 10-7. Illustration of a two-stage Interest Rate Swap

Stage (1)

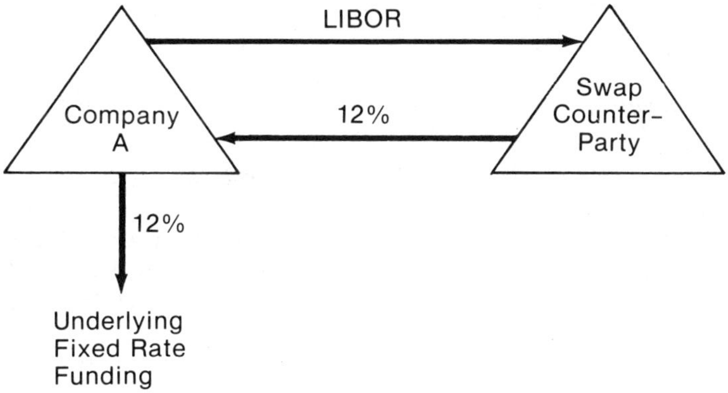

Stage (2)

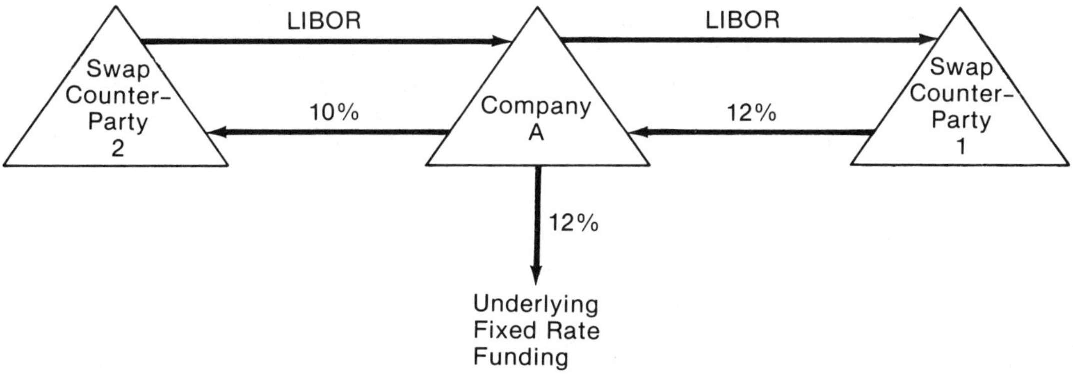

Source: *Euromony,* special supplement, March 1986, p. 96. Reproduced with permission from *Euromoney.*

step (1) may be either physical or notional, that is, established for the purpose of calculating interest payments exchangeable in step (2).

The net effect of the fixed-rate currency swap is to transform a debt raised in one currency into a fully hedged fixed-rate liability in another currency. In this respect its objective is similar to the forward foreign exchange contract. However, the swap structure has more flexibility than the conventional forward exchange contract with respect to both maturities and amounts desired by the counterparties. While the interest rate differential between the two currencies in the forward market is reflected in the forward premium (or discount), which is payable in one lump sum, the swap structure allows for periodic settlement of interest differentials.

The fixed-rate currency swap with the intermediation of a bank is illustrated in Exhibit 10-8. The objective of the U.S. firm is to provide financing in pounds sterling to its British subsidiary without incurring exchange risk, and with a minimum of delays and administrative problems. In step (1) the bank exchanges with the U.S. parent company an amount of British pounds equal to the principal of the intracompany loan (made to the subsidiary) in return for an equivalent amount of U.S. dollars based on the spot exchange rate. In step (2) interest payments are exchanged over the life of the swap based on rates established in step (1). The U.S. firm uses interest payments in pounds sterling received from its British subsidiary to pay the bank, while receiving from the latter fixed-rate interest in U.S. dollars. In step (3), the principal amount is reexchanged by the parties on the maturity date. The British subsidiary pays back the principal of the loan to its U.S. parent in sterling. The U.S. parent uses this amount to pay the bank, receiving in return the principal amount in U.S. dollars.

On the other side of the swap deal, the bank arranged an asset swap with a British corporation which was looking for a U.S. dollar security for investment. The flows generated by this swap exactly match the payments or receipts which the bank is obligated to make to the U.S. firm. In effect the British firm, through the intervention of the bank, is enabled to obtain a fixed-rate U.S. dollar investment. This investment is converted, through the use of the currency swap, into a fully hedged sterling investment providing a higher rate of return than a sterling investment of a similar quality available to the British firm at the time.

Currency Coupon Swap

The currency coupon swap is a combination of the interest rate swap and the fixed-rate currency swap. The only difference between this arrangement and the fixed-rate currency swap is that in step (2) the fixed-rate interest in one currency is exchanged for a floating-rate interest in another currency.

This arrangement offers the corporate treasurer the opportunity to avail himself or herself of favorable financing (or leasing terms) available in another country without incurring the exchange risk and the exposure to floating rates. A foreign-currency-denominated floating-rate liability (such as lease payments) would be converted, through a swap arranged with a financial institution, into a fully hedged fixed-rate dollar liability.

Basis Rate Swap

The basis rate swap is an interest rate swap whereby a floating-interest liability linked to LIBOR, for example, is exchanged for an equivalent liability denominated in the same currency but linked to a different benchmark, such as the U.S. dollar prime rate. An example of such a swap

Exhibit 10-8. Illustration of a Fixed-Rate Currency Swap

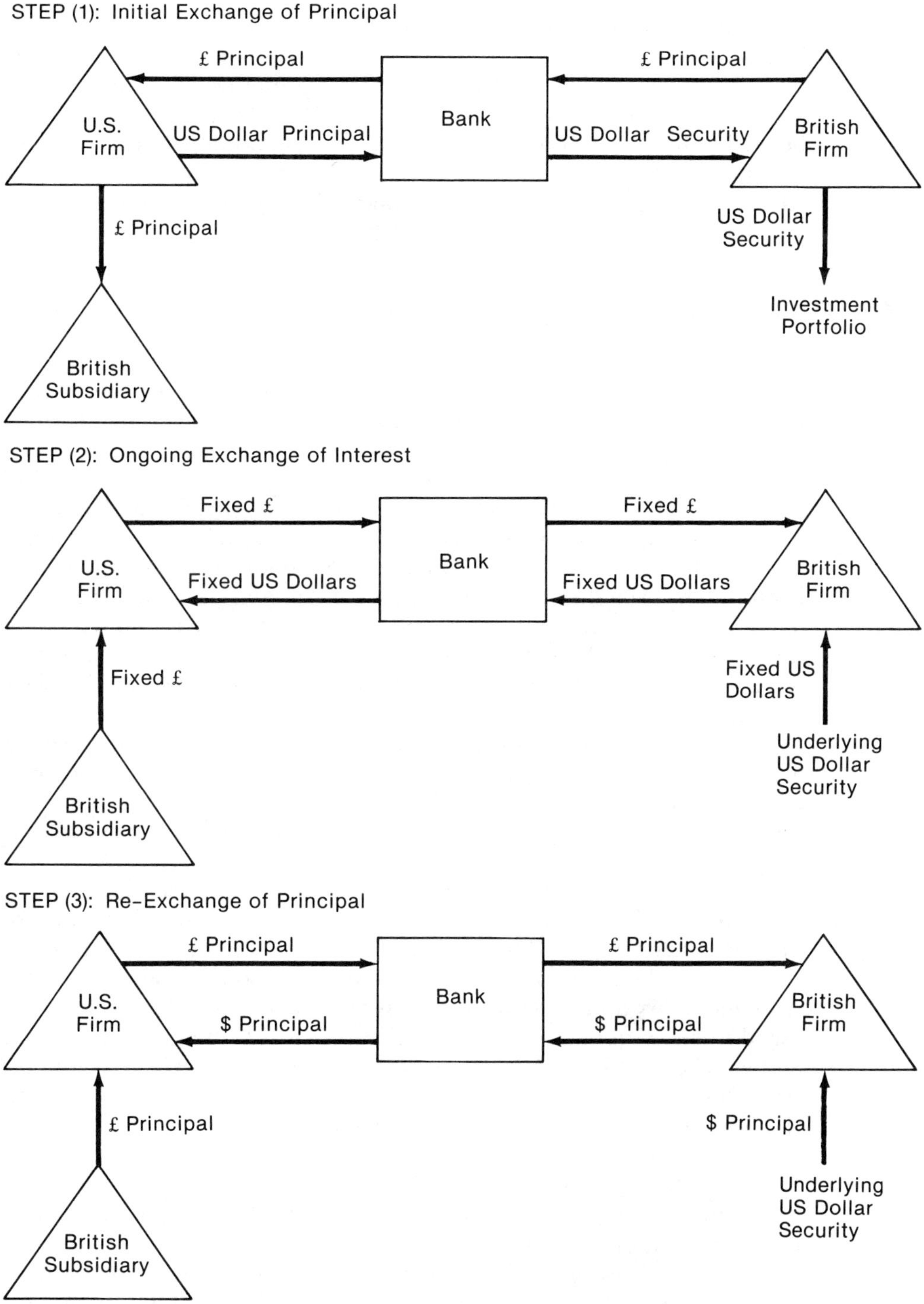

Source: Based on illustrations in *Euromoney*, special supplement, March 1986, p. 97. Reproduced with permission from *Euromoney*.

arrangement which is fairly common is the exchange of a U.S. dollar debt instrument linked to LIBOR for U.S. dollar commercial paper.

Basis swaps, like most other swaps, are motivated primarily by the ability of each of the two counterparties, say two banks, to obtain relatively better lending terms on loans based on one or another short-term interest benchmark. By having each bank providing short-term loans on the basis which offers the most relative advantage, both banks emerge after swapping with a somewhat higher rate of return.

ORGANIZATION OF THE SWAP MARKET AND RISK ASPECTS

Despite its phenomenal growth in recent years, the swap market remains a relatively new and untested innovation in the capital market. The market operates largely informally with little in the form of organizational and regulatory framework. The International Swap Dealers Association (ISDA) has 42 members, consisting mainly of large commercial and investment banks which are actively involved in the swap market. There is no uniform documentation, and attempts to develop standardized documents have been stalled over the fear that such documentation may stifle the market. There has been, however, some movement in this direction. A code was developed by ISDA in 1985 to help writers of swaps and encourage them to use standardized terminology. Also, the British Banking Association prepared a standard contract applicable to interest rate swaps.

Knowledge of the market and its dynamics is limited, since transactions are not reported to any central body. Most swap transactions are effected over the telephone and later confirmed in writing. There is no secondary market proper, because swaps are not securities; they can only be assigned, not traded.

There is growing concern on the part of the central banking and regulatory authorities (such as the SEC) over the proliferation and growth of swap transactions and their interaction with other facets of international financial markets. Central bankers are worried about the swap market both from monetary and supervisory points of view. The questions that are being asked more frequently are how much risk is involved in swap transactions, and who bears this risk? Another concern is the disruptive impact of large-scale default on the functioning of the international capital markets. Although the swap itself is a risk-management tool, it gives rise to some risk elements. The exposure of a party to a swap is the risk that the counterparty may default on its obligation, and that the interest or currency rate may move counter to the interests of the nondefaulting party. Both events have to occur for an actual loss to materialize.

There is also a market risk involved in the interest rate swap. The "swap spread," that is, the difference between the two rates quoted in the swap transaction, may move adversely, creating an unfavorable situation for a counterparty in relation, for example, to the movement of the yield on U.S. Treasury bills or notes. A technique commonly used to "assess the market risk of a swap is to calculate the replacement cost of hypothetical swap in hypothetical default under various interest rates (and for currency swaps, exchange rates) possibilities."[15]

Most interest rate swaps are intermediated by commercial banks or other financial institutions. In this role, they effectively guarantee the swap payments, and thus enable their clients to avail themselves of swaps that otherwise would not have been possible. The financial institutions are in effect market makers and have been instrumental in the development of depth and innovation in this market. What about the risk implications to the banks themselves? Bankers normally execute swaps for their clients, rather than arranging them for speculative purposes. Thus, they are in a position to eliminate or reduce their total exposure by arranging opposite underlying swaps.

Swaps involve essentially arbitraging imperfect markets. This implies that those who can correctly identify and exploit market imperfections will profit in so doing, at the expense of those who gauge them incorrectly. Some experts in the swap market have likened it to a "zero sum game, if some are making (money), others are losing."[16]

REVIEW QUESTIONS

1. Contrast the New York Stock Exchange with a typical stock exchange in a developing country with respect to:
   a. Listing requirements
   b. Depth and breadth of market
   c. Price determination process
   d. Continuity of price changes
   e. Orderly behavior of stock prices
2. Why did non-U.S. MNCs resort to issuing ADRs to tap the U.S. equity market? What are the advantages to the issuing firms in using this instrument? What are the advantages to the U.S. investor in buying an ADR issued by a foreign company? Are there disadvantages?
3. Why was the performance of foreign equity markets in Exhibit 10-1 corrected for changes in the exchange rate (dollar/foreign currency) during the period? From whose viewpoint should the adjusted performance (combined change) be interpreted?

[15]*Euromoney*, special supplement, p. 107.
[16]*Euromoney*, special supplement, p. 105.

4. What accounts for the growing interest of large pension funds in the United States in acquiring foreign stocks? Why is acquisition of foreign stocks by U.S. investors discouraged by a decline in the value of the dollar and a rise in interest rates in the United States?
5. How meaningful is a global stock index that tracks on a daily basis the movements of a large number of equities in 16 major equity markets, including the United States? Who will find this index useful and for which purposes?
6. Explain briefly the major factors behind the innovations in the international capital markets during the first half of the current decade. In particular, which specific needs and circumstances of the issuers and investors have been addressed by these innovations? Substantiate your answers with illustrations.
7. Differentiate between a dual-currency convertible Eurobond and a Eurobond with warrants exchangeable into equity of the issuing firm. Under what circumstances would a U.S. investor in a yen/dollar bond issued by a Japanese industrial firm find it advantageous to convert into the common stock of the firm?
8. What accounts for the increasing popularity of such quasi-equity instruments as ADRs and PCs? How have these and other innovations contributed to the internationalization of the equity markets? Why has the integration of such markets lagged considerably behind the integration of the international market for debt securities?
9. Cite briefly the major objectives behind an MNC seeking to list its stock in other than the country of its incorporation. How does multiple listing contribute to the profitability of multinational firms? What specific advantages would accrue to a U.S. high-tech firm, for instance, by listing on the Tokyo Stock Exchange?
10. Why are financial swaps considered a form of arbitrage? List the main factors behind the phenomenal growth in the swap market in recent years.
11. Explain in each of the following cases how a swap transaction would benefit the party in question:
    a. A U.S. corporate treasurer who is qualified to borrow funds from the firm's bankers at the prime rate, but desires to obtain floating-rate funds based on LIBOR.
    b. A medium-sized U.S. firm which is able to raise long-term funds in the U.S. at favorable rates by issuing bonds at home, but is unable, because of lack of recognition in international capital markets, to enjoy more favorable borrowing terms available in the Eurobond market.

  c. A German firm wishing to raise fixed-rate dollar funds for its affiliate in New York, but unwilling to expose itself to the exchange risk.
  d. The same German firm as in c with the additional constraint that it can obtain the best terms at home by a floating-rate loan linked to LIBOR.

12. The World Bank, which raises funds continuously in international capital markets to finance its loans to member countries, has resorted frequently to the use of swaps in recent years. In particular, these swaps have enabled the Bank to benefit from the favorable terms in the Swiss market, which otherwise would not have been available. Explain briefly the circumstances and situations which cause an international financial organization, such as the World Bank, to use the swap market.
13. Are swaps securities which can be exchanged by two counterparties? If not, in what sense can one speak of trading in swaps?
14. Swaps are risk-management instruments; yet they give rise to certain risks themselves. Comment on this statement, indicating how such risks may be contained or minimized by participants.

BIBLIOGRAPHY

DREXEL BRUNHAM LAMBERT, INC., *International Investment Monthly,* New York.

DUFEY, GUNTER, "Innovations in the International Financial Markets," *Journal of International Business Studies,* Fall 1981.

Euromoney, special supplement, March 1986.

Euromoney, Annual Financial Report, March 1986.

International Monetary Fund, *International Capital Markets: Developments and Prospects,* Occasional Paper 43, February 1986.

PARK, YOON S. and JACK ZWICK, *International Banking in Theory and Practice.* Addison-Wesley Publishing Company, 1985.

The World Bank, *Annual Report 1985,* pp. 75–84.

11

Multinational Banking

The expansion of international banking has paralleled if not outpaced the growth of the multinational firm. British banks were quick to establish presence in British colonies in the second half of the nineteenth and the early part of the twentieth centuries, mainly to finance trade and business activity created by British firms in these colonies. American banks, which initially followed their clients, the U.S. MNCs, have later sought to generate new banking business from depositors and borrowers in foreign countries.[1]

ORGANIZATIONAL ASPECTS OF INTERNATIONAL BANKING

A bank may conduct business outside its home country in a variety of forms. It need not establish a presence outside its home country to engage in international banking transactions on behalf of its clients. *Correspondent banking* provides the vehicle whereby a bank which does not have an office in a foreign country maintains a correspondent account with a bank in that country. Foreign correspondents facilitate international payments and collections, and arrange foreign exchange and other transactions as requested by the home bank.

[1]For an excellent background on international banking and its regulations, see: Richard Dale, *The Regulation of International Banking* (Englewood Cliffs, N.J.: Prentice-Hall, Inc., 1986).

If a U.S. bank desires to establish a presence abroad, this presence may take one or more of the following forms:

Foreign Branches

A foreign branch is a full-fledged office of the home bank which operates subject to banking rules of the home as well as the host countries. The transactions of a branch are incorporated with those of the parent bank, and claims on the branch are legal claims on the head office. This form enables the parent bank to exercise full control over the operations of the branch. The branch also offers local customers faster check clearing through the parent bank, as well as the other services which may not be available from local banks.

Foreign Agencies

Agencies are virtually identical to branches, except that they are not authorized to accept ordinary deposits (although they may accept credit balances of customers doing business with the agency). Agencies deal mainly in the money and foreign exchange markets and clear dollar settlements. An agency may also arrange loans for customers acting on behalf of the home office.

Foreign Subsidiary Banks

Unlike a branch bank, which is an integral part of the parent institution, a foreign subsidiary is a bank incorporated in the host country. Foreign subsidiaries operate under exactly the same rules as the local domestic banks. Although the foreign bank has operational control over the subsidiary, this control is somewhat circumscribed by the existence of a separate board of directors. The subsidiary form has an advantage in some countries over the branch form, in that it may engage in activities which are not allowed to branches of foreign banks.

Edge Act Corporations

Through an amendment to the Federal Reserve Act in 1919, U.S. banks were authorized to establish subsidiaries whose activities are restricted to financial operations in foreign countries. Banks are allowed to have a maximum of five such subsidiaries, each of which may have one office in the United States. Edge Act corporations in foreign countries can engage in almost any line of banking business, including dealing in government and corporate securities and owning equity in foreign banks. U.S. offices of such subsidiaries are not permitted to conduct domestic banking business, though they often serve as referral or loan production offices.

Representative Offices

These offices are not operating banks. They cannot accept deposits nor make loans, nor conduct any other banking activity, such as check clearance and foreign exchange transactions. The primary function of these offices is to supply the parent bank with information on local business conditions, cultivate contacts, and solicit potential customers. The resident representative, who is an employee of the parent bank, also keeps close working relationships with local correspondent banks.

GROWTH OF INTERNATIONAL BANKING

The growth of international banking, particularly during the 1965–1980 period, has been phenomenal. Offices of American banks operating in foreign countries rose dramatically in the twenty-year span between the early 1960s and the early 1980s. From a modest beginning in 1960 (only seven U.S. banks operated a total of 132 foreign branches and offices), U.S. banking presence abroad increased to some 800 offices operated by 130 U.S. banking organizations by 1980. In terms of assets, the growth was even more dramatic. From only $9 billion in 1965, total assets held by offices of American banks abroad increased to $150 billion by 1974, and rose sharply to $495 billion by the end of 1981.[2]

Operations of American banks abroad are concentrated in international money centers, tax haven countries, and locations in the Caribbean and the Far East, where most Eurocurrency operations are transacted. In mid-1984 European branches accounted for about 44 percent of total assets held by branches of U.S. banks abroad, dominated by the United Kingdom (primarily London) which alone accounted for over 19 percent of total assets. Branches in Latin America and the Caribbean held about 18 percent of total assets, while Japan, Hong Kong, and Singapore together accounted for about 16 percent of the total (Exhibit 11-1).

Apart from the rapid growth of multinational business operations, the expansion of U.S. banks in foreign countries may be traced to the controls instituted during the 1960s on outflow of capital from the United States, and to regulation Q, which imposed ceilings on interest paid by U.S. banks and other financial institutions on savings and time deposits.[3] Other factors include the enormous banking opportunities opened up by the vast surpluses of OPEC countries during the 1970s and early 1980s, and the consequent mushrooming of the syndicated Eurocurrency loan business. Just

[2]See Richard K. Abrams, "Regional Banks and International Banking," Federal Reserve Bank of Kansas City, *Economic Review* (November 1980), pp. 3–14; and James V. Houpt and Michael G. Martinson, *Foreign Subsidiaries of U.S. Banking Organizations*, Staff Economic Study, Board of Governors of the Federal Reserve System, 1982.

[3]Regulation Q was phased out by the Depository Institutions Deregulation Act of 1982 (the so-called Garn-St. Germain Act) in stages which ended on March 31, 1986.

Exhibit 11-1. Geographical Distribution of Assets and Liabilities of Major Foreign Branches of U.S. Banks[1] as of June 30, 1984 (in millions of U.S. dollars)

COUNTRY	ASSETS	%	LIABILITIES	%
Europe	110,171	43.5	72,010	34.6
of which:				
Belgium-Luxemborg	7,752	3.1	4,683	2.3
France	10,180	4.0	5,113	2.5
Germany	10,546	4.2	2,696	1.3
United Kingdom	48,254	19.1	29,173	14.0
Canada	4,228	1.7	3,413	1.6
Latin America and the Caribbean	45,089	17.8	23,464	11.3
of which:				
Bahamas	4,942	2.0	5,049	2.4
Brazil	9,195	3.6	2,180	1.0
Cayman Islands	4,423	1.7	2,000	1.0
Mexico	8,615	3.4	2,561	1.2
Panama	4,783	1.9	2,366	1.1
Asia	67,338	26.6	52,485	25.2
of which:				
Hong Kong	10,351	4.1	10,315	5.0
Japan	20,072	7.9	8,911	4.3
Singapore	9,341	3.7	4,701	2.3
Middle East (oil-exporting countries)[2]	5,960	2.4	10,708	5.1
Africa	9,017	3.6	3,189	1.5
Oceania	4,203	1.7	108	
Unallocated[3]	13,041	5.2	53,314	25.6[4]
Total[5]	253,096	100.0[6]	207,983	100.0[6]

[1]Table includes only the assets and liabilities of major foreign branches of U.S. banks which have total assets in excess of the reporting threshold. It does not include the assets and liabilities of affiliates and subsidiaries of U.S. banks abroad.

[2]Bahrain, Iran, Iraq, Kuwait, Oman, Qatar, Saudi Arabia, and the United Arab Emirates.

[3]Including international organizations.

[4]Negotiable CDs issued by the branches are included in the "unallocated" line.

[5]Excludes branches in Puerto Rico and U.S. possessions.

[6]Due to rounding percentages, totals are not exactly 100.0.

Source: Federal Reserve Bank of Chicago.

like its counterpart, the multinational firm, the multinational bank also sought to obtain tax advantages by establishing "shell" or nonoperating branches in tax havens.[4]

[4]"Shell" bank branches in offshore centers, such as the Caymans and Bahamas, are offices that have little more than a nameplate and a telephone. They are used by parent U.S. banks as addresses for booking transactions, thus avoiding U.S. banking regulations.

While branching abroad has opened wide vistas of new business for U.S. banks in the areas of "merchant banking,"[5] syndicated Eurocurrency loans, and international leasing, among others, it has also exposed them to higher risks. The volatility of exchange markets since 1973 and the increased need of their clients for foreign currencies have exposed international banks on occasion to substantial losses. Multinational banks as a group loaned excessively large amounts to LDCs, which since the early 1980s have been experiencing serious debt servicing problems (see Chapter 20).

The growth of foreign bank offices in the United States has been even more phenomenal than the expansion of the U.S. bank presence abroad. From a modest beginning in 1972, foreign banks have succeeded in gaining a sizable foothold in the U.S. market. Based on Federal Reserve Board statistics, as quoted by Bellanger,[6] 52 foreign banks had 104 offices in the United States with assets of about $25 billion in 1972. As of the end of 1983, 230 banks from 53 nations had 495 offices in the United States with assets of $330 billion. Foreign banks held 14 percent of U.S. banking assets and 10 percent of commercial and industrial loans to domestic customers.

U.S. offices of foreign banks are predominantly located in New York, California, and Illinois, which together account for 98 percent of foreign bank operations in the United States.[7] Eight other states permit foreign banks to operate: Florida, Georgia, Hawaii, Massachusetts, Oregon, Pennsylvania, Texas, and Washington. Initially, Western European banks dominated the scene and have tended to cluster in New York, and to a lesser extent in Chicago. In the early 1980s, Japanese banks, which have tended to cluster in California, emerged as by far the leading foreign bank operation in the United States. In terms of assets, Japanese banks accounted for about 46 percent of the total assets of U.S. offices of foreign banks at the end of 1984 (see Exhibit 11-2).

There are six identifiable banking operations which offices of foreign banks are conducting in the United States. These are: (1) financial services to subsidiaries of foreign corporations, (2) financial services to U.S. corporations, (3) money market operations based primarily in New York, (4) foreign exchange operations, also primarily based in New York, (5) clearing of dollar settlements on behalf of their respective head offices, and (6) retail banking services. The last activity is still relatively limited

[5] "Merchant banking" refers to activities which include long-term financing and the sale and purchase of corporate securities, in addition to the regular commercial banking functions. Institutions that combine these activities are referred to as "merchant banks." Merchant banking is a European phenomenon, concentrated mainly in London.

[6] Serge Bellanger, "Foreign Banks in America," *The Bankers Magazine* (May-June 1985), p. 19.

[7] Samuel Rabino, "Foreign Competition for the U.S. Banking World," *Long Range Planning* (United Kingdom), Vol. 17, no. 3, p. 116.

Exhibit 11-2. Total Assets of Foreign Banks by Country of Origin, December 1984 (billions of U.S. dollars)

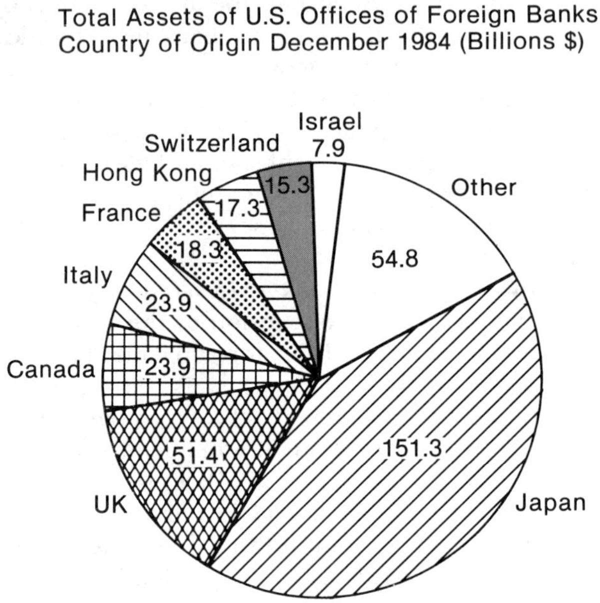

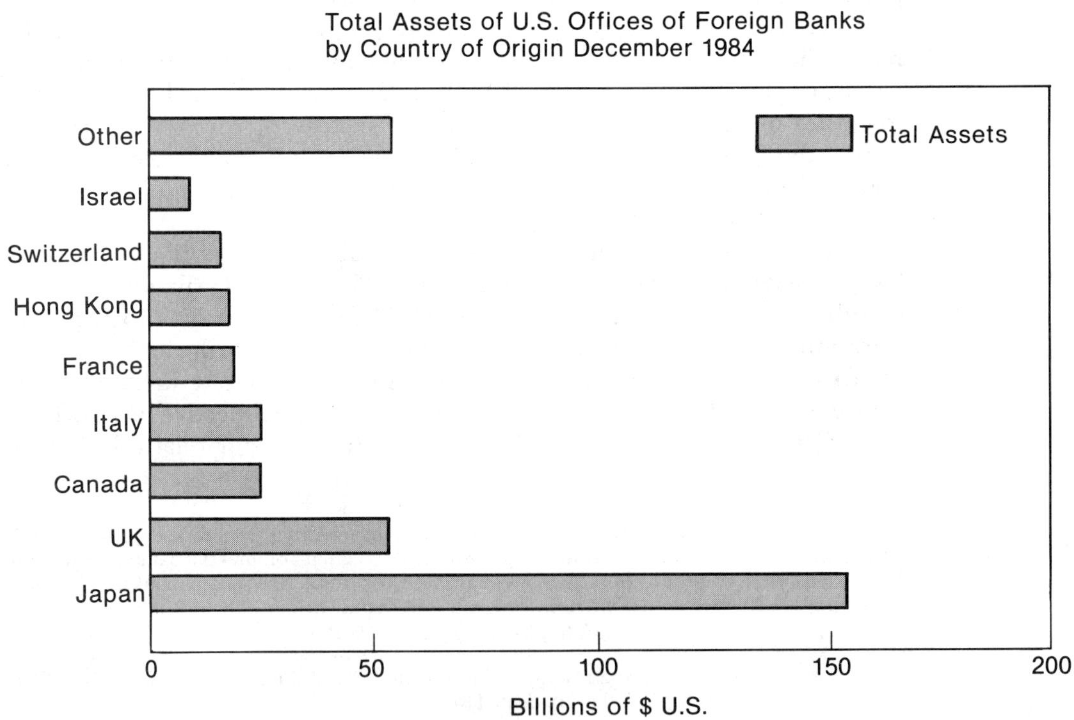

Ideas based on Nick Gilbert, "Foreign Banks in America: They're Still Coming," *Euromoney* (August 1985), p. 152.

in scope and confined to British banks (New York) and Japanese banks (California.)[8]

The growth of multinational banking in recent years has been characterized by both a fast rate of growth in total assets, and the displacement of U.S. banks by foreign banks in the list of the top twenty banks. In 1984, three of the top five banks (ranked on the basis of total assets) and five of the top 10 were Japanese banks. The top 20 banks and their ranking in 1983 and 1984 are shown in Exhibit 11-3.

THE INTERNATIONAL BANKING ACT

Until the passage of the International Banking Act of 1978 (IBA) foreign banks operating in the United States were regulated by the individual states which licensed them. The IBA sought essentially to place operations of

Exhibit 11-3. Multinational Commercial Banks Ranked by Assets

Bank and Head Office	Assets at End-December 1984 (in billions of U.S. dollars)	RANK 1984	RANK 1983
Citicorp, New York	142.7	1	1
Dai-Ichi Kangyo Bank, Tokyo	119.1	2	3
Fuji Bank, Tokyo	115.1	3	4
Bank America Corporation, San Francisco	113.7	4	2
Mitsubishi Bank, Tokyo	110.7	5	7
Sumitomo Bank, Osaka	107.6	6	5
Banque National de Paris, Paris	99.0	7	6
Sanwa Bank, Osaka	96.5	8	9
Crédit Agricole, Paris	92.4	9	10
Crédit Lyonnais, Paris	90.5	10	11
Société Générale, Paris	87.1	11	13
Barclays, London	85.2	12	8
Norinchukin Bank, Tokyo	83.1	13	17
National Westminister Bank, London	82.7	14	12
Industrial Bank of Japan, Tokyo	81.7	15	18
Chase Manhattan, New York	81.6	16	16
Tokai Bank, Nagoya	76.1	17	22
Deutsche Bank, Frankfurt	73.4	18	14
Manufacturers Hanover Corporation, New York	73.1	19	23
Midland Bank, London	71.1	20	15

Source: International Monetary Fund, *International Capital Markets: Developments and Prospects,* Occasional Paper No. 43, February 1986, p. 102.

[8]Serge Bellanger, "The Foreign Challenge to U.S. Banks," *The Banker* (October 1978), pp. 38–39.

foreign banks in the United States on the same footing with U.S. banks. The IBA addressed six areas which affect the operations of foreign banks in the United States: interstate banking, federal branches for foreign banks, Edge Act corporations, deposit insurance, Federal Reserve powers, and nonbanking activities.[9]

Although the 1978 legislation left the licensing of foreign banks with the states, a foreign bank was required to declare a "home state," and the branching activities of the bank were subjected to the regulations of that state. The act allowed for a one-time change in this "home state" designation. Multistate operations of foreign banks which existed at the time the act was passed (July 27, 1978) were "grandfathered." Forty of the 50 largest foreign bank operations in the United States had multistate facilities on that date.

The IBA gave all agencies and branches that were operating under state charters the opportunity to obtain federal charters from the Comptroller of the Currency. The requirement that all directors of a national bank be U.S. citizens was waived. It also permitted foreign banks to set up Edge Act corporations or subsidiaries to engage in international trade and finance, an activity which has been allowed to U.S. banks since 1919.

The act provided that FDIC insurance would be open to those foreign banks that would like to have it. This was viewed as a benefit to foreign banks, especially those conducting retail business. The deposit insurance was made compulsory for federal branches of foreign banks and for state banks if other domestic banks in that state were required to take it. If a foreign bank did not accept deposits of less than $100,000, this requirement would not apply.

The act also broadened the supervisory powers of the Federal Reserve System over foreign banking operations in the United States. All branches and agencies of foreign banks with a minimum of $1 billion in total assets worldwide are required to maintain the same reserve requirements which are observed by U.S. depository financial institutions under existing legislations. Foreign banks are granted access to the "discount window," as well as other services provided by the FED for which fees are charged, on par with U.S. depository institutions.

The Federal Reserve Board was also granted the ability to examine the operations of foreign banks. To make such examinations, the Federal Reserve was to use any existing reports already required by the Comptroller of Currency, the FDIC, or any state authority.

The last issue addressed by the IBA was that of nonbanking activities. The act basically subjected foreign banks to the Bank Holding Company Act of 1956 as amended in 1970. It further restricted foreign banks' com-

[9]For a good article on the IBA and regulation of foreign banks, see: Betsy B. White, "Foreign Banking in the United States: A Regulatory and Supervisory Perspective," Federal Reserve Bank of New York, *Quarterly Review* (Summer 1982), pp. 48–58.

petition with domestic banks for loans and deposits not closely related to international finance. Branches and agencies of foreign banks may not engage in underwriting or the purchase and sale of stocks, an activity which has been denied U.S. banks since 1933 by the Glass-Steagall Act.

INTERNATIONAL BANKING FACILITIES

U.S. banks and other depository financial institutions, as well as foreign banks, were permitted under a 1981 legislation to establish international banking facilities (IBFs). IBFs are U.S.-based subsidiaries of the financial institutions which establish them to engage exclusively in international banking activities. IBFs do not represent new physical banking facilities; instead, they are merely separate sets of books of the existing banking facilities which establish them. Because they do not transact domestic banking business, they are exempt from the reserve and deposit insurance requirements, as well as from interest rate limitations, such as regulation Q.

The central idea behind the IBFs was to attract Eurodollar deposits from offshore centers back to the United States, while insuring that the facilities will not compete with the U.S. domestic banking systems. The exemption features outlined above and the perceived lower country risk were thought to be sufficient attractions. Provisions designed to guard against competition with domestic banking business (such as minimum transaction size of $100,000, and inability to issue negotiable CDs) may have placed IBFs at some disadvantage vis-a-vis their offshore counterparts.[10]

Despite the limiting provisions, IBFs have enjoyed a fast rate of growth since their inception in December 1981. Total assets of IBFs reached over $200 billion in the first two years after they started operation. Of the 477 IBFs in the United States at the end of 1984, 264, or 55 percent, were facilities established by foreign banks. The remainder were facilities set up by U.S. banks (144) and by Edge Act Corporations (69). Almost half of the IBFs are in New York; California, Florida, and Illinois account for most of the rest.[11]

IBFs' operations are closely linked to the Eurocurrency market, as evidenced by the high proportion of both assets and liabilities due to other banking institutions. Interbank transactions conducted through IBFs are predominantly in the form of "swap" arrangements, which enable banks to reduce either exchange risk or interest rate risk. Funds attracted to IBFs were mainly shifted from offices of U.S. banks in offshore centers and from U.S. branches of foreign banks which typically maintain a high proportion of assets eligible for shifting to IBFs.[12]

[10]Dale, *Regulation of International Banking,* pp. 29–30.

[11]K. Alec Chrystal, "International Banking Facilities," Federal Reserve Bank of St. Louis, *Economic Review* (April 1984), pp. 6–7.

[12]*Ibid.,* pp. 9–10.

THE BORROWING-INVESTMENT DECISION

The MNC faces a more complex, yet a more flexible, task in financing its operations than its domestic counterpart. This arises from the multiplicity of international sources of finance as well as the need to incorporate the exchange risk in the calculation of the cost of funds. Moreover, the borrowing and investment decision has to take into account the political risk attendant upon such a decision. MNCs have been known to favor local financing for their affiliates as a means of reducing the political risk and to avoid keeping excess balances in countries deemed to have a high degree of such risk. Another complicating factor is the need to coordinate the borrowing-investment decision with the MNC's overall cash management policies, which were discussed in Chapter 8.

CASE STUDY

The International Food and Confectionary Corporation

The nature of the borrowing-investment decision, considering the multiple sources of financing and outlets for investment of excess balances and the need to take into account the MNC's overall exchange exposure management policies in making such a decision, can be best understood in a case study context.

International Food and Confectionary Corporation (IFCC) is a multinational enterprise based in Philadelphia, Pennsylvania, with total sales in excess of $500 million in 1983. IFCC manufactures and distributes several lines of breakfast cereals, tea biscuits, and hard candy, operating from three plants in the United States as well as three wholly owned affiliates located in Italy, Singapore, and Switzerland.

IFCC's current manual dealing with foreign exchange exposure management and choice of financing sources for the affiliates leaves considerable leeway to the affiliates' managements. However, major hedging decisions are subject to consultation with the Vice President of Finance in the headquarters (Philadelphia), and prior approval for transactions exceeding $10 million is required. In the early 1970s, soon after IFCC moved from relying on exports from its U.S. plants to meet foreign demand to manufacturing and distribution from three foreign affiliates, its financing and currency exposure policies were centralized. The management, moreover, was adhering closely to the dictum of local financing of affiliates' operations to the extent possible, and minimizing currency exposure risks by hedging such exposure whenever possible. However, a decade of unfavorable experiences in an environment of increasingly volatile exchange and interest rates has convinced the management that a more decentralized and flexible approach may be more appropriate.

In the early 1980s, acting on a memorandum prepared jointly by the staff of the International Finance and Foreign Exchange Division of the company and the Foreign Department of its main bank (First Continental Bank of Pennsylvania), IFCC's management revamped its policies and incorporated the changes in the company's manual dealing with foreign operations. The memorandum in question argued for a decentralized and more imaginative approach to the borrowing-investment decision in light of the world monetary and financial developments.

The memorandum noted that there are basically *four* sources of financing an affiliate: (1) local financing, (2) Eurocurrency financing in the country of the affiliate, (3) Eurocurrency financing outside the country of the affiliate, and (4) parent company financing. Similarly, there are four outlets for the investment of temporary excess funds: (1) local investment, (2) Eurocurrency deposits or securities in the country of the affiliate, (3) Eurocurrency deposits or securities outside the country of the affiliate, and (4) transfer of funds to the parent for investment in the U.S. money market.

The memorandum also noted that alternative financial policies to be considered depend to some extent on the efficiency of the financial markets and IFCC's exposure management posture. Two basic postures may be distinguished:

1. *Conservative posture,* which aims at eliminating or minimizing currency risk. This posture dictates that borrowing should be made in the currencies in which funds will be generated by the company's affiliates. In addition, all residual exposure should be hedged.
2. *Aggressive posture,* which aims at minimizing the cost of financing, taking into account the company's own forecast of future exchange rates, rather than the market forecast which is embedded in the forward rates. Hedging will be confined to situations where the cost of hedging is less than the expected loss entailed in maintaining currency positions; that is, hedging operations are conducted only when they are deemed to be cost effective.

There are several other possible alternatives falling between these two extremes. For example, IFCC could finance in the currencies that will minimize exposure, but refrain from hedging residual exposure. Conceivably, an MNC may decide on the financial policies which will minimize the overall cost of funds, without regard to currency exposure implications of such policies, or rely on the company's diversity of operations to provide a natural hedge against such exposure.

IFCC'S CASH FLOW FORECAST FOR 1984

IFCC's analysis of financial policies under the new strategy begins with a quarterly cash flow forecast prepared by Mr. Munyon, manager of the International Finance and Foreign Exchange Division, working closely with the managements of the affiliates (Exhibit 1). This forecast becomes the basis of decisions to be made by the affiliates to borrow needed funds, invest excess funds, and cover exchange risks (when necessary) each quarter. Affiliates are empowered to introduce changes in these forecasts in the light of current developments, subject to clearing transactions exceeding the equivalent of $10 million with the Vice President of Finance in Philadelphia.

Exhibit 1. IFCC—Projected Cash Flow of Affiliates for 1984 (millions of U.S. dollar equivalents at initial exchange rates)

	Q_1	Q_2	Q_3	Q_4	OVERALL 1984
Italian Affiliate					
Net cash flow other than profit (or loss) on operations	20	(70)	30	(90)	(110)
Net profit (loss) from operations	15	5	10	15	45
Total net cash flow	35	(65)	40	(75)	(65)
Cumulative net cash flow	35	(30)	10	(65)	(65)
Singapore Affiliate					
Net cash flow other than profit (or loss) on operations	(15)	(40)	55	32	32
Net profit (loss) from operations	15	15	15	15	60
Total net cash flow		(25)	70	47	92
Cumulative net cash flow		(25)	45	92	92
Swiss Affiliate					
Net cash flow other than profit (or loss) on operations	17	(25)	(27)	(29)	(64)
Net profit (loss) from operations	(20)		5	(35)	(50)
Total net cash flow	(3)	(25)	(22)	(64)	(114)
Cumulative net cash flow	(3)	(28)	(50)	(114)	(114)

To illustrate alternative financial policies and their costs under varying interest and exchange rates assumptions, Mr. Munyon prepared, in consultation with the managements of the affiliates and the Foreign Exchange Department of the First Continental Bank of Pennsylvania, the data shown in Exhibit 2. The data in this exhibit were used by Mr. Munyon and his staff to illustrate the cost and other consequences of alternative financial policy options under both a *conservative* and an *aggressive* posture. To simplify the presentation, he used annual cash flow data outlined in Exhibit 1. However,

Exhibit 2. Market and Forecast Exchange Rate and Interest Data

		ITALIAN LIRA (LIT)	SWISS FRANC (SF)	SINGAPORE DOLLAR (S$)
Spot rate		\$0.005728	\$0.4145	\$0.5269
Forward 1-year rates		\$0.005212	\$0.4238	\$0.5006
Forward premium (discount) against U.S. dollar		−9.0%	+2.2%	−5.0%
Interest Rates Per Annum	**U.S.**	**Italy**	**Switzerland**	**Singapore**
Euromarket	12.5%	20.5%	7.5%	15.8%
Domestic	11.5%	18.0%	9.0%	14.0%
FORECAST EXCHANGE RATE AND EFFECTIVE INTEREST RATES				
Scenario I—Market Forecast[1]				
Spot rate—1 year later		\$0.005212	\$0.4238	\$0.5006
Effective interest rates				
Euromarket	12.5%	11.5% (20.5 − 9.0)	9.7% (7.5 + 2.2)	10.8% (15.8 − 5.0)
Domestic	11.5%	9.0% (18.0 − 9.0)	11.2% (9.0 + 2.2)	9.0% (14.0 − 5.0)
Scenario II—IFCC's Management Forecast				
Spot rate—1 year later		\$0.05327	\$0.4311	\$0.5374
Forecast change in exchange rate		−7.0%	+4.0%	+2.0%
Effective interest rates				
Euromarket	12.5%	13.5% (20.5 − 7.0)	11.5% (7.5 + 4.0)	17.8% (15.8 + 2.0)
Domestic	11.5%	11.0% (18.0 − 7.0)	13.0% (9.0 + 4.0)	16.0% (14.0 + 2.0)

[1]This scenario assumes that market expectations embedded in the currently quoted forward rates will actually materialize. In other words, it is assumed that forward rates are not only *unbiased* but also *exact* predictors of future spot rates.

he made it clear that policy actions by the affiliates and parent company should be based on quarterly cash flow projections, using market data prevailing at the beginning of each quarter.

Before the possible outcome of alternative strategies can be calculated, a number of relevant observations need to be made with respect to IFCC's financial policies:

1. Like other MNCs, IFCC reflects the outcome of foreign exchange transactions in accordance with FASB Rule #52. This rule stipulates that exchange conversions for accounting (balance sheet exposure) and transaction exposures should be made at the current rates (the rates prevailing at the date the financial statements are prepared, and the dates of the actual transactions, respectively).
2. As a policy, IFCC's management has refrained from covering accounting exposure. As for transaction and economic exposure, hedging operations have been done on a *selective* basis, primarily when the expected cost of the unhedged positions exceeds the cost of such hedging operations. The protection of cash flows generated by the affiliates in the current and subsequent accounting periods, that is, managing economic exposure, is the focus of IFCC's exposure management strategy.
3. For the purpose of the exercise outlined in Exhibits 1 and 2, economic exposure is defined as the net profit from operations generated by the affiliates, while transaction exposure is confined to the investing and borrowing operations conducted in currencies other than the U.S. dollar.
4. Transaction costs, other than the cost of the forward cover and interest cost, are ignored in this exercise. However, IFCC'S financial policies, as outlined in the new manual, emphasize that other transaction costs, such as the cost of transferring currencies and the bid-ask spread in currency conversion, as well as other costs, should be considered by the decision maker.
5. While IFCC's financial policies preclude creating positions for outright speculative purposes, the management does not discourage leaving positions in foreign currencies, which are generated in the normal course of business, uncovered if, in the judgment of the decision maker, such positions will be advantageous to the company. Flexibility in the management of foreign exchange exposure is encouraged even if such judgments are not in accord with the market's expectations.

EVALUATION OF ALTERNATIVE FINANCIAL POLICIES

The next step in this exercise is to evaluate the cost and other implications of alternative financial policies. Although there obviously are a fairly large number of options, the evaluation process is to be confined to only four options: the cost implications of an aggressive policy and a conservative policy under each of the two exchange rate forecasts: the market's and IFCC's.

Under the aggressive posture, the objective of the decision maker is to borrow funds at the lowest possible cost and invest excess funds at the highest possible rate of return, subject to the limitation that only domestic markets can be used by affiliates; that is, the affiliate in Singapore, for example, can not use the Singapore Eurocurrency market for borrowing or investing.

Under the conservative approach, the emphasis is primarily on reducing exchange exposure. Borrowing is primarily undertaken in the currencies in which funds will be generated by the affiliates. Additionally, all residual positions are hedged in the forward market.

Mr. Munyon is anxious to impress the Chief Operating and Chief Financial Officers with the merits of IFCC's new flexible approach to the borrowing-investment decision and exchange rate exposure management policy. With the assistance of his staff in the International Finance and Foreign Exchange Division, he is preparing a detailed analysis of the cost of alternative financial policies based on the data in Exhibits 1 and 2 and the current company's guidelines. His objective is to demonstrate to his superiors that the new strategy will prove beneficial to IFCC, and will not only contribute to lower overall cost of financing, but also reduce the cost of hedging operations.

BIBLIOGRAPHY

ABRAMS, R. K., "Regional Banks and International Banking," Federal Reserve Bank of Kansas City, *Economic Review* (November 1980), pp. 3–14.

ARESKOUG, K., "Exchange Rates and the Currency of Denomination in International Bonds," *Economica* (May 1980), pp. 159–163.

BAUGHN, W. H., and D. R. MANDICH, *The International Banking Handbook.* Homewood, Ill.: Dow-Jones-Irwin, 1983.

BELLANGER, S., "The Foreign Challenge to U.S. Banks," *The Banker* (October 1978), pp. 37–44.

______, "Foreign Banking in America," *The Bankers Magazine* (May-June 1985), pp. 18–22.

BLANDEN, M., "Joint Venture and Consortium Banks: Why Banks Choose to Work Together," *Banker* (March 1981), p. 93.

Business Week, "Here Come the Foreign Banks Again" (June 26, 1978), pp. 76–86.

CASSIDY, R. F., "The International Banking Act's Cost Impact on Foreign Banks," *American Banker* (March 23, 1979).

CATES, D. C., "Foreign Banks are Cracking the Facade of U.S. Banking," *Fortune* (August 28, 1978), pp. 94–99.

CHRYSTAL, K. A., "International Banking Facilities," Federal Reserve Bank of St. Louis, *Economic Review* (April 1984), pp. 5–11.

DALE, R., *The Regulation of International Banking.* Englewood Cliffs, N.J.: Prentice-Hall, Inc., 1986.

DEAN, J. W., and I. H. GIDDY, "Six Ways to World Banking Safety," *Euromoney* (May 1981), p. 128.

DE FARO, C., and J. V. JUCKER, "The Impact of Inflation and Devaluation on the Selection of an International Borrowing Source," *Journal of International Business Studies* (Fall 1973), pp. 97–104.

DUFEY, G., and I. H. GIDDY, "International Financial Planning: The Use of Market-Based Forecasts," *California Management Review* (Fall 1978), pp. 69–81.

EDWARDS, F. R., "The New International Banking Facility: A Study in Regulatory Frustration," *Columbia Journal of World Business* (Winter 1981), pp. 6–18.

FOLKS, W. R., JR., "Optimal Foreign Borrowing Strategies with Operations in Forward Exchange Markets," *Journal of Financial and Quantitative Analysis* (June 1978), pp. 245–254.

GRANT, C., "Back to Basics in International Banking," *Euromoney* (May 1983), pp. 181–182.

GURWIN, L., "Foreign Banking in America," *Institutional Investor* (September 1978), pp. 128–144.

HANEY, S., "Foreign Banks: More New Names in New York," *The Banker* (March 1985), pp. 109–113.

HIRSCH, A. A., "Edge Act Banks: Edges Hit Big Times," *American Import/Export Management* (October 1982), p. 12.

HOUPT, J. V., "Performance and Characteristics of Edge Corporations," *Federal Reserve Bulletin* (January 1981), pp. 13–14.

HOUPT, J. V. and M. G. MARTINSON, *Foreign Subsidiaries of U.S. Banking Organizations,* Staff Economic Study, Board of Governors of the Federal Reserve System, 1982.

JACOBS, D. P., "Foreign Takeovers Spurred by Obsolete Merger Laws," *American Banker* (August 16, 1979), pp. 78–86.

JUCKER, J. V., and C. DE FARO, "The Selection of International Borrowing Sources," *Journal of Financial and Quantitative Analysis* (September 1975), pp. 381–407.

KEY, S. J., "International Banking Facilities," *Federal Reserve Bulletin* (October 1982), pp. 565–577.

LINN, Q. P., "The Big Shift in Bank Strategies," *Euromoney* (November 1982), pp. 16–18.

MATHIS, F. J., "International Banking: An Outlook for the 1980's," *Journal of Commercial Bank Lending* (July 1980), pp. 25–32.

MEADOWS, E., "The U.S. Pushovers Push Back," *Fortune* (August 24, 1981), pp. 106–107.

NAUMANN-ETIENNE, R., "A Framework for Financial Decisions in MNC," *Journal of Financial and Quantitative Analysis* (November 1974), pp. 859–874.

O'BRIEN, L., "United States Sets the Boundaries for Foreign Banks," *The Banker* (December 1978), pp. 15–19.

OSBORN, N., "Will Foreign Takeovers of U.S. Banks be Stopped?", *Institutional Investor* (September 1978), pp. 157–168.

______, "Is International Banking Still in Fashion?", *Euromoney* (October 1984), pp. 252–253.

______, "Foreign Banks Keep Rolling Along," *Institutional Investor* (September 1980), pp. 223–227.

PEAGAM, N., "Florida: Why the Foreign Banks Have Slowed Down," *Euromoney* (January 1984), pp. 74–75.

RABINO, S., "Foreign Competition for the U.S. Banking World," *Long Range Planning* (June 1984), pp. 115–124.

REIMNITZ, J., "German Banks Follow German Investment," *Euromoney* (June 1978), p. 91.

REMMERS, H. L., "A Note on Foreign Borrowing Costs," *Journal of International Business Studies* (Fall 1980), pp. 123–144.

ROBBINS, S. M., and R. B. STOBAUGH, "Financing Foreign Affiliates," *Financial Management* (Winter 1972), pp. 56–65.

ROUSSAKIS, E. N., *International Banking: Principles and Practices.* New York: Praeger, 1983.

SANDLER, L., "Foreign Banks Learn in U.S.," *The Wall Street Journal* (June 20, 1984), p. 34.

SEVERN, A. K., "The Use of Multicurrency Financing by the Financial Manager," *Financial Management* (Winter 1978), pp. 45–53.

SOLOMON, L. D., "Multinational Business: New Approaches to Financing and Structuring Ventures," *Case Western Reserve Journal of International Law* (Spring 1980), pp. 363–382.

STARR, D. W., "Opportunities for United States Borrowers in the International Bond Markets," *Financial Executive* (June 1979), pp. 50–59.

TEETERS, N. H., and H. S. TERRELL, "The Role of Banks in the International Financial System," *Federal Reserve Bulletin* (September 1983), pp. 663–671.

THOMPSON, I. B., "International Banking Act: for Regional Banks a New Challenge and Opportunity," *ABA Banking Journal* (January 1980), pp. 45–46.

U.S. Statutes at Large, 95th Congress, 2nd Session 1978, Vol. 92, Part 1, Public Law 95-369, *"The International Banking Act,"* September 17, 1978.

WALMSLEY, J., "International Banking Facilities—We have Lift Off," *Banker* (February 1982), pp. 91–92.

WHITE, B. B., "Foreign Banking in the United States: A Regulatory and Supervisory Perspective," Federal Reserve Bank of New York, *Quarterly Review* (Summer 1982) pp. 48–58.

CASE STUDY

International Banking and Trust Corporation (New York)

COUNTRY RISK ANALYSIS AND EXPOSURE TO FOREIGN LOANS

In early April 1986, Mr. F. W. Wheeler, Senior Vice President of International Banking and Trust Bank (IBT) New York, was called to the office of Mr. Richard Buchanan, the Chairman of the bank. Mr. Buchanan told Mr. Wheeler that he had just received an urgent request from the government of Zaire for a loan of up to $250 million. He asked Mr. Wheeler to leave for Kinshasa immediately to conduct a preliminary investigation of the loan request. The chairman indicated that if the findings based on Mr. Wheeler's preliminary investigations as well as on economic and political prospects in Zaire are favorable, IBT might consider being the lead manager for a syndicated Eurocurrency loan to that country.

BACKGROUND

IBT, owned by International Banking and Trust Corporation (a one-bank holding company), ranked fourteenth in the United States in terms of total assets at the end of 1985, is a large money center bank with substantial international activities. The present bank was formed in early 1969 by a merger of two New York banks: New York Security and Trust Company, with strong retail operations, and International Metropolitan Bank, a fast-growing bank with a large number of foreign branches and agencies. The new bank had a spectacular rate of growth during the 1970s, pursuing fairly aggressive policies, particularly in liability management and participation in the international syndicated loan business.

Despite its aggressive stance, IBT has pursued a cautious policy in extending or participating in loans to developing countries. Country exposure limits are established and revised periodically by the bank's research division, which keeps current data on economic, financial, and political developments in about 50 LDCs which are either current or potential clients. Exposure in any one country is normally limited to 20 percent of the bank's capitalization (including long-term notes and debentures). In exceptional cases, by action of the board of directors, loans to a few selected countries were approved on a case-by-case basis which raised the bank's exposure in these countries to 25 percent of capitalization.

In the early 1980s, when major debtor LDCs developed debt servicing problems which cast some serious doubts on the foreign loan portfolio of major U.S. and foreign international banks, IBT's nonperforming loans and reserves for loan losses remained well below that of the ten largest U.S. banks. IBT's capital adequacy ratio, the ratio of stockholders' equity/total assets, has remained well above the corresponding ratio for the ten largest banks.

IBT'S FORMULA FOR CALCULATING COUNTRY EXPOSURE LIMITS

IBT uses a rather simple approach to calculate the maximum amount that it is willing to lend to any prospective borrowing LDC. A country's capacity to repay debt obligations is primarily a function of the level of exports in recent years and the growth potential of these exports. The formula developed by IBTs research division to calculate a country's maximum global debt burden incorporates the following features:

1. A country's total foreign debt should not exceed five times its average expected annual exports and (net) earnings on the services account. Barter transactions or exports involving special concessions are excluded.

2. Average earnings from exports and services (net) are calculated over a seven-year period centered in the year in which the evaluation is made. For example, if the evaluation were being conducted in 1986, the period for calculating the average would be 1983–1989. Actual figures would be used for 1983–1985, estimated figures for 1986, and projected figures for 1987–1989.
3. The country's debt service payments plus imports in the latest year for which data is available should not exceed 1.5 the total value of exports in that year.
4. To determine the maximum loan eligibility of a certain country for IBT loans, the current global indebtedness of the country is netted out [with the exception of soft bilateral loans that are expected to be changed into grants, and long-term soft loans provided by the International Development Association (IDA), an affiliate of the World Bank].
5. Total exposure by IBT in any one country is limited to 20 percent of the bank's primary capital (stockholders' equity plus long-term notes and debentures).
6. The research division uses exports and (net) services earnings data published by the International Monetary Fund, and debt data compiled by the World Bank and the Bank for International Settlements for the purpose of computing a country's maximum loan eligibility.[1]

THE ECONOMY AND FINANCES OF ZAIRE[2]

The Republic of Zaire is the third largest country in Africa after Sudan and Algeria; its population was estimated at 32 million in mid-1984. The country is located in equatorial central Africa and has a 25-mile coastline on the Atlantic Ocean. Zaire obtained independence from Belgium in 1960. Its currency, the zaire (Z), floats independently. At the end of 1985, US$1.00 = Z55.793.

Zaire's economy and its exports earnings are heavily dependent on mineral resources, which include copper, cobalt, zinc, silver, cadmium, and

[1]The actual formula is

$$D_m = 5\left[\frac{\Sigma_{t-3 \text{ to } t+3}\,(X + s_n)}{7}\right] - D_o$$

provided that: $DSP_0 + IM_0 < 1.5X_0$

where

D_m = The calculated maximum eligibility for IBT loans
D_0 = Existing total foreign debt of the country (excluding soft loans and quasi-grants)
X = Exports
IM_0 = Import payments for the year of calculation (the center year)
S_n = Earnings on services (net)
DSP_0 = Debt service payments for the year of calculation (the center year)

[2]Material on Zaire is based on "Economic Adjustment Efforts of Zaire Require Support of External Creditors," *IMF Survey,* March 3, 1986, pp. 72–75.

gold. Its principal exports are copper, cobalt, oil, industrial diamonds, zinc, and coffee. Total export earnings in 1985 amounted to $936 million, half of which was copper and cobalt. Exports of minerals and oil accounted for over 80 percent of total exports.

At the end of 1985, Zaire's medium and long-term debt (excluding drawings on the IMF) amounted to $4.5 billion.[3] The country's heavy debt burden has resulted in the accumulation of arrears, frequent rescheduling of debt by creditors, as well as some debt relief in recent years. The overall balance of payments deficit in 1985 (before rescheduling of debt) amounted to SDR 423 million, or about 10 percent of GDP. However, after rescheduling of debt, the overall balance of payments was only in a small deficit (about SDR 12 million).

Prospects for economic growth and higher export earnings are constrained by the limited potential of increase in mineral products and oil, as well as the depressed prices of Zaire's major exports. Some scope remains for increasing agricultural production. Coffee is emerging as the second largest export earner, after copper.

The floating of the zaire has resulted in a sizable depreciation of the currency, particularly in 1983 and again in 1985, when the zaire declined by over 50 percent. The depreciation reflected for the most part the weakening balance of payments situation, as export earnings declined by about 6 percent in 1985 while debt service payments increased by 8 percent.

Zaire has been pursuing monetary and fiscal reforms, as well as exchange rate rationalization programs, in support of which the IMF has extended additional credit. As of April 30, 1986, Zaire outstanding drawings from the IMF amounted to SDR 664.80 million, or 228 percent of its quota of SDR 291 million. Debt service payments in 1985 amounted to $565 million.

The data needed for evaluating Zaire's international debt position and its eligibility for loans from IBT are given in Exhibit 1.

COMPARISON OF IBT'S FOREIGN LENDING AND OTHER POLICIES WITH SIX MAJOR U.S. BANKS

Exhibit 2 presents selected financial and market data for IBT Corp. and six major U.S. banks which have extensive foreign operations. The data are derived from *Moody's Bank and Finance Manual* (1985) and covers the period 1982–1984. For reasons related to data availability, the figures represent the operations of the holding companies rather than the operating banks.

[3]The breakdown of this figure by sources is not available. World Bank figures for December 31, 1983 (*World Bank Annual Report,* 1985) show that the total external public debt owed by Zaire on that date amounted to $4,022 million and consisted of: $2,569 million bilateral official, $583 million multilateral, $163 million suppliers' credit, and $706 million from financial institutions.

Exhibit 1. Zaire: Selected Financial and Economic Data

EXCHANGE RATE: ZAIRES PER U.S. DOLLAR (END OF QUARTERS)				
	1st Q	2nd Q	3rd Q	4th Q
1983	5.896	5.956	27.316	30.120
1984	35.288	36.340	37.930	40.450
1985	47.200	50.650	53.550	55.793
1986	56.000			
		Consumer Prices (1980 = 100)		
1983	245.27	267.98	337.82	451.09
1984	465.98	485.36	510.38	520.52
1985	540.92	577.52	635.04	700.94

FOREIGN TRADE (MILLIONS OF ZAIRES)			
	Exports	Imports	Average Exchange Rate (zaires per U.S. dollar)
1980	4,554	2,328	2.800
1981	2,385	2,951	4.384
1982	2,295	2,751	5.750
1983	13,921	6,818	12.889
1984	36,300	24,754	36.129
1985	46,696	38,651	49.873

Source: International Monetary Fund, *International Financial Statistics,* several issues.

This, however, should not present a problem, since in each case the holding company is a one-bank holding company, and the operations of the bank account for the predominant part of total operations.

The comparison focuses essentially on the degree of exposure to foreign loans and capital adequacy, normally measured by the ratio of equity to total assets. Stock market and dividend data are provided to show the market valuation of different banks' stocks in light of these and other policies, reflecting the degree of aggressiveness in managing the bank's assets and liabilities, particularly with respect to overall lending operations.

Among the seven banks in Exhibit 2, IBT has the lowest proportion of foreign loans to total loans, just over 25 percent in 1984. The other banks, particularly Bankers Trust New York Corp. and Chemical New York Corp., have significantly more exposure to foreign loans than IBT. Moreover, IBT has successfully implemented a policy of reducing its exposure to foreign loans since 1982 in view of the increasing frequency of payments interruptions by debtor nations (see Chapter 20). This trend is also visible, though not as clearly as in the case of IBT, by the declining

Exhibit 2. International Banking and Trust Corporation (New York)
Comparison of Selected Financial and Market Data with Six Major U.S. Banks, 1982–1984

	IBT Corporation			Bank America Corporation			Citicorp		
	1984	1983	1982	1984	1983	1982	1984	1983	1982
	(in millions of U.S. dollars)								
Total assets	50,450	47,385	44,176	117,680	121,176	122,405	150,586	134,655	129,997
Total deposits	32,792	31,274	27,830	94,048	95,751	94,407	90,349	79,794	76,538
Total equity capital	2,623	2,417	2,165	5,119	5,136	4,596	6,426	5,771	4,815
Total loans	31,783	30,800	29,156	76,627	82,357	85,046	102,707	90,283	86,891
Foreign loans	8,136	8,562	8,746	26,794	25,637	27,674	38,425	38,677	38,387
Net income	459	394	336	346	390	457	890	860	723
	(U.S. dollars per share)								
Net income	7.50	7.25	6.80	1.77	2.18	2.60	6.45	6.48	5.60
Dividends	2.20	2.00	1.80	1.54	1.54	1.54	2.06	1.88	1.72
Common Stock Price Range									
High	57¾	60¼	48⅝	28⅛	25½	26¼	40½	46⅛	40
Low	39⅝	41	29¾	14⅜	18	15⅝	27⅜	30½	21½
Close	50½	44¾	40¼	18⅛	20⅞	20⅛	38¾	37⅛	32½
	(in percent)								
Selected ratios									
Stockholders' equity as percentage of year-end assets	5.2	5.1	4.9	4.4	4.2	3.7	4.3	4.3	3.7
Net income on year-end stockholders' equity	17.5	16.3	15.5	6.8	7.6	10.0	13.8	14.9	15.0
Foreign loans as percentage of total loans	25.6	27.8	30.0	35.0	31.2	32.6	37.4	42.8	44.2
P/E ratio (year end)	6.7	6.2	5.9	10.2	9.6	7.7	6.0	5.7	5.8

Exhibit 2. *(continued)*

	Chemical New York Corporation			Bankers Trust New York Corporation			Continental Illinois Corporation			Manufacturers Hanover Corporation		
	1984	1983	1982	1984	1983	1982	1984	1983	1982	1984	1983	1982
	(in millions of U.S. dollars)											
Total assets	48,167	51,165	52,236	45,208	40,003	42,427	30,413	42,097	42,899	75,714	64,332	64,041
Total deposits	27,998	32,452	33,698	25,559	22,829	24,492	15,056	29,431	28,175	44,206	42,284	43,825
Total equity capital	1,945	2,305	2,545	2,104	1,790	1,556	1,737	1,821	1,710	3,287	2,671	2,474
Total loans	30,598	33,328	36,882	23,513	23,651	21,330	23,970	30,777	33,339	53,847	45,336	42,222
Foreign loans	12,174	13,227	13,639	10,330	10,411	9,401	8,269	10,203	10,817	22,764	22,483	21,531
Net income	341	306	241	307	261	239	(1,087)	108	78	353	337	295
	(U.S. dollars per share)											
Net income	6.48	6.33	5.61	9.52	8.55	8.34	(26.99)	2.63	1.95	7.12	8.37	7.78
Dividends	2.36	2.16	1.92	2.51	2.30	2.10	.50	2.09	2.15	3.17	3.07	2.95
Common Stock Price Range												
High	35⅞	37½	31⅝	—	—	—	—	—	—	—	—	—
Low	23½	25⅝	17⅝	—	—	—	—	—	—	—	—	—
Close	34½	29⅜	27	54¾	45⅛	37⅛	5⅝	22⅜	21⅝	36⅝	38	41⅝
	(in percent)											
Selected ratios												
Stockholders'equity as percentage of year-end assets	4.8	4.5	4.0	4.7	4.5	3.8	5.7	4.3	4.0	4.2	4.2	3.9
Net income on year-end stockholders' equity	17.5	13.3	9.5	13.6	14.6	14.8	(d)	6.0	4.6	10.7	12.6	11.9
Foreign loans as percentage of total loans	39.8	39.7	37.0	43.9	44.0	44.1	34.5	33.2	32.4	42.3	49.36	51.0
P/E ratio (year end)	5.3	4.6	4.8	5.8	5.3	4.5	(d)	5.7	11.1	5.1	4.5	5.4

(d) = deficit

Source: *Moodys Bank and Finance Manual* (1985), Vol. 1, and (1984), Vol. 1.

proportions of foreign loans to total loans for some of the major banks during the period covered.

Potential vulnerability of major financial institutions, particularly multinational banks, to loan default, both domestic and foreign, has led to increasing emphasis on the capital adequacy ratio. Capital adequacy, usually measured by the ratio of stockholders' equity to total assets, represents the cushion available to sustain possible loan defaults before such default impinges on the financial integrity of the institution and safety of depositors' money. Data in Exhibit 2 show that this ratio has been steadily rising for all the covered banks in response to the criteria established by the regulatory authorities. IBT's capital adequacy position is significantly stronger than the other six banks.

There is some evidence that policies pursued by IBT's management with respect to foreign operations, capital adequacy, and dividends have been well received by the market. Market valuation data indicate that, with the exception of Bank America Corp., IBT's price/earning ratio has been higher than the other banks during the period covered in this study. The policies pursued by IBT also resulted in the highest return on stockholder's equity of all the banks covered in Exhibit 2. The performance of banks with respect to the parameters indicated for 1984 are summarized in Table 1.

EVALUATION OF LOAN REQUEST BY IBT STAFF

Upon his return from Kenshasa, Mr. Wheeler reported to Mr. Buchanan that Zaire needs fresh funds to reduce its current arrears and to maintain the current level of essential imports. While the government is determined to turn things around and continue to observe the performance targets specified in programs negotiated with the IMF, the prospects for a substan-

Table 1.

Bank	Ratio of Foreign Loans to Total Loans	Stockholders' Equity/ Year-end Assets	Net Income/ Stockholders Equity	P/E Ratio
IBT	25.6	5.2	17.5	6.7
Bank of America	31.2	4.4	6.8	10.2
Citicorp	37.4	4.3	14.5	6.0
Chemical New York	39.8	4.8	14.4	5.3
Bankers Trust	43.9	4.7	16.0	5.8
Continental Illinois	34.5	5.7	(d)	(d)
Manufacturers Hanover	42.3	4.2	10.7	5.1

(d) = deficit

tial improvement in the financial and economic situation are not bright. Mr. Wheeler, however, reserved final judgment on the merits of the loan request pending the analysis of data compiled by the staff and application of IBT's loan assessment criteria.

In a meeting with his staff attended by staff members from the research division, Mr. Wheeler went over the data compiled for the evaluation exercise. Following some discussion, it was agreed to ignore net earnings on services, since the data are difficult to obtain and the amounts are small. It was further agreed to project a small growth rate for exports for 1986–1988 in dollar terms (10–15 percent). Mr. Wheeler was hoping to complete his report and recommendations by the end of June.

12

Direct Foreign Investment Motivating Forces and Strategies of MNCs

WHY DIRECT FOREIGN INVESTMENT?

Direct foreign investment, the acquisition by a firm of physical assets in the form of plants and equipment in other countries, has long intrigued economists and writers in the field of international business finance. The literature abounds with theories and hypotheses which attempt to explain why a firm based in a certain country would seek direct investment in other countries.

The question that is usually asked is under what conditions does direct foreign investment become preferable to its alternatives: namely, exporting, licensing arrangements, and management contracts? Stated alternatively, if a firm enjoys a competitive edge in manufacturing a certain product, why not produce it at home and then export it, instead of setting up a plant to produce it in other countries? Similarly, if it enjoys a technological advantage or management and marketing expertise, why not utilize them in the form of licensing arrangements, or management contracts, respectively, instead of direct foreign investment?

A number of hypotheses have been advanced to explain the foreign expansion sequence from exporting to production overseas, as if these stages are distinct organic phases in the growth of the MNC. Yet we find a large number of MNCs today which undertake exporting and licensing activities side by side with foreign manufacturing activities. What is confusing, and perhaps misleading, is that some of these hypotheses try to explain the evolution of the MNC as a carefully designed process, rather than the outgrowth of response, over time, to an array of competitive and financial challenges. Attempting to fit actual corporate behavior into the mold of investment theory may be intellectually stimulating, but it fails to capture the complexities of the real world of international finance.

Approaches to understanding the motivating factors behind direct foreign investment are most useful when applied to explain the foreign investment decision in lieu of, or in addition to, the traditional capital budgeting approach. There is empirical evidence that financial criteria, such as those presented in Chapter 13, are often subordinated to strategic and behavioral consideration in the foreign investment decision. However, one should not jump to the conclusion that, in so doing, the financial manager has departed from the norms of financial theory for maximizing the value of the firm, or share prices in the market. Strategic and behavioral factors which influence investment activities may very well be consistent with these norms over the long run.

This chapter will examine these issues, citing the major contributions in the literature advanced for explaining the direct foreign investment decision. We propose to discuss the topic in the following order:

1. Strategic and behavioral motivations
2. Economic and competitive motivations
3. Financial and related considerations
4. Synthesis of the various factors involved, attempting to demonstrate that the nonfinancial factors are, in most instances, reconcilable to, or consistent with, the mainstream of financial theory

The reader will probably recognize that various arguments or hypotheses advanced in explaining the investment behavior of MNCs are often related. The investment decision is ultimately influenced by a number of various considerations simultaneously, rather than one such motivation at a time. The chapter will conclude with a statistical presentation and analysis of U.S. direct foreign investment abroad, and direct foreign investment in the United States.

STRATEGIC AND BEHAVIORAL CONSIDERATIONS

The strategic and behavioral factors motivating MNCs to invest outside their home country are closely interrelated. Strategic factors, despite their diversity, center on the desire of the firm to preempt its competitors, or gain a strategic advantage over them in its search for markets, raw material sources, or technological know-how. Behavioral factors attempt to explain the foreign investment decision in terms of the reaction of the firm to various stimuli originating from within or outside the firm. Both approaches purport to explain why, at various stages of its growth, an MNC may undertake direct foreign investment irrespective of, though not necessarily contrary to, the traditional financial tests of the profitability of these undertakings.

Strategic Factors

The most commonly cited strategic patterns are "preempt the competition" and "follow the leader," sometimes referred to as the "bandwagon effect." While the initial motivating force impelling the firm to seek investment abroad is essentially strategic, the ultimate objective must be the achievement of favorable pecuniary results sometime during the life cycle of the investment. It is difficult to explain why international oil companies moved early in the twentieth century to obtain oil concessions in the Middle East without invoking the favorable impact such investments have on their profitability. Obviously these firms, like other firms which sought early to establish mining businesses in Latin America or tea and rubber plantations in Asia, were motivated by a strong desire to establish a foothold in their respective host countries, to the exclusion of their rivals. Nevertheless, managers of these firms must have carefully estimated the eventual impact of these ventures on their financial performance. To presume that their moves were primarily motivated by a burning desire to preempt their competitors, irrespective of the financial implications of their decision, would be unrealistic.

The decision of these early pioneers seeking a strategic foothold in lucrative extractive industries abroad was understandably a lot easier than that of their counterparts later in this century attempting to preclude their competition in manufacturing industries, banking, or financial services. The latter was perhaps a more difficult and more calculating decision, but the initial motivating force may have been essentially similar.

"Follow the leader" or the "bandwagon effect" types of strategic behavior have been a predominant motive in post-World War II foreign investments by MNCs. Examples of this pattern of strategy are plentiful among the big three U.S. automobile manufacturers, major chemical companies (Dow Chemical and Union Carbide), office machine and data processing firms (IBM, Honeywell, and National Cash Register), soft drink companies (Coca-Cola and Pepsi Cola), and big money center banks (Citibank, Chase Manhattan Bank, and Morgan Guaranty).

The behavioral approach to understanding direct foreign investment has been articulated by Yair Aharoni's study published in 1966.[1] Aharoni's thesis is that the foreign investment decision is typically a response to a specific opportunity arising from stimulating forces inside or outside the

[1]Yair, Aharoni, *The Foreign Investment Decision Process* (Boston: Harvard Graduate School of Business Administration, 1966).

firm, rather than a systematic search for profitable investment opportunities abroad. The external stimulus may originate with the host country, the MNC's clients, or distributors of its products. Irrespective of whether the stimulus originates within the firm or without, strategic motivations, such as the fear of losing a market, the "bandwagon effect," or strong competition from abroad in the home market, would impel the firm to seriously consider the opportunity.[2]

Other factors come into play and act as catalysts reinforcing the initiating force. These are usually production and technological factors which in themselves would have provided an impetus for investing in a foreign project. A check list of these factors include:

1. Technological superiority and the desire of the firm to spread the cost of heavy investment in research and development.
2. Intensity of competition for the firm's domestic sales and exports, eroding the profit margin on these sales.
3. The desire of the firm to recapture lost markets through direct investment in a country possessing preferential treatment in those markets.
4. Capitalizing on the firm's intensive promotion and consumers' identification with its differentiated product line.

Aharoni emphasized that once interest in the foreign project is triggered, the investigative process is set in motion at different levels of the organization.[3] This diametrically reverses the sequence of traditional project evaluation in which interest in the investment develops following a favorable outcome of the investigative process. Information on the project is accumulated by the organization, which would form the basis for a full-dress analysis of the foreign investment for final decision.

ECONOMIC JUSTIFICATION OF DIRECT FOREIGN INVESTMENT

The classical theory of comparative cost advantage and factor endowment explains the patterns of specialization and trade among countries, under competitive conditions in both the product and factor markets. While comparative advantage offers a good explanation of import-export patterns among trading nations, it fails to answer the crucial question: Why direct foreign investment? The answer to this question must be sought outside the framework of classical economic theory, particularly as the conditions in the product and factor markets which underlie the behavior of the modern MNC have departed sharply from the competitive structure assumed by the classicists.

[2]*Ibid.*, pp. 54–55.
[3]*Ibid.*, pp. 80–81.

Several attempts were made in the last two decades to explain the phenomenon of direct foreign investment in a modern economic context. The common thread among these theories has been to use market imperfections as an explanation of economic motives impelling firms to attempt direct investment abroad. The pioneers in this field are Stephen Hymer,[4] Charles Kindelberger,[5] Raymond Vernon,[6] and Richard Caves.[7]

The common denominator among economic hypotheses is that the multinational firm operating as an oligopolist undertakes direct foreign investment to capitalize on imperfections in the product and factors markets. These imperfections may have been created by policies of host governments, or by the firm itself through product differentiation supported by aggressive promotion. The essential element is that there is a protected market which discourages competitive approaches by other firms.

Protected markets can result from customs or economic union agreements, such as the Common Market, created in 1957 among six European countries, and the European Free Trade Association (EFTA), established in 1958. These arrangements typically dismantle gradually tariff barriers among member countries and erect a tariff wall against imports from third countries, resulting in a large protected market. An MNC which had an export market in these countries prior to the establishment of the customs union finds itself virtually shut off, unless it moves to establish a facility inside the new market. Opportunities to establish local manufacturing or assembly facilities may also arise due to tax incentives provided by host countries, or other preferential nontax provisions provided by these countries.

Opportunities created for the firm by these arrangements, however, are often deemed a necessary but not a sufficient condition for undertaking direct investment abroad. The firm, to successfully operate in the protected environment, must possess other advantages which would enable it to compete effectively against local firms and discourage other entrants to the market from outside. Oligopolist firms with highly differentiated projects are uniquely situated to muster such an advantageous position. These firms move to inhibit competition from local firms and to preempt their multinational competitors, once they are firmly established in their new habitat.

Large firms with oligopolistic powers are particularly well situated to assume this role. In addition to highly differentiated products, per-

[4]Stephen H. Hymer, *The International Operations of National Firms: A Study of Direct Foreign Investment* (Cambridge, Mass.: MIT Press, 1976). This study, which was originally presented by the author as a doctoral dissertation at MIT, is believed to be the earliest among economic works linking multinationality with oligopolistic behavior.

[5]Charles P. Kindelberger, *American Business Abroad: Six Lectures on Direct Investment,* (New Haven, Conn.: Yale University Press, 1969).

[6]Raymond Vernon, "International Investment and International Trade in the Product Cycle," *The Quarterly Journal of Economics* (May 1966), pp. 190–207.

[7]Richard E. Caves, "International Corporations: The Industrial Economics of Foreign Investment," *Economics* (February 1971), pp. 1–27.

petuated by intensive investment in research and development and massive advertising, these firms also enjoy some or all of the following features:

1. Economies of scale in production, marketing, purchasing, and several other areas of operation.
2. Managerial know-how accumulated by their operations at home and in foreign countries and by their hiring policies.
3. Technological excellence, which is the product of their amply funded research and development programs, as well as (for the U.S. MNCs) their long involvement with the military and/or space programs.
4. Well-diversified structure, both as to product and as to country presence, enables them to capitalize on risky undertakings, with the assurance that they can absorb such risks should these undertakings fail to measure up to their expectations.
5. Intimate knowledge of foreign markets by virtue of their long experience in exporting to these markets.
6. Ability to mobilize their worldwide information-gathering apparatus to analyze and evaluate the merits and limitations of foreign investment opportunities.
7. Financial strength, which permits them to obtain needed funds and invest excess funds at relatively favorable terms.

These advantages possessed by large oligopolistic firms which have the resources and capacity to assume a multinational role do not in themselves explain why such firms seek direct foreign investment. Most of these features, such as economies of scale and technological and managerial know-how, can easily justify export activities, licensing arrangements, or management contracts. Attempts were made by a number of economists to explain the circumstances under which the firm finds it profitable or necessary to locate production facilities abroad rather than engage in these type of activities. The following section addresses itself to these issues.

PHASES OF PENETRATING FOREIGN MARKETS

The figure in Exhibit 12-1 presents an illustrative, though not necessarily typical, sequence of a firm expanding into foreign markets. Most MNCs began their penetration of foreign markets by exporting to these markets. The growth of such markets and the increasing familiarity of the firm with their nature and competitive conditions may eventually justify setting up a sales and distribution affiliate. Note that XYZ, Inc. moved to Phase II to cover the requirements of the markets in countries A and B, but continued to export to country C directly.

While the penetration of markets in countries A and B was carried out to Phase II only, the penetration of country C's market moved directly from the export phase to local production under a licensing arrangement.

Exhibit 12-1. Illustrative Sequence of Phases of Penetrating Foreign Markets

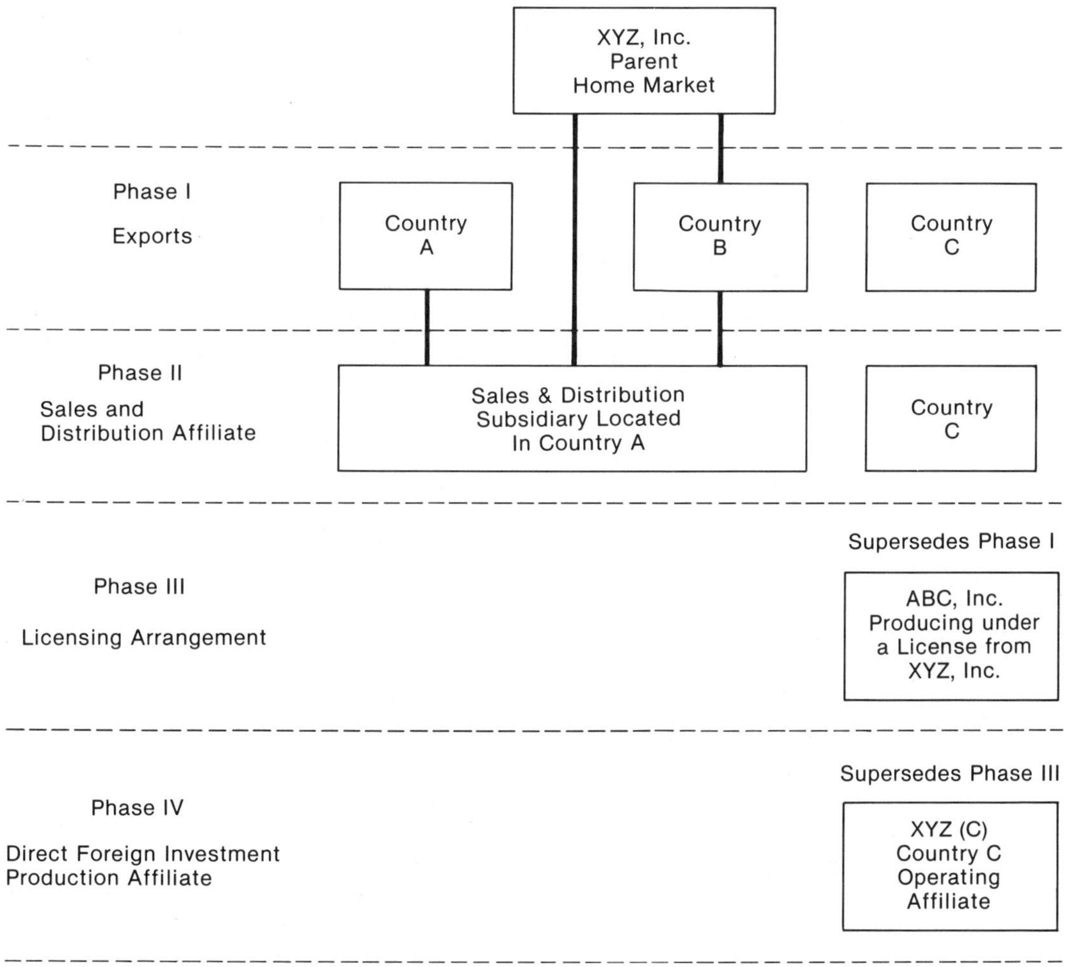

The initiative may have been taken by a local firm which probably possessed the capacity and managerial know-how to produce and distribute the product in country C. For XYZ, Inc. to consent to the licensing agreement, it must have made a favorable assessment of the prospects of licensing fees compared to export profits, and must have also concluded that the licensed firm was capable of serving well the market in country C. Licensing, as compared with direct foreign investment, requires little or no initial investment on the part of XYZ, Inc., but suffers from the disadvantage that the licensing firm may not be able to effectively control quality standards.

In Phase IV, XYZ terminated the licensing agreement and acquired the operation in country C as a wholly owned affiliate. This development could have been triggered by unsatisfactory performance by the licensee and consequent decline in sales in the market. XYZ Inc. may have decided that it was time to exercise direct control over the quality of the product and utilize its superior managerial and marketing techniques to expand the market. Its move into country C may have also been encouraged by tax and other incentives offered by country C's government.

This illustration demonstrates several important points:

1. Expansion into foreign operations is typically a gradual phase-by-phase process commencing with export activities.
2. The process of expansion may not necessarily be parallel in all foreign markets; that is, an MNC may establish an operating affiliate in one country, while at the same time it continues to meet the requirements of the markets in other countries by exports.
3. The process of moving from one phase to the next in a particular market may be accelerated, or even made inevitable, by unforeseen developments, adverse or favorable, in that market.

The evolutionary approach to direct foreign investment is generally accepted as a reflection of the risk aversion behavior of a typical firm. Before embarking on higher-risk investment opportunities in an uncertain and relatively unfamiliar foreign environment, the firm strives to acquire information about the environment which would enable it to move to the succeeding phase.

The expansionary pattern, however, may be different for different firms, depending on the nature of the product, the technology involved, and the importance of maintaining direct managerial and marketing control. Caves advanced the notion that these circumstances, that is, the nature of imperfections in the product and factors markets and the type of intangibles possessed by the management would determine which approach to the penetration of foreign markets would be preferable.[8] If the firm's technological superiority and managerial skills can be embodied in the product without adaptation to the local environment, then exporting should be the preferable method of market penetration.

When the firm's unique knowledge and intangible capital take the form of a process or a formula (such as the Coca-Cola recipe) that can be easily transmitted to others, licensing would provide the logical approach to expansion into foreign markets. In situations where the managerial skills can be unbundled from the intangible capital and technological aspects of the process, management agreement may prove to be the right approach, particularly if management fees offered by the host company exceed the profits derived from exporting to that particular market.

In many situations, however, the unbundling of the various elements that make for successful penetration of foreign markets may prove intrac-

[8]Caves, "International Corporations: The Industrial Economies of Foreign Investment," pp. 1–27.

table. The firm needs to maintain direct control over the production process to insure that quality standards are met, and to use its marketing and managerial skills as well as its proprietary knowledge to serve dynamic foreign markets. In these situations, direct foreign investment may be the only viable approach.

PRODUCT CYCLE THEORY

The product cycle theory, developed first by Vernon,[9] suggests that direct foreign investment is a natural and climactic stage in the life cycle of a new product introduced to the market by oligopolistic firms, capitalizing on product and factor markets imperfections. The stages in the life cycle of a new product are:

1. The initial stage, when the product is first introduced in the home market. The product, a creature of intensive investment in research and development, is highly differentiated by massive promotional and marketing techniques to establish a firm foothold in the home market.
2. After the product is perfected and standardized to benefit from economies in production and distribution, output would begin to outstrip the requirements of the home market. The firm starts looking for foreign markets.
3. The export stage provides the firm with outlets to market excess output, and to spread out massive investments in research and development, as well as marketing and promotion outlays.
4. As the product reaches maturity, patents expire and technological know-how becomes available to competitors at home and abroad, and the market is eventually flooded with similar or look-alike products. Profit margins begin to erode not only in the home market, but also in export markets as well.
5. At this stage the firm begins to search for manufacturing locations abroad, particularly where imperfections in the factor market (low labor cost, for example) hold the promise of lower production costs in an attempt to protect the eroding profit margins.

Vernon's theory thus viewed direct investment as a *defensive* mechanism or a solution to the problem of intensifying competition in both the home and export markets. The most widely quoted example illustrating the product cycle theory is the manufacturing of electronics. The final stage in the development of this product was the establishment by major U.S. producers of offshore plants in an attempt to survive the intense competition from other producers of electronics, particularly Japanese firms. Richard

[9]Raymond Vernon, *Storm Over the Multinationals* (Cambridge, Mass.: Harvard University Press, 1977).

Moxon's study of these offshore plants, located primarily in Mexico and Taiwan, revealed interesting observations which lend some credence to product cycle theory,[10] although these plants could have also been explained in terms of the strategic and behavioral approaches. Moxon's study of the electronics industry reached the following conclusions:

- The offshore plants are predominantly owned by 20 U.S. parent firms. These firms chose to locate their plants outside the United States, primarily as a defensive strategy to achieve lower production costs, in an attempt to remain competitive with low-priced imports from Japan.
- Not all products and operations in the electronics industry are adaptable for offshore production and shipment back to the parent firms. Offshore plants specialize in lightweight assembly products that are standardized and capable of being mass-produced in a labor-intensive type of operation. Products that require special skills, capital intensive technology, or bulky products are not adapted to this operation.
- Export of these products to the U.S. parents is facilitated by the relatively low shipping cost and favorable treatment under U.S. tariff schedules.[11]

Although the electronics industry may serve as a good illustration of the successive stages of development postulated by the product cycle theory, it is difficult to see how it can satisfactorily explain multinational behavior in most industries. In the first place oligopolistic MNCs operating in a variety of industries, such as the automobile, chemical, and drugs and pharmaceutical industries, seem to operate in different foreign markets using different market penetration approaches simultaneously. For example, the Ford Motor Company continues to rely on direct exports to a large number of countries, while it has manufacturing and assembly plants in some countries, and sales and distribution centers in still other countries. Second, a large number of MNCs continue to maintain profitable international operations long after the maturity of the product and the loss of their innovative lead. Contrary to product cycle theory, the last stage in the evolutionary process, namely, decline and eventual disappearance of the product, does not often materialize.

The survival of MNCs' foreign operations in the same standardized product line would seem to indicate that factors other than technological lead must have acted as barriers to entry. These barriers are generally not much different from the barriers which protect oligopolistic firms in their own domestic markets. Large MNCs, such as Coca-Cola, Eastman Kodak,

[10]Richard Moxon, "The Motivation for Investment in Offshore Plants: The Case of the U.S. Electronics Industry," *Journal of International Business Studies* (Spring 1975), pp. 51–66.

[11]Exports to U.S. parents from their offshore plants are subject to Items 806.30 and 807.00 of the U.S. Tariff Schedule under which duties are levied only on the foreign value added. This is typically a small fraction of the value of such products, as in most cases offshore plants start with materials imported from the parent companies.

Colgate-Palmolive, and Bayer, rely primarily on superior marketing skills and intensive advertising to remain entrenched in their markets.

It is difficult to explain direct foreign investment in terms of one theory, considering the complex nature of the behavior and strategies of MNCs. It would take probably several of these theories and motivations to explain multinational behavior in any product line or an industry. It is obvious that not all foreign investments are defensive. Some of them are preemptive, designed to discourage the entry of potential competitors in the same market. Others are disruptive in nature, such as when an MNC moves into a market to prevent a competitor from achieving sufficient experience and economies of scale to dominate it. Despite the usefulness of product cycle theory, it has not been found to offer an adequate explanation for multinational behavior in penetrating foreign markets.[12]

INTERNATIONAL DIVERSIFICATION

We suggested earlier that the achievement of diversification benefits provides a strong motive for direct foreign investment. Diversification by country not only provides the MNC with a natural hedge against the foreign exchange and political risks, but also reduces the variability of the overall cash flow, thus contributing to the increased valuation of the firm as a whole. There is little doubt that diversification through direct investment in foreign markets reduces the systematic risk facing the firm, since economic cycles are likely to be in different phases.[13]

The issue that has attracted considerable attention in international financial theory is to what extent an investor can improve his or her risk/return performance by holding an internationally diversified portfolio as compared with a domestic portfolio. This section addresses itself to this issue, and the related question of whether or not an investment in the shares of a well-diversified MNC would serve as a surrogate for an internationally diversified portfolio.[14] International financial theory relating to the cost of capital of the multinational firm is developed in Chapter 15.

[12]Ian H. Giddy, "The Demise of the Product Cycle Model in International Business Theory," *Columbia Journal of World Business* (Spring 1978), pp. 90–97.

[13]Alan R. Rugman, "Risk Reduction by International Diversification," *Journal of International Business Studies,* Vol. 7, no. 2 (1976), pp. 75–80.

[14]There is a considerable body of literature on the theory of international portfolio diversification. Among the pioneers in this field are Herbert G. Grubel [see "Internationally Diversified Portfolios, Welfare Gains and Capital Flow", *American Economic Review* (December 1968), pp. 1299–1314], Haim Levy and Marshall Sarnat [see "International Diversification of Investment Portfolios," *American Economic Review* (September 1970), pp. 668–675], B. H. Solnik [see "Why Not Diversify Internationally?" *Financial Analysis Journal* (July-August 1974), pp. 48–54], and D. R. Lessard [see "World, National and Industry Factors Through International Diversification," *Financial Analysis Journal* (January–February 1976), pp. 32–38].

This section is largely based on Lessard's "Principles of International Portfolio Selection," reprinted in Donald R. Lessard, ed., *International Financial Management: Theory and Application,* 2nd ed. (New York: John Wiley and Sons, 1985), pp. 16–30.

The ratio of total risk that is systematic (nondiversifiable in a portfolio context) to total risk is about 0.50 for the United States, but is somewhat higher in other countries.[15] This reflects their less diversified economies and narrower industrial base, as well as relatively unstable and volatile political regimes. However, when diversification is extended across boundaries, the proportion of total risk that is systematic can be reduced considerably.

Exhibit 12-2 reflects the risk reduction achieved by an internationally diversified portfolio, compared with a diversified U.S. portfolio. The percentage of nondiversifiable or systematic risk (measured by the ratio of portfolio standard deviation to the standard deviation of a typical stock) is reduced from 0.50 to about 0.33.

The beneficial impact of international diversification on the portfolio's risk arises from the diversity of economic and financial conditions in different countries, and the fact that business cycle phases in different countries are often not synchronized.

Comparative valuation data of equity markets in different countries (Exhibit 12-3) show a wide divergence of price/earning ratios and yields. It is interesting to note that the U.S. market is undervalued against a number of foreign equity markets, particularly Austria, Italy, and Japan.

Exhibit 12-2. Risk Reduction Through National and International Diversification

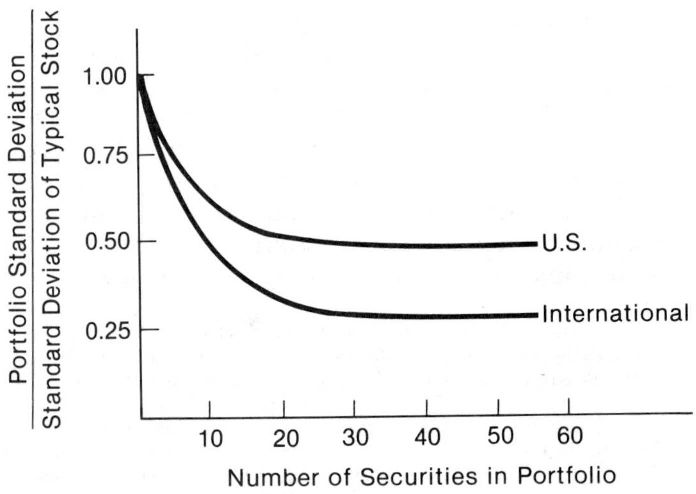

Source: Donald R. Lessard, "Principles of International Portfolio Selection,"reprinted in *International Financial Management: Theory and Application* (New York: John Wiley and Sons, 1985), p. 18. Chart was originally developed by Solnik; see footnote 14.

[15]*Ibid.*, p. 17.

Exhibit 12-3. Comparative Valuation in Selected Equity Markets, August 30, 1985

INTERNATIONAL INDICES	P/BV[a]	P/CE[b]	P/E	YIELD
The World Index	1.61X	6.2X	13.2X	3.5%
Europe, Australia, Far East	1.76	6.1	15.5	2.6
Europe	1.36	5.0	11.1	4.0
NATIONAL INDICES				
U.S.A.	1.50	6.2	11.8	4.3
Australia	1.32	7.4	12.1	4.0
Austria	1.95	11.0	56.5	1.8
Belgium	0.99	3.1	8.0	10.3
Canada	1.52	6.9	14.8	3.2
Denmark	1.28	6.3	14.5	2.2
France	1.35	3.7	11.7	4.1
Germany	2.17	4.8	13.3	3.2
Hong Kong	1.88	12.7	14.8	3.7
Italy	1.44	4.6	22.1	2.5
Japan	2.63	8.7	26.1	1.0
The Netherlands	0.91	3.1	7.0	4.6
Norway	1.46	3.2	5.4	3.8
Singapore/Malaysia	1.36	12.5	19.4	3.0
Spain	0.43	3.0	10.0	8.7
Sweden	1.23	4.8	7.9	3.1
Switzerland	1.35	5.7	11.5	2.4
United Kingdom	1.44	6.5	11.4	4.4

[a]BV = book value
[b]CE = cash earnings
Source: Capital International, Geneva, September 1985. Reprinted in Drexel Burnham Lambert, Inc., *International Investment Monthly* (September 1985), p. 6.

Obstacles to International Portfolio Investment
The Exchange Rate and Political Risks

If there were no barriers to investments across national boundaries, internationally diversified portfolios would dominate national portfolios, since they offer more favorable risk-return relationships. It is a fact of life, however, that national capital markets are segmented by barriers which allow the diversities in returns and valuation shown in Exhibit 12-3 to persist.

Aside from the barriers which impede the flow of portfolio investment across borders, the higher rate of return or valuation realized in some countries than in U.S. equity markets may not be obtainable in the future. For one thing, such superior returns in most cases reflect, in part, higher economic growth rates in these countries compared to the United States, which could reverse in the years ahead.

Another key consideration is the foreign exchange risk. Improving the risk-return tradeoff by international diversification may be offset by adverse exchange rate movements for the investor. For example, a U.S. investor, attempting to raise the performance of his or her portfolio by investing in foreign stocks, may discover that the higher return through this strategy is more than offset by the appreciation of the U.S. dollar against the currencies of the countries of investment.

The crucial question is whether or not an internationally diversified portfolio can produce a higher rate of return on a fully hedged basis. This hedge may be accomplished by either borrowing currency in the local market, or by selling the currency of investment in the forward market. In either case, the return differential in favor of foreign portfolio investment is reduced by the cost of hedging. The cost of hedging in the money market is the interest differential between the two money market rates (the home country and the country of investment) and the expected percentage change in the exchange rate. The cost of hedging through forward contracts is the difference between the forward discount or premium and the expected percentage change in the exchange rate. In efficient money and exchange markets, these two costs will be equated by the interest parity relationship.

Political risk is a major factor not only in direct foreign investment, but also in international portfolio investment. MNCs have the capacity and resources to assess the political risk factor and incorporate it in the evaluation process. Moreover, they have the option of buying insurance against certain types of political risk (See Chapter 17). The average portfolio investor is typically not in a good position to evaluate political risk, and is likely to lack the resources and expertise to undertake this evaluation. As interest in foreign investment has increased in recent years, a number of international brokerage houses and multinational banks are making available to their clients data relevant to the assessment of the political risk.

A key question is whether or not the political risk is reflected in securities prices. Lessard points out that little empirical research has been done on this and other areas relating to foreign portfolio investment.[16] The only available evidence is the relative overall efficiency of securities markets. In major markets, such as the United States and industrial countries, information is quickly embedded in securities prices which consequently bear a reasonable relationship to the risks taken by investors. Such is not the case in the small and shallow securities markets of most countries, particularly those of LDCs.

[16]Lessard, "Principles of International Portfolio Selection," p. 24.

A well-diversified international portfolio benefits from spreading out the political risk, as this risk is essentially unsystematic and is, therefore, amenable to be diversified away. As such, political risks may favor foreign investors relative to domestic investors, since the former have more flexibility to diversify their portfolios than the latter. Overall, political risk, although an important variable in the foreign portfolio decision, does not seem to greatly inhibit purchase of foreign securities.

Other Barriers to Foreign Portfolio Investment

Aside from the currency and political risks, a major hindrance to foreign portfolio investment is the smallness and the inefficiency of foreign markets relative to that of the United States. Small and thin markets lack liquidity, an essential property of all money and capital markets. There has been, however, a marked growth of foreign equity markets in the last two decades. As a percentage of world stock market capitalization, foreign markets accounted for 44 percent of the total in 1980 (the U.S. market accounting for 56 percent), as compared with 29 percent (71 percent for the U.S. market) in 1966. The growth in turnover is even more impressive, increasing from 24 percent of world total turnover in 1966 to 46 percent in 1980.[17]

Despite this growth, the equity markets outside the United States, a number of Western European countries and Japan remain too small and their turnover too limited to offer realistic investment opportunities to U.S. institutional investors. Even in such countries as Switzerland, the Netherlands, and Germany, there are constraints on diversification, since a small number of shares typically account for a large proportion of total trading.

There are also other institutional restrictions that make investing in foreign markets costly, inconvenient, and even sometimes impossible. These restrictions include limitations on foreign ownership of shares in some countries, difficulties of accessing certain foreign equity markets, governmental controls governing capital flows, and the tax aspects explained in Chapter 18. These obstacles make the diversification benefits of an international portfolio less realizable in practice, or, in effect, offset these benefits, inasmuch as a number of these restrictions involve an explicit or implicit cost.

Investment in the Shares of Diversified MNCs

If international portfolio diversification proves difficult or impractical, because of the barriers and restrictions discussed in the previous section, can

[17]*Ibid.,* p. 25.

investment in the shares of a diversified MNC deliver the same diversification benefits to the investor? This question has been addressed by a large number of theoreticians in recent years. By buying the shares of multinationals, it is postulated, investors can overcome imperfections and barriers in the national securities market and share in the profits realized by these firms through capitalizing on imperfections in the product and factors markets.

Despite the seeming reasonableness of such an inference, studies testing this hypothesis reached different conclusions. If shares of MNCs provide the diversification benefits which can be realized by an internationally diversified portfolio, should they not sell at a premium? If the answer to this question is positive, then these firms should enjoy a lower cost of equity. Empirical evidence on the lower cost of equity hypothesis has been divided.[18]

MULTINATIONAL BUSINESS—THE STATISTICAL EVIDENCE

Multinational business has experienced a fairly rapid and steady growth in recent years. Aggregate worldwide statistical data on the size and growth of MNCs are not available. A fairly good picture of the dimensions of multinational business can be formed by examining U.S. data on U.S. direct investment abroad and foreign direct investment in the United States.

Although multinational business is dominated by U.S. firms, non-U.S. multinationals have been increasing in number and importance. Data in Exhibit 12-4 show that there were in 1981 67 firms with capitalization in excess of $2 billion outside of North America, compared with 93 in the United States and nine in Canada.

U.S. Direct Investment Abroad

Data in Exhibit 12-5 show that U.S. direct investment abroad increased by 39 percent in the 1978–1984 period. These data represent equity investments in foreign affiliates and subsidiaries measured at book value, as well as net loans outstanding to foreign business in which U.S. investors own at least 10 percent of the voting stock. About 75 percent of total investments as of year end 1984 is located in developed countries. This concentration of investments in developed countries, primarily in Canada and

[18]Tamir Agmon and Donald Lessard ["Investor Recognition of Corporate International Diversification," *Journal of Finance* (September 1977), pp. 1049–1055], and Raj Aggarwal, [Multinationality and Stock Market Valuation," *Management International Review,* Vol. 19 (February 1979), pp. 5–21], among others, reached evidence supporting this hypothesis. Their conclusions were challenged by Bernard Jacquillat [see "Multinationals are Poor Tools for Diversification," *Journal of Portfolio Management* (Winter 1978), pp. 8–12].

Exhibit 12-4. Nationality of Firms with Capitalization in Excess of $2 Billion

United States	93
Japan	35
United Kingdom	9
Canada	9
West Germany	9
Switzerland	5
South Africa	3
Hong Kong	2
Australia	1
France	1
Italy	1
The Netherlands	1

Source: *Capital International Perspective,* Geneva, Switzerland, 1981. Reprinted in Lessard, "Principles of International Portfolio Selection," p. 26. Also, reprinted with permission from Donald R. Lessard.

Western European countries, seems to have increased in the last decade. Investments outside developed countries, which have been traditionally located in Latin American countries, have recently become more diversified as to country of location.

United States investment abroad is concentrated in manufacturing and petroleum, accounting in 1983 for about 40 percent and 26 percent of total investment, respectively (Exhibit 12-6). Banking and finance ranks third as a major area of U.S. foreign investment.

Direct Foreign Investment in the United States

Total direct foreign investment in the United States at the end of 1984 amounted to about $138 billion, or about 58 percent of U.S. direct foreign investment abroad. Western European countries dominate the investment scene in the United States, accounting for over 77 percent of total foreign investment in the United States, of which the United Kingdom, the largest single investor in the United States, accounted for about 28 percent in 1984. Japan and Canada rank next, accounting each for just over 10 percent of the total. Investments of other countries outside Western European countries, Canada, and Japan are insignificant (Exhibit 12-7).

Direct foreign investment in the United States is also concentrated in manufacturing industries (32.8 percent), followed by trade (20.4 percent), petroleum (17.6 percent), real estate (8.2 percent), and banking (6.4 percent).

Exhibit 12-5. U.S. Direct Investment Position Abroad, Year End 1978, 1980, and 1984

	IN MILLIONS OF U.S. DOLLARS		
Item	1978	1980	1984
Developed countries			
Canada	37,071	44,640	50,467
Ten European Community countries[a]	55,228	76,588	78,867
Other Europe[b]	14,325	19,098	24,796
Japan	4,972	6,274	8,374
Australia, New Zealand, and South Africa	8,876	10,484	11,554
Total developed countries	120,472	157,084	174,058
Developing countries			
Latin America	32,662	38,275	28,094
Africa[c]	3,175	3,730	6,247
Middle East	−2,194	2,281	3,435
Asia and Pacific[d]	6,757	8,397	16,156
Total developing countries	40,400	52,683	53,932
International and unallocated	6,934	3,701	5,423
Total for all countries	167,806	213,468	233,413

	AS PERCENT OF TOTAL		
Item	1978	1980	1984
Developed countries			
Canada	22.1	20.9	21.6
Ten European Community countries[a]	32.9	35.2	33.8
Other Europe[b]	8.5	9.1	10.6
Japan	3.0	3.3	3.6
Australia, New Zealand, and South Africa	5.3	5.1	5.0
Total developed countries	71.8	73.6	74.6
Developing countries			
Latin America	19.5	17.9	12.0
Africa[c]	1.9	1.8	2.7
Middle East	−1.3	1.1	1.5
Asia and Pacific[d]	4.0	3.9	6.9
Total developing countries	24.1	24.7	23.1
International and unallocated	4.1	1.7	2.3
Total for all countries[e]	100.0	100.0	100.0

[a]Belgium, France, Germany, Luxembourg, the Netherlands, Denmark, Ireland, United Kingdom, and Italy. Greece became a member in 1981.

[b]Includes Norway, Spain, Sweden, Switzerland, and other European countries.

[c]Excludes South Africa, which is classified as developed.

[d]Excludes Japan, which is classified as developed.

[e]Due to rounding, totals do not add up to 100.0.

Source: U.S. Department of Commerce, *Survey of Current Business* (August 1980), pp. 27–28, and (June 1985), pp. 30–32.

Exhibit 12-6. U.S. Investment Position Abroad, by Industrial Area, Year End 1983 (in millions of dollars)

INDUSTRY	DEVELOPED COUNTRIES	DEVELOPING COUNTRIES	ALL COUNTRIES	PERCENT OF ALL COUNTRIES
Manufacturing:				
Food and kindred products	6,834	2,244	9,078	4.0
Chemicals and allied products	16,000	4,220	20,220	8.9
Primary and fabricated metals	4,025	2,021	6,046	2.7
Machinery, except electrical	13,963	1,693	15,656	6.9
Electrical and electronic equipment	5,671	2,045	7,716	3.4
Transportation equipment	9,606	1,693	11,299	5.0
Other manufacturing	15,646	4,464	20,110	9.0
Total manufacturing	71,745	18,380	90,125	39.9
Mining	3,962	2,780	6,742	3.0
Petroleum	38,879	16,572	59,785	26.4
Trade	22,676	5,858	28,534	12.6
Banking	5,195	6,294	11,489	5.1
Finance (except banking, insurance, and real estate)	20,585	−3,347	17,238	7.6
Other industries	6,540	4,441[a]	12,205	5.4
Unallocated & international		5,557		
Total all industries	169,582	56,535	226,117	100.0

[a]Excludes data suppressed by Department of Commerce to avoid disclosure of data of individual companies.

Source: U.S. Department of Commerce, *Survey of Current Business* (August 1984), p. 29.

New direct foreign investments in the United States in 1984 amounted to just over $13 billion. Exhibit 12-8 shows the distribution of this investment by industry and by country of foreign parent. Petroleum and manufacturing accounted for the largest shares, followed by trade, banking, and real estate. United Kingdom, Canada, and Japan were the largest investing countries, but developing countries as a group were fairly large investors in the United States, accounting for over 20 percent of the total in 1984.

Exhibit 12-7. Total Direct Foreign Investment Position in the United States, Year End 1984 (in millions of U.S. dollars)

SOURCE OF INVESTMENT	TOTAL	PETROLEUM	MANUFACTURING	TRADE	BANKING	FINANCE EXCLUDING BANKING	INSURANCE	REAL ESTATE	OTHER
Canada	14,001	1,419	3,888	1,651	1,093	547	982	2,717	2,126
United Kingdom	38,099	10,917	9,347	6,708	2,337	943	2,573	4,008	1,879
Europe, excluding United Kingdom	68,468	11,980	29,337	9,768	3,554	1,947	4,558	3,880	3,806
Japan	14,817	−178	2,262	9,940	1,778	−312	175	663	984
Other	2,336	43	317		42			72	
Total	137,751	24,181	45,151	28,067	8,804	3,125	8,288	11,340	8,795
Percent of total	100.0	17.6	32.8	20.4	6.4	2.3	6.0	8.2	6.3
As a Percent of Total									
Canada	10.2	5.9	8.6	5.9	12.4	17.5	11.8	24.0	24.2
United Kingdom	27.6	45.1	20.7	23.9	26.5	30.2	31.0	35.3	21.4
Europe, excluding United Kingdom	49.7	49.5	65.0	34.8	40.4	62.3	55.0	34.2	43.3
Japan	10.8	−0.7	5.0	35.4	20.2	−10.0	2.2	5.9	11.1
Other	1.7	0.2	0.7		0.5			0.6	
Total	100.0	100.0	100.0	100.0	100.0	100.0	100.0	100.0	100.0

Source: U.S. Department of Commerce, *Survey of Current Business* (June 1985), p. 32.

Exhibit 12-8. **New Direct Foreign Investment in the United States (1984) by Industry of Acquired or Established U.S. Business Enterprise and by Country of Foreign Parent**

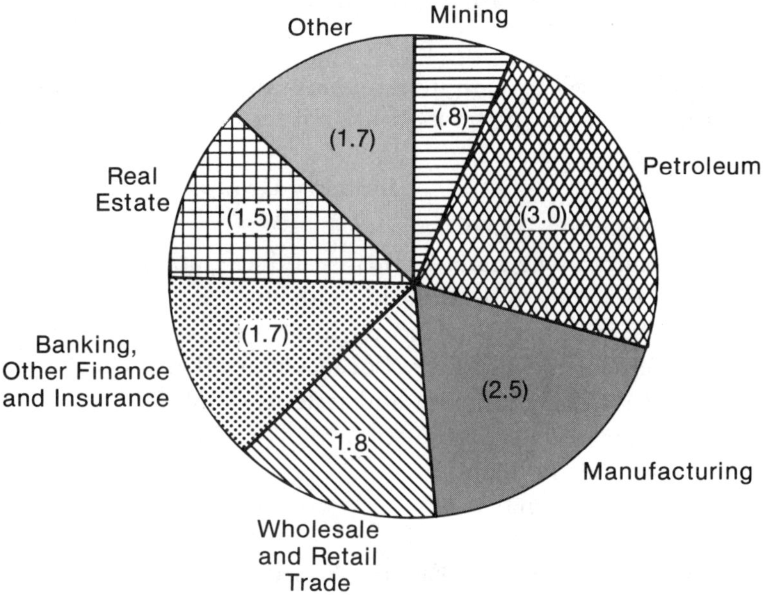

(a) By Industry, 1984 ($13 Billion)

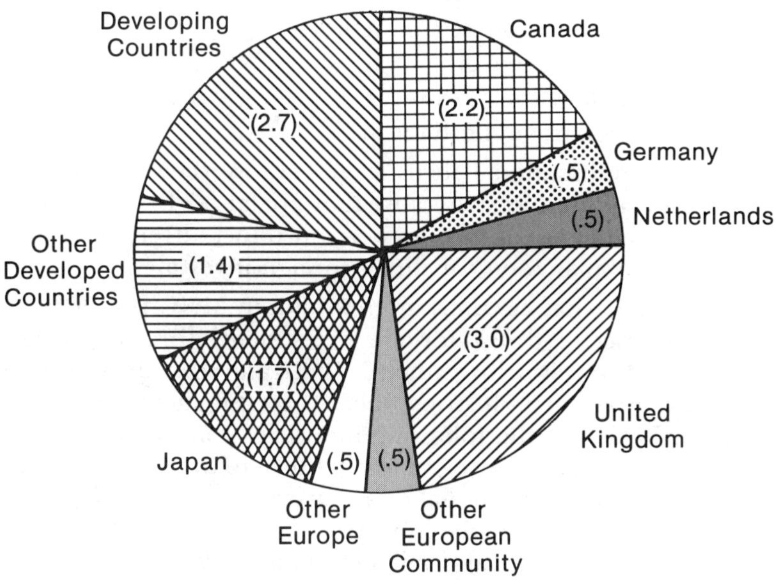

(b) By Country, 1984 ($13 Billion)

Source: U.S. Department of Commerce, *Survey of Current Business* (May 1985), pp. 19, 21.

REVIEW QUESTIONS

1. Explain direct foreign investment in the following industries in terms of one or more of the motivational factors listed.

Industry Groups

Accounting firms
Automobile manufacturing and assembly
Electronic and microchip industry
Oil industry (prospecting for oil)
Soft drinks industry (Coca-Cola and Pepsi Cola)
Business equipment and systems (IBM, DEC, etc.)
Pharmaceutical industry
Rubber industry
International banks

List of Motivational Factors (Strategic, Behavioral, and Economic)

Follow the leader "bandwagon effect"
Raw material seekers
Efficiency seekers
Cutting cost, that is, taking advantage of lower labor or input cost in other countries
Preemption of competitors
Market seekers
Follow the customers
Defensive mechanism

2. Are multinational firms large because they are multinational, or are they multinational because they are large? Do such interrelated factors as size, oligopolistic power, and product differentiation provide a plausible explanation for direct foreign investment?
3. Under what circumstances would an MNC prefer (a) a management contract to direct foreign investment? (b) a licensing agreement to direct foreign investment? Illustrate your answer by citing specific examples or industries where these practices are common.
4. a. Which of the following industries conforms closely in its historical growth and development pattern to the *product cycle theory?* Explain.
   the international oil industry
   the automobile industry
   electronics and microchip industry
   the soft drinks industry

b. What are the major weaknesses of the product cycle theory? Illustrate your answer by referring to specific industries which have had a pattern of development not consistent with the theory.

5. How does international diversification help explain in part direct foreign investment? Can the benefits of diversification (such as reducing the systematic risk and stabilizing the overall cash flow pattern of the firm) be achieved by other forms of market penetration?
6. From Exhibit 12-3 compare and contrast equity markets in the United States (from the standpoints of valuation and yield) with each of the following countries: (a) Canada, (b) Japan, and (c) Sweden. What are the implications of divergencies in equity valuation for international portfolio investment?
7. Can investment in the stock of a well-diversified multinational firm afford the investor the same benefits of diversification obtainable from a portfolio of stocks selected from different countries? If that is the case, why do portfolio managers incur the cost, and perhaps the inconvenience, of buying shares of foreign firms to diversify their portfolios? Is the jury still out on this particular controversy?

BIBLIOGRAPHY

ADLER, M., and B. DUMAS, "Optimal International Acquisitions," *Journal of Finance* (March 1975), pp. 1–19.

AGMON, T., and S. HIRSCH, "Multinational Corporations and the Developing Economies: Potential Gains in a World of Imperfect Markets and Uncertainty," *Oxford Bulletin of Economics and Statistics,* Vol. 14 (1979), pp. 333–344.

AGRARWAL, J. P., "Determinants of Foreign Direct Investment: A Survey," *Weltwirtschaftliches Archiv,* no. 4 (1980), pp. 739–773.

AHARONI, Y., *The Foreign Investment Decision Process.* Boston: Harvard Graduate School of Business Administration, Division of Research, 1966.

ALIBER, R. Z., "A Theory of Foreign Direct Investment," *The International Corporation,* Charles P. Kindleberger, ed. Cambridge, Mass.: MIT Press, 1970, pp. 17–34.

ARPAN, J. S., E. B. FLOWERS, and D. A. RICKS, "Foreign Direct Investment in the United States: The State of Knowledge in Research," *Journal of International Business Studies* (Spring-Summer 1981), pp. 137–154.

BANKER, P., "You're the Best Judge of Foreign Risks," *Harvard Business Review* (March-April 1983), pp. 157–165.

BAROVICK, R. L., "Bilateral Investment Treaties: Ensuring Fair Treatment for U.S. Investors in the Third World," *Business America* (August 23, 1982), pp. 3–5.

BERGSTEN, C. F., T. HORST, and T. H. MORAN, *American Multinationals and American Interests.* Washington, D.C.: The Brookings Institution, 1978.

BODDEWYN, J. J., "Foreign and Domestic Divestment and Investment Decisions: Like or Unlike?" *Journal of International Business Studies* (Winter 1983), pp. 23–35.

BROOKE, M. Z., and H. L. REMMERS, *The Strategy of Multinational Enterprise.* London: Longmans, 1970.

BUCKLEY, P. J., and M. CASSON, *The Future of the Multinational Enterprise.* London: Macmillan, 1976.

Business America, "Foreign Investments in U.S. at New High During 1981" (February 7, 1983), p. 18.

Business Week, "Investment Abroad: Foreign Markets Turn More Hazardous" (December 28, 1981), pp. 129–131.

CALVET, A. L., "A Synthesis of Foreign Direct Investment Theories and Theories of the Multinational Firm," *Journal of International Business Studies* (Spring-Summer 1981), pp. 43–59.

CAO, A. D., "Foreign Acquisition in the U.S.," *California Management Review* (Summer 1980), pp. 47–55.

CARTER, E. E., "The Behavioral Theory of the Firm and Top-Level Corporate Decisions," *Administrative Science Quarterly* (December 1971), pp. 413–428.

CAVES, R. E., "Causes of Direct Investment: Foreign Firms' Shares in Canadian and United Kingdom Manufacturing Industries," *Review of Economics and Statistics* (August 1974), pp. 270–293.

CONTRACTOR, F. J., "The Role of Licensing in International Strategy," *The Columbia Journal of World Business* (Winter 1981), pp. 73–83.

DANIELS, J., and P. SATISHKUMAR, "U.S. Foreign Acquisitions: An Endangered Species?", *Management International Review* (1980/2), pp. 25–34.

DAVIDSON, W. H., "The Location of Foreign Direct Investment Activity: Country Characteristics and Experience Effects," *Journal of International Business Studies* (Fall 1980), pp. 9–22.

______, *Experience Effects in International Investment and Technology Transfer.* Ann Arbor, Mich.: UMI Research Press, 1981.

DUNNING, J. H., "Explaining Changing Patterns of International Production in Defense of the Eclectic Theory," *Oxford Bulletin of Economics and Statistics,* Vol. 41 (1979), pp. 269–296.

______, "Explaining the International Direct Investment Position of Countries: Towards a Dynamic or Developmental Approach," *Weltwirtschaftliches Archiv,* 117/1 (1981), pp. 30–64.

Economist, "Foreign Investment in America: Twilight's Last Gleaming" (October 16, 1982), pp. 97–98.

Economist, "Buying Up America" (May 21, 1983), pp. 104–105.

FISHER, W. H., *Technology Transfer as a Motive for U.S. Direct Investment by European Firms.* Columbus, Ohio: Battelle Memorial Institute, 1977.

FLOWERS, E. B., "Oligopolistic Reactions of European and Canadian Direct Investment in the United States," *Journal of International Business Studies* (Fall-Winter 1976), pp. 43–55.

FRANKO, L. G., "Foreign Direct Investment in Less Developed Countries: Impact on Home Countries," *Journal of International Business Studies* (Winter 1978), pp. 55–65.

GIDDY, I. H., "The Demise of the Product Cycle Model in International Business Theory," *Columbus Journal of World Business* (Spring 1978), pp. 90–97.

HARTMAN, D. G., "Foreign Investment and Finance with Risk," *Quarterly Journal of Economics* (May 1979), pp. 213–232.

HENMART, J. A., *Theory of Multinational Enterprise.* Ann Arbor, Mich.: University of Michigan Press, 1982.

HIGGINS, P. W., "U.S. Market Attracts Foreign Investors," *National Underwriters* (December 1980), pp. 44–45.

HORST, T., "Firm and Industry Determinants of the Decision to Invest Abroad: An Empirical Study," *Review of Economics and Statistics* (August 1972), pp. 258–266.

HYMER, S. H., *The International Operations of National Firms: A Study of Direct Foreign Investment.* Cambridge, Mass.: MIT Press, 1976.

JUHL, P., "On the Sectoral Patters of West German Manufacturing Investment in Less Developed Countries: The Impact of Firm Size, Factor Intensities and Protection," *Weltwirtschaftliches Archiv,* Vol. 115 (1979), pp. 508–521.

KELLY, M. W., *Foreign Investment Practices of U.S. Multinational Corporations.* Ann Arbor, Mich.: UMI Research Press, 1981.

KILLING, P., "Technology Acquisitions: License Agreement or Joint Venture," *The Columbia Journal of World Business*" (Fall 1980), pp. 38–46.

KIM, S. H., "Financial Motives of U.S. Corporate Investment in Korea," *California Management Review* (Summer 1976), pp. 60–68.

KNICKERBOCKER, F. T., *Oligopolistic Reaction and the Multinational Enterprise.* Boston: Harvard Graduate School of Business Administration, 1973.

KOBRIN, S. J., "The Environmental Determinants of Foreign Direct Manufacturing Investment: An Ex Post Empirical Analysis," *Journal of International Business Studies* (Fall-Winter 1976), pp. 27–42.

______, "Foreign Enterprise and Forced Divestment in the LDCs," *International Organization* (Winter 1980), pp. 65–88.

KOHLHAGEN, S. W., "Exchange Rate Changes, Profitability, and Direct Foreign Investment," *Southern Economic Journal,* Vol. 44 (1977), pp. 43–52.

KOJIMA, K., *Direct Foreign Investment: A Japanese Model of Multinational Business Operations.* London: Groom Helm, 1978.

KRAVIS, I. B., and R. E. LIPSEY, "The Location of Overseas Production and Production for Export by U.S. Multinational Firms," *Journal of International Economics* (May 1982), pp. 201–223.

LALL, S., "Monopolistic Advantages and Foreign Involvement by U.S. Manufacturing Industry," *Oxford Economic Papers,* N.S., Vol. 32 (1980), pp. 102–122.

LOMBARD, F. J., "Screening Foreign Direct Investment in LDCs: Empirical Findings of the Columbian Case," *Journal of International Business Studies* (Winter 1978), pp. 66–80.

LOUIS, A. M., "Investing in Richer Returns Abroad," *Fortune* (August 19, 1985), pp. 72–73.

MAGEE, S. P., "Information and the Multinational Corporation: An Appropriability Theory of Direct Foreign Investment," in *The New International Economic Order: The North-South Debate,* Jagdish N. Bhagwati, ed. Cambridge, Mass.: MIT Press, 1977, pp. 317–340.

______, "Multinational Corporations, the Industry Technology Cycle and Development," *Journal of World Trade Law* (July/August 1977), pp. 297–321.

Management Review, "Foreign Acquisitions of U.S. Firms: Blessing or Curse?" (October 1982), pp. 61–62.

MANTELL, E. H., "How to Measure Expected Returns on Foreign Investments," *Journal of Portfolio Management* (Winter 1984), pp. 38–43.

MAZZOLINI, R., "Creating Europe's Multinationals: The International Merger Route," *Journal of Business* (January 1975), pp. 39–51.

MILLER, R. R. and D. R. WEIGEL, "The Motivation for Foreign Direct Investment," *Journal of International Business Studies* (Fall 1972), pp. 67–79.

MILLMAN, A. F., "Licensing Technology," *Management Decisions,* no. 3 (1983), pp. 3–16.

MIRUS, R., "A Note on the Choice Between Licensing and Direct Foreign Investment," *Journal of International Business Studies* (Spring-Summer 1980), pp. 86–91.

MOXON, R. W., "The Motivation for Investment in Offshore Plants: The Case of the U.S. Electronics Industry," *Journal of International Business Studies* (Spring 1975), pp. 51–66.

NEHEMKIS, P., "Business Payoffs Abroad: Rhetoric and Reality," *California Management Review* (Winter 1975), pp. 5–20.

ORLIN, H. J., and T. M. BROWNE, "Investment Incentive in the United Kingdom," *Financial Executive* (August 1978), pp. 48–49.

OZAWA, T., "International Investment and Industrial Structure: New Theoretical Implications from the Japanese Experience," *Oxford Economic Papers* (March 1979), pp. 72–92.

RADEZ, R. E., "Applying Industry Specialization Internationally," *Columbia Journal of World Business* (Summer 1978), pp. 95–104.

RAGAZZI, G., "Theories of Determinants of Direct Foreign Investment," *IMF Staff Papers* (July 1973), pp. 471–498.

RAVEED, S., "Foreign Investment in the U.S.: Looking Beyond Productivity Statistics," *Management World* (August 1981), pp. 40–41.

REDDY, A. C., "International Licensing May Be Best Bet for Companies Seeking Foreign Markets," *Marketing News* (November 1982), p. 6.

ROEMER, J. E., "Japanese Direct Foreign Investment in Manufactures: Some Comparisons with the U.S. Pattern," *Quarterly Review of Economics & Business* (Summer 1976), pp. 91–111.

ROOT, F. R., and A. A. AHMED, "The Influence of Policy Instruments on Manufacturing Direct Foreign Investment in Developing Countries," *Journal of International Business Studies* (Winter 1978), pp. 81–93.

RUGMAN, A. R., "Motives for Foreign Investment: The Market Imperfections and Risk Diversification Hypothesis," *Journal of World Trade Law* (September–October 1975), pp. 567–573.

______, "A New Theory of the Multinational Enterprise: Internationalization Versus Internalization," *Columbia Journal of World Business* (Spring 1980), pp. 23–39.

______, "Internalization as a General Theory of Foreign Direct Investment: A Re-Appraisal of the Literature," *Weltwirtschaftliches Archiv,* Vol. 116, no. 2 (1980), pp. 365–379.

______, "Internationalization Theory and Corporate International Finance," *California Management Review,* Winter 1980, pp. 73–79.

SEVERN, A. K., and M. M. LAURENCE, "Direct Investment, Research Intensity, and Profitability," *Journal of Financial and Quantitative Analysis* (March 1974), pp. 181–190.

STOPFORD, J., "German Multinationals and Direct Investments in the United States," *Management International Review* (1980/1), pp. 7–15.

STULZ, R. M., "On the Effects of Barriers to International Investment," *Journal of Finance* (September 1981), pp. 231–232.

TSURUMI, Y., *The Japanese Are Coming: A Multinational Interaction of Firms and Policies.* Cambridge, Mass.: Ballinger, 1978.

VERNON, R., *Storm Over the Multinationals: The Real Issues.* Cambridge, Mass.: Harvard University Press, 1977.

WALDMAN, R. J., and J. VICTOR, "European Investment Incentives," *Financial Executive* (September 1978), pp. 16–21.

WILKINS, M., ed., *Foreign Investment in the United States.* New York: Arno Press, 1977.

WILSON, B. D., *Disinvestment of Foreign Subsidiaries.* Ann Arbor, Mich.: UMI Research Press, 1980.

______, "The Propensity of Multinational Companies to Expand Through Acquisitions," *Journal of International Business Studies* (Spring–Summer 1980), pp. 59–65.

YOSHIHARA, K., *Sogo Shosha: The Vanguard of the Japanese Economy.* Oxford: Oxford University Press, 1982.

ZAGARIS, B., *Foreign Investment in the U.S.* New York: Praeger, 1980.

13

Multinational Capital Budgeting—The Basic Framework

INTRODUCTION

Multinational firms engaged in evaluating foreign projects face a number of variables, many of which are encountered in the domestic capital budgeting decision-making process. There are, however, a number of factors that are unique to international capital budgeting. The purpose of this chapter is to delineate the second set of variables that impact the project evaluation process, and the alternative methods of treating them in the analysis. Chapter 14 incorporates these variables in the standard discounted cash flow (DCF) technique used by firms to weed out unprofitable projects and rank profitable ones in the order of their contribution to the profitability of the firm.

A checklist of the variables that are unique to multinational capital budgeting includes:

1. Cash flows from foreign projects must be converted into the currency of the parent firm.
2. Cash flows from foreign projects may be subject to various restrictions that are imposed by the host country.
3. Initial investment in the host country may benefit from a partial or total release of blocked funds.
4. Profits generated from projects undertaken in other countries are subject to two taxing jurisdictions: the host country and the parent country.

5. Cash flows generated from foreign projects may replace revenue-producing exports to the host country.
6. Profitability of foreign projects may be enhanced from concessionary financing arrangements and other benefits provided by the host country.
7. Foreign investment may produce diversification benefits to shareholders of the parent firm.
8. Foreign investment may contribute to the corporate overall strategy of growth and gaining foothold in markets to preempt competitors.
9. Terminal value is more difficult to estimate than in the case of domestic projects. Such value to the parent company may differ from the valuation put on the facilities by potential buyers in the host country or from third countries.

ISSUES IN FOREIGN INVESTMENT ANALYSIS

The Foreign Exchange Risk

Multinational firms investing in affiliates abroad must contend with the foreign exchange risk. Management of this risk was explained in Chapter 5. The treatment of the foreign exchange risk in a multinational capital budgeting context focuses on how to handle it in the evaluation of cash flows generated by the foreign project over its life cycle.

Cash flow estimates must be converted to the parent firms currency if the project is to be evaluated from the standpoint of its contribution to the earnings per share that will accrue to the shareholders of the parent company. Hedging through the forward market is not relevant in this process for two reasons. First, cash flows will materialize over the project's life cycle, which extends beyond the time period, normally a maximum of two years, for which such hedging is available. Second, the capital budgeting exercise involves calculation of projected cash flows long before any actual investment is undertaken.

The foreign exchange risk is incorporated in cash flow estimates in the same manner as the inflation projection. This would require first an estimate of the inflation rate in the host country during the life span of the project. After cash flows in terms of local currency are adjusted upward for the inflation, they are then converted into the parent's currency at the spot exchange rate multiplied by an expected depreciation or appreciation rate calculated on the basis of purchasing power parity. If markets are deemed inefficient, conversion into the parent's currency is made on the basis of exchange rate forecast accepted by the management.

To illustrate, let us assume that inflation rate in the host country over the next five years (the expected life cycle of the project) is 12 percent annually, and the expected inflation rate in the parent country over the same period is 5 percent per annum. Then, according to PPP, the currency of the host country is expected to depreciate vis-à-vis the currency of the parent country by about 7 percent annually.[1] Indeed if PPP holds, the entire adjustment process, first for inflation in the host country, then for depreciation of the host country's currency, would be unnecessary. Over the long run, the ratio of domestic and foreign prices will equal the change in the equilibrium exchange rate.[2]

The multinational firm, however, is more likely to encounter situations when PPP does not hold due to inefficient exchange markets and/or restrictions on capital and trade flows. Under these circumstances, it must rely on its estimates of likely inflation and exchange rates. Foreign projects, particularly those engaged in manufacturing, often market their products in countries outside the domestic market where they are located. When this is the case, forecast changes in exchange rates in third country currencies in terms of either the host country's or the home country's currency must be provided.

Restrictions on Transfer of Cash Flows to the Parent Firm

There are a number of factors which cause a substantial difference between project cash flows and cash flows received by the parent firm. Host countries, particularly among LDCs, impose a variety of restrictions on transfer of profit, depreciation, and other fees accruing to the parent company (see Chapter 6). Project cash flows consist of profits and depreciation charges, whereas parent's cash flows consist of the amounts that can be legally transferred by the affiliate. In most instances a certain fraction of realized profits and all depreciation charges are not remittable. On the other hand, certain compensation items, such as management fees and royalties, which are part of the project's operating cost, are part of the parent firm's cash flow when transferable.

Another factor which causes the cash flows accruing to the parent to differ from that of the project is the tax provisions of the host country. This factor is examined in a subsequent section in this chapter. The entire subject of the taxability of the multinational firm and accounting for taxes imposed by more than one jurisdiction will be covered in Chapter 18.

Initial investment in the foreign project, though not necessarily its cash flows, is impacted by the possible release of all or part of the blocked

[1]More precisely, using the formula on p. 59, the currency of the host country is expected to depreciate by 6.25 percent vis-à-vis the home currency as shown below:

$$\frac{0.05 - 0.12}{1.12} = -0.0625$$

[2]Ian H. Giddy, "An Integrated Theory of Exchange Rate Equilibrium," *Journal of Financial and Quantitative Analysis* (December 1976), pp. 883–892.

funds which the parent already owns in the host country. Accounting for freed blocked funds in the capital budgeting process depends on the opportunity cost of blocked funds. If such blocked funds have no other remunerative use, that is, if their opportunity cost is zero, the entire amount released for the project should be considered as a reduction in the initial investment. If, on the other hand, blocked funds do have an opportunity cost, as is the case, for example, if they can be sold at a fraction of their face value to another multinational firm, an appropriate downward adjustment in the initial investment is warranted.

The general principle that governs the determination of appropriate cash flows for evaluating a foreign project is that the project should be credited with the incremental revenues that accrue directly, or indirectly, because of its implementation.

The Tax Issue

Capital budgeting principles postulate that only after-tax cash flows are relevant for project evaluation, a principle that is valid both for domestic and foreign projects. The tax issue for multinational capital budgeting purposes is complicated by the existence of two taxing jurisdictions, as well as a host of other factors. These include, in addition to the foreign corporate income tax rate, the form of remittance to the parent (dividends, loan repayments and interest, management fees, royalties), tax withholding provisions in the host country, tax credit provisions in the home country, and the existence of tax treaties between home and host countries. The tax issue is further complicated by the fact that tax laws in most host countries discriminate against transfer of realized profits as against local reinvestment of these profits. The ability, or potential ability, of the multinational firm to reduce its overall tax burden through the transfer pricing mechanism must also be considered in the evaluation exercise.

To circumvent the complexities surrounding the determination of actual after-tax cash flows accruing to the parent, it has been suggested that the higher of the home or host country rate be used.[3] The reasoning behind this simplifying procedure is that, in most cases, it represents a worst-case scenario. If the project proves acceptable under this procedure, then it will certainly be acceptable under the more favorable tax scenarios, where the parent firm manages to reduce the overall tax burden. If, on the other hand, the project does not qualify under the parent's acceptability standards, tax savings may be reintroduced in the calculation to determine whether or not such savings are sufficient to push the project's profitability past the hurdle rate.

[3]Alan C. Shapiro, "International Capital Budgeting," reprinted in *International Financial Management: Theory and Application,* 2nd ed. (New York: John Wiley & Sons, 1985), p. 552.

Lost Exports

The issue of lost exports is straightforward. Most MNCs have profitable export markets long before they consider direct foreign investment. The motivation for switching from exports to direct foreign investment was examined in Chapter 12. In the context of the capital budgeting decision, profits from lost exports represent a reduction from the cash flows generated by the foreign project for each year of its life span.

This generalization must, however, be modified by examining the considerations that led the parent firm to undertake the project. There are a number of reasons which may prompt a multinational firm to decide to set up a plant in a certain country to meet the market needs in that country and, possibly, neighboring countries. If this step is taken due to protective policy by the host government in the form of tariffs or other trade restrictions that will threaten the continuity of exports to that country, cash flows from the project should not be penalized by profits from lost exports. Under these conditions, exports will be lost whether or not the project under consideration is carried out.

The downward adjustment in cash flows may be total, partial, or nil depending upon whether the project will replace all projected exports, only a proportion of such exports (the remainder will be eroded by competition and/or by restrictive practices introduced by the importing country), or none of them.

Amenities and Concessions Granted by Host Country

A considerable number of countries offer foreign investors a variety of concessions and incentives to encourage direct investment. These concessions take many forms, but they may be grouped under two categories: tax or tax-related incentives, and nontax concessions. The first group includes income-tax holidays for a stated number of years, exemption from or reduction in custom duties on imported parts and raw materials (permanent or temporary), exemption from, or preferential treatment of, tax withheld on net income, and lower stamp or other types of duties and government fees on certain transactions. The second category includes provision of loans (for initial investment and/or working capital purposes) on concessionary terms, subsidized utility rates, and provision of free or inexpensive land to serve as the project site.

The reader will recognize that most of these benefits require no special adjustment in the capital budgeting exercise, because they are, or should be, already reflected in the estimated project's cash flows. The only notable exception is the concessionary financing arrangement, which requires an adjustment, since such financing will replace financing by the parent or from other higher-interest sources.

Diversification and Strategic Benefits from Foreign Investment

In addition to the quantifiable variables that are unique to the foreign investment decision, there are a number of less tangible and often non-quantifiable factors. Investments in foreign projects are believed to produce diversification benefits to the shareholders of the parent firm. Foreign projects may also contribute to the growth strategy of the multinational firm, particularly as it relates to gaining footholds in certain markets to the exclusion of its competitors.

These aspects of the foreign investment decision were discussed at some length in Chapter 12. For the purpose of multinational capital budgeting we need to show how these factors are handled in the process of evaluating a foreign project. Since a typical MNC is likely to undertake many projects in a number of diverse countries, it would be difficult, if not impossible, to quantify such benefits which can be attributed to a particular project.

The general consensus on how to deal with such and similar non-quantifiable variables is to initially ignore them in the capital budgeting exercise. If the project in question proves unacceptable or marginal on its own merits, management may bring these other factors to bear on the final decision. A marginal project may prove attractive when its salutary diversification impact on the overall pattern of cash flow generation by the MNC is brought into the picture.

CHOICE OF FRAMEWORK FOR ANALYSIS

All MNCs encounter the following two major questions early in the capital budgeting process:

1. Should the foreign project be evaluated on the basis of its own cash flows, or on the basis of cash flows received by the parent company?
2. Should the impact of the variables discussed in the previous section, which are unique to the evaluation of foreign projects, be reflected in cash flow estimates or in adjusting the discount rate?

The answers to both questions raise a number of fundamental as well as methodological issues relating to the goals of the multinational firm, its capital structure, and cost of capital. A number of these issues will be analyzed in later chapters; others were already covered in earlier chapters. The purpose of this section is to examine the alternative procedures and point out their merits and drawbacks. It is also useful to refer to the actual practice of MNCs. The material presented in this and the next chapter will show that, in most situations, the best approach is not to select one methodology or framework to the exclusion of the others. Rather, an approach combining two or more methodologies would perhaps prove most effective in the decision-making process.

Project Versus Parent Cash Flows

In most situations a substantial difference exists between project and parent cash flows due to the factors explained earlier in this chapter. Given this appreciable difference, on what basis should the project be evaluated? There are only three possible answers to this question: It should be evaluated on the basis of (1) its own cash flows, (2) cash flows accruing to the parent company, or (3) both.

Evaluating a foreign project on the basis of its own cash flows has much merit. The project must be able to compete successfully with domestic or regional firms for the host country's and neighboring countries' markets. Moreover, the project should yield a risk-adjusted rate of return in excess of its locally based competitors. If the project fails to do so, shareholders of the parent company would be better off investing in the equity of local firms. While this criterion is theoretically valid, it would be difficult in most cases to find such local benchmarks for comparison. Most foreign investment projects replace imports rather than compete with existing local firms. As such, a foreign project must be able to effectively compete with imports disregarding tariffs, since tariffs may be reduced or eliminated by the host country.

Evaluating projects on the basis of local cash flows has the advantage of avoiding currency conversions, thus eliminating the margin of error involved in forecasting exchange rates over the life cycle of the project. This approach will also appeal to the local managers, local joint venture partners, and host governments.

Financial management theory provides a strong basis for evaluating a foreign project from the viewpoint of the parent company. The ultimate yardstick of corporate performance is level of earnings per share and dividends distributed to the stockholders of the parent firm. These are determined ultimately by the net present value of funds which are actually remitted to the parent and converted into the parent's currency. It is these funds that actually make it possible to pay dividends to shareholders and make interest and principal payments to lenders. It is the financial viability of the foreign project, from the viewpoint of the operations of the MNC as a whole, that provide the basis for raising equity and debt resources to finance foreign operations.

The problem with cash flows remitted to the parent company is that they consist not only of project operating cash flows, but also often financial cash flows, such as fees and royalties, and interest on loans provided by the parent. These flows are in many cases lumped together, rather than unbundled. Capital budgeting theory stipulates that an investment should be evaluated only on the basis of net after-tax operating cash flows generated by that investment.

A three-stage financial analysis of foreign investment has been suggested.[4] In the first stage, project cash flows are computed and analyzed from the viewpoint of the subsidiary or the affiliate as if it were a separate entity. The second stage involves evaluation of the project on the basis of forecasts of cash flows which will be transferable to the parent company. In the third and last stage, the analysis from the viewpoint of the parent company is widened to include indirect benefits or costs for the company as a whole (including other affiliates) which are attributable to the foreign project in question.

Several surveys conducted over the period 1968–1981 confirm that MNCs tend to evaluate foreign projects from both the parent and project viewpoints.[5] A more recent survey conducted by Bavishi showed that among 155 respondent MNCs, 42 percent measured cash flow from the foreign subsidiary's viewpoint, 21 percent from the U.S. parent's viewpoint, and 37 percent were using both perspectives together in one form or another.[6]

It would seem that analyzing cash flows from each viewpoint reveals important aspects about the project's competitiveness and its contribution to the company as a whole. An approach combining project evaluation from both viewpoints would, therefore, seem recommended. The crucial question that is missing in most of the cited surveys is on what basis the final capital budgeting decision is made. If a project passes the hurdle rate on the basis of its own cash flows, is this sufficient to make it acceptable to the parent firm? If the question was put in this form, most respondents would have answered in the negative.

Alternatively, if a foreign project proved unviable on the basis of its own cash flows denominated in the host country's currency, does that necessarily imply that it would also fail to meet the acceptance criteria from the parent's viewpoint? Not necessarily, because the parent may be in a position to receive management fees and royalties that are not part of the cash flow of the project. Indeed, such payments are treated as operating expenses for the affiliate, and thus reduce the net cash flow from the project's viewpoint. The parent could also benefit from the diversification advantage derived from the foreign project, as well as from other nonquantifiable variables

[4] *Ibid.*, p. 552.

[5] A. Stonehill and L. Nathanson, "Capital Budgeting and the Multinational Corporation," *California Management Review* (Summer 1968), pp. 39–54. J. C. Baker and L. J. Beardsley, "Multinational Companies' Use of Risk Education and Profit Measurement for Capital Budgeting Decisions," *Journal of Business Finance* (Spring 1973), pp. 38–43. D. J. Oblak and R. J. Helm, Jr., "Survey and Analysis of Capital Budgeting Methods Used by Multinationals," *Financial Management* (Winter 1980), pp. 37–41.

[6] V. B. Bavishi, "Capital Budgeting Practices at Multinationals," reprinted in *International Finance, Concepts and Issues,* G. D. Gay and R. W. Kolb, eds. (Richmond, Va.: Robert F. Dame, Inc., 1983), pp. 520–527.

that would not be normally considered if the project is to be evaluated on the basis of its own cash flow. The sum of fees, royalties, and other payments to be received by the parent, when added to the nonquantifiable benefits that could accrue, may well tip the balance in favor of adopting the project.

Cash Flow Versus Discount Rate Adjustment for Risk and Other Variables

The issue of whether to adjust cash flows or the discount rate to reflect the unique risks and other variables impacting on the foreign investment decision has occupied a prominent place in multinational capital budgeting theory. It has also been addressed in the survey of MNCs' capital budgeting practices referred to earlier.

MNCs have traditionally translated incremental risks by adjusting the hurdle rate upwards for riskier projects. Indeed, a large number of firms that employ one variant of the discounted cash flow (DCF) approach or another in evaluating domestic projects assign different hurdle rates for different projects, depending on their risk categories. The attraction of this adjustment is simply an extension of a method long applied to domestic projects to analysis of foreign investment.

Surveys confirm that calculating a risk-adjusted discount rate to be applied to foreign projects is popular with MNCs. In the Bavishi survey, well over 50 percent of respondent companies indicated that they evaluate their foreign projects on the basis of uniquely determined discount rate, rather than using the weighted average cost of capital for the company as a whole.[7] Thirty percent of responding firms indicated that they determined discount rates subjectively. An earlier survey found that about 50 percent of respondents add a premium percentage for risk to their required rate of return on foreign investments.[8]

There are several theoretical and practical advantages in favor of this method of adjustment. First, it is in accord with the tenets of investment theory which postulate that the required rate of return should be commensurate with the degree of risk. It also provides a rigorous test for the foreign project, thus weeding out marginal projects that could possibly involve the MNC in substantial losses. Its biggest attraction, however, is its simplicity. Adjusting the discount rate for the incremental risk of the foreign project does away with elaborate and time-consuming cash flow forecasting based on various assumptions, which may involve, among others, probability analysis.

[7] *Ibid.*, p. 525.

[8] J. C. Baker and L. J. Beardsley, "Multinational Companies' Use of Risk Evaluation and Profit Measurement for Capital Budgeting Decisions," *Journal of Business and Finance* (Spring 1973), p. 39.

There are several drawbacks to this method as well. Reliance on this technique may cause the MNC to overlook analysis of crucial uncertainties that surround a foreign project. Moreover, if raising the discount rate is considered, as it often is, as a blanket equalizer for the added political and exchange rate risk, cash flows in earlier years tend to be disproportionately penalized. Such risks are normally low in the earlier years of the project, and tend to increase sharply in the later years of the project's life span.

Political risk management (Chapter 17) provides the MNC with several options to reduce its impact on project's cash flow (including insuring against such risks). Moreover, political uncertainties pose a threat to the entire investment, not just the annual cash flows. Losses arising from the political risk depend on a number of factors which include financing policies, terminal value, recovery from insurance policies, and post expropriation compensation arrangements.

Adjusting the discount rate to offset the exchange risk is an oversimplification, since it assumes that only adverse exchange rate movements are expected, irrespective of the markets where products are sold and inputs are sourced. It is entirely possible for an MNC with a multimarket foreign project whose inputs are obtained from diverse sources to face favorable overall currency movements, even if the host country's currency depreciates against the parent's currency during the life span of the project.

The alternative is adjusting the annual cash flows, and then discounting them using the applicable rate for that type of project either at the host country or at the parent country. Adjustment of cash flows requires an elaborate set of projections backed by thorough research and analysis, as well as use of probability analysis techniques. Two techniques generally used in making such adjustments are explained below.

1. Uncertainty absorption consists of reducing each year's cash flow by an amount equivalent to a risk or an insurance premium, even if such protection is not actually purchased by the management. For example, certain political risks which could impact the cash flow and recovery of the entire investment are insurable with the Overseas Private Investment Corporation (Chapter 17). Premiums paid to secure this insurance are appropriate deductions from cash flows. Similarly, if the exchange risks can be covered in the forward market, the cost of this coverage should be charged against the cash flow of the appropriate time period. The adjustment is made irrespective of whether the insurance or hedging programs are actually undertaken.

   There are conceptual and practical difficulties involved in cash flow adjustment using the uncertainty absorption principle. In the first place, although political risk insurance is available, such insurance covers normally only a fixed proportion of the book value of the firm (in the event of expropriation, for example). The economic value of expropriated assets, as measured by future cash flows to be generated by such assets, normally far exceeds the book value. Second, there are a number of political risks which impact on the operation and profitability of the MNCs' affiliates for which no insurance is available. These include restrictions imposed by the host country on imports of raw materials and component parts, higher tariff rates on such inputs and/or exports to neighboring markets, as well as a variety of measures designed to harass the affiliate and intervene in its operations.

The forward exchange market, versatile and efficient as it is, is not equipped to provide cover for cash flows to be generated by the foreign project beyond the first two years of its life span. Moreover, MNCs undertake foreign projects in many countries where a forward exchange market does not exist.

2. Probability and Certainty Equivalents Techniques. Probability analysis techniques have long been used in economic and financial forecasting. According to this technique, cash flows generated by the foreign affiliate and remitted to the parent during each time period are adjusted for political risk, exchange rate, and other uncertainties by converting them into certainty equivalents.

To illustrate, the MNC may employ a statistical technique called decision tree analysis[9] to estimate the probability of expropriation, the extreme form of the political risk. Once this is done, the next step is to forecast at what point of time expropriation is likely to materialize. Aided with these projections, the MNC will be in a position to determine an NPV for the foreign project based on cash flows adjusted for the probability of expropriation at the fifteenth year, for instance. It should be pointed out that, in the event of expropriation, cash flow will not cease in most situations. Additional cash flows may materialize in the form of compensation paid by the host expropriating authorities and tax write-offs by the parent in the home country, but such post-expropriation cash flows are difficult to estimate.

Shapiro offered an alternative method to estimate the probability of occurrence of the political risk.[10] An alternative to assigning probabilities to certain events is to use a form of break-even analysis to calculate the probability of expropriation at which the project will break even. For example, on the basis of the management's anticipation of the timing of the occurrence of expropriation, they calculate two values for NPV, one if it does not occur (let us say—$7 million), and another if it does occur (let us say—$3 million). The probability of expropriation which will render the project marginal

[9]See Chapter 16 for a discussion of decision tree analysis and other statistical techniques used for measurement of the political risk.

[10]Shapiro, *op. cit.*, p. 558.

may be then calculated as follows:

$$-3P + 7(1 - P) = 0$$

$$10P = 7, \quad \text{and} \quad P = \frac{7}{10} \times 100 \text{ or } 70\%$$

The result should be interpreted that a probability of expropriation of less than 70 percent would render the project financially viable. This result is based on the premise that expropriation would take place at some projected time period during the project's life cycle, or would not occur at all. It is also assumed that once it does occur, cash flow would cease totally.

The advantage of this method over alternative techniques is that it is easier to ascertain whether the probability of expropriation is lower or higher than 70 percent than to estimate it. There are, however, serious questions about the ability of this approach to cope with various degrees and forms which the political risk may take during the life span of the project. MNCs in most cases encounter various degrees of intermittent or temporary blockages of funds and restrictions on transfers which cannot be satisfactorily dealt with by this approach.

Probability analysis could also be used to estimate the foreign exchange rate (or the host versus parent currency) for each time period. For example, several exchange rate scenarios may be prepared by the capital budgeting staff over the project's life cycle. Projected cash flows in each year would be converted into home currency equivalents for each of these scenarios. Finally, cash flows would be converted to expected or certainty equivalent cash flows by applying the assigned probability for each of the scenarios. Alternatively, an expected exchange rate could be calculated each year, by using the probabilities of the various scenarios. These expected rates are then applied to the estimated cash flows denominated in the host country's currency.

These same approaches could be used for sales forecasts or export projections, or any other aspect of the project's cash flow for which the management expects a range of values, depending on the materialization of an alternative set of assumptions or scenarios. There are, however, some limitations to the application of the expected value approach in managerial decisions. Although the expected value of cash flows may prove acceptable in terms of meeting the criteria for investment, the management may not be willing to invest in a losing foreign project, even if the probability of the loss is very small. The management may be concerned not only with the expected values of cash flows, but also with the range of possible outcomes. Moreover, insofar as exchange rate forecasting is concerned, there is no reason to believe that a forecast based on calculating the expected values of alternative scenarios is superior to one based on purchasing power parity assumption, or any other forecasting technique.

STRATEGIC CONSIDERATIONS IN INTERNATIONAL CAPITAL BUDGETING

MNCs establishing affiliates abroad have been persuaded to take this step, rather than being contented with exporting or licensing arrangements, by a number of considerations which go beyond the variables of the DCF evaluation process. The motivation and theories which attempt to explain direct foreign investment, which is defined as the acquisition of physical assets abroad (as contrasted with financial assets), are covered in Chapter 12. For the purpose of rounding out the basic framework of the multinational capital budgeting decision, this chapter will conclude with a brief discussion of strategic considerations which modify the outcome yielded by the project evaluation process.

It has been suggested that in seeking profitable projects abroad, the MNC is capitalizing on product or market imperfections which it recognizes or is able to exploit better than its competitors. This would suggest that by virtue of its possession of knowledge of specific markets, managerial skills, or technological expertise, an MNC can derive benefits from direct foreign investments that are not available to its competitors.

An MNC possessing these and other similar advantages may be in a better position to identify potentially lucrative projects. If the project meets the acceptance criteria when subjected to DCF analysis, then that MNC had an identification advantage over its competitors. The crucial question is that, if such a project fails to meet the acceptance criteria, could these specific advantages induce the MNC to undertake the investment anyway in expectation of potential profitability? Such an outcome is possible if the MNC exploits its distinctive advantages once it establishes a foothold in the host country.

Equally important perhaps is the desire of the MNC to gain a strategic advantage over its competitors by preempting them from certain markets. This consideration might be sufficient for the management to embark on a foreign project, even if it fails initially to pass the hurdle rate. The project could fit well strategically in the company's overall expansion program, and provide an effective barrier to potential competitors. MNCs, particularly broadly diversified ones, foresee future dividends from being strategically placed in certain geographic locations.

Another strategic aspect of direct foreign investment already alluded to in this chapter is the beneficial impact of diversification on the MNC's cash flow as a whole. This stabilizing effect on the operation of the MNC as a whole, which would enhance its market value, should not be overlooked, although it is difficult to incorporate in the capital budgeting evaluation process.

Traditional capital budgeting techniques often are not adequate to perform the acceptability test for foreign projects. More sophisticated techniques have been developed to allow the variables discussed in this chapter to exert their appropriate weight in the evaluation process. These techniques will be discussed and illustrated in the next chapter. However, it should be emphasized that the foreign investment decision should not hinge only on the outcome of the capital budgeting techniques. It is often necessary to look beyond the rates of return derived from these techniques to incorporate the impact of strategic and other considerations which influence the overall risk-return pattern of the operations of the MNC as a whole.

REVIEW QUESTIONS AND PROBLEMS

See end of Chapter 14.

14

Multinational Capital Budgeting Application and Interpretation of Discounted Cash Flow Analysis

INTRODUCTION

The preceding chapter was devoted to the complex problems facing MNCs in evaluating foreign projects. The emphasis was placed on isolating the variables that are unique to the international capital budgeting decision, and on the options available to MNCs for incorporating these variables in the evaluation process. These variables included the foreign exchange risk, the political risk, multiple layers of taxation, the availability of concessionary arrangements, impact on existing exports, and strategic considerations which influence the capital budgeting decision. Chapter 13 was intended to focus on the complexities surrounding the foreign investment decision, and on the inadequacies of traditional capital budgeting techniques to allow relevant factors to exert their due influence on its outcome.

The focus of this chapter is on the application of the conceptual framework developed in Chapter 13 to the evaluation of a foreign project, involving all or most of the relevant variables and simulating the institutional and financial environment that confronts the MNC. Step-by-step analysis will be used to illustrate the impact of the various variables in an attempt to overcome the complexities characteristic of the foreign investment evaluation process. Before proceeding with an illustrative capital budgeting example, we will first develop the analytical framework that will be used in the evaluation process.

DISCOUNTED CASH FLOW ANALYSIS (DCF)

DCF analysis involves the use of the time-value-of-money principle to project evaluation by discounting project's cash flow using an appropriate discount rate. Results yielded by this technique are used, together with other considerations developed by the management, to evaluate projects. The evaluation process culminates in accepting or rejecting the project under consideration, as well as ranking accepted ones by some index based on the rate of return or profitability.[1]

The most widely used criteria based on DCF analysis are the net present value (NPV) and the internal rate of return (IRR). The NPV is defined as follows:

$$\text{NPV} = -I_0 + \sum_{t=1}^{n} \frac{\text{CF}_t(1 - T)}{(1 + k)^N}$$

where I_0 = initial investment

CF_t = expected before tax cash flow in year t

T = applicable tax rate

k = a risk-adjusted discount rate

N = life span of the project

IRR is calculated by solving for r in the following equation:

$$\sum_{t=1}^{n} \frac{CF_t(1 - T)}{(1 + r)^N} - I_0 = 0$$

that is, finding the discount rate which would equate the present value of the cash flow generated by the project with the initial investment, or the rate which would equate the present value of all cash flows to zero.

The acceptance-rejection decision is based, *inter alia,* on the ability of the project to generate a positive NPV, or an IRR which exceeds the cost of capital or any risk-adjusted hurdle rate adopted by the firm. The IRR or a profitability index, derived by dividing the PV of cash flows by the initial investment, is used for ranking projects for the purpose of determining the cutoff point of the capital budget. Both NPV and IRR yield the same acceptance-rejection signal; that is, if a project is acceptable when the NPV criterion is used, it is also acceptable when the IRR criterion is used.[2]

[1]For a thorough discussion of the DCF application to capital budgeting and its limitations, see any good introductory textbook in financial management. See, for example, Van Horne, *Financial Management and Policy,* 6th ed. (Englewood Cliffs, N.J.: Prentice–Hall, Inc., 1983).

[2]The IRR is the rate of return that equates NPV of cash flows to zero. Therefore,

if NPV is positive	$\text{IRR} > k$
NPV is negative	$\text{IRR} < k$
NPV = 0	$\text{IRR} = k$

However, the two criteria may give different ranking of projects in situations where the projects being compared differ significantly in size, cash flow pattern, or life span. There are techniques which are more sophisticated extensions of the DCF approach for evaluating projects which differ in these parameters. Introductory textbooks in financial management advise that, in the event of conflict between the NPV and IRR criteria in choosing among mutually exclusive projects, the NPV criterion should be relied upon.

THE ADJUSTED PRESENT VALUE APPROACH

A DCF technique better adapted to accommodate the unique aspects of evaluating foreign projects is the adjusted present value (APV).[3] The APV is essentially a method which allows different components of the project's cash flow to be discounted separately, thus providing the needed flexibility to allow the various variables and other features of the project to impact the outcome. The APV approach also makes possible the use of different discount rates for different segments of the total cash flow, depending on the degree of certainty of the eventual materialization of each segment. Moreover, the APV framework enables the capital budgeting analyst to test the profitability of the foreign project prior to accounting for all the complexities. If the project proves acceptable, no further evaluation based on accounting for other cash flows will be necessary. If it fails to meet the acceptance criteria, then an additional segment is added, and the evaluation in process is repeated.[4] For example, the analysis may be conducted on the basis of the contractual cash flows which are remittable to the parent company under existing foreign exchange regulations of the host country. If the project does not pass the hurdle rate, another cash flow component, such as the cash flow the MNC can unblock through the transfer pricing mechanism, will be added to ascertain whether or not it could nudge the project toward profitability.

We turn now to an examination of the components of the APV technique.

Initial Investment

Initial investment consists of the cost of the project (denominated in dollars) representing cash, equipment, and other assets contributed by the parent U.S. company plus local loans (if any) for working capital purposes. The latter part is to be converted into U.S. dollars at the spot exchange rate. In

[3]The technique developed in this chapter is based on D. R. Lessard, "Evaluating Foreign Projects: An Adjusted Present Value Approach," in *International Financial Management: Theory and Application,* (Boston: Warren, Gorham, and Lamont, 1979).

[4]L. D. Booth, *Capital Budgeting Frameworks for the Multinational Corporations,* unpublished manuscript, University of Toronto, 1980.

the event that the foreign project will release blocked funds the parent owns in the host country, the face value of the blocked funds which are activated by the project (if it is assumed that such funds have a zero opportunity cost)[5] will be treated as a reduction in initial investment. This component may be expressed as follows:

$$-[I_0(\text{U.S.}) + I_0(\text{local}) \times S_0(\text{H/L}) - \text{UF} \times S_0(\text{H/L})]$$

where $I_0(\text{U.S.})$ = initial investment of parent company in U.S. dollars

$I_0(\text{local})$ = initial local investment expressed in local currency

$S_0(\text{H/L})$ = spot exchange rate at period zero (year of initial investment) expressed in home currency per unit of local currency

UF = unblocked funds expressed in local currency

Project's Remittable Cash Flows

Project's cash flows consist of several components. The major component is the cash flows generated by sales in the host country, adjusted downward by the lost income on sales previously realized on exports made by the parent to the host country market. It also includes cash flows generated by sales from the new project to third country markets, also reduced by profits on lost exports to these markets (if any). In addition, remittable cash flow includes royalties and fees agreed upon by the parent and the affiliate for the use of patents and services, respectively, provided by the parent. Contractual payments to the parent also include interest on loans advanced to the affiliate by the parent. It should be emphasized that this component of the APV formula includes only those cash flows which are legally remittable to the parent. It may be expressed as follows:

$$\sum_{t=1}^{n}\left[\frac{[S_t^*(\text{H/L})CF_t^* - \text{L}][1-T]}{(1+\text{DR}_1)^N}\right] + \left[\frac{CF_{t_2}^* S_t^*(\text{H/L})}{(1+\text{DR}_2)^n}\right][1-T] + \left[\frac{(CF_{t_3}^*)\,(S_t^*(\text{H/0}) - L_{t_3})}{(1+\text{DR}_1)^N}\right][1-T]$$

where: CF_t^* = cash flows generated by expected sales in the host country in time period t.

$S_t^*(\text{H/L})$ = expected exchange rate in period t (home currency per one unit of local currency).

Lt = loss profits on exports to host country in time period t expressed in home currency.

[5]If such funds have an opportunity cost, the amount which will be deducted from initial investment is the face value of the released funds minus their value in the next best use.

T = applicable tax rate in host country or home country, whichever is higher.

$CF^*_{t_2}$ = expected cash flows from royalties and fees and other contractually remittable transfers in time period t.

$CF^*_{t_3}$ = net cash flows generated by expected sales in third country markets in time period t.

$S^*_t(\mathrm{H}/0)$ = expected exchange rate in time period t – home country currency in terms of one unit of third country currency.

L_{t_3} = lost profits on exports to third countries in time period t expressed in home currency units.

DR_1 = discount rate applicable to project's cash flows from sales in host and third country markets. This rate reflects discount rates applied to projects of similar risk in host country or home country.

DR_2 = discount rate applicable to transfer of contractual payments. DR_2 is lower than DR_1, because both the materialization and transfer of such flows are subject to less uncertainty than the cash flows generated by sales.

N = life expectancy of the project, i.e., number of years over which cash flows are expected to materialize.

Contribution of Concessionary Arrangements to Project

It was indicated in Chapter 13 that most of the special concessions and other benefits granted by the host country will automatically impact cash flows. These may include provision of free land for the site of the project (to be treated as a reduction in the initial investment), tax holidays, lower tariffs on imports, and lower utility rates. As such, there is no need to assign a separate term of the APV formula to incorporate these benefits in the evaluation process.

A concessionary arrangement that would require a separate treatment in the APV format is when the project can obtain a loan at a low interest rate from a local financial institution. Such a loan, which is usually provided to meet all or part of the working capital requirements of the foreign project, represents a one-time contribution to the APV of the project. This contribution is measured by the difference in home currency terms between the face value of the loan and the amount of repayments, discounted to the present at the rate of interest (probably home country borrowing rate) that would have been incurred had the concessionary loan not been available.

This may be expressed as follows:

$$S_0(\mathrm{H/L})\left[CL - \sum_{t=1}^{n} \frac{R_t}{(1 + \mathrm{DR}_3)^N}\right]$$

where: CL = face value of concessionary loan in local currency.
R_t = loan repayments on concessionary loan in local currency.
DR_3 = applicable discount rate; an appropriate rate is the borrowing rate in the home country or Eurocurrency market.

Accounting for Other Transfers to Parent and for Tax Savings

This term of the APV formula is somewhat conjectural and is not normally added unless the project proves unacceptable on the basis of remittable cash flows and the contribution of the concessionary arrangements.

In Chapter 6 we explained how MNCs, through the transfer pricing mechanism, are often able to move funds from high-tax locations to low-tax locations, as well as to defer tax payments by transferring funds to tax havens. Tax savings realized from these operations contribute to the viability of the project by lowering the effective tax rate for the determination of net cash flows.

The transfer pricing mechanism also enables an MNC to effect transfers over and above the legally remittable cash flows. It can also serve as a tool for overcoming to some extent future obstruction of transfers of legally remittable contractual cash flows.

Potential contribution of tax savings and extra remittable income should be discounted at a substantially higher rate than contractually remittable income, in recognition of the higher degree of risk involved.

This term may be expressed as follows:

$$\sum_{t=1}^{n} \frac{S_t^*(\mathrm{H/L})\,(\mathrm{ATTS}_t^*)}{(1 + \mathrm{DR}_4)^N}$$

where: ATTS_t^* = additional expected transfers and tax savings in period t.

DR_4 = appropriate discount rate for such transfers.

Accounting for Terminal Value

Estimation of terminal value is perhaps the most subjective part of the multinational capital budgeting process, unless there exists a prior arrangement with the host country's government or local private investors. In some cases, the host government stipulates that the projects will revert to it after a stated number of years for a nominal sum. If such is the case, or where the management of the parent company deems the terminal value to be insignificant, no adjustment is needed in the evaluation process.

In practice, MNCs view foreign affiliates as a continuing venture just like their operating facilities at home. Nevertheless, accounting for the terminal value may prove to be as crucial a step in determining the financial viability of foreign projects as in the evaluation of domestic projects. The problem lies in arriving at a reasonable estimate of the terminal value, based on the most realistic assumptions possible. The range of possible values may be very wide, depending on whether the estimate is based on the project's potential value if retained as a going concern or if liquidated and sold to local investors.

The importance of estimating a realistic terminal value is especially crucial when the capital budgeting process is based on a relatively short project life span and in capital-intensive undertakings. MNCs have used several techniques to arrive at an acceptable estimate for the terminal value. Our approach is to assume that net cash flows generated at the terminal year are to continue at the same level for a stated number of years. The terminal value will thus be the present value of this annuity at the terminal year discounted at an appropriate rate, probably reflecting local interest rates. Alternatively, a *break-even terminal* value may be computed. This value is defined as the value which would result in an APV of zero; that is, the project is just barely acceptable. Thus calculated, the terminal value is examined by the management to ascertain whether the projected market values are likely to attain or exceed that figure. In any event, if the project can achieve a positive APV without allowance for the terminal value, this adjustment would not be necessary.

The estimated terminal value is the last term of the APV equation and will be discounted at DR_1, the same rate applied to discounting cash flows generated by sales in the host country,[6] thus:

$$\frac{S_t^*(\mathrm{H/L})(\mathrm{TV}_t^*)}{(1 + \mathrm{DR}_1)^N}$$

where TV* denotes the expected terminal value.

The various terms of the APV formula are now aggregated as follows:

APV = − initial investment reduced by the value of unblocked funds

Term 1 − $[I_0(\text{U.S.}) + I_0(\text{local})S_0(\mathrm{H/L}) - (\mathrm{UF})(S_0\mathrm{H/L})$

+ present value of project's remittable cash flows

[6]Capital budgeting analysts argue that in cases where terminal value estimates are highly conjectural a higher discount rate than the one used for projected flows should be applied to terminal value. For purposes of the APV technique, however, an appropriately risk-adjusted rate used for cash flows generated by sales in the host country is also adequate for discounting the terminal value.

$$\textbf{Term 2} + \sum_{t=1}^{N} \frac{[S_t^*(\text{H/L})CF_t^* - L_t][1 - T]}{(1 + \text{DR}_1)^N} + \frac{[CFt_2^* S_t^*(\text{H/L})][1 - T]}{(1 + \text{DR}_2)^N}$$

$$+ \frac{(CF_{3t}^* S_t^*(\text{H/0}) - L_{t3})(1 - T)}{(1 + \text{DR}_1)^N}$$

+ present value of concessionary loan arrangement

$$\textbf{Term 3} + S_0(\text{H/L})\left[CL - \sum_{t=1}^{N} \frac{R_t}{(1 + \text{DR}_3)^N}\right]$$

+ present value of additional transfers and tax savings

Term 4 achieved by the transfer pricing mechanism

$$+ \sum_{t=1}^{N} \frac{S_t^*(\text{H/L})(\text{ATTS}_t^*)}{(1 + \text{DR}_4)^N}$$

+ present value of cash flow from estimated terminal value

$$\textbf{Term 5} + \frac{(S_t^*(\text{H/L})(\text{TV}_t^*)}{(1 + \text{DR}_1)^N}$$

The last two terms of the formula are added, in the shown or reverse sequence, if the project being evaluated fails to meet the acceptability criteria on the basis of terms 1–3. Under these circumstances, the project is reevaluated, wih the so-called two- or multiple-stage approach, by adding the remaining terms sequentially.

CASE STUDY

Illustrating the Use of the APV Technique—International Diversified Technologies

To illustrate the application of the APV technique, an evaluation of a foreign project will be undertaken in this section. The illustration will proceed on a step by step basis, highlighting the various components or terms of the APV formula in the order they were discussed in this chapter. These components will then be pulled together to meassure the APV of the project, in an attempt to reach an overall assessment. While most of the data and assumptions are contrived so as to simulate conditions facing MNCs in real-life situations, a number of simplifying assumptions will be used

These are primarily intended to focus the analysis on the crucial variables and to reduce the complexities involved in the illustration to manageable proportions.

International Diversified Technologies Inc. (IDT) is a manufacturer of small office systems and minicomputers suited for small enterprises. The company and its research and manufacturing facilities are based in Philadelphia, Pennsylvania; it uses the Port of Philadelphia for its exports, which accounted in 1984 for about 35 percent of its sales. Total sales have grown rapidly since the company was established in 1974, reaching $130 million in 1984.

The company's major domestic market is concentrated mainly in southeastern Pennsylvania and the Delaware Valley industrial area. Most of its exports in recent years have been to Greece and a few countries in the Middle East. An affiliate of IDT in Spain, organized as a joint venture with local investors, produces several of the company's product lines under a licensing agreement for the Spanish and Portuguese markets.

IDT's performance both in the domestic and exports markets was adversely affected in 1983–1984 by increasing competitiveness in the minicomputer and office systems industry, a reflection in part of overproduction and saturation of markets which plagued the high-technology industry as a whole during this period. Although IDT's markets in Greece, Egypt, and a number of Middle Eastern countries are well established, some inroads in its share of the market in these countries were made by a British competitor.

Realizing that it must make a defensive move to protect its lucrative export markets, IDT has been seriously looking into the possibility of setting up a wholly owned affiliate located in Greece. The facility will manufacture, distribute, and service the full line of IDT's products in Greece and the Middle Eastern market. The staff of the Capital Budgeting Division has just completed the compilation of the necessary cost and market projection data for the evaluation of the project.

The facility, to be located in a suburb of Athens, Greece, and to be called IDT (Greece), will be a wholly owned subsidiary of IDT, Inc. (U.S.). The land on which the facility is to be erected is state land which will be assigned to the project rent-free for a period of 10 years. The Greek government, to induce IDT to locate the project in Greece, has also offered the project a 10-year exemption from customs duties on parts and components imported from the parent company, as well as a preferential 20 percent income tax rate on net profits plus 10 percent withholding tax on dividends transferred to IDT (U.S.).

In addition, the draft agreement with the Ministry of National Economy of Greece contains the following provisions:

1. Seventy-five percent of profits less tax withholding, and all royalties and service fees are freely transferable to IDT (U.S.).

2. Payments for parts and components imported from IDT (U.S.) are also freely transferable.
3. Proceeds of all exports and royalties for sales outside Greece are to be remitted to IDT (Greece), and are subject to the same transfer provisions governing profits on sales made in Greece.
4. A concessionary loan not exceeding Dr500,000,000 (500 million Greek drachmas) is to be made available to IDT (Greece) carrying an interest rate of 8 percent per annum. This loan, together with accrued interest, is to be paid back in five equal annual installments.
5. The facility will be sold to a joint venture of public and private Greek investors 11 years after the project becomes operational. The sale price will be five times the net profit realized by IDT (Greece) from its domestic operations during the tenth year. The terminal value is transferable to the parent company.

INITIAL INVESTMENT

Initial investment in the project consists of cash and equipment contributed by the parent company according to the schedule in Table 14-1.

Working capital requirements of the project are to be met from the proceeds of the concessionary loan, as well as other local loans if necessary.

IDT (U.S.) was offered Dr100 million in blocked accounts in local banks by the Universal Canning Co., a U.S. firm which discontinued operation of its plant in Greece. The blocked amount was to be exchanged into U.S. dollars at the rate of U.S. $1.00 = drachmas 200.

CASH FLOW FROM OPERATIONS

Sales in Greece. The projected sales, operating expenses, and net profits from operations in Greece for five years beginning in 1988 are shown in Exhibit 1.

Equipment bought locally and that shipped by IDT (U.S.) as part of the initial investment, valued at cost based on the exchange rate which

Table 14-1.

	1986	1987
Local construction cost (millions of drachmas)	Dr210.4	73.3
Local purchase of equipment (millions of drachmas)	Dr12.5	80.0
Equipment shipped by IDT (U.S.) (millions of U.S. dollars at cost)	$0.5	2.5

Exhibit 1. Projected Sales, Operating Expenses, and Net Income

A. SALES IN GREECE	(IN MILLIONS OF DRACHMAS)				
	1988	1989	1990	1991	1992
Sales	510.3	550.8	610.5	640.0	675.5
Cost of goods sold and operating expenses (excluding depreciation)	130.0	145.3	151.8	158.3	160.2
Depreciation	100.0	100.0	100.0	100.0	100.0
Gross operating income	280.3	305.5	358.7	381.7	415.3
Selling, general, and administrative expenses	41.0	45.1	51.1	54.0	57.6
Interest on concessionary loan	40.0	32.0	24.0	16.0	8.0
Royalties and service fees to IDT (U.S.)	45.5	47.5	50.5	52.0	53.8
Net income from local sales	153.8	180.9	233.1	259.7	295.9
B. SALES IN MIDDLE EASTERN MARKETS	**(IN MILLIONS OF U.S. DOLLARS)**				
Sales	1.25	1.47	1.75	1.95	2.19
Cost of goods sold and allocated expenses[1]	0.52	0.61	0.72	0.82	0.92
Net income from exports before royalties	0.73	0.86	1.03	1.13	1.27
Royalty to IDT (U.S.) 10% of sales	0.13	0.15	0.18	0.20	0.22
Net income from exports	0.60	0.71	0.85	0.93	1.05

[1]Exports' share of operating, general, and administrative expenses, with the exception of depreciation. Depreciation is charged against production for sales in Greece only.

prevailed at the time of the initial investment, is to be depreciated by the straight-line method to a zero salvage value.

The agreement between IDT (U.S.) and IDT (Greece) stipulates that the affiliate is to compensate the parent for the use of patents and for the technical assistance to be provided by the parent's staff in the form of a royalty equivalent to 5 percent of sales in Greece (10 percent for exports) plus Dr20 million annually. These amounts are to be transferred to the parent company, together with the dividends allowable under the agreement with the Ministry of National Economy of Greece. A schematic cash flow chart involving IDT (U.S.) and its affiliate in Greece is shown in Exhibit 2.

Sales in Middle Eastern Countries. Sales in Middle Eastern markets, mainly Egypt and Sudan, are denominated in U.S. dollars. According to the

Exhibit 2. IDT (U.S.) and IDT (Greece) Cash Flow Chart

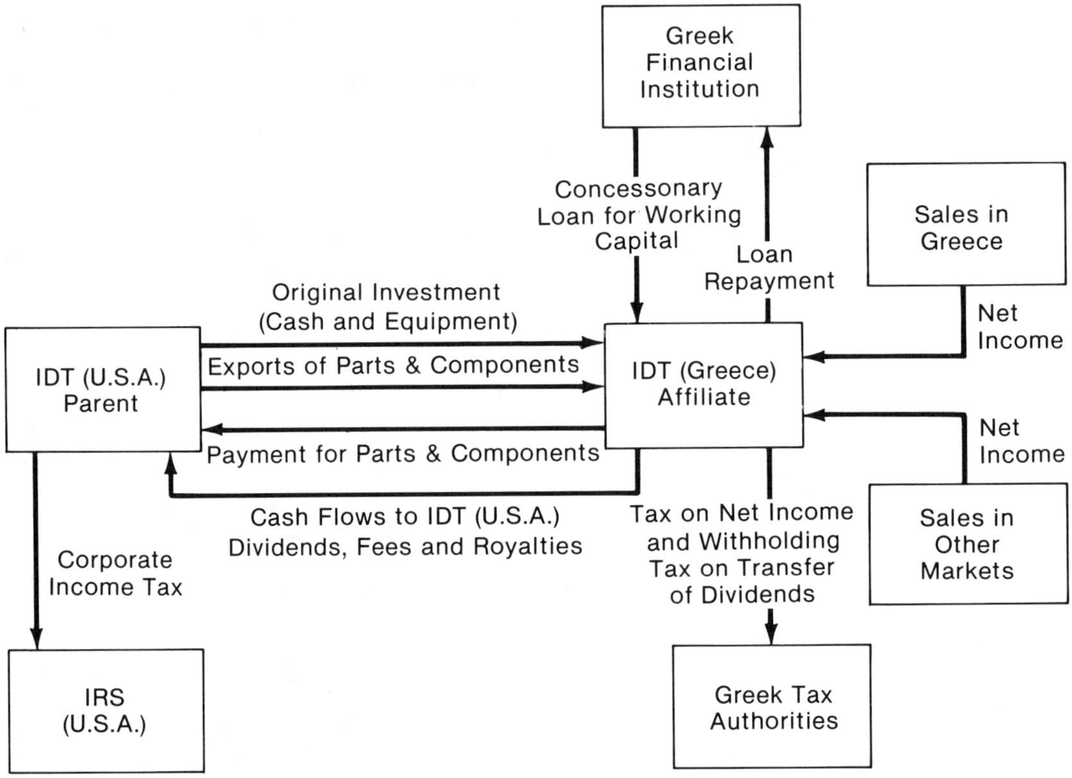

agreement with the Greek Ministry of National Economy, proceeds of these sales are remittable to IDT (Greece), and are to be lumped with sales in Greece for accounting and tax purposes. These sales are shown in part B of Exhibit 1.

Remittable Cash Flows and Exchange Rate Forecast. Remittable cash flows to IDT (U.S.) include royalties, service fees, and dividends, which represent 75 percent of net after-tax profit of IDT (Greece) less withholding tax on dividends transferred to the parent.

Calculation of IDT (Greece) profit would require a forecast of the drachma-U.S. dollar exchange rate for the 1988–1992 period, since sales to Middle Eastern countries are denominated in dollars. These same rates should also be used in converting drachma cash flows into U.S. dollars in accordance with the APV formula.

While the project was still in the planning stage, a special committee from the staff of the Financial and Foreign Exchange Division of IDT developed two sets of forecasts of the drachma/dollar exchange rate. These forecasts were based on the spot rate of drachma 135 = U.S. $1.00 which prevailed on June 28, 1985.

The first forecast was based on purchasing power parity with the assumption of an annual inflation rate differential of 10 percent between the two countries (5 percent for the U.S. and 15 percent for Greece). The second forecast was based on a number of international financial projection models and studies prepared by multinational banks and international financial institutions. The drachma/U.S. dollar rates according to these two forecasts are shown in Table 14-2.

The rates derived from international forecasting models are based on a scenario having the U.S. dollar weaken vis-à-vis currencies of the U.S. trading partners in the early years of the period and then appreciate steadily thereafter. Using these two sets of forecasts, the management of IDT (U.S.) developed its own set of figures for the purpose of evaluating the project under consideration.

Remittable cash flows to the parent company are calculated in Exhibit 3. They consist of transferable dividends [75 percent of IDT (Greece) after-tax profit less withholding tax], royalties (5 percent of sales in Greece and 10 percent of sales elsewhere), and a flat Dr20 million service fee per year.

Table 14-2.

DRACHMA/U.S. DOLLAR RATE		FORECAST BASED ON PPP[1]	FORECAST BASED ON INTERNATIONAL FORECASTING MODELS	MANAGEMENT'S OWN FORECAST
Spot rate 6-28-	1985	135.00	135.00	135.00
Average rate for	1986	153.13	125.00	145.00
	1987	166.45	120.00	145.00
	1988	180.93	145.00	155.00
	1989	196.67	155.00	160.00
	1990	213.78	175.00	175.00
	1991	232.28	185.00	185.00
	1992	252.60	200.00	205.00

[1]According to PPP formula, the drachma should depreciate vis-à-vis the U.S. dollar by 8.7 percent per annum.

$$\text{Expected change in exchange rate} = \frac{\text{inflation rate in U.S.} - \text{inflation rate in Greece}}{1 + \text{inflation rate in Greece}} \times 100$$

or

$$= \frac{5 - 15}{1.15} \times 100 = -8.7\%$$

Exhibit 3. Calculation of Remittable Cash Flows to IDT (U.S.) (in millions of Greek drachmas)

	1988	1989	1990	1991	1992
Net income from sales:					
In Greece (from Exhibit 1)	153.8	180.9	233.1	259.7	295.9
In Middle Eastern markets (U.S. million) (Exhibit 1)	0.60	0.71	0.85	0.93	1.05
Exchange rate					
Drachma per U.S. $	155	160	175	185	205
Drachmas	93.0	113.6	148.8	172.1	215.3
Total net income	246.8	294.5	381.9	431.8	511.2
Income tax at 20%	49.4	58.9	76.4	86.4	102.2
Net income after tax	197.4	235.6	305.5	345.4	409.0
Transferable dividends (75% of net after tax income)	148.1	176.7	229.1	259.1	306.8
Less tax withholding (10% of transferable dividends)	14.8	17.7	22.9	25.9	30.7
CALCULATION OF REMITTABLE CASH FLOWS					
Dividends less withholding	133.3	159.0	206.2	233.2	276.1
Royalties on sales in Greece (5% of sales)	25.5	27.5	30.5	32.0	33.8
Royalties on sales in Middle East (10% of sales)	19.4	23.6	30.6	36.1	44.9
Service fees	20.0	20.0	20.0	20.0	20.0
Total remittable cash flows	198.2	230.1	287.3	321.3	374.8

Lost Sales on Exports. IDT (U.S.)'s initial decision to consider the possibility of setting up an affiliate in Greece is predicated on its assessment of market developments during the 1980s. The project is envisioned as a defensive move to preclude loss of export markets in Greece and Middle Eastern countries due to imminent increase in tariffs on office computers and systems by these countries, as well as stiffening competition. Based on its intelligence sources, IDT's management is confident that at least two European competitors are considering plans to establish manufacturing subsidiaries in the area.

IDT's marketing staff estimate that the company stands to lose 50 percent of its net profits on exports in the base year (1985), to lose 75 percent in 1986, and to lose the market entirely thereafter. No adjustment for lost exports is needed since IDT (Greece) started operations in 1988.

Calculation of NPV of Remittable Cash Flows Net of Lost Exports. IDT's policy for evaluation of all minicomputer and office system projects (domestic and foreign) assumes a life cycle of five years, and employs a discount rate of 16 percent. Its capital budgeting policy with respect to foreign investment is based on reflecting the exchange and political risks primarily in cash flows rather than in adjusting the discount rate for the higher perceived risks. This policy also tacitly acknowledges the diversification and flexibility benefits which accrue from foreign projects. Such benefits are considered adequate to offset other risks which are inherent in foreign investment.

The net present value of remittable cash flows from IDT (Greece) taking into account foregone profits from replaced exports are presented in Exhibit 4.

CONTRIBUTION OF CONCESSIONARY LOAN TO THE PROJECT

The loan arrangement negotiated with the Greek Ministry of National Economy allows IDT (Greece) to borrow up to Dr500 million at 8 percent to finance the working capital requirements of the project. If such a concessionary loan had not been made available, IDT (Greece) would have had to borrow from local private commercial banks at 18 percent.

The contribution of the concessionary arrangement to the project is measured by the face value of its loan minus the present value of repayments (consisting of interest and principal) discounted to the present at 18 percent (Exhibit 5).

Overall Evaluation

We will now proceed to evaluate IDT (Greece) from the viewpoint of the parent firm on the basis of the first three terms of the APV formula, as of the end of 1985. APV is calculated as follows:

APV (in millions of U.S. dollars) = − adjusted present value of investment in project
+ present value of remittable cash flows
+ present value of concessionary loan

$$= -\left[\frac{1.85}{1.16} + \frac{3.56}{(1.16)^2}\right] + 4.90 + 0.77$$

$$= -4.24 + 5.67 = \$1.43 \text{ million}$$

Exhibit 4. PV of Net Profits Generated by IDT (Greece)[1] (millions of Greek drachmas)

	1988	1989	1990	1991	1992
Total remittable cash flows from Exhibit 3	198.2	230.1	287.3	321.3	374.3
Estimated profits on the sale of parts and components to IDT (Greece)	65.0	70.0	75.0	80.0	85.0
Income tax paid in Greece[2] (Exhibit 3)	49.4	58.9	76.4	86.4	102.0
Withholding tax on dividends[2] transferred (Exhibit 3)	14.8	17.7	22.9	25.9	30.7
	327.4	376.7	461.6	513.6	592.7
Exchange rate forecast (drachmas per U.S. dollar)	155	160	175	185	205
(MILLIONS OF U.S. DOLLARS)					
Taxable income generated from IDT (Greece)	2.11	2.35	2.64	2.77	2.88
U.S. corporate income tax (40%)	0.84	0.94	1.06	1.11	1.16
Less credit for taxes paid in Greece	(0.41)	(0.48)	(0.57)	(0.61)	(0.65)
Net income generated from IDT (Greece)	1.68	1.89	2.15	2.21	2.38
PV factor at 16%[3]	.6407	.5523	.4761	.4104	.3528
PV of net income generated by IDT (Greece)	1.08	1.05	1.02	0.91	0.84
Cumulative PV of net income (IRR 21.3%)	1.08	2.13	3.15	4.06	4.90

[1]Includes remittable cash flows and estimated profits on the sale of parts and components to IDT (Greece) excluding depreciation charges, which are not transferable.

[2]Income tax paid in Greece on net income of IDT (Greece) plus withholding tax on dividends transferred to the parent company are "grossed up" before U.S. corporate income tax liability is calculated. See Chapter 18.

[3]PV in 1985, the base year for evaluating the project.

The project has a positive APV of $1.43 million and appears to have passed the acceptability criterion easily.

The figures in the APV solution require some explanation. The first term relating to the initial investment consists of the following:

1. Investment outlays in 1986. The drachma portion of the investment was converted into dollars at the rate of 200 drachmas = U.S. $1.00 for the first 100 million drachmas to reflect the purchase of blocked drachma accounts from the Universal Canning Co. The remaining drachma investment was converted at the rate of 145 drachmas = U.S. $1.00, which is the applicable rate in the company's forecast in 1986. As the in-

Exhibit 5. IDT (Greece) Repayment of Concessionary Loan from Greek Financial Institution (millions of drachmas)

YEAR	LOAN OUTSTANDING	INTEREST APPLIED	APPLIED TO PRINCIPAL	TOTAL PAYMENT	PRESENT VALUE OF PAYMENT[1]
1	500.0	40.0	100.0	140.0	118.7
2	400.0	32.0	100.0	132.0	94.8
3	300.0	24.0	100.0	124.0	75.5
4	200.0	16.0	100.0	116.0	59.8
5	100.0	8.0	100.0	108.0	47.2
					396.0

Contribution of loan to project = 500 − 396 = 104/135 = $0.77

[1]Discounted at 18 percent, the rate at which IDT (Greece) would have borrowed working capital funds from local financial institutions had the concessionary loan not been made available.

vestment outlays are projected for 1986, while the evaluation is undertaken in 1985, the outlays were discounted to the present for one year at 16 percent.

2. Investment outlays in 1987. The drachma portion of this investment was converted into dollars at the rate of 145 drachmas = U.S. $1.00, which is the projected rate for 1987 in the company's own forecast. These outlays were discounted for two years at 16 percent.

The second term is the present value of remittable cash flows to IDT (U.S.), after payment of U.S. taxes and adjustment for foregone profits on lost sales. This term is the sum of cumulative PV of net profits shown in the last line of Exhibit 4. The last term represents the difference between the face value of the concessionary loan and the present value of repayments, converted to dollars at the applicable rate of the base year, that is, 135 drachmas per U.S. dollar (Exhibit 5).

Readers may have noted that IDT (U.S.) used the same discount rate for cash flows representing royalties and service fees and cash flows arising from sales in Greece and exports to third country markets. The APV formula provided for the use of a lower discount rate for the former, since they represent flows which are less risky and more definitive than the latter. IDT's policy is to lump these two components together and discount them at the rate applicable to projects of similar grade risk at home and abroad.

Other Terms of the APV Equation

In accordance with the two-step analysis approach, the fourth and fifth terms of the APV equation would have been introduced had the APV outcome been negative. However, IDT's evaluation team decided to ascertain how accounting for terminal value would impact the project.

According to the agreement with the Greek government, IDT (Greece) and its facilities will be sold to Greek investors 11 years after the project becomes operational. The sale price will equal five times the net profit realized by the affiliate from its domestic operations during the tenth year. A reasonable terminal value estimate for purposes of APV analysis is five times net income from domestic operations in 1992 discounted back to 1985 at an appropriate rate.

With reference to Exhibit 3, net income from sales in Greece in 1992 less 20 percent local income tax amounts to Dr236.7 million, equivalent to \$1.15 million at the forecast exchange rate for that year. The present value of U.S. \$5.75 million (5 × \$1.15 million) discounted at 20 percent for 7 years (from 1992 to 1985, the base year for evaluation) is \$1.60 million. A 20 percent discount rate was chosen for the potential cash flow from terminal value due to the uncertainties surrounding the evaluation process, which might result in a substantial margin of error. Furthermore, the actual turnover of the project to local investors will not take place until 1998, which casts some doubts about the eventual sale price (which will be based on 1997 net profits), as well as about political developments that might compromise transferability at that time.

Irrespective of the uncertainties which surround the estimation and the eventual transferability of the terminal value, its inclusion in the evaluation process greatly enhances the attractiveness of the project. If the impact of other transfers and tax savings made possible by the transfer pricing mechanisms is also included, the APV of the project will look still more favorable.

The IRR of the project cash flows, including terminal value, may be calculated by solving for r in the following equation:

$$-\frac{1.85}{(1+r)} - \frac{3.56}{(1+r)^2} + \frac{1.68}{(1+r)^3} + \frac{1.89}{(1+r)^4}$$

$$+\frac{2.15}{(1+r)^5} + \frac{2.21}{(1+r)^6} + \frac{2.38}{(1+r)^7} + \frac{5.75}{(1+r+.04)^7} = 0$$

$$r = \text{IRR of the project} = 29.31 \text{ percent}$$

EVALUATING THE PROJECT FROM THE AFFILIATE'S VIEWPOINT

The project could have been evaluated from the viewpoint of the affiliate to ascertain its financial viability, quite apart from the provisions of transferability of cash flows to the parent company. Such evaluation will answer questions such as whether or not it will be able to compete with local or other foreign firms should such competitive situations arise in the future.

This evaluation is performed in Exhibit 6 employing a risk-adjusted discount rate of 18 percent, which is assumed to be the applicable rate for a local project in the same risk category.

Exhibit 6. Calculation of NPV of IDT (Greece) (in millions of Greek drachmas)

Year	Investment	Net Income after tax	Depreciation	CF net Income + Dep.	PV Factor at 18%	PV
1985					1.0000	
1986	−294.5			−294.5	.8475	−249.6
1987	−515.8			−515.8	.7192	−371.0
1988		197.4	100.0	297.4	.6086	181.0
1989		235.6	100.0	335.6	.5158	173.1
1990		305.5	100.0	405.5	.4371	177.2
1991		345.4	100.0	445.4	.3704	165.0
1992		409.0	100.0	509.0	.3139	159.8
1992				1,000[1]	.3139	313.9
						549.4

NPV = Dr.549.4 million
(IRR = 39.9%)

[1]Assumed terminal value.

Viewed as a domestic project, IDT (Greece) appears to be a very lucrative project with considerable ability to withstand potential competition from local or foreign sources. The evaluation in Exhibit 6, however, overestimates the projects' NPV and IRR, since no allowance was made for the concessionary arrangements (free land, lower utility rates, exemption from tariffs on imported parts and components, and the like) and for the management services provided by the parent.

SENSITIVITY ANALYSIS

The analysis performed on the foreign project so far has been based on what the management considered to be the most likely assumptions. Evaluation of all investment projects, domestic and foreign, cannot be complete unless they are subjected to a series of tests under several less likely, but possible, scenarios. There are several probabilistic techniques which can be used to test the sensitivity of a foreign project to political and foreign exchange risks, such as certainty equivalent cash flows and decision trees. Another method consists of subjecting the cash flows to a series of changed assumptions, then reevaluating the project on the basis of the changed cash flows. Still another way of testing the viability of the project is to vary the discount rates used in the APV technique, depending on the degree of perceived risk for each type of cash flows.

The use of sophisticated techniques may not necessarily produce the best results, since they invariably involve estimating probabilities of occurrence of certain events which are essentially subjective in nature. In this section, sensitivity analysis is performed by reevaluating the project on the basis of changed cash flow assumptions. Four sensitivity tests will be performed on IDT (Greece) involving (1) lower sales levels, (2) a different exchange rate forecast based on a sharper rate of depreciation of the Greek drachma than the one used in the original investigation, (3) partial blockage on transfer of dividends imposed by the Greek government, and (4) expropriation of IDT (Greece) by the Greek government at the end of the fourth year of operation.

Sensitivity Test (1) Lower Sales Projections

Working with a lower sales forecast would necessitate redoing Exhibits 1, 3, and 4. To simplify the presentation, Exhibit 7 skips some intermediate steps, but the reader can follow the analysis by tracing back these steps in the original exhibits.

Recalculating APV with the investment and concessionary loan remaining unchanged will yield:

$$\text{APV} = -4.24 + 3.61 + 0.77 = \$.14 \text{ million}$$

$$[\text{IRR} = 19.6\%]$$

The foreign project barely meets the acceptability criteria with the lower sales forecast, excluding the impact of the terminal value and other possible transfers and tax savings. The next step is to reestimate the terminal value on the basis of the revised net profit figure for 1992. Valued at five times net income from local sales after tax, or Dr160.7 million (Exhibit 7), terminal value equals Dr803.5 million, or U.S. \$3.92 million. Discounting back to 1985 at 20 percent, or \$1.09 million, will increase the APV value from \$0.14 million to \$1.23 million.

Sensitivity Test (2) Using a Less Favorable Exchange Rate Scenario

The exchange rate forecast used by the project evaluation team was based on IDT's management assessment of future exchange developments. That forecast, which was influenced by projection models prepared by some multinational banks, embodied a much slower rate of depreciation of the drachma than justified by the differential in the inflation rate between Greece and the United States. In Exhibit 8, IDT (Greece) is reevaluated on the basis of the exchange forecast based on purchasing power parity formula. This exercise will result in reducing the present value of income generated by the affiliate from \$4.90 million to \$4.27 million. The APV of the project will now be

$$\text{APV} = -3.96 + 4.27 + 0.77 = \$1.08 \text{ million}$$

Exhibit 7. Reevaluating IDT (Greece) on the Basis of a Lower Sales Forecast

(IN MILLIONS OF GREEK DRACHMAS)	1988	1989	1990	1991	1992
Sales	410.3	450.8	610.5	640.0	675.5
Net income from local sales	58.8	85.9	138.1	164.7	200.9
Total net income after tax (local sales and income from exports)[1]	121.4	159.6	229.5	269.4	333.0
Calculation of remittable cash flows					
Dividends less withholding	82.0	107.7	154.9	181.8	224.8
Royalties on sales in Greece	20.5	22.5	25.5	27.0	28.8
Royalties on sales in the Middle East	19.4	23.6	30.6	36.1	44.9
Service fees	20.0	20.0	20.0	20.0	20.0
Total remittable cash flows	141.9	173.8	231.0	264.9	318.5
Estimated profits on sale of components	50.0	55.0	60.0	65.0	70.0
Taxes paid in Greece (income and withholding)	39.5	41.9	58.6	87.6	108.2
	231.4	270.7	349.6	417.5	496.7
Exchange rate forecast (Dr/$)	155	160	175	185	205
(IN MILLIONS OF U.S. DOLLARS)					
Taxable income generated from IDT (Greece)	1.49	1.69	2.00	2.26	2.42
U.S. corporate income tax (40%)	0.60	0.68	0.80	0.90	0.97
Less credit for taxes paid in Greece	(0.25)	(0.26)	(0.33)	(0.47)	(0.53)
Net income after tax	1.14	1.27	1.53	1.83	1.98
PV factor at 16%	0.6407	0.5523	0.4761	0.4104	0.3528
PV of net profits generated by IDT (Greece)	0.73	0.70	0.73	0.75	0.70
Cumulative PV of net profits (IRR = 10.7%)	0.73	1.43	2.16	2.91	3.61

[1]Assumes that sales outside Greece will remain unchanged.

The initial investment in 1986 and 1987 was converted into dollars at exchange rates based on purchasing power parity, taking into account that Dr100 million were exchanged in 1986 for $0.5 million. Once again IDT (Greece) is able to meet the acceptability criterion demonstrating a relatively low degree of sensitivity to adverse exchange rate developments. As in the case of the first test, the fairly sizable impact of the terminal value term makes the project still more attractive financially.

Exhibit 8. Reevaluating IDT (Greece) on the Basis of Exchange Rate Forecast Based on Purchasing Power Parity

(IN MILLIONS OF GREEK DRACHMAS)	1988	1989	1990	1991	1992
Total remittable cash flows and profits on sale of components, including taxes paid in Greece (Exhibit 4)	327.4	376.7	461.6	513.6	592.7
Exchange rate forecast (Dr/$)	180.93	196.67	213.78	232.38	252.60
(IN MILLIONS OF U.S. DOLLARS)					
Taxable income generated from IDT (Greece)	1.81	1.92	2.16	2.21	2.35
U.S. corporate income tax (40%)	0.72	0.77	0.86	0.88	0.94
Less credit for taxes paid in Greece	(0.41)	(0.48)	(0.57)	(0.61)	(0.65)
Net income generated from IDT (Greece)	1.50	1.61	1.87	1.94	2.06
PV factor at 16%	0.6407	0.5523	0.4761	0.4104	0.3528
PV of net income	0.96	0.89	0.89	0.80	0.73
Cumulative PV of net income (IRR = 18.7%)	0.96	1.85	2.74	3.54	4.27

Sensitivity Test (3) Partial Blockage on Transfer of Dividends

Foreign projects have a high degree of sensitivity to the political risk. Although the provisions of transfer of dividends and other payments to IDT (U.S.) are clearly spelled out in the agreement with the Greek Ministry of National Economy, foreign exchange stringencies might arise which would lead to restrictions on various transfers.

The impact of blockage on the project's rate of return from the viewpoint of the parent company depends on when the blockage is imposed, opportunities for investing blocked funds in the host country, and the possibility of subsequent repatriation of blocked funds. Let us assume that due to a foreign exchange crisis experienced by the Greek government, all transfers, except payment for imported parts and components from the parent company, were blocked after the second year of operations of the project. Let us also assume that blocked funds can be invested in Greece to yield 10 percent per annum, and that 50 percent of the blocked funds are transferable at the end of 1992.

With reference to Exhibit 4, blocked funds in each of 1990, 1991, and 1992 consist of total remittable cash flows in those years. The amounts, in millions of Greek drachmas together with accumulated interest, will be as shown in Table 14-3.

At the end of 1992, only Dr537.9 million, or 50 percent of blocked funds, can be remitted. The impact of this blockage on the project's APV is calculated in Exhibit 9. APV may now be recalculated as follows:

$$\text{APV} = -4.24 + 3.91 + 0.77 = \$0.44 \text{ million}$$

The partial blockage, though temporary, appears to hurt the project's profitability somewhat, although it still meets the acceptability criterion. The adverse impact of the blockage is due to delaying the cash flow until the end of 1992, when both the continued depreciation of the drachma and the longer discounting period reduce the present value of cash flows.

Sensitivity Test (4) Expropriation of IDT (Greece)

Expropriation, action by the host government to take over a foreign affiliate, represents the highest degree of political risk. As in the case of partial blockage of transfers, the impact of expropriation on the foreign project depends on a number of factors, such as: (1) the stage in the project's life cycle when expropriation occurs, (2) possibilities of recovering foreign cash flows through compensation, (3) the extent of the use of local financing, and (4) the ability of the parent company to recover losses sustained by expropriation through tax write-offs.

If the probability of expropriation by the Greek government of IDT (Greece) is high, particularly in the early years of its operations, the project's viability will be seriously compromised. We should point out that although the capital budgeting analysis is done on the assumption of a five-year life cycle, IDT (U.S.) anticipates operating the Greek affiliate for 11 years before turning it over to a local joint venture. Expropriation will not only interrupt cash flow generated by operations, but also will jeopardize the chances of receiving the sale price stipulated in the agreement with the Greek Ministry of National Economy.

If we assume expropriation at the end of the fourth year of operation, the project's APV turns negative by \$0.18 (−4.24 + 4.06), disregarding the

Table 14-3.

YEAR	AMOUNT	INTEREST AT 10%		TOTAL AMOUNT
1990	287.3	60.3		347.6
1991	321.3	32.1		353.4
1992	374.8	—		374.8
			Total	1075.8

Exhibit 9. Reevaluating IDT (Greece) with Partial Blockage on Transfers[1]

	1988	1989	1990	1991	1992
(IN MILLIONS OF GREEK DRACHMAS)					
Total remittable cash flows	198.2	230.1	—	—	537.9
Estimated profits on the sale of parts and components to IDT (Greece)	65.0	70.0	75.0	80.0	85.0
Income tax paid in Greece	49.4	58.9	76.4	86.4	102.2
Withholding tax on dividends[2]	14.8	17.7	—	—	—
	327.4	376.7	151.4	166.4	725.1
Exchange rate forecast (Dr/$)	155	160	175	185	205
(IN MILLIONS OF DOLLARS)					
Taxable income generated from IDT (Greece)	2.11	2.35	0.87	0.90	3.53
U.S. corporate income tax (40%)	0.84	0.94	0.35	0.36	1.41
Less credit for taxes paid in Greece	(0.41)	(0.48)	(0.47)	(0.47)	(0.50)
Net income generated from IDT (Greece)	1.68	1.89	0.96	1.01	2.62
PV factor at 16%	0.6407	0.5523	0.4761	0.4104	0.3528
PV of net income generated by IDT (Greece)	1.08	1.04	0.46	0.41	0.92
Cumulative PV of net income	1.08	2.12	2.58	2.99	3.91

[1]See explanatory notes in Exhibit 4.
[2]No taxes are withheld on dividends in 1990 through 1992, since no dividends are remitted to the parent in those years.

contribution of the concessionary loan to APV which has to be reworked to reflect the event of expropriation prior to the settlement of the local loan. Further, expropriation will make the eventual transfer of the terminal value highly questionable.

Overall Assessment of Sensitivity Tests

IDT (Greece) appears to be only moderately sensitive to both the exchange rate and political risks, barring expropriation. Some degree of sensitivity also exists with respect to the level of sales in the host country. In all three cases—that is, a lower assumed level of sales in Greece, a sharper rate of depreciation of the Greek currency vis-à-vis the U.S. dollar, and partial blockage of transfers—the project's APV was reduced considerably but remained positive. In none of the three tests did the adverse scenarios prove damaging to the project, particularly when cash flow generated by the terminal value is taken into account. Expropriation, if it is assumed to take place at a relatively early stage in the project's life cycle, appears to damage its chances of acceptance. In this highly adverse scenario, the acceptability of the project clearly hinges on expectation of recovery of lost cash flows through some form of compensation.

REVIEW QUESTIONS

1. How does the adjusted present value technique (APV) differ from other techniques of discounted cash flow analysis?
2. Why is the APV format more suitable for evaluating foreign projects than the conventional NPV format?
3. Explain briefly at least two approaches to reflect the exchange rate and political risks in the multinational capital budgeting exercise. How did the illustration relating to International Diversified Technologies accommodate these risks?
4. Discuss the pros and cons of reflecting the exchange rate and political risks in the discount rate. Would the expected life cycle of the project affect the choice of the appropriate vehicle for incorporating these risks in the quantitative exercise of the project evaluation process? Are there variables other than the project's life cycle which could influence the choice of the appropriate technique?
5. Under what circumstances would an assumption of blockage of transfers of dividends from an affiliate to the parent company hurt the project's viability most? Incorporate the following concepts in your answer:
    a. Timing of assumed blockage or restrictions on transfers.
    b. The expected or projected behavior of the exchange rate (the host country's currency against the parent's currency).
    c. The reinvestment assumption, that is, the rate at which intermediate cash flows can be reinvested locally, if they are not expected to be used in financing the activities of the project.
    d. The expected cash flow pattern of the project.
    e. The expected life cycle of the project on the basis of which the foreign project is being evaluated.
    f. The estimated terminal value (if any) of the project, and the size of the terminal value in relation to the initial investment and annual cash flows.
6. Show how facilities for financing on concessional terms offered by the host government improve the likelihood of a foreign project's accept-

ability. Is there an alternative procedure to measure the contribution of such financing to the project to the one used in the APV formula? Does this procedure reflect the full contribution of such a facility to the project's present value? (How would you deal with the political risk reduction aspect of local financing?)

7. Evaluate the treatment of profits on exports lost or foregone in the local and third-country markets suggested in the APV format presented in this chapter. How realistic is the assumption that lost exports in physical terms (based on exports prior to the coming into operation of the foreign project) remain unchanged irrespective of changes in exchange rates over the life cycle of the project? Should we invoke the concept of the price elasticity of demand for imports?

8. Discuss the two-step approach in the process of evaluating foreign projects using the APV technique. Which components of the cash flow are likely to be considered last in the overall evaluation process?

9. Suggest at least four discount rates used in the APV technique and discuss the rationale for using these different rates in discounting the several components of the cash flow.

REVIEW PROBLEMS

1. Widgets International, a U.S. MNC, is considering setting up a widget manufacturing plant in Neverneverland. The plant will cost the equivalent of $10,000,000 and will have a salvage value of the equivalent of $2,000,000 at the end of 10 years (the expected life cycle of the project).

   Use the following data:

   - Widget sales are projected at 500,000 units annually at a unit price of Rupees 35 and a unit cost of Rupees 15, including allocation for overhead. Both sale price and unit cost are expected to rise in line with the rate of inflation in Neverneverland.
   - Widgets International has been exporting widgets to meet most of the requirements of Neverneverland. However, unless it takes immediate action to establish a plant in that country, all exports will be lost to competitors exporting low-priced widgets soon to be manufactured in nearby Fantasyland.
   - The project will add $4,000,000 to the borrowing capacity of Widget's International. Borrowing rate at home is 12 percent per annum.
   - The government of Neverneverland does not grant concessionary loans to foreign projects, but allots free land to such projects. Land will revert back to the government at the end of the life cycle of the

project. Moreover, the government stipulates that foreign projects be sold to domestic investors at the indicated salvage value.

- Foreign exchange regulations in Neverneverland permit transfer of net profits in their entirety, but not the depreciation allowances. However, Widget International will have no problem in using intersubsidiary transfer pricing to get the depreciation proceeds out of Neverneverland at exchange rates roughly equivalent to those prevailing in the market.
- Tax rate in Neverneverland is 30 percent on net income, while Widgets International is subject to a 40 percent tax in the United States with full credit allowed for the tax paid in Neverneverland.
- The expected inflation rate in the United States is 5 percent per annum compared to 15 percent in Neverneverland.
- So ($/Rupees) = $0.195
  S* ($/Rupees) will adjust to the differential rate of inflation between the two countries in accordance with the purchasing power parity (PPP) principle.
- Widgets International employs an all equity discount rate of 25 percent for foreign projects, which includes a premium for the political risk. The risk-free rate in the United States is 8 percent per annum.

  a. Evaluate the project from the standpoint of the parent company, using the APV (adjusted present value) approach.
  b. Using sensitivity analysis, reevaluate the project under the following changed assumptions:
     (1) The rupee is projected to depreciate against the U.S. dollar by 5 percent annually, rather than by the percentage derived from the PPP principle.
     (2) Sales of widgets in Neverneverland are projected to increase by 10 percent annually.
     Perform the sensitivity analysis in three steps, using assumptions (1) and (2) separately and assumptions (1) and (2) together.
  c. Does the sensitivity analysis in (b) change your recommendation as to the acceptability of the project? Explain.

2. *Short Case Study Problem—Akida Motor Co. (Japan)*

Akida Motor Co., a Japanese multinational firm, is evaluating a project to build and market a modified version of its subcompact "the comettail" in Spain. If the project proves viable, an agreement is to be signed with a Spanish government corporation.

The Market

Japanese share of the car market in Spain has been declining steadily in recent years due to stiff competition from the European Economic

Community (EEC). Imported cars from countries inside the EEC, such as the United Kingdom, France, and Italy, enjoy substantially lower tariffs than cars imported from outside the EEC. Akida's share of the market has always been relatively small, and has been declining since 1982. The management is of the viewpoint that unless they establish a wholly owned affiliate in Spain, they will have to abandon this market altogether.

If approved, Akida Motors (S.A. Spain) is projected to produce and market 10,000 cars in the first year of operation (1987). Local sales in units are projected to rise by 10 percent annually over the next four years. The increase in output and sales is to be accommodated by the initial capacity built into the project. The project has a fairly long life, extending up to 20 years. However, the Spanish government corporation, with which Akida will be negotiating the concession agreement, has indicated that the agreement will be subject to renegotiation at the end of 1991. At that time, Akida Motor Co. may be asked to turn over the affiliate either to the corporation, or to a joint venture involving the corporation, Akida Motors, and local private sector interests. In that eventuality, the project will be given a terminal value equal to five times the after-tax net profit actually realized in 1991.

Initial Investment and Working Capital Requirements

The initial investment in plants and equipment, to be entirely provided by the parent company in 1986, was estimated at Pts14 billion (fourteen billion Spanish pesetas). Because Akida Motors will be building the plant in a depressed and high unemployment province of Spain, the concession agreement will include three concessional features:

a. Financing for working capital requirements (estimated at Pts5 billion needed at the outset of operations) may be provided by a local financial institution at 6 percent per annum. In the absence of this facility, Akida will have had to raise the funds from Eurocurrency markets at an estimated rate of 12 percent. The concessional loan facility is to be repaid in five equal annual installments plus accrued interest. The first installment is due at the end of 1987.

b. During the first five years of operations, Akida Motors' (S.A. Spain) applicable corporate income tax and withholding tax rates will be 25 percent and 10 percent, respectively.[1]

c. A rent-free plot of land will be assigned to house the operating facilities and the administrative offices of the project.

[1]The corporate income tax and withholding tax rates in effect in Spain are 35 percent and 18 percent, respectively. See: Ernst and Whinney *(International Series) 1984 Foreign and U.S. Corporate Income and Withholding Tax Rates,* 1985, p. 26.

Price and Cost Data

To insure its competitiveness with comparable European subcompacts, Akida is planning to price the "comettail" at Pts800,000 to be adjusted upward by 5 percent annually. Production costs are as follows:

VARIABLE COST PER UNIT

	Pts
Materials and Components	
Domestic component	125,000
Imported component (from the parent)	120,000
Labor	80,000

FIXED COSTS (ANNUALLY)

Royalties and fees to the parent	250,000,000
General, selling, and administrative expenses	300,000,000
Depreciation (plant and equipment to be depreciated over a ten-year period to Pts4 billion salvage value)	1,000,000,000

The domestic component of raw materials and components as well as labor are subject to an upward adjustment by the average projected rate of inflation in Spain (see below). General, selling and administrative costs are estimated to rise by 5 percent annually, while the other two components of fixed costs (royalties and fees to the parent company and depreciation) will remain unchanged. The parent company provides the affiliate with components priced on a cost basis.

Inflation and Exchange Rate Data

The volatility of exchange rates which characterized exchange markets in late 1985 presents perhaps the greatest risk facing the project. This period witnessed a sharp decline in the value of the U.S. dollar vis-à-vis the Japanese yen and currencies of major industrial countries, due to in part to sustained intervention by central banks in a concerted effort to weaken the U.S. dollar. As a result of these operations, the Japanese yen tended to appreciate against the Spanish peseta in the period when the project was being considered. This would seem to suggest that, when such massive intervention activities cease, the peseta will tend to appreciate somewhat against the yen.

The evaluating team compiled the inflation and exchange rate data in Table 1, which are projected to prevail during the life cycle of the project.

Table 1.

	EXCHANGE RATES			INFLATION RATES		
	Y/$	Pst/$	Pst/Y		SPAIN	JAPAN
Spot Rate 12/31/85	202	160	0.79	Actual 1985	10.5	2.5
Average 1986	190	170	0.89	1986	9.0	2.0
Average 1987	215	175	0.81	1987	8.0	3.5
Average 1988	229	180	0.79	1988	11.0	4.0
Average 1989	235	200	0.85	1989	12.0	5.0
Average 1990	240	211	0.88	1990	13.5	5.5
Average 1991	245	215	0.88	1991	15.0	6.0

The forecast assumes further strengthening of the Japanese yen against the dollar in 1986, but a resumption of the dollar's appreciation against most currencies (including the yen and the peseta) beginning in 1987. The peseta-yen rate is projected to depreciate in 1986, due to expected continuation of intervention by Japan to prop the yen, but remains fairly steady thereafter.

Inflation rates are forecasted to decline further in 1986 (and through 1987 in Spain), but to accelerate somewhat in later years.

Tax Provisions in Japan

Japanese tax laws distinguish between distributed and undistributed income of domestic corporations, which apply also to branches of foreign corporations doing business in Japan. Corporations with capitalization of Y100,000,000 and over are subject to 33.3 percent on distributed income and 43.3 percent on undistributed income.[2] This distinction is intended primarily to lessen somewhat the incidence of double taxation in the case of distributed profits.

For the purpose of this case problem, Akida Motors follows a policy of distributing one-half of realized profits. Consequently, the effective tax rate is 38.3 percent. Japanese corporations operating overseas can claim full credit for corporate income tax and withholding tax paid to foreign tax jurisdictions.

Project Evaluation

As a member of the project's evaluation team you have been asked to prepare and analyze the cash flow data, and to test the acceptability of the project, using standard DCF techniques (NPV and IRR). Akida Motors requires a 20 percent return on car manufacturing and assem-

[2]*Ibid.*, p. 14.

bly plants established in foreign countries. Similar projects in Spain employ a hurdle rate of 18 percent.

The project is to be evaluated from the standpoint of the Spanish affiliate (in pesetas) as well as from the standpoint of the parent firm (in Japanese yen).

You are also given the following additional information:

a. All profits after tax realized by the Spanish affiliate are freely transferable to Japan. Royalties and management fees are also freely transferable.
b. Only one-half of depreciation charges is transferable. The other half is to be maintained in a local noninterest-earning escrow account, pending renegotiation of the status of the affiliate in 1991.
c. The terminal value, which is estimated to equal five times the projected after-tax net profit of the affiliate in the fifth year of operation (1991), is also transferable to Japan. However, capital gains on the transaction are taxable in Japan at the rate of 25 percent. Because of the uncertainty of the amount, the terminal value is to be discounted at five percentage points above the discount rate applicable to regular cash flows.

Sensitivity Analysis

It is the policy of Akida Motors to subject foreign-project proposals to a series of tests to ascertain the sensitivity of those projects to adverse developments, particularly those relating to sales projections, the exchange risk, and the political risk. You have, therefore, been also asked to perform the following tests on the project's cash flow in yen separately:

a. Projected sales are 8000 units annually (instead of 10,000 units), rising by 10 percent annually.
b. Exchange rates adjust to the projected average inflation rates in Spain and Japan during the 1986–1991 period in accordance with the PPP principle (instead of using the projected rates given in the text of the problem).
c. Blockage of transfers from Spain affects 50 percent of profits after tax and the 50 percent of depreciation charges that is transferable. Blocked amounts can be invested in Spain at 10 percent and are to be transferred to Japan at the end of 1991.

You may also want to consider subjecting the project to both (b) and (c) simultaneously. (Blockage hurts the project's viability more if the currency of the host country is expected to depreciate against the parent's currency.)

3. *Short Case Study—Consolidated Engines and Agricultural Equipment, Inc.*

Background

Consolidated Engines and Agricultural Equipment, Inc. (CEAE), a leading U.S. manufacturer of small engines and related equipment, was recently approached by the Minister of Economic Development of San Hectador (SH) to set up a plant to manufacture small irrigation pumps in that country. CEAE is not currently exporting its products to SH, and the establishing of a manufacturing facility in that country is not expected to cut into current CEAE exports to other countries in the region.

SH is a small republic in Latin America with a fairly stable and democratic system. The favorable political climate has been fostered by an open and constructive economic policy which favors foreign investment. The inflation rate has averaged 20 percent in recent years, a very reasonable rate by Latin American standards.

Investment

The facility in SH is to be a wholly owned affiliate of CEAE which will provide all funds needed to build the manufacturing facility, as well as equipment. Total initial investment is estimated at SHP (San Hectadoran pesos) 50,000,000. Working capital requirements, estimated at SHP20,000,000, would be provided by a local financial institution at 6 percent per annum, repayable in five equal installments beginning on December 31 of the first year of operation. In the absence of this concessional facility, CEAE would have financed these requirements by a loan from its bankers in the United States at 15 percent per annum.

The cost of the entire manufacturing facility is to be depreciated over five years on a straight-line basis. At the end of the fifth year of operation, all remaining assets would be taken over by a public corporation to be designated by the government of SH with no compensation.

Sales, Prices, and Exchange Rate Data

Sales, price, and exchange rate projections are presented in Table 1.

- Variable costs are SHP500 per unit in year 1 and are expected to rise by 20 percent each year.
- Fixed costs (other than depreciation) are SHP25 million in year 1 and are expected to rise by 10 percent per year.

Table 1.

YEAR	SALES IN UNITS	UNIT PRICE	EXCHANGE RATE SH/$
0			Spot rate SHP4.50/$
1	100,000	SHP 1,000	5.50
2	125,000	1,200	6.50
3	150,000	1,440	7.50
4	175,000	1,728	8.50
5	200,000	2,074	9.50

- Sale price per unit already reflects the annual inflation rate of 20 percent.
- All initial investment is to be made at the spot rate.

Other Data

- All profits after tax realized by the affiliate are transferable to the parent at the end of each year. Depreciation funds are to be blocked until the end of year 5. These funds may be invested in local money market instruments, yielding a tax-free 10 percent per annum. When the operating assets are turned over to a local corporation, the balance of these funds including interest, may be repatriated.
- SH taxes corporate income at the rate of 35 percent, but has no withholding tax on transfer of dividends. Dividends received by CEAE in the United States would be subject to a 45 percent tax with credit allowed for taxes paid on affiliate's income abroad.
- CEAE uses a 20 percent weighted average cost of capital for evaluating domestic projects similar to the ones planned in SH. For foreign projects in developing countries a 5 percent political risk premium is added.

    a. Perform DCF analysis on the data to compute both the APV and the IRR for the project from the standpoint of the parent company. What are your recommendations for the proposal?

    b. Test the sensitivity of the project to the political and exchange risks by reperforming the analysis on the assumptions that all dividends are blocked until the end of year 5. Blocked funds (like depreciation funds) are investable locally in money market instruments, yielding a tax-free rate of 10 percent per annum.

    c. Briefly evaluate the political risk in this project and indicate the extent to which it has been allowed for in the planning phase (as reflected in the assumptions or data given in the question). What other measures are available to the management of CEAE to reduce the political risk?

(*Hint:* The present value of the concessional loan facility may be viewed as a reduction in initial investment in year 0.)

BIBLIOGRAPHY

BAKER, J. C., and L. J. BEARDSLEY, "Multinational Companies' Use of Risk Evaluation and Profit Measurement for Capital Budgeting Decisions," *Journal of Business Finance* (Spring 1973), pp. 38–43.

BARTLEY, J. W., "NPV Model Modified for Inflation," *Management Accounting* (December 1980), pp. 49–52.

BAVISHI, V. B., "Capital Budgeting Practices at Multinationals," *Management Accounting* (August 1981), pp. 32–35.

BOADWAY, R., "A Note on the Treatment of Foreign Exchange in Project Evaluation," *Economica* (November 1978), pp. 391–398.

BRUNO, C. J., and M. R. EAKER, "Further Evaluation of Financing Costs for Multinational Subsidiaries," working paper. Dallas, Texas: Edwin L. Cox School of Business, Southern Methodist University, 1981.

CARTER, E. E., *Portfolio Aspects of Corporate Capital Budgeting*. Lexington, Mass.: D. C. Heath and Company, 1974.

CARTER, W. G., "National Support of International Ventures," *Columbia Journal of World Business* (September–October 1972), pp. 6–12.

DAVIDSON, W. H., "The Location of Foreign Direct Investment Activity: Country Characteristics and Experience Effects," *Journal of International Business Studies* (Fall 1980), pp. 9–22.

DURAND, D., "Comprehensiveness in Capital Budgeting," *Financial Management* (Winter 1981), pp. 7–13.

EZZELL, J. R., and W. A. KELLY, "An APV Analysis of Capital Budgeting Under Inflation," *Financial Management* (Autumn 1984), pp. 49–54.

FOSTER, E. M., "The Impact of Inflation on Capital Budgeting Decisions," *Quarterly Review of Economics and Business* (Autumn 1980), pp. 19–24.

GADDIS, P. O., "Analyzing Overseas Investment," *Harvard Business Review* (May/June 1966), pp. 115–122.

KIM, S. H., and T. CRICK, "Foreign Capital Budgeting Practices Used by the U.S. and Non-U.S. Multinational Companies," *The Engineering Economist* (Spring 1984), pp. 207–215.

______, "How Non-U.S. MNC's Practice Capital Budgeting," *Management Accounting* (January 1984), pp. 28–31.

LESSARD, D. R., "Evaluating International Projects: An Adjusted Present Value Approach," in *International Financial Management: Theory and Application,* Donald R. Lessard, ed. Boston, Mass.: Warren, Gorham & Lamont, 1979, pp. 577–592.

LUMBY, S., "APV or NPV: A Matter of Complexity," *Accountancy* (February 1985), p. 124.

MCCABE, G. M., and G. N. SANDERSON, "Abandonment Value in Capital Budgeting: Another View," *Management Accounting* (January 1984), pp. 32–36.

MEHTA, D. R., "Capital Budgeting Procedures for a Multinational," in *Management of Multinationals,* P. Sethi and R. Holton, eds. New York: Free Press, 1974, pp. 271–291.

OBLAK, D. J., and R. J. HELM, "Survey and Analysis of Capital Budgeting Methods Used by Multinationals," *Financial Management* (Winter 1980), pp. 37–41.

PIPER, J. R., "How U.S. Firms Evaluate Foreign Investment Opportunities," *MSU Business Topics* (Summer 1971), pp. 11–20.

RIZZI, J. V., "Capital Budgeting: Linking Financial Analysis to Corporate Strategy," *Journal of Business Strategy* (Spring 1984), pp. 81–84.

SHAPIRO, A. C., "Capital Budgeting for the Multinational Corporation," *Financial Management* (Spring 1978), pp. 7–16.

SHAPIRO, A. C., and A. I. STONEHILL, "Capital Budgeting with Segmented Capital Markets," working paper, University of Pennsylvania, 1976.

STANLEY, M., and S. BLOCK, "An Empirical Study of Management and Financial Variables Influencing Capital Budgeting Decisions for Multinational Corporation in the 1980's," *Management International Review,* no. 3 (1983), pp. 61–72.

STOBAUGH, R. B., JR., "How to Analyze Foreign Investment Climates," *Harvard Business Review* (September/October 1969), pp. 100–108.

STONEHILL, A., and L. NATHANSON, "Capital Budgeting and the Multinational Corporation," *California Management Review* (Summer 1968), pp. 39–54.

THOMSEN, C. T., "Danger in Discounting," *Management Accounting* (January 1984), pp. 37–39.

WESTON, J. F., and B. W. SORGE, *Guide to International Financial Management.* New York: McGraw-Hill, 1977, Chapter 15.

CASE STUDY

Delicious Foods and Confectionery Corporation of the United Kingdom—DFC (U.K.)

Background

DFC (U.K.) is a producer and exporter of a diversified line of packaged food products, sweets, and soft drinks based in Devonshire, U.K. The company is organized in three divisions: (1) Packaged Foods Division, (2) Sweets and Confectionery Division, and (3) Soft Drinks Division. Sales in the United Kingdom (U.K.) and exports for 1980–1985 were as shown in Table 1.

DFC (U.K.) has an arrangement with Bon Bon Swisse, S.A., a Swiss confectionery company, to manufacture and sell a selected line of its products in Western Europe and in the Middle East under a licensing agreement. It also has a 49 percent interest in DFC (Kenya), a joint venture with private local investors to produce and market a limited line of its products in Kenya and other East Africa countries. Sales of Bon Bon Swisse S.A., and DFC (Kenya) for 1980–1985, which are not included in DFC (U.K.) exports listed above, are as shown in Table 2. DFC (U.K.)'s overall net profits for the indicated period are calculated in Table 3.

Investigating Establishing a Plant in Italy

The management has been considering for some time terminating its licensing agreement with Bon Bon Swisse (S.A.) and the joint venture in

Table 1.

(IN MILLIONS OF POUNDS STERLING)				
	U.K. Sales	Exports	Total Sales	Percentage of Exports to Total Sales
1980	127.4	258.4	385.8	67.0
1981	125.3	256.3	381.6	67.2
1982	121.2	260.7	381.9	68.3
1983	130.3	300.9	431.2	69.8
1984	145.9	350.2	496.1	70.6
1985	142.0	410.0	552.0	74.3

Table 2.

	(IN MILLIONS OF POUNDS STERLING)			
	Bon Bon Swisse (S.A.)		DFC (Kenya)	
	Sales	*Royalties Paid to DFC (U.K.)*	*Sales*	*Dividends Transferred to DFC (U.K.)*
1980	34.2	3.4	20.0	1.7
1981	38.5	3.9	23.9	1.9
1982	29.6	3.0	34.5	2.8
1983	37.2	3.7	36.8	4.2
1984	45.9	4.6	40.2	3.8
1985	50.0	5.0	36.7	4.0

Table 3.

(IN MILLIONS OF POUNDS STERLING)	1980	1981	1982	1983	1984	1985
1. Net income from sales in U.K.	10.8	10.0	9.5	11.3	13.5	12.9
2. Net income from exports	20.0	19.2	21.5	27.5	30.8	35.2
3. Total net income from DFC (U.K.) (1 + 2)	30.8	29.2	31.0	38.8	44.3	48.1
4. Royalties from Bon Bon Swisse	3.4	3.9	3.0	3.7	4.6	5.0
5. Dividends from DFC (Kenya)	1.7	1.9	2.8	4.2	3.8	4.0
6. Total net income from operations (3 + 4 + 5)	35.9	35.0	36.8	46.7	52.7	57.1
7. Income tax at 40%	14.4	14.0	14.7	18.7	21.1	22.8
Net Profit	21.5	21.0	22.1	28.0	31.6	34.3

Kenya, and setting up a wholly owned affiliate in Milan, Italy.[1] A committee headed by the Vice President of Marketing has concluded that the company's profits from sales in these markets can be tripled or even quadrupled within a few years, given aggressive marketing and direct control on activities. These have been lacking under the present arrangements. The committee, which was entrusted with investigating the project, is impressed by the favorable investment climate in Italy, but is concerned over the prospects of the exchange rate of the Italian lira against the pound sterling.

[1]The management of DFC (U.K.) has been dissatisfied with their sales and profits originating from Europe, Africa, and the Middle East. Both the royalty arrangement with Bon Bon Swisse and the joint venture in Kenya have been disappointing, relative to management's expectations and the potential of those markets.

In its preliminary report submitted in September 1985, the committee indicated the following advantages for going ahead with the proposed project:

1. Virtually free land offered by Milan's city government for the erection of the plant, and relatively low construction costs.
2. Availability of high-quality ingredients and skilled labor in the Milan area.
3. Accessibility to markets in Europe, Africa, and the Middle East, which would reduce the need for maintaining high inventory levels.
4. Availability of concessionary financing arrangements for financing most, if not all, of the working capital requirements.
5. Reduced income tax rate for the first five years of operation on profits generated from sales in Italy and from export sales.
6. Present foreign exchange regulations, which permit transfer of 90 percent of dividends during the first five years of operation, and 75 percent during the next five years. There is no withholding tax on dividends transferred to the parent firm.

Although these favorable factors, particularly 5 and 6, may change in the future, the committee expressed the view that the investment climate would remain favorable due in part to the affiliation of both Italy and the United Kingdom in the European Economic Community (EEC).

Assessment of Political Risk and Foreign Exchange Risk

Italy has been considered in recent years the Western European country with the highest political risk, with the probable exception of Greece, following the assumption of political power by the Socialists in the latter country. This assessment has been due more to the control of labor unions by the communists and the size and influence of the communist party, than to the restrictive nature of the economy and the financial process. The increasing violence caused by extremist groups, such as the Red Brigade, during the late 1970s and early 1980s further added to the fluidity of the political situation.

The investigating committee noted that these circumstances notwithstanding, Italy has remained a loyal member of NATO and the EEC. The economic and financial systems were essentially control-free, and restrictions on transfers and foreign exchange transactions were minimal. The committee also noted that, despite the chronic political instability caused by the multiparty system characteristic of such countries as Italy and France, the political risk has declined over the last two or three years. The control of communists over labor unions has weakened, and the incidence of politically motivated strikes has decreased considerably. Moreover, there has been a marked decrease in the terrorist activities carried out by extremist factions. The committee expected this improving trend to continue in the foreseeable future.

The exchange rate risk presented the committee with a more difficult problem. Italy is a member of the European Monetary System, which includes Belgium, Denmark, France, the Federal Republic of Germany, Ireland, Luxembourg, and the Netherlands. Every member, except Italy, maintains maximum margins of 2.25 percent for exchange rates in transactions in the official markets between their currencies and those of the other countries in the group. Italy maintains maximum margins of 6 percent, in view of the greater volatility of the Italian lira. The pound sterling is floating independently, as the United Kingdom, although an EEC member, has not joined the European Monetary System.

The committee prepared Table 4 to show the degree of volatility of the sterling pound/Italian lira exchange rate in recent months. The period under review, end of 1983 to mid-1985, shows a pattern of relatively high volatility. When both the Italian lira and the pound sterling were depreciating against the U.S. dollar, the pound sterling was depreciating at a faster rate. When both currencies began appreciating vis-à-vis the U.S.

Table 4.

EXCHANGE RATES

Date	Italian Lira per U.S. Dollar	U.S. Cents per Pound Sterling	Italian Lira per Pound Sterling	Percentage Change*
Year end 1983	1655	145.25	2404	
4/30/84	1679	139.80	2347	−2.4
5/31/84	1688	138.65	2340	−2.7
6/30/84	1709	135.70	2319	−3.5
7/31/84	1774	130.70	2319	−3.5
8/31/84	1788	130.85	2334	−2.9
9/28/84	1897	123.45	2342	−2.6
10/31/84	1882	122.00	2296	−4.5
11/30/84	1915	119.80	2294	−4.6
12/31/84	1933	115.92	2241	−6.8
1/31/85	1950	113.10	2205	−8.3
2/28/85	2075	108.25	2246	−6.6
3/31/85	1965	124.00	2437	+1.4
4/30/85	1981	124.40	2464	+2.5
6/30/85	1932	130.41	2520	+4.8

*Percentage change from year end 1983. A negative change denotes depreciation of pound sterling against Italian lira, and vice versa.

Source: Drexel Burnham Lambert Incorporated, *International Investment Monthly,* various issues. Reproduced with permission from Drexel Burnham Lambert Incorporated, New York.

dollar (beginning March 1985), the pound was appreciating at a faster rate than the lira. During the 18-month period covered by the table, the pound swung from a depreciation of 8.3 percent against the lira at the end of January 1985 to an appreciation of 4.8 percent at the end of June 1985, a swing of over 13 percent in five months.

The committee looked next into growth and inflation data for Italy in recent years and the comparable data for the United Kingdom. These data are presented in Table 5.

As was the case in all major industrial countries, the inflation rate in Italy decreased sharply from its peak in 1980. However, it remained about six percentage points higher than the U.K. rate in 1984. This differential was projected to narrow down considerably over 1985–1986. Economic growth in Italy rebounded somewhat after the 1981–1983 recession, with growth rates projected to be sluggish over the 1985–1986 period, but comparable to the rates projected for the United Kingdom.

In its recommendations on the exchange rate risk, the committee indicated that the lira-pound exchange rate would remain volatile over the intermediate term. However, the committee felt that, barring a sharp acceleration in Italy's inflation rate not accompanied by a similar resurgence of the inflation rate in the United Kingdom, the exchange risk would be manageable, and would probably be primarily influenced by long-term factors such as purchasing power parity over the time horizon of the contemplated project. Current projections are for inflation rates to average 5 percent in the United States, 6 percent in the United Kingdom, and 7.5 percent in Italy over the next five or six years.

Table 5.

	ANNUAL GROWTH OF REAL GNP (PERCENT)		INFLATION RATE (PERCENT CHANGE IN CPI)	
Year	U.K.	Italy	U.K.	Italy
1980	(1.9)	3.8	18.0	21.2
1981	(2.8)	(0.2)	11.0	18.7
1982	(0.9)	(0.3)	8.6	16.3
1983	3.0	(1.5)	4.6	14.7
1984	2.5	2.8	4.6	10.8
1985*	3.5	2.5	5.5	7.5
1986*	2.5	2.5	6.0	7.0

*Projections by Drexel Burnham Lambert International Research Department.

Source: Drexel Burnham Lambert Incorporated, *International Investment Monthly,* May 1985, p. 9. Reproduced with permission from Drexel Burnham Lambert Incorporated, New York.

DFC (U.K.) Foreign Projects Evaluations Policy

DFC's foreign-project-evaluation policy calls for the use of the APV technique over a life span of seven years. The discount rate for the operational cash flows (cash flows generated from sales and exports) is the same rate used for evaluating similar projects at home on the basis of an all-equity capitalization. The company currently uses an 18 percent rate for this purpose. Discount rate for riskier and less predictable components of the APV formula, such as transfer of terminal value and tax savings achieved through the transfer pricing mechanism, is established by adding a risk premium of two to three percentage points to the base rate.

Foreign project evaluation starts with an investigation committee which probes the overall feasibility of the project without going into detailed projections of cash flows and APV calculations. The major task of the investigating committee is to formulate a recommendation to continue or discontinue further evaluation of the project. This recommendation focuses primarily on data relating to the size and expected growth of domestic and export markets, and the investment environment of the host country. The committee is to investigate carefully and make specific assessments of both the exchange and political risks.

Following the presentation of the investigating committee's final report to the Vice President of Financial Operations, and if the green light is given for further evaluation, the Vice President of Financial Operations will form a task force, usually headed by the General Manager of the Capital Budgeting Division, to compile cash flow and all other required data, perform the APV analysis, and make its recommendations in the light of its findings. The final decision on the project is to be made by the Board of Directors, based on the recommendations of the Chief Financial Officer.

Compilation of Data for APV Evaluation of DFC (Italy)

The task force entrusted with the evaluation of the project, DFC (Italy), compiled data on projected sales and exports, profit margins, taxable income, transferable dividends and other payments to DFC (U.K.), concessionary arrangements made available by the city of Milan, and terminal value estimates.

Sales and Income Data. Sales and profit margin projections covering the period from 1987, the year the project will commence operations, to 1993, and projected exports by DFC (Italy) to Europe, Africa, and the Middle East during the same period are given in Table 6. Export projections are denominated in U.S. dollars, since all exports to these areas will be billed in U.S. dollars, and are payable in the same currency.

Table 6.

	Italy (in billions of Italian lira)		Europe, Africa, and the Middle East (in millions of U.S. dollars)	
	Sales	Profit Margin	Exports	Profit Margin
1987	17.8	.13	180.5	.11
1988	20.2	.14	200.3	.12
1989	24.7	.14	225.8	.13
1990	30.3	.15	275.7	.13
1991	35.9	.16	320.5	.14
1992	40.0	.16	380.5	.14
1993	47.5	.17	420.7	.15

Sales and exports by DFC (Italy) will replace, to some extent, sales and exports currently undertaken as follows:

1. Sales currently made to Europe by Bon Bon Swisse (S.A.) under a licensing agreement. These sales were projected to grow at the average growth rate realized during 1980–1985, at a profit margin equaling the average margin realized during this period.
2. Sales currently made by DFC (Kenya). These sales were projected to increase at the average growth rate of 1980–1985, and to realize a profit margin equivalent to the average margin during the same period.
3. Ten percent of exports made by DFC (U.K.) worldwide (except Europe, Africa, and the Middle East). These exports were projected to increase at the average growth rate attained during 1980–1985, at a profit margin equivalent to the average margin realized during the same period.

The Investment Environment, Transferability, Tax, and Other Provisions

The operations of DFC (Italy) will be subject to the following provisions:

1. Profits originating from domestic sales will be subject to 25 percent income tax for the first five years, rising to 30 percent thereafter. Profits originating from exports by DFC (Italy) will be subject to 15 percent income tax rate during the first five years, rising to 20 percent thereafter.
2. Up to 90 percent of net profits of DFC (Italy) will be transferable to DFC (U.K.) during the first five years of operation, falling to 75 percent of net profits thereafter. Depreciation charges are to be used for replacement of fixed assets and are, therefore, not transferable. There is no withholding tax on dividends transferred to the parent company.

3. All royalties and management fees are freely transferable to the parent. It is planned that the agreement between DFC (U.K.) and DFC (Italy) will stipulate a royalty of 10 percent and a management fee of 5 percent on all combined domestic sales and exports.
4. DFC (Italy) can borrow up to Lit25 billion from local financial institutions with a guarantee from the Italian government. It is anticipated that Lit10 billion will be drawn in 1986 to finance part of the fixed investment, and Lit15 billion will be drawn in 1987 to finance working capital requirements. Borrowed funds are repayable in seven equal annual installments with interest at five percentage points below a reference money market rate. It is projected that the reference rate will be 19 percent in January 1986 and 18 percent in January 1987. In the absence of the concessionary financing arrangement, DFC (Italy) would have had to borrow at two percentage points above the reference rate.

Initial Investment and Terminal Value Assumption

Estimates for the initial investment on the project broken down by currency and by year are as shown in Table 7.

All funds, with the exception of the local concessionary loan of Lit25 billion, are to be provided by the parent company as an equity investment in DFC (Italy).

The terminal value in 1993 is estimated at five times the after-tax profits generated by the affiliate from domestic sales and exports in that year.

Mr. Melvin Huit, manager of the Capital Budgeting Division and chairman of the task force entrusted with evaluating DFC (Italy), is hoping to finalize his report on the project, supported by APV calculations and appropriate recommendations. Mr. Huit is planning to present in his report a brief description of the project, followed by a synopsis of the investigating committee's report on the exchange rate and political risks. This will be

Table 7.

YEAR	CURRENCY	AMOUNT	PURPOSE
1986	Italian lira	30 billion	Construction of plant
1986	U.S. dollar	35 million	Equipment shipped from the U.S.
1987	Italian lira	18 billion	Equipment purchased locally
1987	Italian lira	15 billion	Working capital

followed by the APV calculations under the most likely conditions. He is also planning to perform at least two sensitivity tests, one dealing with adverse exchange risk and the second with adverse political risk assumptions. An overall assessment and recommendations of the task force will conclude the report.

15

Cost of Capital and Capital Structure of the Multinational Firm The International Capital Asset Pricing Model

Financial theory has made significant strides in the past two decades, particularly in the area of measuring the firm's cost of capital and the related derivation of the optimal capital structure. A milestone in this progress is the development of the capital asset pricing model (CAPM) and its use for pricing securities and the computation of the required rate of return on equity. These developments have been extended to the international finance area, with consequent impact on multinational capital budgeting, as well as on direct foreign and international portfolio investment.

This chapter consists of two parts. The first part contains a brief presentation of the concepts of the optimal capital structure and cost of capital as they apply to the domestic firm. The second part highlights the adaptation of these concepts to the multinational firm. Certain aspects relating to improving the risk/return trade-off through international portfolio diversification, and investing in the shares of the multinational firm as a proxy to achieve this improvement, are examined in Chapter 12.

THE OPTIMAL CAPITAL STRUCTURE AND COST OF CAPITAL THEORY—THE DOMESTIC FIRM[1]

Financial theory states that for each firm there is a combination of financing encompassing debt, equity, and other forms (preferred stock) which maxi-

[1]Only a brief discussion of the basic theory is presented in this section. For more detailed analysis of the assumptions behind cost of capital theory and major contributors, see Van Horne, *Financial Management and Policy,* 6th ed. (Englewood Cliffs, N.J.: Prentice-Hall, Inc., 1983) or Weston and Copeland, *Managerial Finance,* 8th ed. (Hinsdale, Ill.: Dryden Press, 1986).

mizes the value of the firm, while simultaneously minimizing the cost of capital. The financial manager is in constant search for the optimal proportion of debt and equity that will achieve this objective. This point is theoretically determined by solving for the proportion of debt and equity which will maximize share prices[2] in the marketplace. The financial manager in practice, however, can at best only approximate it by choosing a capital structure that is located somewhere within the optimal zone, avoiding excessive leverage (to the right of the zone) or inadequate leverage (to the left of the zone). See Exhibit 15-1.

Weighted Average Cost of Capital

Once the optimal point is established, the cost of capital is solved for by the traditional method of computing the weighted average cost of debt and equity, thus:

$$k = k_d(1 - T)W_d + k_e W_e$$

where k is the weighted average cost of capital

k_d is the cost of debt measured by the cost of new borrowings by the firm

T is the applicable marginal corporate income tax rate

W_d is the proportion of debt in the capital structure, or $\frac{D}{D + E}$

k_e is the cost of equity (from internal sources or new flotations of common stock)

W_e is the proportion of equity in the capital structure, or $\frac{E}{D + E}$

$$\frac{D}{D + E} + \frac{E}{D + E} = 1$$

There are two important observations with respect to the use of the cost of capital thus determined in evaluating new projects undertaken by the firm:

1. The firm must maintain the optimal proportion of debt and equity in financing new projects as long as the new investments have the same degree of risk as the average risk of its present project mix. Venturing into riskier (or less risky) undertakings or new lines of business, which are inevitably encountered when firms diversify their activities or acquire other businesses, will necessitate re-

[2]Theoretically, maximization of EPS occurs at a debt ratio which is higher than that which maximizes share price in the market. This is due to the decline of the price/earning ratio (P/EPS) in recognition of the increased riskiness of the firm.

Exhibit 15-1. Cost of Capital: Location of Optimal Capital Structure

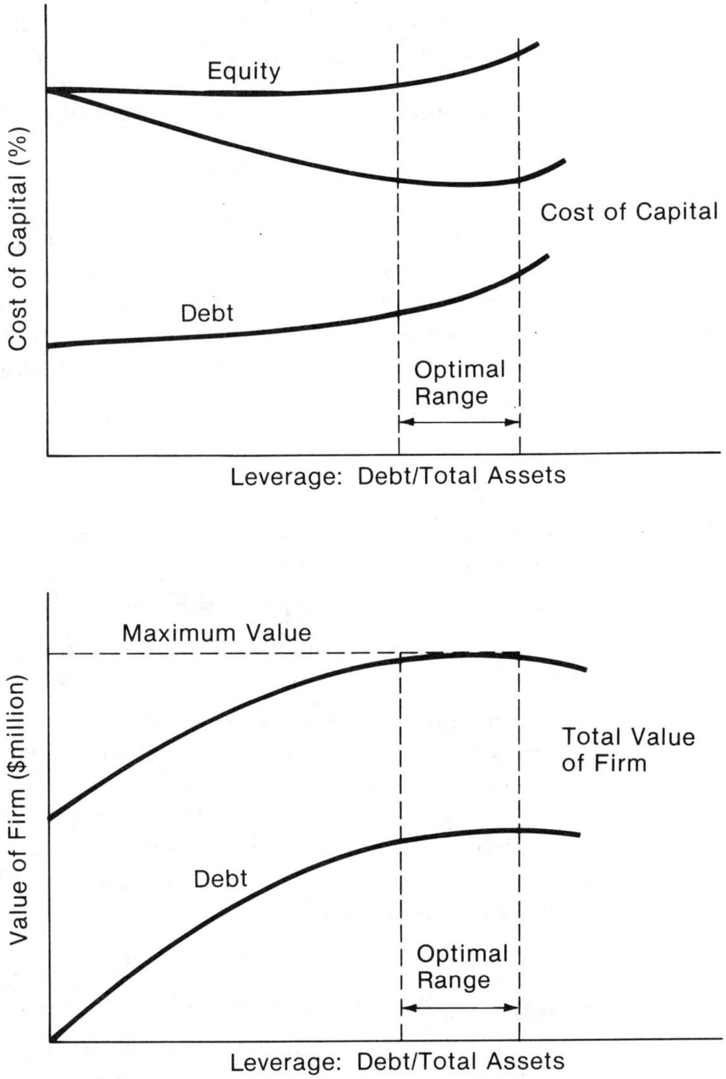

computing the optimal capital structure and, subsequently, recalculation of the cost of capital.

2. As more financing is undertaken for expansion, higher cost of equity and debt sources will have to be tapped, while the same proportions indicated in the optimal capital structure are maintained. When internal equity resources are exhausted, new common stock issues will involve flotation cost. New loans above a

certain point will also involve higher interest rates in recognition of the higher riskiness of the firm. Consequently, as the firm expands, the weighted average cost of capital will rise in discrete steps, resulting in a stepladder cost of capital function. This function is often referred to as the marginal cost of capital (MCC) which is encountered as the capital budget of the firm increases.

Derivation of the Cost of Equity

Conceptually, measuring the cost of equity, or the required rate of return by investors in the firm's stock, poses more problems than estimating the cost of debt. For firms which have an established record of earnings and dividends, the cost of equity may be computed by the dividend discount method (also called the Gordon-Shapiro formula) by using the following equation:

$$K_e = \frac{d_1}{P_0} + g$$

where d_1 is the amount of dividend in the subsequent period, i.e., $d_1 = d_0(1 + g)$

P_0 is the current market price of the stock

g is the compounded annual rate of growth in dividends or earnings

The formula essentially uses the historical rate of return earned by the investors as a proxy for the required rate of return for equity. When the shares of the firms are widely held and actively traded, the historical rate of return serves as a close approximation to the required rate that investors, given the risk involved in the investment, would deem acceptable.

Alternatively, the cost of equity may be calculated by the CAPM (Exhibit 15-2) by using the following formula:

$$E(R)_j = R_F + \beta_j(E(R)_M - R_F)$$

where $E(R)_j$ is the expected rate of return on stock of firm j or security j.

R_F is the rate of return on riskless investment measured by the current rate of return or yield on Treasury bonds.

$E(R)_M$ is the expected rate of return on a broad market index, such as the Standard and Poors index of industrial stocks, comprising 425 companies.

β_j is the beta of stock j, measured by the relative variability or volatility of the rate of return on the stock compared to the variability of the return on a broad market index. A beta of 1 (unity) denotes a risk equivalent to the one entailed in an invest-

Exhibit 15-2. The Capital Asset Pricing Model

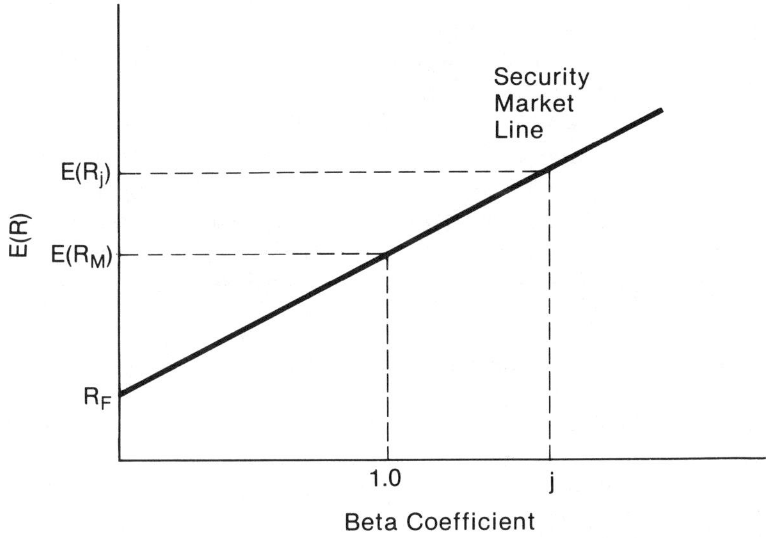

ment in a diversified portfolio of stocks exemplified by a broad market index.

Both the Gordon-Shapiro Model and CAPM yield a risk-adjusted rate of return on equity. The major difference is that the latter utilizes beta, which is a measure of the market-related or systematic risk, rather than total risk, which is traditionally measured by the standard deviation. Both methods yield acceptable and conceptually defensible estimates of the rate required by the investors given the degree of risk inherent in the investment. For firms with no established track record and for which beta coefficients are not available, the cost of equity may be derived by adding an arbitrary risk premium (ranging between four to six percentage points) to the firm's recent borrowing rate.

Choosing an Appropriate Discount Rate for Evaluation of Investment

Once the financial manager arrives at the optimal capital structure, which is essentially long-term in nature, the object is to raise debt and equity funds, in the proportion established by the capital structure, so as to finance new investments. The manager may depart in the short run from these proportions so as to avoid issuing securities at high costs or when market conditions are unfavorable. But over the long run, adherence to the optimal capital structure should be approximated.

All new investments involving risk comparable to the average risk of the firm's current investments are to be evaluated by the cost of capital thus calculated, irrespective of how they are individually financed. When a firm attempts projects of riskier nature, a risk premium is sometimes added to the established hurdle rate based on the weighted average cost of capital. However, the riskiness of individual projects, just like that of stocks or other financial investments, should be ascertained in conjunction with how their returns correlate with that of the portfolio of existing investments, rather than in isolation. A project whose cash flow pattern departs sharply from existing investments undertaken by the firm may be assigned a lower hurdle rate than when it is being considered in isolation.

COST OF CAPITAL FOR THE MULTINATIONAL FIRM

In evaluating foreign investments, the MNC is faced with a wide array of options as to the choice of an appropriate discount rate. The simplest choice is to use the same rate adopted by the firm for discounting the returns from a comparable domestic project. This choice is conceptually valid where the capital markets are efficient (rather than segmented—see below) and if the MNC opts for reflecting the exchange and political risks in adjustments to expected cash flows rather than adjustments to the discount rate. Efficient markets would insure that the differentials in the cost of raising funds between the home and foreign capital markets are offset by the forward premium (discount) of foreign currencies against the home currency. Where markets are segmented due to barriers on capital movements, government restrictions, or otherwise, the firm may be able to finance foreign projects at a higher (or a lower) cost than is available for domestic projects. If such is the case, the management must make a determination whether or not the particular foreign project should bear the burden (or benefit) from a different cost of capital attributable to market segmentation.

Another option is to use the required rate of return on equity in the host country as a hurdle rate. The use of this rate would subject the foreign project to the same test of viability used for competing projects initiated by local or other foreign investors. If this rate is chosen, the project's cash flow analysis should benefit from the project's contribution to the firm's borrowing capacity determined by the proportions of debt and equity in its optimal capital structure.[3]

Alternatively, an MNC's management may decide to change the project-specific required rate of return to reflect foreign risks. This choice complicates the task of arriving at the appropriate discount rate, since it depends in part on how the shareholders of the parent firm view or

[3]Refer to the adjusted present value approach in Chapter 13.

appraise the foreign risks. Adjusting the project-specific hurdle rate to foreign risks may be analyzed under the following subheadings:

1. Adjustment for the exchange risk
2. Adjustment for the political risk
3. Adjustment for segmentation of capital markets
4. Adjustment for the international diversification effect
5. Adjustment for country differences in the optimal capital structure

Factoring in the impact of taxation policies of the home and host countries will not be considered in this context, since it influences the investment decision irrespective of whether the firm opts to adjust the cash flows of the project or the cost of capital. Tax considerations are discussed in Chapters 14 and 18.

Adjusting for the Exchange Risk

The cost of capital of a foreign project may be adjusted by the average rate of appreciation (depreciation) of the host country's currency against the home country's currency during the life cycle of the project. To illustrate, let's assume that a U.S. firm which has an optimal capital structure of 35 percent debt and 65 percent equity is considering a project in Egypt which intrinsically has the same degree of risk as the average risk of projects undertaken in the United States.

Let us assume further that the shareholders in the U.S. firm require a return of 20 percent (measured in U.S. dollars), while the cost of borrowed funds is 12 percent and 18 percent per annum in the United States and Egypt, respectively. If exchange markets are efficient, the Egyptian pound is expected to depreciate by 6 percent against the U.S. dollar during a time span of one year.

We can calculate the cost of capital in U.S. dollars and in Egyptian pounds, using a marginal corporate tax rate of 40 percent:

(Cost of capital in U.S. dollars)

$$\$k = (0.35)(0.12)(0.60) + (0.65)(0.20) = 15.5 \text{ percent}$$

(Cost of capital in Egyptian pounds £.E.)

$$k_d \text{ before tax (in £E)} = 12\% \ (1 + 0.06) + 6\% = 18.72 \text{ percent}$$

$$k_e \text{ (in £E)} = 20\% \ (1 + 0.06) + 6\% = 27.\ 20 \text{ percent}$$

$$\text{£Ek} = (0.35)(0.187)(0.60) + (0.65)(0.272) = 21.6 \text{ percent}$$

Alternatively,

$$£Ek = 15.5\% (1 + 0.06) + 6\% = 22.4 \text{ percent}$$

The small discrepancy between the two computations of the cost of capital in Egyptian pounds (0.8 percent) is due to the greater tax savings on the higher-cost debt component in the first method. Note also that the cost of capital expressed in Egyptian pounds exceeds the cost in terms of U.S. dollars by approximately the expected rate of depreciation in the pound against the dollar, or 6 percent. This would suggest that if markets are efficient the choice of the currency for computing the cost of capital would not affect the investment decision. Computed either way, the project's return in U.S. dollars has to exceed the hurdle rate of 15.5 percent to be accepted.

Adjustment for the Political Risk

Reflecting the political risk in the cost of capital consists of adding an arbitrary risk premium to the domestic cost of capital for a project of comparable risk. Because political risk is likely to be higher in the later years of the investment life cycle, this procedure tends to penalize cash flows which materialize in earlier years (see Chapter 13).

Segmented Capital Markets

The cost of capital for an MNC could differ from the firm's domestic cost of funds if there are market imperfections. Such imperfections may affect the availability as well as the cost of the debt and equity components of the capital structure. Segmented capital markets are, by definition, inefficient markets which are characterized by persistent differentials in the cost of raising funds in different countries which are not offset by exchange rate movements. Segmentation arises from controls on the flow of capital across boundaries and from the varying degrees of depth and development of capital markets in different countries. It may also result from lack of accurate information on investment and lending opportunities in different markets.

Market segmentation impacts the cost of capital of the MNC upward or downward, depending on a number of factors, which include: the interest elasticity of the supply and demand for loanable funds in the domestic market, access to international sources of funds, the degree of segmentation in the home or host country capital markets, and transaction costs.

A segmented host country capital market may provide lower cost of funds, as restrictions on capital outflow prevent these funds from seeking higher returns outside the country. In this case, an MNC's cost of capital in the host country of the project may be lower than its cost of capital at home. The management must decide in this case whether the local project should benefit from the lower cost of funds, or if it should be evaluated on the basis of the MNC's worldwide cost of capital.

More often segmentation of capital markets leads to higher cost of capital than if such markets were fully integrated. A common form of segmentation in many countries takes the form of unavailability or limited availability of equity financing. Many U.S. multinationals find it difficult to raise substantial amounts of equity capital even in many industrial countries, perhaps with the exception of the United Kingdom. Investors in many countries have an aversion to buying shares of foreign companies, and often lack sufficient information about these investments. Other determinants include controls which restrict purchase of foreign securities, difficulties of listing on foreign stock exchanges, and stiff and lengthy registration and disclosure requirements. Such requirements in the United States, for example, discourage non-U.S. multinational firms from raising equity funds in the United States.

Where the foreign investment faces a unique cost of capital due to excessive segmentation, the financial manager must make a determination as to the appropriate hurdle rate for purposes of evaluation. One possible rate is what the project should earn if it were to be competitive in its own environment.

Adjustment for the International Diversification Effect

MNCs, by virtue of their diversified operations, are able to reduce their cost of capital compared to domestic firms for at least two reasons:

1. Diversification should contribute to the stability of the overall cash flow. Less cash flow variability causes the firm to support a higher debt ratio, which is the lower cost component in computing the weighted average cost of capital.
2. International diversification (by country and by product) should lower the systematic risk of the firm, thus lowering its beta coefficient and consequently the cost of equity.

The improvement in the risk/return trade-off resulting from international portfolio diversification was discussed in Chapter 12. The beneficial effect of geographically diversified direct foreign investment on the cost of capital of MNCs has been the subject of wide investigation in the financial literature. The reduction in the systematic risk through such diversification has been analyzed through the mechanism of the international capital asset pricing model.[4]

[4]Among the major contributors to this field of inquiry are Donald Lessard, Bruno Solnik, and Raj Aggarwal. See bibliography at the end of this chapter for references to this topic listed under these authors.

An example of the application of CAPM to risk reduction through international diversification was provided by Lessard.[5] He computed the risk premium for eight countries from domestic perspective, as well as the risk premium for the same countries from world perspective. The risk premium from a world perspective was substantially lower for all eight countries than the domestic premium. This is because the correlation between the returns of a project with domestic market portfolio is invariably higher than the average correlation of the same project with world market portfolio. The risk reduction is greater for countries like Japan or Spain, whose markets have low correlation with world market, than the United States, where correlation with world markets is relatively high.[6]

Adjustment for Differences in Capital Structure Among Countries

The theory of the optimal capital structure when applied to the multinational firm requires some elaboration. Answers to such questions as the following should be sought. Should the MNC aim at maintaining its capital structure which minimizes cost of capital at home, or should it seek to minimize its consolidated worldwide cost of capital? Should it adjust the capital structure for its affiliates to suit the norms prevailing in the host countries? Should it adjust its capital structure to recognize the increased riskiness of overall operations attributable to foreign investments?

In the first place, the optimal capital structure is not sacrosanct. Although its underlying determinants are relatively long-term in nature, the firm should review its capital structure periodically to reflect changes in the risk mix of its operations. This is particularly important when it enters entirely new lines of business, or when it merges with or acquires other

[5]Donald R. Lessard, "World, Country, and Industry Relationships in Equity Returns: Implications for Risk Reduction Through International Diversification," *Financial Analyst Journal* (January–February 1976), pp. 32–38.

[6]Restating the value of $\beta_j = P_{jm}(\sigma_j/\sigma_m)$, we have

where P_{jm} is the correlation of the returns on j and m (market portfolio)

σ_j is the standard deviation of j

σ_m is the standard deviation of m

Lessard expressed

the domestic risk premium $= \sigma_j \times p_{dm} \times (R_M - R_F)/\sigma_m$

and the global risk premium $= \sigma_j \times p_{wm} \times (R_M - R_F)/\sigma_m$

where P_{dm} = correlation of project with the domestic market portfolio

P_{wm} = correlation of the project with the world market portfolio

Assuming values of .30 and .5 (market price of one unit of nondiversifiable risk) for σ_j and $(R_M - R_F)/\sigma_m$, respectively, based on U.S. data, he arrived at the following values for the United States:

Domestic risk premium = .30 × .55 × .5 = 8.25%

Global risk premium = .30 × .44 × .5 = 6.6%

firms which have radically different operations. A firm in the process of transforming its operations from predominantly domestic to increasingly multinational would, by necessity, encounter significant changes in the capital structure.

Theoretically an MNC should aim at maximizing the value of the firm worldwide by opting for a globally optimal capital structure. The cost of capital consistent with the globally determined capital structure should, therefore, be the yardstick for evaluating all investments, home and abroad. In practice financial managers have been known to depart from the norms of optimality to take advantage of favorable financing terms, or to postpone certain financing (such as issuance of common stock) when the cost is high.

Managers of U.S. and non-U.S. multinationals have indicated in a number of surveys that factors other than minimizing the cost of capital may play a more important role in determining the optimal capital structure. Factors such as the coverage of fixed charges under variable business conditions, availability of capital, as well as management of the exchange and political risks have been mentioned.[7] The reader should recognize, however, that these are not noncost factors, and that taking such factors into account is not necessarily in conflict with the objective in minimizing the cost of capital.

Debt ratio norms (debt/total assets) differ significantly among countries (Exhibit 15-3). While it hovers around 50 percent for all manufacturing industries in the United States, it is about 75 percent in Japan, and in the range of 65 to 70 percent in France and Scandinavian countries. The substantially higher debt ratio in Japan, for example, is a reflection of the close association between the government and the business sector. The government-owned Bank of Japan guarantees debt provided by commer-

Exhibit 15-3. Debt Ratios in Selected Industries and Countries

Country	No. of Firms	Metals	Chemicals	Electronics	Motor Vehicles	Pharmaceuticals
France	41	64.4	63.6	71.4	74.6	—
Germany	37	57.6	40.5	37.9	45.1	28.1
Japan	79	83.5	81.1	58.7	78.3	40.5
United Kingdom	90	51.5	48.2	53.2	54.0	42.1
United States	326	45.9	42.3	46.8	48.2	36.8

Note: Debt ratios are average total debt as a percentage of total assets based on book value for year end 1980.

Sources: Prepared by Vinod Bavishi, Frederick Choi, and Hany Shawky from the data bank at the Center for Transnational Accounting and Financial Research, University of Connecticut, Storrs, Connecticut, 1981.

[7]See Arthur Stonehill, et al., "Financial Goals and Debt Ratio Determinants: A Survey of Practice in Five Countries," *Financial Management* (Autumn 1975), pp. 27–41.

cial banks to major industrial firms, particularly those producing primarily for export.

In view of the significant differences in debt ratio norms among different countries, should the MNC localize the financial structure of its affiliates abroad? As in many areas of cost of capital theory, particularly as it applies to multinational operations, there is no clear-cut answer to this question.

There are obvious advantages accruing from a localized capital structure. It permits the affiliate to be evaluated on the same basis as its local competitors, and makes foreign affiliates more acceptable by their host environments. They are viewed as abiding by the same rules of the game governing local business, rather than, for instance, operating with little equity and a high proportion of debt from local sources. Localizing the capital structure also allows the firm to reap the benefits of financial leverage, where debt ratios are substantially higher than that of the parent company.

Conforming to local financial structures may cause the affiliates to operate at a higher cost of capital, compared with the worldwide consolidated cost of capital of the parent. MNCs have access to international capital markets, which may enable them to raise funds at more favorable terms than in the local markets of the affiliates. They also enjoy the cost-reduction benefit of diversification. Why should they not pass these advantages to their affiliates, instead of conforming to local norms and patterns of financing? In theory, minimizing the worldwide cost of capital would occur only if the overall consolidated capital structure conforms to the optimal structure.

An argument against localizing capital structure is that it is purely cosmetic, even if it seemingly results in lowering the cost of capital for the affiliate. Potential lenders, particularly outside the host country, look for the firm's worldwide cash flow generation to service their loans, rather than the resources of the borrowing affiliate. Lenders realize that the parent stands behind the obligations of its affiliates, even if no direct guarantee of such loans has been given by the parent. According to this argument, an MNC has in fact an internationalized capital structure even if it departs from this norm in financing its affiliates.

To summarize, an MNC should aim to conform to the principles of cost capital theory and rationalize its capital structure on a worldwide basis. This rationalization process is not necessarily inconsistent with allowing for such variables as the exchange and political risks, the impact of diversification, and adjustment wherever possible to norms and conditions in host countries. Neither is it inconsistent with its obligation (to its own shareholders) to use its size and resources to raise funds worldwide at the lowest possible cost.

REVIEW QUESTIONS

1. Is it possible to ignore localized financial structures in estimating the cost of capital for foreign affiliates? What reasons may be advanced for ignoring them? Are there some drawbacks in taking such a position?
2. "The securities of firms with relatively large international operations are more closely related to the rest of the world market factor and less to their home country factor than the domestic firms." Do you agree? Explain why you would expect the first group to have a lower systematic risk than the second group.
3. Is investor perception or recognition of diversification opportunities necessary for improving the risk/return performance of MNCs? If these diversification effects are accurately assessed by investors, should you not expect this to be reflected in higher share prices for MNCs?
4. Why has the extension of the CAPM to a world context proven to be difficult? What are the major problems which hinder a complete integration of world capital markets?
5. How does increased availability of capital to multinational firms impact their cost of capital? Does market segmentation result invariably in a higher cost of capital for an affiliate in a segmented market?
6. Why are parent loans to affiliates often considered an equity investment? Would such a treatment distort the capital structure of the affiliate? Is such a treatment as acceptable to host governments as to multinational financial managers?
7. Did the Interest Equalization Act of 1963 result in a segmented market for U.S. multinationals? How did this legislation affect the cost of capital of these firms, and how did they get around it?
8. Could a U.S. investor benefit from an internationally diversified portfolio even if some of the foreign securities added to the portfolio have a lower yield than U.S. securities which they replaced?
9. Why is a U.S. MNC likely to derive a better risk/return performance by locating an affiliate in Japan than in the United Kingdom? Do you think that decision makers consider the diversification effect in locating their affiliates?
10. How is the optimal structure of a Japanese multinational firm likely to be affected by large direct foreign investment in the United States and the United Kingdom? What would be the consequences of this firm's insisting that its affiliates in these two countries conform to

norms of the parent country, rather than those of the host countries? What is likely to be the position of its competitors in these two countries?

REVIEW PROBLEMS

1. You are in charge of the capital budgeting division of a U.S. diversified multinational firm. The parent company's cost of capital is 16.5 percent, assuming a current borrowing interest rate of 14 percent, a marginal tax rate of 40 percent, and an optimal capital structure of 0.45 debt and 0.55 equity.

   You are considering an investment in a subsidiary incorporated in country X. Your firm's policy is to reflect risk of foreign undertakings in the hurdle rate, rather than to adjust projected cash flows of these projects.

   What hurdle rate would you apply to the proposed investment under each of the following situations? If no specific rate can be calculated from the data given, you may express the appropriate rate as being higher or lower than the parent's stated cost of capital, stating in each case your reasons. You are to treat each case separately, rather than cumulatively. In situations where you think that not enough information is provided, you may so state, but the missing data should be indicated in each case.

   a. The project in country X has a risk comparable to your firm's overall risk in its domestic investments. Political risk is deemed to be insignificant, but you expect the currency of country X to depreciate by an average of 1.5 percent annually against the U.S. dollar in the next four or five years (assume efficient exchange markets).
   b. Same assumptions as in situation (a) except that you can borrow in local financial markets at 10 percent, but you have reason to believe that exchange and capital markets are not efficient.
   c. Your subsidiary in country X will be facing intense competition from local firms, which consider a 20 percent return on investment as the minimum rate needed to attract funds from investors. (Assume here that both the exchange and political risks are negligible.)
   d. Your subsidiary in country X will be involved in new lines of business that are riskier, and in which your management has had no past experience. Your beta is currently 1.4, while betas of firms involved in the same activities as the project in country X

is 1.8. Moreover, country X has been known to impose restrictions and blockage on transfers by affiliates to their parent firms. (Disregard the exchange risk in this case.)

e. The debt ratio norms for manufacturing industries in country X are radically different. For subsidiary X, a capital structure consisting of 0.65 debt and 0.35 equity would not be unusual. (Disregard both exchange and political risks in this situation.)

f. Cash flows to be generated by subsidiary X are negatively correlated with the company's present cash flow pattern. Moreover, as stated in situation (e), the subsidiary could support a higher debt ratio than indicated in the parent's optimal capital structure. There is a small political risk involved, but in your judgment, it will be more than offset by these features. (Ignore the exchange risk in this situation.)

2. TRW, a U.S. MNC, floated in 1971 a deutsche-mark-denominated bond issue in Germany with a coupon rate of 7.5 percent. The issue sold at par. In 1972, the deutsche mark appreciated against the U.S. dollar by 4.5 percent. What was the effective borrowing cost in 1972, given that TRW had a marginal income tax rate of 0.48? If at the time TRW could have sold a similar bond issue in the U.S. (denominated in U.S. dollars) at par with a coupon rate of 11 percent, which market would have afforded TRW a lower borrowing cost? (*Hint:* The appreciation of the mark affects not only the amount of interest in terms of U.S. dollars, but also the repayment of the principal.)

BIBLIOGRAPHY

AGGARWAL, R., "Multinationality and Stock Market Valuation: An Empirical Study of U.S. Markets and Companies," *Management International Review,* no. 2 (1979), pp. 5–21.

______, "Investment Performance of U.S.-Based Multinational Companies: Comments and a Perspective of International Diversification of Real Assets," *Journal of International Business Studies* (Spring–Summer 1980), pp. 98–104.

______, "International Differences in Capital Structure Norms: An Empirical Study of Large European Companies," *Management International Review* (1981/1), pp. 75–88.

AGMON, T. and D. LESSARD, "Investor Recognition of Corporate International Diversification," *Journal of Finance* (September 1977), pp. 1049–1055.

BERTONECHE, M. L., "An Empirical Analysis of the Interrelationships Among Equity Markets Under Changing Exchange Rate Systems," *Journal of Banking and Finance,* no. 4 (1979), pp. 397–405.

BIGER, N., "Exchange Risk Implications of International Portfolio Diversification," *Journal of International Business Studies* (Fall 1979), pp. 64–74.

BLACK, F., "International Capital Market Equilibrium with Investment Barriers," *Journal of Financial Economics* (December 1974), pp. 337–352.

BREWER, H. L., "Investor Benefits from Corporate International Diversification," *Journal of Financial and Quantitative Analysis* (March 1981), pp. 113–127.

CHOI, F. D. S., "Financial Disclosure and Entry to the European Capital Market," *Journal of Accounting Research* (Autumn 1973), pp. 159–175.

______, "Financial Disclosure in Relation to a Firm's Capital Costs," *Accounting and Business Research* (Autumn 1973), pp. 272–282.

______, "European Disclosure: The Competitive Disclosure Hypothesis," *Journal of International Business Studies* (Fall 1974), pp. 15–23.

COHN, R. A., and J. J. PRINGLE, "Imperfections in International Financial Markets: Implications for Risk Premia and the Cost of Capital to Firms," *Journal of Finance* (March 1973), pp. 59–66.

DE FARO, C., and J. V. JUCKER, "The Impact of Inflation and Devaluation on the Selection of an International Borrowing Source," *Journal of International Business Studies* (Fall 1973), pp. 97–104.

DUFEY, G., "Institutional Constraints and Incentives on International Portfolio Investment," *International Portfolio Investment,* U.S. Department of the Treasury OASIA, 1975.

DUFEY, G., and I. H. GIDDY, "International Financial Planning: The Use of Market-Based Forecasts," *California Management Review* (Fall 1978), pp. 69–81.

EAKER, M. R., "Denomination Decisions for Multinational Transactions," *Financial Management* (Autumn 1980), pp. 23–29.

ELTON, E. J., and M. J. GRUBER, eds., *International Capital Markets.* Amsterdam: North-Holland, 1975.

ERRUNZA, V. R., "Gains from Portfolio Diversification into Less Developed Countries," *Journal of International Business Studies* (Fall–Winter 1977), pp. 83–99.

______, "Determinants of Financial Structure in the Central American Common Market," *Financial Management* (Autumn 1979), pp. 72–77.

______, "Financing MNC Subsidiaries in Central America," *Journal of International Business Studies* (Fall 1979), pp. 88–93.

ERRUNZA, V., and L. W. SENBET, "The Effects of International Operations on the Market Value of the Firm: Theory and Evidence," *Journal of Finance* (May 1981), pp. 401–417.

FINDLAY, M. C., III, A. E. GOODING, and W. Q. WEAVER, JR., "On the Relevant Risk for Determining Capital Expenditure Hurdle Rates," *Financial Management* (Winter 1976), pp. 9–16.

FINNERTY, J. E., and T. SCHNEEWEIS, "The Co-Movement of International Asset Returns," *Journal of International Business Studies* (Winter 1979), pp. 66–78.

FOLKS, W. R., JR., "Analysis of Short-Term, Cross-Border Financing Decisions," *Financial Management* (Autumn 1976), pp. 19–27.

______, "Optimal Foreign Borrowing Strategies with Operations in Forward Exchange Markets," *Journal of Financial and Quantitative Analysis* (June 1978), pp. 245–254.

GRUBEL, H. G., and K. FADNER, "The Interdependence of International Equity Markets," *Journal of Finance* (March 1971), pp. 89–94.

HILLIARD, J., "The Relationship Between Equity Indices on World Exchanges," *Journal of Finance* (March 1979), pp. 103–114.

HUGHES, J. S., D. E. LOGUE, and R. J. SWEENEY, "Corporate International Diversification and Market Assigned Measures of Risk and Diversification," *Journal of Financial and Quantitative Analysis* (November 1975), pp. 627–637.

JACQUILLAT, B., and B. H. SOLNIK, "Multinationals Are Poor Tools for Diversification," *Journal of Portfolio Management* (Winter 1978), pp. 8–12.

JUCKER, J. V., and C. DE FARO, "The Selection of International Borrowing Sources," *Journal of Financial and Quantitative Analysis* (September 1975), pp. 381–407.

KENEN, P. B., "Capital Mobility and Financial Integration: A Survey," *Princeton Studies in International Finance,* no. 39 (1976).

KOHERS, T., "The Effect of Multinational Operations on the Cost of Equity Capital of U.S. Corporations: An Empirical Study," *Management International Review* (February 1975), pp. 121–124.

KOHLHAGEN, S. W., "Overlapping National Investment Portfolios: Evidence and Implications of International Integration of Secondary Markets for Financial Assets," paper presented at the New York University Conference on Internationalization of Financial Markets and National Economic Policy, New York, April 10–11, 1980.

KORNBLUTH, J. S. H., and J. D. VINSO, "Capital Structure and the Financing of the MNC: A Fractional Multiobjective Approach," *Journal of Financial and Quantitative Analysis* (June 1982).

LAN, S. G., S. R. QUAY, and C. M. RAMSEY, "The Tokyo Stock Exchange and the Capital Asset Pricing Model," *Journal of Finance* (May 1974), pp. 507–514.

LEE, W. Y., and K. S. SACHDEVA, "The Role of the Multinational Firm in the Integration of Segmented Markets," *Journal of Finance* (May 1977), pp. 479–492.

LESSARD, D. R., "International Portfolio Diversification: A Multivariate Analysis for a Group of Latin American Countries," *Journal of Finance (June 1973), pp. 619–633.*

______, "World, National, and Industry Factors in Equity Returns," *Journal of Finance* (May 1974), pp. 379–391.

______, "World, Country, and Industry Relationships in Equity Returns: Implications for Risk Reduction Through International Diversification," *Financial Analysts Journal* (January–February 1976), pp. 32–38.

______, "The Structure of Returns and Gains from International Diversification," in *International Capital Markets,* E. J. Elton and M. J. Gruber, eds. Amsterdam: North-Holland, 1975, pp. 207–220.

LOGUE, D. E., M. SALANT, and R. J. SWEENEY, "International Integration of Financial Markets: Survey, Synthesis, and Results," in *Eurocurrencies and the International Monetary System,* Carl H. Sten, John H. Makin, and Dennis E. Logue, eds. Washington, D.C.: American Enterprise Institute, 1976, pp. 91–137.

MCCABE, G. M., "The Empirical Relationship Between Investment and Financing: A New Look," *Journal of Financial and Quantitative Analysis* (March 1979), pp. 119–135.

MALDONADO, R., and A. SAUNDERS, "International Portfolio Diversification and the Inter-Temporal Stability of International Stock Market Relationships," *Financial Management* (Autumn 1981), pp. 54–63.

MEHRA, R., "On the Financing and Investment Decisions of Multinational Firms in the Presence of Exchange Risks," *Journal of Financial and Quantitative Analysis* (June 1978), pp. 227–244.

MIKHAIL, A. D., and H. A. SHAWKY, "Investment Performance of U.S. Based Multinational Corporations," *Journal of International Business Studies* (Spring–Summer 1979), pp. 53–66.

MINOT, W. G., "Tests for Integration Between Major Western European Capital Markets," *Oxford Economic Papers* (November 1974), pp. 424–439.

NAUMANN-ETIENNE, R., "A Framework for Financial Decisions in MNC," *Journal of Financial and Quantitative Analysis* (November 1974), pp. 859–874.

PROFFITT, D., and N. SEITZ, "The Performance of Internationally Diversified Mutual Funds," *The Journal of Financial and Quantitative Analysis* (July 1978).

REMMERS, H. L., "A Note on Foreign Borrowing Costs," *Journal of International Business Studies* (Fall 1980), pp. 123–134.

REMMERS, L., A. STONEHILL, R. WRIGHT, and T. BEEKHUISEN, "Industry and Size as Debt Ratio Determinants for Manufacturing Internationally," *Financial Management* (Summer 1974), pp. 24–32.

ROBBINS, S. M., and R. B. STOBAUGH, "Financing Foreign Affiliates," *Financial Management* (Winter 1972), pp. 56–65.

______, *Money in the Multinational Enterprise.* New York: Basic Books, 1973.

ROBICHEK, A. A., and M. R. EAKER, "Debt Denomination and Exchange Risk in International Capital Markets," *Financial Management* (Autumn 1976), pp. 11–18.

ROLL, R., "A Critique of the Asset Pricing Theory's Tests," *Journal of Financial Economics* (March 1977), pp. 129–176.

ROLL, R., and B. H. SOLNIK, "A Pure Foreign Exchange Asset Pricing Model," *Journal of International Economics,* no. 7 (1977), pp. 161–179.

ROSS, S. A., "The Current Status of the Capital Asset Pricing Model (CAPM)," *Journal of Finance* (June 1978), pp. 885–901.

RUGMAN, A. M., "Risk Reduction by International Diversification," *Journal of International Business Studies* (Fall 1976), pp. 75–80.

______, "International Diversification by Financial and Direct Investment," *Journal of Economics and Business* (Fall 1977), pp. 31–37.

______, *International Diversification and the Multinational Enterprise.* Lexington, Mass.: Lexington Books, 1979.

SAUNDERS, A., and R. S. WOODWORTH, "Gains from International Portfolio Diversification: U.K. Evidence 1971–1975," *Journal of Business Finance and Accounting* (Autumn 1977), pp. 299–309.

SENBET, L. W., "International Capital Market Equilibrium and the Multinational Firm Financing and Investment Policies," *Journal of Financial and Quantitative Analysis* (September 1979), pp. 455–480.

SEVERN, A. K., "Investor Evaluation of Foreign and Domestic Risk," *Journal of Finance* (May 1974), pp. 545–550.

SEVERN, A. K., and D. R. MEINSTER, "The Use of Multicurrency Financing by the Financial Manager," *Financial Management* (Winter 1978), pp. 45–53.

SHAPIRO, A. C., "Evaluating Financing Costs for Multinational Subsidiaries," *Journal of International Business Studies* (Fall 1975), pp. 25–32.

______, "Financial Structure and Cost of Capital in the Multinational Corporation," *Journal of Financial and Quantitative Analysis* (June 1978), pp. 211–226.

SOLOMON, L. D., "Multinational Business: New Approaches to Financing and Structuring Ventures," *Case Western Reserve Journal of International Law* (Spring 1980), pp. 363–382.

SOLNIK, B. H., "Note on the Validity of the Random Walk for European Stock Prices," *Journal of Finance* (December 1973), pp. 1151–1159.

______, "The International Pricing of Risk: An Empirical Investigation of the World Capital Market Structure," *Journal of Finance* (May 1974), pp. 365–378.

______, "Why Not Diversify Internationally Rather Than Domestically?" *Financial Analysts Journal* (July/August 1974), pp. 48–54.

______, "An Equilibrium Model of the International Capital Market," *Journal of Economic Theory* (August 1974), pp. 500–524.

______, "An International Market Model of Security Price Behavior," *Journal of Financial and Quantitative Analysis* (September 1974), pp. 537–554.

______, "Testing International Asset Pricing: Some Pessimistic Views," *Journal of Finance* (May 1977), pp. 503–512.

STANLEY, M. T., "Capital Structure and Cost of Capital for the Multinational Firm," *Journal of International Business Studies* (Spring/Summer 1981), pp. 103–120.

STAPLETON, R. C., and M. SUBRAHMANYAM, "Market Imperfections, Capital Market Equilibrium, and Corporation Finance," *Journal of Finance* (May 1977), pp. 307–319.

STARR, D. W., "Opportunities for United States Corporate Borrowers in the International Bond Markets," *Financial Executive* (June 1979), pp. 50–59.

STEHLE, R. F., "An Empirical Test of the Alternative Hypothesis of National and International Pricing of Risk Assets," *Journal of Finance* (May 1977), pp. 493–502.

STONEHILL, A., T. BEEKHUISEN, R. WRIGHT, L. REMMERS, N. TOY, A. PARES, A. SHAPIRO, D. EGAN, and T. BATES, "Financial Goals and Debt Ratio Determinants: A Survey of Practice in Five Countries," *Financial Management* (Autumn 1975), pp. 27–41.

SUBRAHMANYAM, M. G., "On the Optimality of International Capital Market Integration," *Journal of Financial Economics,* no. 1, 1975, pp. 3–28.

TOY, N., A. STONEHILL, L. REMMERS, R. WRIGHT, and T. BEEKHUISEN, "A Comparative International Study of Growth, Profitability, and Risk as Determinants of Corporate Debt Ratios in the Manufacturing Sector,"

Journal of Financial and Quantitative Analysis (November 1974), pp. 875–886.

VINSO, J. D., "Financial Planning for the Multinational Corporation with Multiple Goals," *Journal of International Business Studies* (Winter 1982).

WHITE, B. B., and J. R. WOODBURY, III, "Exchange Rate Systems and International Capital Market Integration," *Journal of Money, Credit and Banking* (May 1980), pp. 175–183.

APPENDIX F

International Capital Asset Pricing Model

INTRODUCTION

The capital asset pricing model (CAPM) developed briefly in Chapter 15 as a risk-adjusted pricing mechanism underlying cost of capital theory has been extended to multinational cost of capital theory. The question of international portfolio diversification and its impact on the risk/return tradeoff, as well as impediments to such diversification, was covered in Chapters 12 and 15. The related issue of whether investments in the stocks of geographically diversified MNCs may perform the same diversification function to investors by proxy was also addressed.

This appendix reviews briefly recent contributions to financial theory in this area as well as empirical tests of the International Capital Asset Pricing Model (ICAPM). The discussion of ICAPM is inseparable from the degree of market segmentation, since the assumption of perfect or integrated markets is central to the working of this model. Nevertheless, a multinational firm based in a country with a segmented capital market can lower its cost of capital by accessing equity and debt financing in capital markets outside its country. To what extent this can be achieved and the limitations of ICAPM are also important issues. The integration of international capital markets, including a survey of recent innovations in these markets, was reviewed in some depth in Chapter 10 because they impact in a very fundamental way the cost of capital of today's MNCs.

FINANCIAL THEORY—ICAPM RESTATED

CAPM as a tool for pricing financial assets was developed by Sharpe (1964) and Lintner (1965), as an extension of the basic mean-variance model for equilibrium optimal portfolio choice developed by Markowitz (1959). There are two major conclusions advanced by CAPM with respect to risk/return tradeoff in investment in financial assets:

1. The return on an asset consists of the risk-free rate of return plus a risk premium that is a function of the asset's covariance with the market portfolio (the beta coefficient).
2. It is optimal for each investor to hold a linear combination of the riskless asset and the market portfolio so as to achieve maximum possible return within the limitation of the investor's resources, given his or her risk aversion pattern.

The ICAPM, like its domestic counterpart, is a risk-pricing mechanism in a portfolio context in which all firm specific (or unsystematic) risk is virtually eliminated. It is the pricing of the beta coefficient (the measure of the systematic risk) that is measured along the Capital Market Line. In applying ICAPM to cost of capital theory, there are two basic issues: (1) the impact on beta and the rate of return of the multinational firm's geographically diversified operations, and (2) whether MNCs have a higher debt capacity than their domestic counterparts by virtue of this diversity through direct foreign investment. Alternatively stated, does direct foreign investment result in lowering the cost of capital of the MNC both by decreasing the required rate of return on equity (raising equity prices) and by increasing the debt capacity of the firm?

ICAPM has been empirically tested by a large number of studies, producing conflicting evidence as to its impact on the cost of capital of the MNC compared to the domestic firm. Most of the conflict relates to data problems and testing designs used by financial theorists. There is considerable disagreement as to what constitutes a "world model" in testing equity pricing and risk/return relationships. There is also controversy on how the exchange rate risk should be treated. The incorporation of the exchange risk in the capital budgeting process impacts the acceptance (or rejection) of foreign projects and, therefore, the rate of return from foreign operations. In Chapter 14, the exchange risk was reflected in the periodic cash flows accruing from foreign investment. The alternative of incorporating the exchange risk in the firm's cost of capital may trigger different capital budgeting decisions.

Another problem with ICAPM is that empirical testing of the model has been largely confined to industrial countries with highly developed financial and exchange markets. The applicability of the model's conclusions to LDCs that lack such markets is questionable.[1] The validity of conclusions postulated by financial theory to cost of capital of firms operating in such countries is further clouded by joint venture arrangements required

[1]Marjorie T. Stanley, "Capital Structure and Cost-of-Capital for the Multinational Firm," in *International Finance: Concepts and Issues,* Gerald D. Gay and Robert W. Kolb, eds. (Richmond, Va.: Robert F. Dame, Inc., 1983), p. 568.

by many of these countries. These arrangements affect dividend policy and sourcing of funds, and ultimately the cost of borrowed funds and pricing of equity issues.

The conclusions of ICAPM studies with respect to impact of diversification through direct foreign investment on the capital structure and cost of capital of MNCs are summarized below:

1. International diversification through direct foreign investment has been found to result in some risk reduction by stabilizing the firm's cash flow pattern. Rugman, who tested this hypothesis by using the ratio of foreign sales/total sales as a measure of international diversification, and earnings variance as a proxy for risk, concluded that the former was statistically significant and inversely related to variance of profits. He also found that the ICAPM was not a useful tool for testing diversification through direct foreign investment because of its perfect market assumption, which is not consistent with conditions motivating this investment.[2]

2. A major issue of contention is the degree to which financial and exchange markets are segmented or integrated. If the markets are integrated, a broadly diversified world model would be the relevant one for determining an MNC's cost of capital. The general consensus seems to suggest that such markets are sufficiently integrated among industrial countries to validate the working of ICAPM. The model does not seem to extend to MNCs' operations in LDCs. However, MNCs can reap some of the benefits of capital market integration through intracompany transfer of funds and transfer pricing.

3. Most of the empirical studies on market integration have concentrated on the degree of correlation among return on equity investments located in different countries. The crucial test of market integration is not the degree of correlation among such returns, but rather the degree to which assets located in different countries are priced on the basis of common criteria.

The problem of interpreting high correlation among the rates of return (and cost of capital) in different markets as an evidence of integrated markets has been frequently addressed in the literature. While zero (or low) correlation indicates the existence of market segmentation, high or strong correlation cannot be used as a proof of integrated markets. Neither can rising or falling correlation among markets indicate higher or lower integration among those markets.[3]

4. Irrespective of the theoretical and empirical difficulties that surround this area of investigation, none of the studies presents evidence

[2]Alan M. Rugman, *International Diversification and the Multinational Enterprise* (Lexington, Mass.: Lexington Books: D. C. Heath and Company, 1979), pp. 11–13, 16–17.

[3]Steven W. Kohlhagen, "Overlapping National Investment Portfolios: Evidence and Implications of International Integration of Secondary Markets for Financial Assets," in *Research in International Business and Finance,* Hawkins and Levich, eds., Vol. 3 (Greenwich, Conn.: JAI Press, 1983), p. 117.

indicating that the cost of equity is higher for the multinational firm than for the purely domestic one, other things being equal.[4]

5. Although diversification through direct foreign investment appears to increase the debt capacity of the MNC, the concept of the optimal capital structure for the MNC is much more complex than it is for the purely domestic firm. Factors which could influence the optimal structure include the foreign exchange risk, tax differentials, and local norms for operating subsidiaries, among others. The consensus is that available evidence through empirical testing does not "provide a definitive answer to the question of optimum capital structure for the multinational firm, nor to how it is determined."[5]

6. The most serious methodological problem with empirical testing of ICAPM undertaken by financial theorists is that they use *ex-post* data to test *ex ante* hypotheses. Critics of the design of these tests and conclusions drawn from them pointed out that not only the hypothesis (of the ICAPM) was being tested, but also of the existence of risk premium and the rationality of investors' expectations. Because of these and other problems alluded to earlier, these critics see little possibility that a correct empirical test of the ICAPM can ever be devised.[6]

BIBLIOGRAPHY

COHN, RICHARD A., and JOHN J. PRINGLE, "Imperfections in International Financial Markets: Implications for Risk Premia and the Cost of Capital to Firms," *Journal of Finance* (March 1973), pp. 59–66.

ELLIOTT, J. WALTER, "The Cost of Capital and U.S. Capital Investment: A Test of Alternative Concepts," *Journal of Finance* (September 1980), pp. 981–999.

HUGHES, JOHN S., DENNIS E. LOGUE, and RICHARD J. SWEENEY, "Corporate International Diversification and Market Assigned Measures of Risk and Diversification," *Journal of Financial and Quantitative Analysis* (November 1975), pp. 627–637.

KOHERS, THEODORE, "The Effect of Multinational Operations on the Cost of Equity Capital of U.S. Corporations: An Empirical Study," *Management International Review,* (February 1975), pp. 121–124.

KOHLHAGEN, STEVEN W., "Overlapping National Investment Portfolios: Evidence and Implications of International Integration of Secondary

[4]Stanley, "Capital Structure and Cost-of-Capital for the Multinational Firm," p. 569.
[5]*Ibid.,* p. 569.
[6]Kohlhagen, "Overlapping National Investment Portfolios," p. 116.

Markets for Financial Assets," in *Research in International Business and Finance,* Hawkins and Levich, eds., Vol. 3. Greenwich, Conn.: JAI Press, 1983, pp. 113–137.

LEE, WAYNE Y., and KANWAL S. SCHDEVA, "The Role of the Multinational Firm in the Integration of Segmented Capital Markets," *Journal of Finance* (May 1977), pp. 479–492.

LINTNER, JOHN, "Security Prices, Risk, and Maximal Gains from Diversification," *Journal of Finance* (December 1965), pp. 587–615.

LOGUE, DENNIS E., MICHAEL A. SALANT, and RICHARD J. SWEENEY, "International Integration of Financial Markets: Survey, Synthesis, and Results," in *Eurocurrencies and the International Monetary System,* Carl H. Stem, John H. Makim, and Dennis E. Logue, eds. Washington, D.C.:American Enterprise Institute for Public Policy Research, 1976, pp. 91–137.

MEHRA, RAJNISH, "On the Financing and Investment Decisions of Multinational Firms in the Presence of Exchange Risk," *Journal of Financial and Quantitative Analysis* (June 1978), pp. 227–244.

RABICHEK, ALEXANDER A., "Foreign Exchange Hedging and the Capital Asset Pricing Model," *Journal of Finance* (June 1978), pp. 1011–1018.

ROLL, RICHARD, "A Critique of the Asset Pricing Theory's Tests," *Journal of Financial Economics* (March 1977), pp. 129–176.

RUGMAN, ALAN M., "Discussion: Corporate International Diversification and Market Assigned Measures of Risk and Diversification," *Journal of Financial and Quantitative Analysis* (November 1975), pp. 651–652.

SHAPIRO, ALAN C., "Financial Structure and the Cost of Capital in the Multinational Corporation," *Journal of Financial and Quantitative Analysis* (June 1978), pp. 211–226.

SOLNIK, BRUNO H., "Testing International Asset Pricing: Some Pessimistic Views," *Journal of Finance* (May 1977), pp. 503–512.

STANLEY, MARJORIE T., "Capital Structure and Cost-of-Capital for the Multinational Firm," in *International Finance: Concepts and Issues,* Gerald D. Gay and Robert W. Kolb, eds. Richmond, Va.: Robert F. Dame, Inc., 1983, pp. 550–570.

STEHLE, RICHARD, "An Empirical Test of the Alternative Hypothesis of National and International Pricing of Risky Assets," *Journal of Finance* (May 1977), pp. 493–502.

STONEHILL, A., and K. DULLUM, *Internationalizing the Cost of Capital.* New York: John Wiley, 1982.

CASE STUDY

Alpha Beta Aircraft, Inc.

Alpha Beta Aircraft, Inc. (ABA, Inc.) is a major aerospace firm based in Seattle, Washington, with total sales of $22.2 billion in 1984. The company has manufacturing and assembly operations in ten countries outside the United States, with foreign operations accounting for upward of 45 percent of total revenue. ABA, Inc. makes military and civilian aircraft and is a recognized pioneer in space research and technology. Worried over the prospects of declining sales (total sales declined in each of 1984 and 1983) and stiffening competition in the industry, ABA, Inc. has been looking into opportunities to diversify into electronic communication systems, construction and operation of airport facilities, and systems management.

Most of the international expansion program was accomplished in the 1970s, as the company sought to offset the sharp decline in sales of military and civilian aircraft. The slump faced by all aircraft companies was due to a drop in defense orders (following the end of hostilities in Vietnam) and sharply higher oil prices, which adversely affected most airlines.

Capital Structure and Cost of Capital Policies

ABA, Inc. maintains a capital structure which is roughly in line with the norm prevailing in the aircraft and aerospace industry. Measured in terms of long-term debt as a ratio of long-term debt and equity ($D/D + E$), the ratio has been in the range of 40 to 45 percent during the past ten years. The company strives to adhere, to the extent possible, to these ratios in structuring the finances of its affiliates abroad. On occasion, where debt financing is available on favorable terms, the target debt ratio may be exceeded, but in no case has it been allowed to go over 60 percent. In these situations, it has been the policy of the company to gradually reduce the debt ratio (through debt retirement, income retention, or both) back to the target level.

ABA, Inc. uses discounted cash flow analysis (DCF) to evaluate all projects. Domestic projects must pass a hurdle rate based on the marginal cost of capital (MCC) as long as they have a degree of risk comparable to its overall domestic operations. For entirely new product lines and processes and for projects which belong to a higher risk category, a risk premium ranging between two to five percentage points is added to the hurdle rate. For foreign projects it uses an all-equity rate measured by the acceptable rate of return on equity on similar or comparable investment in the host country (if available), or the rate of return required by its own stockholders, whichever is higher.

Capital budgeting policy requires that all risks that are unique to foreign investments be reflected in cash flow forecasts, rather than in the discount rate. The capital budgeting evaluation process also credits the projects' cash flow with the present value of the tax savings attributable to the increased borrowing capacity of the firm (since an all-equity rate is used in discounting future cash flows). All of the firm's foreign projects have so far been in industrial countries, where the political risk was judged to be minimal.

Financing Policies

ABA's policy in financing expansion has been to rely primarily on internal financing to generate equity funds, avoiding dilution of shareholders' interest engendered by issuing new common stock. This policy has frequently resulted in sharp cuts in dividend payments whenever operational results were disappointing. For debt financing, either domestic U.S. bonds or Eurobond issues have been used, depending on which source proved to offer the lower overall cost at the time.

ABA's investment bankers, The First Morgan Corporation, have recently (early 1985) informed the Chief Financial Officer, Mr. Eugene McCladden, that despite the company's disappointing performance in recent years, future borrowing operations are likely to be less costly than the company's last bond issue in 1981. In that year, a dollar-dominated 15-year Eurobond issue was sold to European investors. The issue was priced at par and carried a 15 percent coupon rate. The investment bankers indicated that if a comparable issue were to be sold in 1985 or early 1986, the coupon rate would probably be around 12 percent.

The New Venture

In early 1985 ABA, Inc. was contacted by Zublin A. G., a large West German firm based in Dusseldorf, to form a joint venture with ABA for constructing complete airports in developing countries. The objective of the new firm, to be based in Dusseldorf, is to join ABA's expertise in electronic communication systems and airport facilities with Zublin's wide experience in a number of countries in the construction of port terminals, grain silos, and other types of terminal facilities over the past 30 years.

ABA's Chief Executive Officer became increasingly enthusiastic about the joint venture, particularly after a preliminary investigation committee strongly recommended the association with Zublin A. G. The committee's recommendation was primarily based on the German firm's remarkable record in constructing large facilities in a number of developing countries, particularly in the Middle East. His enthusiasm was also due in part to the realization that the venture fitted well ABA's current thrust to diversify out of the aerospace business and revitalize the company's sagging profitability.

Realizing that the proposal needed thorough investigation, the CEO assigned the task to a committee headed by Mr. McCladden which included the vice president in charge of foreign operations, the treasurer, the head of the Systems Management Division, and the head of the Capital Budgeting Division. The committee delegated the task of obtaining detailed information (from Zublin A. G.) on capitalization, projected cash flows and costs over a 10–15-year period, and of evaluating the viability of the venture to Ms. Hilda Skillstadt, head of the Capital Budgeting Division. Mr. McCladden himself took the responsibility of looking into the financing of ABA's share of the initial investment which was estimated at $1.2 billion, including working capital requirements.

Ms. Skillstadt spent most of June 1985 in Germany assembling background data on the proposed firm and compiling cost and cash flow data needed for final evaluation. During the course of discussions with the staff of Zublin's capital budgeting division, she learned that Zublin has somewhat different cost of capital criteria for evaluating projects. For domestic projects, it uses a hurdle rate of 30 percent based on cash return on net assets (CRONA).[1] For foreign projects, the discounted cash flow method is used. Projects have to meet a basic hurdle rate of 20 percent plus a risk premium, depending on its assessment of the political risk in the host country.

The committee met twice during September to examine the reports of Mr. McCladden and Ms. Skillstadt. Before the formal task of subjecting the project's cash flows to the firm's established capital budgeting procedure, the committee needed to determine ABA's current cost of capital and the appropriate hurdle rate for the new venture.

Mr. McCladden's Report

On the basis of extensive consultation with ABA's investment bankers, Mr. McCladden proposed to raise $600 million from a 15-year Eurobond issue denominated in U.S. dollars priced at 102 (2 percent above par) with a coupon rate of 13.5 percent. The First Morgan Corporation agreed to underwrite the issue at or about par, depending on the exact timing of the flotation.

[1]CRONA relates cash flow to average net investment computed for each year, as well as over the life cycle of the project. CRONA disregards the time value of money in computing the average rate of return on investment. For a project with even cash flows (an annuity) CRONA is the reciprocal of the payback period.

There are two alternatives to the Eurobond issue. A domestic U.S. bond issue could be floated at approximately the same terms as the Eurobond issue. Both issues have a sinking fund provision, retiring annually 5 percent of the total face value of the bonds to take effect one year from the date of issue. Both are callable beginning five years from the date of issue at 106 with the premium sliding by one-half of 1 percent annually.

Alternatively, a deutsche mark convertible 15-year bond issue may be sold in Germany. The investment bankers indicated that, if such issue was to be floated in late 1985, it would be priced at 98 at an 8 percent coupon. However, the issue would be sold to investors on a best-effort basis, costing ABA 2 percent in management and distribution fees. The bonds are callable at 105 beginning at the third anniversary with no sinking fund provisions. They are convertible into ABA's shares at a price which exceeds the closing price in the New York Stock Exchange on the date of the issue or three months from the issue date, whichever is lower, plus a premium of 15 percent. The conversion is to take place at the spot U.S. dollar/deutsche mark exchange rate on the date of conversion.

The investment bankers advised that the equity portion of financing be raised in two separate common stock issues to take place three months and six months after signing the agreement with Zublin A. G., respectively. This proposal was justified by the improving trend in equity prices in the United States, and the fact that not all funds would be required by the new firm at the outset.

While the investment bankers could not make a commitment at the time, they indicated their willingness to underwrite these issues at a share price equal to the closing price on the New York Stock Exchange on the day prior to the signing of the underwriting agreement less 7 percent. ABA's shares closed on September 15, 1985, at $20.25.

Ms. Skillstadt's Report

In her report Ms. Skillstadt outlined the company's existing policy for evaluating the proposed joint venture with Zublin A. G. She listed three unique aspects of the new venture which differentiate it from ABA's present operation in foreign countries:

1. All existing foreign operations were carried out by wholly owned affiliates of ABA, Inc.
2. All these affiliates were located in industrial countries where the political risk was deemed to be minimal. Business with firms or governments of developing countries was confined to export transactions denominated in U.S. dollars against confirmed irrevocable letters of credit. Although the new firm was to be based in Germany, it would undertake construction and contracting activities in developing countries with considerably higher political exposure.

3. Existing foreign operations were primarily confined to the aerospace and aircraft business, in which ABA had long experience. The new venture would involve the firm for the first time in the construction of airport and other terminal facilities, as well as in other areas where ABA had little expertise.

Ms. Skillstadt also reported that the capital budgeting criteria used by large contracting and construction firms in Germany vary widely. Zublin uses a CRONA hurdle rate of 30 percent for domestic projects and an internal rate of return (IRR) of 20 percent plus a political risk premium for foreign projects. A number of large firms with considerable contracting work in developing countries use a hurdle rate based on the MCC adjusted upward for an appropriate risk premium. A number of other firms with large foreign projects still employ the payback period as the primary evaluation criterion, generally requiring a fairly short duration of three to four years.

At the end of her presentation, Ms. Skillstadt sought directives from the committee as to the appropriate hurdle rate for evaluating the new project. She also sought the committee's approval to proceed with the evaluation process along the following lines:

1. The MCC based on the weighted average cost of capital (with appropriately calculated proportions of debt and equity) should be the basis for deriving the hurdle rate.
2. The new venture represented a unique risk situation for ABA, not only in terms of moving into activities which are unfamiliar to its management, but also because its operations will be conducted primarily in developing countries.
3. Whatever risk premium is eventually decided upon, the decision must take into account the potential stabilizing impact of the new project on ABA's overall cash flow.
4. The hurdle rate must also take into account the current practices of German construction firms (Zublin A. G. and others) which have had experience in major contracting work in the same markets where the proposed joint venture will be operating.

The committee charged Ms. Skillstadt with the task of investigating and recommending an appropriate hurdle rate for ABA, Inc.-Zublin A. G. proposed joint venture. Her findings were due by the end of November, so that capital budgeting evaluation and final recommendation on the proposal could be made before the end of the year.

Additional Data

As she was pondering the task assigned to her by the committee, Ms. Skillstadt was aware that she needed additional information apart from the financial statements and the market and financial data shown in Exhibits 1 and 2. She was also wondering whether ABA's erratic and poor per-

Exhibit 1. Alpha Beta Aircraft, Inc. Consolidated[1] Balance Sheets for Years Ending December 31 (in millions of dollars)

	1984	1983	1982	1981	1980
Cash and marketable securities	476.9	826.1	592.2	760.1	546.2
Notes and accounts receivable	1,352.7	1,391.0	959.1	985.9	571.9
Receivables under government contracts	1,195.6	1,064.1	992.6	902.8	932.7
Inventories	10,608.9	12,826.2	13,951.7	13,062.5	9,586.0
Prepayments	63.8	60.0	64.6	112.0	120.6
Total current assets	13,697.9	16,167.4	16,560.2	15,823.3	11,757.4
Leased aircraft	2,594.2	2,657.8	2,955.3	2,793.5	2,783.0
Property, plant, and equipment	9,914.5	10,083.1	10,337.6	10,348.5	9,657.3
Less: Depreciation reserve	6,335.2	5,881.0	5,356.4	4,646.2	3,782.6
Net property account	6,173.5	6,859.9	7,936.5	8,495.8	8,662.7
Other assets	41.0	39.8	39.2	39.7	42.1
Total assets	19,912.4	23,067.0	24,535.9	24,358.8	20,462.2
Notes payable to banks	1,002.0	2,355.9	1,075.9	1,387.6	—
Notes and accounts payable	3,044.5	4,931.1	7,112.3	6,890.4	5,560.0
Accrued wages and taxes	1,404.3	1,218.4	1,256.5	1,457.4	1,688.8
Current portion of long-term debt	1,333.6	1,158.7	969.5	374.0	137.5
Total current liabilities	6,784.4	9,664.1	10,414.2	10,109.4	7,386.3
Deferred income taxes and investment credit	328.5	574.7	711.4	878.9	1,087.1
Long-term debt	4,704.7	4,937.9	5,834.0	5,919.9	4,403.8
Capital stock ($10 par)	4,185.4	4,184.3	4,184.3	4,184.3	4,171.0
Retained earnings	3,909.3	3,705.9	3,392.0	3,266.4	3,414.0
Total stockholders' equity	8,094.7	7,890.2	7,576.3	7,450.7	7,585.0
Total claims	19,912.3	23,067.0	24,535.9	24,358.8	20,462.2

[1] All accounts of foreign affiliates were fully consolidated in the parent's financial statements.

Exhibit 2. Alpha Beta Aircraft, Inc. Selected Consolidated[1] Income Statement Items for Years Ending December 31 (in millions of dollars)

	1984	1983	1982	1981	1980
Sales (net)	22,179.3	28,452.7	34,417.4	26,531.7	30,644.4
Operating profit	542.8	391.8	575.6	145.1	1,556.6
Other income	502.9	882.6	486.2	470.7	221.8
Total income	1,045.7	1,274.4	1,061.8	615.8	1,778.4
Interest expense	528.2	528.9	717.1	456.3	313.1
Taxable income	517.5	745.5	344.7	159.5	1,465.3
Federal income tax	232.9	350.4	137.9	63.8	688.7
Net income	284.6	395.1	206.8	95.7	766.6
Retained earnings, beginning of period	3,705.9	3,392.0	3,266.4	3,414.0	2,880.4
Dividends	81.2	81.2	81.2	243.0	243.0
Retained earnings, end of period	3,909.3	3,705.9	3,392.0	3,266.4	3,414.0

SELECTED FINANCIAL DATA AND RATIOS

	1984	1983	1982	1981	1980
Market share price ($) H	$13\frac{1}{2}$	$11\frac{3}{8}$	15	$30\frac{3}{4}$	$35\frac{1}{2}$
L	$8\frac{1}{4}$	$5\frac{1}{8}$	$6\frac{1}{2}$	$17\frac{1}{8}$	$20\frac{5}{8}$
Year end	$12\frac{1}{8}$	9	$6\frac{7}{8}$	$19\frac{7}{8}$	$26\frac{1}{8}$
Earnings per share ($)	$0.68	$0.94	$0.49	$0.22	$1.86
Dividend per share ($)	$0.20	$0.20	$0.20	$0.58	$0.58
Return on stockholders' equity (%)	3.5	5.0	2.7	1.3	10.2
Long-term debt/long-term debt + equity (%)[2]	29.4	32.3	39.1	42.7	36.0

[1]Includes operations of all foreign affiliates.
[2]Long-term debt minus the current portion of long-term debt divided by long-term debt plus stockholders' equity.

formance in recent years (which forced a sharp dividend cut in 1982) had invalidated the use of the Gordon Shapiro Model in calculating the required rate of return by shareholders.

At her request, the staff of the capital budgeting division compiled the following data:

- The average rate of return on equity for ABA during the period 1974–1984 (based on changes in market price of shares plus dividends) amounted to 13.7 percent, compared to 15.5 percent for 15 aerospace companies.
- The average rate of return on equity for Zublin A. G. during the five-year period 1980–1984 (calculated on the same basis) was 21 percent. For ten large German contracting firms (including Zublin) for which foreign operations account for more than half of total revenue, the average rate of return during the same period was about 25 percent.
- A recently released study by a major investment research organization showed that the average rate of return on equity for 2500 diversified manufacturing firms over the five years ended December 31, 1984, was 13.1 percent.
- The rate of return on the stocks included in the S & P 500 index for the year ended September 30, 1985, was 14.5 percent. The yield on Treasury bonds on September 30, 1985, was 10.6 percent.
- The most recent beta for ABA, Inc. (June 30, 1985) published by Value Line was 1.78, compared to an average beta of 1.58 for 15 aerospace firms. The corresponding measure of systematic risk for ten large German contracting firms (including Zublin) at the end of 1984 was about 1.95.
- The staff also produced an overall assessment of prospects for interest rates and equity markets for 1986. On the basis of available forecasts at that time, the staff reported that interest rates were projected to hold steady at the prevailing levels or decline slightly. They also indicated that the majority of investment analysts expected the bull equity market to continue well into 1986.

16

Assessment and Forecasting of the Political Risk

INTRODUCTION

All international trade and finance transactions involve a political risk in varying degrees. Goods and services moving across boundaries may be subjected to various forms of controls and restrictions by different political jurisdictions. However, since foreign trade transactions involve essentially short-term claims, their exposure to the political risk is marginal. The political risk impacts to a significant degree direct foreign investment as well as portfolio investment. The long-term nature of these financial decisions and the cash flows they generate over a number of years make them especially susceptible to this risk. We are not suggesting that short-term capital flows, such as time deposits and short-term Eurocurrency loans, are immune to the political risk. Rather, because of the short time span involved in these financial transactions, the variables underlying this risk are not likely to change significantly.

Political risk encompasses a wide spectrum of events or occurrences initiated by host governments, ranging from temporary restrictions or controls imposed on affiliates of foreign firms, to an outright expropriation of these firms. The genesis of the political risk is often traced to the presumed inevitable conflict between the interests of MNCs and those of the host countries. We have suggested in Chapter 1 that, as profit-maximizing organizations, MNCs' strategies and policies in managing their affiliates may run afoul of economic priorities of their hosts. This is much more likely to be the case if the host country is a typical LDC afflicted with limited resource base and financial imbalances. This basic conflict is not inevitable, nor is political risk confined to the confrontation between profit-maximizing MNCs and development-oriented host countries.

Political risk has long been a major consideration in international lending. Banks have always factored in the sovereign risk and established country lending limits in evaluating loan requests by foreign private and public borrowers. Country risk evaluation is a major factor in the Eurocurrency syndicated loan market, which was discussed in Chapter 9. Nevertheless, it is the sharp increase in direct foreign investment in the post-WWII era, and the rising incidence of nationalization and expropriation of foreign firms that has given prominence to the assessment of political risk. Several approaches involving statistical and quantitative techniques have been developed to forecast and measure political risks.

This chapter will examine the various types or forms of political risk, methods of forecasting political risk, as well as a number of quantitative approaches to measure this risk. It will also look briefly at the historical record of expropriation by host governments of foreign affiliates operating under their jurisdiction.

TYPES OF POLITICAL RISK

Political risks may be grouped into the following categories:

1. Discriminatory practices that subject affiliates of foreign firms to requirements which are not imposed on domestic firms.
2. Operational restrictions which, although they are theoretically applicable to foreign and domestic firms alike, impinge primarily on the freedom of operations of foreign firms.
3. Expropriation, that is, the seizure of assets of foreign firms by the host government, or forced sale of their business assets to local interests.

This list does not cover damage to properties or earning capacity by riots, revolutions, and other acts of violence, or strikes. Some of these actions, particularly strikes, are sometimes instigated by authorities of the host government.

Discriminatory Practices

Host governments may choose to subject affiliates of foreign MNCs to payments of certain fees or taxes, or restrictive practices which are not applicable to domestic firms. In addition to discriminatory taxes or fees for certain transactions, these include higher tariffs on their imports, quantitative restrictions on imports of raw materials and components, and higher prices for utilities and other services than those charged to domestic firms. Another form of discriminatory practice is allowing foreign firms to operate only as joint ventures, with local investors holding a majority position.

These actions are usually taken by host governments when changes in the local political environment are such that would result in their characterizing foreign firms as hostile to the government's economic interests. Frequently such practices are a prelude to confiscation or nationalization. Although the motivation behind such practices is often political, some authorities may justify them as a means of raising badly needed revenues, or in the case of restrictions on imports, economizing on scarce foreign exchange resources.

Some of these actions may involve revoking a number of earlier concessions or incentives accorded to foreign firms to induce them to establish affiliates in the host country. Although such actions are not discriminatory, since such concessions were not extended to domestic firms in the first place, they do constitute a breach of agreements reached between the parent company and the host government.

Operational Restrictions

These restrictions impinge on the ability of an affiliate to conduct its business in a profitable manner, or limit the ability of the parent company to receive regular transfer of funds from its affiliates. This category also includes imposition of certain employment policies on foreign firms, such as staffing a stated proportion of supervisory or managerial positions with local employees.

Host governments may justify these restrictions on the grounds that they are in the best interests of the national economy and that they are not discriminatory, since they apply to all firms. In practice, however, only affiliates of foreign firms find such practices restrictive, since domestic firms need not make regular transfer of funds and use mostly local managerial talent anyway.

The most common form of operational restrictions is the *blockage* of funds, defined as restricting transfer of funds to the parent company, which may be total or partial, temporary or permanent. The most usual form of blockage is the restriction, most often permanent, on the percentage of the net profits of the affiliate which can be remitted to the parent firm. Blockage may be extended to other transfers such as royalties and management fees, as well as payments of interest and principal on loans advanced by the parent. Countries, particularly LDCs experiencing a severe foreign exchange shortage, may block all transfers during a period of stringency, even when the right to remit funds is spelled out in the agreement negotiated with the investing MNC. A total blockage of funds that is permanent is tantamount to sequestering of business assets. This is sometimes referred to as "creeping expropriation," since the return on these assets cannot be received by the shareholders of the parent firm.

Expropriation

Expropriation, the seizure of foreign assets by a host country, is a right of sovereign states recognized by international law. This right is circumscribed by the obligation of the expropriating entity to make adequate and prompt compensation in convertible currencies. Expropriation is sometimes distinguished from confiscation in that the latter denotes seizure *without* a fair compensation. While expropriation singles out foreign firms in a certain industry, nationalization is an act whereby the state takes over all privately owned firms in a certain industry, domestic and foreign. In practice, this distinction is often rendered insignificant by the fact that all firms in the nationalized industry are foreign-owned.

ANALYSIS OF PAST PATTERNS

Analysts of political risk attempt to discern host countries' propensity to expropriate foreign firms by examining the historical record. The record may also throw some light on industries or economic activities which are more likely to be expropriated than others. There is no comprehensive record covering all instances of expropriation or nationalization. An obvious problem is that control over foreign assets by a host country often takes the form of a forced sale to domestic private investors, or a planned divestment, rather than an officially proclaimed act of expropriation.

There are obvious pitfalls in attempting to forecast future expropriation patterns on the basis of the historical record. Political risk patterns are highly changeable. The rise of nationalism among newly independent LDCs dominated the political climate of the 1960s and 1970s, which witnessed a flurry of expropriation acts in Latin America, Africa, and the Middle East. The political climate of the early and mid-1980s has been characterized by a more sober and realistic assessment of the role of foreign investment in the process of economic development.

Past patterns of takeovers in terms of geographic region, industry, operating characteristics, and form of seizure were examined in two fairly comprehensive studies.[1] These studies delineated the following major patterns in takeovers during the periods covered:

[1]The study by Hawkins, Mintz, and Provissiero included 170 takeovers occurring between 1946 and 1973; see "Government Takeovers of U.S. Foreign Affiliates," *Journal of International Business Studies* (Spring 1976), pp. 3–16. The second study, by David G. Bradley, covered 114 takeovers in the 1960–1976 period; see "Managing Against Expropriation," *Harvard Business Review* (July–August 1977), pp. 75–83.

1. Almost all takeovers occurred in LDCs, with Latin America accounting for about half, followed by Africa and the Middle East. LDCs in Asia had the least incidence of expropriation.
2. Governmental takeovers, except in a few countries, have been selective and targeted at natural resource-based extractive industries, financial institutions, and public utilities in that order. Affiliates of foreign firms engaged in manufacturing activities were less prone to takeover.
3. There has been an increasing vulnerability of foreign manufacturing firms to expropriation in recent years. Among manufacturing industries, those which are large, in relation to the size and resources of the host country, highly visible, or enjoy a monopoly situation are considered likely candidates for expropriation.

Expropriation does not mean a total loss to investors in the parent country. Some form of compensation is paid to the parent company in 90 percent of takeovers,[2] although the fairness and adequacy of the compensation are difficult to gauge. In a large number of past takeovers, the parent company retained relationship with the host country market in the form of management contracts. The continuing stream of profits from this source offset to some extent losses sustained by the parent. Moreover, the parent company may be in a position to write off losses sustained by expropriation against their overall profits, thus reducing the financial burden of the takeover. Dealing with imminent expropriation and post-expropriation strategies will be examined in Chapter 17.

FORECASTING THE POLITICAL RISK

Forecasting political risk is a complex undertaking involving first a thorough collection of relevant economic and sociopolitical data, and then subjection of the collected data to a careful analysis for the purpose of reaching an overall appraisal or assessment. Multinational banks and other financial institutions involved in international lending maintain and update country reports for the purpose of evaluating risks of foreign loans and establishing country exposure limits. These reports contain a capsule of relevant financial, economic, and political data, followed by an overall assessment of likely trends. Financial institutions rely both on data gathered by their own staff, and on reports prepared and published by international financial institutions and other agencies.

MNCs face a more difficult task in forecasting political risk than international bankers, due to the long-term nature of direct foreign investment and the higher probability of conflict between their own interests and those

[2]J. D. Daniels, E. W. Ogram, Jr., and L. H. Radebaugh, *International Business Environments and Operations,* 3rd ed. (Reading, Mass.: Addison-Wesley, 1982), p. 449.

of the host country. It is the interface with host countries over a long period of time, under changing economic and political circumstances, that makes political risk forecasting for the MNC a complex yet necessary task.

MNCs have different approaches to the task of political risk forecasting. Large MNCs with extensive foreign operations rely primarily on their in-house intelligence gathering, supplemented in some difficult and volatile situations by outside expert opinion. Smaller MNCs rely heavily on data gathered by international banks, and often obtain needed information from specialized firms which regularly prepare and update political risk assessment reports on a large number of countries.

What to Look For

Irrespective of how the data is gathered and the format in which it is presented, the key factors or variables the MNC's manager should be looking for include:

1. The country's attitude and policies toward foreign investment
2. The country's financial and economic conditions and potential for development
3. The country's political stability, as reflected by its sociopolitical structure, system of government, and level of achievement of the people's aspirations
4. The relation of the project under consideration to the country's economic development and goals, its visibility, and the degree of its indispensability

Each of these main variables encompasses a large number of subvariables, of which some can be quantified, or expressed in a definitive manner, but most call for a subjective and judgmental evaluation. This is true particularly for variables 1, 3, and 4. The focus of the data collection process should be such as to throw light on three key issues: (1) the country's present discriminatory and restrictive practices, (2) the country's propensity to impose restrictions or expropriate the project under consideration in the future, and (3) the project's propensity to be expropriated by the host country.

Analysis and Appraisal of Data

Once data on the key variables are collected, the next task is to subject the data to a painstaking analysis with a view to reaching an overall assessment of the political risk. The finished product may range from a brief country report highlighted by the analyst's appraisal of trends and expected developments, to an elaborate quantitative index of political stability.

A technique which is often used to assess the political risk is to conduct a survey in which experts from within the MNC and outside are asked to evaluate the variables that have been identified. These evaluations are then combined, some system of weights being used, to produce a composite index of political risk. The experts are also asked to assign confidence estimates for the index so as to gauge its degree of reliability. While both the evaluation and confidence estimation stages are subjective and judgmental in nature, this method allows a large number of variables to be combined in a meaningful overall composite which can provide an intelligent basis for the investment decision.

Alternatively, to economize on the resources needed to complete this process, the MNC may opt for indices prepared and published by independent organizations such as Business International Corporation's Country Assessment Service and Frost and Sullivan's World Political Risk Forecasts. The former surveys some 75 countries twice a year, while the latter surveys 60 countries every month. Indices prepared by these and similar organizations have the advantage of being based on up-to-date data collected by their vast networks. They may also reduce the cost of political risk assessment, particularly for relatively small MNCs which do not compile data on a regular basis. They have, however, a basic disadvantage compared to in-house political risk analysis. The latter relates the political risk attributes of the host country to the particular vulnerabilities of the specific project that the MNC is contemplating. In view of the varying degree of sensitivity of different industries to political risk, it provides a better basis for judgment than an overall country rating. The in-house approach also enables the parent firm to factor in its geographic diversification pattern in the analysis process by integrating the new project in its worldwide foreign investment strategy.

Quantitative Methods of Political Risk Analysis

We will now examine three quantitative and somewhat sophisticated approaches to political risk analysis. These approaches have in common the measurement and ranking of complex and interrelated economic and sociopolitical factors in a certain country to arrive at an overall index of political stability, or the probability of its expropriating foreign firms. A word of caution is in order here. The use of statistical and quantitative techniques in the area of political risk analysis does not guarantee that the outcome is more accurate, or more usable for decision-making purposes, than the simpler methods. As stated earlier, their principal advantage lies in summing up an array of complex variables into a meaningful overall quantitative index. The margin of error in these indices is difficult to estimate, but is obviously large. A helpful supplement to the indices produced by these methods is an estimate of the degree of confidence placed on them by those who participate in the process of evaluating the component variables.

The quantitative methods will be illustrated by three models: (1) Stobaugh's analysis of probability of nationalization, (2) the Haendel-West-Meadow Political System Stability Index, and (3) Knudsen's National Propensity to Expropriate Model.

Stobaugh's Analysis of Probability of Nationalization

Exhibit 16-1 illustrates the application of the decision tree technique, a form of probability analysis, to appraise the chances of expropriation occurring in year one. Probabilities of events' occurring are indicated along the tree branches. Probabilities are then multiplied along the branches and summarized in the right-hand column, which adds up to 1.00. The probabilities of certain events' occurring are subjectively determined by an analysis based largely on past patterns of events. The analysis indicates that the probability of the affiliate's not being nationalized is .810, and the probability of its being nationalized with no compensation is .095, that is, less than 10 percent.

The analysis demonstrates that a government overthrow in the host country does not automatically lead to expropriation, as the host country must weigh the pros and cons of such a move. The probability of expropriation is higher if the new government is dominated by socialists or radical elements. An act of expropriation, if it occurs, may be followed by some form of compensation which may or may not be adequate. The probability of expropriation's occurring without any compensation may be calculated as follows:

Probability of expropriation without compensation

= Probability of government overthrow × Probability of new government's being left wing × Probability of affiliate's being expropriated by new government × Probability of no compensation's being paid after expropriation + Probability of government overthrow × Probability of new government's being right wing × Probability of affiliate's being expropriated by new right wing government × Probability of no compensation after expropriation

or

$$= [.500 \times .600 \times .500 \times .500] + [.500 \times .400 \times .200 \times .500]$$

$$= .075 + .020 = .095$$

The Haendel-West-Meadow Political System Stability Index

The Haendel-West-Meadow (H-W-M) Political System Stability Index (PSSI) represents an attempt to overcome a major weakness of probability

Exhibit 16-1. Probability Analysis — Year 1: Government Overthrow

[000] = Probability

Regrouping Outcomes:	
Plant not Nationalized	[.810]
Plant Nationalized	
—with adequate compensation	[.034]
—with inadequate compensation	[.061]
—with no compensation	[.095]
Total	[1.000]

Source: Reprinted by permission of the *Harvard Business Review.* An exhibit from "How to Analyze Foreign Investment Climates" by Robert Stobaugh (Steptember/October 1969).

analysis and survey approaches, namely, their reliance on subjective estimates of probability of certain events' occurring, or attitude inputs on the part of respondents to surveys. The H-W-M technique breaks down the variables impacting on political stability into components that are measurable objectively, then reaggregate these measures into an overall index.

The H-W-M index (Exhibit 16-2) is composed of three equally weighted subindexes encompassing (1) socioeconomic characteristics, (2) social conflict characteristics, and (3) governmental processes characteristics. These subindexes are in turn derived from 15 underlying indicators

Exhibit 16-2. Formation of Political System Stability Index (PSSI)

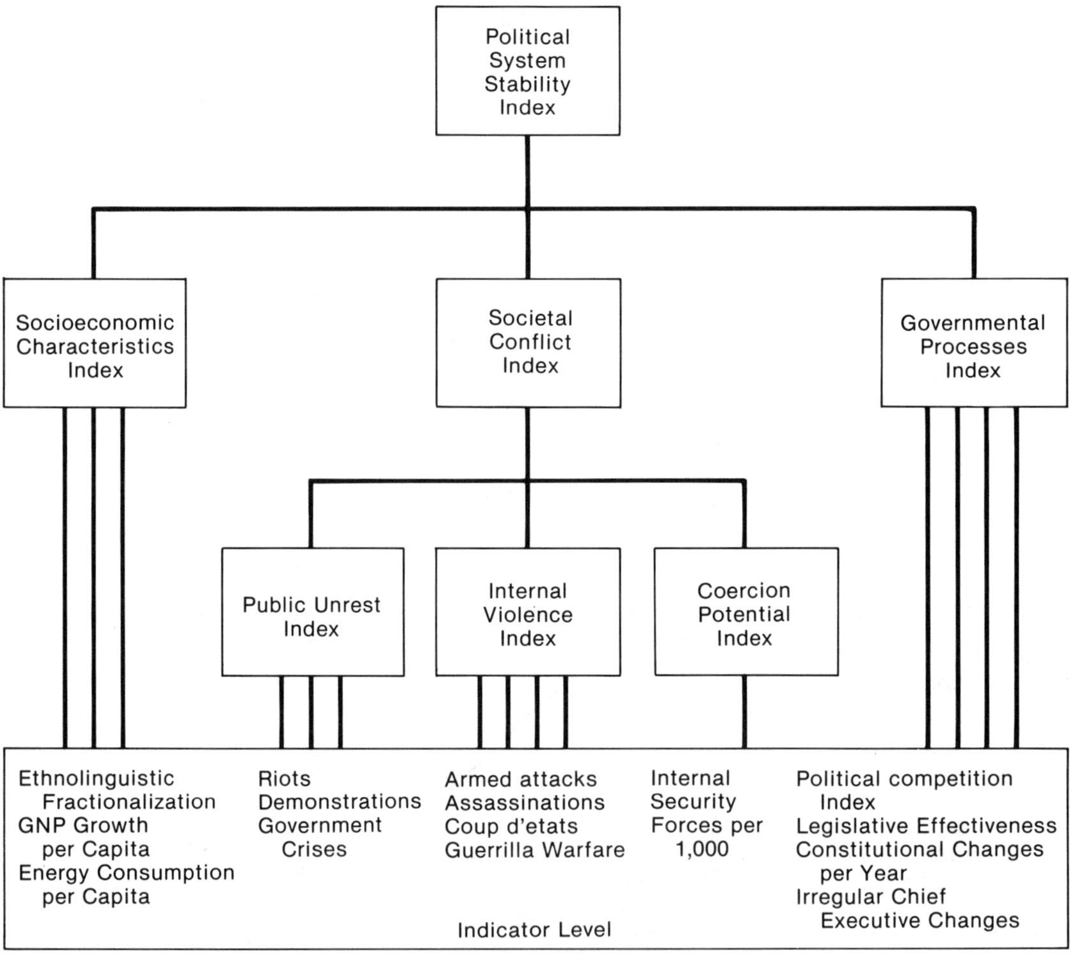

Source: D. Haendel, G. T. West, and R. G. Meadows, *Overseas Investment and Political Risk,* (Philadelphia, Pa.: Foreign Policy Research Institute, Monograph Series Number 21, 1975), pp. 70–71.

which can be measured either in terms of value (such as GNP growth, energy consumption per capita) or in terms of frequency (such as riots, constitutional changes per year). Each of the three subindexes is also given a confidence estimate, on a scale from 1 to 5, ranging from very high confidence to minimal confidence in the accuracy and reliability of the score. The confidence estimates are subjective in nature.

The PSSI scores and confidence estimates are presented in Exhibit 16-3 for the ten highest scoring countries and the ten lowest scoring countries among 65 countries rated on the basis of conditions that existed in 1961–1966.

Knudsen National Propensity to Expropriate Model

Like H-W-M's PSSI, Knudsen's approach uses measurable variables rather than subjective judgments about the host country's investment climate. The key to his model is that a high level of national frustration combined with a high level of foreign investment presence results in a relatively high probability of expropriation by the host country.

As shown in Exhibit 16-4, the level of frustration consists of people's aspirations minus welfare expectations, the difference between what people hope for and what they expect to get. The variables used to measure aspirations and welfare expectations are listed below.

Aspirations

1. Degree of urbanization
2. Literacy rate
3. Number of newspapers
4. Number of radios
5. Degree of labor unionization
6. National resources endowment

Expectations

1. Infant survival rate
2. Calorie consumption
3. Number of doctors per population size
4. Number of hospital beds per population size
5. Percentage of housing with piped water supply
6. Per capita GNP

Foreign investment presence, which would serve as a scapegoat to allay national frustrations, is measured by: (1) the ratio of aggregate U.S. investment to the GNP of the host country, and (2) concentration of U.S. investment in sensitive industries, such as extractive industries and utilities, which reflects the visibility of foreign investment in the host country's vital economic activities and exports.

Knudsen tested his model on Latin American countries for the period 1968–1971. The model correctly identified Chile, Mexico, and Venezuela as countries with a high propensity to expropriate, while Argentina and Brazil were among a number of Latin American countries having the least propensity to expropriate.

Exhibit 16-3. Political System Stability Rankings and Confidence Estimates

HIGHEST SCORING COUNTRIES			LOWEST SCORING COUNTRIES		
Country	Score	Confidence	Country	Score	Confidence
Israel	+4.56	2.3	Dominican Republic	−5.98	2.3
Trinidad	+3.70	4.3	Zaire	−5.20	4.3
Venezuela	+2.84	2.3	Yemen	−3.48	3.3
Malagasy Republic	+2.51	3.3	Ghana	−3.23	3.0
Romania	+2.53	2.3	Guatemala	−2.12	3.0
Costa Rica	+2.44	2.3	Indonesia	−1.92	3.7
Philippines	+2.42	3.0	Ecuador	−1.85	2.7
Sri Lanka	+2.27	3.0	Liberia	−1.84	3.0
Greece	+1.99	2.7	Dahomey	−1.81	3.3
Panama	+1.72	2.7	Haiti	−1.73	3.3

Source: D. Haendel, G. T. West, and R. G. Meadows, *Overseas Investment and Political Risk,* (Philadelphia, Pa.: Foreign Policy Research Institute, Monograph Series Number 21, 1975), pp. 70–71.

Exhibit 16-4. National Propensity to Expropriate Model

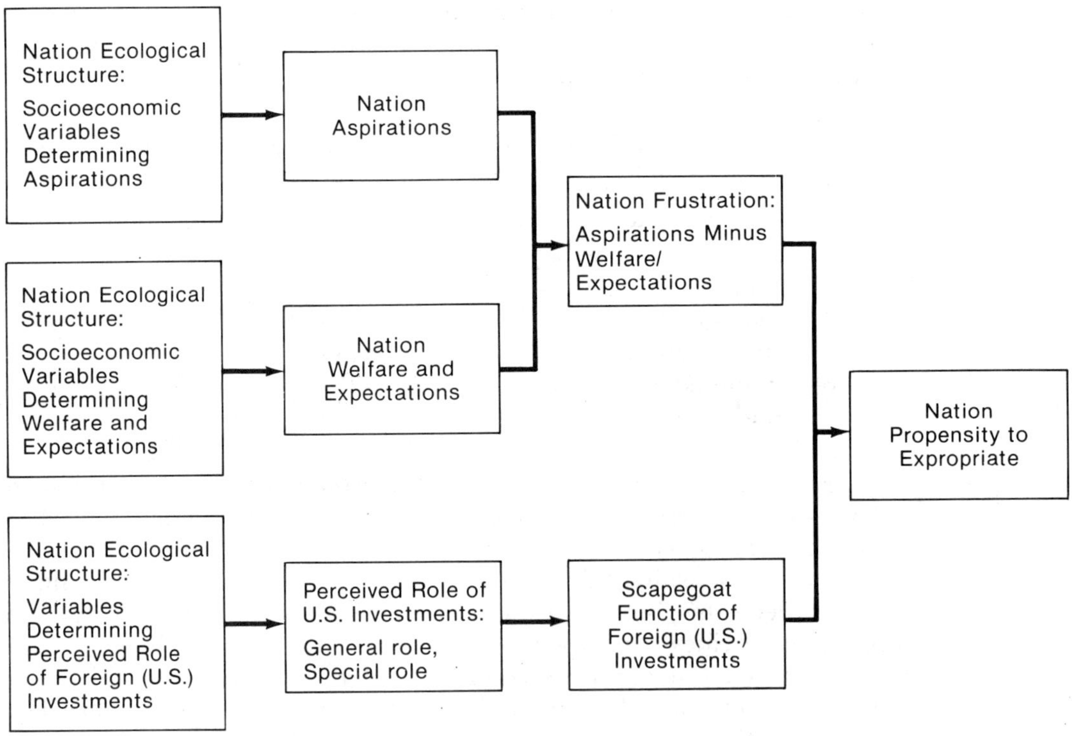

Source: Harald Knudsen, "Explaining the National Propensity to Expropriate: An Ecological Approach," *Journal of International Business Studies,* Spring 1974, p. 54.
Note: Double line denotes measurable entities.

A note of caution about the use of these and other models in forecasting political risk. Although the variables underlying indices are measurable, the choice of these variables, to the exclusion of others, and the weighting system remain subjective and judgmental in nature. Discriminant analysis (such as that used by Knudsen) would help to isolate the relevant and crucial variables. To the extent that such an analysis is used, the choice of the underlying variables will be less arbitrary. Another point is that testing the models successfully over a certain period of time does not necessarily make them usable for subsequent time periods. Changing patterns of political behavior and country alignments would trigger different reactions from host countries to the same social, economic, and financial circumstances.

POLITICAL RISK RELATED TO FOREIGN DEBT

Analysis of political risk in this chapter has ignored the difficult debt-servicing burden which has plagued most LDCs in the 1980s. The variables underlying the quantitative models discussed in the previous section did not include the impact on host governments' behavior of the massive foreign debt accumulated by them during the 1970s and 1980s. These models were based on conditions which prevailed mostly during the 1960s. The global debt-servicing issue did not emerge in serious proportions until the early 1980s.

The global debt issue and its implications to the MNC is addressed in Chapter 20. LDCs' vulnerability to interruption of debt-servicing payments will be measured by an index which reflects the variables that underlie their inability to meet their international obligations. Countries facing difficult debt-servicing problems must be considered as having a higher political risk, irrespective of the traditional factors that have been addressed in this chapter. These countries are more likely to impose exchange and import controls, and restrictions on transfers of dividends and other payments to parent companies from affiliates operating in their boundaries. On the other hand, these countries may be less likely to expropriate or nationalize foreign firms, because such drastic measures may anger the international financial community and cut off their sources of financing.

AN ILLUSTRATION—HOW DOES BORG-WARNER ASSESS COUNTRY RISK?[3]

Borg-Warner (BW) is a $2.3 billion firm whose major businesses are industrial products, air conditioning, chemicals, transportation equipment, and

[3]Business International, *International Risk Management* (Morristown, N.J.: Financial Executives Research Foundation, 1983), pp. 38–41. Reprinted with permission from the Financial Executive Research Foundation.

financial services. About 30 percent of its total sales and assets are in 20 countries outside the United States. Recognizing the growing role of these overseas operations, BW began in 1977 to conduct an annual survey of political and economic conditions worldwide.

Unlike many other companies that carry out similar surveys, BW interviews only its own managers and executives; no outsiders are contacted. In 1979, over 120 BW executives were polled. They provided ratings for 37 countries (including some in which the firm does not have major investments) based on five factors: political stability, economic conditions, labor situation, government controls, and external considerations (such as diplomatic and IMF relations, risk of war or boycott, and the like). Each country was then ranked according to its investment attractiveness.

The United States topped BW's list, followed by Germany, Canada, Japan, and Switzerland. This order usually matched that of other surveys, which also place India, Turkey, and Iran near the bottom. But several "medium-risk" countries were rated differently from what might have been seen in a more general survey, reflecting BW's particular perspective. For example, "overall Europe" was considered less attractive than some developing countries (for example, Mexico and Taiwan). And Italy, Argentina, and South Africa were ranked near the bottom, below the Philippines and Indonesia. The most desirable countries were those offering, in general, political stability with low inflation and, in particular, mild tax policies and generous investment incentives. Controls of various sorts were deemed the most worrisome factor, followed closely by poor labor conditions.

BW integrated its country-risk evaluations and its overall strategic planning system by applying the survey results to an investment risk matrix. Having used matrices for several years in its long-term planning program, BW was able to adapt the concept to risk measurement after identifying its foreign strategic business units (SBUs). Each SBU represents a real or potential organizational unit within a BW division and serves only one market. The status of an SBU is plotted against two scales, each graded high, medium, or low on the matrix: The investment attractiveness of its country (derived from the survey) and the business strengths of the unit itself (that is, ability to compete in its market). The SBU's strategy will depend on its position in the nine-box matrix (see Exhibit 16-5).

Most BW operating units fall in the medium range of the matrix, with only one unit located in a low-ranking country: South Africa. Different SBUs within the same country were usually found to rank similarly. However, the matrix highlighted specific products that were not doing well even though they were located in attractive countries.

The most obvious limitation of BW's survey approach is its total reliance on the views of company employees, whose self-interest might compromise their objectivity. Moreover, the exclusion of outside opinions could reduce the "richness" of the final assessments. A BW executive emphasized, however, that since the system is designed primarily as a practical manage-

Exhibit 16-5. Borg-Warner's Risk Matrix

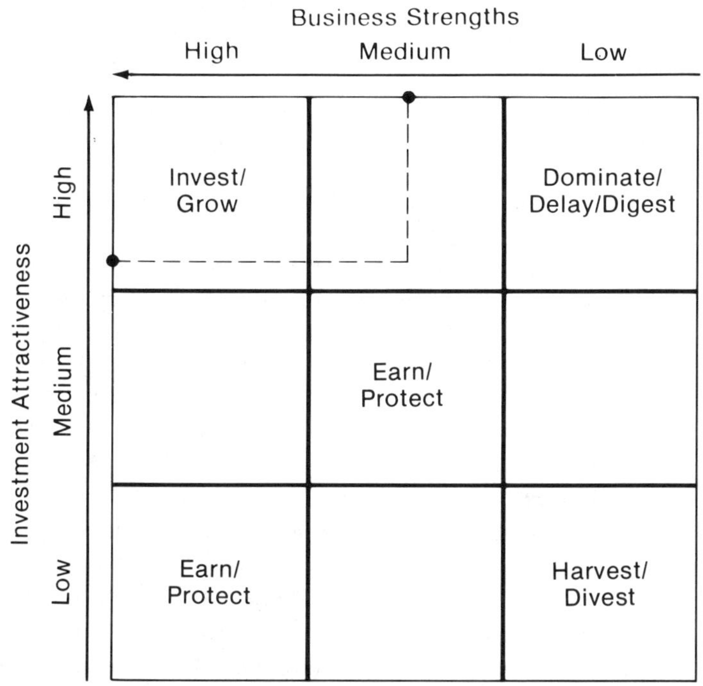

ment tool, it offers a number of advantages. First, it enables the firm to pinpoint conditions and risks most pertinent to its particular operations. As for objectivity, BW has found that most of its corporate respondents, as citizens of the places they evaluate, usually rate their own countries very rigorously.

BW regards the survey exercise itself as a positive planning tool. Its basic purpose is to encourage managers to participate in the planning process. While some factors measured by the survey may already be considered in daily operations, others are not; therefore, executives must keep in mind a wider range of long-term planning criteria than they might otherwise think about.

The format requires, for example, analytical comments on each country to supplement the numerical ratings. BW is not yet satisfied with the number of comments received, and it plans to encourage more qualitative feedback, particularly for the many factors that are difficult or impossible to quantify.

REVIEW QUESTIONS

1. Why were large commercial banks among the first institutions to develop strong interest in assessing and quantifying country risks?

2. The methodology of country risk assessment has become increasingly structured in recent years, and in some ways more quantitative. Why are qualitative judgments difficult to integrate in today's decision-making process?
3. Several large MNCs base their country risk assessment on a periodic (usually once a year) survey of their own managerial personnel stationed abroad. Some of these surveys take the form of a checklist of the risk variables. The staff are asked to indicate (for a particular country) the variables that are relevant and to rate the country on a scale (let us say from 1 to 5) that reflects how favorable or unfavorable is the score of the country with respect to each of the variables.

   For an LDC of your own choosing, develop a checklist of what you consider to be the salient political risk variables. Rate that country with respect to each variable on a scale of 1 to 3 (three is very unfavorable). Can you construct a country risk index using the data which you have developed?
4. Is it correct to assume that affiliates of MNCs located in industrial countries, such as Canada or France for example, are not exposed to political risk? What type of restrictions or government controls could conceivably disrupt the operations of foreign firms in these countries?
5. Why is the task of political risk forecasting more difficult for MNCs than for multinational banks? If you were the financial manager of a small firm which is looking into operating in an LDC, how would you go about assembling the information needed for overall risk assessment? Which sources of data (financial, economic, and political) would you rely on?
6. What are the major objections against using probability analysis in forecasting certain political risk events, such as expropriation? Would the same objections apply to the use of expected value theory, or mathematical expectations, in the managerial decision-making process?
7. What can be said about the usability of quantified political risk assessment techniques (such as Knudsen's model) in forecasting propensities of certain countries to nationalize foreign firms in the future? If the model was successfully tested on past data, does that demonstrate its usefulness in predicting future events?

BIBLIOGRAPHY

See end of Chapter 17.

17

Management of Political Risk

INTRODUCTION

Understanding the circumstances and factors which give rise to the political risk, as well as its measurement with as precise techniques as possible, are essential to an intelligent and foresighted management of such risk. While no MNC, no matter how large and diversified its operations may be, can immunize itself against the political risk, good management can reduce the exposure of the MNC to such risk and reduce its disruptive impact on the operations of the firm.

There are three well-recognized phases of managing the political risk:

1. Planning prior to direct foreign investment
2. Managing the political risk during the life cycle of the foreign project
3. Managing the political risk subsequent to expropriation or nationalization

The various measures and techniques of political risk management are not necessarily appropriate for every MNC contemplating foreign investment and in all circumstances. Each MNC must strive to adapt these techniques to its own requirements and scale of foreign operations so as to fashion an optimal policy consistent with the achievement of its goals. As is the case with the management of the foreign exchange risk, political risk management entails two types of costs: (1) direct costs in the form of outlays to obtain protection against various types of political risks, or to implement specific techniques and measures to reduce them, and (2) indirect costs in the form of management time devoted to forecasting, measuring, and coping with these risks.

PLANNING PRIOR TO DIRECT FOREIGN INVESTMENT

An MNC can reduce considerably its exposure to political risk by thorough planning of the project and careful investigation of the economic, financial, and political conditions of the host country. The planning and investigating phase will yield certain known or expected variables which must be incorporated in the capital budgeting evaluation process. It will also yield other variables which, while they cannot be fully integrated in the capital budgeting exercise, should be considered in the final acceptance or rejection decision.

Planned measures before actual investment include: (1) integrating the political risk, to the extent possible, in the capital budgeting process, (2) negotiating precise and definitive agreements with the government of the host country and/or the local joint venture partners, (3) planned divestment to insure gradual and orderly repatriation of invested capital and reduce the risk of expropriation, and (4) adaptation to host country goals and economic priorities.

Integrating the Political Risk in the Capital Budgeting Process

It is axiomatic that the known aspects of the political risk must be integrated in the capital budgeting exercise and in the management's final decision on the project. What is less axiomatic, and perhaps difficult, is how to incorporate the various aspects of this risk in the project evaluation stage. Our discussion of multinational capital budgeting has illustrated the conceptual and practical difficulties of accommodating the exchange risk in this exercise. The reader should recognize that it is much more difficult to incorporate the political risk in the same exercise. Political risk is far less recognizable, predictable, and measurable than the foreign exchange risk.

In Chapter 14, we pointed out that there are two ways of integrating the political risk in the traditional DCF evaluation technique: either by impacting the cash flows or by adding an appropriate risk premium to the discount rate. The APV technique has the versatility, through breaking out the cash flow into separately determined components, to do both. For example, the cash flow originating from the local sales and exports of the foreign affiliate can be adjusted for conditions of transferability, while other components, such as tax savings and transfers effected through the transfer pricing mechanism, may be discounted at a higher rate than the one used for discounting the operational cash flows, in recognition of the greater degree of risk entailed in these transfers. The principal argument against using a higher hurdle rate for operational cash flows is that they penalize flows in the earlier years of operation, whereas political risk impacts more heavily on receipts in later years.

Another facet of incorporating the political risk in the initial evaluation process is the way an MNC plans for financing the fixed investment and the working capital requirements of the foreign project. Exposure to political risk can be significantly reduced by minimizing the contribution of the parent company to project financing, and by meeting all or most of the working capital needs of the affiliate from local sources. Judicious planning in financing the foreign project will deter future actions against the affiliates by involving local interests and local financial institutions in the success or failure of the enterprise.

Financing part of the initial investment and/or all or most of the working capital from local sources may run counter to the principle of seeking the least costly sources of finance developed in Chapter 11. The financial manager in this situation, as in most financial decisions, must strike a balance in the trade-off between higher financing cost and a lower political risk.

Negotiating Specific Arrangements with the Host Government

Although an agreement negotiated with a host government may be repudiated in the event of a revolution or a radical change in the political order, MNCs with definitive agreements have fared better than those operating without one or with loosely defined ones. The historical record confirms that host governments are less likely to block transfers of debt repayments and royalties, for example, than dividends transfer. Fronting loans, for instance, where the loan to the affiliate is made by an international financial institution in consideration of a deposit made by the parent company, is a case in point. Host governments will be damaging their access to credit from multinational banks by restricting the freedom of the affiliate to service its debt to these institutions.

A carefully negotiated concession agreement must address itself to a large number of crucial provisions which affect almost every phase of operation of the affiliate. A checklist includes the following key provisions:

- Unbundling potential transfers to the parent company into specific and well-defined components, such as dividends, royalties, management fees, interest, and loan repayments. Bundling hurts the prospects of smooth transfers, as most host governments usually construe such bundled transfer as dividends, the segment which is most susceptible to future restrictions. Management fees and compensation for services rendered by the staff of the parent to the affiliate have often been controversial. Host governments, particularly among the LDCs, have viewed such compensation as exorbitant, and amounting to what they deem to be illegal transfer of profits (bilking the host country—a phrase often used). By spelling out these fees at the outset, the parent company would be in a better bargaining position should disputes arise in the future.

- Transfer pricing, the pricing of inputs exchanged in intracorporate transactions, is perhaps the most controversial aspect of an MNC's worldwide operations. Stating the bases for pricing such transfers in the concession agreement would contribute to lessening the extent of disagreements over such transactions during the operational phase.
- Employment policies and limitations on employment of foreign personnel. Most host countries, particularly among the LDCs, have labor laws which limit employment of foreign workers and stipulate procedures for granting permission for hiring nonlocal personnel.
- Requirements of the host country as to construction of social overhead capital and facilities to promote the local economy.
- Access to local financing and limitations on the use of local financing.
- Price controls on sales in the host market, and any limitations on export to third-country markets.
- Laws and regulations relating to taxation of income and property of the affiliate, and methods of estimating taxable income and properties.
- Provision for arbitration of disputes.

Planned Divestment

Planned divestment and orderly turning over of ownership and control of the business to local investors is an effective technique to reduce the probability of expropriation. It is also conducive to smooth working relationships within the local environment. Planned divestment may be negotiated at the outset with the host government, or subsequently offered as a defensive measure to counteract local hostility against the affiliate. Divestment in some countries is required by host governments as a condition of entry to their markets. The Cartagena Agreement of 1969 requires that foreign firms operating in the Andean countries of South America allow local investors over time to acquire at least 51 percent ownership in these firms.

Planned divestment has some drawbacks. Management of the affiliate may develop acquiescent attitudes over time as the prospect of turning over the helm to local managers undermines their motivation and dedication to the affiliate. The parent company, in anticipation of the planned turnover, may neglect vital maintenance work or allow the operations of the affiliate to drift along aimlessly. These situations could trigger the sort of confrontation with the host government that planned divestment initially sought to prevent. Where planned divestment is carefully designed with a residual major role for the parent company, such as a management contract, these potential problems could be avoided, and an effective partnership with local investors may prove rewarding to both parties.

Joint ventures have been thought to provide a vehicle of reducing political risk, by sharing ownership with local private and public investors at the outset, rather than through gradual divestment. MNCs have mixed feelings about joint ventures, and some, as a matter of corporate policy, refuse to operate in foreign countries where a joint venture is a precondition for such operation.

The record of joint ventures as a means of reducing the risk of expropriation is inconclusive. When ownership and management are shared with private local partners, it is argued that the host government would be reluctant to hurt local business and financial interests. This, however, may not be the case if a change of government takes place and the new leaders view the local partners with skepticism, or when firms associated with falling regimes provide them with easy and convenient targets to consolidate their power. Joint ventures with public firms or agencies of the host government may also tend to encourage or accelerate expropriation rather than deter it. Conflicting interests and divergent motivation may quickly lead to confrontation between local and foreign managers. This confrontation may hasten expropriation, which will be viewed by the host government as the only means of resolving the perceived conflict of interest.

Insuring the Political Risk

Political risk insurance is available for U.S. as well as non-U.S. multinational firms in most industrial countries. Investment insurance programs are offered in various forms by public agencies in Australia, Canada, Denmark, France, Germany, Japan, the Netherlands, Norway, South Korea, Sweden, Switzerland, the United Kingdom, and the United States. In addition to insuring the political risk, a number of these programs offer financing facilities and export promotion services.[1]

The U.S. investment insurance and guarantee program is carried out by the Overseas Private Investment Corporation (OPIC), a U.S. government corporation, organized in 1971.[2] OPIC operates two main programs: Insurance of qualifying U.S. private investment in less developed countries and project financing.[3]

[1]See Appendices G and H at the end of this chapter.

[2]Prior to 1971, the insurance function was performed by the Agency for International Development (AID).

[3]Material relating to the investment insurance and project financing programs in the United States is based on two pamphlets issued by OPIC: *Investment Insurance Handbook* and *Investment Finance Handbook*.

OPIC provides insurance of U.S. direct investment in developing countries against the following political risks:

1. The risk of inconvertibility, that is, inability of investor to convert funds received in local currency (dividends, royalties, other fees, and repatriation of original investment) into U.S. dollars.
2. Loss of investment due to expropriation, nationalization, or confiscation by action of foreign host governments.
3. Loss due to war, revolution, or insurrection. Coverage against civil strife is also available.

Investment insurance is extended only to "eligible investors," which are defined as "citizens of the U.S.; or corporations, partnerships, or other associations created under the laws of the U.S., or of any state or territory of the U.S., which are substantially beneficially owned by U.S. citizens, or a foreign business at least 95% owned by eligible investors."[4] A corporation is considered substantially owned by U.S. citizens if more than 50 percent of each class of its issued and outstanding stocks is owned by U.S. citizens.

OPIC also restricts its insurance coverage to investments in eligible countries, defined as those countries or areas with a per capita gross national product of $2950 (in 1979 dollars) or less. The eligibility list includes only those countries with which the United States has an intergovernmental agreement, usually referred to as "friendly" countries. Investments in countries with a per capita gross national product of over $2950 are eligible if the projects are sponsored by U.S. small businesses or cooperatives, or if they involve minerals or energy and construction projects. Small businesses are defined as industrial companies having less than $122 million of consolidated revenues, or businesses with stockholders' equity of less than $42 million.

OPIC's policy is to insure new investments only. Enlargement or modernization of existing plant and equipment, as well as additional working capital for an expanded business are also covered. The form which an eligible investment may take covers equity, loans, and other forms of investment, such as licensing and technical assistance agreements.

OPIC's insurance typically covers only 90 percent of the cost of a proposed investment. In addition, standby commitments of up to 180 percent of the face value of an eligible investment are available to cover accrued earnings and interest. In countries where OPIC has a substantial exposure, particularly in sensitive industries, coverage may be limited to less than 90 percent.

The cost of insurance varies as to the risks covered, form of investment (equity or loan), and type of industrial activity. Exhibit 17-1 shows the base premium rates in effect on July 30, 1985. Rates are higher for risky projects, projects in sensitive areas, and industries or countries in which

[4]OPIC, *Investment Insurance Handbook,* pp. 2–3.

Exhibit 17-1. Premiums for Political Risk Insurance Provided by OPIC (percent per annum of current insured amount)

	COVERAGE			
Type of Investment and Industry	Inconvertibility	Expropriation	WRI[1]	WRI & Civil Strife
Equity				
Manufacturing & services (including leasing)	.30	.60	.60	.75
Natural resource projects	.30	.90	.60	.75
Oil and gas projects	.30	.40	.60	.75
Contractors and exporters	.30	.60	.60	.75
Loans (institutional)	.25	.30	.60	.70

[1]War, revolution, and insurrection.
Source: OPIC, *Investment Insurance,* October 1985, pp. 6–7.

OPIC maintains a relatively high degree of exposure. In general, base rates may be increased or decreased by up to one-third, depending on the risk profile of the specific project. Rates for natural resource and hydrocarbon projects, and large projects (costing $50 million or more) may vary by more than one-third of the base rates.

In addition to insuring private U.S. investments abroad, OPIC provides financing of projects in developing countries in conjunction with U.S. private investment through loans and loan guarantees. OPIC participation usually takes the form of medium- and long-term loans for projects in countries where such financing is not available from local financial institutions. OPIC does not offer financing on concessional terms, nor does it engage in financing or insuring export sales, where such exports are not related to long-term investment in overseas business. OPIC does not make equity investments in qualified foreign projects, but may purchase convertible notes and certain other debt instruments with equity participation features.

MANAGEMENT OF POLITICAL RISK DURING LIFE CYCLE OF PROJECT

Planning at the preinvestment stage may lessen the probability of expropriation and assures the parent company of a strong negotiating position in future disputes. Political risk management, however, does not end at that phase. The parent company and the affiliates' managements have the continuing responsibility of conducting operations with a view to reducing the impact of the various manifestations of political risk on the profitability of the project. This phase of managing political risk is all-pervasive, and manifests itself in every aspect of operation from the day-to-day relations with the host environment to the formulation of marketing and production policies.

Political risk management strategies in this phase may be grouped into three main areas:

1. Flexibility and keen understanding of the host country priorities
2. Production and marketing strategies
3. Financial policies

Maintaining Smooth Relationship with Host Country

An affiliate would serve the interests of the project best by understanding the host country's requirements and priorities, and by being flexible and adaptive to these priorities. A rigid and noncompromising posture, which is often exemplified by clinging tenaciously to the provisions of the initial investment agreement, hardly serves its interests or that of the parent firm. Host governments have been able to scrap or sidestep concession agreements negotiated with foreign investors, or to introduce new legislation which preempts provisions of these agreements. Local management must always endeavor to anticipate evolving conditions in the host country and show sufficient flexibility to adapt to these conditions wherever possible. Maintaining a smooth and mutually beneficial relation with the host government is not a concession; it is good business. An important prerequisite for pursuing a dynamic and adaptive strategy is the degree of latitude allowed the affiliate's management. If local management has to gain prior approval of the parent company for making adjustments in all operational matters, pursuance of such a strategy is hardly possible.

Production and Marketing Strategies

An MNC, particularly if it is geographically diversified, has a great deal of latitude in shaping its production and marketing strategies with a view to discouraging expropriation by the host country. The key to the use of these strategies in political risk management is to make expropriation unprofitable or counterproductive for the host government. Should the host government seize the business, it will be unable to operate the facility or market the end products.

In the *production area,* the relevant strategies that could contribute to reducing political risk are

1. Control of raw materials and component sources. An expropriating authority cannot operate the facility unless it can secure the required raw materials or components. This realization will act as a deterrent

to expropriation. MNCs operating assembly-type manufacturing operations in high-risk LDCs usually resort to this strategy to discourage their hosts from taking over the plants. One or more vital parts of the products are manufactured by the parent company or a subsidiary elsewhere, and are then imported to complete assembly.

Sourcing raw materials presents local management with some difficult options, each of which has political risk implications. Sourcing materials locally has the advantage of cutting down shipment time and transport costs, but exposes the project to supply interruptions in the event of a strike or other forms of politically motivated action. Local sourcing also has the advantage of improving working relationships with the host country's authorities, but may compromise adherence to quality standards. Sourcing materials and components from outside the host country is costly and time-consuming, but affords the management of a more assured source of supply and enables better control over quality standards. This policy, however, usually does not sit well with host country authorities, who usually aim at prodding foreign investors to maximize the value added generated by local manufacture.

2. Controlling patents or secret processes, normally at the parent company's level. An obvious example is the secret formula for Coca-Cola, which has never been made available to locally organized bottling plants across the world. High-technology operations such as computers, business communication systems, and copiers have a certain degree of immunity against expropriation by host governments, since such an action would be counterproductive.

In the *marketing area,* MNCs can discourage expropriation or nationalization by either controlling to an effective degree the means of transporting the product to its markets, or controlling the markets themselves. This control, real or contrived, enabled international oil companies to operate in the Middle East and other producing countries for almost 60 years (from the turn of the century until the mid-1950s) without the threat of nationalization. Host countries thought that such a course of action was unthinkable for several reasons. In the first place, they could not operate the oil wells without the technical expertise of the company's staff and workers. Second, even if they somehow succeeded in producing crude oil, they did not know what to do with it. Refineries were owned and operated by the same companies, and they were located outside the oil-producing countries (in Aden or Rotterdam, for example). Finally, host countries were not in a position to export crude oil, because the companies owned and operated the pipelines and oil tankers. They also controlled most markets outside the eastern European countries, which are net oil exporters themselves.

These impediments, however, later proved surmountable as Iraq nationalized the oil industry in the mid-1950s, followed by a number of other Middle Eastern countries. Producing countries on the whole demonstrated that they were capable of producing and marketing their oil resources, with the help in some cases of hired expatriates. The formation of OPEC in the 1960s contributed to the strengthening of the position of producing countries vis-à-vis the international oil companies and led to the sharp increase in prices during the 1970s. OPEC, however, began to weaken in the early 1980s due to rising oil supplies, in relation to world demand, and price undercutting by some members in violation of production quotas imposed by the cartel.

Another example where control of transportation proved effective in discouraging expropriation is the control exercised for a long number of years by United Fruit Company over the export of bananas from Latin American countries. The company owned and operated the refrigerator ships and had a tight grip on market outlets.

Financial Policies

We have suggested earlier that the method of financing a foreign project and its sources of funds have a great impact on its susceptibility to political risk. This risk can be significantly reduced by localizing the affiliate's capital structure, that is, by meeting most of its funds requirements from local sources. Appropriate working capital management strategies can also contribute to reducing political risk. This has been covered in Chapters 6 and 8 under positioning of funds, the use of leads and lags, and the transfer pricing mechanism.

As in the case of production and procurement policies, the use of financial policies in political risk management has its costs and limitations. Overdependence on local financing or starting foreign operations with a thin equity base is not conducive to constructive working relationships with host governments. Most host countries view suspiciously firms that are not adequately financed by parent firms. Reliance on local financing sources may be risky, as loans from local banks may not be renewed, or credit lines may be suspended or terminated, perhaps at the suggestion of the host government. Such financing may also be more costly compared to other sources. The use of working capital management techniques are also subject to limitations imposed by host governments. The use of such techniques as transfer pricing for political risk management purposes may expose the MNC to more drastic measures on the part of the host government.

STRATEGIES FOLLOWING EXPROPRIATION AND NATIONALIZATION

The MNC must evolve a strategy aiming at maximum recovery of the value of the foreign investment following expropriation. Irrespective of how the action of taking over the assets is characterized by the host government (expropriation, nationalization, or confiscation), the affected firm has, with few exceptions, a right to compensation under international law. However, the complexity of the definition of expropriation and these exceptions often render this right questionable or subject to dispute. OPIC's definition of expropriation throws some light on the complexity of the concept, and defines a number of exceptions. Expropriation is any action authorized or conducted by the host government "that prevents the investor or the foreign enterprise from exercising effective control over the use or disposition of property owned, or the rights accruing from the property, for at least one year."[5] The focal point of the definition is the effect of the host government's action on the foreign firms, not its expressed purpose. A series of steps which seriously impede and interfere with the functioning of a foreign firm is considered expropriatory (sometimes referred to as "creeping expropriation"), even if the host government has not purported to take over the firm.

OPIC's definition provides for a number of exceptions. An action by a host government is not considered expropriatory if it results from a law or regulation that "(1) is reasonably related to constitutionally sanctioned government objectives; (2) is not arbitrary; (3) is based upon a reasonable classification of the entities to which it applies; and does not violate generally accepted principles of international law."[6] In addition, expropriation is deemed not to have taken place in such situations as the failure of the foreign investor to take appropriate remedial measures, insolvency of the foreign investor, or the implementation of a voluntary agreement made by the foreign investor with the host government (gradual divestment).

The complexity of the issue of expropriation and the recognized exceptions to the definition, together with the relative ambiguity of international law on this question, explain the frequent disputes that arise subsequent to such action and the protracted and expensive negotiations that usually ensue. The question, therefore, arises as to what is the optimal strategy an MNC should follow under these circumstances?

Search for an Optimal Post-Expropriation Strategy

An MNC faced with an act of expropriation must first make a quick but thorough assessment of the situation to determine if the action is reversible. If that is the case, its strategy should focus on achieving such an outcome, since preserving the affiliate as a going concern is invariably more favorable than compensation based on some valuation of the assets taken over by the host government.

[5]Business International Corporation, *International Risk Management* (Morristown, N.J.: Financial Executives Institute, 1983), p. 145.

[6]*Ibid.,* p. 145.

Hoskins suggested that an affected MNC resort first to rational negotiations with the host government with the serious intention of making acceptable concessions to preserve the continued operation of the firm.[7] He suggested that the firm prepare three sets of concessions: Group A includes steps which it is willing to take (such as hiring national managers, or accepting a local company as minority partner). Group B includes steps that it is willing to take under duress (such as investing more capital, or supporting government programs). Group C is steps which it will not take (such as suspending payment of dividends or surrendering majority control). The strategy is to use the concessions in Groups A and B to dissuade the host government from its decision.

If rational negotiations fail to achieve their objective, Hoskins suggests that the firm move to Phase II, which is essentially mixing bargaining with some power tactics. These consist of threats, explicit or implied, to apply political and economic pressure on the host country, perhaps seeking support from the home country government and possibly from neighboring countries. This approach has its serious drawbacks, and may irretrievably damage the relationship between the MNC and the host government.

It may, on the other hand, prove effective, particularly if the MNC's bargaining position is strong by virtue of its control of technological skills, component parts, and export markets. The experience of the international oil companies nationalized in the Middle East and Latin America in the 1950s and 1960s suggests that this approach was of little value in reversing nationalization decisions. In some of these cases economic sanctions were applied by the United States by refusing to approve EXIMBANK loans to these countries, as well as withholding support of World Bank loans to them.

In certain situations, where the host country is heavily dependent on aid and loans from the parent country of the nationalized firm, threatening to withhold assistance could prove effective in averting takeover of properties or in settlement of valuation disputes. Use of such high-pressure tactics may, however, deepen the rift between the two countries, and further polarize the dispute.

Constructive negotiations with the expropriating authority may produce some favorable accommodation for the MNC even if they fail to reverse the expropriation decision. This accommodation may guarantee the firm continued presence in the host market, which could prove in some cases as profitable as the original arrangement. Accommodation may take the form of providing technical and managerial expertise to the nationalized firm under a management contract, and/or handling its exports on a commission basis. Good examples of this accommodation are the arrangements reached by the governments of Saudi Arabia and Kuwait with the

[7] William R. Hoskins, "How to Counter Expropriation," *Harvard Business Review* (September/October, 1970), pp. 102–112.

international oil companies following the "friendly" nationalization of the oil industry in these two countries in the mid-1960s.

Resort to Legal Remedies

When the MNC is convinced that negotiating with the expropriating authority is fruitless, or that the expropriation decision is irreversible, it should seek legal remedies. There are several options available, depending on the circumstances of the case and the underlying agreement between the firm and the host government. Seeking redress through the judicial system in the host country would normally be less costly and more expeditious; however, it is highly unlikely that judgment rendered by such a system would provide relief to the litigant firm. The judicial system in most LDCs, where such situations often arise, is not truly independent of the executive branch of government, and, as a consequence, it is hardly expected to render a decision against the confiscating authority.

Redress is more often sought in the courts of the parent country, or through enlisting the support of government agencies or financial institutions in the parent country to seize assets owned by the expropriating country to satisfy the firm's claim. Legal remedy in the courts of the parent country is proscribed by a principle of international law which makes actions of sovereign nations within their own borders not subject to review or question by foreign courts. An amendment to the U.S. Foreign Assistance Act (the Sabbatino amendment) attempted to override this principle in cases of confiscation or other taking over of properties in violation of international law.

A case in point was the use of part of the frozen Iranian assets to satisfy the claims of firms which sought damages for losses of properties or profits as a result of measures taken by the Iranian government. Following the negotiations which led to the release of U.S. hostages in 1981, the frozen Iranian bank balances and other assets were gradually released through intermediaries. Of the total amount (about $12 billion), $4 billion was transferred to the Bank of England and placed in a security account to satisfy some 300 disputes filed by foreign firms which were to be settled by arbitration.[8]

Binding arbitration is also available to MNCs through the International Center for the Settlement of Investment Disputes (ICSID). The Center, established by the World Bank in 1966 and based in Washington, D.C., provides a mechanism for settlement of disputes arising between a member state (countries which signed the convention creating the institution)[9] and foreign investors who are nationals of another member state. The

[8]Herman Nickel, "The Iran Deal Doesn't Look Bad," *Fortune* (February 23, 1981), pp. 57–59.

[9]As of January 31, 1985, 91 countries had signed the convention.

ICSID can have jurisdiction only when both parties to the dispute consent to use its arbitration mechanism. Such consent may be expressed by the parties at the outset, and incorporated in the investment agreement. This consent is binding and cannot be revoked even if one of the contracting states subsequently withdraws from the Center. The ICSID has experienced limited success in resolving the cases which have been referred to it since its formation. The institution is somewhat handicapped by the fact that a fairly large number of countries, including most Latin American countries, have not yet joined the convention. Moreover, prospects of success of legal proceedings against sovereign member states are small. Decisions on cases arbitrated by the Center have been often rendered ineffective by lengthy and prolonged appeals and protestations by the losing side.

Settlement with the Expropriating Authority (Compensation)

The final phase in the post-expropriating strategy, following the exhaustion of other avenues, is for the MNC to seek settlement with the expropriating authority, usually by direct negotiation. These negotiations are often difficult and prolonged, particularly if the situation is charged with political and emotional factors. Settlement or determination of compensation amount under friendly expropriation (such as Saudi Arabia's nationalization of its oil industry) is an exception, as compensation amounts in such cases are pre-agreed upon by both parties.

The usual pattern in such negotiations is for the MNC to propose a compensation figure based on capitalizing (or discounting) the future income stream from the expropriated affiliate as a going concern. Authorities of the expropriating country are most likely to take the position that compensation should reflect the value of the affiliate to the country, rather than to the surrendering MNC. The two amounts are usually so far apart that prospects of an agreement are often dim if not altogether nonexistent.

A settlement based on the present value of future cash flows, which is in line with capital budgeting theory, has considerable theoretical appeal. However, such cash flows are difficult to ascertain, and are likely to depend on from whose standpoint they are estimated. From the viewpoint of the MNC, such cash flows are inseparably tied to the operation of the firm as a whole, and are difficult, if not impossible, to estimate in isolation. Expropriating countries, on the other hand, often contend that future cash flows from expropriated firms are likely to be small due to the loss of markets and/or loss of efficiency. They also advance the argument that the MNC has recouped the initial investment and reaped substantial profits from previous years' operations. The initial estimates put forward by the two sides are likely to be far apart, and negotiations may drag on for a number of years.

It is in the interest of the MNC to arrive at a swift settlement, as prolonged negotiations are costly and may impose a high demand on management's time to the detriment of the overall operation of the firm. Moreover, a settlement would enable the MNC to write off part of the sustained losses against its operating income in the parent country. A reasonably fair settlement is also in the best interests of the expropriating country. Authorities are likely to be concerned about irreparably damaging their relations with the international financial and business community. The process of negotiations may also produce some basis of future cooperation between the host country and the parent company, such as operating the expropriated affiliate under a management contract, or exporting parts and components to enable continued operation.

Eiteman suggested an alternative approach to achieve settlement which is based on capital budgeting, in an attempt to break the impasse which the two sides often reach. The approach consists essentially of "unwinding" all historical cash flows from the parent to the host country, and all cash flows remitted to the parent by the affiliate.[10] These cash flows in opposite directions are netted for each year to ascertain the net annual flows for each year since the inception of operations. The third step is to use a discount rate to find the compounded value at present of all past net cash flows. This process runs in the opposite time direction from traditional capital budgeting, which consists of discounting expected future cash flows to the present. A positive sum of the net compounded value of past flows would indicate the appropriate compensation to be paid by the country to the firm, as it had put in the venture (cash inflows) more than it had gotten out (cash outflows). A zero outcome would indicate that the parent had earned a rate of return commensurate with the degree of risk involved in the venture (as embedded in the discount rate), and that no further compensation is warranted.

Although this approach could provide a useful framework for eventual settlement, it has some serious limitations. The central part of the exercise is to produce a mutually agreeable discount rate which truly reflects the particular mix of risk and efficiency of the venture. Negotiations may be stalemated over agreeing on such a rate, as the host country is likely to argue for a rate which would show that the parent has obtained more than a fair return on the investment. The main drawback of this approach, however, is the penalty it imposes on successful and efficient affiliates, which by virtue of their successes must have transferred back to the parent more than they received in initial investment and other flows. Such affiliates when expropriated, according to this approach, would end up paying compensation to the host country, rather than the other way around. Less

[10]David K. Eiteman, "A Model for Expropriation Settlement," *Business Horizons* (April 1970), pp. 85–91.

successful affiliates (losing and inefficient ones) would be rewarded when expropriated by compensation paid by the host country.

The road to a fair and just settlement is a long and bumpy one. In the end a compromise will be hammered out, as the basic interests of the two parties would finally prevail to put an end to costly haggling and move on to other pursuits.

REVIEW QUESTIONS

1. Some argue that planned divestment is self-defeating and may often result in anticipatory deterioration of the physical assets of the operating affiliate. Do you agree? State briefly the main arguments for and against planned divestment.
2. Why has the transfer of dividends to the parent company been the major target of controls and restrictions by host countries? Does unbundling work as an overall strategy to facilitate the smooth flow of funds to the parent company?
3. Joint ventures with host governments have in some instances encouraged rather than deterred expropriation. How can we explain this pattern of behavior on the part of the host governments?
4. Some argue that when an MNC buys OPIC insurance against the political risk, why bother about taking other measures to manage this risk (such as integrating the risk in the capital budgeting process, negotiating a specific concession agreement, and planned divestment). Do you agree? Is there such a thing as overmanaging the political risk, or devoting an unduly large amount of time and resources to such management?
5. Can you buy OPIC insurance against expropriation for new investments in (a) Iran? (b) United Kingdom? (c) China? (d) South Korea? Explain.
6. You are about to enter a joint venture agreement with a Middle Eastern oil-producing country to produce petrochemicals, primarily for export markets. Outline briefly some key production, marketing, and financial policies which you would pursue in order to minimize the probability of expropriation.
7. State whether you agree or disagree with the following statements, indicating in each case your reasons:
   - The record of negotiating with expropriating authorities is so dismal that an MNC faced with this situation should not even attempt it.

- MNCs prefer an explicit and final act of expropriation to a prolonged process of controls and restrictions which paralyze the operations of their affiliates. (Refer to such factors as compensation under OPIC policies, tax write-offs.)
- Resort to legal remedies has historically proved to be ineffectual. Using political muscle and threats has a better chance of succeeding.
- An MNC should pack and leave after expropriation, rather than negotiate to continue to do business with the expropriated venture in some different capacity.

BIBLIOGRAPHY

AMERASINGHE, C. F., "Model Clauses for Settlement of Foreign Investment Disputes," *Arbitration Journal* (December 1973), pp. 232–257.

______, "Submissions to the Jurisdiction of the International Centre for Settlement of Investment Disputes," *Journal of Maritime Law and Commerce* (January 1974), pp. 211–250.

BANKER, D., "You're the Best Judge of Foreign Risks," *Harvard Business Review* (March-April 1983), pp. 157–165.

BLANK, S., J. BASEK, S. J. KOBRIN, and J. LAPALOMBARA, *Assessing the Political Environment: An Emerging Function in International Companies.* New York: The Conference Board, 1980.

BODDEWYN, J. J., *International Divestment: A Survey of Corporate Experience.* New York: Business International, 1976.

______, "Divestment: Local vs. Foreign and U.S. vs. European Approaches," *Management International Review* (1979/1), pp. 21–28.

______, "Foreign Divestment: Magnitude and Factors," *Journal of International Business Studies* (Spring-Summer 1979), pp. 21–27.

BRADLEY, D., "Managing Against Expropriation," *Harvard Business Review* (July/August 1977), pp. 75–83.

BREWER, T. L., "Political Sources of Risk in the International Money Markets: Conceptual, Methodological, and Interpretative Refinements," *Journal of International Business Studies* (Spring-Summer 1983), pp. 161–164.

BULCKE, D. V., and J. J. BODDEWYN, *Investment and Divestment Policies in Multinational Corporations in Europe.* London: Saxon/Teakfield; New York: Praeger, 1979.

BUNN, D. W., and X. MUSTAFAOGLU, "Forecasting Political Risk," *Management Science* (November 1978), pp. 1557–1567.

Business International, *International Risk Management.* Morristown, N.J.: Financial Executive Foundation, 1983.

CHOPRA, J., J. J. BODDEWYN, and R. TORNEDEN, "U.S. Foreign Divestment: A 1972–1975 Updating," *Columbia Journal of World Business* (Spring 1978), pp. 14–18.

COPLIN, W. D., and M. O'LEARY, "Forecasting Risk in the International Marketplace," *Security Management* (August 1983), pp. 81–87.

DANIELS, J. D., E. W. OGRAM, JR., and L. H. RADEBAUGH, *International Business Environments and Operations,* 3rd ed. Reading, Mass.: Addison Wesley, 1982.

DAVIS, R. R., "Alternative Techniques for Country Risk Evaluation," *Business Economics* (May 1981), pp. 34–41.

DONATH, B., "Handicapping and Hedging the Foreign Investment: Political Risk Analysis," *Industrial Management* (February 1981), pp. 56–58.

DOZ, Y. L., C. A. BARTLETT, and C. K. PRAHALAD, "Global Competitive Pressures and Host Country Demands," *California Management Review* (Spring 1981), pp. 63–74.

DOZ, Y. L., and C. K. PRAHALAD, "How MNCs Cope with Host Country Demands," *Harvard Business Review* (March/April 1980), pp. 149–160.

FRANK, I., *Foreign Enterprise in Developing Countries.* Baltimore, Md.: Johns Hopkins University Press, 1980.

GLADWIN, T. N., and I. WALTER, *Multinationals Under Fire.* New York: John Wiley & Sons, 1980.

GOLDSTEIN, E., and J. VANOUS, "Country Risk Analysis: Pitfalls of Comparing the Eastern Bloc Countries with the Rest of the World," *Columbia Journal of World Business* (Winter 1983), pp. 10–16.

GREEN, R. T., "Political Structures as a Predictor of Radical Political Change," *Columbia Journal of World Business* (Spring 1974), pp. 28–36.

GREEN, R. T., and C. M. KORTH, "Political Instability and the Foreign Investor," *California Management Review* (Fall 1974), pp. 23–31.

GRIFFIN, J. P., "Transfer of OPIC's Investment Insurance Programs to Private Insurers," *Law and Policy in International Business,* no. 3 (1976), p. 631.

GULLANDER, S., "Joint Ventures and Corporate Strategy," *Columbia Journal of World Business* (Spring 1976), pp. 104–114.

HAENDEL, D., *Foreign Investment and the Management of Political Risk.* Boulder, Col.: Westview Press, 1979.

HAENDEL, D., and G. T. WEST, with R. G. MEADOW, *Overseas Investment and Political Risk.* Philadelphia, Pa.: Foreign Policy Research Institute, 1975.

HANER, F. T., "Rating Investment Risks Abroad," *Business Horizons* (April 1979), pp. 18–23.

HAWKINS, R. G., N. MINTZ, and M. PROVISSIERO, "Government Takeovers of U.S. Foreign Affiliates," *Journal of International Business Studies* (Spring 1976), pp. 3–15.

HOSKINS, W. R., "How to Counter Expropriation," *Harvard Business Review* (September/October 1970), pp. 102–112.

HU, HENRY T. C., "Compensation in Expropriations: A Preliminary Economic Analysis," *Virginia Journal of International Law* (Fall 1979), pp. 61–95.

INGRAM, G. M., *Expropriation of U.S. Property in South America.* New York: Praeger, 1974.

JOHNSON, H. C., *Risk in Foreign Business Environments: A Framework for Thought and Management.* Cambridge, Mass.: Arthur D. Little, 1980.

KNUDSEN, H., "Explaining the National Propensity to Expropriate: An Ecological Approach," *Journal of International Business Studies* (Spring 1974), pp. 51–71.

KOBRIN, S. J., "When Does Political Instability Result in Increased Investment Risk?" *Columbia Journal of World Business* (Fall 1978), pp. 113–122.

______, "Political Risk: A Review and Reconsideration," *Journal of International Business Studies* (Spring-Summer 1979), pp. 67–80.

______, "Foreign Enterprise and Forced Divestment in LDC's," *International Organization* (Winter 1980), pp. 65–88.

______, "Political Assessment by International Firms: Models or Methodologies?" *Journal of Policy Modeling* (May 1981), pp. 251–270.

______, *Environmental Assessment in the International Firm: Politics as a Problem of Managerial Process.* Berkeley, Cal.: University of California Press, 1982.

KOBRIN, S. J., J. BASEK, S. BLANK, and J. LAPALOMBARA, "The Assessment and Evaluation of Noneconomic Environments by American Firms: A Preliminary Report," *Journal of International Business Studies* (Spring-Summer 1980), pp. 32–47.

KORTH, C. M., "Management of International Lending Risk by Regional Banks," *Journal of Commercial Bank Lending* (October 1981), pp. 27–36.

KRAAR, L., "The Multinationals Get Smarter About Political Risks," *Fortune* (March 24, 1980), pp. 86–100.

MICALLEF, J. V., "Political Risk Assessment," *Columbia Journal of World Business* (Summer 1981), pp. 47–52.

MULLER, M. H., "Compensation for Nationalization: A North-South Dialogue," *Columbia Journal of Transnational Law,* no. 1 (1981), pp. 35–78.

NAGY, P. J., "Quantifying Country Risk: A System Developed by Economists at the Bank of Montreal," *Columbia Journal of World Business* (Fall 1978), pp. 135–147.

______, *Country Risk—Banker Point of View.* London: Euromoney, 1980.

NEHEMKIS, P., "Expropriation Has a Silver Lining," *California Management Review* (Fall 1974), pp. 15–22.

NEHRT, L. C., "The Political Climate for Private Investment," *Business Horizons* (June 1972), pp. 51–58.

NEVILLE, M. K., JR., "Present Status of Compensation by Foreign States for the Taking of Alien-Owned Property," *Vanderbilt Journal of Transnational Law* (Winter 1980), pp. 51–74.

NIGH, D., "The Effect of Political Events on United States Direct Foreign Investment: A Pooled Time-Series Cross-Sectional Analysis," *Journal of International Business Studies* (Spring 1985), pp. 1–17.

PERLITZ, M., "Compensatory Arrangements in International Licensing Agreements: Effects on Market Penetration Abroad, Foreign Pricing Policy, and Conflict Areas Between Licensee and Licensor," *Management International Review* (1980/1), pp. 75–82.

PORTER, M. E., "Please Note Location of Nearest Exit: Exit Barriers and Planning," *California Management Review* (Winter 1976), pp. 21–33.

ROBINSON, J. N., "Is It Possible to Assess Country Risk?" *Banker* (January 1981), p. 71.

ROBINSON, R. D., *National Control of Foreign Business Entry.* New York: Praeger, 1976.

ROBOCK, S., "Political Risk: Identification and Assessment," *Columbia Journal of World Business* (July/August 1971), pp. 6–20.

RUMMEL, R. J., and D. A. HEENAN, "How Multinationals Analyze Political Risk," *Harvard Business Review* (January/February 1978), pp. 67–76.

RYANS, J. K., and J. C. BAKER, "The International Centre for Settlement of Investment Disputes," *Journal of World Trade Law* (January-February 1976), pp. 65–79.

SACHDEV, J. C., "Disinvestment: A Corporate Failure or a Strategic Success?" *International Studies of Management and Organization* (Spring-Summer 1976), pp. 112–130.

______, "Disinvestment: A New Problem for Multinational Corporation Host Government Interface," *Management International Review* (March 1976), pp. 23–35.

SHAPIRO, A. C., "Managing Political Risk: A Policy Approach," *Columbia Journal of World Business* (Fall 1981), pp. 63–70.

SIMON, J. D., "Political Risk Assessment: Past Trends and Future Prospccts," *Columbia Journal of World Business* (Fall 1982), pp. 62–71.

SINNOTT, J. T., "Four Commandments for Wary Multinationals," *Industry Week* (April 5, 1982), p. 13.

STOEVER, WILLIAM A., *Renegotiations in International Business Transactions.* Lexington, Mass.: Lexington Books, 1981.

______, "LDC Governments: Takeovers and Renegotiations of Foreign Investments," *California Management Review* (Winter 1979), pp. 5–14.

THUNELL, L. H., *Political Risks in International Business: Investment Behavior of Multinational Corporations.* New York: Praeger, 1977.

TIPGUS, M. A., "Compliance with the Foreign Corrupt Practices Act," *Financial Executive* (August 1981), pp. 38–48.

TORNEDON, R., and J. J. BODDEWYN, "Foreign Divestment: Too Many Mistakes," *Columbia Journal of World Business* (Fall 1974), pp. 87–94.

TRUITT, F. J., *Expropriation of Private Foreign Investment.* Bloomington, Ind.: Graduate School of Business, Indiana University, 1974.

VAN AGTMAEL, A. W., "How Business Has Dealt with Political Risk," *Financial Executive* (January 1976), pp. 26–30.

VUYLSTEKE, C., "Foreign Investment Protection and the ICSID Arbitration," *Georgia Journal of International and Comparative Law* (Spring 1974), pp. 343–361.

WEEKLY, J. K., "Expropriation of U.S. Multinational Investments," *MSU Business Topics* (Winter 1977), pp. 27–36.

WELLS, L. T., JR., "Negotiating with Third World Governments," *Harvard Business Review* (January/February 1977), pp. 72–80.

WILSON, B. D., *Disinvestment of Foreign Subsidiaries.* Ann Arbor, Mich.: UMI Research Press, 1980.

WRIGHT, R. W., and C. S. RUSSEL, "Joint Ventures in Developing Countries: Realities and Responses," *Columbia Journal of World Business* (Summer 1975), pp. 74–80.

YONAH, A., and R. A. KILMARX, *Political Terrorism and Business: The Threat and Response.* New York: Praeger, 1979.

ZINK, D. W., *The Political Risks for Multinational Enterprise in Developing Countries.* New York: Praeger, 1973.

APPENDIX G

Chart of Insurable Risks

Exhibit 1 contains a summary and comparison of the types of risks that can be insured by OPIC, EXIMBANK, FCIA, and private insurers. The chart reflects the status of the various political risk insurance markets as of August 1, 1983. These data are updated on a regular basis by the firm indicated in the footnote.

Notes to Political/Export Credit Risks

1. OPIC's confiscation insurance is available only for those new investments or significant expansions of existing investments that satisfy a number of public policy eligibility requirements. As a condition precedent to the payment of a claim the insured usually will be required to assign its entire interest in the investment to OPIC.
2. The confiscation insurance programs of private insurers are available both for new and existing investments, subject only to risk-oriented underwriting considerations with no public policy eligibility requirements. These private insurers are willing to cover the takeover of all or a portion of a foreign investment.
3. Private insurers can cover direct physical damage caused by war under ocean marine and aviation policies. (Chubb offers a war damage coverage as an extension of its expropriation coverage.) Under the confiscation insurance arrangements of these insurers, however, coverage is afforded for the takeover of an insured asset or enterprise by a de facto or the de jure government, even if installed by force.
4. OPIC and Eximbank insurance and guarantees covering overseas contracts are usually tied irrevocably to the terms of the underlying contract—this could be a particularly significant factor if the underlying contract calls for arbitration in the country of the buyer.
5. Under political contingency coverages written by private insurers, any issue between the insured and the insurers may be submitted to specified neutral arbitration.
6. Private insurers may be expected to make available coverage for contract cancellations (and, perhaps, for payment defaults) by private buyers, where such cancellations or payment defaults are caused by the termination of contracts by foreign governmental agencies.
7. Neither OPIC, Eximbank, nor FCIA offers a specific coverage for loss arising out of the force majeure termination of a con-

Exhibit 1. Political/Export Credit Risks. Principal Causes of Loss; Insurance Facilities Available to U.S. Corporations.

[\\\\ hatched] Insurance normally available | [blank] Insurance may be negotiable | [//// hatched] Insurance generally not available

Foreign Investments

Causes of Loss	Insurance Facilities			
	OPIC	EXIMBANK	FCIA	Private Insurers
Confiscation, Expropriation,* Nationalization	Insurance normally available (1)	Insurance generally not available	Insurance generally not available	Insurance normally available (2)
"Creeping" Expropriation†	Insurance normally available	Insurance generally not available	Insurance generally not available	Insurance may be negotiable
Inconvertibility—Earnings, Debt Service, Fees	Insurance normally available	Insurance generally not available	Insurance generally not available	Insurance may be negotiable
War Damage	Insurance normally available	Insurance generally not available	Insurance generally not available	Insurance may be negotiable (3)

Overseas Contracts

Causes of Loss	Insurance Facilities			
	OPIC	EXIMBANK	FCIA	Private Insurers
On-Demand Bank Guarantees or Forfeiture Bonds‡	Insurance normally available (4)	Insurance generally not available	Insurance generally not available	Insurance normally available
Contract Repudiation—Public Buyers	Insurance normally available	Insurance generally not available (4)	Insurance generally not available	Insurance normally available (5)
Contract Cancellation—Private Buyers	Insurance generally not available	Insurance generally not available	Insurance generally not available	Insurance generally not available (6)
Contract Termination—Force Majeure▲	Insurance normally available (7)	Insurance generally not available (7)	Insurance generally not available (7)	Insurance may be negotiable (8)
Payment Default—Private Buyers	Insurance generally not available	Insurance normally available	Insurance normally available	Insurance may be negotiable
Confiscation, Deprivation—Mobile Equipment	Insurance normally available	Insurance generally not available	Insurance generally not available	Insurance normally available
Exchange Transfer	Insurance normally available	Insurance normally available	Insurance normally available	Insurance normally available
War Contingencies	Insurance normally available	Insurance normally available	Insurance normally available	Insurance normally available (9)

Source: The chart in this appendix was prepared by Alexander & Alexander of New York, Inc. (Foreign Credit Division, 1185 Avenue of the Americas, New York, N.Y. 10036). It was published in Business International Corporation, *International Risk Management*, a publication of the Financial Executives Institute, New Jersey, 1983, pp. 162–165. The chart and explanatory notes are reproduced by permission of the publisher and Business International Corporation.

Sale of Specialized Products—Pre-Shipment Risks

Causes of Loss	*Insurance Facilities*			
	OPIC	EXIMBANK	FCIA	Private Insurers
On-Demand Bank Guarantees or Forfeiture Bonds‡				
Contract Repudiation—Public Buyers				(6)
Contract Cancellation—Private Buyers				(6)
Contract Termination—Force Majeure▲		(7)	(7)	(8)
Export Embargo				
Import Embargo				
War Contingencies				(9)
Confiscation—Business of Private Buyers				
				(10)

Sale of Products or Services—Post-Shipment Risks

Causes of Loss	*Insurance Facilities*			
	OPIC	EXIMBANK	FCIA	Private Insurers
Exchange Transfer				
Default—Political Causes				
Default—Commercial Causes (Private Buyers)				(10)

*Expropriation refers essentially to the taking of an asset or enterprise by a foreign government without prompt, adequate, and effective compensation.

†"Creeping" Expropriation refers herein to a series of acts by a foreign government which are discriminatory in nature and which have the cumulative effect of being expropriatory—other meanings are often assigned to this term; underwriting acceptability is likely to vary with these meanings.

‡On-Demand Bank Guarantees or Forfeiture Bonds are callable at the sole discretion of the beneficiaries. Potential causes of political risk loss include the calling of these guarantees or bonds following specified political events and their unfair calling when the insured is not in material default on contractual obligations.

▲Force Majeure is a contractual provision which usually creates a right to terminate the contract after an agreed upon waiting period in the event of specified types of natural disasters or political events.

tract. These insurers, however, implicitly afford limited protection against this risk as an inherent part of an insured political risk peril, such as a war situation.

8. Some of the factors to be considered when analyzing a force majeure clause (as well as other terms of a contract) include: (a) circumstances to be insured (natural disasters, political events); (b) possibility of loss in excess of the buyer's liability; (c) ability of the insured to collect amounts owed; (d) termination by the buyer; and (e) termination by the insured.
9. Under their political contingency coverages, private insurers provide a significant degree of protection for losses attributable to war. This result is achieved by limiting the "war" exclusion under these coverages (a) to a war between the "Five Great Powers" or (b) to a war between the country of the buyer and the country of the insured.
10. As of August 1983, private-sector comprehensive export credit risks insurance protection (covering both political and commercial losses) is available only through AIG and AFIA.

The information contained here is explanatory and illustrative only. It does not control the interpretation of the various policies discussed, nor does it purport to identify all possible causes of political/export credit losses. Revised as of August 1, 1983, this information is subject to change at any time.

APPENDIX H

Foreign Investment Guarantee Programs[1]

This appendix contains a rundown of non-U.S. investment guarantee programs. Most industrial countries, particularly members of the Organization of Economic Cooperation and Development (OECD), provide investment insurance that has to some extent been patterned after OPIC. U.S. multinational firms with affiliates in these countries have the choice of insuring the political risk with OPIC, or of having their affiliates take out the insurance in the host country. The decision ultimately hinges on the relative coverage and cost of such insurance.

[1]Source: Business International Corporation, *International Risk Management,* a publication of the Financial Executives Institute, New Jersey, 1983, pp. 166–173. Reproduced by permission of the publisher and Business International Corporation. The data are compiled and updated by Alexander & Alexander of New York, Inc. (Foreign Credit Division, 1185 Avenue of the Americas, New York, N.Y. 10036). The information reflects the status of the investment guarantee programs as of August 1, 1983.

Exhibit 1. Rundown of Non-U.S. Investment Guarantee Programs

	AUSTRALIA	CANADA	DENMARK
Agency	Export Finance and Insurance.	Export Development Corp (EDC).	Danish International Development Agency (DANIDA).
Risk covered— (A) Political (B) Commercial	(A) Expropriation, war, revolution, currency inconvertibility. (B) Not covered.	(A) Coverage is available for loss due to expropriation, war, revolution, and insurrection, or inconvertibility.	(A) A comprehensive policy against nationalization, obstacles to the transfer of funds, and belligerent actions in the host country. Guarantees are not given to projects in areas where political risk is imminent. (B) Not covered.
Eligible countries	In principle, all countries; however, each application is treated on its individual merits.	In principle, all countries; however, EDC reserves option to restrict coverage to any country at any time.	Low-income developing countries.
Eligible investments	All new direct investment (equity and loan), which is of social and economic assistance to the development of the overseas country and in Australia's national interest. Coverage is now available for comfort letters and "third country" investments.	Almost any right that an investor might acquire in a foreign enterprise is covered, including equity, loans, management contracts, royalty and licensing arrangements. Investment may be in the form of cash, contribution in kind, or the issuance of a guarantee. Insurance is only available for new investments that include a significant expansion, modernization, or development of an existing enterprise.	All new direct (not portfolio) investments, loans, and know-how. No guarantee is given for takeover of an existing enterprise.
Eligible investors	Australian companies or residents. Foreign-owned subsidiaries have rarely been given cover under recent government guidelines.	Any person, partnership corporation, government agency, or other legal entity carrying on business in Canada.	Danish resident companies (including foreign-owned subsidiaries).
Indemnification— (A) Amount (% of loss) (B) Term	(A) 90% of actual loss. EFIC's maximum liability on all policies: \$200 million. (B) 15 years (minimum five).	(A) 85% of the actual loss up to an insured amount of C\$10 million; for insured amounts over C\$10 million, 75%. (B) 15 years maximum.	(A) Normally 85% of the guaranteed investment plus dividends up to 24% of the investment (equal to three years' dividends at 8% per year). (B) 15 years.

Exhibit 1. *(continued)*

	AUSTRALIA	CANADA	DENMARK
Rates; fees	As a benchmark figure, under 1% for all three risks and a concessional 0.8% for joint ventures. A "standby premium" of half of each respective cited rate, payable annually for the difference between the maximum insured amount elected and the current (each year) amount. Standby coverage cannot exceed 200% of the original investment and is for the purpose of insuring future profits.	The premium for the coverage of the three risks calculated on the current amount is 1% p.a. The investor, however, has a wide range of flexibility in his selection of coverage. This usually results in a substantial reduction in premium costs to the investor. There is a one-time handling fee of 1/10 of 1% of the proposed investment, to cover administrative expenses. The maximum and minimum are $1000 and $200 respectively.	0.5% p.a. of the insured amount.
Other stipulated requirements	To qualify, the investment must make a worthwhile contribution to the host country's development. Joint ventures are specifically encouraged.	The investment should help to maintain or enhance Canada's trade position. It should promote Canadian private-sector involvement in the industrial growth of developing nations.	Investor must generally strongly influence management and operation of the project, which must aid host-country economic development and have host-government approval.

	FRANCE	GERMANY	JAPAN
Agency	(1) Banque Francaise du Commerce Exterieur. (2) Coface.	Treuarbeit A/G.	Ministry of International Trade and Industry (MITI).
Risk covered— (A) Political (B) Commercial	(1) (A) Nationalization, expropriation, confiscation, war, and inconvertibility are covered by a single policy. (B) Not covered. (2) Same.	(A) A single policy covers war, expropriation, confiscation, nationalization, and inconvertibility. (B) Not covered.	(A) War risk. (B) Confiscation risk and remittance risk.
Eligible countries	(1) Developing countries that directly (via agreements) or indirectly (via membership in the Franco-African franc zone) provide sufficient protection to French investment. (2) Most nations.	Developing countries that provide sufficient legal protection for foreign investment.	In principle, all countries; however, each application is treated on its individual merits.

Exhibit 1. *(continued)*

	FRANCE	GERMANY	JAPAN
Eligible investments	(1) Direct or indirect investment (including reinvested profits up to 100% of original investment and repatriation of profits up to 25% of original investment) that not only adds to French activity abroad but has a positive effect on the French economy. (2) Capital investment (including reinvested profits up to 100% of original investment and repatriation of profits up to 50% of original investment) related to a real increase in French exports.	Investments in shares of foreign enterprises and long-term loans pertaining to those investments or capital provided to an overseas branch of a German company. Profits (including interest) may be insured up to 8% p.a. to a maximum loss of 24% of initial investment.	Shares and dividends in subsidiaries or joint ventures; long-term loans to foreign partners in joint ventures; debentures and other long-term loans to foreign-controlled firms; real estate, mining rights, and industrial property rights of Japanese-controlled firms; and loans for long-term contracts to develop and import minerals.
Eligible investors	French-controlled resident companies.	German registered companies (including foreign-owned subsidiaries).	Japan-domiciled firms.
Indemnification— (A) Amount (% of loss) (B) Term	(1) (A) Normally 90%, but this percentage may be reduced in some cases or raised in others to 95%. (B) Up to 15 years but exceptionally extended to 17 years. (2) (A) Normally 95% but can be reduced. (B) 15 years, but exceptionally extended to 20 years.	(A) 95% of net investment. (B) 15 years (extension to 20 years possible).	(A) Up to 80% in cases of commercial risk confiscation and remittance risk. (B) 15 years, may be extended for certain projects.
Rates; fees	(1) Between 0.7% and 0.9% (exceptionally 1%) of the investment guaranteed. (2) Normally 0.4% but exceptionally 0.5% or 0.6%.	0.5% p.a. of the insured amount.	0.55% p.a. of insured amount.
Other stipulated requirements	The guarantee must be applied for before the capital can be invested, and the project must obtain host-country approval.	The investment must be in accordance with host-country laws and all permits granted. Otherwise only partial coverage will be granted.	The investment must be conducive to sound development of Japan's foreign trade, a new outlay, and protected by law or policy of host country.

Exhibit 1. *(continued)*

	NETHERLANDS	SWEDEN	SWITZERLAND
Agency	Netherlands Credit Insurance Co (Nederlandsche Credietverzekering Mattschappij NV–NCM).	Swedish Export Credit Guarantee Board (EKN).	Bureau pour la Garantie Contre les Risques a l'Exportation.
Risk covered— (A) Political (B) Commercial	(A) Nationalization, confiscation, nontransferability of funds, civil war, and other disturbances. (B) Not covered.	(A) Nationalization, war damage, and currency inconvertibility may be covered in one policy or separately. (B) Not covered.	(A) Expropriation, nationalization, war, and nontransferability of funds. (B) Covered only when government defaults or when investment is guaranteed by a government-controlled bank.
Eligible countries	All developing countries that have, or that intend to have, a bilateral treaty protecting Dutch investments; or that provide sufficient guarantees to foreign capital.	Countries receiving official Swedish development assistance and other low-income LDCs. Exceptionally, can be applied to oil-exporting and certain Latin American countries.	All developing countries that agree to protect Swiss investments, either formally or informally.
Eligible investments	All new direct investment and associated proceeds to a maximum of 150% of the original investment. Within this limit the annual maximum profit (including interest) insurable is 8% of the insured amount that year.	All new projects and expansions (investments in cash or kind) where a Swedish company participates in management or control of the investment. Earnings may be covered up to 8% p.a. of original investment to a maximum of 24% of the original value.	Any loan or equity participation in a new investment is eligible for coverage. Profits may also be covered, provided they are allowed for at the time when the scheme starts operating. Profits are freely transferable.
Eligible investors	Any Dutch enterprises (including foreign-owned subsidiaries) manufacturing in Holland.	Swedish companies and residents who are actively engaged in business in Sweden.	Companies controlled at least 51% by Swiss citizens domiciled or resident in Switzerland.
Indemnification— (A) Amount (% of loss) (B) Term	(A) 90% of the amount insured (but no more than the actual loss, interest excluded), reduced by 10% p.a. 10 years after investment is completed. (B) usually 15 years after investment is completed.	(A) 80–90% of actual loss. (B) 15 years (extendable to 20 years in exceptional cases).	(A) 70% of initial outlay. However, after 1–5 years the guaranteed amount will be reduced by 5% p.a. Profit compensation is limited to 24% of guaranteed amount. (B) Up to 15 years.

Exhibit 1. ***(continued)***

	NETHERLANDS	SWEDEN	SWITZERLAND
Rates; fees	0.2% per quarter of insured amount. There is also a registration fee of 0.1% of the investment (minimum G1,000, maximum of G10,000).	0.7% p.a. for full cover. Lower premiums apply for limited cover in exceptional cases.	1.25% p.a. on equity or loan; (loan rate raised by 0.5 percentage points to 1.75% if no government guarantee is available); 4% on guaranteed profits.
Other stipulated requirements	The investment must further the economic development of the recipient country and must improve trade relations. Protection must be offered to the investor, and the host government must approve the project.	The host country must recognize the investment as contributing to its economic development. The investor must provide host-country employees with satisfactory working conditions.	The new investment must contribute to the host country's economy and must have close ties with the Swiss economy.

	UK	EEC (Proposed)
Agency	Export Credits Guarantee Department (ECGD).	National agencies administering common guarantees by delegation.
Risk covered— (A) Political (B) Commercial	(A) Expropriation, war and insurrection, and currency inconvertibility. (B) Not covered.	(A) War and revolution, nationalization, expropriation, confiscation, transfer of profits and capital. (B) None.
Eligible countries	All countries.	Any LDC, on a specific project basis (see below).
Eligible investments	Equity capital, which may include plant or know-how. Acquisition of existing enterprises, provided "new" capital is involved. Portfolio investment where participation is greater than L50,000 and 10% of the venture.	Equity investments intended by host country and EEC to create or increase a permanent holding in manufacturing or trading facilities. Long-term loans and advances to such establishments are also eligible. Minimum investment of UA50 million and participation of firms from at least two member states is required.

Exhibit 1. *(continued)*

	UK	EEC (Proposed)
Eligible investors	All UK-based companies, including foreign-owned subsidiaries.	EEC companies, EEC subs of non-EEC companies, or joint ventures with EEC companies.
Indemnification— (A) Amount (% of loss) (B) Term	(A) 90% of the claim. (B) 15 years (minimum 3 years).	No details provided.
Rates; fees	1% p.a. on the current amount (less 20% of premium if one type of risk is excluded from the policy) plus 0.25% on the difference between the current amount and the maximum, which is normally twice the equity value.	To be worked out.
Other stipulated requirements	The investor is responsible for obtaining all necessary approval from the host government. ECGD is granted considerable flexibility in deciding whether or not to accept a policy, to change the terms offered or to remove a country from the eligibility list if necessary.	Projects must be of interest to EEC as well as to host country, be approved by host country, benefit host country in terms of economic development, foster intra-LDC economic and trade cooperation, and leave "adequate" participation opportunities to local capital.

CASE STUDY

International Machine Corporation An Analysis of a Foreign Investment Project in Mexico*

*Prepared for Business International Corporation by Vinod B. Bavishi, Director, Center for Transnational Accounting and Financial Research, University of Connecticut: and Hany A. Shawky, School of Business Administration, State University of New York at Albany. Published in Business International Corporation, *International Risk Management,* a publication of the Financial Executives Institute, Morristown, New Jersey 1983, pp. 127–137.

INTRODUCTION

International Machine Corporation (IMC) is a large, established manufacturer of a wide variety of food processing and packaging equipment. IMC has been exporting its products to Mexico for several years and is considering setting up a Mexican subsidiary. The company's international division believes that demand warrants a Mexican investment at this time; management believes that the Mexican market for IMC products is expanding, that the economy is growing, and that producing such products locally is consistent with the national aspirations of the Mexican government.

FINANCIAL ANALYSIS OF THE PROJECT

IMC believes that a project must result in a positive net present value (NPV) from the parent's point of view and will therefore add to the overall value of the firm. Exhibit 1 shows the projected cash flow.

ANALYSIS OF POLITICAL RISKS

While everyone will agree that political risk is inherent in any overseas investment, few can agree as to how this risk should be incorporated into the investment decision. Political risk can range from outright expropriation by the host government to simple interference or lack of cooperation by local officials.

The following is an examination of how political risk is analyzed and incorporated into the investment decision. Several quantitative techniques are suggested to deal with and assess the political risk in Mexico. In order

Exhibit 1. Projected Cash Flows: Parent's View

	YEARS/EXPECTED EXCHANGE RATE										
Cash Flow Items	0 P22:$1*	1 P24.2:$1	2 P26.6:$1	3 P29.3:$1	4 P32.2:$1	5 P35.4:$1	6 P39.0:$1	7 P42.9:$1	8 P47.2:$1	9 P51.9:$1	10 P57.1:$1
1. Initial investment in $ millions	(6.0)										
2. Licensing fees											
a. in millions of pesos		14	18	24	32	43	56	74	98	129	170
b. in $ millions		0.6	0.7	0.8	1.0	1.2	1.4	1.7	2.1	2.5	3.0
c. less: US taxes @ 42%, in $ million		(0.3)	(0.3)	(0.3)	(0.4)	(0.5)	(0.6)	(0.7)	(0.9)	(1.1)	(1.3)
d. net after tax, in $ millions		.3	.4	.5	.6	.7	.8	1.0	1.2	1.4	1.7
3. Dividends received											
a. in millions of pesos		0	0	0	50	71	97	134	183	247	334
b. in $ millions					1.6	2.0	2.5	3.1	3.9	4.8	5.9
4. After-tax effects of lost exports in $ millions		(1.0)	(1.2)	(1.5)							
5. Terminal payment, in $ millions											12.6†
6. Total cash flows 1 + 2d + 3b + 4 + 5, in $ millions	(6.0)	(0.7)	(0.8)	(1.0)	2.2	2.7	3.3	4.1	5.1	6.2	20.2
7. Discount factor @ 12%‡	1.0	0.893	0.797	0.712	0.636	0.567	0.507	0.452	0.404	0.361	0.322
8. Present value, in $ millions	(6.0)	(0.6)	(0.6)	(0.7)	1.4	1.5	1.7	1.9	2.1	2.2	6.5
9. Cumulative present value, in $ millions	(6.0)	(6.6)	(7.2)	(7.9)	(6.5)	(5.0)	(3.3)	(1.4)	0.7	2.9	9.4

*For the life of the project, inflation in Mexico is expected to average 20% annually; in the United States, it is expected to be 10%. The 10-percent-point difference represents expected decline in the value of the peso vis-à-vis the dollar. Thus, project cash flow is adjusted for expected changes in exchange rates.

†IMC's share of the Mexican subsidiary's net worth
= 60% (beginning equity + net income years 1 to 10—dividend distributed years 4 through 10)
= 60% (220 + 2835 − 1860)
= P717 million
= $12.6 million

‡The discount rate of 12% is the world-wide weighted average cost of capital.

to incorporate this element in the capital budgeting process, this analysis examines two broad categories of adjustments. The first category adjusts the cash flow figures, while the second adjusts the discount rate used to evaluate the project's cash flow.

Adjusting Cash Flow

The Use of Certainty-Equivalent Coefficient. In this approach, a certainty-equivalent coefficient for political risk is assigned for the project's cash flow for each year. This coefficient is a function of the expected political risk in any given year and will vary from a value of 1, denoting complete certainty, to 0, denoting the complete confiscation of the cash flow in that year.

In light of the political risk summary presented in this case, estimates of the certainty-equivalent coefficient for the 10-year cash flow are 1 for the first three years; .9 for years four, five, and six; .8 for years seven and eight; and .7 for years nine and ten.

The net present value (NPV) for the project will then be calculated as follows:

$$\text{NPV} = \sum_{t=1}^{3} \frac{X_t}{(1+k)^t} + (.9)\sum_{t=4}^{6} \frac{X_t}{(1+k)^t} + (.8)\sum_{t=7}^{8} \frac{X_t}{(1+k)^t} + (.7)\sum_{t=9}^{10} \frac{X_t}{(1+1)} - \text{I}$$

where: x_t represents the cash flow in period t (Exhibit 1)
k is the firm's worldwide weighted average cost of capital (12%)
I is the investment outlay (Exhibit 1)

Applying the project's cash flows per the above formulation results in:

$$\text{NPV} = 1.0(-.6 - .6 - .7) + .9(1.4 + 1.5 + 1.7) + .8(1.9 + 2.1) + .7(2.2 + 6.5) - 6.0$$

$$= -1.9 + 4.1 + 3.2 + 6.1 - 6.0$$

$$\text{NPV} = \$5.5 \text{ million}$$

On the basis of the above adjustment procedure, and subject to the appropriateness of the estimated certainty-equivalent coefficients, IMC should proceed with the project, since it provides a positive NPV after political risks are taken into consideration.

Advantages of Method

- adjusts cash flow
- specific to each country
- specific to the project
- adjusts for the risk in each year separately

Disadvantages of Method

- the certainty-equivalent coefficients are difficult to estimate
- does not incorporate cumulative risk effects

Adjusting for the Possibility of Expropriation/Nationalization. In this approach, a simple NPV formula is introduced to account for the possibility of expropriation. Let the probability of expropriation be equal to Ph in year h and 0 in all other years. Accordingly, the NPV of the projects can be calculated as follows:

$$\text{NPV} = \sum_{t=1}^{h=1} \frac{x_t}{(1+k)^t} + (1 - \text{Ph}) \sum_{t=h}^{n} \frac{x_t}{(1+k)^t} + \text{Ph} \frac{\text{Gh}}{(1+k)^h} - \text{I}$$

where n is the expected project life and Gh is the expected dollar compensation should expropriation/nationalization occur.

Past experience indicates that there has never been expropriation activity by the Mexican government. However, a trend toward self-sufficiency and nationalization exists. As far as IMC is concerned, nationalization during the life of the project is equivalent to a compensated expropriation. Thus, the application of this model might shed some light on the desirability of the project in light of Mexico's political climate.

Based on recent experience in Mexico (and consistent with declared national goals), the probability of IMC seeing its subsidiary nationalized in its seventh year of operation is approximately 50 percent. In this event, IMC can expect compensation from the Mexican government amounting to \$5 million. The above discussion can thus be summarized as: Ph = 50%, h = 7, and Gh = \$5 million.

We now apply the above-described approach to the cash flow of the Mexican project as follows:

$$\text{NPV} = \sum_{t=1}^{6} \frac{x_t}{(1+k)^t} + \frac{(.5)\,{}^x7}{(1+k)^7} + \frac{(.5)\,{}^x8}{(1+k)^8} + \frac{(.5)\,{}^x9}{(1+k)^9} + \frac{(.5)\,{}^x10}{(1+k)^{10}} + \frac{.5\,{}^G7}{(1+k)^7} - \text{I}$$

Applying the appropriate cash flow from Exhibit 1 (line 8), we obtain:

$$\begin{aligned}\text{NPV} &= 1.0(-.6 - .6 - .7 + 1.4 + 1.5 + 1.7) + 0.5(1.9 + 2.1 \\ &\quad + 2.2 + 6.5) + 0.5(5.0 \times .452) - 6.0 \\ &= 2.7 + 6.4 + 1.1 - 6.0 \\ \text{NPV} &= \$4.2 \text{ million}\end{aligned}$$

Based on a 50 percent probability that nationalization will occur in year 7, and an estimated government compensation of \$5 million in such case, IMC can still realize a positive net present value. This indicates that, even with the given percentage of political risk, the Mexican project is a good investment.

Advantages of Method

- treats cash flow
- treats years independently
- gives a good perspective regarding the desirability of a project, taking into consideration the possibility of nationalization

Disadvantages of Method

- difficult to estimate quantitatively the probability of expropriation
- difficult to obtain a good approximation of when expropriation might occur
- treats expropriation or nationalization exclusively, therefore not a good indicator of total political risk
- difficult to estimate compensation from the host government

The Use of Decision Trees (Conditional Probabilities). Often economic losses due to political risk occur as a result of a sequence of events beginning with economic problems, political instability and change of power which may result in a new regime that may exercise expropriation or nationalization. The problem of assessing political risk may be approached by using a decision tree, as shown in Exhibit 2.

The decision tree in Exhibit 2 demonstrates all the possible conditions that might occur in Mexico. The numbers on the tree branches are the

Exhibit 2.

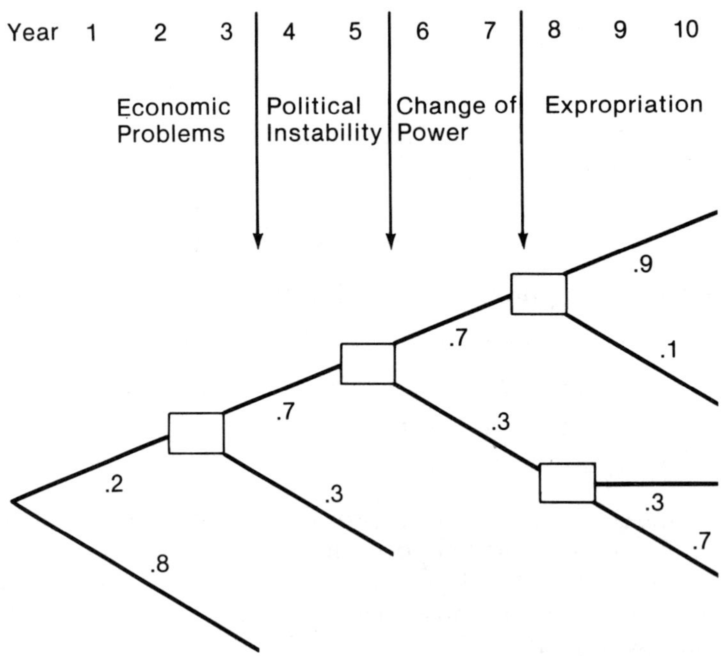

probabilities that the various events will occur. Assessing the project's cash flow is done by asking: What are the expected cash flows if economic problems developed in Mexico? and so on. This will give the appropriate numbers in the first branch of the tree. Assessing the cash flow under all circumstances will provide the necessary numbers on all the tree branches. Then the probabilities are used to obtain values and proceed from the farthest (extreme right) branch of the tree toward the left, giving the expected value of cash flow.

Advantages of Method

- takes into consideration sequential events
- treats all facets of political risk
- easy to apply once the numbers are developed

Disadvantages of Method

- difficult to predict the various conditions in a specific country and their duration
- difficult to estimate the probabilities of these conditions' occurring

Adjusting the Discount Rate

Adjusting the discount rate for risks that are unique to a particular country or a particular project appears at first glance to be harder to justify on purely theoretical grounds. While this is generally the conceptual position, adjusting the discount rates for political risk in a systematic manner can be justified under certain conditions and for various practical reasons.

Many MNCs arbitrarily use a higher discount rate for their foreign projects than that used for domestic projects. The premium or increase in the discount rate is usually arrived at subjectively and is rarely justified. The only reason usually given is that higher risks are associated with foreign operations. Increasing the discount rate seems to be a sensible as well as convenient method used in MNCs' capital budgeting processes.

Rather than increasing the discount rate subjectively, there are two alternative procedures a firm can use to adjust the discount rate for overseas projects in a systematic manner. The basic premise underlying the two approaches suggested here is the following:

- Countries differ significantly with respect to political risk. Thus, the premium should be commensurate with the risk of each country.
- MNCs are well diversified across countries and are interested primarily in ranking the riskiness of their investments in a relative sense.
- Political risk is inherent in foreign operations and thus can be viewed as systematic risk.

The Use of Political Risk Assessment Services. While the use of readily available political risk assessment services is viewed with some suspicion from the business community, these services are relatively new and are likely to become more popular and gain greater acceptance as their procedures are refined and improved.

One service provides an index ranking countries by degree of political risk. The index ranges from 0 to 100—the higher the number, the lower the risk. The number for Mexico is 75. It must be noted that this index (as with all others) is in relative terms—hence, investing in Mexico (75) is riskier than investing in Germany (86), as reflected in the relative magnitude of the numbers.

An approach to systematically incorporating the information provided by a country risk index is suggested below for the case of IMC's Mexican investment.

The added political risk in investing in Mexico rather than investing in the United States is 25 points (on a 100-point scale). Hence, we should expect commensurate compensation for the added risk and thus adjust the discount rate in such a manner as to incorporate the magnitude of the above relative riskiness indicated by the index numbers.

Applying this to IMC's Mexican investment, we have

$$\text{IMC worldwide weighted average cost of capital} = 12\%$$
$$\text{Mexico's risk level} = 75$$

To invest in Mexico, IMC must adjust its required rate of return (12 percent) to account for the added political risk. Required return for Mexican project:

$$= \frac{.12}{.75} = 16\%$$

The 16 percent rate for discounting the Mexican project's cash flow in Exhibit 1 yields:

$$\begin{aligned} \text{NPV} &= -0.7(.862) - 0.8(.743) - 1.0(.641) + 2.2(.552) + 2.7(.476) \\ &\quad + 3.3(.410) + 4.1(.354) + 5.1(.305) \\ &\quad + 6.2(2.63) + 20.2(.227) - 6.0 \\ &= -.6 - .6 - .6 + 1.2 + 1.3 + 1.4 + 1.5 + 1.6 + 1.6 \\ &\quad + 4.6 - 6.0 \end{aligned}$$

$$\text{NPV} = \$5.4 \text{ million}$$

The NPV is positive after adjusting for political risk.

Note: This approach has in essence translated the index number into a systematic way in which to derive risk premiums for different countries. In this case, the premium for Mexico is 4 percent.

Advantages of Method

- the index numbers are readily available
- the adjustment procedure is fairly simple
- the method treats different countries systematically

Disadvantages of Method

- the reliability of any one index is unsure
- all indices cover short-term periods only
- all numbers are simply forecasts

An In-House Index. Many large MNCs have created their own country-evaluation indices. This can usually be done through basic research and the firm's historical experience in the country or region. The objective of the index should be to provide a relative ranking for various countries or geographical regions of the world. Once these evaluations are made, the results must be summarized in such a way as to make a useful and operational tool to be used effectively in the capital budgeting process.

In recent years, IMC has developed an in-house index that subdivides the world into four levels of political risk.

1. the United States and Canada
2. Western Europe and Japan
3. newly emerging industrial countries
4. developing nations

IMC has developed this system of ranking based on a number of factors that are commonly associated with political risk, such as political instability, expropriation experience, etc. While the index is not very detailed, IMC management feels it is sufficient to represent fairly the risk differentials between most, if not all, countries they would be interested in evaluating.

The graph in Exhibit 3, based on the index, represents IMC's assessment.

IMC clearly found that Mexico falls into the newly emerging industrialized group. Thus, a required return of 18 percent would be expected from the Mexican investment.

Applying the 18 percent discount rate to the project's cash flow yields

$$\begin{aligned} NPV &= .7(.848) - .8(.718) - 1.0(.609) + 2.2(.516) + 2.7(.437) \\ &\quad + 3.3(.370) + 4.1(.314) + 5.1(.266) \\ &\quad + 6.2(.226) + 20.2(.191) - 6.0 \\ &= -.6 - .6 - .6 + 1.1 + 1.2 + 1.2 \\ &\quad + 1.3 + 1.4 + 3.9 - 6.0 \end{aligned}$$

$$NPV = \$3.7 \text{ million}$$

Exhibit 3.

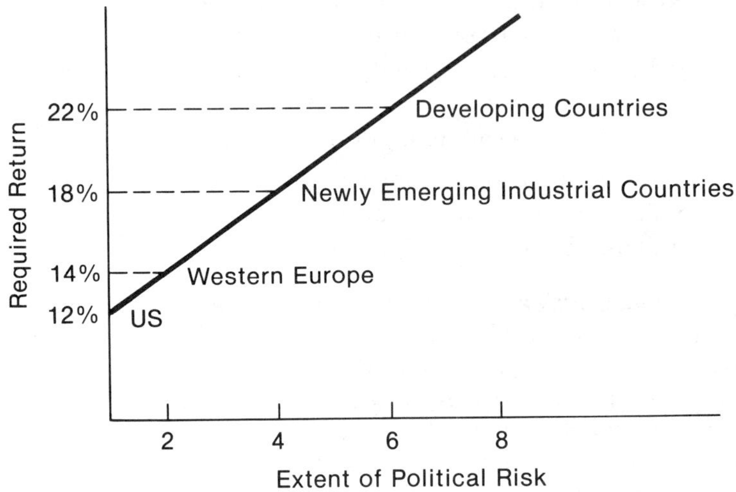

Concluding Comments on Political Risk Assessment

There are very difficult issues to be answered with respect to incorporating political risk into the capital budgeting process. This section was designed to introduce the reader to some of the techniques available to aid the decision maker in assessing political risk. Of primary importance are the following:

1. Political risk assessment should be systematic.
2. It should be incorporated in any new (or expanded) investment decision from the beginning.
3. All information available should be utilized.
4. Firms' experience and the information they generate externally should be evaluated systematically.
5. As many approaches as possible should be used.

For the Mexican investment, IMC found that it had obtained a wide range of evaluation on the project and felt that, in total, the risk inherent in the Mexican project would be worth taking. It is important to note that while the specific estimates employed in any one technique were difficult to obtain with accuracy, collectively they reflect favorably on the investment and provide a basis upon which a sound investment decision can be made.

18

Taxation of the Multinational Firm

INTRODUCTION

The topic of the taxation of the MNC involves a number of complex and dynamic tax issues, as well as knowledge of accounting procedures which vary widely from one country to another. The financial manager of a U.S. MNC, for instance, has to be fully acquainted not only with U.S. tax laws pertaining to the taxation of foreign-based income, but also with the tax policies of host countries. Moreover, he or she has to be cognizant of such issues and practices as:

1. Tax withholding provisions and the extent and procedure of claiming tax credit for taxes paid to foreign taxing jurisdictions.
2. The treatment by the United States' and host countries' tax authorities of transactions involving the parent company and its affiliates, and transactions among affiliates of the same company.
3. Opportunities for reducing the overall tax burden through transfer pricing, and use of tax havens to defer payment of taxes to the home country.
4. The provisions of tax treaties (if any) between the United States and each of the host countries where the MNC conducts operations.
5. Tax incentives available through the formation of special entities geared for exports, such as the Domestic International Sales Corporation (DISC).

Most of these issues are interrelated. For example, tax withholding provisions are spelled out in tax treaties concluded between the United States and a number of countries. The use of tax havens by U.S. MNCs, for purposes of tax deferral, is circumscribed by limitations imposed by tax authorities on the pricing of intracorporate transfer of input and other resources.

The dynamic and ever-changing tax environment is a major challenge for financial managers as they strive to keep abreast of new developments. Data relating to national tax codes and changes in such codes, especially those affecting the operations of MNCs, are published regularly by international accounting firms. The leading publications are Price Waterhouse, *Corporate Taxes: A Worldwide Summary* and *U.S. Corporations Doing Business Abroad;* Ernst and Whinney, *Foreign and U.S. Corporate Income and Withholding Tax Rates;* and Arthur Young, *Financial Reporting and Accounting.*

NATIONAL CORPORATE INCOME TAX CODES

Corporate income tax rates vary widely among countries, ranging from zero in tax haven localities, such as the Bahamas and the Cayman Islands, to maximum marginal rates of 56 percent in Germany (Exhibit 18-1). The leading industrial countries generally have the highest corporate income tax rate, ranging from 40 to 55 percent. Less industrialized countries in Europe and the western hemisphere have somewhat lower rates to stimulate investment by both domestic and foreign firms. LDCs' corporate income tax rates are generally lower than the first tier of industrial countries and the second tier of developed, but less industrialized countries. Although they vary widely, they cluster around 25 to 30 percent. These rates have tended to rise in recent years as their governments continue to seek revenue sources in support of the development effort. A number of LDCs grant tax concessions for a limited number of years to attract foreign firms, particularly in the industrial sector. These concessions may take the form of either a "tax holiday," such as exemption from the corporate income tax for a specified number of years (typically five), or an accelerated depreciation of the initial investment.

Tax haven countries assess very low corporate income tax rates (typically zero to five percent) as part of their overall policy to stimulate the development of their economies by maintaining an open, unrestricted, and virtually tax-free environment. Their economies thrive on attracting financial resources from richer, higher-tax countries, and to a lesser extent, on tourism. MNCs and large international banks maintain "shell" or "tax haven" affiliates in these countries to take advantage of their virtually tax- and control-free environment. Switzerland and Hong Kong, which have traditionally been international financial centers, assess fairly low tax rates (less than 10 percent in Switzerland and 19 percent in Hong Kong) to

Exhibit 18-1. Selected Foreign Income Tax Rate Summaries

	FEDERAL (NATIONAL) CORPORATE TAX RATES			WITHHOLDING RATES ON PAYMENTS TO NONRESIDENTS[3]		
Country	Ordinary Income Rate	Capital Gains Rate	State, Provincial or Local Rate	Dividends	Interest	Royalties
Argentina	33%	15%	None	17.5%	11.25%	18%
Brazil	35%	35%	None	25%	25%	25%
Canada[1]	46%	23%	10–16%	25%	25%	25%
China[2]	33%	33%	None	10%	10%	10%
France	50%	15%	None	25%	45%	33.5%
Germany	56%	56%	15–24.5%	25–30%	25%	25%
Greece	49%	30%	None	None	None	None
Hong Kong	18.5%	None	None	None	None	None
Ireland	50%	40–60%	None	None	35%	35%
Italy	36%	30%	16.2%	32.4%	15%	21%
Jamaica	35–45%	12.5%	None	37.5%	None	None
Japan	43.3%	43.3%	13.2%	20%	20%	20%
Mexico	42%	42%	None	55%	42%	42%
Phillippines	35%	20%	None	15%	15%	25%
Spain	35%	35%	2%	5–15%	5–15%	5–15%
Sweden	52%[4]	0–37.5%	4%	30%	None	52%
Switzerland	9.8%	9.8%	9–24%	35%	35%	None
South Africa	50%	None	None	15%	10%	15%
United Kingdom	45%	30%	None	None	30%	30%
United States	46%	28%	0–12%	30%	30%	30%

[1]Canada allows a 10 percent tax abatement for income earned in the Canadian provinces.
[2]Only joint ventures between the government of China and the foreign investor are allowed to operate in China.
[3]Rates applicable to nontreaty countries. Lower (or nil) rates apply to nonresidents of treaty countries.
[4]Total effective rate including local taxes.

Source: Coopers and Lybrand, *1985 International Tax Summaries,* John Wiley and Sons, New York, 1985.

maintain their status as the meccas of financial resources. Funds flow from all over the world to these two centers for investment and safekeeping, attracted in part by the control-free environment, and the confidentiality with which transactions are conducted.

The disparity in corporate income tax rates among countries is more than matched by the diversity of the national tax codes in defining taxable income and allowable deductions. When this diversity is superimposed on the differences in applicable accounting standards and procedures, it is not difficult to see how complex tax planning is for a wide-flung MNC. Firms operating in high-inflation environments, as is the case in many Latin American countries, face a continuous task of revaluing their price structure and assets, to allow greater write-downs for tax purposes. National tax codes also differ as to the treatment of retained vs. distributed earnings by assessing a lower rate on the latter. In Japan, for example, a 43 percent maximum rate is applied to retained earnings, whereas distributed earnings are assessed only 33 percent. The lower tax assessment on distributed profits partly offsets the double taxation of dividends.

In addition to the diversity of national corporate income tax systems, MNCs face a variety of other taxes and levies in host countries. Indirect taxes, as contrasted with direct taxes on corporate and personal incomes, are an important feature of the tax environment outside the United States. The most prominent of such taxes is the value-added tax applied in most western European countries, including all European Economic Community members, some of the largest Latin American countries (Argentina, Brazil, Chile, Mexico, and Peru), as well as in a number of Asian and Middle Eastern countries.

The value-added tax, typically about 15 percent, is essentially a sales tax which is levied at the value added in each stage of production and distribution until the product reaches the final consumer. In general, this tax is applied to consumer goods, while capital goods and certain products related to medical and health services, as well as educational and religious activities are usually exempt. Being an indirect tax, it is rebated on exports and levied on imports at the borders, under the rules of the General Agreement on Tariff and Trade (GATT). Direct taxes, such as corporate income tax, are not rebatable on export sales under the rules of GATT.

Proponents of the value-added tax, including those who advocate its introduction in the United States, claim that the tax has several advantages compared to alternative indirect forms of taxation, or even compared with corporate income tax. It is broad-based, relatively easy to calculate and levy, and difficult to evade. It is more equitable and less distortive than other forms of indirect taxation, such as the turnover tax, which is assessed and collected every time a product changes hands. It is also less amenable to be evaded, as is the case in corporate income tax, by such practices as tax sheltering, loss-carry-forward provisions, intracorporate transfer pricing, charitable contributions, and plain accounting gimmickry. Critics of this tax point out that it is, just like all indirect taxes, regressive, having a larger incidence on lower income groups. There is also some evidence that the imposition of the value-added tax for the first time increases the rate of inflation. This is probably due to the attempt of the taxpayer at each stage of production and distribution to shift the tax assessed to the next stage.

TAX ISSUES FACING THE MNC

The major tax issues facing the MNC may be summarized under the following points:

1. Tax treatment of its foreign-based income by tax authorities in the home country, and the extent to which it can claim credit for taxes paid or withheld in host countries.
2. Tax treatment of its foreign-based income retained for reinvestment by affiliates, or profits transferred among those affiliates, or from them to another affiliate in a tax haven location.
3. Treatment by host country tax authorities of profits generated by its affiliates, and taxation of such transfers to the parent company as dividends, interest on parent company loans, fees and royalties, and other forms of compensation.
4. Treatment of income received from financial investments outside the home country both by tax authorities of the countries of issue (of financial and capital market instruments) and by the home country.
5. Whether or not a tax treaty exists between the home country and host countries where it maintains operation, and the provisions of the treaty with respect to points 1 through 4.

We will now proceed to examine these issues in some depth, but not necessarily in the order they were presented. There is by necessity a considerable degree of overlapping and interrelationship among them, so discussing one issue inevitably leads to the discussion of one or more other issues. Inasmuch as most major MNCs have the United States as their home country, and a large number of non-U.S. MNCs operate mainly in the United States, the discussion will focus on the taxation of U.S. MNCs at home and abroad, as well as on the taxation of foreign firms operating in the United States.

UNITED STATES INCOME TAXATION OF FOREIGN CORPORATIONS

The ground rules which govern U.S. tax treatment of foreign corporations were established in 1913. The Foreign Investors Tax Act of 1966 made substantial changes in the ground rules, and the Tax Reform Act of 1976 added a few refinements. The test of whether or not a corporation is foreign focuses on the place of organization. A foreign corporation is one which is not organized or created under the laws of the United States, or any state, or the District of Columbia. Corporations created under the laws of U.S. possessions are deemed to be foreign corporations.

The 1966 Tax Act separated the tax treatment of business income from that of investment income. The mechanism adopted for separating the two was the *effectively connected* concept. Income of foreign taxpayers which is "effectively connected with the conduct of a trade or business within the United States" is subject to tax at normal domestic tax rates. All other income is considered passive investment income, subject to a flat or treaty rate of tax. Prior to the 1966 act those engaged in business in the United States were taxed at rates applicable to U.S. corporations on all U.S. source income.[1]

According to this criterion, three categories of foreign corporations engaged in U.S. business may be distinguished:

1. A foreign corporation which has an office or a fixed place of business in the United States is subject to tax at regular corporate income tax rates on its "effectively connected" taxable income and capital gains from U.S. sources. It is taxable on all its other U.S. source determinable income at a 30 percent rate.[2]
2. A foreign corporation which has no office or fixed place of business in the United States is taxed on its "effectively connected" income at regular corporate income tax rates. It is also taxed on its other income at a flat 30 percent rate, except "effectively connected" capital gains, which are taxed at the capital gains tax rate. Capital gains which are not "effectively connected" are not subject to tax.[3]
3. A foreign corporation which is not engaged in U.S. trade or business is taxed on U.S. source fixed or determinable gross income at the 30 percent withholding tax rate, which does not apply to its capital gains. A number of exceptions exist, including treaty modifications.[4]

The test of whether a certain income is U.S. based depends on the type of income. The source of interest income is the residence of the obligor. For example, interest on U.S. government or corporate bonds is considered U.S. source income; so is interest on certificates of deposits which is the obligation of a foreign branch of a U.S. bank. Interest on obligations of

[1]Strick, "The Effectively Connected Concept in the Foreign Investors Tax Act of 1966," *Taxes,* Vol. 45 (1967), pp. 3–5.

[2]*Ibid.,* p. 5.

[3]*Ibid.,* p. 4.

[4]D. Ross, "U.S. Taxation of Aliens and Foreign Corporations: The Foreign Investors Tax Act of 1966," *Tax Law Review,* Vol. 22 (1967), p. 279.

foreign corporations not engaged in U.S. trade or business is considered income from sources outside the United States.

Dividends received from a domestic corporation are U.S. source income except: (1) dividends of domestic corporations incorporated in United States possessions, and (2) dividends of a domestic corporation deriving less than 20 percent of its gross income from U.S. sources for the preceding three-year period.[5] Dividends received from a foreign corporation are U.S. source income unless less than 50 percent of such corporation's gross income for the preceding three-year period was "effectively connected" income. If 50 percent or more of the "effectively connected" income of the dividend paying foreign corporation's income is derived from U.S. sources, the dividend received is apportioned between U.S. and foreign sources in the ratio that "effectively connected" income bears to gross income from all sources.[6]

The source of payment for personal services is the place where the services which give rise to the income are performed, irrespective of the payer's residence, or the place of payment. If the amount is paid for services performed both within and outside the United States, an allocation of the amount is made depending on the proportion performed in the United States. For example, if the managing director of a foreign corporation performs services both in the United States and abroad, the proportion of the services performed in the United States to his or her total services will determine what part of his fees is considered U.S. source income.[7] Similarly, the apportionment principle is applied to other types of income generated from sources partly within and partly outside the United States. The apportionment formula depends on the category of income.

The source of income arising from the rental of real estate or tangible personal property is determined by the site of the property. If the property is located outside the United States, the rentals are considered foreign source income.

The Internal Revenue Code also specifies certain exemptions from U.S. corporate income tax. A foreign corporation's gross income does not include items which are considered exempt items for domestic corporations. Income derived from the operation of ships and aircraft registered under a foreign country's laws is exempt if the foreign country grants a similar exemption to U.S. corporations. This exemption, which dates back to 1921 (for ships) and 1948 (for airlines), was extended to income generated from communication satellites in 1983.[8] Interest received by foreign central banks and the Bank for International Settlements (based in Basle, Switzerland) from deposits held in U.S. banks is also exempt from U.S. tax,

[5]Internal Revenue Code, Section 861, August 1983.
[6]*Ibid.,* Section 861 (a) (2) (B).
[7]U.S. Treasury Regulation 1.861, August 1983.
[8]U.S. Treasury Regulations 1.883.1, August 1983.

unless the deposits are held in relation to commercial transactions. A foreign corporation's income may also be wholly or partially exempt from U.S. income tax under tax conventions negotiated with foreign countries.

TAX TREATIES

Bilateral tax treaties have been negotiated between countries primarily for the purpose of reducing the incidence of double taxation, and granting each other preferential tax withholding provisions and other favorable features on a reciprocal basis.[9]

The provisions of tax treaties vary to some extent. However, they address common issues which are of concern both to MNCs and individual investors. The features highlighted below refer to U.S. tax conventions with other countries, but these are generally common to most treaties binding any two signatories. The main features are

1. Treaties generally exempt "industrial and commercial profits" of foreign corporations except profits to those engaged in business through a "permanent establishment" located in the United States. The intent of this provision is to grant the exemption to firms engaged primarily in export activities rather than manufacturing operations. The term "permanent establishment" refers to a place for carrying on a trade or business. The tax courts have interpreted this provision widely to include an office located in the United States, the presence of directors, officers, and employees, bank accounts, telephone listing, or an agent with a general authority to contract.[10]
2. If a "permanent establishment" exists, treaties address the apportionment of taxable income between the two jurisdictions, as explained, for example, in the preceding section.
3. Treaties typically specify lower tax withholding provisions between the two signatory countries. For example, a number of the treaties between the United States and other countries specify a withholding tax of 15 percent, compared with 30 percent, which apply to not "effectively connected" U.S. source income applicable to corporations or citizens with which no treaty exists. As explained earlier, "effectively connected" income is taxable at the same rate applicable to U.S. corporations.

[9]The United States has tax conventions or treaties in effect with the following countries: Australia, Austria, Barbados, Belgium, Brazil, Canada, Congo, Denmark, Finland, France, Germany, Greece, Honduras, Ireland, Israel, Italy, Jamaica, Japan, Luxembourg, Malawi, The Netherlands, Netherlands Antilles, New Zealand, Nigeria, Norway, Pakistan, Philippines, Ruanda, the Soviet Union, Sierra Leone, Sweden, Switzerland, Thailand, Trinidad and Tobago, Union of South Africa, United Kingdom, and Zambia. See Coopers and Lybrand, *International Tax Summaries* (New York: John Wiley & Sons, 1983).

[10]Hamlin, "Reconciling Industrial and Commercial Profits, Provisions in Treaty and Code," *Journal of Taxation,* Vol. 14 (1969), p. 31.

4. Treaties deal with credit for taxes paid by a foreign corporation. Taxes paid by a foreign corporation to a foreign country, or a possession of the United States, may be credited against U.S. tax on "effectively connected" income. Generally, these credits are available to foreign corporations even if they are domiciled in countries with which the United States does not have tax treaties.

TAXATION OF THE U.S. MNC

United States taxation of its own firms on their foreign source income would seem to be a straightforward matter. This income should be lumped together with domestic income, and the total should be taxed at the applicable rates. Moreover, some of the rules and criteria discussed in connection with taxing of foreign corporations (such as claiming tax credit) are based on the rules that are applicable to domestic corporations. There are, however, several issues which have, over the years, contributed to the complexity and the controversial nature of this area.

Taxation of MNCs' foreign income has been a hotly debated issue over the last 25 years. The most controversial aspect is the tax deferral feature which has long been enjoyed by U.S. MNCs. Deferral means taxing the dividend, but not the retained earnings of a subsidiary. Profits funneled from operating subsidiaries to a "shell" tax haven subsidiary (see below) were also deferred, since the parent company did not recieve these profits in the form of dividends.

There have been several attempts to eliminate the deferral feature with a view to accelerating the repatriation of U.S. investment abroad. These attempts were particularly intense during the late 1960s and early 1970s, when the United States was incurring substantial balance of payments deficits. Both the deferral and tax credit features were fiercely opposed by organized labor, who accused MNCs of "exporting U.S. jobs." Although these features have not been repealed, several measures were introduced to circumscribe the use of the deferral feature and tighten the accounting standards for tax computation. The Tax Reform Act of 1962 required that dividend income from affiliates located in developed countries be "grossed up." "Grossing up" is computing the taxable income for U.S. tax purposes on the basis of dividends received from subsidiaries, inclusive of the foreign income taxes allocable to those dividends. Taxes paid to foreign jurisdictions are then credited against U.S. income tax liability. The act also limited substantially deferral through channeling funds to tax havens.

Another feature of the tax legislation which impacts the computation of the taxable income of U.S. MNCs is the treatment of intracompany transactions, which was introduced by Section 482 of the U.S. Tax Code.[11]

[11]See Appendix I at the end of this chapter.

Tax regulations applying to transfer pricing, that is, the pricing of intra-company transfer of inputs and other resources, were discussed in Chapter 6. A number of other countries also have provisions regulating the appropriate pricing of such transactions which attempt to circumscribe the flexibility which MNCs have to reduce their overall tax burden.

A landmark legislation for MNCs is the Tax Reform Act of 1976. The legislation sets in some detail the computation of foreign tax credits, and describes certain tax incentives available for U.S. firms by forming special-purpose corporations. Regulations relating to creditability of foreign taxes have been revised several times in recent years by the Treasury Department. The last revision is dated October 12, 1983.[12] Application of these regulations is illustrated in a later section.

Tax Havens and the Issue of Tax Deferral

A tax haven is a country or a locality which offers investors, including affiliates of foreign firms, several advantages in addition to zero or low income tax rates. These advantageous features include:

1. A stable currency and absence of exchange controls or other restrictions, thus permitting easy transfer of funds to and from the parent firm.
2. A developed network of banking and other financial services, and an efficient system of communication and other supporting facilities.
3. A stable political regime which encourages the entry of foreign firms, even if such firms compete for business with local establishments.
4. A fairly well-developed Eurocurrency market, thus making possible borrowing and investments of large sums in foreign currencies.

The traditional tax haven country has been Switzerland, a role which it has played for a long time due to its neutrality, strong currency, well developed financial market and services, and the confidentiality which it has guaranteed to financial transactions. Switzerland, which has a corporate income tax rate of about 10 percent, continues to attract foreign MNCs, investors, and borrowers from around the world. However, its preeminent position is being challenged by a number of alternative tax havens, such as Hong Kong, Kuwait, the Bahamas, Cayman Islands, Lichtenstein, and Panama.

MNCs have been traditionally attracted to tax havens due to the tax deferral provisions of the corporate income tax codes of their parent countries. An MNC has typically not been taxed on the foreign source income generated by its operating affiliates around the world, until such income is

[12] Price Waterhouse, *U.S. Corporations Doing Business Abroad* (1985), p. 40.

declared as a dividend and transferred to the parent company. By establishing an affiliate in a tax haven, which is typically 100 percent owned by the parent, an MNC can defer indefinitely the payment of income tax on foreign source income. This is accomplished by channeling profits from operating affiliates to the tax haven affiliate, where they are invested until they are needed to finance the requirements of the operating affiliates.

Deferral is not tax avoidance or tax evasion. Eventually profits are repatriated to the parent company in the form of dividends and other forms of payment by the operating affiliates or tax haven affiliate. The deferral feature is particularly valuable to an MNC with growing foreign operations which would require an increasingly higher level of financing. The tax haven would function as a pool from which these financing requirements are met, thus sheltering this pool from the parent country's tax bite. Tax deferral does not appeal to MNCs that do not face such circumstances, or those which are anxious to repatriate income from foreign affiliates to finance operations at home or reduce their debt burden.

The tax deferral mechanism for U.S. MNCs was originally intended to give U.S. firms the same advantage enjoyed by their competitors from other countries, which also enjoy comparable tax deferral and other subsidies bestowed by their home countries. This feature was, however, frequently abused by a number of MNCs by siphoning all or most of the profits generated by foreign operations to tax haven affiliates. Using artificially rigged transfer prices, such profits on trade and manufacturing activities were diverted to tax haven affiliates, leaving the tax authorities in the parent countries with little or no income base to tax.

The widespread abuse of this defense mechanism by U.S. firms led to the Tax Reform Act of 1962, which attempted to eliminate the tax advantages engineered through "fictitious" or "shell" tax haven affiliates. Although the act was not intended to restrict the deferral incentive to bona fide manufacturing and sales affiliates of MNCs, it virtually denied this privilege to U.S. MNCs. However, a considerable number of these firms have continued to maintain their tax haven affiliates primarily as money centers to coordinate their international cash management strategy. Some of them have retained these affiliates to influence, to some degree, their tax exposure, notwithstanding the Tax Reform Act of 1962.

Tax Withholding and Foreign Tax Credit

Tax withholding is a specified percentage of income levied by tax authorities at the source of such income. An earlier section outlined withholding provisions enforced by the U.S. tax authorities on not "effectively connected" income of foreign corporations. The tax is assessed at 30 percent of such income, unless tax treaties specify a lower withholding percentage. This tax applies also to interest and dividend income received by foreign investors on portfolio investment in U.S. securities. Exhibit 18-1 presented withholding rates on payments to nonresidents enforced by tax authorities in 20 countries. Most countries withhold the same rate on income in the form of dividends, interest, and royalties, although few withhold a higher rate on dividends distributed by affiliates to their parents. Most tax havens have no withholding tax.

Most countries, including the United States, allow tax credit for direct taxes paid to or withheld by other countries on various income payments remitted to the parent. Taxes levied on other than income, such as the value-added tax, the turnover tax, and sales taxes, are not eligible for tax credit, but they are in most instances deductible from pretax income as an expense.

The Tax Reform Act of 1976 also allowed domestic corporations to claim a foreign tax credit for income taxes paid to a foreign country by a foreign firm in which the domestic corporation owns at least 10 percent of its voting stock. The tax paid by the foreign distributing corporation is considered as if it is paid by the U.S. firm. This credit may be applied against dividends paid by the distributing corporation to the U.S. firms on a prorated basis. The amount of creditable foreign tax is measured by the proportion that dividends paid to the U.S. firm bears to the foreign corporation's earnings in the year in which dividends are paid (see illustration in Exhibit 18-2). The same provision is extended to taxes paid by a "second-tier" foreign corporation which is at least 10 percent owned by the "first-tier" foreign corporation, provided that the U.S. firm owns at least 5 percent of the stock of the "second-tier" foreign corporation. The same arrangement is extended further to a "third-tier" corporation. The purpose of extending credit to taxes indirectly paid by U.S. firms is to reduce further the element of double taxation, and to encourage direct and portfolio investment abroad.

Tax credit for taxes paid or withheld on foreign source income is subject to an overall limitation to insure that the total creditable amount

Exhibit 18-2. Computation of Foreign Tax Credit

EXAMPLE 1

	$
Earnings of foreign branch	100
Foreign income tax at 40%	40
Included in U.S. income	100
U.S. tax thereon at 46%	46
Less foreign tax credit	40
Net U.S. tax payable	6

Exhibit 18-2. *(continued)*

EXAMPLE 2

Dividend from foreign corporation	100
Foreign withholding tax at 15%	15
Net amount received	85
Included in U.S. income	100
U.S. tax thereon at 46%	46
Less foreign tax credit	15
Net U.S. tax payable	31

The following example illustrates the method of computing the indirect or deemed-paid foreign tax credit.

EXAMPLE 3

Earnings before tax of foreign corporation for calendar year 1980	1000
Foreign income tax at 30%	300
Earnings and profits for 1980	700
Dividend paid to U.S. parent company	700
Less foreign withholding tax at 15%	105
Net dividend received in U.S.	595
Foreign creditable taxes	
a. Direct credit for withholding tax	105
b. Deemed paid credit for subsidiary's tax:	
$\frac{\text{(Dividend) } 700}{\text{(Earnings and Profits) } 700} \times \text{(Foreign tax) } 300$	300
Total creditable taxes	405
Included in U.S. income	
Gross dividend received	700
Plus foreign deemed paid tax	300
U.S. gross dividend included	1000
U.S. tax at 46%	460
Less foreign tax credit	405
U.S. tax payable	55

Source: Price Waterhouse, *U.S. Corporations Doing Business Abroad* (1985), pp. 41–43.

This example illustrates the following formula for determining the amount of creditable deemed paid tax is:

$$\frac{\text{Dividend (including withholding tax)}}{\text{Net earnings and profits of foreign corporation}} \times \text{Foreign tax}$$

does not exceed what would have been paid in the United States had the entire income been generated domestically. This overall ceiling is determined by multiplying the ratio of foreign source income to total income (foreign and domestic) times the applicable U.S. tax:

$$\frac{\text{Foreign taxable income (after all relevant deductions)}}{\text{worldwide taxable income}} \times \text{U.S. tax liability}$$

SPECIAL-PURPOSE CORPORATIONS

Domestic International Sales Corporation

To encourage U.S. firms engaged in export activities, a further incentive was provided by a 1971 legislation if such activities are undertaken by a special-purpose corporation. The Domestic International Sales Corporation (DISC) is a vehicle for deferral of U.S. corporate income tax on that part of the DISC's taxable income which is not distributed as dividends to shareholders.

If the DISC meets certain requirements (discussed below), a U.S. export firm which owns it (the shareholders) can effectively defer up to 42.5 percent of its gain in export earnings. The remaining 57.5 percent is deemed to be distributed to the shareholders and is taxable to the recipients, irrespective of whether or not a distribution is actually made. The DISC itself is not taxable.

A U.S. nonmanufacturing corporation may qualify as a DISC if it meets certain requirements, of which the most important are the *gross income test* and the *assets test.* To qualify, at least 95 percent of the corporation's gross receipts must be from export activities, and at least 95 percent of its assets must be "qualified export assets." Export receipts are defined to include income from such activities as leasing or rental of export property, and engineering and architectural services for foreign construction projects. "Qualified export assets" are defined to include chiefly exportable U.S. goods and other assets primarily connected with the sale of such goods abroad, such as packaging and storage facilities, accounts receivable arising from export transactions, and securities of certain related foreign corporations.

Prior to the Tax Reform Act of 1976 the U.S. shareholders of a DISC were permitted to defer payment of U.S. taxes on 50 percent of taxable income generated from export activities. The 1976 Act narrowed down the deferral privilege somewhat by limiting the deferral benefits to one-half of the increase in annual export gains from a base period level. The export base level is 67 percent of the annual average export profits in the 1972–1975 period. Beginning with 1981 the base on which average export earnings are calculated moves forward one year. Thus, for 1985 the base period was 1977–1982.

In addition to establishing the incremental approach as a yardstick for determining the tax deferral privilege, the 1976 act narrowed down the definition of qualified export receipts. Such receipts now exclude (1) income from the sale or exchange of property used by DISC for export-related activities, (2) dividends or "deemed distributions" from a "related foreign export corporation," and (3) interest received from funds provided by a producer or a manufacturer. Exports of military products are eligible for half the normal DISC deferral benefit. DISCs with export profits of $100,000 or less are exempted from the incremental base period formula, while those whose export earnings are between $100,000 and $150,000 enjoy somewhat smaller deferral privileges.

Possessions Corporations

A possession corporation is a U.S. corporation incorporated in one of the possessions of the United States, which include the Commonwealth of Puerto Rico, the Panama Canal Zone, Guam, American Samoa, and Wake and Midway Islands. Although they are technically U.S. corporations, these corporations are treated generally as foreign corporations for nearly all tax matters. To qualify as a possession corporation, at least 65 percent of a corporation's gross income must be generated by trade or business in a U.S. possession.

Prior to the 1976 Tax Reform Act, these corporations were not subject to U.S. tax on income earned outside the United States until such income was repatriated to the United States. The 1976 Act liberalized this provision by exempting income repatriated to the United States from U.S. tax. The exemption is granted indirectly by allowing these corporations a credit equivalent to their tax liability.

Possession corporations are in some cases subject to taxes in the possessions where they operate or in foreign countries. These taxes are neither deductible nor creditable against the parent companies' U.S. tax liabilities. Dividends paid by such corporations to their parents in the United States enjoy the 100 percent or 85 percent corporate dividend exemptions which apply to U.S. domestic corporations.

To summarize, possession corporations are treated for the most part as foreign corporations with respect to taxability of income generated in the possession. Such income qualifies for exemption from U.S. tax, but non-qualified income is subject to tax at the appropriate U.S. corporate income tax rate. Like foreign corporations, taxes paid by them to possession or foreign governments are not creditable against their parents' U.S. tax liability. However, for purposes of dividends exclusion from taxable income, they are treated as U.S. corporations.

LDCs' Corporations

U.S. tax laws have permitted special tax provisions for corporations doing business in developing countries (LDCs) as a means of encouraging U.S. investment in these countries. An LDC corporation need not be incorporated in an LDC (it cannot be incorporated in the U.S.), but it must be actively involved in business or trade in an LDC. To qualify for the special tax provisions, a corporation must derive 80 percent of its gross income from LDC operations, and it must commit at least 80 percent of its assets for such operations.

The restrictions on tax deferral of undistributed profits of affiliates, introduced by the Tax Reform Act of 1962, applied only to income generated by affiliates of U.S. firms in developed countries. Affiliates operating in less-developed countries continue to enjoy deferral of U.S. tax on undistributed income. Another provision which favors LDC corporations is the tax rate applicable to gains from the sale of stock in a foreign-controlled corporation. These gains are normally taxed at ordinary income tax rates, but gains from an LDC corporation may qualify, if certain conditions are met, for the capital gains tax.

REVIEW QUESTIONS

1. Do the differentials in corporate income tax rates among countries listed in Exhibit 18-1 reflect faithfully the differences in business tax incidence? Can one say, for example, that German companies pay 10 percent more taxes on their income than Canadian firms?
2. Can a U.S. multinational firm claim credit for value-added taxes paid by its European affiliates? Explain. Why are these taxes sometimes thought of as giving a competitive advantage to European exporting firms over their U.S. counterparts?
3. What is the limit on credit for taxes paid to foreign countries which can be claimed by a U.S. multinational firm? How are taxes paid by foreign corporations which are partially owned by a U.S. firm, the so-called "deemed paid taxes," treated for tax credit purposes?
4. Explain how the United States tax laws treat each of the following:
   a. Interest income received by a resident of a foreign country on investment in U.S. government bonds. (The country has no tax treaty with the United States.)
   b. Interest income received by a resident of a foreign country on investment in U.S. corporate banks. (The country has a tax treaty with the United States.)

c. Income of a foreign corporation which maintains a place of business in the United States generated by activities in the United States.
d. "Effectively connected" income of a foreign corporation which does not maintain a place of business in the United States.
e. Income of a citizen of a foreign country which has a tax treaty with the United States derived from employment in this country.
f. Income of an agency of a foreign airline derived from tickets sold in the United States.
g. Income received by a foreign corporation which maintains a place of business in the United States from sources outside the United States.

5. Does the concept of "effectively connected" income require the maintenance of a "permanent establishment" in the United States? Does the presence of a tax treaty alter the taxation rate for "effectively connected income"? Explain.
6. Is the tax deferral feature which attracts MNCs to tax havens valuable to all such firms? Under what circumstances is tax deferral especially adapted to the MNC's funds transfer pattern? Why do many U.S. MNCs continue to maintain "shell" affiliates in tax havens despite the virtual removal of the deferral feature in recent amendments to the tax code?
7. How does a DISC help to promote U.S. exports? Does the use of DISCs appeal to large MNCs with manufacturing and distribution facilities in foreign countries?

REVIEW PROBLEMS

The data in Table 18-1 describe the operations of a U.S. parent corporation and its subsidiaries for 1986.

- *Subsidiary A* is a fully-owned subsidiary of the parent located in a developed country.
- *Subsidiary B* is 55 percent owned by the parent company, also located in a developed country.
- *Subsidiary C* is a foreign company in which the parent has a 10 percent ownership.

a. Determine the total U.S. tax liability of the parent company in 1986.
b. How would your answer differ from a if subsidiary B is located in a developing country?

Table 18-1.

	U.S. Operations	Subsidiary A	Subsidiary B	Subsidiary C
Earnings before tax ($ million)	1315	200	350	50
Applicable tax rate	45%	50%	35%	20%
Dividends declared	40% of profits after tax	All profits after tax	50% of profits after tax	None
Withholding tax on dividends transfer	–	30%	10%	None

c. How would your answer differ from a if subsidiary C is only 8 percent owned by the parent?

d. How much credit for foreign taxes can be claimed in 1986? Can the U.S. company carry forward excess tax credit to future years?

BIBLIOGRAPHY

BENJAMIN, R. W., "Tax Aspects of Operating Possessions Corporation in Puerto Rico," *International Tax Journal* (Spring 1976), pp. 197–221.

BROWN, R. D., and L. J. LOORAM, "Unitary Tax: At the Crossroads?" *CPA Journal* (May 1985), p. 18.

BURGE, M., "Structuring Foreign Operation in the United States," *International Tax Journal* (Summer 1976), pp. 293–300.

Business Week, "A Lower U.S. Tax Bill for Multinationals" (May 23, 1983), p. 154.

CARLSON, G. N., "International Aspects of Corporate-Shareholder Tax Integration," *Case Western Reserve Journal of International Law* (Summer 1979), pp. 535–555.

CHOWN, J. F., *Taxation and Multinational Enterprise.* London and New York: Longman, 1974.

CONNORS, P. J., and N. KRAUTHAMER, "Reporting on International Transactions: A View of the Current Enforcement System," *Journal of Taxation* (July 1983), pp. 42–46.

COOPERS and LYBRAND, *International Tax Summaries,* New York, various dates.

CPA Journal, "State Taxation of Foreign Source Dividend Income" (September 1980), pp. 64–67.

CPA Journal, "Controversy Over Unitary Tax Method" (March 1984), p. 4.

DICKENSON, H. A., "Recapture of Overall Foreign Loss Under the Foreign Tax Credit Provisions," *Ohio Northern University Law Review,* Vol. 6, no. 2 (1979), pp. 372–391.

Duns Business Month, "Flat Tax Plan: Bad News for Multinationals" (February 1985), p. 14.

FELD, A. L., *Tax Policy and Corporate Concentration.* Lexington, Mass.: Lexington Books, 1982.

FEINSCHREIBER, R., "Maximizing DISC Profits Through Quantitative Pricing Techniques," *International Tax Journal* (November 1975), pp. 28–55.

______, "Analysis of the DISC Report," *International Tax Journal* (Summer 1976), pp. 301–317.

______, "The Foreign Tax Credit Under Siege," *Financial Executive* (October 1979), pp. 56–62.

______, "How to Double DISC Benefits Through FISC and Grouping," *International Tax Journal* (June 1980), pp. 367–372.

______, "Apportioning Interest Expense to the U.S. Branch of a Foreign Corporation," *International Tax Journal* (October 1980), pp. 51–75.

FEINSCHREIBER, R., and C. NACKENSON, "Obtaining Interest and Royalties from Foreign Subsidiaries: The Impact of *Xerox v. Maryland,*" *International Tax Journal* (October 1980), pp. 5–13.

FIALKA, J. J., "Corporate Tax Haven in Netherlands Antilles Is Bracing for a Disaster," *Wall Street Journal* (October 11, 1982), p. 1.

FUERBRINGER, J., "U.S. Drive on Tax Havens," *New York Times* (September 3, 1983), p. D-3.

GELINAS, A. J. A., "Tax Considerations for U.S. Corporations Using Finance Subsidiaries to Borrow Funds Abroad," *Journal of Corporate Taxation* (Autumn 1980), pp. 230–263.

HARRISS, C. L., "Value-Added Taxation," *Columbia Journal of World Business* (July-August 1971), pp. 78–86.

HELLAWELL, R., *United States Taxation and Developing Countries.* New York: Columbia University Press, 1980.

HEYDE, R. D., "Interplay of Capital Gains and Foreign Tax Credits," *Tax Executive* (July 1980), pp. 257–267.

HORST, T., "American Taxation of Multinational Firms," *American Economic Review* (June 1977), pp. 376–389.

HOWARD, F., "Overview of International Taxation," *Columbia Journal of World Business* (Summer 1975), pp. 5–11.

HUFBAUER, G. C., "The Taxation of Export Profits," *National Tax Journal* (March 1975), pp. 43–59.

HUFBAUER, G. C., and D. FOSTER, "U.S. Taxation of the Undistributed Income of Controlled Foreign Corporations" (Washington, D.C.: Office of International Tax Affairs, Department of the Treasury, April 1976).

HUFBAUER, G. C., and J. R. NUNNS, "Tax Payments and Tax Expenditures on International Investment and Employment," *Columbia Journal of World Business* (Summer 1975), pp. 12–20.

ITAGAKI, T., "Systems of Taxation of Multinational Firms under Exchange Risk," *Southern Economic Journal* (January 1982), pp. 708–723.

JOHNSON, A. R., L. NIRENSTEIN, and S. E. WELLS, "Reciprocal Enforcement of Tax Claims Through Tax Treaties," *Tax Lawyer* (Winter 1980), pp. 469–487.

KOPITS, G. F., "Taxation and Multinational Firm Behavior: A Critical Survey," *IMF Staff Papers* (November 1976), pp. 624–674.

KRAUSE, L. B., and K. W. DAM, *Federal Tax Treatment of Foreign Income.* Washington, D.C.: Brookings Institution, 1964.

LAMONT, HOWARD, "Multinational Enterprise, Transfer Pricing, and the 482 Mess," *Columbia Journal of Transnational Law,* Vol. 14, no. 3 (1975), pp. 383–433.

LAWRENCE, W. J., "The Taxation of Americans Living Abroad," *Columbia Journal of Transnational Law,* no. 1 (1981), pp. 79–119.

LENT, G. E., M. CASANEGRA, and M. GUERARD, "The Value-Added Tax in Developing Countries," *IMF Staff Papers* (July 1973), pp. 318–378.

LUNDY, D. F., "Tax and Accounting Effects on Foreign Currency Fluctuations," *Tax Executive* (January 1976), pp. 135–143.

MADERE, G. L., "Analysis of the Final Regulations on Foreign Corporate Interest Deductions," *Journal of Taxation* (July 1981), pp. 44–49.

MCINTYRE, M. J., *United States Taxation of Foreign Income with Special Emphasis on Private Investments in Developing Countries.* Cambridge, Mass.: International Law Program, Harvard Law School, 1975. This is a revision of Arie Kopelman, *United States Income Taxation of Private Investments in Developing Countries.* New York: United Nations Secretariat, 1970.

MIHALOV, J. B., "Retaining the Section 482 Arm's Length Standard," *Taxes* (May 1982), pp. 331–343.

MOORE, M. L., and R. N. BAGLEY, *U.S. Tax Aspects of Doing Business Abroad.* New York: American Institute of Certified Public Accountants, 1978.

MUSGRAVE, P. B., "Exchange Rate Aspects in the Taxation of Foreign Income," *National Tax Journal* (December 1975), pp. 405–413.

______, "The OECD Model Tax Treaty: Problems and Prospects," *Columbia Journal of World Business* (Summer 1975), pp. 29–39.

MUTTI, J., "Tax Incentives and the Repatriation Decisions of U.S. Multinational Corporations," *National Tax Journal* (June 1981), pp. 241–248.

O'CONNOR, W. F., and S. M. RUSSO, "Tax Consequences of the Currency Float," *Financial Executive* (January 1975), pp. 48–52.

OWENS, E. A., *International Aspects of U.S. Income Taxation,* Vol. III. Cambridge, Mass.: Harvard Law School International Tax Program, 1980.

OWENS, E. A., and G. A. HOVEMEYER, eds., *Bibliography of Taxation of Foreign Operations and Foreigners.* Cambridge, Mass.: Harvard Law School, 1976.

PAGAN, J., "Borrowing Abroad: The Tax Problems," *Accountancy* (September 1982), pp. 72–74.

PAULES, E. P., "Guide Through the Tax Maze," *Euromoney* (October 1980), pp. 252–260.

PETERS, J. H., "Supreme Court in Container, Upholds State's Broad Power Under Unitary Taxation Method," *Journal of Taxation* (November 1983), pp. 300–307.

POLK, R. M., "Financial and Tax Aspects of Planning for Foreign Exchange Rate Fluctuations," *Taxes* (March 1978), pp. 131–142.

Prentice-Hall, Inc., *Tax Ideas — Tax Transaction Guide,* two vols., loose-leaf. Englewood Cliffs, N.J.: various dates.

PREST, A. R., *Value Added Taxation.* Washington, D.C.: American Enterprise Institute, 1980.

Price Waterhouse and Company, Information Guide Series, separate booklets. New York: various dates.

RAYMENT, C., "Foreign Anxiety Grows Over U.S. Unitary Tax," *Accountancy* (May 1982), p. 16.

SALE, T. J., "Tax Planning Tools for the Multinational Corporation," *Management Accounting* (June 1979), pp. 37–41.

SAMUELS, L. B., "Federal Income Tax Consequences of Back-to-back Loans and Currency Exchanges," *Tax Lawyer* (Spring 1980), pp. 847–880.

SATO, M., and R. M. BIRD, "International Aspects of the Taxation of Corporations and Shareholders," *IMF Staff Papers* (July 1975), pp. 384–455.

SAUNDERS, M. R., *Tax Planning for Businesses in Europe.* London and Woburn, Mass.: Buttersworth, 1978.

SCHMITZ, M. N., "Taxation of Foreign Exchange Gains and Losses," *Management Accounting* (July 1976), pp. 49–51.

SINGER, S. R., and M. J. A. KARLIN, "Multinationals and New Customs Law Will Have Broad Impact on Intercompany Pricing," *Journal of Taxation* (April 1983), pp. 226–231.

STEIN, H., et al., *Proposals to Modify the Taxation of U.S. Citizens Working Abroad.* Washington, D.C.: American Enterprise Institute for Public Policy Research, 1981.

STONE, L. M., "United States Tax Policy Toward Foreign Earnings of Multinational Corporations," *The George Washington Law Review,* Vol. 42 (1974), pp. 557–567.

TANZI, V., *Inflation and the Personal Income Tax: An International Perspective.* Cambridge, England: Cambridge University Press, 1980.

TECK, A., "Using Computers for Foreign Exchange Tax Planning," *International Tax Journal* (November 1975), pp. 5–27.

United Nations, "Tax Treaties Between Developed and Developing Countries," New York: 1975.

WASSERMAN, M. G., "International Withholding on Corporate Capital Distributions," *International Tax Journal* (October 1980), pp. 27–50.

WILLIAMS, T. J., "The Creditability of Foreign Income Taxes: An Overview," *Taxes* (October 1980), pp. 699–709.

APPENDIX I

Intercompany Transactions[1]

Introduction

Although the U.S. returns of many large U.S. corporations are examined by agents of the Internal Revenue Service (IRS) under normal procedures, these agents have for many years been paying particular attention to U.S. corporations with substantial foreign operations and to the many unique aspects of these operations which might affect the taxpayer's U.S. tax. The area in which agents are making most of their recommendations for adjust-

[1]Price Waterhouse, *U.S. Corporations Doing Business Abroad* (1985), pp. 30–38. Reproduced by permission from Price Waterhouse.

ments is intercompany pricing. Section 482 of the Internal Revenue Code permits the reallocation of income and deductions among associated taxpayers, where such a redistribution of income and expenses is necessary to reflect the true income of each taxpayer.

Using the authority of this provision and detailed regulations thereunder, the agent will examine closely the financial statements of U.S. corporations and their foreign affiliates to make sure that the U.S. corporation is not absorbing expenses which result in increased income to a foreign affiliate or charging unrealistically low sales prices to it. However, a corporation qualifying as a Foreign Sales Corporation (FSC) is subject to special rules which may be more favorable.

A U.S. corporation engaged in foreign operations should be prepared to justify its pricing policies and charges made between domestic and foreign affiliates and should keep adequate records in support of its positions. The regulations are discussed in more detail below.

Purpose of Section 482

Section 482 has been part of the tax law for many years. It consists of the following single sentence:

> In any case of two or more organizations, trades, or businesses (whether or not incorporated, whether or not organized in the United States, and whether or not affiliated) owned or controlled directly or indirectly by the same interests, the Secretary may distribute, apportion, or allocate gross income, deductions, credits, or allowances between or among such organizations, trades or businesses, if he determines that such distribution, apportionment, or allocation is necessary in order to prevent evasion of taxes or clearly to reflect the income of any of such organizations, trades, or businesses.

Detailed regulations have been issued for the purpose of providing additional guidelines and formulas for the allocation of income and deductions particularly relevant for cases involving foreign income. The purpose of the section, as stated in the regulations, is to place a controlled taxpayer on a "tax parity" with an uncontrolled taxpayer, and the interests controlling a group of controlled taxpayers are assumed to have complete power to cause its members to conduct their affairs in such a way that each will state its "true taxable income," as that phrase is used in the regulations.

The concept that a U.S. taxpayer should deal with affiliates on arm's-length terms is central and fundamental to Section 482. The regulations provide guidelines of how the Commissioner would expect related taxpayers to deal with each other on an arm's-length basis and, in a number of instances, also provide for exceptions to this standard in the form of safe havens or formula approaches.

Methods of Allocation

When the Commissioner finds it necessary to make an allocation under Section 482, the allocation can take the form of an adjustment to gross income, deductions, credits, tax base of assets for depreciation and gain or loss purposes, or any other adjustments required to reflect the substance of transactions.

The regulations provide that where the Commissioner has made an adjustment to the income of one member of the group, known as a "primary adjustment," he must also make any "correlative adjustment" to the income of other members involved. Primary adjustments can technically only be made to the income of a taxpayer under U.S. tax jurisdiction. However, the correlative adjustments can involve a foreign affiliate to the extent that U.S. tax consequences could ensue. Thus, if income is allocated from a foreign affiliate to the U.S. taxpayer, the foreign affiliate's earnings and profits would be correspondingly reduced and could affect the amount of deemed paid foreign tax credit for dividends received from that corporation.

Arrangements for Reimbursement

In making allocations with respect to particular transactions, the Commissioner must take into consideration the effect of any arrangements between the members of a group for reimbursement within a reasonable period before or after the taxable year if such an arrangement actually existed in the year in which the transaction took place. Thus, if an agreement exists between members for payment for services, within a "reasonable" period, no allocation is required. For example, an arm's-length sales transaction might require a U.S. corporation to charge a certain sales price plus a royalty for intangibles. The arm's-length standard could be satisfied if the sales price is increased to include the royalty charge.

The Commissioner must also take reciprocal services by members into consideration and give effect to them in the form of a setoff against an allocation. For example, the performance of services at no charge for a member could be recompensed by reciprocal services, by excessive royalties, by intercompany sales at a discount, or by purchases at a premium.

Blocked Income

If reimbursement in any transaction is prevented because of currency restrictions in the other country, the U.S. taxpayer can elect to defer the income until the income ceases to be blocked. However, any expenses attributable to the income must also be deferred.

Unilateral Relief Provisions

Since Section 482 adjustments in the early enforcement years were generally made some years after the relevant taxable year, it was often too late for the U.S. taxpayer to make retroactive charges to its foreign affiliates. To alleviate the burdens of "economic double taxation" and "undue hardship," the Treasury introduced certain novel relief provisions in the form of Revenue Procedures 64-54 and 65-17.

Revenue Procedure 64-54 applied only through taxable years beginning before January 1, 1965. Revenue Procedure 65-17 relief measures are still applicable, provided that the transactions giving rise to the Section 482 allocation were not structured with U.S. tax avoidance motives. Two relief measures are provided. First, the U.S. taxpayer can exclude from U.S. income any dividend received from the subsidiary in the same year up to the amount of the allocation. The income will not be treated as a dividend for U.S. tax purposes, which also means that it will not generate any deemed paid foreign tax credits, although foreign withholding taxes would still be available for credit.

The second relief measure is consistent with the notion that Section 482 allocations generally represent items which should have been charged to affiliates but were not charged. Consequently, the U.S. taxpayer is permitted to charge its subsidiary with the amount of the adjustment after the fact, and this is accomplished by establishing an interest-bearing account receivable from the foreign affiliate as of the last day of the year for which the allocation is made. If the account receivable is paid (in cash or notes) within a certain period, it will not constitute U.S. taxable income.

Procedures Under Tax Treaties

The income tax treaties to which the United States is a party generally provide for the allocation of income and deductions on transactions between related persons in accordance with the arm's-length standard. The treaties also generally show recognition of the problem of international double taxation arising from allocations when countries have different concepts of what constitutes arm's-length dealing and provide for settlement of taxpayers' grievances by consultation between the "competent" tax authorities of the countries involved.

The procedures which are to be followed by a U.S. taxpayer in order to secure consideration of his case by the competent authorities in Section 482 cases, at least from the U.S. standpoint, are detailed in Revenue Procedure 82-29. The taxpayer must show that action of the U.S. or foreign tax authorities will result in double taxation. If the claim is deemed to be worthy of consideration, the competent U.S. tax authority will consult with the competent tax authority in the other country for the purposes of arriving at an agreement which is acceptable to the United States, the treaty country, and the taxpayer.

Specific Guidelines

To illustrate the general principles of Section 482, the regulations attempt to offer guidance on five kinds of intercompany transactions:

1. Intercompany loans and advances.
2. Performance of services by one affiliate for another.
3. Use of tangible property of one affiliate by another.
4. Use or transfer of intangible property.
5. Intercompany sales of personal property.

U.S. taxpayers who hope to avoid subsequent reallocations are, in general, attempting to follow the principles outlined in these guidelines, which are discussed below.

Loans and Advances

If funds are advanced by one member of the group to another, interest will be imputed to the lender unless an arm's-length rate of interest is charged. However, if the lender is not in the financing business, interest at a rate of at least 11 percent and not more than 13 percent will be treated as arm's length. This is known as the "safe haven." If the interest charge is not within this range, an allocation at a 12 percent rate will be made by the Commissioner unless the taxpayer carries his burden of showing that the rate charged was appropriate in the circumstances. In the case of loans existing generally between July 24, 1975, and July 1, 1981, the safe haven rates are 6 percent to 8 percent, and 7 percent in the case of an imputed rate.

Safe haven rates do not apply when the U.S. taxpayer borrows funds at the situs of the borrowing affiliate and relends the funds to the affiliate. In such a case, the interest charged must be at least equal to the interest incurred, plus the costs of the borrowing. In addition, the safe haven rates do not apply to loans denominated in currency other than U.S. dollars. Ostensibly, market interest rates will apply in such cases.

Even if the member is not in the business of lending money, it is permitted to establish an arm's-length rate of interest by reference to the facts and circumstances and without regard to the safe haven range.

Performance of Services

If the U.S. taxpayer performs marketing, managerial, administrative, or technical services for the benefit of one or more affiliates or for the joint benefit of itself and other affiliates without charge, or at less than arm's-length charge, an allocation may be made.

The regulations make a distinction between services which are intended to be of direct benefit to an affiliate, either in its day-to-day activities or in its overall operations. No allocation is required if the benefits to the affiliate are so indirect or remote that an unrelated party would not have charged for the services and if the subsidiary would not have paid a fee had they been performed by an unrelated corporation. This also seems to be a logical consideration from the subsidiary's point of view, because it too must be regarded as dealing with the parent on an arm's-length basis and must generally satisfy this criterion in claiming a tax deduction in its own jurisdiction. No allocation is required if the services are merely a duplication of a service which the other member is performing itself, since the other member would not obtain any benefit from mere duplication.

The regulations provide that the amount of the charge for services may equal the cost of rendering the services, unless the rendering of such services is an integral part of either party's business, in which case, the intercompany charge must include a profit. Cost includes not only the direct expenses identified specifically with a particular service, such as salaries and traveling expenses of employees performing the services, but also any indirect costs which relate to the direct costs.

If the services rendered by or to an affiliate are an integral part of either affiliate's business activity, the charge of the intercompany service must be made at an arm's-length rate and thus include a profit element. This would also apply in cases where both affiliates are in the business of rendering similar services to unrelated parties. A profit must also be included when the services are rendered by a company whose principal activity consists of the rendering of such services to related parties.

In determining whether these services are a company's principal activity, an objective test is provided, although it does not apply in the case of services which constitute a manufacturing, construction, production, or extraction activity. If the costs of services rendered to affiliates do not exceed 25 percent of the renderer's total costs or deductions for a year, such services will not be treated as a principal activity. A profit must also be included where the renderer of the services is peculiarly capable of rendering such services and the recipient is in the business of rendering such services. Similarly, if the recipient has received substantial services from related parties, a profit element must be included in the charge.

Finally, it should be noted that, if the parties so choose, intercompany services of any nature can be priced at arm's-length terms rather than at cost.

Use of Tangible Property

If a U.S. taxpayer transfers possession or use of tangible property to an affiliate at no charge or at less than an arm's-length charge, an allocation may be made by the Commissioner to reflect an arm's-length lease or rental arrangement.

If either party is in the business of leasing tangible property to unrelated parties, an arm's-length rental is required. If neither company is in the leasing business, a rental based on a specific formula set forth in the regulations is considered to be acceptable. The formula rental charge is based on the sum of (1) depreciation computed on a straight-line basis, (2) 3 percent of the original basis of the asset, and (3) current operating expenses, excluding interest.

The taxpayer still retains the right to establish an arm's-length rental not based on the formula, but based on marketplace criteria. If the affiliate leasing the property (lessee) in turn subleases it to another affiliate, the sublease rental must be equal to all the deductions directly or indirectly attributable to the property in the hands of the sublessor.

Use or Transfer of Intangible Property

Where intangible property is transferred or made available in any way to an affiliate for other than an arm's-length consideration, the Commissioner is authorized to propose an allocation.

Intangible property includes patents, trademarks, trade names, brand names, and similar items. The arm's-length consideration should be in a form which would normally be adopted between unrelated parties, and could be in the form of royalties based on the transferee's output, sales, profits, or any other measure, lump-sum payments, or any other form, including reciprocal licensing rights.

No objective guidelines or safe haven rates are given to assist in arriving at an arm's-length sale price or royalty. Transactions with unrelated licensees form the principal basis for determining an arm's-length rate of royalty.

As an alternative to compensating the developer of intangible property for the right to use the property once it has been developed, a group of related entities can enter into a written "cost-sharing" agreement, under which the costs and risks of development can be spread between two or more affiliates in return for each being entitled to a specified interest in the property which may be produced. Since all parties to such an agreement are sharing the risk, no profit element is involved in the charges, which are simply reimbursements of expenses incurred by those parties who incur more than their allocated share thereof. Companies using this method generally allocate the aggregate costs on the basis of each affiliate's proportion of worldwide customer sales.

Sales of Personal Property

One of the most important areas of the regulations deals with prices charged for goods sold to affiliates. If goods are sold to an affiliate at less than an arm's-length price, an allocation can be made. An arm's-length price is the price which an unrelated party would have paid under the same circumstances for similar property. The regulations describe three acceptable methods of pricing goods and the circumstances under which they may be used. The three methods are (1) the comparable uncontrolled price method, (2) the resale price method, and (3) the cost-plus method. There is also, in effect, a fourth method. If the three specified methods are inappropriate or less appropriate than the method which a taxpayer is using, considering all the facts and circumstances, the taxpayer may use the more appropriate method, or a variation of the three specified methods.

The taxpayer does not have the choice of which method to use, because the regulations require the comparable uncontrolled price method to be used if there are comparable uncontrolled sales. This is considered to be the most accurate estimate of an arm's-length price, because it is based on sales to unrelated parties. If it does not apply, the resale price method must be used, because it is considered the second most accurate method, being based on customer sales. If certain requirements under the resale price method are not met, the taxpayer may use either the resale price method or the cost-plus method. The "fourth method" applies only if it is more appropriate than the other three.

Comparable Uncontrolled Price Method

The comparable uncontrolled price is the price which is paid when buyer and seller are unrelated. This includes not only the price charged by a U.S. corporation to its outside customers, but also the price a U.S. corporation or any member of the group pays when buying from an unrelated supplier. It would also include sales between other parties of comparable goods. Sales are comparable if the physical property and the circumstances involved are the same or are so nearly identical that an ascertainable adjustment can be made, e.g., for place of delivery. The terms of sale, intangibles, time of sale, level of the market, and geographic market in which the sale takes place are factors which could influence price comparability. Whether these and other differences render the price noncomparable depends on the facts and circumstances of each case.

Thus, a sale made to unrelated customers in one country would not necessarily be comparable to a sale made in another country. Sales of similar products by other unrelated companies might provide a comparable price if the other facts, such as quality and intangibles, are comparable. In practice, however, the terms of sale to unrelated customers provide strong evidence of an uncontrolled price, and the existence of such sales would normally place the onus of showing incomparability on the taxpayer.

In order not to put U.S. exporters at a disadvantage in establishing new markets, the regulations provide that a lower price may be permitted for a time where sales are made in new geographic locations at less than normal prices for purposes of market penetration or to meet competition.

Resale Price Method

The resale price method assumes a manufacturer selling to a related sales company which sells to an outside customer. The price of goods sold by the manufacturer to the selling company is established by working down from the actual resale price charged to the customer and reducing this resale price by the appropriate markup for the selling subsidiary. Under this method, the taxpayer must determine an appropriate profit margin for the selling company in order to determine the appropriate invoice price from the manufacturer to the sales company. The markup for the selling subsidiary is the missing factor in this method and must be determined on the basis of factors both internal and external to the business. This method is used only if there are no uncontrolled sales with which to compare the manufacturing affiliate's sales price. There must be an uncontrolled customer sales price to compare with the purchasing/reselling company's sales price. A further condition is that the buying/reselling company does not add substantial value to the property in the form of physical alteration or by the use of an intangible.

If the selling company adds substantial value to the product, the resale price method may still be used if this method is likely to result in a more accurate determination of an arm's-length price than the use of the cost-plus method.

Cost-Plus Method

The cost-plus method starts with the manufacturer's costs and adds the appropriate markup to the selling company. Under this method, the manufacturing costs are presumed to be determinable and the markup percentage needs to be established by looking at internal and external trade factors. This method would normally be used if the sales company adds substantial value to the product, which it has bought from the manufacturer.

Other Consequences of Allocation of Income

The allocation of income and the correlative adjustments under Section 482 can have serious tax consequences in other areas of the tax law, particularly where there are objective percentage tests, as in determining if a corporation is a foreign personal holding company. An allocation of income involving a controlled foreign corporation could affect the Subpart F relief provisions. For example, no foreign base company income is imputed to the U.S. shareholder if foreign base company income is less than 10 percent of gross income. An allocation affecting gross income of a controlled foreign corporation could have the effect of making Subpart F income taxable to the U.S. shareholder. Allocations could affect the foreign tax credit, when foreign earnings and profits are adjusted or the source of an item of income is changed; they could affect foreign personal holding company status when income is reclassified.

A more far-reaching collateral consequence of the allocation concept is the possibility of constructive dividend treatment. It has been recognized for many years that the diversion of corporate funds between shareholders and their corporations for the benefit of the shareholders may be treated as a constructive dividend.

In the case of Section 482 allocations between U.S. taxpayers and foreign subsidiaries, the Commissioner has used this theory to explain the movement of the allocated funds into the "wrong" entity. For example, if the U.S. parent company undercharges its foreign subsidiary for goods or services, the "excessive" funds left in the foreign subsidiary, which were allocated as additional income by the Commissioner to the U.S. parent, are regarded as a contribution to the capital of the subsidiary. This is in effect a correlative adjustment. The Commissioner has extended this concept to intercompany transactions between foreign sister subsidiaries of a common U.S. parent. The IRS has met with mixed success with this approach in the U.S. tax courts, which tend to look more closely at the facts and circumstances in each individual case.

19

International Accounting and Control of Foreign Operations

INTRODUCTION

Multinational firms need accurate and timely reporting from their affiliates to formulate policies and to evaluate operating results against plans. Regular financial reporting forms the basis of preparing financial statements required by the authorities and to fulfill management's obligations to the shareholders.

In the preceding chapters, financial reporting was examined in connection with a number of multinational financial management functions. These functions included:

1. Translating the functional currencies of the affiliates into the parent's currency for the purpose of preparing consolidated financial statements (Chapter 4).
2. Preparing currency exposure statements for the firm as a whole which are essential for the formulation and follow-up of foreign exchange exposure management (Chapters 4 and 5).
3. Managing the firm's cash and formulating fund-positioning policies (Chapter 8).
4. Formulating the firm's borrowing-investment policies which are closely coordinated with both cash and currency exposure management strategies (Chapter 11).
5. Determining the firm's tax liability to host countries and the parent country (Chapter 18).

Another area of concern is the valuation of assets and pricing policies, particularly for affiliates located in high-inflation countries. Operating in such an environment poses a serious problem for protecting the firm's assets and the profitability of its overall operations. Although this accounting problem as well as other facets of financial reporting are essential for all profit-maximizing firms, it is especially crucial for the successful management and survival of MNCs.

The task of efficient and policy-oriented financial reporting is considerably more complex for MNCs due to the diversity of accounting standards and methods observed in different countries. MNCs cannot simply settle this issue by adhering to the accounting standards of their parent country. In the first place, these firms have a legal obligation to their host countries to have financial reporting of their affiliates conform to the standards recognized by the local tax authorities and accounting conventions. Second, when operating subsidiaries have joint venture partners, they have an obligation to make their financial statements comprehensible to the local investors. Third, MNCs are likely to have shareholders outside the parent country, particularly if the stock is listed on foreign stock exchanges. Foreign shareholders also have a right to expect financial reporting that is comprehensible to them.

This chapter explores the issues involved in international accounting and the nature of financial reporting that are best suited for furthering the policies and strategies of MNCs. The objective is to pull together the financial and accounting reports developed in the previous chapters to enable MNCs to monitor the operations of their affiliates, and to pursue an overall profit-maximizing strategy.

WHAT IS INTERNATIONAL ACCOUNTING?

Accounting standards and procedures differ from country to country due to diverse social, economic, and legal influences which have shaped the development of accounting in different countries. The evolution of accounting in most countries has been closely linked to local business practices and conventions, the legal framework regulating conduct of trade and business, and national economic and financial policies. Yet there are basic elements of accounting that are common to all countries, mainly the double-entry bookkeeping system, and the requirement to produce periodic financial statements for the investors and for the national tax authorities. Another common characteristic is that the firm is the focal point of the accounting process in almost all countries.

The functions of accounting are basically similar in all countries. These functions are

1. Regular financial reporting to fulfill legally stipulated obligations to the investors and to the tax and other revenue collecting and regulatory agencies

2. Compilation of data on a regular basis to provide the firm's management with the information needed for financial planning and decision making
3. Provision of information needed by the firm to control operations and to verify actual results against preestablished standards of achievement

The development of international accounting has been closely tied to the growth and development of the multinational firm. Because of the diversity of national accounting systems and standards, the MNC has to develop rational and coherent accounting methods which will enable it to perform these functions in a multinational context. Apart from performing these functions, the MNC's accounting system has to address variables that are unique to its operations in a number of countries. Compilation of accounting data and financial reporting have to accommodate:

1. The choice of appropriate (or legally stipulated) exchange rates, as well as reflecting the changes in exchange rates
2. Adopting methods to reflect diverse inflation rates and their impact on pricing policies and reported income
3. Determining net income and tax liability under multiple tax jurisdictions, that is, the home country and each of the host countries where it conducts business
4. Accommodating intracompany transactions, that is, transactions between the parent and each of the affiliates, and transactions among the affiliates

It would seem axiomatic that performing the basic accounting functions in a multinational context would require regular flow of financial reports from the affiliates to the parent company and/or to the centralized funds management centers. These reports are, by virtue of the dynamic nature of the variables involved, more detailed and more complex than those needed by a firm operating within the borders of one country.

APPROACHES TO INTERNATIONAL ACCOUNTING

There are four basic approaches or underlying philosophies which have shaped the development of accounting systems in different parts of the world. These approaches, though not necessarily mutually exclusive, differ basically in their focal point, as well as in the end purpose of recording and measuring the results of business and financial operations.

The *macroeconomic approach* ties the accounting system rather closely to the economic and financial policies of the government. Unlike the accounting system in socialist countries, this approach, typified by the Swedish accounting system, regards the firm as the essential economic unit of accounting. However, the financial goals of the firm are closely integrated with national economic and financial policies.

The *microeconomic approach,* of which the Netherlands is the prototype, focuses on the firm and its survival. Accounting, according to this approach, is a branch of business economics, which aims at maintaining the integrity of the firm's monetary capital. Because of this emphasis, this accounting system focuses on adjusting the earning capacity of the firm for changes in the price level.

Accounting systems prevailing in the United States, Canada, and the United Kingdom typify the so-called *independent discipline approach.* According to this approach, accounting is a discipline whose standards and concepts evolve from the underlying business practices. Accounting standards and concepts are evolved by the business and financial community, which strives to develop systems that would serve its purposes, irrespective of the conformity or nonconformity of these concepts with national economic policies.

Nevertheless, generally accepted accounting practices must be consistent with the overall criteria and guidelines set by taxing authorities and national economic policy. Although uniformity is not an overriding objective of this system, general standards (such as those established by the Financial Accounting Standard Board in the United States) are established and modified to insure fairness, consistency, and compliance with tax laws.

The *uniform accounting approach,* illustrated by the systems adopted in France, Germany, and most developing countries, prescribes uniform and rational yardsticks for recording and measuring commercial transactions that are applicable to all firms. The concepts and practices, which are presumed to be scientific and rational, are determined primarily by the governments rather than evolved, by trial and error, by the business community.

Although uniformity facilitates comparative evaluation of performance, collection of taxes, and compilation of economic data, it has some drawbacks. The major disadvantage is that it may diverge from or conflict with what the business community itself deems as effective or appropriate in conducting its operations. Uniform systems also tend to lack dynamism or ability to adjust to changing circumstances and requirements.

Each of these four approaches may share the characteristics and objectives of one or more of the others. For instance, the macroeconomic and uniform approaches have a lot in common, that is, uniformity of standards and concepts, although their process of evolution and the focal point of the entire system are different. The independent discipline approach is essentially microeconomic in nature, although it does not focus on uniformity as an end in itself. Some measure of uniformity, however, is accomplished by evolving and modifying general standards which govern accounting behavior in selective areas, particularly in those areas where divergence tends to impair competitiveness and fairness in tax treatment. The fundamental difference between this system and standards determined under the uniform and macroeconomic approaches is that the generally accepted conventions are developed by the business community itself, rather than dictated by the government or a central planning agency.

DIVERSITY IN MULTINATIONAL ACCOUNTING

The diversity in accounting systems and methods among countries has posed serious problems to the decision-making process of MNCs, and has distorted communication of financial data across national boundaries. A major question is whether the growth of MNCs in the past two decades has succeeded in bridging the gap among these various systems and has contributed to the development of a core of uniform basic accounting standards.

A recent study by Choi and Bavishi of leading industrial firms in ten major countries noted striking similarities among these firms in the fundamental areas of financial reporting.[1] The study concluded that "fundamental differences between each of the ten countries examined are not as extensive as the accounting literature seems to suggest."[2] Among the similarities noted are

1. All ten countries prepare consolidated financial statements when the parent company enjoys a majority ownership or operating control of local firms. Minority interest is excluded from consolidated income by firms operating in all ten countries except Germany.
2. In nine countries (the exception being Germany) both domestic and foreign subsidiaries are consolidated.
3. In nine countries (the exception being Germany) long-term debt includes maturities longer than one year.
4. All firms, except those operating in Sweden and Switzerland, follow fairly uniform standards in accounting for deferred taxes.
5. Research and development expenditures are expensed by firms operating in all ten countries.
6. Historical cost remains the basic valuation yardstick in most of these countries; however, replacement cost and inflation accounting were gaining dominance, particularly among U.K., U.S., and Australian companies, and some acceptance in a number of other countries.

[1]F. D. S. Choi and V. B. Bavishi, "Diversity in Multinational Accounting.", pp. 45–49. Reprinted by permission from *Financial Executive,* August 1982, copyright 1982 by Financial Executives Institute. The investigation used a checklist of 32 fundamental accounting principles to ascertain the uniformity, or lack of it, among 869 leading industrial firms (with a capitalization in excess of $500 million) in ten major industrial countries. Countries and number of companies included in the study are: United States (413), Canada (36), Japan (111), Australia (17), United Kingdom (107), Germany (66), France (49), the Netherlands (21), Switzerland (18), and Sweden (31).

[2]*Ibid.,* p. 48.

7. The current rate method of foreign currency translation is predominant, replacing the once popular temporal method, particularly since the adoption of FASB #52 in the United States beginning in 1983.

Major differences exist in accounting methods relating to the treatment of goodwill and other intangible assets, long-term leases, discretionary reserves, and the treatment of currency translation gains or losses in the financial statements.

A more recent survey of 250 MNCs in 17 major industrial countries coauthored by David Cairns, a partner in a leading British accounting firm, focused on the quality and uniformity of financial reporting by those firms.[3] Although the focal point of the survey is the usefulness of the financial reports to the international investor, rather than the multinational financial manager, the authors reached a number of interesting conclusions, which are summarized below:

1. Although the authors reported significant overall improvement in international financial reporting since an earlier study (a survey by Cairns and Lafferty prepared in 1980 for *London's Financial Times*),[4] they "found large companies in many countries reporting financial results that seemed likely to mislead would-be investors."[5] In particular, a number of MNCs outside the United States and the United Kingdom apply startlingly liberal definitions to "earnings" and "earnings per share."
2. There is lack of uniformity in the time lapses permitted in the publication of earnings reports. Only in the United States is a 90-day deadline mandated by the SEC observed. In the United Kingdom a voluntary limit of six months for reporting operating results exists. In other countries, deadlines are more liberal or no deadlines are observed.
3. The highest marks were received by companies in the United States, United Kingdom, Sweden, the Netherlands, and Canada. Fifteen of the 25 best companies were U.S. firms. Firms in Belgium, Denmark, Germany, Italy, Switzerland, and Spain received generally low marks. Firms in Australia, France, Hong Kong, Japan, Malaysia, and South Africa received fair marks. The major criterion for ranking is the quality of financial reporting and its intelligibility by the international investor.

Progress toward uniform international accounting standards has been understandably slow, despite efforts by the International Accounting Standards Committee and a committee formed by the United Nations to formulate proposals that would accelerate the movement toward uniformity.

[3]David Cairns, et al., "Survey of Accounts and Accountants 1983–84," quoted in *Management Review* (October 1984), pp. 66–67.

[4]*Ibid.*, p. 66.

[5]*Ibid.*, p. 66.

MAJOR ISSUES IN MULTINATIONAL ACCOUNTING

In the background of diverse national accounting standards and concepts, and apart from the legal, economic, and social values which underlie this diversity, MNCs face three major issues in reporting the results of their operations. These issues are

1. Choosing a system of financial reporting and the degree of consolidation of accounts
2. Choosing an appropriate exchange rate to use when reporting the results of foreign operations
3. Accounting for price changes, particularly in high-inflation countries

Financial Reporting and Consolidation of Accounts

The income statement and the balance sheet are universally recognized as the primary instruments of financial reporting. There are, however, varying degrees of emphasis on one or the other statement in different countries. The focal point of financial reporting in the United States and Canada is the income statement, reflecting primarily the wide public ownership of corporations and the close correlation between stock prices and reported earnings.

Financial reporting in most European countries focuses on the balance sheet as shareholders are more preoccupied than their American counterparts in matters of wealth and position vis-a-vis creditors than in current income. Balance sheets prepared by Europeans reflect this preoccupation in containing substantial details and an elaborate stockholders' equity section. There are a number of legally mandated reserve accounts to which part of current earnings is set aside before dividends are declared. In addition, voluntary reserve accounts are often created to sustain dividend payments in years of poor performance. Unlike the unallocated retained earnings in U.S. balance sheets to which all undistributed profits are credited, all earnings in European balance sheets are either allocated for some specific purposes or paid out in the form of dividends.

An MNC has to decide if it wishes to prepare a single set of financial statements in accordance with the accounting standards of the parent country, or pursue a "dual" accounting approach. Under the latter, the firm prepares in addition to the "primary" financial statements, a number of "secondary" statements for investors and governments of host countries. In a sense, dual accounting is widely used, as evidenced by the practice of a large number of U.S. companies which prepare two sets of financial statements, one for the stockholders and the investment community and the other for the tax authorities. While dual reporting addresses the information needs of investors and financial markets attuned to different standards, it creates some serious problems for users and complicates the process of translating affiliates' operations to the parent's currency.[6]

The MNC has also to decide on the extent of consolidation of accounts it wishes to undertake. Consolidation of affiliates' and subsidiaries' operations, as well as other foreign companies where the firm maintains an investment, into the parent company's financial statements is a complex matter. The complexity arises partly from the existence of mandatory provisions with respect to consolidation in a number of countries, side by side with a relatively wide latitude left to the discretion of MNCs. In some other countries consolidation is completely optional.

In the United States consolidation is mandatory if the parent owns 50 percent or more of the affiliate, unless the affiliate is in an entirely different line of business or in the process of liquidation. Consolidation of affiliates' accounts in which the parent firm has less than 50 percent ownership is optional. Such affiliates are usually reported in the parent's financial statements on an "equity" basis, that is, cost of acquisition plus the parent's share in reinvested earnings, if the percentage of ownership is not less than 20 percent, and on a "cost" basis if it is less than 20 percent.

While consolidation is required in most industrial countries for affiliates in which the parent owns a majority, accounting practices vary considerably with respect to operations of affiliates in which the parent firm has minority interest. Moreover, consolidation remains optional in many countries even for majority ownership affiliates. The exclusion of certain operations from the parent's consolidated financial statements introduces an element of distortion in the operating results of the MNC. A firm, desirous of improving its earnings per share for the purpose of influencing its share price in the market, may consolidate accounts of affiliates which hitherto have been excluded. These practices not only distort the bottom line operating results, but also comparison of earnings over time.

Choosing an Appropriate Exchange Rate

The replacement of the controversial FASB No. 8 by FASB No. 52 in December 1982 (see Chapter 4) injected radically different elements for financial reporting for U.S. MNCs. The temporal method embodied in Rule No. 8, which was once the dominant method of translating accounts of affiliates for the purposes of consolidation, has been virtually replaced by the current method in major industrial countries.

The switch from the temporal to the current method of translating an affiliate's financial statement signaled a change from the parent's perspective to a local perspective. A parent perspective treats the transactions of a foreign affiliate as if they occurred in the currency of the parent, whereas

[6]Gerhard G. Mueller, "The Dual System for Transnational Financial Reporting," *Accounting Forum* (July 1976), pp. 64–74.

a local perspective implies that such transactions should be measured by local currency, or the currency in which they actually occurred.[7] The distortions ascribed to the temporal method, which invited bitter complaints and criticisms from both MNCs and the accounting profession, have given way to the current rate method, which provides results more consistent with changes in the foreign environment.

A recent study attempted to investigate the profound impact of FASB No. 8 on management reporting and control systems of U.S. MNCs since it was introduced in 1975. The study concluded that it had a substantial impact not only on financial reporting practices, but also on managerial policies.[8] The author argued that performance evaluation systems (to be discussed later in this chapter) should be developed internally and independent of FASB external reporting standards.[9]

Choi and Sondhi conducted a survey of corporate translation practices in major industrial countries with floating currencies (outside the United States) based on annual reports available in the English language for 1983. This survey is summarized in Exhibit 19-1. The authors concluded:

> The results of this survey suggest that with the exception of Canada and possibly Sweden, where alternative translation methods employed largely represent a variant of the monetary-nonmonetary method, the trend in corporate reporting for the countries surveyed appears to favor use of the current rate method. As for the accounting treatment of translation gains and losses, most companies examined, excluding Canada, prefer some form of deferral as opposed to recognition in reported earnings.
>
> Part of the popularity of the current rate method, at least in the countries surveyed, may be attributed to its conceptual simplicity and ease of application. Another reason offered here is the nature of a country's foreign operations. In comparison to the United States, most of the countries in Exhibit 19-1 possess relatively small domestic markets. Accordingly, large companies incorporated there are highly dependent on foreign operations as revenue sources. A currency translation method that retains the local currency as a unit of measure seems called for. In short, foreign affiliates are viewed from a local as opposed to a parent company perspective. Interest centers on the status and performance of local operations in the host environment.
>
> In contrast, the United States currently possesses the world's largest domestic market. For many U.S. companies, domestic operations constitute their primary concern; foreign operations are secondary. Under these circumstances, a currency translation method that adopts a U.S. dollar perspective is preferred. This is the perspective that formed the basis of SFAS No. 52's predecessor, SFAS No. 8. Unfortunately, this reporting perspective,

[7]Lee H. Radebaugh, "International Dimension of the Financial Accounting Standards Board: Translation and Disclosure of Foreign Operations," *International Journal of Accounting Education and Research* (Fall 1974), p. 59.

[8]H. Gernon, "The Effect of Translation on Multinational Corporations' Internal Performance Evaluation," *Journal of International Business Studies* (Spring/Summer 1983), pp. 101–112.

[9]*Ibid.*, p. 103.

Exhibit 19-1. International Survey of Corporate Translation Practices

	EEC (EUROPEAN ECONOMIC COMMUNITY)					NON-EEC				
	Country[c]									
Item	*Denmark*	*France*	*Germany*	*Netherlands*	*UK*	*Australia*	*Canada*	*Japan*	*Sweden*	*Switzerland*
Translation Method										
Current rate	4	7	4	8	54	8	8	10	8	5
Current-noncurrent							4			
Monetary-nonmonetary									2	
Temporal			1				5[a]			
Other (hybrids):										
Fixed assets at historical		1	2	2			4		6	2
ST monetary items at current, LT monetary items at historical							1	3		
No disclosure				1				8		1
Nonconsolidation			8	1				11		
Total	4	8	15	12	54	8	17	32	16	8
Disposition of Translation Gains (Losses)										
Current income			3	4	2	2	11[b]	1	5	2
Stockholders' equity/reserves	4	8	3	11	52	6	8	10	10	6
Deferred and amortized				4			3	2	1	
No disclosure			9					19		

[a]These firms adhered to SFAS No. 52 and thus employed both the temporal and current rate methods.
[b]Includes five firms adhering to SFAS No. 52 noted above.
[c]The numbers in each column indicate the number of companies using each method.

Source: F. D. S. Choi, and A. Sondhi, "Accounting for Floating Currencies: An International Perspective," *Journal of Accounting, Auditing, and Finance* (Summer 1985), p. 337.

while appropriate for some, was not suitable for U.S. companies whose operations were truly international. The reporting controversy which surrounded No. 8 is well known.

In adopting a situational approach, the FASB's new currency translation pronouncement recognizes a local currency perspective as a valid reporting framework. It is too early to appraise SFAS No. 52's ultimate success. However, judging from international trends, the new pronouncement appears to be on track.[10]

Accounting for Price Changes

MNCs, like their domestic counterparts, face continuously the difficult question of adjusting the value of their assets and their pricing policies to changes in the price level. The accounting practice of valuing assets, including inventories, at original or historical cost leads to overstatement of profits and corporate income tax liability during periods of a sustained rise in the general price level.

There are several approaches to adjusting the financial statements to reflect changing prices. *Current value accounting* (CVA) adjusts fixed assets and related depreciation, as well as inventories, to reflect changes in the market prices of these assets. The most common form of adjustment is the replacement cost of the asset, based on current market prices or engineering estimates, taking into account the remaining productive capacity of the asset. Alternatively, assets may be valued at the discounted value of future net cash flows which the asset is expected to generate. CVA results in *holding gains or losses,* depending on the relation between the historical cost and current value of the asset however estimated. These gains or losses may be either charged to a *revaluation reserve account,* or directly to retained earnings.

Price level or inflation accounting is more far-reaching. Inflation accounting recognizes the fact that not only fixed assets and inventories are impacted by changes in the price level, but also monetary items (current assets, current liabilities, and long-term liabilities). In essence, this approach modifies the entire financial statement to reflect changes in the purchasing power of money as measured by an appropriate general price index. By necessity, it entails an adjustment of stockholders' equity at the end of each accounting period.

Inflation accounting also impacts pricing policies. The firm's pricing of its products and/or services needs to be changed to reflect current labor cost, replacement cost of inventories, depreciation charges based on revalued fixed assets, and the current level of general, selling, and administrative expenses.

Replacement cost accounting is gradually gaining the ascendance over the traditional historical cost in the United States, the United Kingdom, and

[10]Choi and Sondhi, "Accounting for Floating Currencies," p. 340.

a large number of industrial and developing countries. In the United States both the SEC and the FASB have rulings currently in effect with respect to restatement of financial statements to reflect replacement cost. SEC's Accounting Series Release No. 190 requires companies with over $100 million of inventories and gross properties to reflect the current replacement cost of these assets, and to show depreciation and amortization charges accordingly.

FASB Ruling No. 33 on "Financial Reporting and Changing Prices" requires public companies having either $1 billion of assets or $125 million of inventories and gross properties to provide *supplemental* inflation accounting disclosures both on a constant dollar and a current cost basis. These accounting changes should be accompanied by an adequate narrative explaining the inflation-adjusted information.

MNCs whose affiliates operate in countries experiencing sustained and rapid inflation rates must develop a strategy to deal with this risk dimension. They will have to evolve and implement accounting policies and practices to:

1. Adjust the values of fixed assets, inventories, and monetary assets and liabilities to reflect the inflation rate in the host country, so that reported earnings and, consequently, tax liability are not artificially inflated at the expense of eroding investment in the affiliates.
2. Reflect the rise in inventory cost, depreciation, and other cost components (labor, and the like) in prices of products and services sold by affiliates.
3. Because a sharply higher inflation rate in the host country than in the parent country usually heralds an imminent depreciation of the local currency's exchange rate (against the parent's), local affiliates must consider raising local prices. The success of such a policy in recouping all or part of the decline in receipts in terms of the parent's currency depends primarily on the elasticity of demand for the products in local markets (see Chapter 5).

When both translation of an affiliate's financial statements and accounting for inflation in the affiliate's host country are considered together, a question of methodology has been often raised in international accounting literature. This question is sometimes referred to as the *translate-restate/restate-translate controversy*. The issue is whether to adjust first an affiliate's financial statement to reflect local inflation and then translate it into the parent's currency, or, alternatively, to first translate into the parent's currency and then adjust for host country inflation.

The key issue involved is the maintenance of the affiliate's dividend-paying capacity to the parent. The appropriate approach is, therefore, to first adjust local currency financial statements to reflect current values, and then to translate the adjusted statements to the parent's currency.

CASE STUDY

Barrett Engineering and Electronics, Inc.

The following example illustrates the use of inflation accounting in adjusting the financial statements of an affiliate of an MNC, and the consolidation of the affiliate's accounts with those of the parent company. The object of this exercise is to trace the impact of inflation accounting on the affiliate's earning capacity and the pricing of its products in the local market. Both the balance sheet and the income statements will be impacted by adjustments for inflation. In translating the accounts of the affiliate for the purpose of consolidation, only the balance sheet will be needed. For the purpose of the consolidation process, the affiliate's balance sheet will be adjusted on a replacement-value basis, rather than inflation-adjusted basis. FASB Rule 52 will be used to translate the affiliate's accounts from the functional currency (Spanish pesetas) to the parent's currency (U.S. dollars). The original balance sheet and income statement for the affiliate are shown in Exhibit 1.

Exhibit 1. Barrett Engineering and Electronics (Spain) Statement of Condition as of December 31, 1985 (in millions of pesetas)

ASSETS			LIABILITIES AND NET WORTH	
Cash		500	Current liabilities	2750
Accounts receivable		3500	Long-term debt	5250
Inventory		6250	Equity	5750
Fixed assets (gross)	5000			
Less: accumulated depreciation	1500			
		3500		
Total assets		13750	Total liabilities and net worth	13750

Barrett Engineering and Electronics (Spain) Income Statement Year Ending December 31, 1986 (in millions of pesetas)

Sales	10500
Cost of goods sold	5250
Labor and other costs	1250
Depreciation	500
Profit before tax	3500
Tax at 40%	1400
Net profit after tax	2100

Other Transactions and Assumptions

- Sufficient inventory is purchased to keep ending inventory at the same level as beginning inventory.
- All sales proceeds are collected during 1986.
- Depreciation is 10 percent of fixed assets (straight-line basis).
- Liabilities remain unchanged.
- All earnings are transferred to the parent company.

Inflation and Exchange Rate Assumptions

The inflation rate in Spain in 1986 was 20 percent. The spot peseta/dollar (Pst/$) exchange rate on January 1, 1986 and December 31, 1986 were Pst160 and Pst200, respectively, per $1.00.

The balance sheets of the parent company, Barrett Engineering and Electronics, Inc., on December 31, 1985 and December 31, 1986 (prior to the consolidation of the Spanish affiliate's accounts are shown in Exhibit 2).

Exhibit 2. Barrett Engineering and Electronics, Inc. Balance Sheet (in millions of dollars)

	AS OF DECEMBER 31, 1985	AS OF DECEMBER 31, 1986
Assets		
Cash	75	125
Accounts receivable	410	529
Inventory	724	711
Fixed assets (net of depreciation)	1250	1115
Other assets	150	235
Total assets	2609	2715
Liabilities and Stockholders' Equity		
Bank loans	500	450
Accounts payable	250	350
Long-term debt	450	550
Other liabilities	275	210
Stockholder's Equity		
Capital and paid-in surplus	250	250
Retained earnings	884	905
Total liabilities and stockholders' equity	2609	2715

The analysis will be carried out in steps as follows:

1. Preparation of the affiliate's balance sheet on a historical (non-inflation adjusted) basis on December 31, 1986.
2. Preparation of the affiliate's price level adjusted income statement for 1986.
3. Preparation of the affiliate's opening and closing balance sheets on a price-adjusted basis.
4. Stating the affiliate's closing balance sheet in current value accounting terms.
5. Preparation of consolidated balance sheets for Barrett Engineering and Electronics, Inc. (on December 31, 1985 and December 31, 1986), showing the impact of translation into U.S. dollars using FASB 52.

Step (1)

The ending balance sheet based on historical cost (Exhibit 3) accounting shows three changes compared with the opening position: (1) the increase in cash by Pst2600 million, reflecting Pst2100 million in net profit after tax (prior to transfer of profits to the parent company), and Pst500 million in charges against income for depreciation of fixed assets;

Exhibit 3. Barrett Engineering and Electronics (Spain) Statement of Condition (in millions of pesetas)

	OPENING JANUARY 1, 1986				CLOSING DECEMBER 31, 1986			
Assets		Historical		Price Level Adjusted		Historical		Price Level Adjusted
Cash		500		600		3100		3100
Accounts receivable		3500		4200		3500		3500
Inventory		6250		7500		6250		7500
Fixed assets (gross)	5000		6000		5000		6000	
Less: accumulated depreciation	1500	3500	1800	4200	2000	3000	2400	3600
Total assets		13750		16500		15850		17700
Liabilities and Net Worth								
Current liabilities		2750		3300		2750		2750
Long-term debt		5250		6300		5250		5250
Equity		5750		6900		7850		9700
Total liabilities and net worth		13750		16500		15850		17700

(2) an increase in accumulated depreciation to Pst2000 million from Pst1500 million; and (3) an increase in equity by the amount of profits after tax, or by Pst2100 million. All other accounts have remained unchanged in line with the postulated assumptions.

Step (2)

The adjusted income statement (Exhibit 4) shows a sharp decline in the profitability of the affiliate as selling prices were maintained while costs rose by 20 percent, that is, by the inflation rate. Depreciation charges increased from Pst500 million (in the unadjusted statement) to Pst900 million to reflect not only the current replacement value of fixed assets (Pst6000 million), but also to offset inadequate depreciation charges in the preceding three years. Note that the corporate income tax remained at Pst1400 million, since it was based on the nominal profits in the unadjusted statement, rather than the inflation-adjusted one.

To dramatize the impact of inflation on the profitability of affiliates operating in high-inflation-rate countries, the second column in Exhibit 4 adjusts the income statement to an inflation rate of 25 percent instead of 20 percent. The outcome is a net loss of Pst26 million, since the tax predicated on nominal earnings exceeds profit before tax by that amount. The exercise demonstrates clearly that those affiliates need to adopt a dynamic pricing policy to review prices quickly and frequently, if they were to avoid serious erosion of their profitability and payment of taxes based on nominal rather than real income.

Step (3)

Exhibit 3 also shows Barrett Engineering and Electronics (Spain) opening and closing balance sheets adjusted for inflation. This adjustment

Exhibit 4. Barrett Engineering and Electronics (Spain) Price-adjusted Income Statement—Year Ending December 31, 1986 (in millions of pesetas)

	20% INFLATION	25% INFLATION
Sales	10500	10500
Cost of goods sold	6300	6563
Labor and other costs	1500	1563
Depreciation	900	1000
Profit before tax	1800	1374
Tax at 40% (based on nominal earnings)	1400	1400
Net profit after tax	400	(26)

will make possible a more meaningful comparison with the closing balance sheet, and trace the changes that have taken place.

As both the opening and closing accounts are expressed in the same monetary unit (monetary unit with the same purchasing power), the improvement in equity by Pst2800 million may seem puzzling, particularly as the affiliate realized a profit of only Pst400 million (on a price-adjusted basis). The bulk of the improvement in net worth is due to the gain on net monetary assets, i.e., monetary assets less monetary liabilities, representing the affiliate's purchasing power gain. This gain is computed as shown in Table 1.

In addition, 1986 net income was charged with Pst300 million of additional depreciation to offset the failure of depreciation charges during the preceding three years (Pst100 million annually) to reflect the increased replacement value of fixed assets. Had it not been for this adjustment, net income for 1986 would have been Pst700 million, which, together with the improvement in net monetary assets as computed above, equals the increase in equity of Pst2800 million.

Step (4)

The affiliate's balance sheets need to be expressed in current value terms before they are translated into U.S. dollars and consolidated with the parent, Barrett Engineering and Electronics, Inc. (U.S.). Adjusting for inflation, or by the increase in the general price level, may fall short of reflecting the actual increase in the current replacement value of inventories and fixed assets in domestic currency terms. Exhibit 5 is prepared on the assumption that the replacement value of the inventory and fixed assets are Pst8000 million and Pst7500 million, respectively (compared with Pst7500 million and Pst6000 million, respectively, on a price-adjusted basis).

Table 1.

	VALUES IN PST MILLIONS	
Net monetary assets (January 1)	= Pst4800 − 9600	= −4800
Net monetary assets (December 31)		
Net monetary assets (January 1) + Sales	= −4800 + 10500	= 5700
Less (inventory purchases + labor + taxes)	= 6300 + 1500 + 1400	= −9200
		−3500
Actual monetary assets (December 31)	= Pst6600 − 8000	= −1400
Gain in purchasing power = Actual net monetary assets (Dec. 31) − projected net monetary assets (Dec. 31)	= (−1400) − (−3500)	= 2100

Exhibit 5. Barrett Engineering and Electronics (Spain) Statement of Condition December 31, 1986 (in millions of pesetas)

ASSETS		HISTORICAL		CURRENT VALUE ADJUSTED
Cash		3100		3100
Accounts receivable		3500		3500
Inventory		6250		8000
Fixed assets (gross)	5000		7500	
Less accumulated depreciation	2000	3000	3000	4500
Total assets		15850		19100
LIABILITIES AND NET WORTH				
Current liabilities		2750		2750
Long-term debt		5250		5250
Equity		7850		11100
Total liabilities and net worth		15850		19100

Step (5)

The final step in this case study is the consolidation of the balance sheet of Barrett Engineering and Electronics, Inc. (U.S.) and Barrett Engineering and Electronics (Spain) in one statement using FASB #52. First, the parent's balance sheet on December 31, 1985 shown in Exhibit 2 is consolidated with the opening balance sheet of the affiliate on historical basis shown in Exhibit 3. Second, the parent's balance sheet as of December 31, 1986 (Exhibit 2), is consolidated with the affiliate's CVA adjusted balance sheet on the same date (Exhibit 5).

The consolidation is shown in Exhibit 6. Translation of the affiliate's account into U.S. dollars was carried out at the exchange rate of Pst160 and Pst200 per $1.00 for December 31, 1985 and December 31, 1986, respectively. According to FASB Rule #52 (see Chapter 4), all assets and liabilities are exposed to the exchange risk, and all are to be translated at the exchange rate prevailing at the date when financial statements are prepared. Exchange gains (losses) resulting from the translation process are to be shown as an adjustment to stockholders' equity account on the balance sheet, rather than charged to current income.

Assuming that the Pst/$ exchange rate prevailing at the beginning of 1985 was Pst140 per $1.00, the exchange translation loss shown on the year-end consolidated balance sheet = (total of exposed assets − total of exposed liabilities) (change in the exchange rate) = (Pst13,750 million − Pst8000 million)($0.007143 − $0.00625) = $5.13 million. Similarly, the translation loss shown in the consolidated balance sheet at the end of

Exhibit 6. Barrett Engineering and Electronics, Inc. and Affiliates Consolidated Balance Sheet (in millions of U.S. dollars)

	DECEMBER 31, 1985			DECEMBER 31, 1986		
	Parent	Spanish Affiliate	Consolidated	Parent	Spanish Affiliate	Consolidated
Assets						
Cash	75.0	3.1	78.1	125.0	15.5	140.5
Accounts receivable	410.0	21.9	431.9	529.0	17.5	546.5
Inventory	724.0	39.1	763.1	711.0	40.0	751.0
Fixed assets (net)	1250.0	21.9	1271.9	1115.0	22.5	1137.5
Other assets	150.0	—	150.0	235.0	—	235.0
Total assets	2609.0	86.0	2695.0	2715.0	95.5	2810.5
Liabilities and Net Worth						
Current liabilities	750.0	17.2	767.2	800.0	13.8	813.8
Long-term debt	450.0	32.8	482.8	550.0	26.3	576.3
Other liabilities	275.0	—	275.0	210.0	—	210.0
Stockholders' Equity						
Capital and paid in surplus	250.0	10.0[1]	260.0	250.0	10.0	260.0
Retained earnings	884.0	26.0	910.0	905.0	45.4	950.4
Adjustment for exchange gains (losses) on consolidation	—	—	(5.1)	—	—	(19.0)[2]
Total liabilities and stockholders' equity	2609.0	86.0	2695.0	2715.0	95.5	2810.5

[1]Barrett Engineering and Electronics, Inc. had an original equity investment of $10 million in the Spanish affiliate.

[2]Consisting of exchange losses of $5.1 million in 1985 and $13.9 million in 1986. Adjustments for exchange gains (losses) are not charged to retained earnings in the years they are incurred (FASB 52).

1986 = (Pst19,100 million − Pst8000 million)($0.00625 − $0.00500) = $13.9 million. Both figures appear as an adjustment to stockholders' equity account. Recasting the affiliate's accounts in terms of current value accounting has considerably increased the affiliate's exposure to the exchange risk, since the exposure (using FASB #52) is measured by the value (in local currency) of total assets less total liabilities. Liabilities have remained fixed in local currency monetary units, while the values of inventory and fixed assets were adjusted upward to reflect their current replacement value.

EVALUATION AND CONTROL OF FOREIGN OPERATIONS

Introduction

Closely linked to the development of international accounting standards and systems is the need for MNCs to design and enforce a company-wide system to evaluate and control foreign operations. In many respects, developing and perfecting such a system is an essential managerial function for all firms, domestic and multinational. While the complexity of corporate evaluation and control systems is related to the size and the geographic dispersion of operational activities, international dispersion of operations entails additional challenges, as well as rewards, for monitoring worldwide activities.

There are no generally recognized criteria for an effective system that would meet the needs of all MNCs. Managerial and financial control is essentially a task that seeks to fashion a system that suits the particular needs and conditions of the firm, and helps the management achieve certain clearly defined objectives. The ingredients of a successful system have to be sought and sorted out from the particular experiences of the firm, and have to be molded to suit its overall goals. The constituent elements involve several disciplines, including management principles, international accounting and financial management techniques, psychology (incentive and motivation), as well as a thorough knowledge of how these standards of behavior and accomplishment differ in the various localities of operation.

Design of an optimal evaluation and control system for a large MNC must take into consideration a number of complicating factors that are not encountered in divisions or subsidiaries of a purely domestic operation. The following is a checklist of these factors:

1. The impact on performance of currency fluctuations which are beyond the control of the local managers, particularly if exposure management and hedging operations are centralized at the head office or at designated money centers.

2. Impact of political risks which are beyond the control of the local managers on profitability of affiliates, except to the extent that those managers can predict or forestall actions taken by host governments.
3. The use of reinvoicing centers, whereby inputs and components shipped to an affiliate are billed using internal or administrative prices and exchange rates, seriously interferes with the measurement of the financial performance of the affiliate.
4. The use of transfer pricing in intracompany transactions (Chapter 6) not only distorts the performance of each profit center, but also weakens the incentives of local managers and clouds accountability for actions or inactions of those managers.
5. In situations where local joint-venture partners participate in managing an affiliate, the motivation of managers to achieve corporate goals, as well as their performance, are difficult to ascertain by conventional control and evaluation yardsticks.
6. Affiliates' performance and profitability are often influenced by the terms of the agreement negotiated at the outset with host countries. Local management, for example, cannot take credit for the favorable impact of such features as tax holidays or concessional financing arrangement, nor should they be penalized by excessive royalty and service fees specified in these agreeements.

Elements of an Effective Control and Evaluation System

Control and evaluation systems are evolved over time by MNCs to suit their special circumstances and are adapted for the fulfillment of the overall corporate goals. Each system is by necessity custom-tailored to its particular style of management and environmental factors peculiar to its multinational activity. It is, therefore, difficult to delineate the elements that must be included in the making of an effective system. The following paragraphs attempt to outline the basic constituent elements.

Performance standards represent the most essential element of any evaluation and control system. These standards, if they are to serve as an effective managerial yardstick, must be objective and measurable. Standards which are not measurable or those which are influenced by subjective judgment of the reviewers are not workable. Affiliates' or managers' performances must also be measurable against these predetermined standards.

Standards are often designed or predetermined primarily in the form of budgets which provide the basis with which actual performance may be evaluated. Some firms also use historical standards to monitor an affiliate's performance over time, or, alternatively, external standards to measure its performance against other firms operating under comparable conditions. External standards are often misleading, since it is exceedingly difficult, if not impossible, to find another firm whose performance is affected by the same factors so as to permit valid comparison.

Another basic element of an effective control system is the gathering, processing, and dissemination of *timely information* from the operating units to the parent company and back. A well-designed system of reporting and communication of information provides management with the data to take corrective action, if necessary, to steer the operational units toward the achievement of the firm's objectives. Information also provides the basis for the evaluation of the decision-making centers and local managers by the top management.

A third element of a good evaluation and control system is a well-understood and carefully implemented *set of rewards and penalties* which will motivate local managers. Without this component the system would not function in directing the efforts of all units towards the fulfillment of the firm's declared objectives.

The three essential elements of an effective evaluation and control system—objective performance standards, adequate flow of information, and a set of rewards and penalties for managerial behavior—are common to all such systems, domestic or multinational. However, design and implementation of a system for an MNC must reflect its geographic dispersion and exposure to diverse local environments. Therein lies the difference between domestic and multinational control systems and their adequacy to serve the wide-flung activities of a typical MNC.

The following section addresses the basic question of whether MNCs have succeeded in fashioning evaluation and control systems that suit the nature of their operations, or whether their design of such systems has been merely an extension of their domestic systems.

Multinational Evaluation and Control Systems

In addition to the basic elements that go into the making of an effective evaluation and control system developed in the preceding section, several key questions need to be addressed in designing a multinational system. The key questions are

1. Does the system factor in the degree of decentralization in the decision-making process? Admittedly, this issue is also important in a domestic control system, but it is crucial and more pervasive in a multinational one.
2. Does the system recognize the distortions to the performance standards resulting from such practices and mechanisms as transfer pricing, reinvoicing centers, and tax haven "shell" financial affiliates? The more extensive the use of these practices, the more crucial the need to adapt performance standards to take into account their impact on measurable performance.
3. Does the system recognize the distortions to the performance standards arising from the local conditions under which an affili-

ate operates? Conditions relating to the local environment include such variables as: tax holidays and concessional financing and similar arrangements, the role of local joint-venture partners in the decision-making process, and discriminatory practices of the host government which influence the operation and/or the cost structure of the affiliate.

4. Is financial reporting the backbone of the system? The diversity of multinational operations and the geographic distance separating the center from local operations render conventional managerial evaluation and control techniques less effective and, perhaps, unreliable. Gauging the performance of affiliates, therefore, requires the timely flow of adequate financial data.

Have the MNCs succeeded in developing adequate evaluation and control systems capable of achieving their overall objectives? A recent assessment of such systems by Jacques and Lorange suggests that MNCs have adopted systems which have generally failed to support management evaluation of operations under highly changing and volatile circumstances. To quote the authors:

> MNCs generally seem to have opted for benign simplicity in developing worldwide congruent and motivational control systems. Indeed, recent empirical studies by Bursk, et al. (1977), Choi and Czechowicz (1983), McInnes (1971), and Morsicato and Radebaugh (1979) have found consistent bias toward "exporting" the domestic control system to foreign operations. Excessive reliance on such simplistic financial criteria as ROI and budgets has seemingly continued unabated, however, in spite of a structurally more volatile international monetary system. The heightened turbulence of the international monetary environment during the last decade (a result of the breakdown of the Bretton Woods system) has not been translated into "environmentalized" control systems. Specifically, MNCs have generally not found it necessary to differentiate substantively between the hypoinflationary conditions of the majority of foreign countries and the unique hyperinflationary conditions of countries such as Argentina, Brazil, Israel, Mexico, and Turkey.[11]

An important consideration which seems to have contributed to the inadequacy of multinational evaluation and control systems is their continued reliance on the return on investment criterion (ROI) as the key performance criterion. The ROI has been the chief measure of corporate performance in the United States as well as in most industrial countries. Yet there have been serious questions about whether a strict adherence to this yardstick is appropriate for MNCs, particularly those operating under dynamic and turbulent environments.

[11]Laurent L. Jacques and P. Lorange, "The International Control Conundrum: the Case of 'Hyperinflationary' Subsidiaries," *Journal of International Business Studies* (Fall 1984), p. 185. FASB #52 defines a "hyperinflationary" country as any country having experienced a cumulative rate of inflation of 100 percent or more over three consecutive years.

The "ROI" as a Criterion of Performance

What are the pitfalls in relying on "ROI" as the principal criterion of measuring long-run profit performance of foreign affiliates? And if this yardstick is unusable, what other performance criteria may be utilized for this purpose?

The answer to the first question is that "ROI" is as valid a measure of performance for foreign entities as it is for domestic entities, provided that the relevant investment base and relevant returns can be identified. The problems involved in correctly identifying the investment base and returns associated with the operation of foreign affiliates are of two types:

1. Accounting problems related to the measurement of the investment base which we addressed earlier in this chapter. These include historical cost vs. current replacement cost accounting for valuation of inventory and fixed assets, treatment of working capital as part of the base (should intracompany accounts be excluded?), and defining the parent's investment. (Should long-term loans provided by the parent be considered part of the equity base?)
2. Conceptual and operational problems in measuring the returns from foreign affiliates. Returns consist of several components: dividends, royalties, rentals, service fees, licensing fees and commissions. Some of these represent payment for services performed by the parent at a cost, while others, such as dividends or royalties, constitute part of the relevant return on foreign investment. With the exception of dividends, these payments are also part of the operational cost of the affiliates which are deducted before taxable income is determined.

This would suggest that returns from affiliates may be influenced by the "unbundling" of such returns or their breakdown into various components. Internal transactions, through the use of transfer prices, distorts the cost structure of foreign affiliates, while the use of such practices as reinvoicing centers distorts effective exchange rates applicable to transactions among them, and between them and the parent company. The combined effect of these distortions often invalidates the accounting returns from these units as a measure of their performance.

If "ROI" is an unreliable yardstick due to the problems associated with measuring the relevant investment base and returns from affiliates, what other evaluation standards are appropriate?

Evaluating performance of affiliates operating in a fast-changing and uncertain environment requires frequent monitoring of operations and a dynamic strategy to cope with these developments. Alternative and more appropriate measure of performance include, depending on the nature of operations, such criteria as sales growth, market share, gross or net operating margin, unit production cost, and total and fixed asset turnover. If "ROI" or some other measures of overall profitability is to be used, management must make appropriate adjustments in the investment base and/or returns, so that the measure would truly reflect the outcome of local operations.

Another device for evaluating and controlling operations of foreign affiliates is the use of operating budgets. Budgetary control, when flexibly and appropriately used, can impart an element of objectivity in the evaluation process and provide the head office with an effective control mechanism. A major issue in budgetary control is the selection of an exchange rate. The distinction is between an approach that favors the parent company's perspective (ethnocentric) and one which favors the perspective of the operating affiliates (polycentric). According to the first approach, the reference currency for budgetary evaluation and control is the U.S. dollar (for U.S. MNCs). The second approach recognizes that foreign operations take place in a foreign environment, and, therefore, should be evaluated in terms of local currency. A compromise between these extremes is a budgetary system that combines both local and parent currencies (geocentric).[12]

REVIEW QUESTIONS

1. Given the diversity of accounting standards under which MNCs operate, would you advocate the development of internationally recognized standards? How does the adoption of such standards help investors in the stocks of MNCs with worldwide operations? What are the major obstacles to the development of these standards?
2. Why is the uniformity and consistency in consolidating affiliates' operations with the parents' an important issue to international investors in the shares of MNCs? Could an MNC manipulate earnings per share by consolidating previously unconsolidated operations? As an investor, how would such practices influence your ability to assess the quality of your investment?
3. Fundamentally, the move to a local currency perspective embodied in the current rate method should appeal more to European MNCs, which have relatively small domestic markets, than to U.S. MNCs. Do you agree? As a financial manager of a large and widely diversified U.S. MNC, would you regret the switch from the temporal method to the current rate method?
4. How does inflation accounting differ from CVA accounting? Which approach is more valid in recasting the affiliate's accounts to preserve its dividend-paying ability to the parent? Demonstrate how failure to

[12]Jacques and Lorange, "The International Control Conundrum," p. 186.

adjust pricing policies for inflation rate in the host country can be injurious to the parent company's investment in its affiliate.

5. Why is CVA accounting more appropriate as a basis for consolidating the affiliate's accounts with the parent's? Does this approach invariably increase the exposure of the affiliate to the exchange risk under FASB #52? Could the same thing be said if an alternative rule (such as monetary-nonmonetary, or current-noncurrent) is used?
6. If you were the financial manager of an MNC's affiliate located in a Latin American nation experiencing a "hyperinflation" situation (say the price level increases by some 150 percent monthly), how would you adjust your accounting, financing, and price policies to cope with this situation? Could you visualize circumstances which may lead you to advise your principals to cease operating in that turbulent environment?
7. Why is the return on investment (ROI) often suspect as a valid measure of overall corporate performance? Why is the ROI an even less reliable performance measure for wide-flung MNCs?
8. Critics of MNCs, particularly among financial management experts, contend that they have failed on the whole to develop effective evaluation and control systems. Most of them have merely extended the system in use for domestic operations to encompass their worldwide operations. Do you agree? What sort of evidence must one produce to justify this contention?
9. Why is financial reporting the backbone of a good multinational evaluation and control system? Why do MNCs require a more frequent and more detailed flow of financial reports and other data from their affiliates than do domestically based firms from their divisions and subsidiaries?
10. How can carefully prepared operating budgets and financial plans provide an adequate basis for a multinational control and evaluation system? In what areas of financial management covered in this book can these budgets and financial plans prove most useful for this purpose?

REVIEW PROBLEM

The MCO Corporation (Philippines) is a wholly owned subsidiary of MCO, Inc. (U.S.), uses the calendar year as its accounting period, and maintains its books in local currency (pesos). Its balance sheet at the end of 1985 was as shown in Table 19-1.

Table 19-1. The MCO Corporation (Philippines) Balance Sheet as of December 31, 1985 (in thousands of pesos)

Cash		70,000
Accounts receivable		180,000
Inventory		350,000
Fixed assets	1,000,000	
Less accumulated depreciation[1]	200,000	800,000
Total assets		1,400,000
Current liabilities		180,000
Long-term liabilities		300,000
Capital stock		800,000
Retained earnings		120,000
Total liabilities & stockholders' equity		1,400,000

[1]Straight line depreciation of fixed assets over 10 years.

Activities During 1986 (all figures are in local currency)

During 1986, MCO Corporation had annual sales of 1,470,000, total wages and other expenses of 252,000, and inventory purchases of 910,000 (closing inventory on December 31, 1986 was 418,000). It also purchased additional assets amounting to 430,000 against a long-term note.

MCO's net income in the Philippines is taxable at the rate of 30 percent. The Philippines experienced an inflation rate of 25 percent during 1986.

Assume that no other transactions had taken place during the year, and that the company's policy is to maintain accounts receivable and accounts payable at the same level.

1. Prepare MCO Corporation's (Philippines) income statement for 1986 on a historical cost basis. Also, prepare a price-adjusted income statement:
   a. Assuming that the firms made no adjustment in sales prices.
   b. Assuming that the firm raised prices by an average of 15 percent during the year.
2. Prepare MCO Corporation's (Philippines) balance sheet as of end of 1986 on a historical-cost basis, assuming that the firm made no adjustment in sales prices. Prepare another balance sheet on a price-adjusted basis, using the same assumption.
3. Assume that the Peso/U.S. $ rate declined from 20 pesos per U.S. dollar at the end of 1985 to 28 pesos per U.S. dollar at the end of 1986. If MCO, Inc. (U.S.) uses the current rate for translation,
   a. Calculate translation gains (losses), assuming that the affiliate prepared its closing balance sheet on a historical-cost basis.

b. How much would these gains (losses) be if the affiliate had prepared its closing balance sheet on a price-adjusted basis?
c. How would these translation gains (losses) appear on the parent's end-of-1986 consolidated balance sheet?

BIBLIOGRAPHY

AGGARWAL, R., and J. C. BAKER, "Using Foreign Subsidiary Accounting Data: A Dilemma for Multinational Corporations," *Columbia Journal of World Business* (Fall 1975), pp. 83–92.

ALHASHIM, D. D., "Internal Performance Evaluation in American Multinational Enterprises," *Management International Review* (1980), pp. 33–39.

ARNOLD, J., W. W. HOLDER, and M. H. MANN, "International Reporting Aspects of Segment Disclosure," *International Journal of Accounting* (Fall 1980), pp. 125–135.

ARPAN, J., and L. H. RADEBAUGH, *International Accounting and Multinational Enterprises.* Boston, Mass.: Warren, Gorham & Lamont, 1981.

BARRETT, M. E., "Financial Reporting Practices: Disclosure and Comprehensiveness in an International Setting," *Journal of Accounting Research* (Spring 1976), pp. 10–26.

BARRETT, M. E., and J. ROY, "Financial Reporting Practices in France," *Financial Analysts Journal* (January-February 1976), pp. 39–49.

BAVISHI, V. B., and H. E. WYMAN, "Foreign Operations Disclosures by U.S.-Based Multinational Corporations: Are They Adequate?", *International Journal of Accounting* (Fall 1980), pp. 153–168.

BENSTON, G. J., "Public (U.S.) Compared to Private (U.K.) Regulation of Corporate Financial Disclosures," *Accounting Review* (July 1976), pp. 483–498.

BLOCK, D. J., and E. J. ODOMER, "Enforcing the Accounting Standards Provisions of the Foreign Corrupt Practices Act," *Financial Executive* (July 1979), pp. 19–26.

BURNETT, R. ANDREW, "The Harmonization of Accounting Principles in the Member Countries of the European Economic Community," *International Journal of Accounting* (Fall 1975), pp. 23–30.

Business International, *Solving Accounting Problems for Worldwide Operations.* New York: Business International Corporation, 1974.

______, *Coping with Worldwide Accounting Changes: Successful Strategies and Techniques for the 1980s.* New York: Business International Corporation, 1985.

______, "Evaluating Foreign Operations: The Appropriate Rates for Comparing Results with Budgets," *Business International Money Report* (May 20, 1977), pp. 153–154.

CASTLE, E. F., "The Problems of Consolidation of Accounts of a Multinational Enterprise: Shell Group of Companies—Shell Transport and Trading Company, Limited, U.K.," *International Journal of Accounting* (Fall 1980), pp. 209–219.

CHEN, C. N., and T. W. TSAUR, "Currency Substitution and Foreign Inflation," *The Quarterly Journal of Economics* (February 1983), pp. 177–184.

CHOI, F. D. S., "Analyzing Foreign Financial Statements: The Use and Misuse of International Ratio Analysis," *Journal of International Business Studies* (Spring/Summer 1983), pp. 113–131.

______, "Financial Disclosure and Entry to the European Capital Market," *Journal of Accounting Research* (Autumn 1973), pp. 159–175.

______, "European Disclosure: The Competitive Disclosure Hypothesis," *Journal of International Business Studies* (Fall 1974), pp. 15–24.

______, "Price-Level Adjustments and Foreign Currency Translation: Are They Compatible?", *International Journal of Accounting* (Fall 1975), pp. 121–143.

______, "Global Finance and Accounting Uniformity," *University of Michigan Business Review* (September 1976), pp. 23–26.

CHOI, F. D. S., and V. B. BAVISHI, "Diversity in Multinational Accounting," *Financial Executive* (August 1982), pp. 45–49.

CHOI, F. D. S., and G. G. MUELLER, *An Introduction to Multinational Accounting*. Englewood Cliffs, N.J.: Prentice-Hall, Inc., 1978.

______, *Essentials of Multinational Accounting: An Anthology*. Ann Arbor, Mich.: UMI Press, 1979.

CHOI, F. D. S., and I. J. CZECHOWICZ, "Assessing Foreign Subsidiary Performance: A Multinational Comparison," *Management International Review* (1983), pp. 14–25.

CHOI, F. D. S., and A. SONDHI, "Accounting for Floating Currencies; An International Perspective," *Journal of Accounting, Auditing, and Finance* (Summer 1985), pp. 335–340.

COBURN, D. L., "Dilemmas in MNC Transfer Pricing," *Managerial Accounting* (November 1981), pp. 8–10.

CUMMINGS, J. P., and W. L. ROGERS, "Developments in International Accounting," *CPA Journal* (May 1978), pp. 15–19.

CUNNINGHAM, G. M., *An Accounting Research Framework for Multinational Enterprises*. Ann Arbor, Mich.: UMI Press, 1978.

DA COSTA, R. C., J. FISHER, and W. M. LAWSON," "Linkages in the International Business Community: Accounting Evidence," *Journal of International Business Studies* (Fall 1980), pp. 92–102.

DAVIDSON, S., C. P. STICKNEY, and R. L. WEIL, *Inflation Accounting, A Guide for the Accountant and Financial Analyst.* New York: McGraw-Hill, 1976.

______, "The International Dimension of the Financial Accounting Standards Board: Translation and Disclosure of Foreign Operations," *International Journal of Accounting* (Fall 1974), pp. 55–70.

DRURY, D. H., "Effects of Accounting Practice Divergence: Canada and the United States," *Journal of International Business Studies* (Fall 1979), pp. 75–87.

EICHENSEHER, J. W., "The Effects of Foreign Operation on Domestic Auditor Selection," *Journal of Accounting, Auditing, and Finance* (Spring 1975), pp. 195–209.

ERNST and WHINNEY, *1984 Foreign and U.S. Corporate Income and Withholding Tax Rates,* International Series, New York, 1985.

FARAG, S. M., "The Problem of Performance Evaluation in International Accounting," *International Journal of Accounting* (Fall 1974), pp. 45–53.

FRANK, W. G., "Empirical Analysis of International Accounting Principles," *Journal of Accounting Research* (Spring 1981), pp. 593–605.

GERNON, H., "The Effect of Translation on Multinational Corporations' Internal Performance Evaluation," *Journal of International Business Studies* (Spring/Summer 1983), pp. 103–112.

HAUWROTH, W. P., "Problems in the Development of Worldwide Accounting Standards," *International Journal of Accounting* (Fall 1973), pp. 23–34.

HAYES, D. J., "The International Accounting Standards Committee—Recent Developments and Current Problems," *International Journal of Accounting* (Fall 1980), pp. 1–10.

HOLE, RODERICK C., and M. A. ALKIER, "German Financial Statements," *Managerial Accounting* (July 1974), pp. 28–34.

IMICKE, L., and C. SMITH, "International Financial Control Problems and the Accounting Control System," *Management International Review* (April 5, 1975), pp. 13ff.

INTERNATIONAL PRACTICE EXECUTIVE COMMITTEE, *Professional Accounting in 30 Countries.* New York: American Institute of Certified Public Accountants, 1975.

JACQUES, L. L., and P. LORANGE, "The International Control Conundrum: The Case of Hyperinflationary Subsidiaries [Financial Controls of Multinational Corporations' Foreign Subsidiaries]," *Journal of International Business Studies* (Fall 1984), pp. 185–201.

JONES, E. H., "Decision-Making Based on Foreign Financial Statements," *Financial Executive* (February 1981), pp. 32–35.

KANAGA, W. S., "International Accounting: The Challenge and the Changes," *Journal of Accountancy* (November 1980), pp. 55–60.

LESSARD, D. R., and P. LORANGE, "Currency Changes and Management Control: Resolving the Centralization/Decentralization Dilemma," *Accounting Review* (July 1977), pp. 628–637.

LORANGE, P., and L. L. JACQUES, "Hyperinflation and Global Strategic Management," *The Columbia Journal of World Business* (Summer 1984), pp. 68–75.

MENSAH, Y. M., and L. F. BIAGIONI, "The Predictive Ability of Financial Ratios Using Alternative Translation Methods for Foreign-Currency Financial Statements: A Simulation Study," *International Journal of Accounting* (Fall 1980), pp. 221–245.

MORRIS, M. H., and D. RICKETTS, "The Relevance of Inflation-Adjusted Accounting Data in the Assessment of Systematic Risk," *Review of Business and Economic Research* (Spring 1984), pp. 90–101.

MUELLER, G. G., "The Dual System for Transnational Financial Reporting," *Accounting Forum* (May 1976), pp. 17–25.

MUELLER, G. G., and L. M. WALKER, "The Coming of Age of Transnational Financial Reporting," *Journal of Accountancy* (July 1976), pp. 67–74.

PAKKALA, A. L., "Foreign Exchange Accounting of Multinational Corporations," *Financial Analysis Journal* (March–April 1975), pp. 32–41, 76.

POMERANZ, F., "International Auditing Standards," *International Journal of Accounting* (Fall 1975), pp. 1–13.

PRICE WATERHOUSE and COMPANY, *Guide for the Reader of Foreign Financial Statements, A List of Differences in Accounting Principles and Practices Between the United States and 24 Foreign Countries,* 1975.

RADEBAUGH, L. H., "Accounting for Price-Level and Exchange-Rate Changes for U.S. International Firms: An Empirical Study," *Journal of International Business Studies* (Fall 1974), pp. 41–55.

———, "Foreign Inflation and Management Decisions," *Management Accounting* (June 1977), pp. 21–27.

———, "Multinational Financing and Accounting Harmony," *Management Accounting* (March 1974), pp. 14–17.

RADEBAUGH, L. H., and G. G. MUELLER, *An Introduction to Multinational Accounting.* Englewood Cliffs, N.J.: Prentice-Hall, Inc., 1978.

ROBBINS, S. M., and R. B. STOBAUGH, "The Bent Measuring Stick for Foreign Subsidiaries," *Harvard Business Review* (September–October 1973), pp. 80–88.

RODNEY, E., "Financial Control for Multinational Operations," *Financial Executive* (May 1976), pp. 22–28.

RUESCHLOFF, N. G., *International Accounting and Financial Reporting.* New York: Praeger, 1976.

SCHWEIKART, J. A., "We Must End Consolidation of Foreign Subsidiaries," *Management Accounting* (August 1981), pp. 31–35.

SCOTT, G. M., "Financial Control in Multinational Enterprises: The New Challenge to Accountants," *International Journal of Accounting* (Spring 1972), pp. 55–68.

SHOVEN, J. B., and J. I. BULOW, "Inflation Accounting and Nonfinancial Corporate Profits: Financial Assets and Liabilities," *Brookings Papers,* no. 1 (1976), pp. 15–16.

TAYLOR, N. T., and M. E. BARRETT, *Introduction to European Accounting,* ICH 9-174-043. Boston, Mass.: Harvard Business School, 1974.

TREUHERZ, R. M., "Re-evaluating ROI for Foreign Operations," *Financial Executive* (May 1968), pp. 64–71.

TURNER, J. N., "The Need for International Harmony in Accounting Standards," *CA Magazine* (January 1983), pp. 40–44.

WATT, G. C., R. M. HAMMER, and M. BURGE, *Accounting for the Multinational Corporation.* Homewood, Ill.: Dow-Jones Irwin, 1978.

WOO, J. C. H., "Accounting for Inflation: Some International Models," *Management Accounting* (February 1978), pp. 37–43.

WYMAN, H. E., "Analysis of Gains or Losses from Foreign Monetary Items: An Application of Purchasing Power Pariety Concepts," *Accounting Review* (July 1976), pp. 545–558.

CASE STUDY

International Hotel and Lodges, Inc.

W. A. Klausen, Chief Executive Officer of International Hotel and Lodges, Inc. (Canada), was in the process of reviewing a comprehensive evaluation of the company's foreign operations in 1985. The report, which he requested from his financial staff, was prompted by the company's increasing problems in controlling the financial reporting by its worldwide hotel and services affiliates and subsidiaries. Mr. Klausen had suspected that the decreasing profitability of its foreign operations was in no small measure attributable to the lack of effective control over these operations and the deteriorating quality of its services.

BACKGROUND

International Hotel and Lodges, Inc. (IHL, Inc., Canada), a diversified services firm based in Toronto, Canada, was formed in 1967 by a merger between a family-owned chain of hotels and motels located in North America, and a hotel-services company which operated hotels, food-catering services for airlines, and uniform supply units in Canada, and a number of European and Asian countries.

As of year-end 1985, IHL owned and operated 250 hotels and lodges in North America (Canada, the United States, and Mexico) and 74 hotels in Europe, the Middle East, and Asia. In addition, it managed 45 locally owned hotels in foreign countries under a management contract and royalty arrangement. The company is organized into five divisions: North American Hotel and Lodges Division, International Hotel and Lodges Division, Hotel Services and Supplies Division, Airline Catering Division, and Hotel Training and Management Division, which operates centers for formal schooling and training in hotel management in 21 countries. Exhibit 1 shows total revenue generated by each of the five divisions for the last five fiscal years ended December 31, 1985.

IHL enjoyed a steady growth in its early years, particularly in the late 1960s and the early 1970s. The growth was interrupted by the sharp increases in oil prices in 1973–1974 and again in 1978. The dampening effect of this factor on international travel and tourism severely impacted the

Exhibit 1. IHL, Inc. (Canada) Revenue by Reporting Division (in millions of $ Canadian)

	1981	1982	1983	1984	1985
North American Hotel and Lodges	372.5	315.7	295.7	300.1	295.7
Percentage of total	(58.3)	(53.4)	(53.3)	(51.3)	(49.2)
International Hotel and Lodges	114.9	110.5	105.7	120.3	125.0
Percentage of total	(18.0)	(18.7)	(19.1)	(20.6)	(20.8)
Hotel Services and Supplies	75.0	78.3	71.7	73.9	79.8
Percentage of total	(11.7)	(13.2)	(12.9)	(12.6)	(13.3)
Airline Catering	42.9	46.8	50.2	55.4	60.2
Percentage of total	(6.7)	(7.9)	(9.1)	(9.5)	(10.0)
Hotel Training and Management	33.6	40.2	31.3	35.0	40.1
Percentage of total	(5.3)	(6.8)	(5.6)	(6.0)	(6.7)
Total revenue from operations	638.9	591.5	554.6	584.7	600.8
	(100.0)	(100.0)	(100.0)	(100.0)	(100.0)

revenues of IHL, which reported losses in five of the eight years between 1973 and 1980. After a modest increase in overall revenues in 1980 and 1981, they declined by about 7.5 percent and 9.4 percent in 1982 and 1983, respectively. The decline was associated in part with the recession experienced by the industrial countries during this period. Operations of the North American Hotel and Lodges Division (the largest revenue producer, accounting for well over 50 percent of total revenues) continued to stagnate during 1983–1985 despite the sharp depreciation of the Canadian dollar against the U.S. dollar during this period. A large proportion of the income of this division is derived from hotels and lodges operated in the United States.

Balance sheet and income statement data in summary form are presented in Exhibits 2 and 3. Exhibit 3 also contains share price data. IHL shares are listed both on the American and Toronto Stock Exchanges.

CONTROL OF OPERATIONS—FINANCIAL REPORTING

Control over operations and financial management at IHL are performed by four centers: (1) Toronto looks after operations in Canada and the operations of the Hotel Training and Management Division worldwide; (2) an affiliate in Chicago supervises all operations in the United States and Latin America; (3) an affiliate in London is responsible for operations in Europe and the Middle East; (4) an affiliate in Hong Kong controls operations in Asia.

Although the three foreign affiliates are the focal point of financial control and supervision of operations within their respective areas, they do not function as profit centers. Exchange exposure and cash management decisions, as well as those relating to financing and investing, are centralized at the four centers. Management of individual hotels and lodges and operating affiliates report cash positions and results of operations monthly to the supervising affiliate in the center. These in turn file monthly financial and operational reports with the home office in Toronto.

The financial reporting system is so designed that profitability is measured and evaluated on an overall divisional basis. Thus, neither the local managers of hotels or service units nor the managements of the regional affiliates have a direct incentive to improve performance or reduce costs.

In the last annual meeting, a dissenting group of shareholders, disappointed with the poor performance of IHL, Inc. in recent years, strongly criticized the current financial reporting system, which emphasizes the division rather than the operating units as the focal point of measurement of performance. Although they failed in their attempt to select their slate of directors, they succeeded in thrusting this issue to the forefront of management priorities in 1986.

Exhibit 2. IHL, Inc. (Canada) Balance Sheets for Years Ended December 31 (in millions of $ Canadian)

ASSETS	1981	1982	1983	1984	1985
Cash and marketable securities	18.4	23.3	21.7	15.2	17.5
Accounts and notes receivable	120.3	131.7	125.8	119.2	113.5
Inventories and work in process	39.2	40.5	43.5	40.6	47.8
Other current assets	20.0	25.2	19.1	16.7	22.8
Fixed assets other than hotel properties and real estate (net)	100.9	105.7	110.9	100.3	112.7
Hotel properties and real estate (net)	651.5	720.7	704.5	703.3	689.6
Total assets	950.3	1023.8	1025.5	995.3	1033.9
LIABILITIES					
Current liabilities					
Accounts payable	52.2	54.4	58.3	60.2	56.6
Notes payable (banks)	100.0	135.7	145.7	150.5	166.5
Accrued expenses	70.9	77.3	75.8	80.2	83.5
Current portion of long-term debt	20.5	22.8	20.2	18.3	16.5
Total current liabilities	243.6	290.2	300.0	309.2	323.1
Long-term debt					
First mortgages on hotel properties	220.0	235.6	218.7	203.4	190.6
Debentures (several maturities)	50.0	42.7	38.6	33.1	30.5
Deferred income taxes	17.5	17.8	18.4	18.9	20.0
Total long-term debt	287.5	296.1	275.7	255.4	241.1
Stockholder's equity					
Common stock $2.00 par (25 million issued)	50.0	50.0	50.0	50.0	50.0
Capital surplus	287.5	287.5	287.5	287.5	287.5
Retained earnings	102.5	107.9	116.1	107.7	102.2
Capital stock treasury at cost	(20.8)	(7.9)	(3.8)	(14.5)	—
Total stockholders' equity	419.2	437.5	449.8	430.7	439.7
Total liabilities and stockholders' equity	950.3	1023.8	1025.5	995.3	1003.9

In a recent meeting with Mrs. Lillian Elener, Vice President of Finance and Chief Financial Officer, Mr. Klausen raised the following questions:

1. To what extent is the slump in operations, particularly since 1981, due to general economic conditions affecting the industry as a whole?
2. Is there hard evidence that performance at the operating level, particularly hotels and lodges, has been deteriorating? If so, is the deterioration clearly related to the absence of sufficient incentives and/or highly centralized decision-making process?

Exhibit 3. IHL, Inc. (Canada) Income Statements for Years Ended December 31 (in millions of $ Canadian)

	1981	1982	1983	1984	1985
Revenue from operations	638.9	591.5	554.6	584.7	600.8
Operating costs	511.2	490.5	477.0	520.4	516.6
Depreciation and amortization	44.3	46.6	43.5	40.6	39.6
Interest	35.9	39.4	33.6	30.1	28.4
Income from continuing operations	47.5	15.0	0.5	−6.4	15.2
Income from discontinued operations and extraordinary items	(13.0)	12.7	29.2	11.5	(3.2)
Total income from all operations before income taxes	34.5	27.7	29.7	5.1	12.0
Provision for income taxes	16.0	9.8	9.0	1.0	5.0
Net income	17.5	17.9	20.7	4.1	7.0
Dividends	12.5	12.5	12.5	12.5	12.5
Increase (decrease) in retained earnings	5.0	5.4	8.2	(8.4)	(5.5)

EARNINGS AND MARKET DATA ($ CANADIAN PER SHARE)

		1981	1982	1983	1984	1985
Earning per share		$0.70	$0.72	$0.83	$0.16	$0.28
Dividend per share		0.50	0.50	0.50	0.50	0.50
Price (AMEX)	H	$12\frac{1}{8}$	14	$9\frac{1}{8}$	$7\frac{3}{4}$	$6\frac{3}{8}$
	L	$4\frac{1}{2}$	$3\frac{1}{2}$	$2\frac{1}{2}$	2	$1\frac{3}{8}$
	Close	$6\frac{1}{4}$	$5\frac{3}{4}$	$4\frac{1}{8}$	$2\frac{1}{2}$	$3\frac{1}{4}$
P/E ratio	H	17.3	19.4	11.0	48.4	22.8
	L	6.4	4.9	3.0	12.5	4.9
	Close	8.9	8.0	5.0	15.6	11.6

3. If there is strong evidence supporting the linkage between poor performance in the past few years and the present system of financial reporting and performance evaluation, what changes should be instituted to correct the situation?

Mr. Klausen and Mrs. Elener recognized that the troublesome aspects of the firm's operation are confined primarily to the declining profitability of the two hotel and lodges divisions, whereas the operations of the other three divisions seem to be progressing fairly well. They agreed that a thorough analysis and cross-industry comparisons, particularly with their major competitors, should yield useful insights into the nature of the problems.

HOTEL MANAGEMENT AND THE FINANCIAL DECISION-MAKING PROCESS

IHL, Inc. owns and operates directly upwards of 85 percent of its hotels and lodges. The remaining units are owned by local investors and are operated by IHL under a management contract. The company has no direct control over the financial operations of those units, but has control over personnel matters and procurement of supplies. With few exceptions, IHL requires that all hotels managed by it obtain supplies and materials, whenever possible, from its affiliates.

The financial centers at Toronto, Chicago, London, and Hong Kong exercise total control over the financial operations of operating units within their jurisdiction. This includes cash management, borrowing and investment, hedging against currency exposure, and format and frequency of financial reporting required from the operating units. These decisions, as well as overall financial policies, are reviewed quarterly by the Vice President of Financial Affairs and the Central Corporate Treasurer at Toronto.

Financial centers require that receipts be deposited daily at designated banks where the operating units are located. These balances are either invested in the local money market or transferred to the financial centers as instructed by IHL's bankers, The Imperial Bank of Canada and its correspondents, which supervise the company's international cash management system. Payments to suppliers and payroll are made directly by a designated local bank. Unforeseen expenses are met by a small line of credit at a local bank at the discretion of the hotel or unit manager. A sketch of the cash management system is shown in Exhibit 4.

In addition to controlling financial operations, the centers control managerial and key personnel appointments and promotions. Unit managers are responsible for hiring and firing other personnel. There is no incentive program in force, other than an annual bonus declared by the home office in December each year. The amount of the bonus is determined by the overall performance of the company.

THE DATA

Mrs. Elener and her staff recognized that to provide adequate answers to the questions raised by the Chief Executive Officer, and to formulate proposals for corrective action, a substantial amount of data gathering and investigative work is needed. She asked her staff to compile the following data:

1. Operating and financial data on the operations of two competitive international hotel chains which are comparable to the worldwide operations of IHL, Inc. For this purpose, Holiday Inns, Inc., and Trusthouse Forte P.L.C. (based in London) were selected.

Exhibit 4. IHL, Inc. Sketch of Cash Management System

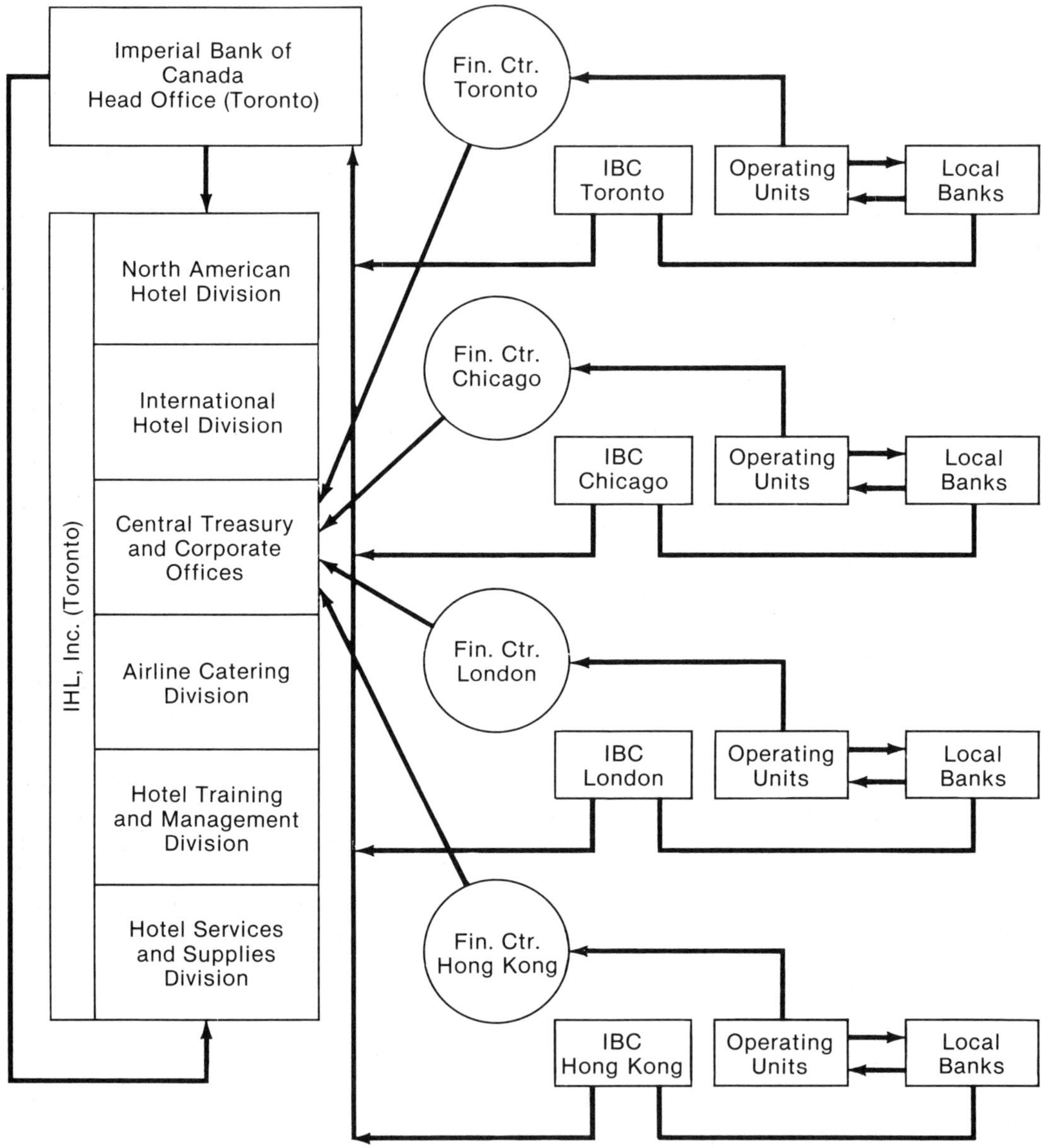

2. Economic data for the countries which account for the major proportion of IHL's revenues.
3. Exchange rate data, particularly relating to the movement of the Canadian dollar against the U.S. dollar.

4. Intelligence data relating to the cash management systems and financial reporting systems, as well as the incentive programs currently used by IHL's main competitors.

Mrs. Elener was pondering her recommendations to Mr. Klausen in late May 1986. The data she requested from her staff (summarized in Exhibits 5 and 6 and the report of a special committee—see below) fell somewhat short of her expectations. Realizing the time constraint and the urgency of the situation, she decided to terminate the investigative process and to proceed to formulate her report, which consisted of two parts: (1) analysis of the reasons behind the relatively poor performance of IHL in recent years, and (2) preparation of a blueprint for future operations. She had a strong feeling that her recommendations would prove crucial to the ability of IHL, Inc. to overcome the current problems and resume a healthy rate of expansion.

REPORT ON CASH MANAGEMENT SYSTEMS, FINANCIAL REPORTING, AND PERFORMANCE EVALUATION MAINTAINED BY MAJOR COMPETITORS

A committee was formed by Mrs. Elener to gather data on practices by major competitors, particularly with respect to financial reporting and performance evaluation systems. The committee encountered a number of problems in obtaining data on these aspects of operation in the hotel industry, mainly because such data are not published. Trade associations in the industry do not compile and publish these data on a regular basis.

Within the short time frame allotted, the committee was able, nevertheless, to present some useful ideas and guidelines utilizing mainly intelligence data gathered about the operations of IHL's major competitors. The findings and observations of the committee are summarized in the following points contained in the committee's report:

1. IHL's international cash management system is more formalized and sophisticated than most of the competing hotel chains. While the company is deriving substantial benefits from this system, an investigation should be undertaken to determine if these benefits justify the cost of maintaining this system. There have also been complaints on the part of the operating units that adequate cash balances have not been available for normal working capital purposes.
2. The decision-making process of IHL is on the whole more centralized than its major competition. This is particularly the case in personnel and procurement matters. While this question obviously requires further investigation, it may explain in part the reported deterioration in the quality of the physical facilities and services provided by the operating units.

Exhibit 5. Operating and Financial Data—Holiday Inns, Inc. and Trusthouse Forte P.L.C. (London)

	HOLIDAY INNS, INC. (MILLIONS OF U.S. DOLLARS)			TRUSTHOUSE FORTE[1] (MILLIONS OF POUNDS STERLING)	
	1984[2]	1983	1982	1984	1983
Revenue from operations	1759.8	1585.1	1425.3	1148.6	1012.0
Operating income	336.5	291.6	234.3	124.7	102.7
Net income from continuing operations	131.0	124.4	97.2	73.6	62.0
SELECTED BALANCE SHEET DATA					
Total assets	2348.0	1936.5		1418.9	1116.4
Current assets of which (cash and marketable securities)	269.7 (65.2)	207.4 (53.7)	209.0 (32.5)	270.5 (50.4)	224.6 (50.7)
Current liabilities	350.6	291.6	232.4	307.1	256.4
Long-term debt	789.6	482.7	436.4	283.0	263.5
FINANCIAL AND MARKET DATA ($ PER SHARE)				**(P PER SHARE)**	
Earnings	3.59	3.28	2.50	9.43	7.95
Dividends	0.90	0.84	0.80	9.48	8.25
Share price range H	$51\frac{3}{4}$	$38\frac{3}{4}$	59	147	199
L	$35\frac{1}{4}$	$23\frac{3}{8}$	$34\frac{1}{4}$	93	147
P/E ratio H	14.4	11.8	23.6	15.6	25.0
L	9.8	7.1	13.7	9.9	18.5
RATIOS (PERCENT)				**PERCENT**	
Return on sales—continuing operations	6.8	7.8	7.4	6.4	6.1
Return on average equity	11.3	12.5	12.8	14.7	17.5

[1]Trusthouse Forte, P.L.C. is incorporated in the United Kingdom and is engaged in the business of hotel operations, catering, and leisure activities. It is listed on the London Stock Exchange.

[2]The breakdown of revenues in 1984 is as follows (in millions of U.S. dollars):

Hotel operations	$1003.7
Gaming	644.1
Restaurant	107.0
Other	5.0
Total	$1759.8

Source: Holiday Inns, Inc., *Annual Report,* 1983, 1984, and 1985; Trusthouse Forte, P.L.C., *Moody's International Manual,* 1985, Vol. 2.

Exhibit 6. IHL, Inc.—Exchange Rates (quarterly data)[1]

	CANADIAN DOLLARS PER U.S. DOLLAR	U.S. DOLLARS PER POUND STERLING	JAPANESE YEN PER U.S. DOLLAR
1981			
1st Qtr.	1.1868	2.2442	251.00
2nd Qtr.	1.2005	1.9428	225.80
3rd Qtr.	1.2068	1.8005	232.70
4th Qtr.	1.1859	1.9080	219.90
1982			
1st Qtr.	1.2303	1.7817	246.50
2nd Qtr.	1.2903	1.7382	254.00
3rd Qtr.	1.2362	1.6927	269.50
4th Qtr.	1.2294	1.6145	235.00
1983			
1st Qtr.	1.2339	1.4790	239.40
2nd Qtr.	1.2273	1.5304	239.70
3rd Qtr.	1.2323	1.4957	236.10
4th Qtr.	1.2444	1.4506	232.20
1984			
1st Qtr.	1.2765	1.4426	224.70
2nd Qtr.	1.3194	1.3527	237.50
3rd Qtr.	1.3180	1.2480	245.50
4th Qtr.	1.3214	1.1565	251.10
1985			
1st Qtr.	1.3670	1.2430	252.50
2nd Qtr.	1.3587	1.2951	248.95
3rd Qtr.	1.3710	1.4010	217.00
4th Qtr.	1.3975	1.4445	200.50

[1]Source: International Monetary Fund, *International Financial Statistics,* several issues.

3. The committee was unable to assemble meaningful data on the financial reporting system followed by IHL's major competitors. Nevertheless, there is sufficient grounds to suggest that performance and profitability should be measured and evaluated on a more decentralized basis. The four financial centers, or some other geographic basis such as region or country, may be used for ascertaining performance in addition to, or in lieu of, the present system of measuring performance on a divisional basis.
4. Inasmuch as the managers of the operating units are in a better position to evaluate the performance of their staff than managers located in the centers or the headquarters, the bonus scheme

should be administered within the operating units. However, the total amount of bonuses and their apportionment among the operating units should be left to the regional financial centers, taking into account the profitability of operations in each region.

20

The Global Debt Issue[1]

BACKGROUND

The combined external debt of developing countries (LDCs) is estimated at over $700 billion with roughly 50 percent of the total owing to commercial banks (mainly in the form of Eurocurrency credits). The balance is owed to official sources and international financial institutions. About one-fourth of the global debt consists of short-term debt with current maturities (as contrasted with original maturities) of one year or less. The bulk of the debt is accounted for by 21 major LDC borrowers in Latin America, Asia, Africa, and the Middle East (Exhibit 20-1).

The rate of growth of external debt for these countries in recent years substantially exceeded the growth of gross earnings on the current account (export of goods, services, and private transfers) with resultant erosion of their debt-servicing capacity. This, together with the recession which has engulfed industrial countries during 1981–1983, have adversely affected the export performance of LDCs and have led to the emergence of serious debt-servicing problems. The problem, which assumed critical proportions in the fall of 1982 and again in recent months, was dealt with mainly by stop-gap measures in the form of short-term bridge financing provided in

[1]This study was prepared by the author in early 1984. A condensed version of the study dealing primarily with the "Development of an Advance Warning Indicator of Debt Servicing Vulnerability," was published in the *Journal of International Business Studies* (Fall 1985), pp. 135–141.

Exhibit 20-1. External Debt Statistics for Major Borrowing LDCs (in billions of U.S. dollars)

	EXTERNAL DEBT END 1982		GROWTH RATES (1976–1982)[1]		
	Total	Short-Term	Total Ext. Debt	Exports	Exports[2] as % Nominal GNP (1982)
21 Major LDC Borrowers	514.5	132.5			22
Latin America	288.1	75.7			15
Argentina	38.1	7.3	25.6	15.1	16
Brazil	86.3	16.7	21.4	13.5	8
Chile	17.2	3.2	18.4	17.7	24
Colombia	10.2	3.3	14.2	12.8	13
Ecuador	6.6	1.3	37.0	12.8	19
Mexico	84.6	25.8	23.3	24.8	17
Peru	11.2	3.2	8.3	13.3	20
Venezuela	33.2	15.0	17.1	10.5	30
Asia	108.8	29.0			34
Indonesia	21.9	2.9	13.0	16.5	22
Korea	37.2	10.4	23.9	25.0	44
Malaysia	8.6	1.7	27.1	17.3	53
Philippines	20.7	7.8	27.4	13.7	21
Taiwan	9.3	4.0	15.8	22.2	55
Thailand	11.1	2.2	33.2	17.4	25
Middle East & Africa	117.6	27.8			26
Algeria	14.8	0.7	17.5	15.2	35
Egypt	21.8	3.2	21.5	17.6	23
Israel	28.0	13.5	15.8	12.9	49
Ivory Coast	8.4	2.0	35.0	9.3	32
Morocco	10.8	1.0	28.7	5.9	26
Nigeria	11.2	3.0	35.6	7.0	22
Turkey	22.6	4.4	25.0	16.2	17

[1]Percent per annum.
[2]Exports of goods, services and private transfers.
Sources: International Monetary Fund, *International Financial Statistics* (several issues). International Monetary Fund, *Yearbook 1982*. Bank for International Settlements, *Distribution of International Bank Lending*. Morgan Guaranty Trust Company, N.Y., *World Financial Markets* (several issues).

connection with or pursuant to the adoption of stabilization programs negotiated with the IMF. Recent measures, which increased the lending resources of international financial institutions, were believed to provide an adequate basis for additional liquidity to cope with emerging debt-servicing problems. Along with the expected pickup in LDCs' exports to industrial countries as the recovery process gains momentum, they were expected to provide a temporary respite while the international monetary system seeks a more lasting solution.

The IMF has been shouldering an increasing share of financing LDCs' deficits, particularly since mid-1982, when it became obvious that the recession in the industrial countries had cut deeply into their exports. Total net drawings from the IMF amounted to $10.2 billion in the year ended June 30, 1984, financing approximately 20 percent of the combined current account deficit of all nonoil LDCs.[2] IMF's resources, which have been strained by these operations, were augmented by a general increase in quotas of 47 percent. This increase, coupled with an expansion of the General Agreement to Borrow (GAB), added about $28 billion in credit available to meet emerging situations. In addition, the IMF had negotiated earlier $6 billion in new loans, of which half is to be advanced by Saudi Arabia and the rest from a group of European countries.

The international financial community, particularly the multinational banks, seem to be reacting on a piecemeal basis to this problem. The syndicated Eurocurrency market which packages most of the loans to LDCs was jolted in mid-1982 by the interruption in Argentina's debt-service payments. That was followed later in the year by Mexico's problems, which were substantially larger in proportion. Interruption of payments (principal or interest or both) has in the past led to a virtual cessation of bank credit to the country in question, as well as a decline in overall lending to LDCs in general. Resumption of credit flows has been contingent upon successful restructuring or rescheduling of the problem country's foreign debt, a lengthy process which requires the endorsement of a committee or a consortium representing the creditor banks. In most cases, this process accompanied or followed the willingness of the problem country to address the economic and financial problems underlying the imbalance, usually articulated in a financial program agreed upon with the IMF.

The world financial community has been hoping that the problem can be kept from getting out of control in the foreseeable future by:

1. The beneficial impact of the expected acceleration of economic growth in the major industrial countries on the exports of the LDCs.
2. The augmentation of the resources of the IMF.
3. Economic adjustment programs pursued by some of the problem countries.

There has been some discussion in recent years about a long-term strategy to deal with the worsening global debt problem. Such a strategy was discussed and endorsed in principle by leaders of the major industrial countries at the Williamsburgh summit conference in early 1983, and was

[2]International Monetary Fund, *Annual Report 1983,* Washington, D.C., 1983.

again addressed in the 1985 meeting of the Board of Governors of the IMF and the World Bank in Seoul, South Korea. The key elements of the strategy consist of a coordinated approach involving major donor countries, international financial institutions, major lending banks, and debtor countries. The LDCs on their part must pursue restrictive demand management policies in the near term to achieve reasonable current account adjustment, although over the longer term, adjustment efforts must emphasize export-oriented policies. Another important part of this strategy is to gradually supplant commercial bank financing by additional official assistance, not merely to address temporary balance of payments need, but also for longer-term development.

RECENT DEVELOPMENTS IN INTERNATIONAL BANK LENDING TO LDCS

Bank lending to nonoil developing countries declined sharply in 1982 and 1983 to about one half of the 1981 level (Exhibit 20-2). The large decline was due largely to heightened perception of risk in the aftermath of the emergence of debt-servicing problems in Argentina, Brazil, and Mexico. Lending to centrally planned economies, other than to those which are IMF members, was also curtailed. This was attributable to diminished willingness on the part of banks to commit new funds to Eastern European countries following Poland's debt-servicing problems in 1981. Resumption of bank lending to these countries on a significant scale is unlikely in the near future.

Exhibit 20-2. External Lending by International Banks (in billions of U.S. dollars)

	1978	1979	1980	1981	1982	1983
Industrial countries	38	69	96	99	117	95
Oil exporting developing countries	15	7	6	2	9	5
Nonoil developing countries	24	40	49	51	41	27
Centrally planned economies	7	6	5	5		
International organizations and unallocated	6	3	4	8	−5	11
Total	90	125	160	165	162	138
Lending to LDCs as percent of total	26.7	32.0	30.6	30.9	25.3	19.6

Source: International Monetary Fund, *Annual Report 1983,* p. 77, and *Annual Report 1984,* p. 68. Figures include external lending by banks in the Bank of International Settlements (BIS) reporting area which comprises all banks in the Group of Ten countries, Austria, Denmark, Ireland, and Switzerland and the branches of U.S. banks in the Bahamas, Cayman Islands, Hong Kong, Panama, and Singapore.

The decline of bank lending to LDCs was accompanied by an increasing preference of international banks for curtailing medium-term syndicated sovereign lending in favor of project-related and trade-related financing, and loans organized through private placement.

Primary data for 1984 show a further albeit a small decline in lending to LDCs. The future willingness of banks to lend to this group will depend in part on successful completion and observance of the terms of renegotiated debt by the LDCs, as well as on the effectiveness of economic adjustment programs of a number of major debtor countries. The scale of future lending also depends on the banks' own assessment of their overall risk position in different regions and their concern about bank capital adequacy.

LDCs have relied heavily on external borrowing to finance current account deficits which have been rising in recent years. External borrowing has also contributed to some buildup in these countries' external reserves (Exhibit 20-3). However, despite a fairly large decrease in their combined deficit in 1982, the group as a whole used up more than $7 billion in reserves due to the sharp drop in external borrowing. 1982 also witnessed a considerably higher amount of reserve-related credit facilities, such as IMF credit facilities and short-term borrowing from other monetary au-

Exhibit 20-3. Nonoil Developing Countries: Current Account Financing, 1978–1983 (in billions of U.S. dollars)

	1978	1979	1980	1981	1982	1983
Current account deficit[1]	− 41.3	− 61.0	− 89.0	− 107.7	− 86.8	− 54.2
Financing						
Change in reserves						
Use of reserves (− increase)	− 17.4	− 12.6	− 4.5	− 2.1	7.1	− 10.0
Nondebt creating flows[2]	17.9	23.9	24.1	28.0	25.1	22.6
Net external borrowing	40.8	49.7	69.3	81.8	54.6	41.6
of which						
Long-term	(37.2)	(36.5)	(47.2)	(62.7)	(41.0)	(54.1)
Use of reserve-related facilities[3]	(0.3)	(0.4)	(1.8)	(5.9)	(10.7)	(6.1)
Other short-term borrowing[4]	(3.3)	(12.8)	(20.4)	(13.2)	(2.9)	(18.6)

[1]Net total of balances on goods, services, and private transfers.

[2]Includes net official transfers, SDR allocations, valuation adjustments, gold monetization, and direct investment flow (net).

[3]Comprises use of IMF credit facilities and short-term borrowing by monetary authorities from other monetary authorities.

[4]Includes errors and omissions.

Source: International Monetary Fund, *Annual Report 1983,* Washington, D.C., *Annual Report 1984,* p. 28, and *Annual Report 1986,* p. 237.

thorities. Their combined current account deficit, as well as net external borrowing, declined further in 1983. Overall, the group's reserve position, which reflects the international liquidity, improved by $10 billion. For the group as a whole, the ratio of reserves to imports of goods and services at the end of 1982 amounted to about 17 percent, which is considered abnormally low in comparison with recent years.

A key factor is the future ability of this group to bring about further reductions in their combined current account deficit in the wake of a decline of some $50 billion from 1981 to 1983. This sizable reduction must have been accomplished at the expense of a sharp curtailment of the development effort. Moreover, the problem must have been exacerbated by the relatively high level of interest rates in the major industrial countries, and the use of loan agreements bearing floating interest rates that are adjusted at frequent intervals.

In view of the above considerations, further sizable reduction in current account deficits may trigger severe economic and political crises in many countries in the group. Signs of such turbulence occurred during the second half of 1983 and in 1984 in such countries as Brazil, the Philippines, Chile, and Israel. Adaptation to a lower level of aggregate demand required in many cases stringent demand management policies and various kinds of import and exchange restrictions. The most severe adjustment was experienced by Latin American countries which, as a group, reduced the 1982 imports in real terms to about the 1975 level.

MEASURES OF DEBT SERVICING CAPACITY

An important aspect of the global debt issue is to develop a leading indicator of external debt servicing vulnerability that would serve as an advance signal of probable or imminent payments interruption. This would entail, *inter alia,* an examination of the structure of global debt to ascertain the degree of concentration in that structure both from the standpoint of borrowing countries and that of lending institutions. This degree of concentration, which has been increasing in recent years, is a serious challenge to the ability of the international financial system to absorb the disruptive impact resulting from the default of one or more major borrowing countries.

Several measures of debt servicing capacity have been used. The most widely used is the ratio of the balance on current account (net export of goods and services and net unilateral transfers) to debt service payments (interest and the maturing portion of external debt). This is analogous to the ratio of corporate earnings to interest, which is referred to as the interest coverage ratio.[3] Other measures are the ratio of external debt to

[3]Ratio of earnings before interest and taxes (EBIT) to interest payments.

exports and the rate of growth in external debt relative to the rate of growth in exports or GNP. The latter ratio gives an overall indication of the recent trends in external debt in relation to the nation's capacity to produce goods and services for exports. Most of these and other indicators have been extensively used by international banks and other financial institutions to calculate country exposure limits and otherwise determine their lending policies to LDCs.

While these ratios measure the capacity of an LDC to handle its international obligations, they generally fail to test the potential vulnerability of debtor countries to debt-servicing difficulties, or the imminence of interruption in debt service payments. The problem with these ratios is that they ignore a key determinant of oncoming debt-servicing difficulties, namely, the country's overall international liquidity position, including availability of drawings on international financial institutions, and emergency financing from private lending institutions. Erosion of liquidity and deterioration in the country's political outlook are perhaps the most crucial manifest indicators of debt-servicing problems. Moreover, while each measure in itself may throw some light on one aspect of an LDC's potential vulnerability, it would probably require an index combining several key measures to predict this vulnerability with an acceptable degree of accuracy. This is analogous to forecasting prospective changes in the level of overall economic activity by using the "Index of Leading Economic Indicators." Although none of the eight components is a dependable guide to future trends, the composite index provides a reliable basis for forecasting economic activity.

Concentration of Outstanding External Debt

Total external debt is unevenly distributed among nonoil LDCs, with 20 major borrowers accounting for over 70 percent of total outstanding debt at the end of 1982.[4] This pattern of concentration, particularly in short-term debt, is evident in Exhibit 20-4, which shows that this group accounted for over 88 percent of total outstanding short-term debt. By contrast, their share of long-term debt which is guaranteed to official creditors is less than 50 percent. This substantiates the tendency of major borrowers to obtain funds from banks at market-related terms, while the rest of the LDC group prefers to tap long-term concessional sources of credit. The low-income group, in particular, resorts mostly to long-term borrowing under official development assistance programs. This pattern of concentration of the bulk of external debt in a relatively small number of major borrowers has intensified in recent years. A handful of major bor-

[4]This grouping of countries differs slightly from the 21 countries listed in Exhibit 20-1. See footnote 1, Exhibit 20-4.

Exhibit 20-4. Distribution of Outstanding Debt Among Nonoil Developing Countries, End 1982 (in billions of U.S. dollars and percentages)

	MAJOR BORROWERS[1]	LOW-INCOME COUNTRIES[2]	ALL OTHER[3]	TOTAL
I. In billions of U.S. dollars				
Total debt	447.0	56.6	108.8	612.4
Short-term debt	99.7	3.0	10.0	112.7
Long-term debt	347.3	53.6	98.8	499.7
Guaranteed to official creditors	(93.7)	(44.8)	(54.7)	(193.2)
Other	(253.6)	(8.8)	(44.1)	(306.5)
II. In percent of corresponding totals for all nonoil developing countries				
Total debt	74.0	9.2	17.8	100.0
Short-term debt	88.4	2.7	8.9	100.0
Long-term debt	69.5	10.7	19.8	100.0
Guaranteed to official creditors	(48.5)	(23.2)	(28.3)	(100.0)
Other	(82.7)	(2.9)	(14.4)	(100.0)

[1]The 20 countries with the largest estimated external debt to private creditors: Mexico, Brazil, Argentina, Chile, Peru, Ecuador, Colombia, Korea, Philippines, Thailand, Malaysia, Greece, Morocco, Egypt, Yugoslavia, Israel, Turkey, Portugal, Romania, and Hungary.

[2]Excluding China and India.

[3]Residual group (including China and India).

Source: International Monetary Fund, *Annual Report 1983,* Washington, D.C.

rowers in Latin America have the highest debt/export ratio (about 250 percent at end 1982) and account for 45 percent of total external debt outstanding. In sharp contrast, Asian developing countries have relatively low debt service ratios, because a large proportion of their debt consists of long-term obligations to official creditors that are subject to relatively low annual amortization payments. While almost all nations in the first group are currently experiencing severe debt servicing problems, none of the countries in the second group, with the recent exception of the Philippines, has interrupted payments.

The concentration of external debt on the borrowing side is matched by even a higher degree of concentration on the lending side. While data as to distribution of external debt among lending institutions are difficult to track down, it is evident that almost the entire global debt is owing to private and official lenders in the leading industrial countries and to international financial institutions (notably the IMF, the IBRD Group, and The Bank for International Settlements).

The real problem lies in the overexposure of a small number of large U.S. and overseas banks to a concentration of credits extended to a few countries. The growth of bank lending to LDCs averaged about 20 percent annually since 1975, far outstripping the rate of growth in banks' capital. Growth of capital of U.S. banks has been running about nine to ten percent per annum since the mid-1970s.[5] As a result, as of year end 1982, credits to Mexico represented almost 50 percent of the combined capital of the nine largest U.S. banks. Even more disturbing is the fact that credits to Mexico, Brazil, and Argentina constituted about 115 percent of the combined capital of the nine largest U.S. banks and roughly half of the banks' claims on all LDCs.[6] Given this degree of overexposure, the possibility of a failure of a major U.S. or foreign bank cannot be realistically dismissed. Such a failure might trigger a domino-type effect with serious consequences to the U.S. banking and the international financial systems.

DEVELOPMENT OF AN ADVANCE WARNING INDICATOR OF EXTERNAL DEBT SERVICING VULNERABILITY

William J. Gasser and David L. Roberts of the Federal Reserve Bank of New York developed recently a "vulnerability index"[7] to reflect mainly the erosion of liquidity among developing countries with substantial external debt. This indicator combines the effects of rising imports (including interest payments), increasing short-maturity bank debt, and falling reserves, weighted by exports of goods and services. While the index provides an indication of a country's vulnerability to debt-servicing problems via liquidity erosion, it is not intended to measure the probability of interruption in payments. For one thing, the indicator does not account for the likelihood of unforeseen shocks that would impair the payments position. Larger values of the index indicate less liquidity and a greater degree of sensitivity to unexpected shocks. A high value for the indicator (above 200) has almost always been accompanied by debt-servicing problems (Exhibit 20-5). Both Argentina and Mexico interrupted debt service payments in late 1982, while Poland has been in default since 1981, pending resumption of suspended rescheduling discussions. The index reflects, on the other hand, Korea's stable debt-servicing profile owing to its relatively strong current account position. Turkey's sharply improved position in

[5]Morgan Guaranty Trust Company of New York, *World Financial Markets* (June 1983), p. 6.

[6]*Ibid.*, p. 6.

[7]William J. Gasser and David L. Roberts, "Bank Lending to Developing Countries, Problems and Prospects," *Quarterly Review,* Federal Reserve Bank of New York (Autumn 1982), pp. 18–29.

Exhibit 20-5. Selected Developing Countries' "Vulnerability" Indicator[1]

	1978	1980	1982
Argentina	73	121	200
Korea	108	142	140
Mexico	188	166	200
Poland	193	191	225
Turkey	238	263	150

[1]Indicator $= \dfrac{M + A - R}{X} \times 100$

where M = imports of goods and services
A = maturing bank debt
R = international reserves (excluding gold)
X = exports of goods and services

Source: Gasser and Roberts, "Bank Lending to Developing Countries, Problems and Prospects," *Quarterly Review,* Federal Reserve Bank of New York (Autumn 1982), p. 26.

1982 reflected for the most part the impact of debt rescheduling which was completed in that year.

An index combining a number of crucial variables which can signal in advance an imminent or a likely payments interruption situation is yet to be developed. Isolating the crucial variables is an exercise of identifying the common denominators which have preceded payments interruption by a number of countries in recent years. These situations have been preceded with a varying time lead by *all* or *most* of the following developments:

1. A significant erosion in the international liquidity position
2. A sharply faster growth rate of external debt than the rate of growth in export earnings
3. An acceleration in the inflation rate experienced by the country
4. A shortfall in exports or a deterioration in export performance
5. Adverse internal political developments

The above developments may be quantified by means of the following ratios:

1. Ratio of international reserves held by country at the end of a certain quarter to reserves held at the end of the corresponding quarter in the preceding year to avoid seasonality distortions. Also, erosion of liquidity may be measured by the decline in the imports coverage ratio, that is, the ratio of reserves to annual imports.
2. Ratio relating rate of growth in exports during a certain period to rate of growth in external debt during a corresponding period. Deterioration in this ratio signals subsequent difficulties in servicing foreign debt obligations.

3. Ratio of annual inflation rate during a given quarter in the preceding year to annual inflation rate in the corresponding quarter in the current year.
4. Ratio of exports during a given period of time in the current year (such as the first three quarters) to exports during the corresponding period in the preceding year.
5. Although adverse political developments are difficult to quantify, use may be made of political stability indices, which have been computed in recent studies.[8] This would require frequent revision of the political stability index to detect underlying patterns of emerging instability.

It is proposed to combine the ratios suggested above, together with information relating to the direction of change in the political risk, to compile a weighted index which would herald or detect in advance situations of likely or imminent payments interruption on the part of debtor countries.

The weighting of the components of the proposed index, to be called *Payments Interruption Likelihood Index,* or "PILI," presents a conceptual as well as a practical problem. The two crucial components, namely, the liquidity situation and changes in the political equation, should be given a prominence in determining the outcome of the index. However, due to the impracticality of frequently updating any political stability index, it is proposed to compute PILI from the four ratios listed above, somewhat higher weights being given to the first two ratios, that is, the one reflecting changes in the international liquidity position and the one relating the growth in exports to the growth in external debt. The index so computed is then adjusted upward or downward, depending on whether there has been an improvement or a deterioration (or no perceptible change) in the underlying political situation. This test was performed on the countries listed in Exhibit 20-1, and the results are tabulated in Exhibit 20-6.

In interpreting the PILI adjusted for the change in political risk, countries with a score of 10 or around 10 display no imminent deterioration in their debt-servicing capacity. Consequently, payments interruption is not likely in the near future. Countries with higher scores (such as 11 and over) show significant improvement in their debt-servicing profile and payments interruption, in their case, would seem highly unlikely. A score of between 6 and 8 would indicate serious oncoming problems in debt servicing, with a good possibility of these countries interrupting debt-servicing payments in the near future. Countries with a PILI score of below 6 must be considered very likely candidates for payments interruption within a relatively short time span. Countries with a score of over 8 but below ten must be watched for signals of further deterioration in their debt-servicing capacity.

[8]For example, the Haendel, West, Meadow index. See Chapter 16.

Exhibit 20-6. Computation of "PILI" Index

	A[1]	B[2]	C[3]	D[4]	PILI[5]	POLITICAL ADJUSTMENT FACTOR[6]	ADJUSTED PILI[7]
Latin America							
Argentina	0.9341 (2.3353)	0.5898 (1.4745)	0.4941 (0.7412)	0.8527 (1.2791)	5.83	2.00	7.83
Brazil	0.6202 (1.5505)	0.6308 (1.5770)	0.6773 (1.0160)	1.1561 (1.7342)	5.88	1.50	7.38
Chile	0.8804 (2.2010)	0.9620 (2.4050)	0.2852 (0.4278)	1.0640 (1.5960)	6.63	1.50	8.13
Colombia	0.5607 (1.4018)	0.9014 (2.2535)	1.3678 (2.0517)	0.9024 (1.3536)	7.06	2.00	9.06
Ecuador	1.0000 (2.5000)	0.3459 (0.8648)	0.2581 (0.3872)	1.0076 (1.5114)	5.26	2.00	7.26
Mexico	1.6872 (4.2180)	1.0644 (2.6610)	0.5857 (0.8786)	1.3414 (2.0121)	9.77	2.00	11.77
Peru	1.1247 (2.8118)	1.6024 (4.0060)	0.6272 (0.9408)	0.9421 (1.4138)	9.17	2.00	11.17
Venezuela	1.5656 (3.9140)	0.6140 (1.5350)	1.5763 (2.3645)	1.1020 (1.6530)	9.47	2.00	11.47
Asia							
Indonesia	1.0821 (2.7053)	1.2692 (3.1730)	0.6370 (0.9555)	0.8418 (1.2627)	8.10	2.00	10.10
Korea	0.8682 (2.1705)	1.0460 (2.6150)	2.1330 (3.1950)	1.1170 (1.6755)	9.66	2.00	11.66
Malaysia	1.2962 (3.2405)	0.6384 (1.5960)	1.6724 (2.5086)	0.7183 (1.0775)	8.42	2.00	10.42
Philippines	0.5875 (1.4688)	0.5000 (1.2500)	1.3793 (2.0690)	0.8489 (1.2734)	6.06	1.00	7.06
Thailand	1.2281 (3.0703)	0.5241 (1.3103)	0.8958 (1.3437)	0.8039 (1.2059)	6.93	2.00	8.93

Exhibit 20-6. *(continued)*

Middle East and Africa							
Algeria	0.7389	0.8686	0.6250	0.9801	6.42	2.00	8.42
	1.8493	2.1715	0.9375	1.4702			
Egypt	0.9947	0.8186	1.1333	1.0003	7.73	2.00	9.73
	2.4868	2.0465	1.7000	1.5005			
Israel	1.0421	0.8165	1.0071	1.0054	7.67	2.00	9.67
	2.6503	2.0413	1.5107	1.5081			
Ivory Coast	1.3333	0.2657	0.6915	0.8853	6.36	2.00	8.36
	3.3333	0.6643	1.0373	1.3280			
Morocco	0.7043	0.2056	2.1190	1.0465	7.02	2.00	9.02
	1.7608	0.5140	3.1785	1.5698			
Nigeria	0.9581	0.1966	1.1515	0.8620	5.91	1.50	7.41
	2.3953	0.4915	1.7273	1.2930			
Turkey	0.9343	0.7168	0.8545	1.1058	7.07	1.50	8.57
	2.3358	1.7920	1.2818	1.6587			

[1] Ratio of international reserves held at the end of September 1983 to reserves held at the end of September 1982.

[2] Growth rate per annum in exports during the period 1976–1982 related to the growth rate per annum in external debt during the same period.

[3] Ratio of inflation rate during 12 months ended September 1982 to inflation rate during 12 months ended September 1983.

[4] Ratio of exports during the second quarter of 1983 to exports during the second quarter of 1982.

[5] Weighted average of the preceding four ratios using the following weights: 2.5 for the ratio indicating the change in the overall liquidity position, 2.5 for the ratio relating the growth in exports to the growth in external debt, 1.5 for the ratio measuring the change in the inflation picture, and 1.5 for the ratio measuring the change in recent exports performance. With a total weight of 10.0, the above weights add up to 8.0, leaving 2.0 for the political stability index.

[6] The political adjustment factor will be basically judgmental in nature. Points will be allotted as follows, depending on the change in the underlying political situation during 1982–1983:

- 2.0 No perceptible change in the political situation
- 1.5 Deterioration in the political situation
- 1.0 Seriously adverse political developments in the country

[7] Column 5 plus column 6.

Source: Based on data compiled from International Monetary Fund, *International Financial Statistics* (December 1982 and December 1983), and *Yearbook 1982;* Bank for International Settlements, *Distribution of International Bank Lending* and *International Banking Developments* (1983).

Exhibit 20-7. Grouping of Countries by "PILI" Score

CATEGORY	"PILI" SCORE	COUNTRIES
I. Countries signalling significant improvement	11 and over	Mexico, Peru, Korea and Venezuela
II. Countries signalling no significant change	9–under 11	Colombia, Indonesia, Malaysia, Egypt, Israel and Morocco
III. Countries signalling possible oncoming deterioration (must be watched)	8–under 9	Chile, Thailand, Algeria, Ivory Coast, and Turkey
IV. Countries signalling likely payments interruption	6–under 8	Argentina, Brazil, Ecuador, Philippines, and Nigeria
V. Countries signalling imminent (highly likely) payments interruption problems	Under 6	None

According to the above criteria, countries listed in Exhibit 20-6 may be grouped in five categories, shown in Exhibit 20-7.

Among the countries listed above, six (Argentina, Brazil, Chile, Ecuador, Nigeria, and the Philippines) are currently in the process of formal multilateral debt restructuring with commercial banks or have recently completed such a process. All countries listed in the fourth category are in this group. Mexico, Peru, Turkey, and Venezuela, which completed the process of restructuring in late 1982 or early 1983, have recently shown a considerable improvement in their debt-servicing capacity (perhaps with the exception of Turkey). Typically, a country's debt profile would show a noticeable improvement upon completion of debt restructuring negotiations, due mainly to the infusion of new lending by banks and drawings on the closely linked IMF stabilization program. Subsequently, however, a number of countries tend to show a rapid deterioration, which would probably set the stage for another round of negotiations. Argentina, Brazil, and Turkey are typical of this group. On the other hand, other countries, typified in Exhibit 20-7 by Mexico, Peru, and Venezuela, seize the opportunity accorded to them by debt restructuring to further improve their debt-servicing profile.

CONCLUSIONS

The rapidly rising global debt and the increasing degree of concentration in its distribution pose a serious threat to the international financial system. While there has been little done in the way of finding a comprehensive long-term solution to the global debt problem, the world financial community has dealt with debt-servicing problems on a case-by-case basis as they reach critical proportions. There is need to improve the capability of forecasting oncoming situations of serious payments difficulties which major debtor LDCs have been experiencing with increasing frequency.

This chapter developed an index combining a number of crucial variables which can signal in advance an imminent or a likely payments interruption situation. These variables include the key changes that usually precede payments interruption, namely, erosion of international liquidity, a substantially faster growth in external debt compared to exports, an acceleration in the inflation rate, a deterioration in export performance, and adverse internal political developments. The index was applied to 20 major debtors among the LDCs which account for the bulk of outstanding external debt, producing results that seem to bear out its ability to detect the likelihood of oncoming payments interruption situations.

BIBLIOGRAPHY

ABDULLAH, F. A., "Development of an Advance Warning Indicator of External Debt Servicing Vulnerability," *Journal of International Business Studies* (Fall 1985), pp. 135–141.

Bank for International Settlements, *Distribution of International Bank Lending,* Basle, Switzerland, 1983 and 1984.

______, *International Banking Developments,* Basle, Switzerland, several issues.

BARTLETT, S., "How an LDC Default Would Hit the U.S. Economy," *Business Week* (June 4, 1984), p. 27.

DHONTE, P., "Describing External Debt Situations: A Roll Over Approach," *IMF Staff Papers* (March 1975), pp. 159–186.

EVANS, M. K., "Third World Debt to Haunt U.S., Too," *Industrial Week* (October 4, 1982), p. 70.

EUH, Y., *Commercial Banks and the Creditworthiness of Less Developed Countries.* Ann Arbor, Mich.: UMI Research Press, 1979.

FEDER, G., and R. JUST, "A Study of Debt Servicing Capacity Applying Logit Analysis," *Journal of Development Economics,* March 1977, pp. 25–38.

FIELEKE, N. S., "International Lending in Historical Perspective," *New England Economic Review,* Federal Reserve Bank of Boston (November–December 1982).

FRANK, C. R., and W. R. CLINE, "Measurement of Debt Servicing Capacity: An Application of Discriminant Analysis," *Journal of International Economics,* Vol. 1 (1971), pp. 327–344.

GASSER, W. L., and D. L. ROBERTS, "Bank Lending to Developing Countries: Problems and Prospects," Federal Reserve Bank of New York, *Quarterly Review* (Autumn 1982), pp. 18–29.

"How Serious is the Third World Debt Problem?" *OECD Review* (November 1981), pp. 9–12.

International Monetary Fund, *International Capital Markets, Developments, and Prospects,* Occasional Paper No. 23, Washington, D.C., 1983.

______, *International Capital Markets, Developments, and Prospects,* Occasional Paper No. 31, Washington, D.C., 1984.

______, *World Economic Outlook,* Washington, D.C., 1984.

______, *World Economic Outlook,* Washington, D.C., 1985.

______, *Foreign Private Investment in Developing Countries,* Occasional Paper No. 33, Washington, D.C., 1985.

______, *Annual Report 1983,* Washington, D.C., 1983.

______, *Annual Report 1984,* Washington, D.C., 1984.

______, *International Financial Statistics* (several issues).

KAHLEY, W., JR., "Assessing Economic Country Risk," Federal Reserve Bank of Atlanta, *Economic Review* (June 1981).

KIM, Y. H., and A. ERTENU, "Beyond the Measurement of Political Risk," *Academy of International Business Proceedings,* Montreal (October 1981).

MAKIN, J. H., "World Debt Crisis," *Center for the Study of Banking and Financial Markets Digest* (Winter 1984).

MAYNARD, G., and P. A. DAVIS, "Evolving Problems of International Financial Intermediation," *Bank Management in a Changing Domestic and International Environment,* Martin Nijhott Publishers (1982), p. 168.

MAYO, A. L., and A. G. BARRETT, "An Early Warning Model for Assessing Developing Country Risk," in Steven H. Goodman, ed., *Financing and Risk in Developing Countries.* New York: Praeger, 1978, pp. 81–87.

MCDONALD, D. C., "Debt Capacity and Developing Country Borrowing: A Survey of Literature," *IMF Staff Papers,* Vol. 22, no. 1 (March 1975).

NAGY, P., "Quantifying Country Risk: A System Developed by Economists at the Bank of Montreal," *Columbia Journal of World Business,* Vol. 13 (Fall 1978).

NOWZAD, B., "Managing External Debt in Developing Countries," *Finance and Development* (September 1980), pp. 24–27.

______, "Debt in Developing Countries: Some Issues for the 1980's," *Finance and Development* (March 1982), pp. 13–16.

ROBERTS, D. L., "LDC Debt Burden," Federal Reserve Bank of New York, *Quarterly Review* (Spring 1981), pp. 33–41.

SARGEN, N., "Economic Indicators and Country Risk Appraisal," Federal Reserve Bank of San Francisco, *Economic Review* (Fall 1977).

SCHMIDT, R., "Early Warning of Debt Rescheduling," Eastern Finance Association Proceedings, New York (April 1983).

STERLING, J., "A New Look at International Lending by American Banks," *Columbia Journal of World Business* (Fall 1979), pp. 61–69.

"Taking a Second Look at Third World Debt," *Citibank* (January 1981), pp. 10–14.

THORNBLADE, J. B., "A Checklist System: First Step in Country Evaluation," EXIM Bank Symposium on Outlook on Private Market Financing and Risk in Developing Countries (April 1977).

______, "Evaluating Country Risk at a Major Commercial Bank," *Academy of International Business Northeastern Meeting Proceedings* (March 1980).

WATKINS, A. J., *Till Debt Do Us Part.* Washington, D.C.: Roosevelt Center for American Policy Studies, 1985.

WESTERFIELD, J. M., "A Primer on the Risks of International Lending and How to Evaluate Them," Federal Reserve Bank of Philadelphia, *Business Review* (July–August 1978).

WILLOUGHBY, J., "Buying Time [World Bank to Aid IMF]," *Forbes* (October 21, 1985), pp. 42–43.

World Bank, *Annual Report 1985,* Washington, D.C.

"World Debt Crisis," A Special Report, *The Wall Street Journal* (June 25, 1984), pp. 25–29.

Currencies and Symbols

Afghanistan	afghani	Af
Algeria	dinar	DA
Antigua and Barbuda	dollar	EC$
Argentina	austral	₳
Australia	dollar	A$
Austria	schilling	S
Bahamas	dollar	B$
Bahrain	dinar	BD
Bangladesh	taka	Tk
Barbados	dollar	BdS$
Belgium	franc	BF
Belize	dollar	BZ$
Benin	franc	CFAF
Bhutan	ngultrum	Nu
Bolivia	peso	$b
Botswana	pula	P
Brazil	cruzado	Cr$
Burkina Faso	franc	CFAF
Burma	kyat	K
Burundi	franc	FBu
Cameroon	franc	CFAF
Canada	dollar	Can$
Cape Verde	escudo	C.V.Esc.
Central African Republic	franc	CFAF
Chad	franc	CFAF
Chile	peso	Ch$
China (People's Republic)	renminbi	Cy
Colombia	peso	Col$
Comoros	franc	CF
Congo	franc	CFAF
Costa Rica	colon	₡
Cote d'Ivoire	franc	CFAF
Cyprus	pound	£C
Denmark	krone	Dkr
Djibouti	franc	DF
Dominica	dollar	EC$
Dominican Republic	peso	RD$
Ecuador	sucre	S/
Egypt	pound	£E
El Salvador	colon	₡
Ethiopia	birr	Br
Fiji	dollar	F$
Finland	markka	Fmk

France	franc	F
Gabon	franc	CFAF
Gambia	dalasi	D
Germany	deutsche mark	DM
Ghana	cedi	¢
Greece	drachma	Dr
Grenada	dollar	EC$
Guatemala	quetzal	Q
Guinea	franc	GS
Guinea-Bissau	peso	PG
Guyana	dollar	G$
Honduras	lempira	L
Hungary	forint	Ft
Iceland	krona	ISK
India	rupee	Rs
Indonesia	rupiah	Rp
Iran	rial	Rls
Iraq	dinar	ID
Ireland	pound	£Ir
Israel	new shekel	IS
Italy	lira	Lit
Jamaica	dollar	J$
Japan	yen	¥
Jordan	dinar	JD
Kampuchea	riel	KR
Kenya	shilling	K Sh
Korea	won	W
Kuwait	dinar	KD
Laos (People's Democratic Republic)	kip	KN
Lebanon	pound	LL
Lesotho	loti	M
Liberia	dollar	$
Libya	dinar	LD
Luxembourg	franc	Lux F
Madagascar	franc	FMG
Malawi	kwacha	MK
Malaysia	ringgit	M$
Maldives	rufiyaa	Rf
Mali	franc	CFAF
Malta	lira	Lm
Mauritania	ouguiya	UM
Mauritius	rupee	Mau Rs
Mexico	peso	Mex$
Morocco	dirham	DH
Mozambique	metical	Mt
Nepal	rupee	NRs
Netherlands	guilder	f.

New Zealand	dollar	$NZ
Nicaragua	cordoba	C$
Niger	franc	CFAF
Nigeria	naira	₦
Norway	krone	NKr
Oman	rial	RO
Pakistan	rupee	PRs
Panama	balboa	B
Papua New Guinea	kina	K
Paraguay	guarani	₲
Peru	inti	I/.
Philippines	peso	₱
Portugal	escudo	Esc
Qatar	riyal	QR
Romania	leu	—
Rwanda	franc	RF
St. Christopher-Nevis	dollar	EC$
St. Lucia	dollar	EC$
St. Vincent	dollar	EC$
Sao Tome' and Principe	dobra	Db
Saudi Arabia	riyal	SRls
Senegal	franc	CFAF
Seychelles	rupee	SR
Sierra Leone	leone	Le
Singapore	dollar	S$
Solomon Islands	dollar	Sl$
Somalia	shilling	So. Sh.
South Africa	rand	R
Spain	peseta	Ptas
Sri Lanka	rupee	SLRs
Sudan	pound	LSd
Suriname	guilder	Sf
Swaziland	ilangeni	E
Sweden	krona	Sk
Switzerland	franc	SwF
Syria	pound	LS
Tanzania	shilling	TSh
Thailand	baht	Bht or Bt
Togo	franc	CFAF
Tonga	pa'anga	PT
Trinidad and Tobago	dollar	TT$
Tunisia	dinar	D
Turkey	lira	LT
Uganda	shilling	USh
United Arab Emirates	dirham	Dh
United Kingdom	pound	£

United States	dollar	\$
Uruguay	new peso	NUr\$
Vanuatu	vatu	VT
Venezuela	bolivar	Bs
Viet Nam	dong	D
Western Samoa	tala	WS\$
Yemen Arab Republic	rial	YRls
Yemen (People's Democratic Republic)	dinar	YD
Yugoslavia	dinar	Din
Zaire	zaire	Z
Zambia	kwacha	K
Zimbabwe	dollar	Z\$

Glossary of Frequently Used Symbols and Acronyms

ADR	American Depository Receipt
ADS	American Depository Share
APV	Adjusted present value
β_j	Beta of security j (a measure of the systematic or market-related risk of the security)
BIS	Bank for International Settlements
B/L	Bill of lading
CAPM	Capital asset pricing model
CF_t	Cash flow in period t
D	Debt
DCF	Discounted cash flow
DISC	Domestic international sales corporation
DR	Discount rate (for projects' cash flows)
E	Equity
ECU	European Currency Unit
EEC	European Economic Community
EMS	European Monetary System
EOQ	Economic order quantity
$E(R)_j$	Expected rate of return from security or project j
$E(R)_m$	Expected rate of return on market (or a broad market index)
EX-IM Bank	Export Import Bank of the United States
F	Forward exchange rate
FASB #8	Financial Accounting Standard Board Rule No. 8
FASB #52	Financial Accounting Standard Board Rule No. 52
FCIA	Foreign Credit Insurance Association
IBA	International Banking Act (of 1978)
IBF	International banking facility
IBRD	International Bank for Reconstruction and Development (World Bank)

ICAPM	International capital and pricing model
IMF	International Monetary Fund
IMM	International Monetary Market
I_0	Initial investment
k	Cost of capital, or a risk-adjusted discount rate
k_d	Cost of debt
k_e	Cost of equity (required rate of return by investors)
L/C	Letter of credit
LDCs	Less developed (or developing) countries
LIBOR	London Interbank Offer Rate
MNC	Multinational corporation
N	Life span (in years) of project
NPV	Net present value
OECD	Organization of Economic Cooperation and Development
OPEC	Organization of Petroleum Exporting Countries
OPIC	Overseas Private Investment Corporation
$\overset{*}{P}$	Expected inflation rate
PC	Participation certificate
PPP	Purchasing power parity
PV	Present value
R	Nominal interest rate
ROI	Return on investment
S or S_0	Spot exchange rate
S_t	Exchange rate in time period t
$\overset{*}{S}_t$	Expected spot exchange rate in time period t
SDR	Special Drawing Right
SEC	Securities and Exchange Commission

Name Index

Subject Index

F

G

H

I

J

K

L

M